ARCHITECTURE EXAM REVIEW

BALLAST'S GUIDE TO THE A.R.E.

VOLUME II: NON-STRUCTURAL TOPICS

David Kent Ballast, A.I.A.

PROFESSIONAL PUBLICATIONS, INC.
Belmont, CA 94002

Architecture Exam Review
Ballast's Guide to the A.R.E.

Volume II: Non-Structural Topics

Printed in the United States of America

ISBN: 0-912045-02-7

Professional Publications, Inc.
1250 Fifth Avenue, Belmont, CA 94002

Current printing of this edition (last number): 6 5 4 3 2 1

TABLE OF CONTENTS

23 MATERIALS AND METHODS—SAMPLE QUESTIONS

24 CONSTRUCTION DRAWINGS AND DETAILS

25 THE PROJECT MANUAL AND SPECIFICATIONS

26 THE PRIMARY CONTRACTUAL DOCUMENTS

27 BIDDING PROCEDURES AND DOCUMENTS

28 CONSTRUCTION ADMINISTRATION SERVICES

29 SOLUTIONS

BIBLIOGRAPHY

INDEX

PROFESSIONAL PUBLICATIONS, INC. ● Belmont, CA

LIST OF ILLUSTRATIONS

LIST OF TABLES

INTRODUCTION

The Architect Registration Examination is a uniform test administered to candidates who wish to become licensed architects after they have served their required internship. It is given in all states, in addition to five other jurisdictions and nine Canadian provinces.

The A.R.E. has been developed to protect the health, safety, and welfare of the public by testing a candidate's entry-level competence to practice architecture. Its content relates as closely as possible to the situations encountered in practice. It tests for the kinds of knowledge, skills, and abilities required of an architect, with particular emphasis on those services that affect public health, safety, and welfare. In order to accomplish these objectives, the exam tests for (1) knowledge in specific subject areas, (2) the ability to make decisions, (3) the ability to consolidate and use information to solve a problem, and (4) the ability to coordinate the activities of others on the building team. It also includes some project management questions.

This guide and the companion book on structural subjects will help you review for the A.R.E. The organization of both books generally follows the divisions of the test, and the chapters of each book are arranged by individual subject matter to help you organize your study effort. In addition, there are sample questions for each subject so you can test yourself on your knowledge of the material. Answers to the sample questions, along with explanations, are provided.

Although the responsibility of professional licensing rests with each individual state, member boards of each state subscribe to the examination prepared by the National Council of Architectural Registration Boards (NCARB). One of the primary reasons for a uniform test is to facilitate reciprocity—that is, to enable an architect to more easily gain a license to practice in states other than the one in which he or she was originally licensed.

The A.R.E. is prepared by committees of the NCARB with the assistance of Educational Testing Service (ETS). ETS helps with production, distribution, and scoring, as well as serving as a consultant for testing format and writing of questions.

The examination is given in each state and jurisdiction at the same time and graded uniformly. All parts except the site and building design divisions are machine-graded. The two design divisions are graded by trained jurors meeting shortly after the test. Although the design grading is somewhat subjective, the jurors follow uniform guidelines, assisted by master jurors, who offer guidance, maintain uniformity, and resolve borderline cases.

In the last several years, the California board has administered its own test. However, beginning in 1990 California will return to the use of the A.R.E., administering a supplemental examination to address the state's special concerns.

The examination is continually evolving. Currently, for example, the NCARB is developing and testing a computer-adaptive exam. Twelve member boards began offering the computerized version of Divisions D/F and E to volunteer candidates in late 1988.

The use of computers will allow the exam to be given more frequently, speed up reporting of grades, and improve reliability. One interesting feature of a computer-based exam is that it will allow ability and knowledge to be demonstrated progressively as the test is taken. The answer to one question can affect the difficulty of the next so that a more competent candidate will answer fewer difficult questions and probably finish earlier.

Although there is no substitute for a good, formal education and broad-based experience provided by your internship with a practicing architect, this review guide will help direct your study efforts to increase your chances of passing the A.R.E.

1 EXAMINATION FORMAT

The Architect Registration Examination is designed to protect the health, safety, and welfare of the public by regulating the practice of architecture. It does this by testing to see if someone has the knowledge, skills, and abilities to perform the services required of an entry-level architect. To this end, the examination is divided into several parts, which test various areas of architectural knowledge and problem-solving abilities.

The examination is administered in June of each year and currently consists of eight divisions given over a period of four days. The divisions are as follows:

Division	
A:	Pre-Design
B:	Site Design
C:	Building Design
D/F:	Structural Technology—General and Long Span
E:	Structural Technology—Lateral Forces
G:	Mechanical/Plumbing/Electrical
H:	Materials and Methods
I:	Construction Documents and Services

The time allotted for each section ranges from about $2\frac{1}{2}$ hours to 12 hours for the full-day, Division C, building design portion. Exact lengths allowed for each division vary and are published in the Pre-Examination Information Booklet sent to applicants by the state registration boards about one month before the exam.

A common breakdown of the divisions given on each of the four days follows:

Day 1: Divisions D/F, E, and G
Day 2: Divisions H and I
Day 3: Divisions A and B
Day 4: Division C

2   HOW TO TAKE THE TEST

A. Types of Questions Asked

In previous exams there has been a single building on which many of the questions in all divisions have been based. Samples of the building's construction drawings, specifications, and other data have been given in the test information package to simulate an actual practice situation. Many questions are based on the information given about this sample building. Other questions are based on memory of facts and general knowledge of the subject matter. Still other questions test the application of facts and general knowledge to specific situations given in the test.

The A.R.E. uses four types of questions and variations of each of these types. In all except the graphic presentation of the site planning and building design divisions, the form of the answer is multiple choice with four answer possibilities.

The first type of question is multiple choice. You are asked to select from four possible answers to a problem that may be based on written, graphic, or photographic material. The problem may require that you perform a calculation to respond correctly, but in the simplest form, a multiple choice question simply gives four choices following the question.

In other multiple choice questions, there may be a list of five choices or statements following the initial written or graphic information, and the four possible answers will be various combinations of the five choices. For example, from the five choices you may be asked to decide which ones are correct or which ones are incorrect. In some of these question types, you may be asked to select the answer which correctly ranks the five choices in some order. Others ask that you match words or phrases from two lists, selecting the answer that provides the proper match.

The second type of question is written identification. This uses a key list of words or phrases around which several questions are based. Written identification questions may simply be definition type questions or they may use written or graphic evidence in presenting a problem. You are asked to look at a diagram or read about a situation and then use the list to select your answer. The list may contain two or more responses that are very similar or seem to be correct, but only one may be selected.

In the third type of question, a written simulation is presented, which is intended to put you in a situation that you might encounter in practice. The written part may be accompanied with drawings, tables, diagrams, forms, or photographs to supplement the question. The simulation is followed by a series of options—single words, phrases, or statements—from which you must select the best one in the context of the given situation.

The fourth type of question is the graphic presentation, in which you are required to create a drawing or series of drawings to complete the problem. These are used for the 12-hour building design problem and the site design problems.

Even though the first three types of questions are structured to allow for multiple choice, for machine grading, they often require that you do much more than simply select an answer from your memory. You must, for example, combine several facts, review data given in the test information package, perform a calculation, or review a drawing.

B. Time Management

One of the biggest problems many candidates have in taking the A.R.E. is simply completing it in time. This is especially true of the 12-hour design problem and the graphic portions of the site design division. Detailed suggestions for the site design graphic test are given in Chapter 5. Because the 12-hour building design problem is particularly unique, guidelines for time management and tips on completing it are discussed in Chapter 6.

For the portions of the exam that consist of multiple choice questions, you may want to proceed in one of two ways.

With the first approach, proceed from the first question to the last, trying to answer each one regardless of its difficulty. Divide the time allotted by the number of questions to give yourself an average time per question. Of course, some will take less than the average, some more. If you are not able to confidently answer a question in your allotted time or a little more, make a note of it and move on to the next one. If you have time at the end, you can go back to the most difficult questions.

With the second approach, go through the test three times. During the first pass, read each question and answer the ones you are sure of and that do not take any lengthy calculations or study of the information packet. Since you will be jumping around, always make sure you are marking the correct answer space. If a question does not fit into the first category of "easy to answer," make a mark by it indicating whether you can answer it with a little thinking or easy calculation or whether it seems impossible and may be a best-guess type of response.

During the second pass, answer the next easiest questions. These should be the ones that you can confidently respond to after some deductive reasoning or with a calculation with which you are familiar. Once again, make sure you are marking the correct numbered spaces on the answer sheet.

During the third pass, answer the questions that remain and that require extra effort or those for which you have to make the best guess between two of the most likely answers. In some cases, you may be making your best guess from among all four options.

Using the three-pass method allows you to get a feeling for the difficulty of the test during the first pass and helps you budget the remaining time for the unanswered questions. One of the tricks to making this method work is not to go back to reread or reanswer any completed question. In most cases, your first response (or guess) is the best response. No matter which approach you use, answer every question, even if it is a wild guess. You are not penalized for guessing.

Remember that you will need time to refer to the drawings, contracts, specifications, building codes, tables, and other background information that is included with the test information package handed out with the test. The test information package is only for reference; you do not have time to read through it completely. This is why it is important in studying for the exam that you know where to find certain types of information in the various sources. For example, if a question asks about what ASTM specification must be satisfied by a brick, you need to be able to quickly turn to the appropriate specification section and the part of the specification that lists test criteria for materials.

C. Tips on Taking the Examination

Even if you are completely familiar with the subject matter, taking the A.R.E. can be an arduous process, simply because of its length and the concentration required to get through it. As with any activity requiring endurance, you should be rested when you start the exam. You should have stopped studying a day or two before the first test day in order to relax as much as possible. Get plenty of sleep the night before and every night between test days.

Allow yourself plenty of time to get to the exam site so you do not have to worry about getting lost, stuck in traffic jams, or other transportation problems. An early arrival at the exam room also lets you select a seat with good lighting and as far away from distractions as possible. Once in the room, arrange your working materials and other supplies so you are ready to begin as soon as you are allowed. The proctor will review the test instructions as well as general rules about breaks, smoking, and other housekeeping matters. You can ask any questions about the rules at this time.

Once the test begins you should quickly review the material given to you in the test information packet. For the non-structural divisions of the test, depending on which division you are taking, this will include such things as contracts, specification sections, portions of zoning ordinances, portions of building codes, contract drawings, and similar items. You do not need to study this material. Simply make a mental or written note about what is included so you know it is available when a question requires that you use it.

Next, check the number of questions and set up a schedule for yourself as described in the previous section. If you plan on tackling the questions one by one in sequence, you should have completed about half the questions when half of your allotted time is up. In your scheduling, leave some time at the end of the period to double-check some of the answers you are most unsure of and to see that you have not marked two responses for any question.

Here are some additional tips:

Make a notation of the answers you are most unsure of. If you have time at the end of the test, go back and recheck these if you really think it may help. Remember, your first response is usually the best.

Many times, one or two choices can be easily eliminated. This may still leave you with a guess, but at least your chances are better between two than among four.

Some questions may appear too simple. While a few very easy and obvious questions are included, more often the simplicity should alert you to rethink all aspects to make sure you are not forgetting some exception to a rule or special circumstance that would make the obvious, easy response not the correct one.

Watch out for absolute words in a question, such as "always," "never," or "completely." These often indicate some little exception that can turn what reads like a true statement into a false statement or vice versa.

Be on the alert for words like "seldom," "usually," "best," or "most reasonable." These indicate that some judgment will be involved in answering the question, so look for two or more options that may be very similar.

Occasionally, there may be a defective question. This does not happen very often, but if you think you have found one, make the best choice you can. The question is usually discovered, and either it is not counted in the test or any one of the correct answers is credited.

As a final thought: try to relax as much as possible during your study for the test and during the examination itself. Worrying too much is counterproductive. If you have worked diligently in school, have obtained a wide range of experience during internship, and have started your exam review early, you will be in the best position possible to pass the A.R.E.

D. Study Guidelines

Your method of studying for the A.R.E. should be based both on the content and form of the exam and your school and work experience. Because the exam covers such a broad range of subject matter, it cannot possibly include every detail of practice. Rather, it tends to focus on what is considered entry-level knowledge and knowledge that is important for the protection of the public health, safety, and welfare. This is not to say that other types of questions are not asked, but it should help you direct your review.

Your recent work experience should also help you determine what areas to study the most. If you have been involved with construction documents for several years, you will probably require less work in that area than in others with which you have not had recent experience.

This review manual was prepared to help you focus on those topics that will most likely be included in the exam in one form or another. As you go through the manual, you will probably find some subjects that are familiar or that come back to you quickly. Others may seem like completely foreign subjects, and these are the ones to give particular attention when using this manual. You may even want to study additional sources on these subjects, take review seminars, or get special help from someone who knows the topic.

The following steps provide a useful structure for organizing your study for the examination.

step 1: Start early. You cannot review for a test like this by starting two weeks before the date. This is especially true if you are taking all portions of the exam for the first time.

step 2: Go through the review manuals quickly to get a feeling for the scope of the subject matter. Although this manual and the companion manual on the structural portions of the exam have been prepared based on the content covered, you may want to review the detailed list of tasks and considerations given in the NCARB study guides.

step 3: Based on this review and a realistic appraisal of your strong and weak areas, set priorities for your study. Determine what topics you need to spend more time with than others.

step 4: Divide the subjects you will review into manageable units and organize them into a sequence of study. Generally, you should start with those subjects least familiar to you. Based on the date of the examination and when you are starting to study, assign a time limit to each of the study units you identify. Again, your knowledge of a subject should determine the time importance you give it. For example, you may want to devote an entire week to earthquake design if you are unfamiliar with that and only one day to timber design if you know that well. In setting up a schedule, be realistic about other commitments in your life as well as your ability to concentrate on studying for a given amount of time.

step 5: Begin studying and stick with your schedule. This, of course, is the most difficult part of the process and the one that requires the most self-discipline. The job should be easier if you have started early and set up a realistic schedule, allowing time for recreation and other personal commitments.

step 6: Stop studying a day or two before the exam to relax. If you do not know the material by this time, no amount of cramming will help.

Here are some additional tips:

Know concepts first, then learn the details. For example, it is much better to understand the basic ideas and theories of waterproofing than it is to attempt to memorize dozens of waterproofing products and details. Once you fully understand the concept, the details and application are much easier to learn and to apply during the exam.

Do not overstudy any one portion. You are generally better off to review the concepts of all the divisions of the test than to become an overnight expert in one area. For example, the test may ask general questions about plate girders, but it will not ask that you perform a complete, detailed design of one.

Try to talk with people who took the test the year before. Although the exam questions change yearly, it is a good idea to get a general feeling for the types of questions asked, the general emphasis, and areas that previous candidates found particularly troublesome.

E. What to Take to the Exam

About a month before the examination, you will receive from your state registration board a Pre-Examination Information Booklet that, in addition to other data, will tell you what materials and supplies to bring to the testing site.

Reference materials are not allowed in the test. The necessary codes, drawings, structural tables, and the like are part of the test information package. However, there are some necessary "survival items" that you will need or that will make things a little easier. A partial list includes:

- calculator
- extra batteries for calculator
- no. 2 pencils and paper
- pencil sharpener or lead pointer
- highlighter markers
- eraser
- watch
- tissue
- aspirin
- snacks

1 MATHEMATICS

Successful completion of the A.R.E. does not require any complex mathematics. Calculations are usually simple and straightforward, requiring the four basic math functions with a few additional bits of knowledge. The following sections should provide you with enough refresher information to let you complete the structural and non-structural portions of the exam.

1 ARCHITECT'S AND ENGINEER'S DIMENSIONING SYSTEM

Architects usually work with units of feet, inches, and fractions of an inch while engineers and landscape architects work with decimals of a foot, and feet and inches. Engineering dimensions are typically found on site drawings, with both elevations and distances being shown in decimal format. You should be able to convert from one to the other.

Calculators are available that allow you to add, subtract, multiply, and divide in feet and inches format, but if you do not have one of these the conversion is fairly simple. Simply remember that the basic unit of measurement is the foot; only the fractions of a foot are different.

To convert from an architectural to an engineering dimension, first divide the fraction of an inch (if any) as it appears to convert to a fraction of an inch. Then combine this with the number of inches. Then divide the inches with the decimal equivalent of the fraction by 12 to obtain the decimal part of a foot.

Example 1.1

Convert 4 feet 5 5/8 inches to decimal format.

First, convert 5/8 of an inch:

$$5/8 = 0.625$$

Combined with the number of inches, the fractional part of a foot (5 5/8 inches) is 5.625 feet.

Dividing by 12,

$$\frac{5.625}{12} = 0.469$$

The number of feet stays the same, so the equivalent decimal dimension is 4.469 feet.

Example 1.2

Convert 15.875 feet to feet and inches format.

First, convert the decimal to inches:

$$0.875 \times 12 = 10.50 \text{ inches}$$

Then, convert the decimal of an inch to a fraction. This can be done to any fractional unit of an inch by multiplying the decimal by the desired unit. For instance, to convert to eighths of an inch, multiply by 8, or

$$0.50 \times 8 = 4/8 \text{ inch } = 1/2 \text{ inch}$$

The complete conversion is then the sum of the pieces, or, 15 feet 10 1/2 inches.

2 TRIGONOMETRY

Trigonometric functions occur frequently in various types of architectural applications. Some of the most common functions, such as the sine, cosine, and tangent, relate to the right triangle. See Figure 1.1. If you have trouble remembering which is which, a useful mnemonic device is to remember the old Indian chief SOH-CAH-TOA. In other words, the sine of an angle, S, is equal to the side opposite the angle, O, divided by the hypotenuse, H. The cosine of an angle, C, is equal to the side adjacent to the angle, A, divided by the hypotenuse, H. Finally, the tangent of an angle, T, is equal to the side opposite the angle, O, divided by the side adjacent, A.

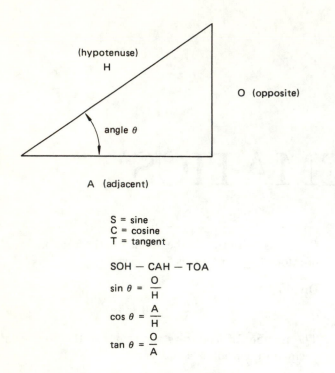

S = sine
C = cosine
T = tangent

SOH — CAH — TOA

$\sin \theta = \dfrac{O}{H}$

$\cos \theta = \dfrac{A}{H}$

$\tan \theta = \dfrac{O}{A}$

Figure 1.1   Functions of a Right Triangle

Knowing any two sides of a right triangle, you can find the other side with the *Pythagorean theorem*, which states that the sum of the squares of the two sides equals the square of the hypotenuse:

$$A^2 + O^2 = H^2 \qquad 1.1$$

3   LOGARITHMS

In the past, logarithms were used to multiply and divide very large numbers. This was because multiplication could be accomplished by simply adding the logarithms of two numbers and converting the resulting logarithm back to a whole number. Logarithms are no longer used for this purpose, but they are used with acoustical calculations and you should be familiar with the concept.

A logarithm of a number, x, is simply a number that, when used as the exponent of another number known as the base, will yield the original number, x. There are two commonly used bases for logarithms: the common and the natural. *Natural logs* are not used in architectural work, but the base of the *common log* is 10. For example, the common log of 100 is 2. This means that if the base of 10 is raised to the second power (2), then the resulting number will be 100. Other even-number logs are:

$$
\begin{aligned}
\log 1 &= 0 \\
\log 10 &= 1 \\
\log 100 &= 2 \\
\log 1000 &= 3 \\
\log 0.1 &= -1 \\
\log 0.01 &= -2 \\
\log 0.001 &= -3
\end{aligned}
$$

For numbers that fall between these even powers, the log is zero or a whole number, known as the *characteristic*, and a decimal, known as the *mantissa*. For example, the log of 78 is 1.89209. Since 78 is between 10 and 100, you would expect the log to be between 1 and 2. Logarithms of numbers can be found in log tables, but any good calculator also has log functions available at the touch of a button.

In performing acoustical calculations, logarithms must be manipulated. The following formulas are useful to remember:

$$\log xy = \log x + \log y \qquad 1.2$$

$$\log \frac{x}{y} = \log x - \log y \qquad 1.3$$

$$\log x^n = n(\log x) \qquad 1.4$$

$$\log 1 = 0 \qquad 1.5$$

2 PRE-DESIGN— ENVIRONMENTAL ANALYSIS

Nomenclature

d	vertical distance between contours	feet
G	slope of land	percent
L	horizontal distance between points of a slope	feet

Competent architectural design depends on a thorough understanding of the environmental factors affecting the selection of a building site and its development. These factors include the larger context of the surrounding community and urban setting as well as the smaller scale influences of the immediate site. This chapter reviews the effects of the larger environmental issues on the planning of a building project. Chapter 4 focuses on site analysis prior to starting design work.

Included here is a review of the historical patterns of urban development, planning concepts, the effect of development patterns on social behavior, land analysis, transportation influences, climatic and ecological considerations, legal constraints, and economic influences and how all of these affect the development of a building site.

1 INFLUENCES ON URBAN DEVELOPMENT

Contemporary city and community planning has antecedents in the historical development of the city and in the theories of many designers and planners who felt that rational development of the land and cities could improve living conditions. Many development concepts and city forms have been tried; some have failed while portions of others have been successfully employed in urban planning.

An architect must have knowledge of the history and theory of planning in order to understand the relationships between an individual building project and the larger context of the community and city in which it is located. The larger environment affects how the site is developed and how the building is designed, and the building, in turn, affects the community of which it is a part.

A. Historical Influences

The first human settlements began as collections of people engaged in agricultural pursuits rather than leading a nomadic life. As surplus food became available and ceremony, religion, and leadership began to develop, the embryonic form of the city was apparent. Living quarters surrounded the archetypes of the granary, the place where food was stored, the temple, where ceremonial rites and social interaction took place, and the palace, where the administration of the village was conducted. For security, villages were often walled in or otherwise situated for protection from other village populations or nomadic tribes seeking to take the food they could not produce.

All of these basic components of the city were present in the Greek cities, but in a more highly developed form. The activities of the palace, which included trade and exchange of goods as well as religious ceremony, had developed to a point where separate places were required for these activities. The temple became the center for religious activity while the agora became the marketplace. The agora was not just a location for the trading of goods but was also a place for meeting people, exchanging news, and conducting other business. The walled Greek cities also had special facilities, such as theaters and stadia, for other activities.

The form of the medieval city was similar to earlier villages; it started at the crossroads of two main streets and was rather irregular in layout. Medieval cities were organized around the church and the market since these represented the two most important aspects of life. The structures were near the center of the city and surrounding them was an informal ring of streets loosely connected, with intersecting streets running from the church to the gates of the city wall. See Figure 2.1.

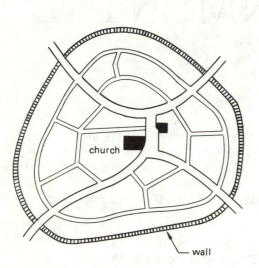

Figure 2.1   Medieval City Form

With the invention of gunpowder, the usual Medieval fortification of the high wall was no longer sufficient to protect the city. The star-shaped city developed with regularly spaced bastions at points around the wall so the entire enclosure and all approaches to the city could be defended before the enemy could get close enough for their cannons to be effective. Streets radiated out from the center, thus allowing the defense to be controlled from one point and making it possible to easily move troops and material. See Figure 2.2.

During the Renaissance, city planning took on greater importance. Although military and defense considerations were still important, planners paid more attention to the aesthetics of urban design. City plans combined symmetrical order with radial layout of streets focused on points of interest. The primary organization of the radial boulevards was overlaid on a grid of secondary streets or over an existing road system.

Christopher Wren's plan for the rebuilding of London after the great fire of 1666 and Haussmann's plan for Paris reflect the Renaissance approach. In the unrealized London plan, Wren proposed main avenues linking major religious and commercial facilities. These were to be superimposed on a gridiron plan for other streets.

In Paris, George-Eugène Haussmann advocated straight, arterial boulevards connecting principal historic buildings, monuments, and open squares. These were designed to create vistas and work in conjunction with the major buildings that were part of the plan. During the period from 1853 to 1869, a large part of Paris was demolished to implement Haussmann's plan. Although the purpose of the plan was to minimize riots, facilitate defense of the city, and clear out slums, the plan also improved transportation and beautified the city.

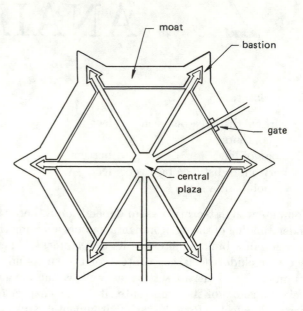

Figure 2.2   Star-Shaped City Form

The Industrial Revolution of the eighteenth and nineteenth centuries in England brought about a fundamental change in the design of cities. The factory system required that the work force be close to the factory and the source of power and transportation. As production expanded, so did the population of the factory towns. The emphasis was on turning out the goods and the cities soon became overcrowded, filthy, and devoid of open space and recreational activities. Although the Industrial Revolution began in England, it rapidly spread to northwestern Europe and the northeastern United States, carrying with it the resulting ills of its environment.

The response to the living conditions brought about by the Industrial Revolution spawned a reform movement. The first concern of many of the reformers was to alleviate the unspeakable housing conditions that existed, to reduce the crowding, and to improve the water supply and sewage systems. Later, the reformers and planners realized that there was also a need for open space and recreation. All of these concerns sparked interest in city planning where factory, housing, and other features of urban life could coexist.

One of the most well-known examples of the reform movement is the *Garden City* concept published by Ebenezer Howard in 1898. Howard's plan attempted to combine the best of city and country living in his town–country idea. He proposed that a 6000-acre tract of land be privately owned by the residents. At the center of his idealized city, there would be civic buildings in a park. These would include a town hall, a concert hall, a theater, a library, and other municipal buildings. See Figure 2.3. Surrounding this core would be housing and shops with industrial facilities in the outermost ring. The urban part of the town would support 30,000 people on 1000 acres of land. The remaining 5000 acres would be reserved for a greenbelt and agricultural use and house 2000 people.

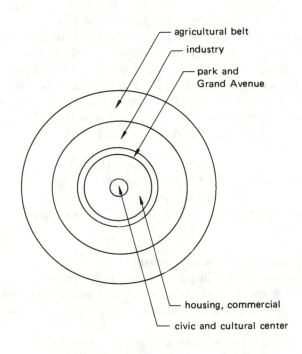

Figure 2.3   Diagram of Ebenezer Howard's
Garden City Concept

Two cities were built in England using Howard's ideas: Letchworth in 1903 and Welwyn Garden City in 1920. Although they followed the Garden City concept, they did not become independent cities but instead were satellite towns.

Another city plan developed as a reaction to the conditions of the Industrial Revolution was the *Cité Industrielle* by Tony Garnier in 1917. This city was to have been built in France and included separate zones for residential, public, industrial, and agricultural use, linked by separated vehicular and pedestrian circulation paths. The buildings would be placed on long, narrow lots with ample open space between them. Garnier's plan was one of the first to emphasize the idea of zoning, an idea which would later become vitally important for city planning.

In the United States, early attempts at city planning reflected the diversity of ideas and styles brought from the Old World. Towns laid out in the colonies were a reaction to the Renaissance ideals and reflected the agrarian life styles of the settlers. They were planned around a central commons, which was the focus of community life. Houses were free-standing structures set back from the front street and the lots included backyards as well. This was one of the influences that helped set a precedent for single-family detached housing, so prevalent even today.

Philadelphia was typical of many of the early towns. Begun in 1682, it was based on a *gridiron street system* with regularly planned public open spaces and uniform spacing and setback of buildings. Its use of the grid system became the model for later planning in America and for the new towns established as the West was settled.

Savannah, Georgia was similarly designed in 1733. It was based on a ward of 40 house lots bounded by major streets in a grid system and contained an interior square, two sides of which were reserved for public use.

The grid system was encouraged by the Ordinance of 1785 that established the rectangular survey system of the United States. This system divided the country into a grid of 24-mile squares, each subdivided into 16 townships, each six miles on a side. These were further subdivided into 36 one-mile-square sections.

One early American city that broke with the grid system was Washington, D.C. Its layout represented a significant step in city planning because of the scale of the project and because Washington was America's capital city. Pierre Charles L'Enfant was the designer. Unlike the simple grid systems of Philadelphia and Savannah, L'Enfant's design was based on the Renaissance and Baroque planning concepts of diagonal and radial streets superimposed on a rectangular grid.

The Washington plan centered on the capitol, the mall, and the executive mansion. Each of these and other, smaller, circles and squares were connected with broad avenues, creating a coherent transportation system based on vistas terminating in either a building or monument. Modifications were made to the original L'Enfant plan over the years, but the basic layout of Washington remains true to his vision.

One of the most profound changes in American urban design began with the *Columbian Exposition* in Chicago in 1893. Designed by architects Daniel Burnham and John Root and by landscape architect Frederick Law Olmstead, the exposition grouped classical buildings symmetrically around formal courts of honor, reflecting pools, and large promenades. It started the *City Beautiful* movement in the United States and revived interest in urban planning. Some of the typical results of emulating the layout cf the Columbian Exposition included civic centers organized around formal parks, a proliferation of classical public buildings, and broad, tree-lined parkways and streets.

In the early part of this decade, architects such as Frank Lloyd Wright and Le Corbusier envisioned cities with vast open spaces. Wright proposed in his plan for Broadacre City that every home should be situated on at least an acre of land. Le Corbusier saw the city consisting of office and housing towers surrounded by large green spaces. Most city planners agree that both schemes would have resulted in very dull cities and a type of urban sprawl probably worse than what exists today.

A fairly recent notion of town planning is the *new town* concept. It is an extension of the idea that entirely new communities can be planned, away from the crowding and ugliness of existing cities. The idea started in Great Britain in the 1940s and soon spread to the United States and elsewhere. New towns were supposed to be autonomous centers including housing, shopping, and business, surrounded by a green belt. Originally, the population was to be limited to about 30,000, but this was later increased to 70,000 to 250,000 people.

Several new towns were built in England. However, they never became truly independent cities because they lacked significant employment centers; they still depended on nearby cities for jobs. In the United States, Columbia, Maryland and Reston, Virginia began as new towns but suffered from the same problems as their British counterparts. They never became truly separate cities; instead, they depended on the jobs of nearby Washington, D.C. and other areas.

These new towns and previous visions of utopia have all suffered from the same problems: they are usually static in their conception and lack the vitality and interest of a city that has evolved over time.

B. Development Patterns

The form of urban development can be viewed at two scales: the larger scale of the city or metropolitan region and the smaller scale of the community and neighborhood. In the twentieth century, the pattern of development at the city scale has generally been determined by geographic features and the layout of transportation, most notably the highway. In some cases where effective city and regional planning has been undertaken, land use plans have also determined, to a certain degree, the form of development.

Cities begun near a major geographic feature such as the junction of two rivers or a large body of water tended to develop along the water and ultimately away from it. When begun in less confining circumstances, cities have grown more or less equally in all directions, usually in a uniform grid pattern.

With the proliferation of the automobile, cities have expanded in a number of typical patterns. These are shown diagrammatically in Figure 2.4. Each of these patterns affects the planning of the smaller-scale communities and neighborhoods and ultimately can have an effect on the design of individual building projects.

The simplest pattern is the *expanding grid*. In this pattern a city is formed at the junction of two roads and laid out in the prevalent pattern exemplified in the initial plan of Philadelphia. Growth simply follows the grid pattern until some natural feature, limiting population, or economics stops it. The strict grid pattern is usually characteristic of smaller cities. Larger United States metropolitan areas follow other patterns but are almost always infilled with some type of grid.

The *star pattern* revolves around the urban core and development follows radiating spokes of main highways or mass transit routes. Higher density tends to form around the spokes with lower density development in between.

The *field pattern* has no central focus or apparent overall organization scheme. Development takes place in an amorphous network of highways and natural features. Los Angeles is a typical example of this type of pattern.

With the *satellite pattern*, there is a central urban core with other major cores surrounding it. The central core is linked to the others with major highways, and often the outer cores are connected with a road system called a *beltway*. It is then possible to travel from center to center or around the city without having to go through the core. The outer cores often begin as major shopping areas, peripheral business centers, or transportation centers. Houston is an example of this type of pattern. Often, a satellite pattern starts out as a star pattern.

Finally, the ultimate in urban development is the *megalopolis*. Here, two or more major urban centers near each other grow together as the space between is

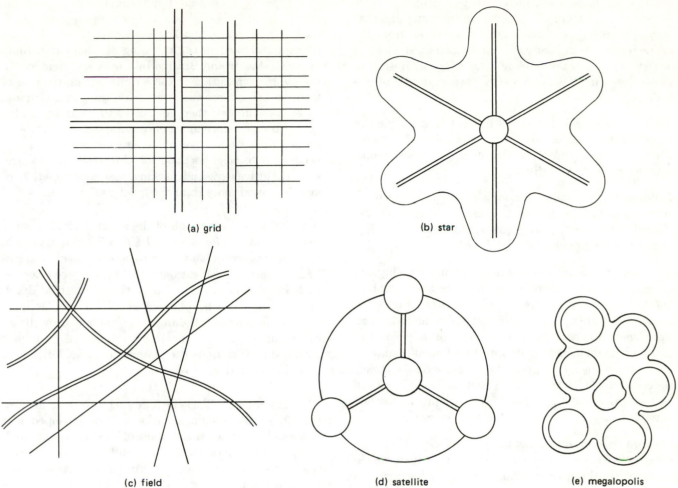

(a) grid

(b) star

(c) field

(d) satellite

(e) megalopolis

Figure 2.4 Patterns of Urban Development

developed. Many sections of the northeastern United States and southern California can be considered a megalopolis.

Although large-scale urban development can affect the way people view the city and how individual parcels of land are developed, it is within the smaller community and neighborhood scale that architects must plan sites and design buildings. One idea that is useful in linking the urban scale with the community scale is the concept of *imageability* proposed by Kevin Lynch.

Imageability is the quality of a physical environment that gives it a high probability of evoking a strong image in the mind of a given observer. For example, the hills of San Francisco are part of the image of that city in the minds of most people who visit it or live there. Everyone maintains a mental image of the environment; it is vital to orientation, way-finding, and general well being.

In *The Image of the City*, Kevin Lynch identified five basic elements of the urban image: paths, edges, dis-

tricts, nodes, and landmarks. These are created by buildings, natural features, roads, and other components of the city. Site planning and building design should respond to existing image elements and enhance them if possible.

A *path* is a way of circulation along which people customarily, occasionally, or potentially move. A path may be a street, pedestrian walkway, railroad, transit line, or river. Since circulation is such an important part of any physical environment, paths are usually at the center of a person's image.

Edges are linear elements other than paths that form boundaries between two districts or that break continuity. An edge may be a shoreline, a line of buildings against a park, a wall, or a similar feature. Sometimes an element is a path if used for circulation and an edge if seen from afar. For example, a highway can be perceived as an edge of one neighborhood and a path when one is traveling on it. Edges may either be solid or penetrable.

Districts are two-dimensional areas that people perceive as having some common, identifying character and that they can enter. A district can be perceived from the inside if you are in it or can be identified as an element of the city if you are outside. Back Bay in Boston or Georgetown in Washington, D.C. are examples of districts.

Nodes are strategic centers of interest that people can enter. They may be the intersection of paths, places where modes of transportation change, plazas, public squares, or centers of districts.

Landmarks are similar to nodes in that they are point references, but people cannot enter them—they are viewed from the exterior. A tower, monument, building, or natural feature can be a landmark.

Many of the large-scale elements of imageability are interwoven with the smaller community and neighborhood. However, there are additional patterns of development that are also intimately related to an individual site. One is the pattern of the street. Initially, community and neighborhood development followed the layout of the street, usually a grid. Blocks between the streets were subdivided into lots and each lot was developed as a separate entity. While this development method persists today, other approaches have emerged.

One of these approaches is the *superblock*, which is an outgrowth of the new town concept. This is shown diagrammatically in Figure 2.5. One of the first trials of this development scheme was in the new town of Radburn, New Jersey by Henry Wright. Here, the attempt was made to plan a large piece of land that limited the intrusion of the automobile. The superblock was surrounded by a continuous street, and vehicular access was provided with cul-de-sacs.

The superblock concept minimizes the impact of the car on housing and allows the development of pedestrian circulation and park space within the block. This concept was used in the planning of Chandigar, India by Le Corbusier and Brasilia by Costa and Neimier. In theory, the separation of the automobile on the side of the house that faces the street from the pedestrian and living area on the other side seems to be an admirable goal. However, since much of contemporary life revolves around the automobile, this separation can be counterproductive to neighborhood social interaction. As a result, the driveways and parking spaces of superblocks are often used more than the quiet park spaces.

A variation and extension of the superblock idea is the *planned unit development*, or *PUD*. With this approach, each large parcel of land can have a mix of uses: residential, commercial, recreational, and open space designed with variable lot sizes and densities. Industrial developments can also be planned as PUDs. PUDs must conform to certain standards as promulgated by the local planning agency and must be approved by it, but within the restrictions the planner has wide latitude in how the site is developed.

The standards for PUDs include such things as the uses permitted, total floor area ratio (ratio of developed floor space to land area), the amount of open space required, the parking spaces required, living space ratio (open space less parking space), maximum heights, and setbacks at the perimeter.

Planned unit developments offer many advantages. They make more efficient use of land by grouping compatible uses without the sometimes unnecessary requirements of setback regulations in zoning ordinances. This grouping allows the extra land to be given over to open space or common use areas. They also provide a variety of housing options, from single family detached to row houses to high-rise apartments and condominiums. PUDs also recapture some of the diversity and variety of urban living that many people find desirable.

C. The Effects of Development Patterns on Social Behavior

The physical environment affects human behavior. This is true at any scale, from the plan of a city to the arrangement of furniture in a room. A great deal of research has been conducted in the field of environmental psychology; some of the results remain inconclusive while other theories have been shown to provide a reliable basis for making design decisions. The following principles are ones with which you should be familiar.

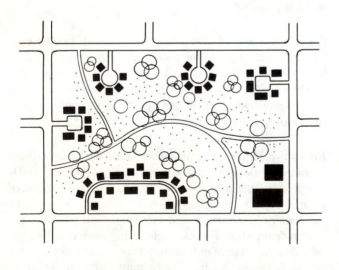

Figure 2.5 Superblock Concept

Density is one characteristic of human settlements that has received a great deal of attention. It refers to the number of people per unit of area. For example, a city might be referred to as having a density of 5000 people per acre. Density refers only to a ratio, not the total number of people or how they are distributed. The 5000 people could be evenly distributed over the acre or they could all be housed in a few high-rise buildings in one part of the land parcel.

For a long time, high density was equated with undesirable living conditions. However, research has shown that there is much more involved when talking about density. The first consideration is that density should not be confused with crowding. Four people sharing a bedroom would be crowding, but if each of the same four people had adequate personal space while still occupying the same overall living space (the same density) they probably would not be crowded.

The perception of crowding also depends on cultural influences and circumstances. Some cultures find living in closer proximity to one another normal and desirable while people from other cultures would find the same density crowded. In a similar way, being densely packed in a restaurant for a few hours would not seem crowded to most people, but trying to relax on a park bench at the same density would be uncomfortable. Regardless of the interpretation of density, however, there are limits to the density under which people can comfortably live, work, and play. Studies have shown that excessive density can cause poor physical and mental health and spawn a variety of antisocial behavior.

Different cultures and socio-economic groups respond to and use physical environments differently. The entire range of a particular group's pattern of living, working, playing, and socializing may flourish under one kind of environment and suffer under another. Taking cultural and social differences into account when designing housing and other facilities is critical to a successful project.

Regardless of the specific culture of a group, all people need and want social interaction with their family, friends, neighbors, and other groups to which they belong. A building, neighborhood, or city can promote or hinder such interaction. Providing spaces to gather, to watch other people, to cross paths, and to meet informally is a way the architect can encourage this vital part of human life. Spaces, buildings, rooms, and even furniture can be considered sociopetal if they tend to bring people together. A group of chairs facing each other, circular gathering spaces, and radial street plans are examples of sociopetal environments. Sociofugal refers to conditions which do just the opposite; they tend to discourage interaction or social contact.

In addition to interaction, people also need a place they can call their own, whether it is their house, a seat at a conference table, or one end of a park bench. This is the concept of *territoriality* and is a fundamental part of animal behavior (humans included). When someone personalizes a desk at the office with family pictures, plants, individual coffee mugs, and the like, he or she is staking a claim to a personal territory, small and temporary as it may be. In a more permanent living environment, such as a house or apartment, territorial boundaries are provided by walls, fences, and property lines. Often, boundaries are more subtle. A street, a row of trees, or something very small such as a change in level may serve to define a person's or group's territory.

Closely related to territoriality is the concept of *personal spaces* that surround each individual. This idea, proposed by Edward Hall, states that there are four basic distances that can be used to study human behavior and serve as a guide for designing environments. The actual dimensions of the four distances vary with the circumstances and with cultural and social differences, but they always exist. The architect should be aware of the fact of personal distance needs and design accordingly, as forcing people closer together than the situation suggests can have a negative effect on them.

The closest is *intimate distance*. This ranges from physical contact to about 6 to 18 inches. People only allow other people to come within this distance under special conditions. If forced this close together, as on a crowded bus, people have other defense mechanisms, such as avoiding eye contact, to minimize the effect of the physical contact.

The next distance is the *personal distance*, from about 1 1/2 feet to 2 1/2 feet (for some cultures) or more. If given the choice, people will maintain this distance between themselves and other people.

Social distance is the next invisible sphere, ranging from about 4 feet to 12 feet. This is the distance at which most impersonal business, work, and other interaction takes place between strangers or in more formal situations.

Public distance is the farthest, ranging from about 12 feet outward. The greatest amount of formality can be achieved at this distance. In addition, this distance allows people to escape if they sense physical danger from another person.

A final principle concerning the effects of development patterns on social behavior is *diversity*. The human animal needs a diverse and stimulating environment. In a monotonous urban setting, community, or building people tend to become depressed, become irritated, or suffer some other type of negative influence. Over a long period of time, living in a dull, non-stimulating environment can even affect personality development.

2 COMMUNITY INFLUENCES ON DESIGN

A. Catchment Areas

Nearly all land development is dependent on or affected by some surrounding base of population within a geographical region. The term used to describe this is the *catchment area*. For example, the developer of a grocery store bases the decision to build on the number of people within a certain distance from the proposed store location. The population within this catchment area is the primary market for the services of the store. In a similar way, a school district is the catchment area for a particular school building.

The boundaries of catchment areas may be determined by physical features such as a highway or river, by artificial political boundaries such as a city line or school district limit, or by nebulous demarcations such as the division between two ethnic neighborhoods. Often, as seen in the example above, when site location studies are being made, a developer knows that a certain number of people must reside within a specified distance from the proposed site to make the project economically feasible. By using population information from census data or other types of surveys, a determination can be quickly made to see if the catchment area will support the land development.

The size and boundaries of a catchment area are dependent on several factors. A residential catchment area, for example, may increase in size with an increase in the population of the surroundings, either through a geographical expansion or with the construction of new housing. Conversely, the expansion of an employment center may create the demand for more workers and increase the employment catchment area. Boundaries are often determined by the availability of transportation. A convenience store that depends on neighborhood customers will have closer boundaries than a shopping center accessible by major highways.

In many cases, the composition of a catchment area must be known in some detail in order to make development decisions. Simple gross population numbers are not enough. The developer of a high-end retail store needs to know how many people or families with an average income over a particular amount reside within a certain distance from the store site. A school district would have to know how many children of a particular age reside within an area. This kind of information is usually available from census data and local planning agencies.

B. Accessibility to Transportation

Transportation of all types is critical to the selection and development of a building site. This is true at all scales, from accessibility by major freeways to the individual road system and pedestrian paths around a small site. Something as simple as a one-way street that makes turning into a site from one direction difficult or impossible may be enough to render the property undesirable for some uses.

The following considerations should be examined when analyzing a site for development.

1. Is there an adequate highway system to bring the catchment area population to the site?

2. Are there adequate traffic counts for businesses that depend on drive-by trade?

3. Would the development create additional traffic that would overload the existing road system or require new roads to be built or expanded?

4. Is there adequate truck access for servicing the site?

5. Does the surrounding transportation network create an undesirable environment for the development? For example, a small site bounded by two freeways may be too noisy for an apartment building.

6. Is there safe and convenient pedestrian access to the site if required?

7. Are there public transportation lines nearby? How can people get from the mass transit stops to the site?

8. Are rail lines available for industrial projects?

C. Neighborhoods

Any development project is an intimate part of the area in which it is located. Architects must be sensitive to the existing fabric of a neighborhood that may influence how a project is designed as well as the impact the project may have on the surroundings. A *neighborhood* can be defined as a relatively small area in which a number of people live who share similar needs and desires in housing, social activities, and other aspects of day-to-day living.

The original concept of the neighborhood as a part of city planning was developed by Clarence Perry in 1929.

Although his ideas had physical design implications, they were primarily proposed as a way of bringing people together to discuss common problems and to become involved in the planning process. He felt that the ideal way to do this was to base the neighborhood on an area within walking distance to an elementary school, which would serve as the community center of neighborhood activity. Additionally, Perry proposed that the district be surrounded by major streets rather than intersected with them.

The neighborhood has become the basic planning unit for contemporary American urban design. This is partly due to the need for a manageable size on which to base city planning and partly to the increased importance placed on citizen participation in the planning process, an idea suggested by Clarence Perry. The neighborhood is the scale most people can readily understand and identify with, the part of a city that people come in contact with on a daily basis and that influences their life the most.

Site development must be sensitive to the existing neighborhood. This can include such criteria as respecting pedestrian paths, maintaining the size and scale of the surrounding buildings, using similar or compatible materials, not creating uses that conflict with the surroundings, respecting views and access to important structures in the area, and trying to fit within the general context of the district.

D. Public Facilities

Public facilities include such places as schools, shops, fire stations, churches, post offices, and recreational centers. Their availability, location, and relative importance in a neighborhood can affect how a site is developed. For example, if a church is the center of social activity in a neighborhood, the designer should maintain easy access to it, surrounding development should be subordinate or compatible with it, and the designer should give consideration to maintaining views or enhancing its prominence in the community. In another case, the path from a school to a recreation center may have special importance. The neighborhood may want the link maintained and improved by any new building along the way.

3 LAND ANALYSIS

A. Topography

A study of a site's topography is an important part of environmental analysis since existing land conditions affect how development can take place, what modifications need to be made, and what costs might be involved. Topography describes the surface features of land. Commonly used in land planning and architectural site development, a topographic map shows the slope and contour of the land as well as other natural and man-made features.

A topographic map is developed from a topographic survey by a land surveyor. In addition to information on the contours of a site, a survey will also include such data as property boundaries, existing buildings, utility poles, roads and other man-made features, trees and other natural features like rock outcroppings and heavy vegetation. Figure 2.6 shows a simplified example of a topographic map.

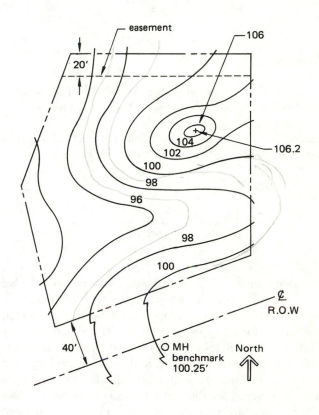

Figure 2.6 Topographic Map

The *contour lines* on a map are a graphic way to show the elevations of the land in a plan view and are used to make a slope analysis to determine the suitability of the land for various uses. Each contour line represents a continuous line of equal elevation above some reference bench mark. The *contour interval* is the vertical distance between adjacent contour lines. The contour interval on a map will vary depending on the steepness of the slope, the scale of the map, and the amount of detail required. Many large-scale maps of individual building sites use 1-, 2-, or 5-foot contour intervals, while small-scale maps of large regions may use 20- or

40-foot contours. The relationship between a contour map and a section through the contours is illustrated in Figure 2.7.

Knowing the contour interval and the horizontal distance between any two contour lines, you can determine the slope of the land at that point. The slope is represented in percent, each percent being one foot of vertical rise for every 100 feet of horizontal distance. Thus, a slope of 6 1/2 percent would rise (or drop) 6 1/2 feet within 100 feet.

The slope is found by using the formula:

$$G = \frac{d}{L}(100) \qquad 2.1$$

Example 2.1

Find the slope between points A and B in Figure 2.7 if the horizontal distance between them is 80 feet.

Since the contour interval is 5 feet, the vertical distance between the two points is 15 feet. The slope is:

$$G = \frac{15}{80}(100)$$
$$= 19\%$$

For slope analysis, the existing contours can be divided into general categories according to their potential for various types of uses. Slopes from zero to 4 percent are usable for all types of intense activity and are easy to build on. Slopes from 4 to 10 percent are suitable for informal movement and outdoor activity and can also be built on without much difficulty. Slopes over 10 percent are difficult to climb or use for outdoor activity and are more difficult and expensive to build on. Depending on the condition of the soil, very steep slopes, over 25 percent, are subject to erosion and become more expensive to build on. Table 2.1 gives some recommended minimum and maximum slopes for various uses.

Respecting the natural contours and slope of the land is important not only from an ecological and aesthetic standpoint but also from an economic standpoint. Moving large quantities of earth costs money and removing from or bringing in soil to a site is not desirable. Ideally, the amount of earth cut away in grading operations should equal the amount required to fill in other portions of the site. Topography and the use of contours is described in more detail in Chapter 4.

Table 2.1
Recommended Grade Slopes for Various Uses

	Slopes in Percent		
	min.	preferred	max.
ground areas for drainage	2.0	4.0	
grass areas for recreation	2.0		3.0
paved parking areas	1.5	2.5	5.0
roads	0.5		8.0
sanitary sewers (depends on size)	0.5–1.5		
approach walks to buildings	1.0		4.0
landscaped slopes	2.0		50.0

B. Natural Features

Every site has natural features that may be either desirable or undesirable. A complete site analysis will include a study of these features.

A view analysis may be required to determine the most desirable ways to orient buildings, outdoor areas, and approaches to the buildings. Undesirable views can be minimized or blocked with landscaping or other man-made features.

Significant natural features such as rock outcroppings, cliffs, caves, and bogs should be identified to determine whether they must be avoided or can be used as positive design features in the site design.

Subsurface conditions of groundwater and rock must be known also. Sites with high water tables (about 6 to 8 feet below grade) can cause problems with excavations, foundations, utility placement, and landscaping. The water table is the level underground in which the soil is saturated with water. Generally, the water follows the slope of the grade above, but it may vary slightly. Boring logs will reveal whether groundwater is present and how deep it is.

Sites with a preponderance of rocks near the surface can be very difficult and expensive (sometimes impossible) to develop. Blasting is usually required, which can increase the site development costs significantly (and may not be allowed by city code restrictions).

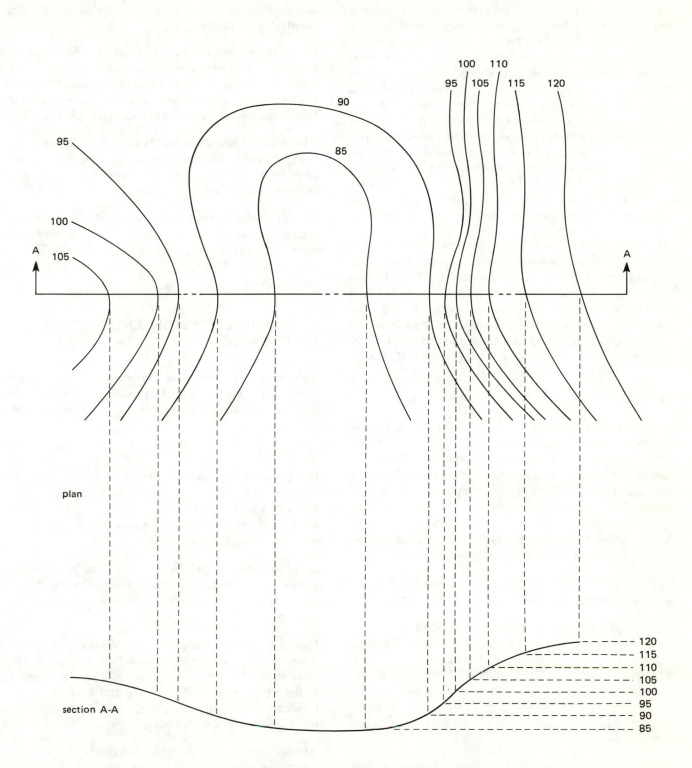

Figure 2.7 Representation of Land Slope with Contour Lines

C. Drainage

Every site has some type of natural drainage pattern that must be taken into account during design. In some cases the drainage may be relatively minor, consisting only of the runoff from the site itself and a small amount from adjacent sites. This type of drainage can easily be diverted around roads, parking lots, and buildings with curbs, culverts, and minor changes in the contours of the land. In other cases, major drainage paths such as gullies, dry gulches, or rivers may traverse the site. These will have a significant influence on potential site development since they must, in most cases, be maintained. Buildings need to be built away from them or bridge them so water flow is not restricted and potential damage is avoided. If modification to the contours is required, the changes must be done in such a way that the contours of the adjacent properties are not disturbed.

The development of a site may be so extensive that excessive runoff is created due to roof areas, roads, and parking lots. All of these increase the runoff coefficient, the fraction of total precipitation that is not absorbed into the ground. If the runoff is greater than the capacity of the natural or man-made drainage from the site, holding ponds must be constructed to temporarily collect site runoff and release it at a controlled rate.

D. Soil

Soil is the pulverized upper layer of the earth, formed by the erosion of rocks and plant remains and modified by living plants and organisms. Generally, the visible upper layer is topsoil, a mixture of mineral and organic material. The thickness of topsoil may range from just a few inches to a foot or more. Below this is a layer of mostly mineral material, which is above a layer of the fractured and weathered parent material of the soil above. Below all of these layers is solid bedrock.

Soil is classified according to grain size and as either organic or inorganic. The grain size classification is:

Gravel: particles over 2 millimeters in diameter.
Sands: particles from 0.05 to 2 millimeters in diameter, the finest grains just visible to the eye.
Silt: particles from 0.002 to 0.05 millimeters in diameter, the grains are invisible but can be felt as smooth.
Clay: particles under 0.002 millimeters in diameter, smooth and floury when dry, plastic and sticky when wet.

All soils are a combination of the types listed above, and any site analysis must include a subsurface investigation to determine the types of soil present as well as the water content. Some soils are unsuitable for certain uses, and layers of different soil types may create planes

of potential slippage or slides and make the land useless for development.

Gravels and *sands* are excellent for construction loads and drainage and for sewage drain fields, but they are unsuitable for landscaping.

Silt is stable when dry or damp but unstable when wet. It swells and heaves when frozen and compresses under load. Generally, building foundations and road bases must extend below it or be elastic enough to avoid damage. Some non-plastic silts are usable for lighter loads.

Clay expands when wet and is subject to slippage. It is poor for foundations unless it can be kept dry. It is also poor for landscaping and unsuitable for sewage drain fields or other types of drainage.

Peat and other organic material are excellent for landscaping but unsuitable for building foundations or road bases. Usually, these soils must be removed from the site and replaced with sands and gravels for foundations and roads.

4   TRANSPORTATION AND UTILITY INFLUENCES

This section reviews some general guidelines for analyzing the transportation and utilities servicing a site. Also review Chapter 4 for more detailed design criteria.

A. Roads

Roads provide a primary means of access to a site. Their availability and capacity may be prime determinants in whether and how a parcel of land can be developed. There are four basic categories of roads: local, collector, arterial, and expressway.

Local streets have the lowest capacity and provide direct access to building sites. They may be in the form of continuous grid or curvelinear systems or be cul-de-sacs or loops.

Collector streets connect local streets and arterial streets. They, of course, have a higher capacity than local streets but are usually not intended for through traffic. Intersections of collector and local roads may be controlled by stop signs, while intersections with arterial streets will be controlled with stop lights.

Arterial streets are intended as major, continuous circulation routes that carry large amounts of traffic on two or three lanes. They usually connect expressways. Parking on the street is typically not allowed and direct access from arterial streets to building sites should be avoided.

Expressways are limited access roads designed to move large volumes of traffic between, through, and around population centers. Intersections are made by various types of ramp systems, and pedestrian access is not allowed. Expressways have a major influence on the land due to the space they require and their noise and visual impact.

Site analysis must take into account the existing configuration of the street system and fit into the hierarchy of roads described above. Entrances and exits from the site must be planned to minimize congestion and dangerous intersections. Figure 2.8 illustrates some general guidelines for road layout.

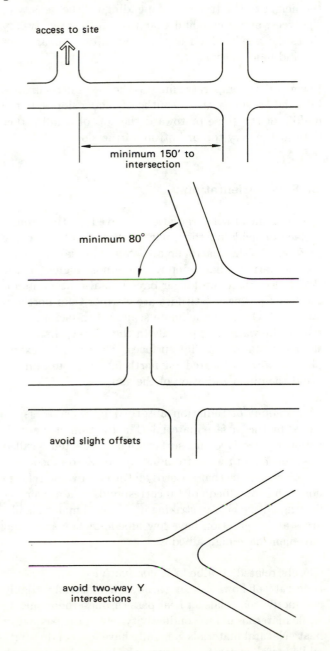

Figure 2.8 Guidelines for Road Layout at Intersections

Roads must be laid out both in the horizontal direction and the vertical direction, called horizontal alignment and vertical alignment, respectively. The straight sections of roads are called *tangents* and the curved portions are *arcs* of a circle so that a vehicle can be steered easily and safely. Simple curves with a uniform radius between tangents are preferred. There should generally be a minimum of 100 feet between curves in opposite directions and 200 feet between curves in the same direction. Multiple radius curves should be avoided.

Vertical alignment must be designed to provide a smooth transition between grade changes and to avoid overly steep grades. Depending on weather conditions and design speeds, streets should not have over a 10 percent grade.

B. Public Transit

The availability and location of public transit lines can influence site design. A site analysis should include a determination of the types of public access available, whether bus, subway, rail line, or taxi stop, and the location relative to the site. Building entrances and major site features should be located conveniently to the public transit. In large cities, site development may have to include provisions for public access to subway and rail lines.

C. Service Access

Service to a site includes provisions for truck loading, moving vans, and daily delivery services. Ideally, service access should be separate from automobile and pedestrian access to a site and a building. Space for large-truck turning and loading dock berths needs to be provided. Local zoning ordinances usually specify the number and size of loading berths, but generally they should be 10 to 12 feet wide, at least 40 feet long and have a 14 foot vertical clearance. A minimum turning radius of 60 should be provided unless some other maneuvering method is possible.

D. Utility Availability

Site analysis must determine the availability, location, and capacity of existing utilities. The development potential of a site is dependent on the availability of the necessary utilities of water, sanitary sewers, storm sewers, telephone service, gas service, electric service, and other public utilities. Utility lines that have to be extended from a considerable distance add greatly to the cost of development.

Generally, utility lines follow the street layout and right-of-way. Sanitary sewers, storm sewers, and water mains are located under the road while electric and communication lines are adjacent to the roads. Gas lines may either be under the road or next to it within the right-of-way. Utilities can also be located in easements, portions of privately owned land that public utility companies can use for the installation and maintenance of their lines.

When new services must be installed, sanitary and storm sewer location takes precedence because they must use the flow of gravity and therefore depend on the natural slope of the land. Collection systems drain to municipal disposal systems or to private, on-site treatment facilities.

E. Municipal Services

Depending on the location of the site, municipal services may include police protection, fire protection, trash removal, and street cleaning. The development site plan must provide access for these services, many of which require large land areas. For example, local fire protection officials may require an unobstructed strip of land around buildings to allow for fire fighting, in addition to suitable access roads from the street to the building. In some climates, adequate provisions must be made for snow removal or snow stacking.

5   CLIMATIC INFLUENCES

For any given site there are two aspects to climatic analysis, the *macroclimate* and the *microclimate*. The macroclimate refers to the overall climate of the region and is reflected in the weather data available from the National Weather Service. From this information a region can be classified as cool, temperate, hot-arid, or hot-humid. The microclimate refers to the site-specific modification of the macroclimate by such features as land slope, trees and other vegetation, bodies of water, and buildings.

The microclimate of a site can have a significant influence on its development; undesirable climatic effects can be minimized by careful planning and desirable effects can be used to enhance the comfort of the inhabitants.

A. Wind Patterns

Both prevailing wind patterns and microclimate wind effects must be studied during site analysis. Buildings can then be located to take advantage of breezes or to avoid cold winds. Wind on the top of a hill, for example, can be about 20 percent higher than on flat ground. On the leeward side of a hill, that side away from the wind direction, the wind will be less than on the windward side. Near large bodies of water, warm air rises over the warmer land during the day and causes a breeze from the water. At night the pattern may be reversed, when cold air flows down a hill and settles in low-lying regions causing pockets that remain colder than higher elevations during the first part of the day. On a large scale, this results in an inversion where warmer air holds colder air below, trapping pollution.

Wind patterns can be modified by buildings and trees. For a line of trees 50 to 150 feet deep, wind velocity can be reduced from 30 to 60 percent to a distance ten times the height of the tree line, depending on the density of the trees, and about half that to a distance of twenty times the tree height. Buildings can affect similar types of wind modification.

In general, in temperate climates the best microclimates for wind are on south- or southeast-facing slopes, in the middle of the slope or toward the top of a hill rather than at the very top or bottom of the slope.

B. Solar Orientation

The amount of solar radiation received on the ground surface depends on the angle of the sun's rays to the surface. At the macroclimate scale, this is why summer is warmer than winter; the sun is higher in the sky. (Also, there are longer days.) It also accounts for the fact that lower latitudes are warmer than northern latitudes. On a microclimate scale, south-facing slopes tend to be warmer, especially in the winter, than other slope orientations or flat surfaces. Ski runs, for example, are always located on north-facing mountains to avoid the direct radiation of the sun.

The amount of radiation absorbed or reflected is affected by the surface material. The fraction of the radiant energy received on a surface that is reflected is called the *albedo* and ranges from 0.0 to 1.0. Zero albedo is a flat black surface that absorbs all the energy and reflects none while an albedo of 1.0 corresponds to a mirror, reflecting all the energy striking it. Natural materials like grass and vegetation have low albedos while snow and pavement have high albedos.

Closely related to albedo is *conductivity*, which is the time rate of flow of heat through a material. Highly conductive materials let heat pass through them quickly while materials of low conductivity retard the passage of heat. Natural materials generally have low conductivity while metal, concrete, and masonry have relatively high conductivities.

Combined, albedo and conductivity affect the microclimate. Ground surfaces with low albedo and high conductivity tend to moderate and stabilize the microclimate because excess heat is quickly absorbed, stored, and released when the temperature drops. Surfaces with grass and other vegetation are cooler in hot weather for this reason. On the other hand, surfaces with high albedo and low conductivity, such as pavements or concentrations of buildings, are much hotter than the macroclimate would normally produce.

6   ECOLOGICAL CONSIDERATIONS

Ecology is the study of living organisms in relation to their environment. Applied to site development the word takes on a slightly broader meaning. There is, of course, the need to understand what impact construction will have on the surrounding natural environment. This concern has been codified in recent years with the requirement to file environmental impact statements that clearly define the effects of construction and how any detrimental effects may be mitigated. There is also the need to be cognizant of the impact of smaller-scale building on the surroundings, whether the environment is rural or in the heart of the city.

Some of the concerns that should be investigated during site analysis for semirural or rural development include the impact on natural landforms, water runoff, wildlife, and existing vegetation. The development should disturb the natural contours of the land as little as possible. Existing drainage patterns must be left intact and additional runoff caused by roofs and paving should not exceed the capacity of the existing drainage paths. The development should also not disturb existing ecological systems of plants and wildlife if possible.

For urban sites, slightly different concerns need to be studied. There is still the relationship of the building and its users to the surrounding environment, but the impact is more on man-made systems than on natural ecosystems. The development should minimize the production of noise, pollution, or other detrimental emissions. Building placement should avoid undesirable wind conditions, either on the site itself or around nearby buildings. The effect of a building on blocking sunlight from adjacent buildings and outdoor spaces should be studied and minimized when possible. Similarly, the development should avoid any possible annoying reflection or glare on neighboring buildings. Finally, the impact of development on the utility and transportation systems must be thoroughly understood.

7   LEGAL AND ECONOMIC INFLUENCES

In the United States today, legal regulations and economic conditions have a great influence on how land is developed. For example, most commercial, for-profit land owners attempt to maximize their return on investment while working within the legal constraints of zoning ordinances and other types of building regulations. This may dictate the best economic uses of the property, how much square footage must be built, and even the overall architectural form of the structure. An architect must have an understanding of these influences and how they affect site development and building design.

A. Zoning

The most common form of legal constraint on land development is zoning. Although human settlements have been informally separated into areas of different uses for centuries, it was not until the first part of the twentieth century that zoning took on legal status. It was originally an attempt to improve the problems of the rapidly expanding cities: crowding, factories being built too close to housing, and tall buildings blocking light and air.

The first zoning ordinance was passed in 1916 in New York City and was the first attempt by a municipal government to control the use and location of buildings throughout a city. Zoning began as a way of regulating land use, but today it has grown into one means of implementing planning policy.

Zoning is the division of a city or other governmental unit into districts and the regulation of the use of land and the location and bulk of buildings on property within those districts. Its legal basis is largely founded on the right of the state to protect the health, safety, and welfare of the public. Municipalities receive the power to zone through the states with enabling legislation.

Zoning primarily regulates the following things:

- the uses allowed on a parcel of land depending on the zoning district

- the area of the land that may be covered with buildings

- the bulk of the structures

- the distances the buildings must be set back from the property lines

- parking and loading space requirements

Other requirements, such as regulation of signs and bonuses for providing plazas and open space, may also be included. Although zoning is primarily used in cities, special types of zoning are sometimes used. These types may include rural zoning to separate agricultural uses from forestry or recreational use, flood plain zoning, airport zoning, and historic area zoning.

Uses are established with the zoning districts and are based on residential, commercial, and industrial occupancies with subdivisions within each of these. Residential zones may include, for example, single-family dwellings, low-density multifamily, and high-density multifamily dwellings. For each zoning district, a list of permissible uses is specified, with single-family zones being the most restrictive. Each zone may be used for the purposes listed for that zone and for any use listed in a less restrictive zone. For instance, a single-family house could be constructed within a dense business zone but probably would not be because of economic and aesthetic reasons.

The amount of land that can be covered is determined by the interrelationship of two zoning restrictions, floor area ratio and setbacks. *Floor area ratio* is the ratio of the gross floor area within a structure to the area of the lot on which it is situated. For example, if the floor area ratio is 1.0, and a lot is 75,000 square feet in area, the maximum permissible gross floor space is 75,000 square feet. Within the constraints of setbacks and bulk planes, this 75,000 square feet of floor space may be configured in any number of ways.

Figure 2.9 (a) shows a structure occupying only 50 percent of the ground area. If the floor area ratio (sometimes referred to as FAR) is 1.0, then a two-story building can be constructed.

Figures 2.9 (b) and 2.9 (c) illustrate two instances where the same floor area ratio can result in two different building forms. In Figure 2.9 (b), the building occupies only 25 percent ground area. If the FAR is 3.0, then a 12-story building can be erected. In Figure 2.9 (c), the building occupies 50 percent of the land so only six stories can be built. In both cases, the building area is three times the land area.

Floor area ratios must always be developed in relation to setbacks. A *setback* is the minimum distance a building must be placed from a property line. Setback distances usually vary depending on which property line is involved. The distance from the property line facing the street or the primary front of the property is known as the *front setback*, usually the greatest setback distance. The distance from the back of the lot is the *rear setback*, and the distance from the side property line is known as the *side setback*. In the example of Figure 2.9 (a), for instance, setbacks might preclude covering

50 percent of the site, so in order to get the maximum floor area ratio, the building would have to be more than two stories.

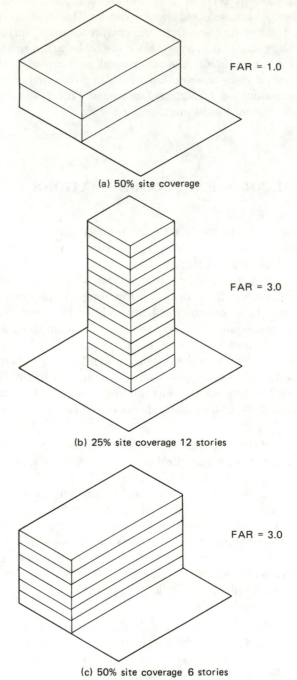

(a) 50% site coverage

(b) 25% site coverage 12 stories

(c) 50% site coverage 6 stories

Figure 2.9　Examples of Floor Area Ratios

In addition to affecting the use of floor area ratios, setbacks also have the effect of regulating the bulk of a building and how much space results between structures. Another common zoning tool is the bulk plane restriction. This sets up an imaginary inclined plane beginning at the lot line or the center of the street and sloping at a prescribed angle toward and over the lot.

The building cannot extend into this plane. The purpose is to ensure adequate light and air to neighboring properties and to the open space and streets around the land.

Sometimes, zoning ordinances will also place maximum limits on the number of stories of a building or the height in feet above grade level.

There are many instances when zoning restrictions create an undue hardship on a property owner or unusual conditions are not completely covered in a zoning ordinance. For these cases, the property owner can apply for a variance, which is a deviation from the zoning regulations. Municipalities have a board to which owners can describe their situation and appeal for a variance. A public hearing is a part of the process so nearby property owners or anyone with an interest can object to the appeal if they wish.

If a new zoning ordinance is being applied to existing development, there may be properties that contain non-conforming uses. These are allowed to remain unless the owner stops using the property in its original fashion, it is demolished, or it is destroyed by fire. Then, any new use must conform to the zoning requirements.

A zoning board may also grant a conditional use permit, which allows a non-conforming use or other violation of the zoning ordinance if the property owner meets certain restrictions. This is often done if the exception is in the public interest. For example, a zoning board may allow a temporary street fair in a location where it would normally be prohibited, or it might allow a church to violate a setback provision with the condition that other open space be provided for the community.

Refer to Chapter 4 for more information on zoning.

B. Easements and Rights of Way

An *easement* is the right of one party to use a portion of the land of another party in a particular way. It is a legal instrument and is normally recorded. There are many types of easements, one of the most common being a *utility easement*. This allows a utility company to install and maintain lines above or below the ground within the boundaries of the easement. Although the land belongs to the property owner, no permanent structures can be erected within the easement without permission from the party holding the easement.

Another type of easement is the *access easement*. If one parcel of land is not served by a public road and another parcel separates it from the street, an access easement may be granted, which allows the public and the owner of the inaccessible land the right to cross.

Other types of easements include *support easements* for the construction of common party walls between properties, *joint use easements* that allow two or more property owners to share a common feature such as a driveway, *scenic easements* that protect views and development in scenic areas, and *conservation easements* that limit land use in large areas. Scenic and conservation easements are often used by public agencies to control land use without the need to purchase large tracts of property.

A *right-of-way* is the legal right of one party or the public to traverse land belonging to another. In its most common form, a right-of-way refers to the public land used for streets and sidewalks. The boundary of a right-of-way usually corresponds to the property line of adjacent property owners. In most cases, the street occupies only a portion of the right-of-way; the remainder is used for sidewalks, landscaping, and utilities. An access easement as described above creates a private or public right-of-way.

C. Deed Restrictions

Deeds to property can contain provisions that restrict the use of the property by the buyer. These are called *restrictive covenants* and are legal and enforceable if they are reasonable and in the public interest. It is quite common for the developer of a large tract of land that is being subdivided to include restrictive covenants in the deeds. They may include such limitations as setbacks, minimum square footage of houses, the types of materials that can and cannot be used on the exterior, and similar provisions.

Since the covenants are in the deed, they are known to the potential buyer before purchase so the buyer can decide not to purchase if the covenants are not acceptable. Restrictive covenants are often used in residential subdivisions to maintain a desired uniformity of appearance, site development, and quality of construction. Most deed restrictions, however, are generally established for a certain period of years such as 10, 15, 20, or 30 years.

D. Land Values

As part of the overall economic analysis of a site for potential development (or adaptive reuse of an existing building), the cost of the property is vital in making a decision concerning site selection. In addition to land acquisition costs, there are also costs of site improvements, building construction, appraisal, financing, professional fees, permits, and maintenance of the completed structure. If all of these cannot be paid off in a reasonable amount of time and yield a profit to the owner or developer, the site is probably a poor economic choice.

Land values are generally based on location, potential profit-making use, and local market conditions, which includes demand for the land. Location includes such things as a potential surrounding market area, population density in the region, special features of the site such as being waterfront property, and proximity to transportation and utilities, which are especially important to residential and industrial development. Land values are based on the concept of "highest and best use," which means that the property is to be used and developed in such a way as to yield the highest return on investment. Property that does not do this is said to be underdeveloped.

There are three basic ways land is valued. A fairly common technique is the market approach. The surrounding neighborhood or region is investigated to find properties that have recently sold or are on the market that are similar to the property being valued. Except for adjustments to reflect the unique nature of the property, it is assumed to have the same value. For example, if three nearby house lots in a subdivision recently sold for around $40,000 and they were all about the same size, then a fourth lot of similar size would also be valued at about $40,000. Quite often, the value is based on a unit quantity that can more easily be applied to another property that is not exactly the same. Land is commonly assigned a value per square foot or per acre and buildings are often valued at a cost per square foot. The assumed value of another property can then be determined simply by multiplying the current market value per square foot times the area of the property being evaluated.

The second method is the *income approach*. Here, the basis is the potential the property has to yield a profit (income). The potential income is estimated (allowing for vacancies and credit losses) and then various expenses such as taxes, insurance, and maintenance are deducted. Since potential income is usually figured on a yearly basis, this amount must be capitalized to estimate the current, total value of the property.

The third method is the *cost approach*. With this method, the value of the land is estimated at its highest and best use. Then, the cost to replace the building or add improvements is calculated. The estimated accrued depreciation is figured and subtracted from the replacement cost or cost of the improvements. This adjusted amount is then added to the land value to give the total value of the property.

E. Tax Structure

As with most aspects of life, the taxes to which a developer is subject can influence whether a project is undertaken and can affect how the site is developed. Although the subject is very complicated, taxes become an ongoing operating cost of a development and can be estimated fairly easily by knowing the tax rate and what it is based on. Many tax rates are based on a mill levy on the assessed valuation of a piece of property. A mill is one-thousandth of a dollar or one-tenth of a cent. The assessed valuation is a percentage of the actual value of the property, and the percentage is set by the taxing authority.

Example 2.2

The assessed valuation of developed property is based on 19 percent of actual value and the mill levy is 0.04931. If a developed piece of property is estimated to have an actual valuation of 150,000, what will the yearly tax be?

The assessed value is

$$0.19 \times 150,000 = \$28,500$$

The yearly tax will be

$$0.04931 \times 28,500 = \$1405$$

Taxing authorities may offer various types of tax incentives to developers as a way of implementing public policy. For instance, tax credits may be given for renovating historic structures as a way of encouraging historic preservation. New business may be encouraged to move to a city by reduction or elimination of taxes for a certain time period. In any case, tax incentives may turn an otherwise uneconomical project into a viable one.

SAMPLE QUESTIONS

1. The accompanying illustration shows a portion of a recreation area. Which area would be best for locating a restaurant and visitors center?

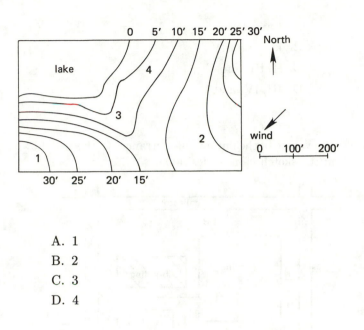

    A. 1

    B. 2

    C. 3

    D. 4

2. The owner of the lot shown in the figure wants to develop a building with the maximum allowable gross square footage. If the FAR is 2.0, how many stories will the building have to be?

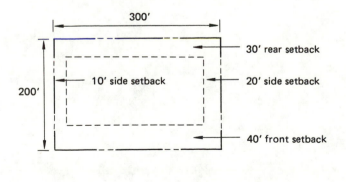

    A. 2 stories

    B. 3 stories

    C. 4 stories

    D. 5 stories

3. Much contemporary city planning in the United States is a result of:

  I. the Columbian Exposition of 1893

  II. the Ordinance of 1785

  III. L'Enfant's plan of Washington

  IV. Garnier's Cité Industrielle

  V. the Industrial Revolution

    A. I, III, and V

    B. I, II, and IV

    C. I, II, IV, and V

    D. all of the above

4. Which of the following would probably not be considered an element of a city's image?

    A. a group of houses

    B. a freeway

    C. a neighbor hangout bar

    D. an area with a high concentration of hospitals

5. Social contact and interaction in a picnic pavilion would be promoted most by which of the following design decisions?

    A. making the dimensions of the pavilion small enough so the anticipated number of users would cross into each other's "personal distance"

    B. designing benches around the support columns so people would have a place to sit and talk

    C. organizing the cooking and serving area distinct from the dining area and entrance

    D. providing an informal variety of spaces of different sizes, locations, and uses

6. If the contour interval on the map shown is two feet, what is the slope between points A and B?

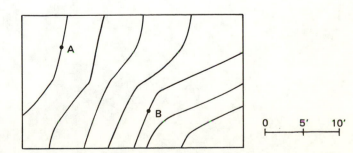

A. 27 percent

B. 53 percent

C. 67 percent

D. not enough information is given to answer

7. A speculative office building probably would not be built if the developer discovered that:

    A. all of the catchment area was not served by arterial streets

    B. the site consisted of mostly sandy soil with a 6-foot top layer of expansive clay

    C. the vacancy rate of office space in the city was three times the national average

    D. the neighborhood community objected to the sight of parking lots

8. Which of the following cause the most foundation problems?

    A. extensive underground rock formations just below the surface

    B. a 5-foot water table

    C. expansive clay and organic soil

    D. all of the above

9. In planning a new building, an architect would have to look at regulations other than the zoning ordinance to find a requirement for the following:

I.   the width of loading berths

II.   the required size of utility easements

III.   minimum lot size

IV.   the size of the parking area

V.   what roof coverings are permissible

    A. I and IV

    B. I, II, and IV

    C. II, III, and V

    D. III, IV, and V

10. Which of the automobile entrances to the site shown in the sketch is most desirable?

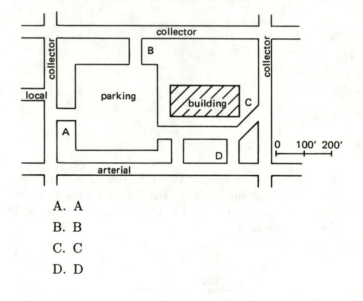

    A. A

    B. B

    C. C

    D. D

3 PRE-DESIGN— BUILDING PROGRAMMING

Architectural programming is a process that seeks to analyze and define an architectural problem along with the requirements that must be met in its physical solution. It is a process of analysis, where design is a process of synthesis once the problem is clearly defined. The process can apply to an individual space or room, a building, or an entire complex of structures.

As building problems have become more complex and construction costs higher, determining the precise needs of the client has become more important than ever before. Programming helps the client understand the real problem and provides a sound basis for making design decisions. Sometimes it is provided by the architect as part of the entire range of design services, and other times it is performed as a separate service.

Thorough programming includes a wide range of information. In addition to stating the goals and objectives of the client, a program report contains a site analysis, aesthetic considerations, space needs, adjacency requirements, organizing concepts, outdoor space needs, codes, budgeting demands, and scheduling limitations. Refer to Chapters 2 and 4 for a review of site analysis, including soil and climatic investigation.

1 FUNCTIONAL REQUIREMENTS

Of all programming information, the amount of space and the relationships between spaces are two of the primary factors in determining building size and configuration. In addition to the primary function of a building in housing a specific use, there are always support spaces required that add to the overall size. These include such areas as mechanical rooms, toilet rooms, storage, and circulation space.

A. Determining Space and Volume Needs

Space needs are determined in a number of ways. Often, when programming is begun, the client will have a list of the required square footages for the new facility in addition to special height requirements. These may be based on the client's past experience or on corporate space standards, or they may simply be a list of what currently exists. For example, space standards of a corporation may dictate that a senior manager have a 225-square-foot office while a junior manager be allotted 150 square feet.

These types of requirements may provide a valid basis for developing space needs or they may be arbitrary and subject to review during programming. Where square footages are not defined by one of these methods, space for a particular use is determined in one of three ways: by the number of people that must be accommodated, by an object or piece of equipment, or by a specific activity that has its own, clearly specified space needs.

People engaged in a particular activity most commonly define the space required. For example, a student sitting in a classroom needs about 15 to 20 square feet. This includes space for actually sitting in a chair in addition to the space required for circulating within the classroom and space for the teacher's desk and shelving. An office worker needs from 100 to 250 square feet, depending on whether the employee is housed in a private office or is part of an open office plan. This space requirement also includes room to circulate around the desk and may include space for visitors' chairs, personal files, and the like.

Through experience and detailed analysis, general guidelines for space requirements for various types of uses have been developed and are commonly used. A representative sample of these is shown in Table 3.1. Occasionally, space needs can be based on something other than the number of people but something which is directly related to the occupancy. For instance, preliminary planning of a hospital may be based on an area per bed, or library space can be estimated based on the number of books.

Table 3.1
Some Common Space Planning Guidelines

offices	100–250	net sq. ft. per person
restaurant dining	15–18	net sq. ft. per seat
restaurant kitchens	3.6–5	net sq. ft. per seat
hotel (1.5 persons/room)	550–600	gross sq. ft. per room
library reading room	20–35	net sq. ft. per person
book stacks	0.08	net sq. ft. per bound volume
theaters with fixed seats	7.5	net sq. ft. per person
assembly areas; movable seats	15	net sq. ft. per person
theater lobbies	30%	of seating area
classrooms	15–20	net sq. ft. per student
stores	30–50	net sq. ft. per person

Whichever way it is done, the number of people that must be accommodated is determined and multiplied by the square footage per person. However, this only includes the space needed for the specific activity, not the space required to connect several rooms or spaces or for support areas such as mechanical rooms. These must be added to the basic area requirements.

The second way space needs are determined is by the size of an object or piece of equipment. The size of a printing press, for example, partially determines the area of a press room. Automobile sizes determine the space needs for parking garages.

The third way space needs are defined is through a built-in set of rules or customs related to the activity itself. Sports facilities are examples of this method. A basketball court must be a certain size regardless of the number of spectators present, although the seating capacity would add to the total space required. A courtroom is an example of an activity where the procedures and customs of a process (the trial) dictate an arrangement of human activity and spacing of individual areas in the courtroom that only partially depend on the number of people.

B. Determining Total Building Area

The areas determined with one of the methods described above result in the net area of a facility. As mentioned, these areas do not include general circulation space between rooms, mechanical rooms, stairways, elevator and mechanical shafts, electrical and telephone equipment rooms, wall and structural thicknesses, and other spaces not directly housing the primary activities of the building. Sometimes the net area is referred to as the net assignable area and the secondary spaces are referred to as the unassigned areas.

The sum of the net area and these ancillary areas gives the gross building area. The ratio of the two figures is called the *net-to-gross* ratio and is often referred to as the *efficiency* of the building. Efficiency depends on the type of occupancy and how well it is planned. A hospital that contains many small rooms and a great number of large corridors will have a much lower efficiency ratio than a factory where the majority of space is devoted to production areas and very little to corridors and other secondary spaces.

Generally, net-to-gross ratios range from 60 to 80 percent, with some uses more or less efficient than these numbers. A list of some common efficiency ratios is shown in Table 3.2. In some cases, the client may dictate the net-to-gross ratio that must be met by the architect's design. This is usually the case where the efficiency is related to the amount of floor space that can be leased, such as in a retail mall or a speculative office building. Increasing the efficiency of a building is usually done by careful layout of the building's circulation plan. A corridor that serves rooms on both sides of it, for example, is much more efficient than one that only serves rooms on one side.

Table 3.2
Some Common Efficiency Ratios

offices	0.75–0.80
retail stores	0.75
restaurants	0.65–0.70
public libraries	0.75–0.80
museums	0.83
theaters	0.60–0.75
hospitals	0.50–0.65

Once the net square footage is determined and the appropriate efficiency ratio established (or estimated), the gross area of the building is calculated by dividing the net square footage by the net-to-gross (efficiency) ratio.

Example 3.1

The net assignable area of a small office building has been programmed as 65,000 square feet. If the efficiency ratio is estimated to be 73%, what gross area should be planned for?

$$\text{gross area} = \frac{65,000}{0.73}$$
$$= 89,000 \text{ square feet}$$

The design portion of the A.R.E. often requires that you provide various unassignable spaces within the context of the problem without giving you the square footages. You are expected to make a reasonable allowance for mechanical rooms, toilet rooms, elevators, and the like if they are not specifically listed in the program. Table 3.3 lists some typical space requirements with which you should be familiar for projects of the size and type normally found in the design portion of the exam.

C. Determining Space Relationships

Spaces must not only be the correct size for the activity they support, but they also must be located near other spaces with which they share some functional relationship. Programming identifies these relationships and assigns a hierarchy of importance to them. The relationships are usually recorded in a matrix format or graphically as adjacency diagrams. See Figure 3.1.

Table 3.3
Space Requirements for Estimating Non-assignable Areas

mechanical rooms, total	5%–9% of gross building area
heating, boiler rooms	3%–5% of gross building area
heating, forced air	4%–8% of gross building area
fan rooms	3%–7% of gross building area
vertical duct space	3–4 sq. ft. per 1000 sq. ft. of floor space available
toilets	50 sq. ft. per water closet
water closets	1 per 15 people up to 55; 1 per 40 people over 55
urinals	Substitute one for each water closet, but total water closets cannot be reduced less than 2/3 of the number required
lavatories	1 per 15 people for offices and public buildings up to 60 people
	1 per 100 people for public assembly use
hydraulic elevator, 2000 lb	7'4'' wide by 6'0'' deep
elevator lobby space	6'0'' deep
main corridors	5 to 7 feet
exit corridors	4'0''; 44 inches minimum by code
monumental stairs	5 to 8 feet
exit stairs	4'0''; 44 inches minimum by code

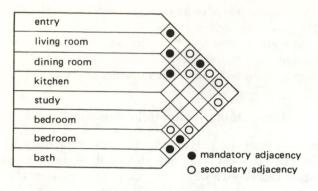

(a) adjacency matrix

● mandatory adjacency
○ secondary adjacency

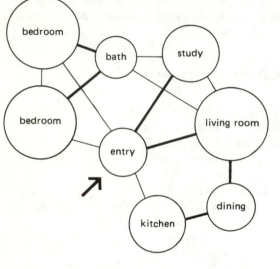

(b) adjacency diagram

Figure 3.1 Methods of Recording Space Relationships

There are three basic types of adjacency needs: people, products, and information. Each type implies a different kind of physical design response. Two or more spaces may need to be physically adjacent or located very close to one another when people need face-to-face contact or when people move from one area to another as part of the building's use. For example, the entry to a theater, the lobby, and the theater space have a particular functional requirement for being arranged the way they are. Because of the normal flow of people, they must be located adjacent to one another. With other relationships, two spaces may simply need to have access to one another, but this can be with a corridor or through another intervening space rather than with direct adjacency.

Products, equipment, or other objects may move between spaces and require another type of adjacency. The spaces themselves may not have to be close to one another but the movement of objects must be facilitated. Dumb waiters, pneumatic tubes, assembly lines, and other types of conveying systems can connect spaces of this type.

Finally, there may only be a requirement that people in different spaces exchange information. The adjacency may then be entirely electronic or with paper-moving systems. Although this is quite frequently the situation, personal, informal, human contact may be advantages for other reasons.

The programmer analyzes various types of adjacency requirements and verifies them with the client. Since every desirable relationship can seldom be accommodated, the ones that are mandatory need to be identified separately from the ones that are highly desirable or simply useful.

2 DESIGN CONSIDERATIONS

During programming, general concepts are developed as a response to the goals and needs of the client. These programmatic concepts are statements about functional solutions to the client's performance requirements. They differ from later design concepts because no attempt at actual physical solutions is made during programming; programmatic concepts guide the later development of design concepts. For example, a programmatic concept might be that a facility should be easily expandable by 20 percent every three years. Exactly how that would happen with a building would be developed as a design concept. It might take the form of a linear building that could be extended by a simple addition to one wing. Some of the more common design considerations that must be addressed during programming are outlined in the following sections.

A. Organization Concepts

The functional needs of a particular type of building most often influence how the physical environment is organized. At other times, the client's goal, the site, the desired symbolism, or additional factors suggest the organization pattern. There are six fundamental organization concepts: linear, axial, grid, central, radial, and clustered. These are shown diagrammatically in Figure 3.2.

Linear organizations consist of a series of spaces or buildings that are placed in a single line. The spaces can be identical or of different sizes and shapes, but they always relate to a unifying line, usually a path of circulation. A linear organization is very adaptable; it can be straight, bent, or curved to meet the requirements of the client, the site, solar orientation, or construction. It is easily expandable and can be built in a modular configuration if desired.

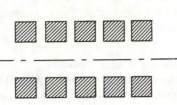

(a) linear

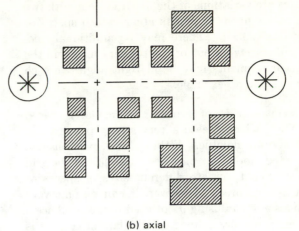

(b) axial

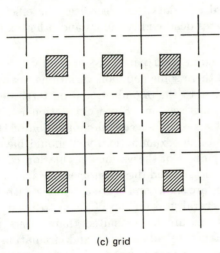

(c) grid

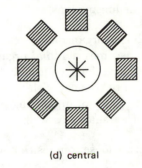

(d) central

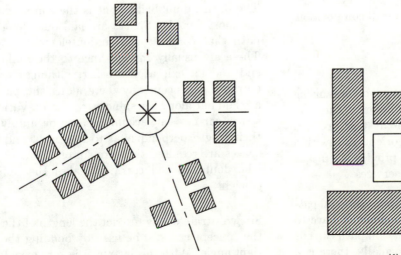

(e) radial

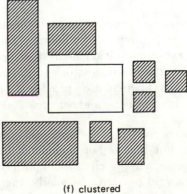

(f) clustered

Figure 3.2 Organization Concepts

PROFESSIONAL PUBLICATIONS ● Belmont, CA

Axial plans are variations of the linear system with two or more major linear segments about which spaces or buildings are placed. There may be additional, secondary paths growing out of the primary axes and the major linear segments may be at right angles to each other or at some other angle.

Grid systems consist of two sets of regularly spaced parallel lines, which create a very strong pattern and one that is quite flexible. Within a grid, portions can be subtracted, added, or modified. The size of the grid can be changed to create different sizes of spaces or to define special areas. However, it can become very monotonous and confusing if not used properly. Since a grid system is usually defined by circulation paths, it is more appropriate for very large buildings and building complexes where a great deal of circulation is required.

Central organizations are based on one space or point about which secondary elements are placed. It is usually a very formal method of organizing spaces or buildings and inherently places the primary emphasis on the central space. Central organizations are often used in conjunction with axial or linear plans.

When more than one linear organization extends from a centralized point, it becomes a *radial* organization. Radial plans have a central focus but also have the ability to extend outward to connect with other spaces, or for expansion. These types of organizing plans can be circular or assume other shapes as well.

Clustered organizations are loose compositions of spaces or buildings related around a path, axis, or central space, or simply grouped together. The general image is one of informality. Clusters are very adaptable to requirements for different sizes of spaces and they are easy to add onto without disrupting the overall composition.

B. Circulation Patterns

Circulation patterns are primary ways of organizing spaces, buildings, and groups of buildings. They are vital to the efficient organization of a structure and provide people with their strongest orientation within an environment. Paths of circulation provide the means to move people, cars, products, and services.

Circulation is directly related to the organizational pattern of a building, but it does not necessarily have to mimic it. For example, a major circulation path can cut diagonally across a grid pattern. Normally, there is a hierarchy of paths. Major routes connect major spaces or become spaces themselves and have secondary paths branching from them. Different sizes and types of circulation are important for accommodating varying capacities and for providing an orientation device for people using them.

Circulation for different functions may need to be separated as well. In a government building, one set of halls for the public may be separated from the internal set of corridors for the workers. A jail may have a secure passage for moving prisoners completely separate from other areas of public movement.

Establishing and maintaining a simple, efficient, and coherent circulation scheme is critical to successfully completing the design portion of the A.R.E. One of the common mistakes is to let the arranging of spaces according to the adjacency requirements take over your design and to connect them with a circulation path as an afterthought. You are then left with a maze of awkward corridors that decreases the efficiency ratio and creates dead end corridors and other exiting problems.

All circulation paths are linear by their very nature, but there some common variations, many of which are similar to the organizational patterns described in the previous section. Since circulation is such an important aspect of successful completion of the design portion of the examination, you should have a good mental picture of the various circulation concepts and the advantages and disadvantages of each. Five basic patterns are shown in Figure 3.3, along with a hypothetical structural grid on top of them to illustrate how some patterns are better suited than others to integration of structure, adjacencies, and circulation system. Also remember that mechanical services can easily follow a logical circulation system.

The linear, dumbbell layout is the simplest and one of the most flexible. Spaces are laid out along a straight path that connects two major elements at the ends. These are usually the entrance to the building at one end and an exit at the other, although the primary entrance can occur anywhere along the path. Spaces are laid out along the spine as required. Various sizes of spaces can be easily accommodated by simply extending their length perpendicular to the path, and if outdoor spaces are required they are simply located as needed. The double-loaded corridor makes the building very efficient.

Site constraints may restrict the length of the spine, but the concept can still be used by bending the path at a right angle. With this layout, it is very easy to establish a regular, one-way structural grid perpendicular to the direction of the path. Simply extending the length of a bay can accommodate larger spaces as the program requires.

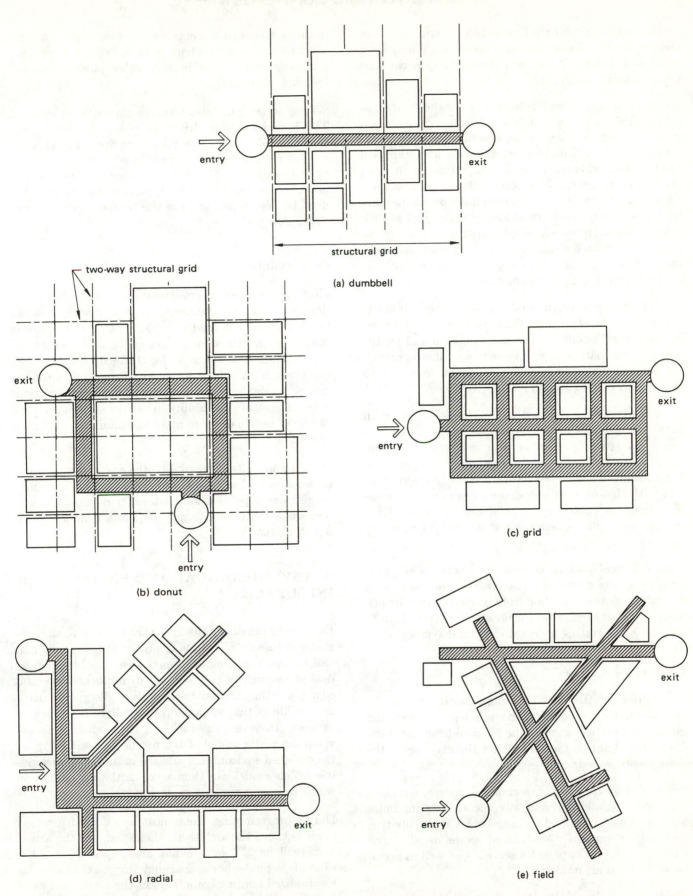

Figure 3.3 Circulation Patterns

Conversely, eliminating a line or two of structure gives you the location for a very large space and a long-span structural system. A two-way structural grid can also be used with this layout.

Making a complete loop results in a doughnut configuration. This is also very efficient because it provides a double-loaded corridor and automatically makes a continuous exit way. Building entries, exits, and stairways can be placed wherever needed. Spaces that do not need exterior exposure can be placed in the middle. Various sizes of spaces are easily accommodated on the perimeter because they can be expanded outward just as with the dumbbell layout. A simple structural grid can be coordinated with the space layout as required. A doughnut pattern is good for square or nearly square sites and for buildings that must be compact.

A grid system is often used for very large buildings where access must be provided to many internal spaces. For the small buildings that are usually found on the A.R.E. examination, a grid system is seldom appropriate because it results in a very inefficient layout, with single spaces being surrounded by corridors.

A radial layout is oriented on one major space with paths extending from this central area. The radial configuration generally requires a large site and is more appropriate for large buildings or building complexes. Establishing a simple structural system is more difficult with this pattern unless the circulation paths extend from the central space at 90 degree angles. Each corridor must also have an exit at the end if it is longer than 20 feet.

Finally, a field pattern consists of a network of paths with no strong direction. There are major paths with secondary routes extending from or connecting the primary routes. Orientation within a field pattern is difficult, as is integrating a logical structural system.

C. Service Spaces

In addition to the primary programmed spaces (the net assignable), secondary spaces such as toilet and mechanical rooms must also be planned from the start. They should not be tacked on after the majority of the design work is done.

Depending on the type of mechanical system, mechanical rooms should be centrally located to minimize lengths of duct runs and piping. This is especially true with all air systems. Mechanical rooms usually need easy access to the outside for servicing as well as provisions for fresh air intakes.

Toilet rooms should be located to satisfy adjacency requirements as stated in the program or in an area that has easy access to the entire floor. Men's and women's toilet rooms should be back to back to share a common plumbing wall and to be near other plumbing in the building, if possible.

Service access must also be given careful consideration. This includes service drives for trucks, the service entrance to the building, and access to mechanical rooms, storage rooms, and other functional areas as required by the program. The A.R.E. design problem usually has a requirement for some type of service access that must be kept separate from the primary entrance and circulation paths.

D. Flexibility

Flexibility is a design consideration that involves a variety of concepts. Expansibility is the capacity for a building to be enlarged or added onto easily as needs change or growth occurs. Convertibility allows an existing building or space to be changed to a new use. For example, a school gymnasium may be converted into classroom space in a second phase of construction. Versatility means the ability to use the same space for a variety of uses in order to make maximum use of limited space.

If a program calls for flexibility, the designer must know or determine what type is required. Expansibility may suggest one type of organizational and structural system while convertibility may require a completely different approach.

3 PSYCHOLOGICAL AND SOCIAL INFLUENCES

Developing physical guidelines that respond to the psychological needs of people is one of the most difficult tasks in programming. Although there has been a great deal of research in the field of environmental psychology, predicting human behavior and designing spaces and buildings that enhance people's lives is an inexact process. However, the architect must attempt to develop a realistic model of the people who will be using the designed environment and the nature of their activities. This model can then serve as the foundation on which to base many design decisions.

During programming, there must be a clear distinction made between the architect's client and who the actual users will be. They are not always the same. For example, a public housing agency may be the client for a subsidized housing complex, but the actual users will be people who probably have an entirely different set of values and lifestyles than those helping to develop the program. Environmental psychology is a very complex subject, but the following concepts are some with which you should be familiar.

A. Behavior Settings

A behavior setting is a useful concept for studying the effects of the environment on human activity. A behavior setting can be thought of as a particular place, with definable boundaries and objects within the place, in which a standing pattern of behavior occurs at a particular time.

For example, a weekly board of directors meeting in a conference room can be considered a behavior setting. The activity of the meeting follows certain procedures (call to order, reading of minutes, discussions, and so forth), it occurs in the same place (the conference room), and the room is arranged to assist the activity (chairs are arranged around a table, audio-visual facilities are present, lighting is adequate).

The idea of a behavior setting is a useful concept for the architect because it connects the strictly behavioral aspects of human activity of interest to the psychologist with the effects of the physical environment on people. Although a behavior setting is a complex system of activities, human goals, administrative requirements, physical objects, and cultural needs, it provides the architect with a definable unit of design. By knowing the people involved and the activities taking place, programmatic concepts can be developed that support the setting.

B. Territoriality

As mentioned in Chapter 2, territoriality is a fundamental aspect of human behavior. It refers to the need to lay claim to the spaces we occupy and the things we own. Although partially based on the biological imperative for protection, territoriality in humans is more related to the needs for self-identity and freedom of choice. In addition to marking out objects and larger spaces in the environment, people also protect their own personal space, that imaginary bubble of distance that varies with different circumstances. (This was also discussed in Chapter 2.)

Territoriality applies to groups as well as to individuals. A study club, school class, or street gang can claim a physical territory as their own, which helps give both the group and the individuals in the group an identity. Environments should allow people to claim territory and make choices about where to be and what activities to engage in.

C. Personalization

One of the ways territoriality manifests itself is with the personalization of space. Whether it happens in one's home, at the office desk, or in a waiting lounge, people need to arrange the environment to reflect their presence and uniqueness. The most successful designs allow this to take place without major adverse affects to other people or to the environment as a whole. At home, people decorate their spaces the way they want. At the office, people bring in personal objects, family photographs, and pictures to make the space their own. In an airport lounge, people place coats and suitcases around them, not only to stake out a temporary territory but also to make the waiting time more personal and a little more comfortable.

Another way people personalize space is to modify the environment. If a given space is not conducive to meeting the needs of the people using it, they can either modify their behavior to adapt to the environment, change their relationship to the environment (leave), or try to change the environment. The simple act of moving a chair to make viewing a screen easier is an example of modifying and personalizing a space. If the chair is attached, the design is not as adaptable to the varying needs of the people using the design.

D. Group Interaction

To a certain extent, the environment can either facilitate or hinder human interaction. In most behavior settings, groups are predisposed to act in a particular way. If the setting is not conducive to the activities, the people will try to modify the environment or modify their behavior to make the activity work. In extreme cases, if the setting is totally at odds with the activity, stress, anger, and other adverse reactions can occur.

Seating arrangement is one of the most common ways of facilitating group interaction. Studies have shown that people will seat themselves at a table according to the nature of their relationship with others around them. For intimate conversation, two people will sit across the corner of a table or next to each other on a sofa. For more formal situations or when people are competing, they will sit across from one another. Where social contact is not desired, two people will take chairs at opposite corners of a table.

Round tables tend to foster more cooperation and equality among those seated around them. Rectangular tables tend to make cooperation more difficult and establish the person sitting at the end in a more superior position. Strangers do not like to share the same sofa or park bench. Knowing the people and activities expected to be in a place can assist the architect in making decisions. For example, individual study carrels in a library will be more efficient than large tables because the tables will seldom be fully occupied by strangers.

In places where informal group interaction takes place, studies have shown that over 97 percent of groups comprise two to four people. Designing to accommodate these sizes of groups makes more sense than anticipating groups of more people, although a plan that allows for the possibility of very large groups while preferring small groups would be the best combination. In most cases, providing a variety of spaces for interaction is the best approach.

E. Status

The physical environment holds a great deal of symbolism that indicates status for some human beings. Some people like colonial houses because such designs symbolize to the occupants the idea of "home." Others prefer banks of classical design with large lobbies, because that is what they think a bank should look like.

The environment can thus communicate status. In the United States, for example, someone with a corner office has more status than someone with only one exterior wall. Office size is also equated with status in many cultures. A house in a better neighborhood provides a higher status than one in other neighborhoods. Status can also operate at the scale of an entire building or complex. The client may want the building to symbolize some quality of the organization and give him or her a physical and psychological status in the community.

An architectural program should investigate the requirements or implications of status. Sometimes clients may clearly state what status-related goals they want to achieve. Other times, the programmer must raise the issue, explore it with the client, and document the response as a programmatic concept.

4 BUDGETING AND SCHEDULING

Establishing a budget and setting up a time frame for design and construction are two of the most important parts of programming because they influence many of the design decisions to follow and can determine whether the project is even feasible. During later stages of design, the initial budget and scheduling are simply refined as more information becomes available.

Budgets may be set in several ways. For speculative or for-profit projects, the owner or developer works out a pro forma statement listing the expected income of the project and the expected costs to build it. An estimated selling price of the developed project or rent per square foot is calculated and balanced against all the various costs, one of which is the construction price. In order to make the project economically feasible, there will be a limit on the building costs. This becomes the budget within which the architect must work.

Budgets are often established through public funding or legislation. In these cases, the construction budget is often fixed without the architect's involvement and the project must be designed and built for the fixed amount. Unfortunately, when public officials estimate the cost to build a project, they sometimes neglect to include all aspects of development, such as professional fees, furnishings, and other line items.

Budgets may also be set by the architect at the request of the owner and based on the proposed project. This is the most realistic and accurate way to establish a preliminary budget because it is based on a particular building type of a particular size on a particular site (or sites if several are being reviewed for selection).

There are four basic variables in developing any construction budget: quantity, quality, the budget itself, and time. There is always a balance among these four elements and changing one or more affects the others. For instance, if an owner needs a certain amount of square footage built (quantity), needs the project built at a certain time, and has a fixed budget amount, then the quality of construction will have to be adjusted to meet the other constraints. In some cases, value engineering can be performed during which individual systems and materials are reviewed to see if the same function can be accomplished in a less expensive way. If time, quality, and the budget are fixed, then the amount of space constructed (quantity) must be adjusted.

A. Cost Influences

There are many variables that affect project cost. The first thing to remember is that construction cost is only one part of the total project development budget. Other factors include such things as site acquisition, site development, and financing. Figure 3.4 lists most of the items commonly found in a project budget and a typical range of percentage values based on construction cost. Of course, not all of these are a part of every development, but they illustrate the things that must be considered.

Building cost is the money required to construct the building, including structure, exterior cladding, finishes, and electrical and mechanical systems. Site development costs are usually a separate item. They include such things as parking, drives, fences, landscaping,

	line item		example
A	site acquisition		1,100,000
B	building costs	sq. ft. times cost per sq. ft.	(assume) 6,800,000
C	site development	10% to 20% of B	(15%) 1,020,000
D	total construction cost	B + C	7,820,000
E	movable equipment	5% to 10% of B	(5%) 340,000
F	furnishings		200,000
G	total construction and furnishings	D + E + F	8,360,000
H	professional services	5% to 10% of D	(7%) 547,400
I	inspection and testing		15,000
J	escalation estimate	2% to 10% of G per year	(10%) 836,000
K	contingency	5% to 10% of G	(8%) 668,800
L	financing costs		250,000
M	moving expenses		(assume) 90,000
N	Total Project Budget	G + H through M	$ 11,867,200

Figure 3.4 Project Budget Line Items

exterior lighting, and sprinkler systems. If the development is a large one that affects the surrounding area, a developer may be required to upgrade roads, extend utility lines, and do other major off-site work as a condition of getting approval from public agencies.

Movable equipment and furnishings include furniture, accessories, window coverings, and major equipment necessary to put the facility into operation. These are often listed as separate line items because the funding for them may come out of a separate budget and because they may be supplied under separate contracts.

Professional services are architectural and engineering fees as well as costs for such things as topographic surveys, soil tests, special consultants, appraisals and legal fees, and the like. Inspection and testing involve money required for special on-site, full-time inspection (if required), and testing of such things as concrete, steel, window walls, and roofing.

Since construction takes a great deal of time, a factor for inflation should be included. Generally, the present budget estimate is escalated to a time in the future at the expected midpoint of construction. Although it is always difficult to predict the future, using past cost indexes and inflation rates and applying an estimate to the expected condition of the construction, the architect can usually make an educated guess.

A contingency should also be added to account for unforeseen changes by the client and other conditions that add to the cost. For an early project budget, the percentage of the contingency should be higher than contingencies applied to later budgets, because there are more unknowns. Normally, from 5 to 10 percent should be included.

Financing includes not only the long-term interest paid on permanent financing but also the immediate costs of loan origination fees, construction loan interest, and other administrative costs. On long-term loans, the cost of financing can easily exceed all of the original building and development costs. In many cases, long-term interest, called *debt service*, is not included in the project budget because it is an ongoing cost to the owner, just as maintenance costs are.

Finally, many clients include moving costs in the development budget. For large companies and other types of clients, the money required to physically relocate, including changing stationery, installing telephones, and the like, can be a substantial amount.

B. Methods of Budgeting

The costs described in the previous section and shown in Figure 3.4 represent a type of budget done during programming or even prior to programming to test the feasibility of a project. The numbers are very preliminary, often based on very sketchy information. For example, the building cost may simply be an estimated cost per square foot multiplied by the required number of gross square feet needed. The square footage cost may be derived from similar buildings in the area, from past experience, or from commercially available cost books.

Budgeting, however, is an ongoing activity for the architect. At each stage of the design process, there should be a revised budget, reflecting the decisions made to that time. As shown in the example, pre-design budgets are usually based only on area basis, but other units can also be used. For example, many companies have rules of thumb for estimating based on items such as cost per hospital bed, cost per student, cost per hotel room, and similar functional units.

After the pre-programming budget, the architect usually begins to concentrate on the building and site development costs. At this stage an average cost per square foot may still be used, or the building may be divided into several functional parts and different square footage prices assigned to each. A school, for example, may be classified into classroom space, laboratory space, shop space, office space, and gymnasium space, each having a different cost per square foot. This type of division can be developed concurrently with the programming of the space requirements.

During schematic design, when more is known about the space requirements and general configuration of the building and site, budgeting is based on major subsystems. Historical cost information on each type of subsystem can be applied to the design. At this point it is easier to see where the money is being used in the building. Design decisions can then be based on studies of alternative systems. A typical subsystem budget is shown in Figure 3.5.

Values for low-, average-, and high-quality construction for different building types can be obtained from cost databases and published estimating manuals and applied to the structure being budgeted. The dollar amounts included in system cost budgets usually include markup for contractor's overhead and profit and other construction administrative costs.

During the later stages of schematic design and early stages of construction documents, more detailed estimates are made. The procedure most often used is the parameter method, which involves an expanded itemization of construction quantities and assignment of unit costs to these quantities. For example, instead of using one number for floor finishes, they are broken down into carpeting, vinyl tile, wood strip flooring, unfinished concrete, and so forth. Using an estimated cost per square

foot, the cost of each type of flooring can be estimated based on the area.

Office Buildings

subsystem	average cost $/sq. ft.	% of total
foundations	3.96	5.2
floors on grade	3.08	4.0
superstructure	16.51	21.7
roofing	0.18	0.2
exterior walls	9.63	12.6
partitions	5.19	6.8
wall finishes	3.70	4.8
floor finishes	3.78	5.0
ceiling finishes	2.79	3.7
conveying systems	6.45	8.5
specialties	0.70	0.9
fixed equipment	2.74	3.6
HVAC	9.21	12.1
plumbing	3.61	4.6
electrical	4.68	6.1
	$76.21	100.0

Figure 3.5 System Cost Budget

With this type of budgeting, it is possible to evaluate the cost implications of each building component and to make decisions concerning both quantity and quality in order to meet the original budget estimate. If floor finishes are over budget, the architect and the client can review the parameter estimate and decide, for example, that some wood flooring must be replaced with less expensive carpeting. Similar decisions can be made concerning any of the parameters in the budget.

Parameter line items are based on commonly used units that relate to the construction element under study. For instance, a gypsum board partition would have an assigned cost per square foot of complete partition of a particular construction type rather than separate costs for metal studs, gypsum board, screws, and finishing. There would be different costs for single-layer gypsum board partitions, one-hour rated walls, two-hour rated walls, and other partition types.

Two additional components of construction cost include the contractor's overhead and profit. Overhead can be further divided into general overhead and project overhead. *General overhead* is the cost to run a contracting business that involves such things as office rent, secretarial help, heat, and other recurring costs. *Project overhead* is the money it takes to complete a job that does not include labor, materials, or equipment. Temporary offices, project telephones, sanitary facilities, trash removal, insurance, permits, and temporary utilities are examples of project overhead. The total overhead costs, including both general and project expenses, can range from about 10 percent to 20 percent of the total costs for labor, materials, and equipment.

Profit is the last item a contractor adds onto an estimate and is listed as a percentage of the total of labor, materials, equipment, and overhead. This is one of the most highly variable parts of a budget. Profit depends on the type of project, its size, the amount of risk involved, how much money the contractor wants to make, the general market conditions, and, of course, whether or not the job is being bid.

During extremely difficult economic conditions, a contractor may cut the profit margin to almost nothing simply to get the job and keep his or her work force employed. If the contract is being negotiated with only one contractor, the profit percentage will be much higher. In most cases, however, profit will range from 5 to 20 percent of the total cost of the job. Overall, overhead and profit can total about 15 to 40 percent of construction cost.

C. Cost Information

One of the most difficult aspects of developing project budgets is obtaining current, reliable prices for the kinds of construction units you are using. There is no shortage of commercially produced cost books that are published yearly. These books list costs in different ways; some are very detailed, giving the cost for labor and materials for individual construction items, while others list parameter costs and subsystem costs. The detailed price listings are of little use to architects because they are too specific and make comparison of alternate systems difficult.

There are also computerized cost estimating services that only require you to provide general information about the project, location, size, major materials, and so forth. The computer service then applies its current price database to the information and returns a cost budget to you. Many architects also work closely with general contractors to develop a realistic budget.

You should remember, however, that commercially available cost information is the average of many past construction projects from around the country. Local variations and particular conditions may affect the value of their use on your project.

Two conditions that must be accounted for in developing any project budget are geographical location and inflation. These variables can be adjusted by using cost indexes that are published in a variety of sources, including the major architectural and construction trade magazines. Using a base year as index 1000, for example, for selected cities around the country, new indexes are developed each year that reflect the increase in costs (both material and labor) that year.

The indexes can be used to apply costs from one part of the country to another and to escalate past costs to the expected midpoint of construction of the project being budgeted.

Example 3.2

The cost index in your city is 1257 and the cost index for another city in which you are designing a building is 1308. If the expected construction cost is 1,250,000 based on prices for your city, what will be the expected cost in the other region?

Divide the higher index by the lower index:

$$\frac{1308}{1257} = 1.041$$

Multiply this by the base cost:

$$1,250,000 \times 1.041 = \$1,300,716$$

D. Scheduling

There are two major parts of a project schedule: design time and construction time. The architect, of course, has control over the scheduling of design and production of contract documents but has practically no control over construction. However, the design professional must be able to estimate the entire project schedule so the best course of action can be taken in order to meet the client's goals. For example, if the client must move by a certain date and normal design and construction sequences make this impossible, the architect may recommend a fast-track schedule or some other approach to meet the deadline.

The design process normally consists of several clearly defined phases, each of which must be substantially finished and approved by the client before the next one can begin. These are generally accepted in the profession and are referred to in the American Institute of Architects' owner–architect agreement as well as other documents.

Following programming, the first phase is schematic design. During this phase, the general layout of the project is developed along with preliminary alternate studies for materials and building systems. Once the direction of the project documented in schematic design drawings is reviewed and approved by the client, the design development phase starts. Here, the decisions made during the previous phase are refined and developed in more detail. Preliminary or outline specifications are written and a more detailed cost budget is made.

Construction documents are produced next, which include the final working drawings as well as the full project manual and any bidding and contract documents required. These are used for the bidding or negotiation phase, which includes obtaining bids from several contractors and analyzing them or negotiating a contract with one contractor.

The time required for these phases is highly variable and depends on the following factors:

- the size and complexity of the project. Obviously, a 500,000-square-foot hospital will take much longer to design than a 30,000-square-foot office building.

- the number of people working on the project. While adding more people to the job can shorten the schedule, there is a point of diminishing returns. Having too many people simply creates a management and coordination problem, and for some phases, only a few people are required, even for very large jobs.

- the abilities and design methodology of the project team. Younger, less experienced designers will usually require a little longer to do the same amount of work as a more senior staff.

- the type of client and the decision-making and approval processes of the client. Large corporations or public agencies are likely to have a multilayer decision-making and approval process. The time required for getting the necessary information or approval on one phase may take weeks or even months, where a small, single-authority client might make the same decision in a matter of days.

The construction schedule may be established by the contractor or construction manager, but it must often be estimated by the architect during the programming phase so the client has some idea of the total time required from project conception to move-in. When the architect does this, it should be made very clear to the client that it is only an estimate and the architect can in no way guarantee an early (or any) estimate of the construction schedule.

Many variables can affect construction time, but most can be controlled in one way or another. Others, like weather, are independent of anyone's control. Beyond the obvious variables of size and complexity the following is a partial list of some of the more common ones.

- the management ability of the contractor to organize his or her own forces as well as those of the subcontractors

- material delivery times

- the quality and completeness of the architect's drawings and specification

- the weather

- labor availability and labor disputes

- new construction or remodeling. For equal areas, remodeling generally takes more time and coordination than new building.

- site conditions. Constricted sites or those with subsurface problems usually take more time to build on.

- the architect. Some professionals are more diligent than others in performing their duties during construction.

- lender approvals

- agency and governmental approvals

There are several methods that are used to schedule both design and construction. The most common and easiest is the *bar chart*. The various activities of the schedule are listed along the vertical axis and a time line is extended along the horizontal axis. Each activity is given a starting and finishing date, and overlaps are indicated by having the bars for each activity overlap. Bar charts are simple to make and understand and are suitable for small to midsize projects. However, they cannot show all the sequences and dependencies of one activity on another.

Another scheduling tool often used is the *critical path method (CPM)* and the CPM chart. The CPM chart graphically depicts all of the tasks required to complete a project, the sequence in which they must occur, their duration, the earliest or latest possible starting time, and the earliest or latest possible finishing time. It also defines the sequence of tasks that are critical or that must be started and finished exactly on time if the total schedule is to be met. A CPM chart for a simple design project is shown in Figure 3.6.

Each arrow in the chart represents an activity with a beginning and end point (represented by the numbered circles). No activity can begin until all activities leading into the circle have been completed. The dashed lines indicate dependency relationships but not activities themselves, and thus they have no duration. They are called *dummies* and are used to give each activity a unique beginning and ending number and to allow establishment of dependency relationships without tying in non-dependent activities.

The heavier line in the illustration shows the critical path, or the sequence of events that must happen as scheduled if the deadline is to be met. The numbers under the activities give the duration of the activity in days. Delaying the starting time of any of these activities or increasing their duration will delay the whole project. The non-critical activities can begin or finish earlier or later (within limits) without affecting the final completion date. This variable time is called the *float* of each activity.

Scheduling is vitally important to any project because it can have a great influence on cost. Generally, the longer the project takes the more it costs. This is due to the effect of inflation on materials and labor as well as the additional construction interest and the lost revenue a client can suffer if the job is not completed in a timely manner. For example, delayed completion of a retail store or office building delays the beginning of rental income. In other cases, quick completion of a project is required to avoid building during bad winter weather, when it costs more to build, or to meet some other fixed date set by the client's needs.

Besides efficient scheduling, construction time can be compressed with *fast-track scheduling*. This method overlaps the design and construction phases of a project. Ordering of long lead materials and equipment can occur and work on the site and foundations can begin before all the details of the building are completely worked out. With fast-track scheduling, separate contracts are established so each major system can be bid and awarded by itself to avoid delaying other construction.

Although the fast-track method requires close coordination between the architect, contractor, subcontractors, owner, and others, it is possible to construct a high-quality building in 10 to 30 percent less time than with a conventional construction contract.

5 CODES AND REGULATIONS

A complete program for a building project will include the various legal restrictions that apply to a project. Two of the most common are zoning ordinances and building codes. Zoning is discussed in Chapters 2 and 4. Building code requirements, including provisions for making buildings accessible to the physically disabled, are reviewed in Chapter 7. In addition to zoning regulations, other land development regulations may apply. Such regulations as deed restrictions and easements are also discussed in Chapter 2.

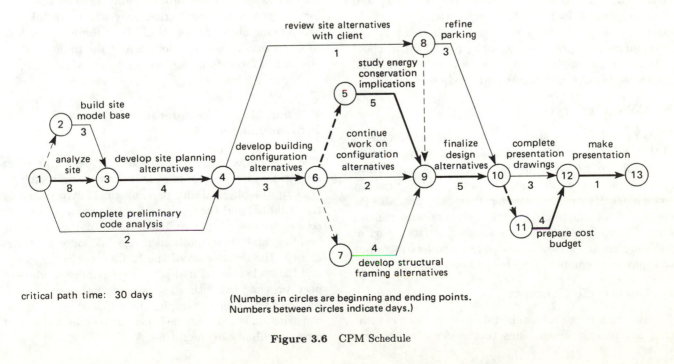

critical path time: 30 days

(Numbers in circles are beginning and ending points. Numbers between circles indicate days.)

Figure 3.6 CPM Schedule

PROFESSIONAL PUBLICATIONS ● Belmont, CA

Other regulatory agency requirements that may be in force, in addition to zoning ordinances and building codes, include special rules of the local fire department, fire zones set by the local municipality, and rules of government agencies like the Federal Housing Authority (FHA) and the Environmental Protection Agency. Additional regulations may include local health and hospital department requirements that spell out needs for restaurants and hospitals. Local and state energy conservation regulations may also be in force.

6   THE PROGRAMMING PROCESS

Programming is an attempt to define the problem and establish all the guidelines and needs on which the design process can be based. It is a time of analysis of all aspects of the problem and a distillation of the problem's complexity into a few clear problem statements.

One popular programming method uses a five-step process in relationship to four major considerations. It is described in *Problem Seeking* by William Peña (AIA Press, 1987). The process involves establishing goals, collecting and analyzing facts, uncovering and testing concepts, determining needs, and stating the problem. All of these steps include the considerations of form, function, economy, and time.

A. Establishing Goals

Goals indicate what the client wants to achieve and why. They are important to identify because they establish the direction of programmatic concepts that ultimately suggest the physical means of achieving the goals. It is not enough to simply list the types of spaces and required square footages the client needs; the client is trying to reach some objective with those spaces and square footages. For example, a goal for a school administration might be to increase the daily informal interaction between students and teachers.

B. Collecting Facts

Facts describe the existing conditions and requirements of the problem. Facts include such things as the number of people to be accommodated, the site conditions, space adjacency needs, user characteristics, equipment to be housed, expected growth rate, money available for construction, building code requirements, and climate facts. There is always a large number of facts; part of the programmer's task is not only to collect facts but to organize them as well so they are useful.

C. Uncovering Concepts

The programming process should develop abstract ideas that are functional solutions to the client's problems without defining the physical means that should be used to achieve them. These are programmatic concepts as discussed earlier in this chapter. They are the basis for later design concepts. To use the previous example described under goals, a programmatic concept concerning increasing the daily interaction between students and teachers might be to provide common spaces for mixed flow in circulation patterns. One possible design concept in response to this could be to provide a central court through which all circulation paths pass.

D. Determining Needs

This step of the programming process balances the desires of the client against the available budget or establishes a budget based on the defined goals and needs. It is during this step that wants have to be separated from needs. Most clients want more than they can afford, so clear statements of true needs at this early stage of the process can help avoid problems later. At this stage, one or more of the four elements of cost (quantity, quality, budget, and time) may have to be adjusted to balance needs against available resources.

E. Stating the Problem

The previous four steps are a prelude to succinctly stating the essence of the problem in just a few statements. The problem statements are the bridge between programming and the design process. They are statements the client and programmer agree describe the most important aspects of the problem and serve as the basis for design and as design criteria by which the solution can be evaluated. There should be a minimum of four problem statements, one for each of the major considerations of form, function, economy, and time.

F. Four Major Considerations During Programming

The four major considerations of any design problem are form, function, economy, and time. Form relates to the site, the physical and psychological environment of the building, and the quality of construction. Function relates to the people and activities of the space or building and their relationships. Economy concerns money: the initial cost of the facility, operating costs, and life cycle costs. Finally, time describes the ideas of past, present, and future as they affect the other three considerations. For example, the required schedule for construction is often a time consideration, as is the need for expansibility in the future.

SAMPLE QUESTIONS

1. The statement "develop a multilevel system of pedestrian circulation" is an example of:

   A. a need
   B. a programmatic concept
   C. a goal
   D. a design concept

2. The developer of a retail shopping complex has estimated through an economic analysis that he can afford to build up to 85,000 square feet of gross building area. If a central, enclosed pedestrian mall is planned to take up about 6 percent of the area and the efficiency ratio is estimated to be 75 percent, about how much net rentable area will be available?

   A. 60,000 square feet
   B. 63,700 square feet
   C. 67,600 square feet
   D. 106,500 square feet

3. A published cost index indicates construction in city A to be 1440 and construction in city B to be 1517. If the same index suggests that inflation will increase by 5 percent by the midpoint of construction and the project is now budgeted to cost $1,500,000 in city A, what should be budgeted for city B?

   A. $1,495,000
   B. $1,650,000
   C. $1,659,000
   D. $1,715,000

4. Contractor's overhead and profit typically amount to what percentage of construction cost?

   A. 5% to 20%
   B. 10% to 20%
   C. 15% to 30%
   D. 15% to 40%

Questions 5 through 7 are based on the following programming situation.

A small medical clinic is being planned for a suburban location on an open, level site. It is to include services of general practice, obstetrics/family planning, testing and laboratories, and dental offices, along with medical offices and an administration area comprising about 70,000 net square feet of space. Access to the building is primarily by automobile.

The group developing the project want the facility to be a comfortable, friendly place that minimizes the anxiety of a visit to the doctor and that makes it as easy as possible to get around. They expect the venture to be successful and each department to grow as the catchment area grows.

5. In order to meet the goals of the client, which of the following design responses would not be appropriate?

   A. Base the size of waiting rooms on a behavior setting where establishing territory should be encouraged.
   B. Group waiting areas and the reception area together to encourage social interaction.
   C. Develop a different color scheme for each of the separate services.
   D. Arrange individual chair seating against walls and other objects so it faces room entries.

6. Which of the following organizational concepts would probably be most appropriate for this facility?

   A. grid
   B. axial
   C. central
   D. radial

7. Which of the following aspects of flexibility related to expected growth of the facility is most important in developing the structural framing concept?

   A. convertibility
   B. versatility
   C. expansibility
   D. all of the above

8. A client discovers shortly after hiring the architect for programming and design services that they must move out of their existing facility sooner than expected. If the new schedule requires that construction and move-in be completed in 18 months instead of the original 21

months, what recommendation from the architect is the most feasible?

A. Consider fast-track construction.

B. Use CPM scheduling and use a negotiated contract rather than bidding.

C. Assign more staff to programming and design and work overtime to get construction started earlier.

D. Suggest that the client streamline its decision-making process and hire a construction manager.

9. Which element of project cost does the architect typically have least control over?

A. the budget for escalation

B. percentage of site work relative to building costs

C. professional fees and consultant services

D. financing costs

10. A school district is planning a new elementary school to replace an outdated facility. A preliminary budget made during programming has shown that the available funds set aside for the school have been exceeded by 8 percent. What should the architect do?

I. Suggest that additional funds from other school building projects be used.

II. Review the design from a value engineering standpoint for approval by the client to see if costs can be reduced without sacrificing quality.

III. Discuss with the client the possibility of reducing the required area.

IV. Modify the statement of need concerning the desired level of finish and construction quality on non-critical portions of the facility after consultation with the client.

V. Propose that building be postponed for a school term until more money can be allocated.

A. V then IV

B. III then IV

C. II then III

D. IV then I

4 SITE ANALYSIS AND DESIGN

This chapter discusses the influences of a specific site on the placement and design of a building and the considerations for site development. Other pertinent topics that apply to site design are reviewed in Chapter 2.

1 TOPOGRAPHY

Topography affects decisions on where to place major site features such as buildings, parking areas, and drives as well as how much soil has to be moved to maintain desired slopes and drainage patterns. Topography is shown with contour lines on the topographic map, as discussed in Chapter 2. Figure 4.1 shows the common conditions contour lines represent. You should be able to immediately recognize these and translate the spacing of the contour lines and the contour interval to a percentage slope using formula 2.1.

Remember that when contour lines represent a ridge they "point" in the direction of the downslope and when they represent a valley, they "point" in the direction of the upslope. Equally spaced contour lines represent a uniform slope. As shown in Figure 4.1, concave slopes have more closely spaced contour lines near the top of the slope while convex slopes have more closely spaced contour lines at the bottom of the slope.

Any site requires some modification of the land, but the changes should be kept to a minimum. There are several reasons for this:

- Earth moving costs money.

- Excavating and building on steep slopes is more expensive than on gentle slopes.

- Excessive modification of the land affects drainage patterns that must be resolved.

- Large changes in elevations can require retaining walls, which add cost to the project.

- Removing or hauling in soil is expensive.

- Large amounts of cutting may damage existing tree roots.

When modifications are made to the contours as part of site design, the amount of material cut away should balance the amount of soil required for fill to avoid the expense and problems with removing or hauling in soil. Generally, it is better to orient the length of a building parallel to the direction of the contours rather than perpendicular to them in order to minimize excavation costs.

Both existing contour lines and new contour lines are shown on the same plan; the existing lines are shown dashed and the new ones solid. See Figure 4.2. At the property lines, the contour lines must match up with the existing contours at adjacent properties or retaining walls must be built.

2 CLIMATE

Solar orientation influences three aspects of site planning: orientation of the building to control solar heat gain or heat loss, the location of outdoor spaces and activities, and the location of building entries. Prior to design, the path of the sun should be located so you know its angle at various times of the day during the seasons. In the northern hemisphere, the sun's angle is lowest on December 22 and highest on June 21. In the northern latitudes, its angle is smaller all year long than in the southern latitudes.

During the winter, the sun rises and sets south of an east-west line through the site, and, depending upon

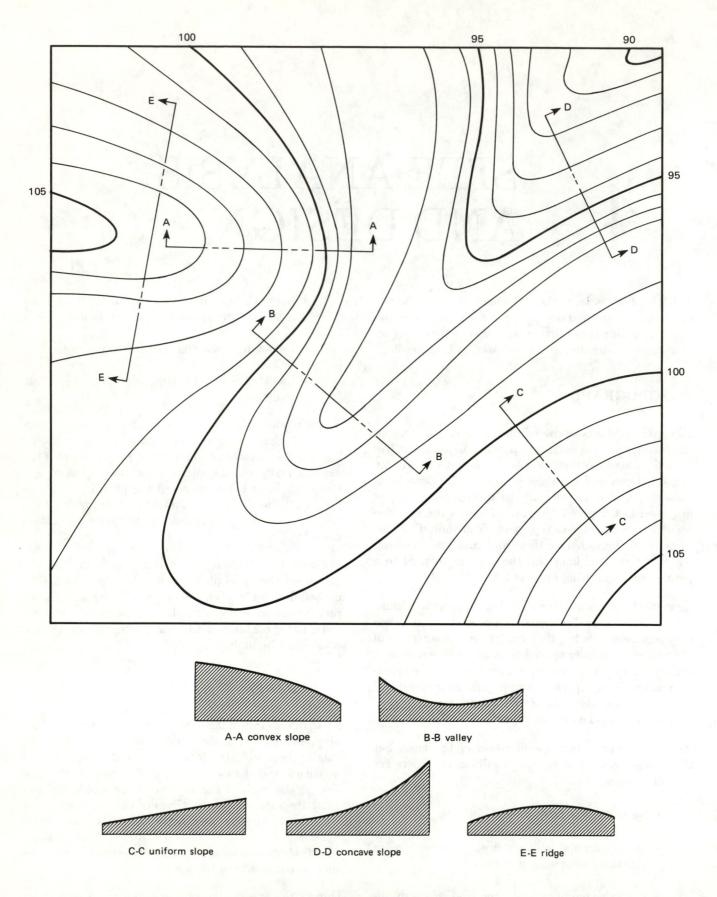

Figure 4.1 Common Contour Conditions

the site location, during the summer it rises and sets north of the same line. On the vernal equinox (March 21) and the autumnal equinox (September 21) it rises and sets due east and west. Some representative values for solar altitude (angle above the horizon) and azimuth (angle north or south from an east-west line) are shown in Table 4.1 for various latitudes and cities.

The orientation of a building—that is, the direction its length faces—has a profound effect on energy gains and losses and on the comfort of the users. For example, for a 40-degree latitude, a southern exposure in the winter receives about three times the solar energy as the east and west sides, while in the summer the east and west facades of a building receive about twice the energy as the north and south combined.

For most northern hemisphere locations, the best over-all orientation for a building is to have its principal facade facing south or slightly east or west of south. An orientation about 25 degrees east of south is considered ideal to balance the desired heat gains in the winter months and to minimize the excessive heat gains on the east and west facades during the summer. Overhangs can be used to control the sun in the summer but let it strike the building and glass areas in the winter for passive solar heating. See Figure 4.3. Deciduous trees can also be used to shield low buildings from the sun in the summer while allowing sunlight through in the winter.

On east and west facades, however, vertical sun baffles are more effective than overhangs because the sun is at a lower angle during the morning and afternoon hours in the summer. Louvers can also be used to shield a building and its interior from the sun. Either exterior or interior louvers and shades are effective, but exterior louvers are more efficient since they block the sunlight before it enters the space.

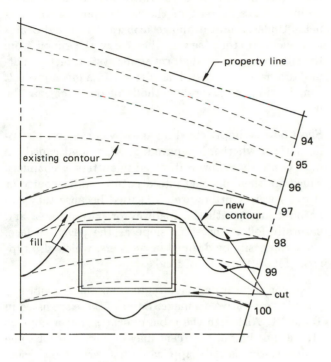

Figure 4.2 New and Existing Contour Lines

Table 4.1
Solar Angles for Representative Latitudes and Cities

| latitude | nearest city | solar altitude, noon, in degrees | | | azimuth at sunrise/ sunset* |
		Dec. 22	Mar/Sept. 21	June 21	
30	Houston	37	60	84	27
34	Los Angeles/Atlanta	32	56	79	28
40	Denver	26	50	73	30
42	Chicago/Boston	24	48	71	32
48	Seattle	18	42	66	34

All angles are approximate to the nearest degree.

* Azimuths in this table are degrees from an east-west line. They are the same for sunrise and sunset. For sunrise on December 21, the azimuth is south of east and for sunset it is the same angle only south of west.

PROFESSIONAL PUBLICATIONS ● Belmont, CA

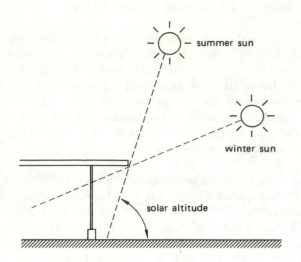

Figure 4.3 South Wall Sun Control

In addition to building position, solar orientation can also influence outdoor activities. In hot, humid climates it is better to locate such activities as patios, outdoor restaurants, and the like where they receive shade from the building or trees. In more temperate climates, the same spaces are best located where they can take advantage of the warming effects of solar radiation in the winter, spring, and fall. In cold climates building entries are best placed on the south where direct sun can melt ice and snow in the winter.

The effects of wind on building location are reviewed in Chapter 2. In addition, the orientation of a building, and locations of windows, plazas, and other elements can either take advantage of cooling breezes in hot, humid climates during the summer or shield the building and occupants from cold winds in the winter. In most temperate climates prevailing wind patterns often change with the seasons so a wind analysis is required to determine the direction of summer and winter winds. Shielding a building as much as possible from winter winds can reduce the heat loss through the walls, while providing for natural ventilation can help cool the building during the summer. Wind breaks can be formed with vegetation, buildings, or other man-made site elements such as screens and fences.

3 DRAINAGE

Any development of a site interrupts the existing drainage pattern and creates additional water flow by replacing naturally porous ground with roof area and paving. The architect must provide for any existing drainage patterns through the site and account for additional storm water that does not seep into the ground, which is called *runoff*. The site design must also create positive drainage away from the buildings, parking areas, and walks to avoid flooding, erosion, and standing water.

The two basic types of drainage are aboveground and underground. Aboveground drainage involves sheet flow, gutters built into roadways and parking areas, ground swales as part of the landscaping, and channels. Underground drainage utilizes perforated drains and enclosed storm sewers that carry the runoff from the site to a municipal storm sewer system or to a natural drainage outlet, such as a river. In a given project, combinations of several methods of drainage may be used.

Sheet flow is simply the drainage of water across a sloping surface, whether it is paved, grass, or landscaped. In most cases, sheet flow is directed to gutters or channels, which are then emptied into a natural water course or storm sewer. Gutters are often used because they can be built along with the roadway or parking area and naturally follow the same slope as the paved surface. They can easily be drained into sewers, which also typically follow the path of roads.

Areas for surface drainage require minimum slopes to provide for positive drainage. Some of these are listed in Table 2.1. Although the table indicates that a slope as little as one-half of 1 percent may be sufficient for some drainage, this is only applicable for very smooth surfaces that have been carefully constructed. Most paved surfaces should have at least a 1 to 1 1/2 percent slope to account for paving roughness and variations in installation tolerances.

Underground systems use piping with a minimum slope of 0.3 percent. The storm drains collect water from roof downspouts, drain inlets, catch basins, and drain tiles surrounding the building foundation. A drain inlet simply allows storm water to run directly into the storm sewer. A catch basin has a sump built into it so that debris will settle instead of flowing down the sewer. Periodically, the sump must be cleaned out. Large storm sewer systems require manholes for service access and are located wherever the sewer changes direction, or a maximum of 500 feet apart. Storm sewers are completely separate from sanitary sewers.

The capacity of a drainage system is based on the size of the area to be drained, the runoff coefficient (that fraction of water not absorbed), and the amount of water to be drained during the most severe storm being used in the design. Frequently, the system is planned for 25-year storms; other times a 10-year storm is used. These periods are simply the average frequency at which storms of a particular magnitude are likely to occur. If the site development creates a runoff in excess of the capacity of the existing municipal storm sewer or natural drainage course, a holding pond may be needed on the site. This collects the site runoff and releases it into the sewer system at a controlled rate without letting the excess water flood other areas.

4   UTILITIES

Determine the location of existing utilities prior to beginning design. These may include, but are not limited to, sanitary sewer lines, storm sewers, water lines, gas, electricity, steam, telephone, and cable television. If possible, the building should be located to minimize the length of utility lines between the structure and the main line.

Sanitary sewers and storm sewers usually take precedence in planning because they depend on gravity flow. The invert, or lowest, elevations of the existing public sewer line should be established, since the effluent must flow from the lowest point where the sewer line leaves the building to the main sewer. This portion of the horizontal piping of the sanitary sewer system outside the building is known as the *building sewer*. The actual connection of the building sewer to the main line must occur above the invert of the main line at any given point in order not to interfere with the free flow.

The minimum slope of the building sewer is 0.5 to 2.0 percent depending on the size of the pipe; a greater slope is required for smaller pipes. In some cases, the run of the building sewer will have to be longer than the shortest distance between the building and the main line simply to intercept the main line at a point low enough to allow for proper slope. See Figure 4.4.

Other utilities, such as water and electricity, do not depend on gravity so there is a little more flexibility in locating the building relative to these services. However, the total distance should still be minimized. In the case of electrical service, the location of the main electric lines may dictate the location of transformers and service entry to the building.

5   CIRCULATION

There are three major types of site circulation: automobile, pedestrian, and service. Both the site design and building design portions of the examination include all three.

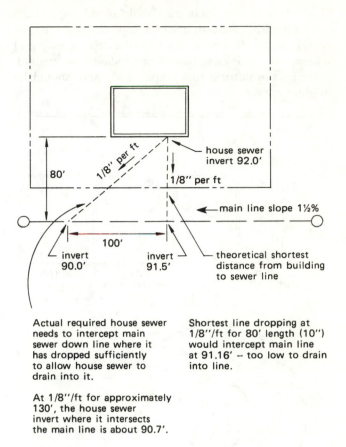

Actual required house sewer needs to intercept main sewer down line where it has dropped sufficiently to allow house sewer to drain into it.

At 1/8"/ft for approximately 130', the house sewer invert where it intersects the main line is about 90.7'.

Shortest line dropping at 1/8"/ft for 80' length (10") would intercept main line at 91.16' -- too low to drain into line.

Figure 4.4   Sewer Layout Based on Slope Required

A. Automobile Circulation

Planning for automobile circulation includes locating the entry drives to the site and providing on-site roads to reach the parking areas and the building drop-off point. The entire automobile circulation system should provide direct, easy access to the parking areas and building without excessive drives, turnarounds, dead ends, or conflicts with service areas and pedestrian circulation.

The size of the site, its relationship to existing public roads, and the expected traffic will help determine whether you should use a one-way loop system with two entry drives or a two-way system with one entry drive. In either case, you should lay out the roads so a driver can go directly to the parking area, drop-off point, or loading area. Forcing traffic through the parking area to get to the loading or the drop-off area should be avoided.

Figure 4.5 gives some design guidelines for on-site roads. Entry drives to the site should be as far away as possible from street intersections and other intersecting roads.

This is to avoid conflicts with vehicles waiting to turn and to avoid confusion about where to turn. Roads should be of sufficient width to make driving easy and to allow two vehicles to pass. Curves should be gradual, following the natural topography and there should be no blind curves.

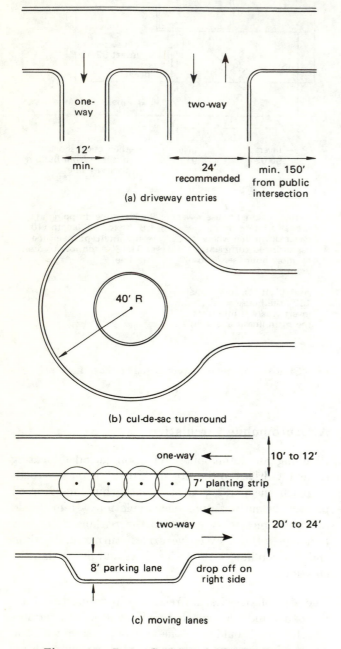

(a) driveway entries

(b) cul-de-sac turnaround

(c) moving lanes

Figure 4.5   Design Guidelines for On-Site Roads

Unless the slope is very gentle, roads should not be laid out perpendicular to the slope but across it slightly to minimize the grade. Limit roads to a maximum slope of 15 percent for short distances, although 10 percent or less is preferable. If a road does slope more than 10 percent, there should be transition slopes of one-half of the maximum slope between the road and level

areas. Ramps crossing sidewalks must have a level area between the ramp and the sidewalk.

Roads should have a gradual slope, a minimum of 1/4 inch per foot, for drainage from the center of the roadway, called the *crown*, to the sides. If the road has a gutter, it should be 6 inches high. Sometimes the representation of roads and gutters on a topographic map or site plan is confusing. Figure 4.6 shows a simple road sloping down, with a uniform pitch from the crown, with gutters on either side. As shown in Figure 4.1, the contours of the road point toward the direction of the slope and the pointed contours representing the gutters point in the direction of the "valley," in this case the gutter.

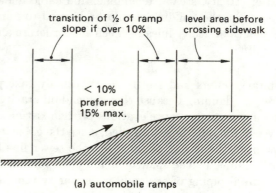

(a) automobile ramps

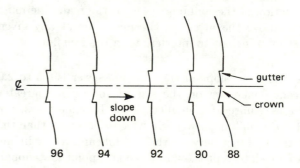

(b) representation of road with gutters on contour map

Figure 4.6   Design Guidelines for Road Grades

B. Pedestrian Circulation

Like roadways, pedestrian circulation should provide convenient, direct access from the various points on the site to the building entrances. If connections with adjacent buildings, public sidewalks, public transportation stops, and other off-site points are required, the circulation system must take these into account as well. Sidewalks should provide for the most direct paths from one point to another since people will generally take the shortest route possible. Pedestrian circulation paths should not cross roads, parking lots, or other areas of potential conflict. There should be collector walks next to parking areas so people can travel from their cars directly to a separate walk.

When these walks are next to parking where cars can overhang the walk, it should be a minimum of 6 feet wide. Required amenities such as seating, trash containers, and lighting should be provided. Walks should slope a minimum of 1/4 inch perpendicular to the direction of the paving for drainage. Figure 4.7 summarizes some of the design guidelines for exterior walks.

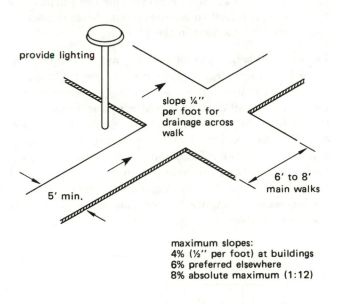
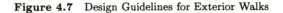

Figure 4.7 Design Guidelines for Exterior Walks

Changes in elevation are accomplished with ramps and stairs. There must be provisions for making the site accessible to the physically disabled. Requirements for curb cutouts and ramps are shown in Figure 4.8, and general guidelines for exterior stairs are shown in Figure 4.9. When a ramp and adjacent stairway serve the same areas, the bottom and top of the ramp and stairway should be adjacent to each other if possible. As with walks, stairways and ramps should be illuminated.

C. Service Circulation

Service and automobile circulation should be kept separate. This is usually stated as a specific program requirement on the A.R.E., but if not it should be done anyway. Service access is typically related to some space in the building program. Service trucks may use the same entry and drives as automobiles (unless specifically stated otherwise), but the loading area should be separate. The examination does not require planning for large trucks. However, sufficient turnaround space or backing areas should be provided to allow for maneuvering. Figure 4.10 shows some common guidelines for service drives for moderate-sized trucks.

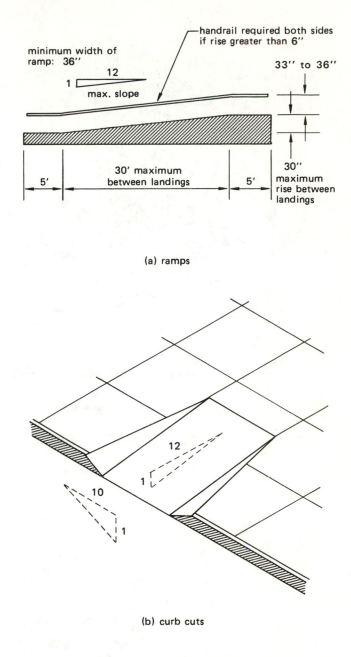

Figure 4.8 Access Requirements for the Physically Disabled

6 PARKING

Plan parking so it is efficient, convenient to the building, and separate from pedestrian circulation. The size of the site, topography, location of entry drives to the property, and relationship to the service drive and building drop-off area will determine the location of the parking area. The number of cars to be parked is determined by requirements of the zoning ordinance or by the building program.

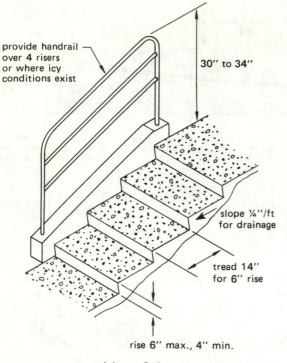

Figure 4.9 Design Guidelines for Exterior Stairs

The basic planning unit for parking is the size of a car stall. The standard size is 9 feet 0 inches wide and 19 feet 0 inches long for standard-size cars and 7 feet 6 inches wide and 15 feet 0 inches long for compact cars. Individual zoning ordinances may have slightly different requirements so you should always verify particular codes, but these dimensions are good ones to use for most planning. Since there is such a large percentage of compact cars today, most zoning ordinances now allow sizing of a certain percentage of required parking spaces for compact cars. However, for the purposes of the A.R.E., it is best to use the standard-size dimension unless otherwise stated in the problem.

Layouts for two types of parking are shown in Figure 4.11. Ninety degree parking is the most efficient in terms of land use, but angled parking is easier to use, forces a one-way circulation pattern, and requires less total width, for either a single- or double-loaded layout. For most parking lots, there should be continuous through circulation. Dead-end parking areas require a back-up space and are only appropriate for parking a few cars. The most efficient layouts are those that use double-loaded configurations or that utilize a drive as the back-up space.

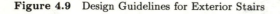

Figure 4.10 Design Guidelines for Service Drives

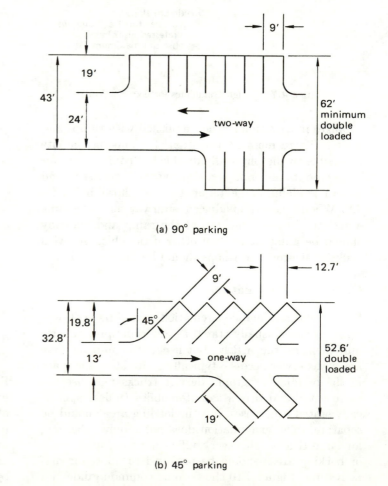

Figure 4.11 Parking Layouts

Unless otherwise required by the program, you must include at least one parking space for the physically disabled. Design guidelines for such a space are shown in Figure 4.12. This space should be located close to the building entrance and be identified with the international symbol for accessibility.

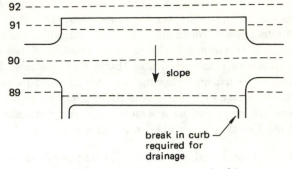

(a) drainage perpendicular to length of lot

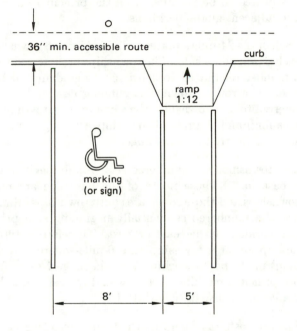

Figure 4.12 Parking for the Physically Disabled

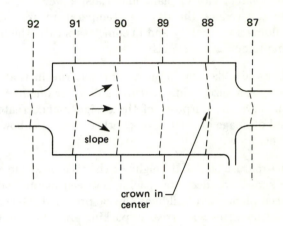

(b) drainage parallel to length

Establish drainage in parking areas as part of the site design. The minimum slope should be 1 1/2 percent with a maximum slope of 5 percent, but for convenience in calculating, use 2 or 3 percent when figuring parking slopes. Water should drain toward the edges of the parking area where it can run off into the landscaping or be collected and diverted to storm sewers or other natural water courses. Figure 4.13 shows three basic drainage patterns, depending on the orientation of the length of the lot to the contour lines. If curbs are used, there must be some way for the water to drain out, either with curb cutouts or drains to a storm sewer.

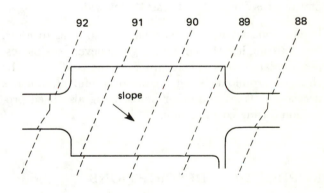

(c) drainage across lot

Figure 4.13 Drainage Patterns in Parking Lots

One useful rule of thumb is that the change in elevation from one side of a double-loaded parking area to the other (62 feet) for a minimum 1 1/2 percent slope is about one foot. With an absolute maximum of a 5 percent slope, the maximum change in elevation for 62 feet is about 3 feet. This is a useful way to quickly check your new contour lines when designing a parking area.

7 LANDSCAPING

Landscaping is a vital part of site development. In addition to its purely aesthetic qualities, landscaping can improve energy conservation, moderate noise, frame desirable views, block undesirable views, create privacy, fashion outdoor spaces, provide shade, retard erosion, and visually connect a building to its site. It is also required in some communities.

The use of landscaping to moderate the microclimate was discussed in Chapter 2 and included the use of deciduous trees to block sunlight in the summer while allowing it to enter a building in the winter. Trees can also moderate the wind and thereby reduce heat loss from wall surfaces. Slowing the normal wind patterns can also make outdoor spaces more pleasant to use. If trees are employed as a windbreak, evergreens should be used so they are still effective in the winter.

Grass, shrubs, and groundcover lower the albedo of the site. *Albedo* is that portion of the radiant energy that is reflected as it falls on a surface. Combined with the low conductivity of plant materials, a well-landscaped site can reduce the daytime temperature around the building significantly and in some cases raise the nighttime temperature slightly.

Plants are like any other design material in that they have form, size, color, texture, and other qualities that can serve the purposes of the designer and create the kind of image desired. Unlike other materials, however, plants grow.

The mature size and height of the tree or shrub must be known so adequate spacing between plants and between plants and buildings can be provided. Generally, planting strips with trees in parking areas and between other paved areas should be at least 7 feet wide while landscaping strips for grass or ground covers between paved areas should be at least 4 feet wide.

Because most trees and shrubs take so long to grow, save existing healthy landscaping whenever possible, especially large trees. The contours of the land cannot be changed around existing trees, so careful planning is necessary. Trees and other landscaping also need protection during construction.

8   PROPERTY DESCRIPTIONS

The boundaries of a site can be described in one of several ways. One of the most common is based on the United States survey system that was begun in 1784. This system laid out the majority of the United States except for those lands surveyed prior to the establishment of the control system and land based on some other system or land grant.

The system starts with a set of east-west lines called *parallels* that follow the lines of latitude of the earth and with a set of north-south lines called *meridians*. There are several meridians and parallels that serve as the basis for the grid layout. These are called the *principal*

meridians and base lines, respectively. Other meridians are called *guide meridians*, and other parallels are called *standard parallels*. They are referred to as being east or west, north or south of the base lines and principal meridians. See Figure 4.14.

The parallels and meridians are 24 miles apart and the squares they form are called *checks*. Since the meridian lines converge because of the shape of the earth, the south line of the first and each successive guide meridian is adjusted to be 24 miles from the principal meridian and adjacent guide meridians.

Each of the 24-mile squares is divided into 16 townships, each 6 miles on a side. The townships are referred to by a number referenced to a principal meridian and base line. The row of townships running east and west is referred to as a *township* (the same term but a different meaning) and the row of townships running north and south is referred to as a *range*.

The townships are numbered sequentially beginning at a base line. Those north of the base line are north townships and those south are south townships. Ranges are also numbered sequentially beginning at a principal meridian, either east or west. Therefore, a typical description of a township (the 6-mile-square parcel of land) might be "township 13 north, range 7 east of the 6th principal meridian." This would typically be abbreviated to T.13N, R.7E, 6th PM.

Each township is then further divided into 36 sections, each section being a 1-mile square. These are numbered sequentially starting in the northeast section, moving west, dropping down, then moving east, and so on from sections 1 to 36 as shown in Figure 4.14.

Sections are commonly further divided into quarter sections and those quarter sections into four more parcels. A complete description of such a portion of a section might read: "The SE 1/4 of the NW 1/4, Section 12, T.13N, R.7E of the 6th PM, located in the County of Merrick, State of Nebraska."

Because so much urbanization has occurred in the past 100 years and subdivision of land has become common, property is often described by its particular lot number within a subdivision, the subdivision having been carefully surveyed and recorded with the city or county in which it is located. Figure 4.15 shows one such property.

In addition to the lot and subdivisions reference, a typical property description will include the bearings of the property lines and their lengths, along with any permanent corner markers set by the original subdivision surveyor.   The property line bearings are

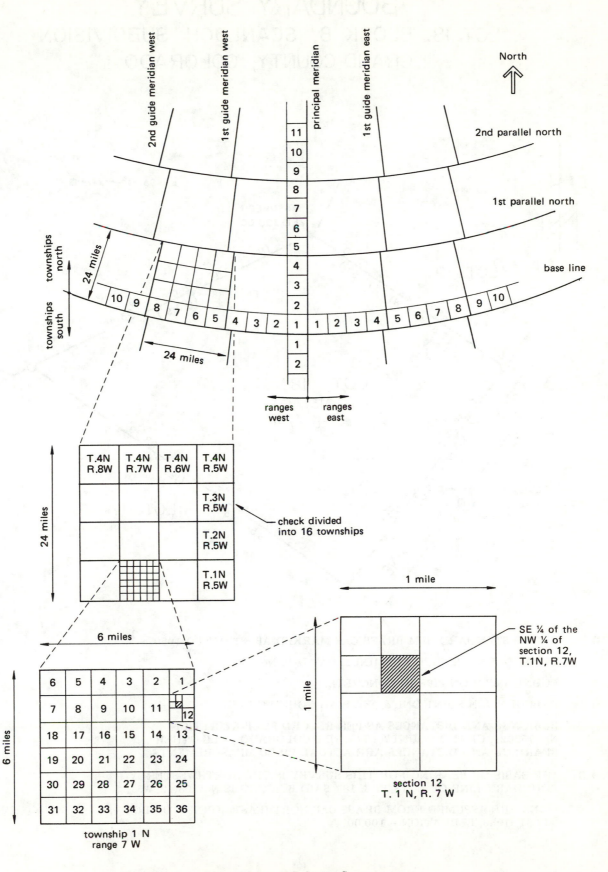

Figure 4.14 U.S. Survey System

PROFESSIONAL PUBLICATIONS ● Belmont, CA

BOUNDARY SURVEY
LOT 18, BLOCK 8, SCANLOCH SUBDIVISION
GRAND COUNTY, COLORADO

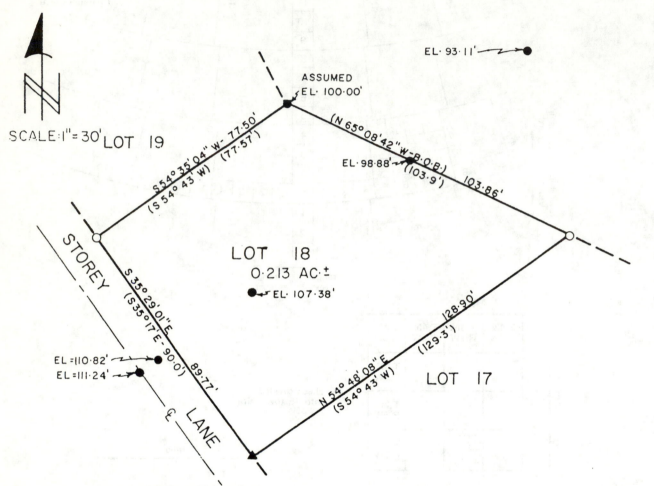

NOTES:

■   FOUND STANDARD BLM BRASS CAP MARKED AP—81 DATED 1950.

○   SET No. 4 REBAR WITH ALUMINUM CAP L. S. No. 11415.

▲   FOUND 1¼" IRON PIPE IN CONCRETE.

●   CALCULATION POINT ONLY, NOTHING FOUND OR SET.

( )   BEARINGS AND DISTANCES AS PER RECORD PLAT RECEPTION
No. 759621, GRAND COUNTY RECORDS, COLORADO. ALL OTHER
BEARINGS AND DISTANCES ARE ACTUAL FIELD MEASUREMENTS.

B.O.B.   THE BASIS OF BEARING FOR THIS SURVEY IS THE NORTHWESTERLY
BOUNDARY LINE OF LOTS 17 & 18. SAID BEARING IS N65°08'42"W.

ELEVATIONS ARE ASSUMED FROM BRASS CAP NORTHEAST CORNER OF LOT 18
AP. 81—1950, ELEVATION = 100.00'.

Figure 4.15   Typical Boundary Survey Description

PROFESSIONAL PUBLICATIONS ● Belmont, CA

referred to by the number of degrees, minutes, and seconds the line is located either east or west of a north-south line.

Another method that is sometimes used is the metes and bounds description. With this approach, the description is a lengthy narrative starting at one point of the property and describing the length and direction of each line around the property boundary until the point of beginning is reached.

With all types of property descriptions, the area of the parcel is also included, usually in acres, one acre containing 43,560 square feet. Remember, too, that one section contains 640 acres and one quarter of a quarter section contains 40 acres.

9   OTHER DESIGN CONSIDERATIONS

In addition to the factors already discussed, many other design considerations can influence the location, orientation, and configuration of a building, as well as other features of the site design. One of the most important is the context of the surrounding development. The design of a building should be sensitive to the scale, massing, and fenestration patterns of nearby buildings. The design should also consider any functional adjacency requirements with other structures or outdoor activities. For example, the entry to a student union building should be located near the existing, primary campus circulation routes.

Views are also an important consideration. Pleasant, desirable views can be used to advantage, either as seen from important spaces within the building or from outdoor spaces. Undesirable views can be avoided by planning the building so service spaces or less important spaces face them. Off-site sources of noise can be similarly avoided by minimizing fenestrations near the noise source.

Quite frequently, buildings are located in order to fall on an important axis with surrounding structures or to complete the enclosure of a major outdoor space. The site-planning process should not overlook these kinds of symbolic criteria.

SAMPLE QUESTIONS

The answers to questions 1 through 3 can be found on the following key list. Select only one answer for each question.

A0 albedo
A1 azimuth
A2 base line
A3 building sewer
A4 catch basins
A5 check
A6 crown
A7 cut and fill
A8 drain inlets
A9 inverts

B0 metes and bounds
B1 principal meridian
B2 runoff
B3 section
B4 sheet flow
B5 solar altitude
B6 storm sewers
B7 township

1. What is especially important in designing roads for drainage?

2. What is a land measure 6 miles on a side known as?

3. Waste water flows because of differences between what?

4. Assuming the building site shown was surrounded on four sides by city streets, which building and road layout would be most appropriate for the site topography?

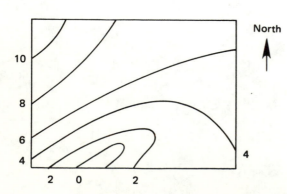

A.

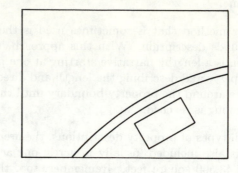

B.

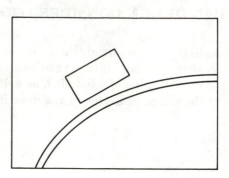

C.

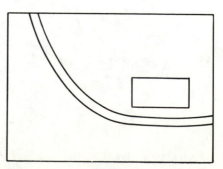

D.

5. Which of the following statements is incorrect?

    A. A 1 1/2% slope is suitable for rough paving.

    B. Landscaped areas near buildings should have at least a 2% slope away from the structure.

    C. A safe sidewalk would slope 2 1/2%.

    D. Roads in northern climates can safely have up to a 12% grade.

6. Which of the following would result in the best site circulation?

    I. planning the service entry drive separate from the automobile entry and drive

    II. making parking areas oversize to accommodate pedestrian circulation

    III. designing all two-way roads at least 24 feet wide

    IV. limiting parking area traffic to a single entrance away from pedestrian walks

    V. laying out walks parallel to parking areas

    A. I, III, and IV

    B. I, III, and V

    C. II, IV, and V

    D. I, III, IV, and V

7. Property can best be described with:

    A. metes and bounds

    B. reference to a section and township

    C. location within a subdivision

    D. all of the above

8. Potential overheating of a medical clinic in a temperate climate could be minimized by:

    A. designing an overhang for the west and east side of the building.

    B. planning a building shape to minimize the surface area of south-facing walls.

    C. having a landscape architect specify deciduous trees near the south elevation.

    D. all of the above

9.

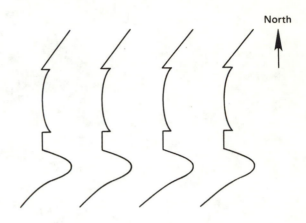

The contour lines in the sketch shown indicate:

    A. a sidewalk sloping down from east to west with a berm on the south side

    B. a road with drainage in the middle and a sidewalk and berm on the south

    C. a swale adjacent to a walking path sloping from northeast to southwest

    D. a curbed street sloping up from west to east next to a drainage ditch

10. If land is limited, which of the following is the best way to plan parking lots?

    A. two-way circulation with 90-degree parking on both sides of a drive

    B. 30-degree parking on both sides of a one-way loop system

    C. combining service circulation with parking at a 45-degree angle

    D. 90 degree parking on one side of a one-way circulation drive

5   SITE DESIGN

The graphic portion of the site design section of the examination tests the candidate's ability to solve a specific site design problem based on given program requirements. Chapter 4 reviewed specific elements of site analysis and design. This chapter discusses how to put all the requirements together with a graphic solution.

This portion of the test focuses primarily on the candidate's ability to understand topography and modify contours, plan site circulation, lay out parking, and incorporate relationships with the site's surroundings into the design.

1   TIPS FOR SOLVING THE SITE DESIGN PROBLEM

The exact content of the site design problem changes slightly from year to year with emphasis placed on different elements of design. However, if you have a good understanding of the following subject areas, you should be able to successfully respond to any type of problem.

Although the following guidelines are intended primarily as a checklist for completing the site design section, they are also helpful for the site planning aspects of the building design portion of the exam.

A. Design Requirements Related to Topography

A thorough knowledge of topography, its representation with contour lines, and how contours are modified to suit the program requirements is mandatory for a successful solution of the site design problem. The graphic techniques of representing topography with contour lines were discussed in Chapter 4. As you work through the problem, keep the following points in mind.

- Although it is unlikely that you will have to locate a building on a site in this portion of the exam, remember that it is better to orient buildings with their length parallel to the contour lines. This makes modifying the contours easier and makes excavating and foundation work less expensive than an orientation perpendicular to the contour lines.

- Driveways and roads are best run parallel to contour lines if little or no change in elevation is required. If a grade change is necessary, run the road at a slight angle to the existing contours and modify the road contour to provide for drainage. An example is shown in Figure 5.1. Roads should be laid out perpendicular to contour lines only if the resulting grade does not exceed recommended limits—usually 8 percent but a more gentle slope is preferred. Calculate the slope after grades have been changed to verify that you are within recommended limits.

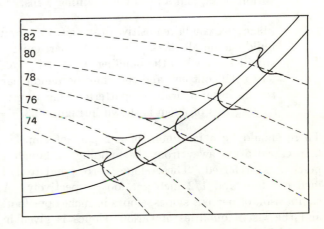

Figure 5.1   Contour Modifications for Roads

- Modify contours to balance cut and fill. During the site exam you do not have to do detailed calculations, but it should appear that you are accomplishing this. One simple method is to draw as many new contour lines on the "fill" side of existing contour lines as you do on the "cut" side at approximately the same distance from the existing lines. See Figure 5.2.

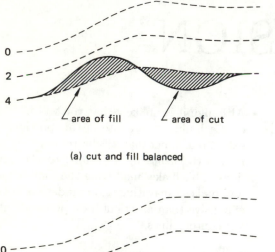

(a) cut and fill balanced

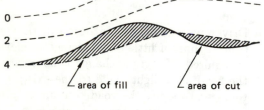

(b) fill exceeds cut

Figure 5.2 Balance Cut and Fill

- Minimize the amount of contour changes, since earth moving costs money and can create other problems such as steep grades, increased excavation costs, and a need for retaining walls.

- Make sure you have positive drainage away from buildings on all sides. This can be particularly troublesome when the building is located parallel to the contours and therefore perpendicular to the natural drainage pattern. One way of solving this problem is shown in Figure 5.3.

There should be a minimum of a 2 percent slope in landscaped areas away from the building, although 4 percent is preferred. These slopes correspond to 1/4 inch per foot and 1/2 inch per foot respectively. A comparison of percent slopes, slopes in inches per foot, and the visual qualities of various slopes is given in Table 5.1.

- Drain approach walks away from buildings as

well as landscaped areas. A minimum of 1 percent (1/8 inch per foot) is required.

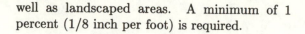
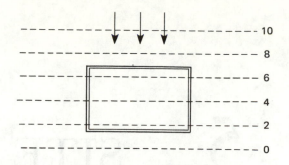

(a) drainage directly into building

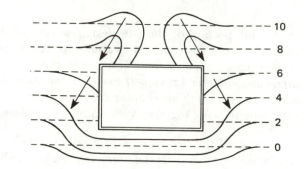

(b) drainage diverted around building

Figure 5.3 Drainage Around Buildings

Table 5.1

Comparison of Percent Slopes and Visual Qualities

percent slope (in inches/foot)		appearance
0.5%	about 1/16	appears flat; use only for smoothest types of pavement
1.0%	about 1/8	slope hardly noticeable
1.5%	about 3/16	good minimum for rough paving
2.0%	about 1/4	noticeable in relation to level construction
2.5%	about 5/16	quite noticeable in relation to level construction
3.0%	about 3/8	very noticeable in relation to level construction

- Try to avoid elaborate drainage patterns or systems of drainage ditches and channels. In most cases, the drainage for the site design problem can be accomplished directly.

- If roads or paths must traverse ditches or drainage swales, make sure you maintain drainage with culverts and call them out on the plan.

- Check parking areas for proper drainage. Ideally, parking lot slopes should be between 1 1/2 percent and 5 percent.

- Avoid very steep slopes that might be susceptible to erosion or make landscaping difficult. A 1 to 3 slope (4 inches per foot) is considered the maximum for a mowed grass slope while a 1 to 2 slope (6 inches per foot) is considered the maximum for unmowed landscaped slopes. Steeper slopes require the use of retaining walls.

B. Planning for Circulation

- Separate pedestrian circulation from vehicular circulation. There should be walks next to parking lots that provide a path to the building.

- Provide ramps accessible by the physically disabled for all changes in elevation. Changes in elevation that cannot be made with a 1 in 20 sloped sidewalk are most efficiently accomplished with a ramp that returns on itself. See Figure 5.4. and refer back to Figure 4.8.

- Be aware of features adjacent to the site that generate pedestrian movement, such as sidewalks, entrances to nearby buildings, and public transportation stops. When the problem mentions these, it is important to provide for them.

- Locate vehicular entries to the site away from intersections. Cars waiting for a stop sign or stop light interfere with cars trying to pull into the site. In most cases, access from a one-way street is preferable to access from a two-way street.

- Driveways into sites facing each other with a street in between should line up exactly or be separated by at least 20 feet.

- If a driveway and a pedestrian path both need to enter a site from a street, they should either be side by side or separated by at least 60 feet. See Figure 5.5.

- Both vehicular and pedestrian circulation should be direct, convenient, and easy to understand. Usually the shortest distance between two points is a good rule of thumb to follow.

- Locate the service drive and loading area close to the areas of the building that need them. Conceal service areas from view as much as possible with vegetation or structures.

- If required, verify that there is emergency access to the building. This may include provisions for fire trucks and ambulances.

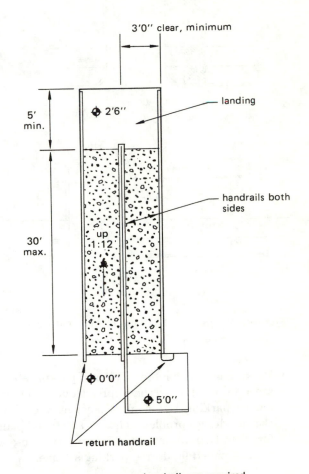

note: most handrails are required to extend 12" beyond the ramp and to wrap a corner.

Figure 5.4 Efficient Handicapped Ramp Layout

C. Parking Requirements

- If a specific number of parking spaces is called for, make sure you provide at least that number. Unless stated otherwise, make each stall 9 feet wide by 19 feet long. Spaces for backing out of a 90-degree parking stall should be at least 24 feet wide.

- There should be at least one parking space for the physically disabled, more if the program specifically calls for it. Design guidelines for parking spaces are shown in Figure 4.12. Arrange the parking spaces and access sidewalks so that people do not have to go behind cars or across the parking drive. Handicapped parking should be as close to the entry as possible, but never more than 125 feet away.

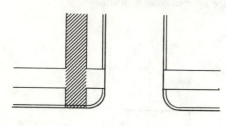

(a) adjacent

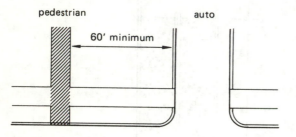

(b) separated

Figure 5.5   Preferred Locations of Automobile and Pedestrian Entries to Streets

- Parking layout is more efficient if parking stalls are grouped rather than spread out. Ninety-degree parking is the most efficient angle. If the site design problem requires a detailed plan for more than about a dozen cars, try to use a double-loaded 90-degree parking scheme.

D. Other Design Considerations

- Entries to buildings and major outdoor areas are best located on the south side of buildings where they will receive sunlight.

- Make every attempt to save existing trees and major vegetation. If it is not possible to keep every tree, at least protect the larger ones. Other major site features, such as rock formations and creeks, should not be altered but used to a design advantage.

- Respect desirable views and incorporate them into the site planning. If views are important, the program usually mentions such a requirement specifically.

- Make sure that no structure or site development occurs outside the limits of zoning setback lines or within easements.

2   DESIGN PROCEDURE AND SCHEDULING

Like the building design section of the exam, the graphic site design section requires that you synthesize a great deal of information and complete a satisfactory drawing in a very short time. You may find the following suggested procedure a useful way to proceed.

step 1: Read the problem thoroughly, twice. Satisfy every statement or requirement, especially those related to topography, drainage, safety, circulation, parking, accessibility for the physically disabled, and relationships with surrounding physical features.

Lay a sheet of tracing paper over the site plan included with the test package and as you read mark the requirements in some graphic format. You should try as much as possible to quickly translate the written word into a graphic form that will make sense to you as you design.

These site influences may include such things as adjacent buildings, pedestrian paths, wind directions, utility locations, traffic volume and direction, views, and similar constraints and design considerations. At this point, some design criteria may simply be a range of locations, such as the most probable areas for vehicle entry onto the site.

step 2: Be careful not to read more into the problem than is there. The test writers are usually very specific about what they want; there is no need to add to the problem requirement and to your work. If a requirement is stated and a particular type of solution is strongly suggested, follow the lead.

For example, a few years ago, the perimeter lines and new spot elevations of a parking area were given. The candidate was supposed to resolve these with the existing grades. The spot elevations indicated a parking lot with a crown one foot higher than either side and gently sloping in one direction parallel to the length of the lot. Although a sheet drainage pattern toward one edge was possible and allowed, candidates were marked down if they did not use the more obvious drainage pattern from the crown of the lot to either side.

step 3: Mark the corners of the site with elevation points. This gives you a quick reference point for checking how your new grading matches up with adjacent property. You may want to mark the midpoints along property lines as well.

If the problem requires the use of storm sewers, find the lowest place where the existing storm sewer can be tapped and work backward from there to determine the invert of any required drain inlets. Unless stated otherwise, use a minimum storm sewer slope of 0.5 percent (1/16 inch per foot).

step 4: Draw schematic sections through the significant slopes. It is usually only necessary to do this in one direction perpendicular to the slope. Draw a section in both directions if the existing contours are complicated. Draw these sections on the same sheet as your markings of site constraints. They can be placed at the top or off to one side as a graphic reminder of the existing slope conditions. Draw the section at the same scale as the site plan.

step 5: Using another sheet of tracing paper over the one you have marked with site constraints, begin laying out roads, walks, parking lots, plazas, or whatever major site features the problem requires. You will find that the site constraints you can read through the tracing paper will resolve many planning questions for you. Others may not be so obvious and will require some study.

step 6: When you have a scheme that works for the major site features, overlay another sheet of tracing paper and begin to study the contour modifications that are needed.

step 7: Work back and forth between the contour sheet and the plan of the site features. If the problem seems to be based more on topography than road and walk design, begin with that sheet. Otherwise, start with the layout of site features. If you have difficulty solving a particular problem with the contours, you may find that you need to change the location or orientation of a plan feature. Or, the required placement of a stairway, sidewalk, or other feature may imply a change in grading.

step 8: When you have solved both major components of the site plan, overlay another sheet of tracing paper and transfer both layout of site features and the new grading plan onto one sheet. As you do this, add other required features, such as landscaping, site furniture, lighting, and so forth.

step 9: Locate spot elevations at building corners, top and bottom landings of stairs and ramps, and other critical locations. Double check that all ramps work with the proper slope and that contour lines are resolved. If abrupt changes in elevation are required,

check to see that you have provided a retaining wall or culverts if natural drainage patterns are covered with roads. Double check all requirements as stated in the program.

step 10: Place your final tracing paper sketch under the paper given to you as part of the test package and trace your solution. Incorporate suitable graphic techniques to clearly communicate your solution. As you do this, you can make minor modifications or corrections to problems that you found in the previous step. Make sure every item is labeled so the graders know you have included what was required.

If you follow a process such as this, you should probably complete the final tracing paper sketch soon enough to allow yourself at least 45 minutes to do the final drawing. By this time you should have solved all the major problems and the final work will be mostly graphics.

3   GRAPHIC TECHNIQUES

Good graphic techniques help you in two ways. First, they help you complete the test in time with the required drawings at the correct level of detail. Second, well-done graphics help communicate your solution to the graders in the short time they have to look at each solution. Part of the trick of finishing on schedule is to budget your time so you have enough left to adequately finish the drawings. However, many candidates fail to finish because they use graphic techniques that take an excessive amount of time for their abilities. This is especially true of the building design portion because there is so much drawing to do.

The goal is to use graphic techniques that are easy to complete yet boldly and clearly show your solution. Before you take the test, you should have a good idea of the tools and techniques you are going to use. Practice making lines, textures, material indications, paving, trees, entourage, and other graphic elements that will be required to draw your solution.

The graphic site design section of the exam is a little easier than the building design portion because there is not so much drawing to do, but similar requirements apply. You need to first get the required lines that show your solution down on paper, and then add rendering techniques that improve the appearance and communication of your work. Keep the following guidelines in mind as you work.

- You can use either hard-line or free-hand techniques or mix them, whichever is faster and easier for you.

- Complete all drawings or portions of one drawing to the same level of detail and appearance. To do this, complete a good line drawing with appropriate line weights. Then go back and add textures, material indications, shadows, and other markings. Since the site design test requires only one drawing, this is easier to do than with the multiple sketches required in the building design portion.

- Use guidelines for lettering.

- Use different line weights to show hierarchy of drawn elements. The outline of an object should be darker and heavier than the lines within the object. Use contrast to show important elements such as walkways.

- Show existing contour lines with dashed lines (usually these are already marked on the base sheet handed out with the test) and new contours with solid lines.

- Do not waste your time or make the drawing hard to read by overrendering. Show what the problem requires you to show. If you are to provide screening for the delivery area, for example, there must be an indication of landscaping or some constructed object to accomplish this.

- Shades and shadows help provide contrast and interest to the drawing, but do these only if you have sufficient time and adding them does not obscure important information within the shadows.

- Use markers that make it easy to lay down a variety of line and texture types. Soft pencils are preferred because they can be erased, while markers may bleed before grading and cannot be erased. Use ink to provide very dark contrast only at the very end of the test session, if you have time and if you are sure nothing will change.

The following examples in Figures 5.6 through 5.10 show some good graphic techniques for the site planning portion of the exam. These are also appropriate for the building design test.

Draw buildings with a heavy outline to clearly identify them on the site plan. A few quick methods are shown in Figure 5.6. At the very least you should show a double line as illustrated in Figure 5.6 (a). A structure with a single outline is too weak and gets lost in the drawing. For buildings with pitched roofs you can shade the top and right sides as though the sun was shining

from the lower left corner of the page [Figure 5.6 (b)]. If you have time, you can completely shadow two sides of the building to achieve the maximum contrast, as shown in Figure 5.6 (c). However, you must be careful not to obscure other lines within the shadow.

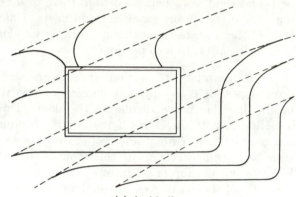

(a) double line

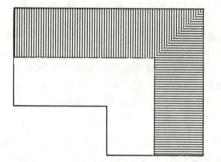

(b) half of pitched roof shaded

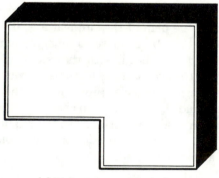

(c) high contrast with shadow

Figure 5.6   Contour Lines and Buildings

Roads can be shown with a single line [Figure 5.7 (a)] but are more prominent with a double line as shown in Figure 5.7 (b). Rendering the background a darker value [Figure 5.7 (c)] makes the road read well but requires much more time to draw.

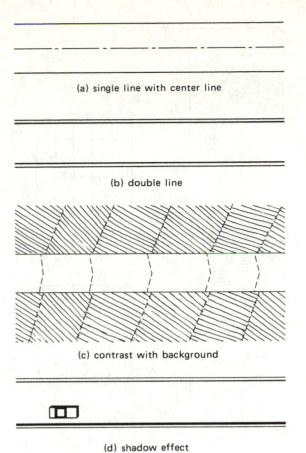

(a) single line with center line

(b) double line

(c) contrast with background

(d) shadow effect

Figure 5.7   Roadways

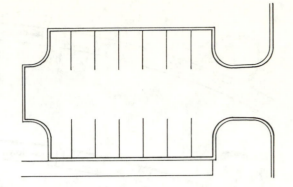

(a) parking at large scale

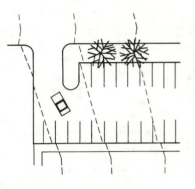

(b) parking at small scale

Figure 5.8   Parking Lots

When drawing parking lots, use guidelines to mark the limits of the width of the parking and driving lanes as well as the width of the stalls. Then outline the lot and use a thin line to mark the individual stalls. If the drawing is on a large scale or actually is intended to show a curb, use a double line as indicated in Figure 5.8 (a).

Since there are usually several walkways in the site design exam, select a technique that is fast and reads well. Figure 5.9 shows three techniques, although drawing the ground with some type of shading takes more time. Use this technique only when there is not a great deal of groundcover. Paving patterns should read well but be simple to draw [Figure 5.9 (b)].

Trees should be simply sketched to indicate their presence but not so detailed as to take too much time or hide lines below them. See Figure 5.10 (a). Drawing shadows is not necessary, but it adds contrast and interest. Figures 5.10 (d) through 5.10 (g) show some possible ways to indicate groundcover. However, all of these are time consuming and their use should be limited to drawings that have limited amounts of groundcover. If you do decide to use a groundcover-rendering technique, you must do the entire area where the groundcover occurs or the drawing will not read properly. The technique shown in Figure 5.10 (e) is quick, but you must make the contour lines heavy so they do not get lost in the pattern. This is also true of Figures 5.10 (f) and 5.10 (g).

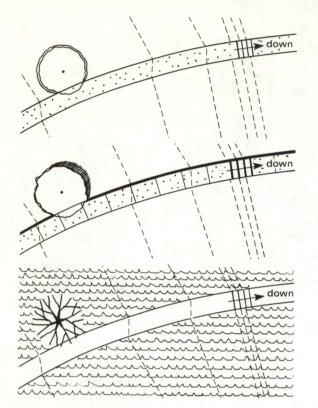

(a) methods of drawing walks

(b) paving pattern techniques

Figure 5.9   Walks and Paving

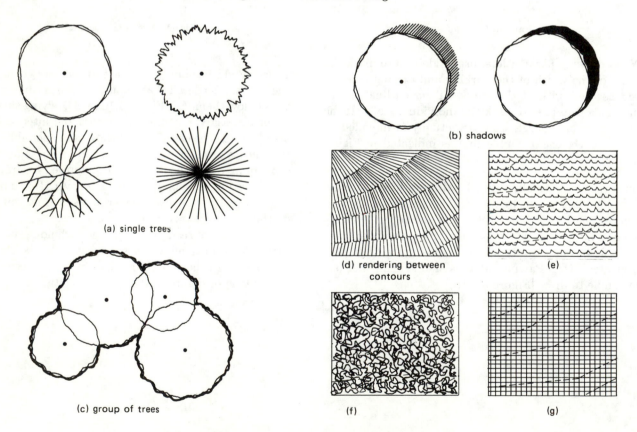

(a) single trees

(b) shadows

(d) rendering between contours

(e)

(c) group of trees

(f)

(g)

Figure 5.10   Trees and Groundcover

SAMPLE PROBLEM

Park and Ride Facility. (See Site Plan.)

A regional transportation district in a midwest city has recently acquired a parcel of land to expand a neighborhood park and ride facility for an express bus stop. The bus shelter and a portion of the waiting platform currently serve a first-phase parking area to the east of the present site. Buses pick up and discharge passengers at an existing pull-off lane on an arterial street on the south edge of the site.

Now that the transportation district has acquired this site, it wants to add more parking, a drop-off area near the bus shelter, and parking for handicapped persons. Since the facility is in a residential neighborhood and acts as a buffer between housing and the busy arterial street, the district would like to minimize the visual impact of the development.

On the site plan given, design the park and ride facility incorporating parking, drives and drop-off area, and handicapped parking using the following design criteria:

Parking

Provide parking for at least 84 cars, half of which may be compact car stalls.

Standard-size car spaces should be 9 feet 0 inches wide and 19 feet 0 inches long. Compact car spaces should be no less than 8 feet 0 inches wide and 15 feet long.

Provide parking for two handicapped persons in addition to the 84 standard spaces. Handicapped spaces should be 13 feet wide and 19 feet long and should be near the waiting platform to avoid excessive changes in elevation with ramps.

Indicate paved parking areas and landscaped areas. Curbs around parking areas are not required.

Connect the parking area with the waiting platform with walks and ramps of suitable widths to accommodate pedestrian traffic.

Drives

Use a one-way drive system with one entrance and one exit from Evans Avenue. The drive should be a minimum of 15 feet wide. Indicate curb cuts.

Separate parking lot circulation from the drive leading to the drop-off area.

Provide a drop-off lane 8 feet wide and at least 80 feet long with suitable transitions for pulling in and out.

Provide a 6-inch curb between the drop-off lane and the waiting platform.

Other Criteria

Existing spot elevations of the waiting platform are shown on the site plan. These are to remain unchanged.

Preserve the existing trees on the site.

The portion of the right of way between the curb and the property line along Evans Avenue can be used for landscaping and drives but not for parking.

Barrier-Free Access

The waiting platform must be accessible to the physically disabled from the handicapped parking areas as well as the main parking lot.

maximum grade on walks with rails: 1:12 (8 1/3%)
maximum grade on walks without rails: 1:20 (5%)
maximum length of ramp between
   landings: 30 feet

Presentation

The final presentation drawing may be in free-hand sketch form. It should be clear and precise to accurately communicate your design concept. All designed elements must be labeled. Show finish contours and provide spot elevations on critical constructed elements.

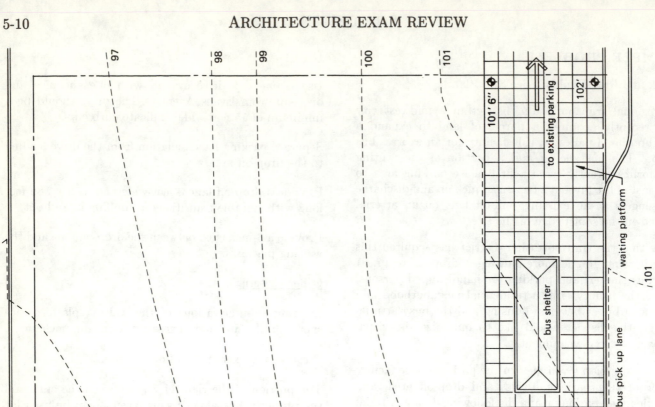

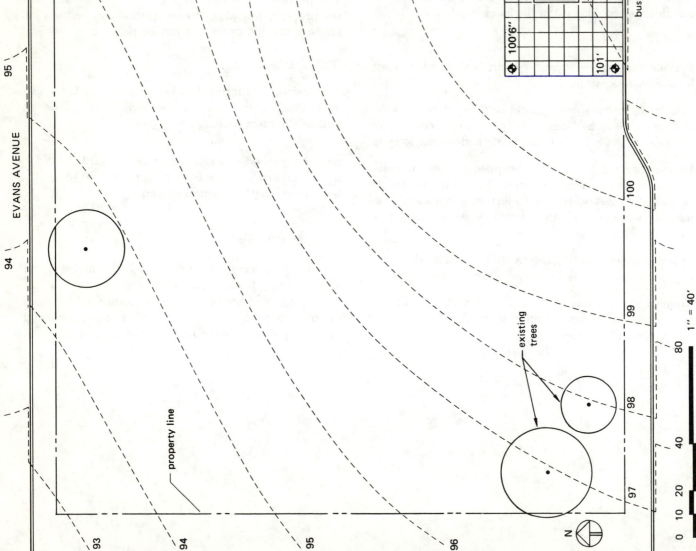

6 BUILDING DESIGN

The building design portion of the A.R.E. is considered one of the most difficult parts of the entire examination. The candidate must synthesize a large amount of information into a comprehensive design solution and do it under severe time constraints in what becomes, at best, an arduous test of endurance. Many candidates fail, not because they cannot solve the problem but because they let it get the best of them. They begin to make the wrong decisions and choices at the wrong time, spend too much time on one part of the problem, then panic and run short on time, and end up either not solving the problem or forgetting to include critical elements.

In the past several years, the design problem has been structured so that there is plenty of time for the candidate to solve it and produce the necessary drawings while still showing his or her ability to design. The key elements of success are to budget your time, stick with your schedule, and follow a logical procedure of solution.

Taking this test requires a different mind set than you may be familiar with either from working in an office during your internship or from school. In an office, you might not have had the opportunity to work through an entire building problem as you must during the examination. In school, the design solution is often idealized, with much of the emphasis devoted to the final form and style. School projects are also developed over a period of weeks or months, not in hours.

The A.R.E. examination demands that the building work in all aspects: function, life/safety, code compliance, structure, mechanical systems, lighting, and so forth. Although it does ask that the building be appropriate for human occupancy in terms of scale, proportion, relationship to its surroundings, use of materials, and other design parameters, it does not demand an award winner. Your emphasis, therefore, should be on solving the stated problem completely with reasonable design decisions.

This chapter presents a suggested approach to the building design section of the examination. This approach can be used on any building type and will allow you to adapt to any surprises the test writers may throw at you. Of course, every candidate has his or her own particular strengths and weaknesses, so you should adapt the process to your own needs. For example, one person may be weak in presentation drawing skills but a good space planner. This person should schedule more time for drafting the final drawings and work from very developed tracing paper sketches that are done from quick, but complete, schematic planning diagrams. Another person good at presentation drawings can afford to allow more time for design work.

The final part of this chapter presents a checklist of critical points of concern for the design test. It is divided into the current groups of grading criteria: program requirements, design logic, code compliance, and technical issues.

1 HOW TO SOLVE THE 12-HOUR DESIGN PROBLEM

A. Strategies for Time Management

Since one of the biggest problems with the design test is finishing on time with a complete solution, your first task should be to quickly read the problem statement and set up your own timetable. Do not read the program in detail the first time through; simply get a feeling for the problem, where major difficulties might be, and how much time you should allow for the final drafting of the solution.

The following timetable might prove useful for you as a starting point:

step 1:	Make a quick overview of the problem statement and a determination of your own timetable.	15 minutes
step 2:	Read the examination information booklet and translate the written data into a programming base sheet.	45 minutes
step 3:	Translate the programmed spaces into graphic form and calculate the maximum allowable gross area.	30 minutes
step 4:	Check areas and functions for each floor.	15 minutes
	total time to this point:	1 hour 45 minutes
step 5:	Begin adjacency/circulation diagrams.	90 minutes
step 6:	Study the structural system.	30 minutes
step 7:	Study the mechanical/plumbing systems.	15 minutes
step 8:	Design the development, including plan, section, and elevations.	120 minutes
	lunch break:	30 minutes
	total time to this point:	6 hours, 30 minutes
step 9:	Make the final drawings.	5 hours
step 10:	Make a final check.	30 minutes
	total time:	12 hours

B. Read Information Booklet and Create a Programming Base Sheet

Reading the examination booklet should not only be an act of looking at words but also a process of reading and simultaneously translating the written word into graphic form as much as possible. This takes a little extra time up front but saves time as you develop your initial plan and results in a better solution.

To do this, put a piece of paper over the first level site plan and schematically mark requirements and facts as given by the program as you read. These are conditions that will (or might) affect the overall conceptual siting of the building and the plan of the major elements. This will become your "*programming base sheet*." See Figure 6.1.

Some of the conditions you should note include:

- views

- probable (or required) entrance location(s)

- any required pedestrian access to adjacent sites or buildings

- service access

- any special circulation requirements: for example, separation of public and private corridors or division of areas for security purposes

- any unusual or apparently important topographic or landscape conditions

- orientation required for energy conservation reasons

- location of utilities, drainage, or any other service that may dictate the location of building elements

As you read the program you should also make quick bubble diagrams of critical adjacency relationships. Place these on the same sheet of tracing paper as your plan diagram of other program requirements, but off to the side so they do not interfere with your later schematic planning. You do not necessarily have to include every detailed adjacency requirement at this point, just those that will affect the overall siting of the building and the planning of its major spaces and circulation paths. Later, you can work on smaller-scale relationships such as the adjacency of two offices within a larger office suite or the position of a steam room near a shower room.

If the site has any significant slope, sketch north-south and east-west sections at the top of your programming base sheet as a constant visual reminder of topographic condition.

When you are through reading the program, you should have your own base sheet of program information in graphic form that is laid over the exam test pad sheet of the site. Your base sheet should include diagrammatic symbols of the critical program requirements more or less to scale on the site plan, diagrammatic adjacency diagrams off to the side where they are clearly visible, section cuts through the site if the topography warrants it, and other notes that you feel are critical but which represent program requirements that cannot be easily shown in graphic form. For example, you might note that your building should be compatible with an adjacent building.

As you develop your programming base sheet, you may want to use different colors to represent various classes of requirements, for example, use red for circulation-related needs, green for relationships with nearby buildings and outdoor spaces, blue for required views and building orientation, and so forth.

If detailed reference information such as building codes or zoning ordinances are reproduced, read only those

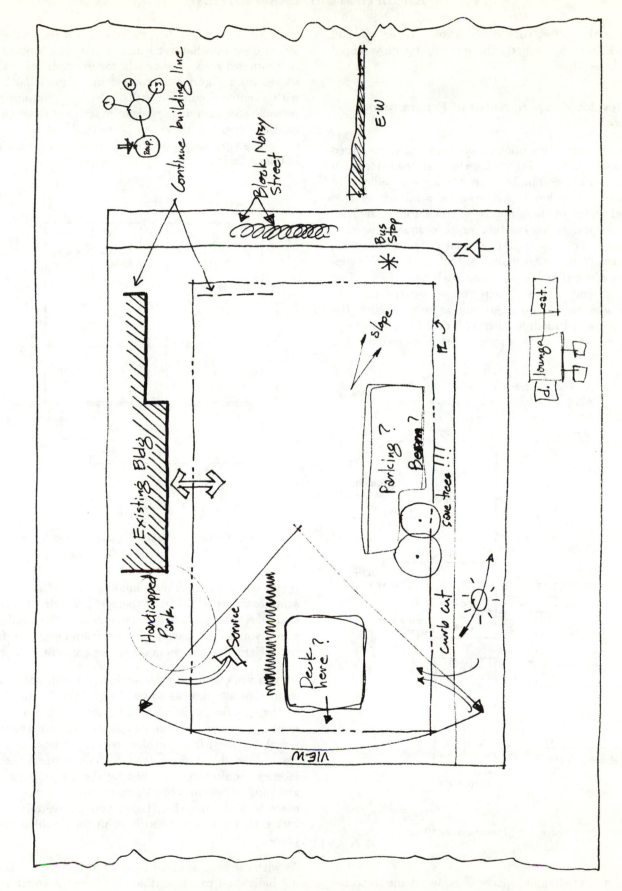

Figure 6.1 Programming Base Sheet

PROFESSIONAL PUBLICATIONS ● Belmont, CA

portions that affect your initial layout. Later, you can go back and select exactly those requirements you need for detailed design.

C. Develop Graphic Notes of Programmed Spaces

The test information booklet will give you the required functional spaces and the square footage needed for each space. However, numbers on a page are difficult to visualize. In order to give yourself a strong, graphic mental image of these numbers, translate the individual programmed spaces into graphic squares or rectangles at the same scale the final drawings must be. Take graph paper to make this job easier. Use consistent dimensional increments such as 5 feet. This will save you time and help you see spatial relationships between functional groupings more easily. Using a standard module such as 5 or 10 feet also helps when you work on a structural system layout. See Figure 6.2.

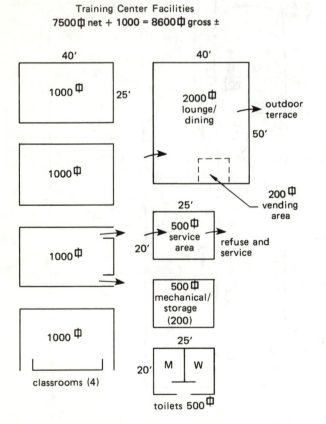

Training Center Facilities
7500 ⊞ net + 1000 = 8600 ⊞ gross ±

Figure 6.2 Programming Blocks

Next, group individual spaces as required and indicated by the program into their most probable, logical shape. For example, several offices that make up an admin-

istrative suite might be grouped into a rectangle two offices deep by whatever length is required to yield the programmed area. Figure 6.3, for example, shows the spaces from Figure 6.2 grouped in a functional block with a center circulation path. Your first grouping may present some planning problems in terms of the required relationships, but these can be worked out later. The size and shape should be enough to help you begin preliminary design.

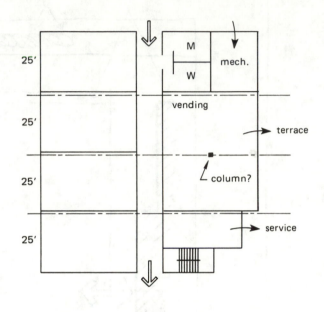

Figure 6.3 Programming Blocks Placed in a Larger Functional Grouping

If you are grouping several small spaces, be sure to add some extra area (15 to 20 percent) for circulation so that when you begin detailed planning of the functional group you do not have to use programmed space from net assignable areas to make up for corridors.

As you work on the building plan, you will need to remain mentally flexible so you can adjust the blocks to fit the specific conditions of site, structure, circulation needs, and so on. You may even need to split the functional block with a corridor, service spaces, and the like, but such divisions need not compromise the adjacency requirements implied by the larger functional grouping. These first block layouts, however, are a good place to start and should give you an overall organization that can be refined later in the detailed design phase.

As with the programming base sheet, the idea in sketching individual rooms and activity areas is to translate them into a visual form that is much easier to comprehend and remember as you work on plan layouts.

D. Check Areas

Add up net assignable square footage if included in the program in the test information booklet. Divide by an efficiency factor to get gross square footage allowed. Use this to check yourself once you get your first layout. If no efficiency factor is given in the program, use 25 percent (0.25).

Next, compare square footage required for each floor. If they are divergent, you know you have to have some setbacks or make other provisions. Be sure to consider any two-story spaces, atriums, mezzanines, and so forth that may balance or unbalance the total square-footage requirements on each floor.

The program will probably state what functions are to be located on each floor. If not, study the adjacency requirements, entrances, and other external access requirements and balance the programmed square footage to approximately even out each floor area.

E. Develop Adjacency Diagrams

Adjacency diagrams should include the entire building, not just the individual bubble diagrams you sketched as visual reminders as you read through the program. Instead of using amorphous, unscaled diagrams, use the square or rectangular blocks of space you have developed as your bubbles. Rough bubble diagrams can mislead you concerning scale and shape. Therefore, beginning directly with approximately sized rectangular shapes saves time and makes it easier for you to see possible structural grid possibilities.

Begin adjacency diagrams using the larger, functional groupings developed earlier. This helps you avoid getting lost in detailed planning too soon. Assuming you grouped smaller spaces into reasonably shaped functional groupings and allowed some extra room for circulation, this approach usually works.

Sketch the adjacency diagrams on a separate sheet of tracing paper over the programming base sheet diagram you developed while you were reading the program. Both of these sheets of tracing paper should be placed over the exam pad provided to you. The diagram serves as a constant reminder of critical program requirements while you do your sketching. The exam pad shows all the given site conditions that you will eventually have to relate to on your final drawing.

As you study and lay out possible adjacencies, make an overall circulation scheme one of your primary concerns. A reasonable circulation scheme must be an integral part of your early planning because it has so much bearing on critical portions of the test. Among other things, the circulation scheme:

- gives overall organization to the building, the spaces, and the required adjacencies

- determines exiting and handicapped access

- provides a logical place to separate long-span spaces from smaller spaces and can make your structural solution easier

See Figure 6.4. Since the long-span spaces are also higher spaces, the circulation path provides a logical place to break the roof line.

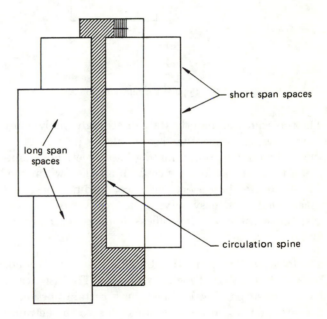

Figure 6.4 Separation of Long-Span and Short-Span Spaces

One of the common mistakes candidates make is to work on adjacencies and locations of spaces and then string them together with a resulting maze of corridors, stairways, and lobbies. If your corridor has more than one change in direction, you may need to replan.

Two common circulation patterns are shown in Figure 6.5. These two types, or some simple variation of them, will almost always work with the type and scale of problem given in the exam.

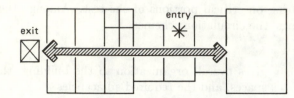

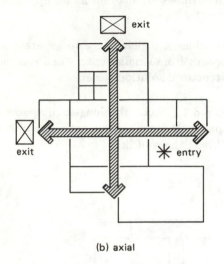

(a) linear, double loaded corridor

(b) axial

Figure 6.5 Typical Circulation Concepts

The program will directly state or strongly imply many conditions for conceptual layout of the plans. These should be on your programming base sheet. For example, a requirement for service from an alley will immediately locate the service entrance, loading dock, and spaces that need easy service; desired views will suggest the location of prime offices, lounges, eating areas, and other rooms.

The location of certain other building elements may not be stated directly but logically implied. For instance, if handicapped parking is shown on a certain portion of the site, you would be wise not to locate the entrance too far from it.

If you work over your programming base sheet using larger blocks of functional spaces, you will be able to try more schematic alternative layouts early in the test just as you would in a normal office situation. Do not get lost in details too soon.

After you have two or three schematic alternatives, take a quick break and then review them with your own mini-critique. Check your solutions against the program requirements, possible problems with or opportunities for structural and mechanical layout, efficiency, and so forth. At this point you should be able to select an alternative that provides a good direction for more detailed development. You may find that you

want to combine the best features of two or more approaches.

F. Study Structural Systems

At some point in the early stages of conceptual design, you should begin to consider a structural system. Trying to apply structure late in the test, after you have locked yourself into a plan, will only cause problems and be obvious to the graders. In the best case, it will be and look awkward; in the worst case, it will result in columns in the middle of spaces, unreasonable spans, and grading marks against you.

The program may make some direct statements concerning structure, for example, either what system has been deemed feasible or unfeasible, or it may say nothing about structure. In any event, keep it simple. The graders will not be looking for innovative structural concepts, just for your understanding of how to integrate structure into your building.

The test will require that you deal with both small spans and long spans so you should have a good grasp of the requirements of both. Unless the program states differently, use a post-and-beam system in steel with exterior bearing walls. If the steel needs to be fireproofed, that is easy to show on the section drawing.

If the program and plan layout suggest it, you might also consider one or two major interior bearing walls. Bar joists with concrete over metal decking usually work for floor and roof systems since different loads and spans can be accomplished by varying the spacing and depth of the bar joists. Bar joists also allow more space for running ductwork, sprinkler piping, and other mechanical services.

As you lay out the programmed spaces, you should begin to see patterns of dimensions that can have implications for a structural bay or grid size while still accommodating different-sized rooms. See Figure 6.6. You will probably have to adjust your preliminary room layout somewhat to work with a structural bay size that makes sense, but this is not too difficult. Once again, remain mentally flexible. A structural bay size does not have to be uniform throughout—just reasonable and arranged so you do not have any impossible spans or columns in the middle of rooms.

There are many ways to logically organize a combination of small spans and large spans so that the solution works structurally, functionally, and aesthetically. Large spaces with long-span structure and higher ceiling heights may be sized to work within two smaller bay sizes or be separated from the small-span structural system with the circulation system or in a separate building wing.

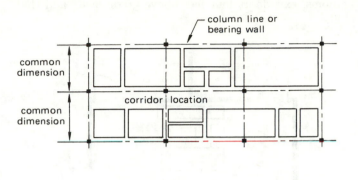

Figure 6.6 Structural Bay Pattern Suggested by Space Layout

Of course, the direction you take will depend on the program, site constraints, and specific spans required. This is one of the reasons why it is useful to develop several schematic alternatives using scaled blocks of space. The adjacency diagrams will begin to suggest a structural grid size and shape that can quickly be checked against what you know is reasonable. You can then draw a regular structural grid and use that to do more detailed layouts of the floor plans. The structural grid may also suggest a way of developing exterior elevations.

If you feel comfortable with your design abilities and have a good idea what the structural requirements are likely to be from the statement of building type known before the test, you may even want to decide on two or three possible structural grids before the test, including needed depths of structural members and thicknesses of bearing walls. Once you read the problem statement, you may be able to select one of these grids and draw it right away as a framework for any subsequent planning.

G. Study Mechanical and Plumbing Systems

After you consider possible structural systems and grid sizes with your preliminary block adjacency diagrams, quickly review how the mechanical system will lay out. This simply means locating the mechanical room and horizontal and vertical spaces for ductwork. Depending on the system stated in the program or selected by you, there may be additional constraints such as outside air or special exhaust needs. If no mechanical system is specifically stated in the program, a variable air volume system usually works. See Chapter 9 for a discussion of mechanical systems.

In most cases, providing space for ductwork is not a great problem because of the size of the building in the test problem. Suspended ceilings usually provide enough flexibility for mechanical services as long as you allow enough room below the bottom of the structure and show this in the section drawing.

At this point, also quickly review provisions for plumbing. Although this is not a critical feature most of the time, you should at least be placing toilet rooms back to back, stacking them on each floor, and locating other plumbing services nearby. Also check that other special plumbing conditions—such as unreasonably long supply or drainage lines or vents that may have to pass through rooms above—do not present obvious problems.

H. Begin Detailed Design

Once you have selected a workable schematic design from your alternatives and know you have a structural grid that works, you can begin more detailed design. Before proceeding, be sure that you have satisfied program requirements that affect the overall siting and planning of the building. For example, if the program states that primary pedestrian access is from the west, your entrance should be on the west. If the exercise gymnasium needs to be directly adjacent to the locker rooms, that is what your schematic should show. You should be sure all major life/safety considerations are satisfied. These include such things as the number of exits, avoiding dead-end corridors, and required distances to exits.

If you do not have all requirements worked out at this point, do not proceed until you do. Of course, there will always be some amount of judgment and compromise. Certain program requirements may have more priority than others, and you may need to make a choice between them. This often happens as you run short on time and you cannot get everything to work out exactly right.

Often, the same requirement is stated in the program more than once: first in the general project statement and again in the detailed program requirements. It is wise to give these highest priority. The next priority should go to requirements specifically stated in the program at least once. Finally, there are priorities that may simply be implied by the program or considered good design practice. For example, if you had to decide between an arrangement to improve energy efficiency or one to satisfy your concern for appearance, you would be wise to choose energy efficiency.

At this point take a short break so you can come back to the test refreshed and able to concentrate on more detailed design.

As you begin detailed development of your schematic plan you will have a very good idea of major elements, organization of the building, siting, major circulation paths, exiting, structure, and provisions for the mechanical system. It should be fairly easy to make minor adjustments to fine tune adjacencies, modify dimensions of spaces to fit within the structural grid, lay out toilet rooms, properly orient exits and stairways, locate doorways, and satisfy the more detailed program requirements. You should still be working on tracing paper at this point so it is easy to make changes.

At this time, you should also be looking at the shape and proportion of individual rooms to make sure they make sense and allow for reasonable furniture arrangement and circulation within the room. Figure 6.7 shows two reception rooms of identical programmed areas. Plan A shows a shape, proportion, and arrangement of doors that would not be reasonable for two secretaries and a small waiting area, while plan B makes more sense for its intended function. The examination instructions often require that you sketch in furniture in some of the major spaces, so this is an important consideration.

Before you proceed too far into detailed development of the floor plan, begin a building section. You may not know at this time exactly what the best location for the section cut will be, but make your best estimate. Beginning a section drawing at this time will help you get out of the two-dimensional floor plan mentality and force your attention on the third dimension. You should also do this with the elevations. You may discover things by working on the elevations and section that will influence how you develop your floor plans. It is better to find this out early than to wait until the last minute to complete the elevations when it is too late to make corrections.

During development of the drawings on tracing paper, remember to draw only what you actually need in order to make decisions. Do not waste time sketching in bar joist framing, exterior material indications, benches, and other items that can just as well be indicated when you do the final drawing.

I. Check, Complete Final Drawings, and Check Again

Once you have finished development of the floor plans and worked on the elevations and section enough to know everything works, take a lunch break and rest. When you come back, go through a final checklist following the same criteria the jurors use: check the

program requirements, look at design logic, verify that building codes and exiting have been satisfied, and review technical issues of life/safety, structure, mechanical systems, energy conservation, and use of materials. Also check for conflicts such as ducts going through rooms, exit doors four feet above grade level, and the like.

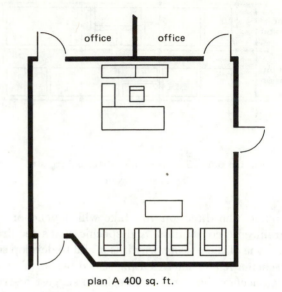

plan A 400 sq. ft.

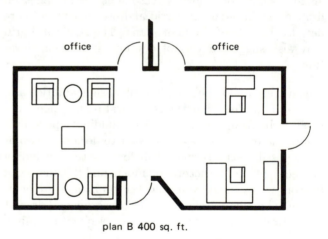

plan B 400 sq. ft.

Figure 6.7 Alternate Room Arrangements

If everything is satisfactory, you are ready to begin your final drawings. You should have decided on a graphic technique before coming to the test and solved the majority of problems during your design development, so this part should go smoothly. Any changes you make at this point will be minor, such as moving a doorway slightly or switching two adjacent spaces of similar size.

You may also be making some final, minor decisions as you draw, such as how wide a walkway should be, or the depth of a window overhang. In addition to these minor design points, concentrate on clarity and completeness of presentation. Make sure the graders can understand your design intent and that you have considered all the necessary requirements. For instance, if you estimate you need a 24-inch deep beam, draw it that deep without over- or underemphasizing it.

Try to leave yourself one-half hour to an hour of time at the end for a final check. Of course, it will be too late at this time to make any major revisions, but you can check for minor omissions and incomplete graphics. If you find you have left out any indication of a required sprinkler system, for example, you can at least show a portion of it on the section and make a note on the drawing. This extra time at the end of the test also allows for making additional explanatory notes to clarify your design.

2 CHECKLIST FOR YOUR DESIGN SOLUTION

One of your primary checklists should be the problem statement itself. When you read through the program and problem statement, underline individual words, phrases, or sentences that you can identify as having a single design consequence. Later, as you work through your solution, use these underlined items as a checklist and make sure you have responded to every one. Omission of any one will count against you, and omission of particularly important requirements will be enough to fail you.

The following list itemizes some of the critical elements that should be included or considered in your final drawings. It includes requirements that are not necessarily expressed in every problem statement but are part of the general grading criteria. It is by no means a complete list, but it outlines the most important evaluation criteria and points out areas where mistakes or omissions are often made by candidates.

A. Program Requirements

_____ solution contains all the required spaces

_____ required spaces contain the correct amount of square footage; solution contains no less than the program requirement but may contain slightly more

_____ efficiency ratio (net-to-gross) not exceeded

_____ required adjacencies satisfied

_____ exterior adjacencies satisfied: service, pedestrian access, entries, and so forth

_____ correct shapes and proportions of spaces for the intended function; reasonable allowances made for furniture

_____ furniture shown if required by problem statement

_____ all desirable views considered

_____ sight lines into toilet rooms considered

_____ relationship to adjacent buildings appropriate in terms of scale, materials, and access

_____ life/safety items addressed

B. Design Logic

_____ circulation efficient, direct, and properly sized

_____ no tight circulation spaces; consideration of handicapped access

_____ direct parking-to-building access

_____ direct access for handicapped from parking to entrance

_____ elevator easily accessible to all users and opens in correct direction on all floors

_____ building entrance or exit avoided through stair vestibules

_____ building zoned as required by program

_____ incompatible traffic types separated

_____ awkward crossing paths avoided

_____ service entrances and access separate from incompatible functions and leading directly to areas they serve

_____ building security shown and noted as required by program

_____ topography utilized appropriately

_____ all major spaces with exterior exposure if appropriate

C. Code Compliance

_____ two exits from each floor remotely located from each other; monumental stairs may not count as required exit

_____ stairs located within minimum and maximum distances from each other

_____ second-level egress exiting directly to outside or as required by program statement

_____ all required exit doors swinging in the direction of travel and not decreasing required corridor width when open

_____ widths of exits appropriate; minimum of 44 inches or as required by program statement

_____ at least two exits from assembly spaces remotely located from each other

_____ maximum travel distances from doors to exit: 150 feet (200 feet in sprinklered buildings) or as indicated in the program

_____ maximum 7-inch riser height; 11-inch minimum tread width

_____ fire separation walls and ceiling/floor assemblies indicated on plan and section

_____ building accessible by the physically disabled according to ANSI 117.1: entrance ramp, corridor widths, vestibule sizes, toilet rooms, and all parts of the building

_____ ramps checked for maximum allowable slope: 1:12

_____ dead-end corridors avoided or limited to 20 feet

_____ guardrails and handrails shown and dimensioned if required

D. Technical Considerations

_____ framing clearly shown and noted: beams, bearing walls, columns, floor, and roof deck

_____ footings and foundations shown under all walls, columns, and elevator shafts both in section and elevations

_____ footings stepped if sloping site

_____ footings at correct bearing or below frost depth

_____ slab on grade construction shown and noted

_____ bearing walls thick enough for loads and unsupported height

_____ all structural elements accurately drawn to scale

_____ mechanical rooms(s) and ductwork routing shown; heating may need to be separate from air conditioning

_____ energy conservation measures shown and noted as appropriate: building orientation, building form, insulation, shading, thermal mass, landscaping, and glazing types

_____ glass type noted in response to solar control and other needs

_____ appropriate solar control on south and west

_____ natural lighting utilized

_____ artificial lighting indicated and described

_____ toilet rooms stacked and other plumbing grouped as appropriate; toilet room ventilation noted

_____ sprinklers indicated if required by program

_____ acoustical control techniques indicated and noted if required by programmed space

_____ all major materials indicated and noted

_____ materials use consistent, cost effective, appropriate for function, and compatible with adjacent buildings as required by program

_____ roof slope and drains indicated on section

_____ fenestrations thought out in terms of view, energy conservation, exterior design, and compatibility with adjacent buildings

_____ foundation and hydraulic shaft indicated under elevator

_____ exterior spot elevations checked on site plan, especially near building, drainage slopes, handicapped ramps, and other areas

_____ natural features such as trees, rock outcroppings, and water used to enhance design

E. General Tips

_____ Do not read anything into the program requirements.

_____ Use only rectangular building shapes and structural systems.

_____ Make exterior design compatible with the surrounding buildings and neighborhood.

_____ Make building spaces and exterior design compatible with the human scale.

_____ Be sure that composition, proportion, texture, materials, and form are appropriate to the building type and surrounding area.

_____ Make elevations on first-floor site plan and second-floor plan, exterior elevations, and section correspond to each other.

3   GRAPHIC PRESENTATION

The final drawings required for the building design portion of the examination add to the difficulty in successfully finishing because you generally have to complete a combination site plan and first-floor plan, second-floor plan, two elevations, and a building section. Since the time required to do this is substantial, you must be skilled in quickly and accurately rendering your design solution. As with the site design problem, an otherwise good solution may be marked down if the graders cannot understand your intent, or a perfect solution may fail if the required drawings are not complete.

The graders take about 10 to 15 minutes to review each submission and may view them closely or from about three to five feet away, so your drawings must be easy to read under those circumstances. Since the required number of drawings will be stated in the problem, they should all be rendered to approximately the same level of detail. Do not spend all your time on three and leave yourself only one-half hour for the last one. You will not finish and not pass. It is better to do good line drawings of all the required sketches along with the necessary notes so you are sure the problem is solved, and then go back and darken walls and add material indications, shadows, entourage, and other graphic elements that make your drawings read better. If you run short of time, at least you will have the absolute minimum required submission.

Some general graphic techniques for site design are described in Chapter 5. These are also applicable to the building design exam. In addition, review the following suggestions for the three types of drawings required.

A. Floor Plans

See Figure 6.8 for a partial floor plan drawn at 1/8-inch scale.

Use double lines for walls and single lines for windows, and poché the walls in with solid black. If time is short, at least do the exterior walls. A heavy marker is good for this task, but wait until the end of the exam period when you know changes are not going to be made.

- Show door swings with a one-quarter circle arc and indicate the door itself with a single line.

- Draw overhangs with dashed lines.

- Indicate all built-in items as well as plumbing fixtures. It is especially important to show the detailed layout of the toilet rooms.

- Show stairways with individual steps drawn in and an arrow indicating direction up or down.

- Draw all required furniture and furniture necessary to explain your design or show a workable plan, using a single line.

- Label all rooms and spaces with the names exactly as given in the program.

- Indicate the location of your section cut with a line through the building and an arrow pointing in the direction of the cut.

- Indicate drainage away from the building with arrows and a note.

- Use a simple paving pattern to indicate circulation both inside and outside the building. Use quick, simple indications for trees, shrubs, and groundcover as discussed in Chapter 5.

- When drawing the second-floor plan and open volumes of high spaces below, label them "open to below."

B. Elevations

See Figure 6.9 for a partial elevation of the floor plan shown in Figure 6.8.

Unless stated otherwise in the problem statement, select elevation views that best represent your design. Although the graders are not looking for award-winning, meticulously detailed elevations, you should show a design that incorporates aesthetic appeal, simple use of materials, and massing of forms that indicate you know how to integrate the internal functions of a building with the structure, fenestration pattern, and human scale. Keep the elevations simple; try not to use more than two exterior materials in addition to glazing. Use simple material indications that are easy and quick to draw. Brick can be shown with closely spaced horizontal lines, stucco, stone, and precast concrete with stipple marks.

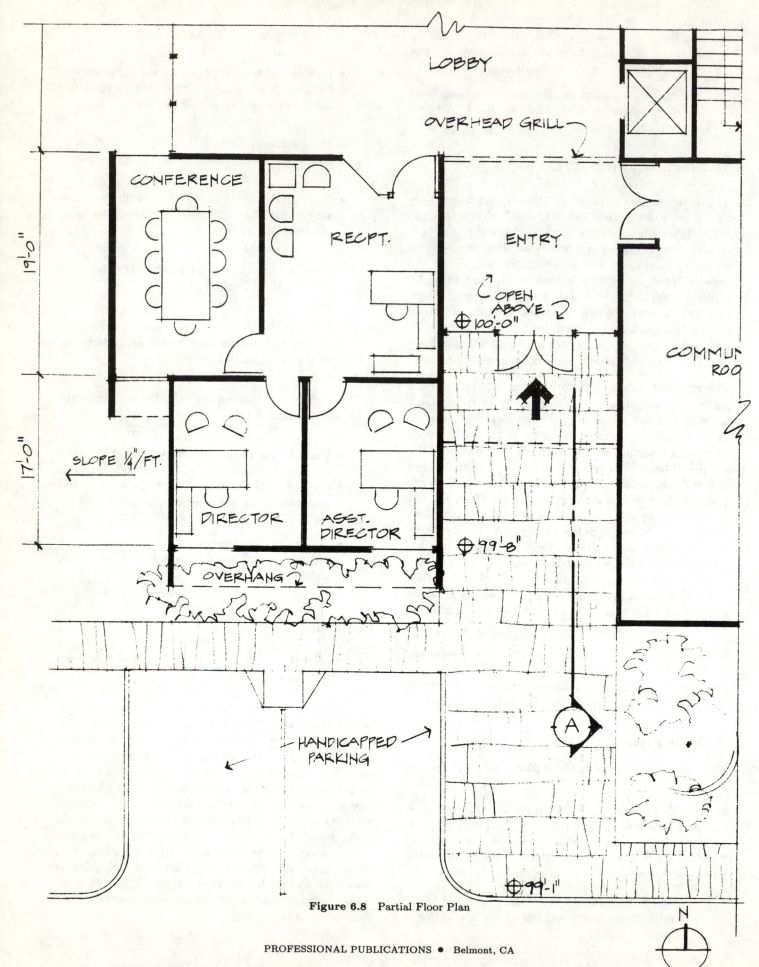

Figure 6.8 Partial Floor Plan

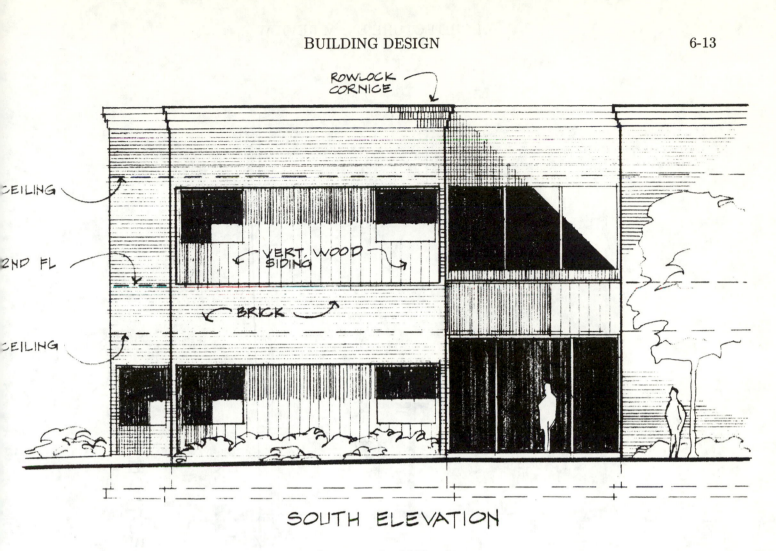

ROWLOCK
CORNICE

CEILING

2ND FL

VERT. WOOD
SIDING

BRICK

CEILING

SOUTH ELEVATION

Figure 6.9 Partial Elevation

Draw a heavy profile line around the perimeter of the elevation, and use varying line weights to indicate those portions of the elevation that are closest to the viewer—heaviest lines close and thinner lines farther away. The base line should be the heaviest and must correspond to the contour lines on the first-floor plan. Show the foundations and floor and ceiling levels with dashed lines.

Use a few scale figures and indicate landscaping if appropriate and if it corresponds to your site plan. However, tree indications and other landscaping must not obscure the other elements of your design.

Use shade and shadowing if time allows. This is a good way to provide contrast to the elevations and to indicate overhangs and the form of the building more distinctly.

C. Section

See Figure 6.10 for a partial section of the floor plan shown in Figure 6.8.

- Take the section cut through your building

where most three-dimensional information will be shown. This includes two-story spaces, changes in topography or levels of the building, areas for mechanical equipment, structure, and typical wall sections.

- Poché the cut sections of walls and foundations with solid black.

- Indicate ceiling heights and finish elevations of both first and second floors.

- Show the existing grade with a dashed line and the new grade at perimeter walls.

- Include a few scale figures.

- Clearly note the mechanical system, structural system, fire rating of walls, roof system and roof drainage, ceiling finish, representative wall finishes, and footing depth.

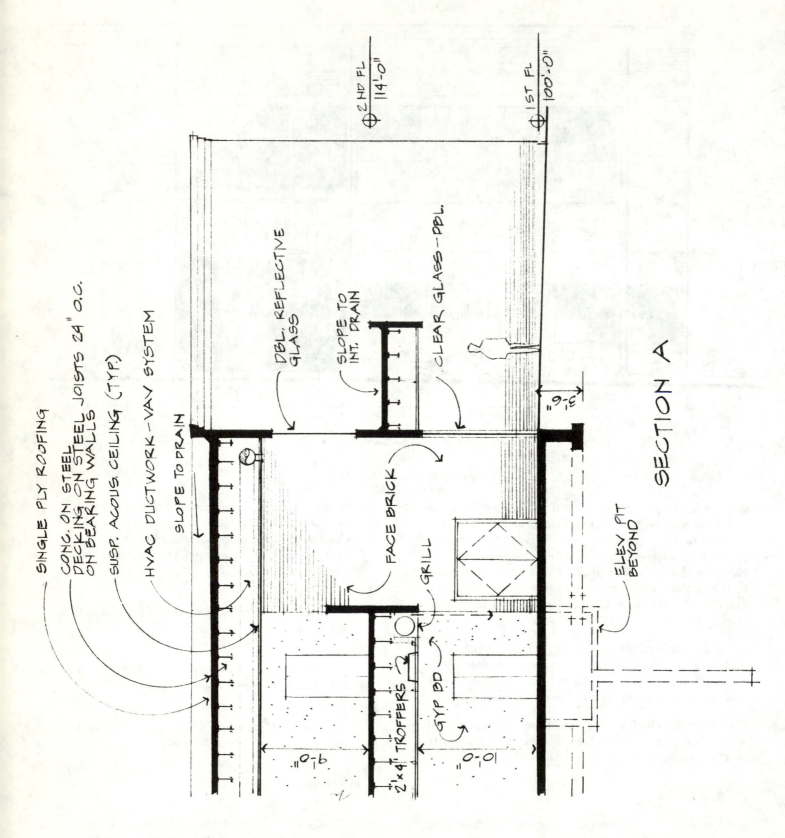

Figure 6.10 Partial Section

D. Drafting Techniques and Final Checks

Before you take the test you should decide on the type of drafting techniques you will use. The test is no time to experiment with new methods or tools. You can complete the sketches with either free-hand or hard-line methods; use the one you feel most comfortable with and the one that is fastest for you. Use simple block lettering on all the drawings and do not overdraft; provide just enough to clearly present all the required information. In the half hour or so you should leave at the end of the test for final checking, make sure you have included everything specifically required by the problem statement. If you discover something is missing from your drawings and you do not have time to make changes, at least make a note on the drawing to show the graders you did not forget it.

7 BUILDING CODES

Knowledge of building codes is a primary requirement of all licensing candidates. There is little else that affects the health, safety, and welfare of the public as much as the various topics dealt with in a typical code. In the broadest sense, building codes set minimum construction criteria to protect life and property.

Building codes differ from zoning ordinances. Zoning regulations deal with the use of a piece of property, the density of building within a district and on a lot, the location of buildings on property, parking, and loading. Refer to Chapter 2 for a more detailed discussion of zoning. Building codes, on the other hand, deal with the structure itself, how it is constructed, and what provisions are required to protect people and property from fire and other hazards.

1 ADMINISTRATIVE PROVISIONS
A. Legal Basis of Codes

Building codes are adopted and enforced at the local level of government, either by a municipality or, in the case of sparsely populated areas, a county. Codes are enacted as laws just as any other local regulation. Prior to construction, a building code is enforced through the permit process, which requires that builders submit plans for checking and approval before a permit is issued that allows construction to proceed. During construction, the local department responsible for enforcement conducts inspections to verify that building is proceeding according to the approved plans.

B. Model Building Codes

Local jurisdictions may write their own building codes, but in most cases one of the model codes is adopted into law by reference. A model code is one that has been written by a group comprising experts knowledgeable in the field, without reference to any particular geographical area. Adopting a model code allows a city or county to have a complete, workable building code without the difficulty and expense of writing its own. If certain provisions need to be added or changed to suit the particular requirements of a municipality, the model code is enacted with modifications. Even when a city writes its own code it is usually based on one of the model codes.

Three model building codes are used in the United States:

1. The Uniform Building Code (UBC) published by the International Council of Building Officials (ICBO). This is used in the western and central portions of the United States.

2. The Basic Building Code published by the Building Officials and Code Administrators International. This is used in the northeastern part of the country.

3. The Standard Building Code (SBC) published by the Southern Building Code Congress International and used in the Southeast.

The Uniform Building Code (UBC) is used by the majority of the states and is the code on which the discussion in this chapter is based. All three codes have very similar provisions, but there are some differences. Of course, building design and construction must conform to whatever code is in force in the locale where the structure is erected. You should be familiar with the code used in your area and the one that will be used on the exam you take.

C. Adjuncts to the Codes

In addition to a building code, there are companion codes that govern other aspects of construction. With the exception of the electrical code, these are published by the same groups that publish the building codes. For example, ICBO also publishes the Uniform Mechanical Code and the Uniform Plumbing Code, among others. The electrical code used by all groups is the National Electrical Code published by the National Fire Protection Association (NFPA).

Model codes also make extensive use of industry standards that are developed by trade associations, government agencies, and standards-writing agencies such as the American Society for Testing and Materials (ASTM), the American National Standards Institute, and the National Fire Protection Association. These are included in the building code by reference name and number.

In addition to building codes and their adjuncts, local jurisdictions may also have required energy conservation codes, health and hospital codes, codes that regulate school buildings, and similar legal requirements for construction.

D. The Organization of the Uniform Building Code

The UBC is divided into ten parts, including a listing of standards used and appendices. Each part contains chapters of similar subject matter. The parts with which candidates should be most familiar include Part III, requirements based on occupancy; Part IV, requirements based on types of construction; Chapter 33 of Part VI; and Part VII, fire-resistive standards for fire protection. The most critical portions of these parts, as well as additional requirements, are discussed in the following sections.

2   REQUIREMENTS BASED ON OCCUPANCY

Chapter 5 of the UBC outlines general requirements for all occupancies and specifies requirements based on occupancy, such as the fire resistance of exterior walls, occupancy separations, allowable floor areas, and building heights. Chapters 6 through 12 give specific requirements for each individual occupancy type.

A. Types of Occupancy

Every building is classified according to its use and is assigned an occupancy group. This is true of all the three model codes although the lettering system may be slightly different. The philosophy behind occupancy classification is that some building uses are more hazardous than others. For example, a building where flammable liquids are used is more dangerous than a

single-family residence. Similarly, a large auditorium holding hundreds of people can be more dangerous than a meeting room that only holds a few dozen people.

The UBC classifies occupancies into seven major groups:

A	assembly
B	business
E	educational
H	hazardous
I	institutional
M	miscellaneous
R	residential

Each of these classifications is divided into categories called divisions to distinguish subgroups that define the relative hazard of the occupancy. Table 5-A in Chapter 5 of the UBC summarizes the occupancy groups and gives a description of each one.

B. Allowable Floor Area and Heights of Buildings

When combined with construction type, the provisions of Chapter 5 and specifically Tables 5-C and 5-D of the UBC determine the allowable floor area in a building as well as the maximum height, both in feet and number of stories. Construction types are based on the fire resistance of building components and are discussed in more detail in the next section. A Type I building is the most fire resistant and Type V the least.

The UBC gives allowable floor areas for one-story buildings based on the occupancy and construction type and then allows increases in floor area if certain conditions are met. Table 7.1 is a reproduction of UBC Table 5-C, which gives the basic allowable floor area for one-story buildings. Buildings over one story may have twice the area permitted by Table 5-C.

If the building is separated with public ways or yards on two, three, or four sides by certain prescribed distances, the allowable floor areas may be increased according to various formulas. If an approved automatic sprinkler system is used, the floor areas may be tripled in one-story buildings and doubled in multistory buildings. Except for Group H, hazardous occupancies, a Type I building may be of unlimited floor area and unlimited height while other construction types are limited.

Tables 5-C and 5-D in the Uniform Building Code can be used in one of two ways. If you know the occupancy and construction type, you simply enter the tables and

Table 7.1
Basic Allowable Floor Area

BASIC ALLOWABLE FLOOR AREA FOR BUILDINGS ONE STORY IN HEIGHT[1]
(In Square Feet)

OCCUPANCY	TYPES OF CONSTRUCTION								
	I	II			III		IV	V	
	F.R.	F.R.	ONE-HOUR	N	ONE-HOUR	N	H.T.	ONE-HOUR	N
A-1	Unlimited	29,900	Not Permitted						
A) 2-2.1	Unlimited	29,900	13,500	Not Permitted	13,500	Not Permitted	13,500	10,500	Not Permitted
A) 3-4[2]	Unlimited	29,900	13,500	9,100	13,500	9,100	13,500	10,500	6,000
B) 1-2-3[3]	Unlimited	39,900	18,000	12,000	18,000	12,000	18,000	14,000	8,000
B-4	Unlimited	59,900	27,000	18,000	27,000	18,000	27,000	21,000	12,000
E	Unlimited	45,200	20,200	13,500	20,200	13,500	20,200	15,700	9,100
H-1	15,000	12,400	5,600	3,700	Not Permitted				
H-2[4]	15,000	12,400	5,600	3,700	5,600	3,700	5,600	4,400	2,500
H-3-4-5[4]	Unlimited	24,800	11,200	7,500	11,200	7,500	11,200	8,800	5,100
H-6-7	Unlimited	39,900	18,000	12,000	18,000	12,000	18,000	14,000	8,000
I) 1-2	Unlimited	15,100	6,800	Not Permitted[8]	6,800	Not Permitted	6,800	5,200	Not Permitted
I-3	Unlimited	15,100	Not Permitted[5]						
M[6]	See Chapter 11								
R-1	Unlimited	29,900	13,500	9,100[7]	13,500	9,100[7]	13,500	10,500	6,000[7]
R-3	Unlimited								

[1]For multistory buildings, see Section 505 (b).
[2]For limitations and exceptions, see Section 602 (a).
[3]For open parking garages, see Section 709.
[4]See Section 903.
[5]See Section 1002 (b).
[6]For agricultural buildings, see also Appendix Chapter 11.
[7]For limitations and exceptions, see Section 1202 (b).
[8]In hospitals and nursing homes, see Section 1002 (a) for exception.

N—No requirements for fire resistance
F.R.—Fire Resistive
H.T.—Heavy Timber

Reproduced from the 1988 edition of the Uniform Building Code, copyright ©1988, with permission of the publishers, the International Conference of Building Officials.

read the permitted area or height and then increase the areas according to percentages allowed. More often, you know the occupancy and the required floor area from the building program and you must determine the required construction type that will allow you to construct the size of building your client needs.

C. Occupancy Separation

When a building contains two or more occupancies, they are considered mixed occupancies. Each occupancy must be separated from other occupancies with a fire-resistive separation of one-, two-, three-, or four-hour construction as specified in UBC Table 5-B. The idea is to increase the fire protection between occupancies as the relative hazard increases. Fire-resistive construction is discussed in more detail in a later section of this chapter.

If the required floor space of a project exceeds that allowed by Chapter 5 of the UBC, the designer can subdivide the building into smaller portions that fall within the allowable floor areas, as long as area separation walls are constructed between the various portions and meet the requirements of Chapter 5. This includes extending the separation wall from the foundation to a point at least 30 inches above the roof. Requirements for openings in area separation walls must be strictly adhered to.

D. Location on Property

One section of UBC Chapter 5 contains requirements for the siting of buildings relative to adjacent property lines. It does this by specifying the fire resistance of exterior walls based on distance from property lines and whether or not openings are allowed in exterior walls based on the same distances. The idea behind these regulations is to prevent the spread of fire from one building to another.

These requirements are given in UBC Table 5-A and are based on the occupancy of the building. For example, an exterior wall of an educational occupancy, E, must be of two-hour construction if it is less than 5 feet from a property line, but it only needs to be of one-hour construction if less than 10 feet. On building walls facing a street or public way, the center line of the public way is considered to be the adjacent property line for the purpose of locating the building. If two or more buildings are on the same property, a line equidistant between them is considered the property line.

3 CLASSIFICATION BY TYPE OF CONSTRUCTION

Every building is classified into one of five types of construction based on the fire resistive protection of its major construction components. The purpose of this is to protect the structural elements of a building from fire and collapse and to divide the building into compartments so a fire in one area will be contained long enough to allow people to evacuate the building and for firefighters to arrive.

Construction type is covered in Chapter 17 of the UBC, and the requirements are summarized in UBC Table 17-A, which is reproduced in Table 7.2 in this chapter. As you can see from Table 7.2, some of the five construction types are subdivided into groups. Reading from the left of the table, Type I is the most fire resistive and the types and groups decrease in resistance until you come to Type V-N, which is the least fire resistive. The table gives the required fire resistance in hours of the various building elements and refers to specific paragraphs in the code for a more detailed explanation.

The major construction elements with which Chapter 17 is concerned include exterior and interior bearing walls, the structural frame, exterior non-bearing walls, permanent partitions, shaft enclosures, floors and ceilings, roofs, and exterior door and window openings. Detailed requirements for the various construction types are contained in Chapters 18 through 22 of the UBC. You should read through these chapters to become familiar with their provisions.

The minimum construction type required of a building is dependent on the occupancy group, the required square footage, the desired height of the building, and the fire zone in which the building will be located. As mentioned above, UBC Tables 5-C and 5-D and UBC Chapter 5 specify the variables of area and height based on occupancy and construction type.

The fire zone is another consideration that is often encountered in urban areas. A municipality may, by action of the local government, divide a city into three fire zones representing the degree of fire hazard. The fire hazard is usually based on such factors as density, access for firefighting equipment, existing building heights, and so forth. The dense, central business district of a city is typically classed as fire zone 1. The local code may then restrict the types of construction that are allowed in the various fire zones.

4 EXITING

Exiting is one of the most important provisions of the building code and one with which the candidate must be intimately familiar. An error in planning for exiting on the building design portion of the examination is usually enough to fail the solution. The examination test booklet will often contain sections of a building code as reference information to be used in completing the building design problem. You should know how to read a building code and extract the data you need for satisfying specific requirements. In addition, you must have a basic understanding of requirements that affect planning. The following sections summarize these requirements.

A. Occupant Load and Number of Exits Required

Chapter 33 of the Uniform Building Code covers exits. You should read and reread this chapter or corresponding chapters in the other model codes in preparation for the exam. Many of the requirements of Chapter 33 are based on the occupant load of a building or portion of a building. Occupant load is determined by taking the area in square feet assigned to a particular use and dividing by an occupant load factor as given in UBC Table 33-A. These load factors range from a low of 7 square feet for certain kinds of assembly areas to a high of 500 square feet for warehouses. These numbers mean that for the purposes of estimating exiting requirements one person is occupying, on average, the number of square feet listed in the occupant load factor column of the table. In determining the occupant load, all portions of the building are presumed to be occupied at the same time.

The number of exits from a space or building is then determined by the occupant load. All buildings or portions of a building must, of course, have at least one exit. When the number of occupants of a use exceeds

Table 7.2
Types of Construction

TYPES OF CONSTRUCTION—FIRE-RESISTIVE REQUIREMENTS
(In Hours)
For details see chapters under Occupancy and Types of Construction and for exceptions see Section 1705.

BUILDING ELEMENT	TYPE I	TYPE II			TYPE III		TYPE IV	TYPE V	
		NONCOMBUSTIBLE			COMBUSTIBLE				
	Fire-resistive	Fire-resistive	1-Hr.	N	1-Hr.	N	H.T.	1-Hr.	N
Exterior Bearing Walls	4 Sec. 1803 (a)	4 1903 (a)	1	N	4 2003 (a)	4 2003 (a)	4 2103 (a)	1	N
Interior Bearing Walls	3	2	1	N	1	N	1	1	N
Exterior Nonbearing Walls	4 Sec. 1803 (a)	4 1903 (a)	1 1903 (a)	N	4 2003 (a)	4 2003 (a)	4 2103 (a)	1	N
Structural Frame[1]	3	2	1	N	1	N	1 or H.T.	1	N
Partitions—Permanent	1[2]	1[2]	1[2]	N	1	N	1 or H.T.	1	N
Shaft Enclosures	2	2	1	1	1	1	1	1 1706	1 1706
Floors-Ceilings/Floors	2	2	1	N	1	N	H.T.	1	N
Roofs-Ceilings/Roofs	2 Sec. 1806	1 1906	1 1906	N	1	N	H.T.	1	N
Exterior Doors and Windows	Sec. 1803 (b)	1903 (b)	1903 (b)	1903 (b)	2003 (b)	2003 (b)	2103 (b)	2203	2203

N—No general requirements for fire resistance.   H.T.—Heavy Timber.

[1] Structural frame elements in the exterior wall shall be protected against external fire exposure as required for exterior bearing walls or the structural frame, whichever is greater.

[2] Fire-retardant treated wood (see Section 407) may be used in the assembly, provided fire-resistance requirements are maintained. See Sections 1801 and 1901, respectively.

Reproduced from the 1988 edition of the Uniform Building Code, copyright © 1988, with permission of the publishers, the International Conference of Building Officials.

the number given in UBC Table 33-A, then at least two exits must be provided. In most situations, and certainly in the building design portion of the exam, you are required to have two exits. The idea is to have an alternate way out of a building if one exit is blocked. Areas above the first floor must always have at least two exits. In addition, three exits are required when the occupant load is from 501 to 1000 persons, and four exits are required for occupant loads over 1001.

For multistory buildings, the number of exits is determined by taking the occupant load of the story under consideration, plus 50 percent of the occupant load of the first adjacent story above, plus 25 percent of the load from the story immediately beyond the first adjacent story. If people below the floor under consideration also exit through the story, then 50 percent of the occupant load of the story below is added to the total.

B. Arrangement and Width of Exits

The code states that when two exits are required they must be placed a distance apart equal to not less than one-half the length of the maximum overall diagonal dimension of the building or area to be served, as measured in a straight line between the exits. See Figure 7.1. When there are two exit stairways, their enclosure walls must be separated by a minimum distance of 30 feet. For sprinklered buildings, the distance between exits may be less than one-half, depending on which model code is being used.

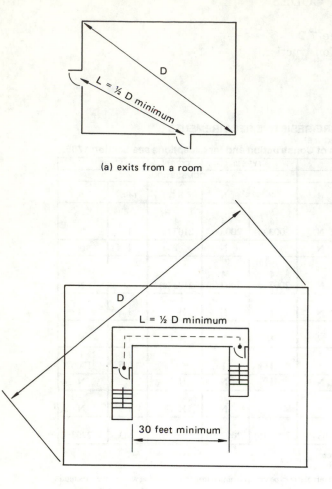

(a) exits from a room

(b) exits from a building

Figure 7.1 Arrangements of Exits

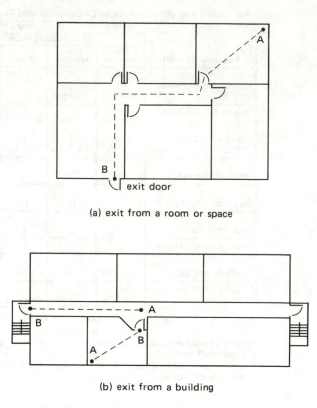

(a) exit from a room or space

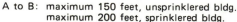

(b) exit from a building

A to B: maximum 150 feet, unsprinklered bldg.
maximum 200 feet, sprinklered bldg.

Figure 7.2 Distances to Exits

the exit may only be through one adjoining room and that room must have a direct and unobstructed means of egress to an exit corridor or other type of approved exit. Exits cannot pass through kitchens, storerooms, restrooms, or closets. Foyers, lobbies, and reception rooms constructed as corridors are not considered as intervening rooms.

If three or more exits are required, they must be arranged a reasonable distance apart so that if one is blocked, the others will be available.

The maximum distances from any point to an exterior exit door, exit corridor, horizontal exit, or stairway are 150 feet in an unsprinklered building and 200 feet in a sprinklered building. See Figure 7.2. These distances may be increased up to 100 feet when such increases are within an exit corridor.

The total width of exits in feet is determined by taking the occupant load and dividing by 50. This total width must be divided approximately equally among the separate exits. For example, if the occupant load from a building is 425, then the total width must be 425/50 or 8.5 feet. This should be rounded up to 9 feet. This could be provided with a pair of 3-foot doors at one exit and one 3-foot door at the other exit, or three exits, each with a 3-foot door.

In some cases, the UBC does allow exiting from one room or space through an intervening space. However,

C. Doors

Doors used as required exits serving an occupant load of ten or more must conform to several provisions of the code. All exit doors serving an occupant load of 50 or more must swing in the direction of travel. This is to avoid a door being blocked in a panic situation when people are trying to get out. Candidates frequently make the mistake of not showing required doors—all building exit doors, stairway doors, and doors from spaces with a high occupant load—swinging in the direction of travel. They must also not swing into a required travel path, such as a corridor. In many instances, you may need to recess doors that swing into corridors.

Exit doors must be a minimum of 3 feet wide and 6 feet 8 inches high. The maximum width is 4 feet. Exit doors must be operable from the inside without the use of any special knowledge or effort and for certain occupancies, such as educational and assembly, panic hardware is required—hardware that unlatches the door when pressure is applied against it.

Exit doors must have a fire rating compatible with the wall in which they are located. Doors are rated in hours—the same way partitions are, and the fire-rating requirements are scattered in various places throughout the UBC. A two-hour partition, for example, must have a 1 1/2-hour-rated door assembly. One-hour partitions acting as occupancy separations must have a one-hour-rated door assembly while a one-hour-rated corridor wall only needs a three-quarter-hour door and in some cases only a tight-fitting 20-minute-rated door.

Exit doors must have automatic closers on them, and all hardware must be tested and approved for use on fire exits. When closed, they must provide a tight seal against smoke and drafts. Glass in exit doors must be wire glass, and its total area is limited depending on the door's fire rating.

In most cases, special doors such as revolving, sliding, and overhead doors are not considered as required exits. Power-operated doors and revolving doors are sometimes allowed if they meet certain requirements. Revolving doors, for example, must have leaves which collapse under opposing pressure and must have a diameter of at least 6 feet 6 inches. There must also be at least one conforming exit door adjacent to each revolving door. A revolving door used as an exit cannot be considered to provide any of the required exit width.

D. Corridors

Corridors and exterior exit balconies provide a safe means of egress from a room or space to a building exit or to another approved exitway such as a stairway. The minimum width of corridors is determined as discussed previously, by taking the occupant load and dividing by 50. However, the absolute minimum width for almost all occupancies is 44 inches. This is based on the basic width required for one person to pass, which is 22 inches. Individual dwelling units may have corridors 36 inches wide. The minimum height of corridors is seven feet. In the UBC, dead-end corridors are limited to 20 feet in length in unsprinklered buildings and 50 feet in sprinklered buildings.

Certain occupancies, most notably educational and institutional in the UBC, require wider corridors. For instance, the UBC requires that corridors in schools must be two feet wider than the width as determined from Chapter 33, but no less than 6 feet.

Corridors must be built of one-hour fire-resistive construction, and this must include walls and ceilings. If the ceiling of the entire story is one-hour rated, then the rated corridor walls may terminate at the ceiling. Otherwise, the one-hour-rated corridors must extend through the ceiling to the rated floor or roof above.

E. Stairways

Since stairways are an important part of any exiting system in a building, all the model codes go to great lengths to specify all required components. Stairways serving an occupant load of 50 or more must be at least 44 inches wide; if a stairway serves an occupant load less than 50, the minimum width is 36 inches. For the exam, the best approach is to make exit stairs 4 feet wide. Any monumental stairs, however, should be wider. The maximum riser height is 7 inches and the minimum tread width is 11 inches. Handrails must be placed on each side of stairways 44 inches wide and wider and may encroach into the required width by 3 1/2 inches. The maximum distance between landings is 12 feet, measured vertically.

In buildings four or more stories in height or of Types I and II, fire-resistive construction stairway walls must be built of two-hour-rated construction. One-hour-rated construction is required elsewhere.

F. Smokeproof Enclosures

When a building height exceeds 75 feet, the UBC requires that stairways be in smokeproof enclosures. These are stairways with vestibules on each floor. Smoke is prevented from entering the stairway either by mechanical or natural ventilation. With mechanical ventilation, the pressure inside the stairway is kept higher than the vestibule. This, along with tight-fitting doors, keeps smoke out of the stairway itself. Using natural ventilation requires that the vestibule be open to the exterior so any smoke is exhausted to the outside before entering the stairway. The minimum size of the exterior opening is 16 square feet.

G. Refuge Areas

High-rise buildings pose a unique kind of problem for fire and life safety. According to the UBC, a high-rise building is any building higher than 75 feet. Fire department apparatus cannot reach above this height so special precautions need to be taken. A section of UBC Chapter 18 deals with high-rise buildings and includes provisions for sprinkler systems, smoke detection and alarms, communications systems, central control stations for use by the fire department, emergency power, and refuge areas.

The UBC requires that high-rise buildings be fully sprinklered or equipped with refuge areas. If the refuge area alternative is selected, each story must be divided into two or more areas separated from each other with two-hour-rated construction. Each area cannot be larger than 15,000 square feet and must contain one elevator and a minimum of one enclosed exit stairway. Refuge areas provide a safe place for people to escape a fire in a high-rise building without having to use the elevators or descend many floors down a stairway. They can wait for firefighters to extinguish the fire and conduct an orderly evacuation.

5 FIRE-RESISTIVE STANDARDS

The requirements contained in UBC Chapters 42 and 43 are intended to protect the primary building elements from weakening or collapse due to fire, to prevent the spread of fire between areas, and to limit the spread of flame and propagation of smoke.

A. Construction Materials and Assemblies

There is no such thing as a fireproof building; there are only degrees of fire resistance. The fire resistance of materials and construction assemblies is measured in hours and is determined by testing materials according to a standard test method. A material or assembly is placed in a test chamber and fire developed with gas jets is applied on one side. The temperature is increased according to a standard time–temperature curve and various criteria are used to determine when the assembly "fails." If an assembly withstands the test for at least an hour it is given a one-hour rating; other ratings include two, three, and four hours. Doors can have a three-quarter-hour or a 20-minute rating as well.

Many materials and assemblies have been tested and carry fire-resistive ratings such as the ones included in UBC Chapter 43 in Tables 43-A, 43-B, and 43-C. Other acceptable references for previously tested assemblies include the Fire Resistance Directory of Underwriters Laboratories, the Fire Resistance Design Manual of the Gypsum Association, and individual ICBO Evaluation Reports. If a material or assembly has not been previously approved, it must be tested according to test method ASTM E-119 of the American Society for Testing and Materials.

Various building elements must be protected with the types of construction specified in UBC Table 17-A (see Table 7.2) and elsewhere in the code. When a fire-resistive barrier is built, any penetrations in the barrier must also be fire rated. This includes doors, windows, and ducts. In most cases a one-hour wall must have a three-quarter-hour-rated door assembly. In some cases

a corridor wall only needs a 20-minute-rated door. A two-hour-rated wall typically requires a 1 1/2-hour-rated door assembly. Duct penetrations are protected with fire dampers placed in line with the wall. If a fire occurs, a fusible link in the damper closes a louver that maintains the rating of the wall.

It is important to remember that many materials by themselves do not create a fire-rated barrier. It is the construction assembly of which they are a part that is fire resistant. A one-hour-rated suspended ceiling, for example, must use rated ceiling tile, but it is the assembly of tile, suspension system, and structural floor above that carries the one-hour rating. In a similar way, a one-hour-rated partition may consist of a layer of 5/8 inch Type X gypsum board on both sides of a wood or metal stud. A single piece of gypsum board cannot have a fire-resistance rating by itself.

B. Finishes

Unlike Chapter 43, Chapter 42 of the UBC regulates interior finishes of single layers of material. Its purpose is to control the rate of flame spread along the surface of a material and to limit the amount of combustible material in a building. It also limits the amount of smoke developed by burning material. The test use to qualify materials is ASTM E-84, also known as the *Steiner Tunnel Test*.

Wall and ceiling finish material are classified into three groups, or classes, with the Tunnel Test. They are known as classes I, II, and III and sometimes classes A, B, and C. Class I is the most restrictive; materials with this rating have the least flame spread. Based on occupancy group, the code specifies which class of interior finish material can be used in enclosed vertical exitways, other exitways, and rooms or areas. In all occupancies except R-3 and M, for example, class I materials must be used in enclosed vertical exitways.

6 OTHER DETAILED REGULATIONS

In addition to the provisions mentioned in the previous sections, all the model building codes regulate many other aspects of construction. These include such things as the use and structural design of individual materials, excavations, demolition, and elevators, among many others. You should be familiar with how the codes regulate the following items.

A. Mechanical System Requirements

The majority of code requirements related to mechanical systems are contained in companion volumes to the primary model codes. The companion volume for the

UBC is the Uniform Mechanical Code, which covers basic design criteria such as minimum ventilation rates and other aspects of health and safety. Also included are requirements for designing mechanical systems so they are safe and effective.

B. Plumbing Systems

The Uniform Plumbing Code is the companion volume to the UBC that regulates plumbing design and construction. In the past, the most notable part of this code for architects that affects building design was the one that specifies minimum plumbing fixtures. Now, Table 5-E in the UBC gives the number of sanitary fixtures required by occupancy. Based on the number of people and the occupancy group, this table gives the minimum number of toilets, lavatories, drinking fountains, and other fixtures required in a building. These should be considered minimum numbers and not necessarily optimum numbers. The Uniform Plumbing Code also outlines detailed requirements for the design of plumbing systems, individual materials, and methods of installation.

C. Electrical Systems and Fire Detection

The National Electrical Code is used throughout the country for the design of electrical systems. It regulates all aspects of electrical system design, installation, and individual materials such as wiring and transformers.

Fire detection and alarm systems have become an important part of a building's overall life safety and fire protection system. Almost all buildings are now required to have some type of detection device, even if it is a single smoke alarm in a residence. Other occupancies, such as high-rise buildings and hotels, must have elaborate detection and alarm systems, including communication devices on each floor to allow firefighters to talk with each other and to occupants in the event of an emergency.

D. Sound Ratings

The Uniform Building Code requires that in Group R occupancies wall and floor-ceiling assemblies separating dwelling units or guest rooms from each other and from public spaces be insulated to provide for the control of sound transmission. For walls, the specification used is a minimum STC rating of 50 (or 45 if field tested).

Refer to Chapter 12 for a definition and review of STC ratings and other acoustical concepts.

Penetrations in sound walls must be sealed or otherwise treated to maintain the required rating. Floor-ceiling assemblies must also meet certain minimum ratings for the impact insulation class (IIC) to control the passage of noise such as footfalls and dropped objects.

E. Glazing

Proper glazing is an important safety feature of any building. The codes specify minimum requirements for window glazing for both energy conservation and strength against wind forces. The use of glass is also regulated in hazardous locations such as doorways, shower doors, glass adjacent to doors, and any place where people are likely to accidentally fall through a piece of glass. In such locations, safety glazing must be used, defined as tempered glass, laminated glass, or wire glass.

Tempered glass is not only stronger than standard glass but safer because it breaks into thousands of small pieces on impact instead of breaking into dangerous shards. Laminated glass is also very resistant to breakage and when it does break it is held in place by the plastic interlayer separating the laminations.

7 PROVISIONS FOR THE PHYSICALLY DISABLED

Practically all public and private buildings are required to be accessible to the physically disabled. Although there are several different standards, especially for government projects, most are based on American National Standard A117.1. The basic approach of this standard is that a building and its site should have an accessible route from parking through the main entrance and to individual building elements that allows people with disabilities to have full access. This includes provisions for elevators and ramps so that all levels of a building are accessible.

Some of the accessibility provisions for site work were discussed in Chapters 4 and 5. Although there are dozens and dozens of detailed requirements for access, some of the basic ones that affect building planning and design are shown in Figure 7.3.

ARCHITECTURE EXAM REVIEW

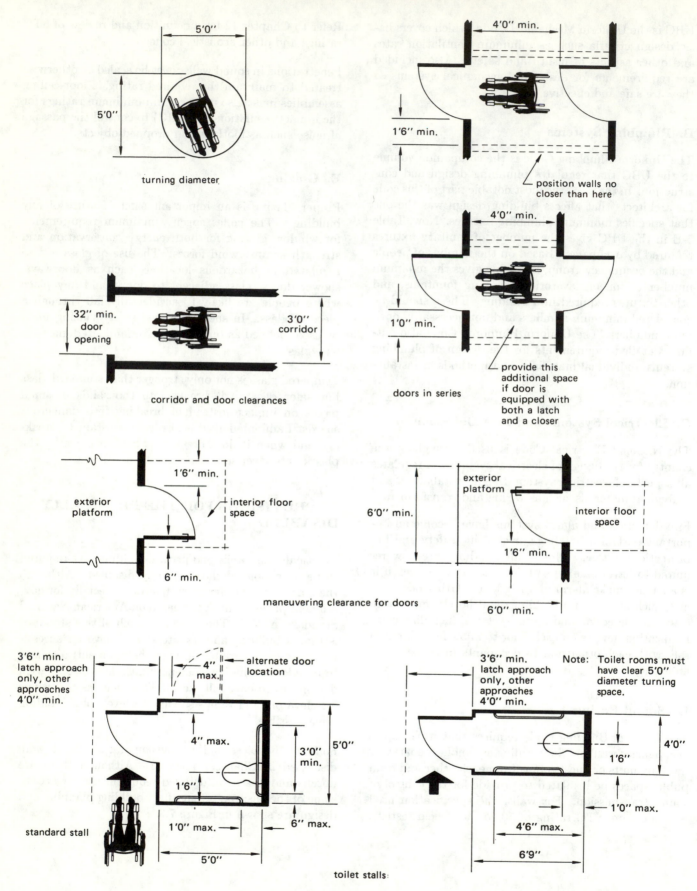

Figure 7.3 Accessibility Requirements

SAMPLE QUESTIONS

1. High-rise buildings must have:

    A. class I interior finishes throughout

    B. at least three stairways

    C. refuge areas or sprinkler systems

    D. all of the above

The answers to questions 2 through 4 can be found on the following key list. Select only one answer for each question.

    A0 fire dampers
    A1 fire rating
    A2 fire resistance
    A3 flame spread
    A4 hour rating
    A5 industry standards
    A6 impact isolation class
    A7 model codes
    A8 occupancy group
    A9 occupant load

    B0 refuge area
    B1 safety glazing
    B2 smoke alarm
    B3 smokeproof tower
    B4 Steiner Tunnel Test

2. What special aspect of construction of residential occupancies is governed by the Uniform Building Code?

3. Exiting from high-rise buildings requires what special provision?

4. What determines the rate at which fire travels on wood wall paneling?

5. Exits may pass through:

    I.   office reception areas

    II. building lobbies

    III. unoccupied storage areas

    IV. hotel lobbies

    V. apartment entries

    A. I, II, IV, and V

    B. I, II, III, and V

    C. II, IV, and V

    D. all of the above

6. Which of the following are correct statements?

    I. Fire zone 3 is the most restrictive.

    II. Fire resistance of exterior walls is determined by type of construction and distance from property lines.

    III. Dead-end corridors up to 50 feet are allowed by the UBC in some circumstances.

    IV. Fire-resistive requirements for interior bearing partitions are found in UBC Chapter 5.

    V. Occupant load is independent of occupancy group.

    A. I, II, and III

    B. II, III, and IV

    C. II, III, and V

    D. III, IV, and V

7. What is the maximum allowable floor area of a sprinklered, three-story, Type III one hour, group B-2 occupancy building that has access only on one side?

    A. 18,000 square feet

    B. 36,000 square feet

    C. 54,000 square feet

    D. 72,000 square feet

8. Which of the following is not true?

    A. A model building code has no legal basis.

    B. Building codes are not the only regulations with which an architect must comply.

    C. A state-adopted building code overrides a city code.

    D. Both zoning ordinances and building codes regulate the allowable floor area of buildings.

9. The abbreviated table shown includes requirements for occupancy loads. A restaurant on the ground floor

contains 3500 square feet of dining area, a 1000-square-foot kitchen, and a 1200-square-foot bar area. What is the total occupant load?

use	occupant load factor
assembly areas, concentrated use (without fixed seats)	7
auditoriums	
dance floors	
lodge rooms	
assembly areas, less-concentrated use	15
conference rooms	
dining rooms	
drinking establishments	
exhibit rooms	
lounges	
stages	
hotels and apartments	200
kitchen—commercial	200
offices	100
stores, ground floor	30

A. 202

B. 318

C. 380

D. 409

10. Which of the following exit door combinations would satisfy the exit width required in the restaurant in the previous problem?

A. a pair of 30-inch entry doors and a 36-inch door remotely located

B. two 36-inch doors on opposite sides of the building

C. three 32-inch doors remotely located

D. three 36-inch-wide doors remotely located from each other

8 HUMAN COMFORT AND MECHANICAL SYSTEM FUNDAMENTALS

Nomenclature

A	area of a building assembly	ft^2
C	conductance	BTU/hr-ft^2-°F
k	conductivity (for one-inch thickness)	BTU/hr-ft^2-°F
q	total heat loss through a building assembly	BTU/hr
q_v	sensible heat loss or gain due to infiltration or ventilation	BTU/hr
R	resistance	hours
Δt	temperature difference between indoor and outdoor air	degrees F
U	coefficient of heat transmission	BTU/hr-ft^2-°F
V	volume flow rate of outside air	ft^3/min

Definitions

British thermal unit (BTU): the amount of heat required to raise the temperature of one pound of water by one degree Fahrenheit.

Coefficient of heat transmission: the overall rate of heat flow through any combination of materials, including air spaces and air layers on the interior and exterior of a building assembly. It is the reciprocal of the sum of all the resistances in the building assembly.

Conductance: the number of British thermal units per hour that pass through one square foot of homogeneous material of a given thickness when the temperature differential is one degree Fahrenheit.

Conductivity: the number of British thermal units per hour that pass through one square foot of homogeneous material one inch thick when the temperature differential is one degree Fahrenheit.

Dew point: the temperature at which water vapor in the air becomes saturated and begins to condense as drops of water.

Dry bulb temperature: the temperature of the air-water mixture as measured with a standard dry bulb thermometer.

Enthalpy: the total heat in a substance, including latent heat and sensible heat.

Latent heat: heat that causes a change of state of a substance, such as the heat required to change water into steam.

Resistance: the number of hours needed for one BTU to pass through a given thickness of a material or assembly when the temperature differential is one degree Fahrenheit. It is the reciprocal of conductance.

Sensible heat: heat which causes a change in temperature of a substance and not its state.

Wet bulb temperature: the temperature of the air as measured with a sling psychrometer. The wet bulb temperature is a more critical measure of heat in high humidity because it indicates the stress when the human body is near the upper limits of temperature regulation by perspiration.

1 HUMAN COMFORT

Human comfort is based on the quality of the following primary environmental factors: temperature, humidity, air movement, temperature radiation to and from surrounding surfaces, air quality, sound, vibration, and light. For each of these factors there are certain levels within which people are comfortable and can function most efficiently. Acoustics and lighting are reviewed in later chapters. This section discusses human comfort relative to the thermal environment. Chapter 9 deals with the mechanical systems used to modify internal environments to maintain human comfort.

A. Human Metabolism

The human body is a heat-producing machine. It takes in food and water and through the metabolic process converts these to mechanical energy and other bodily processes necessary to maintain life. Since the body is not very efficient in this conversion, it must give off excess heat in order to maintain a stable body temperature. At rest, the human body gives off about 400 British thermal units per hour (BTUh). This increases to around 700 to 800 BTUh for moderate activities like walking and work and up to 1300 BTUh for strenuous exercise.

The body loses heat in three ways: by convection, evaporation, and radiation. *Convection* is the transfer of heat through the movement of a fluid, either a gas or liquid. This occurs when the air temperature surrounding a person is less than the body's skin temperature, around 85 degrees Fahrenheit. The body heats the surrounding air, which rises and is replaced with cooler air. Heat loss through *evaporation* occurs when moisture changes to a vapor as a person perspires or breathes. *Radiation* is the transfer of heat energy through electromagnetic waves from one surface to a colder surface. The body can lose heat to a cooler atmosphere or to a cooler surface.

The body loses heat (or is prevented from losing heat) through these three processes in various proportions depending on the environmental conditions. If the body cannot lose heat one way it must lose it another. For example, when the air temperature is above the body temperature of 98.6 °F, there can be no convection transfer because heat always flows from a high level to a low level. This is dictated by the second law of thermodynamics. The body must then lose all its heat by evaporation. Figure 8.1 illustrates how the total amount of heat generated at rest is transferred depending on the surrounding temperature.

The sensation of thermal comfort depends on the interrelationship of air temperature, humidity, air movement, and radiation. Each of these will be discussed separately in the following sections.

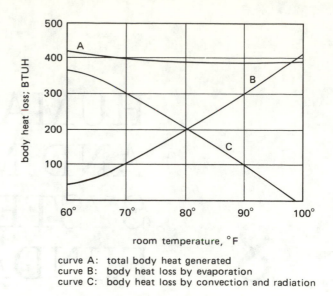

curve A: total body heat generated
curve B: body heat loss by evaporation
curve C: body heat loss by convection and radiation

Figure 8.1 Body Heat Generated and Lost at Rest

fortable temperature limits because the range depends on the humidity levels, radiant temperatures, air movement, clothing, cultural factors, age, and sex, among other factors. However, a general comfortable range is between 69 °F and 80 °F, with a tolerable range from 60 °F to 85 °F.

A value called the *effective temperature* (ET) has been developed that attempts to combine the effects of air temperature, humidity, and air movement.

Dry bulb temperature is measured with a standard thermometer. Wet bulb temperature is measured with a sling psychrometer, a device that consists of a thermometer with a moist cloth around the bulb. The thermometer is swung rapidly in the air causing the moisture in the cloth to evaporate. In dry air, the moisture evaporates rapidly and acquires latent heat, which produces a low wet bulb temperature. The large difference between the wet bulb temperature and the dry bulb temperature indicates low relative humidity. In moist air, less moisture evaporates from the cloth so the wet bulb temperature is higher.

B. Air Temperature

Temperature is the primary determinant of comfort. It is difficult to precisely state a normal range of com-

C. Humidity

Relative humidity is the percent of moisture in the air compared to the maximum amount the air can hold at

a given temperature without condensing. Comfortable relative humidity ranges are between 30 and 65 percent with tolerable ranges between 20 and 70 percent. Relative humidity is particularly important in the summer months because as the air temperature rises the body can lose less heat through convection and must rely mostly on evaporation. However, as the humidity rises, it is more difficult for perspiration to evaporate and hence you feel much hotter than the air temperature would indicate.

D. Air Movement

Air movement tends to increase evaporation and heat loss through convection. This is why you will feel comfortable in high temperatures and humidities if there is a breeze. It also explains the wind chill effect when a tolerable cold air temperature becomes unbearable in a wind. Wind speeds of from 50 feet per minute to about 200 feet per minute are generally acceptable for cooling without causing annoying drafts.

E. Radiation

Since the body gains or loses heat through radiation, the temperature of the surrounding surfaces is an important factor in determining human comfort. If the surroundings are colder than the surface temperature of the skin, about 85 °F, the body loses heat through radiation; if the surroundings are warmer than the skin, the body does not lose heat this way. The *mean radiant temperature* (MRT) is the value used to determine this aspect of comfort. The MRT is a weighted average of the various surface temperatures in a room, the angle of exposure of the occupant to these surfaces, and any sunlight present.

The MRT is an important factor in comfort in cold rooms or in the winter because as the air temperature decreases the body loses more heat through radiation than by evaporation, as shown in Figure 8.1. Even a room with an adequate temperature will feel cool if the surfaces are cold. Warming these surfaces and providing radiant heating panels are two ways to counteract this effect.

F. Ventilation

Ventilation is required to provide oxygen and remove carbon dioxide, to remove odors, and to carry away contaminants. The amount of ventilation required in a room depends on the activity involved, the size of the room, and whether smoking is involved. For example, a gymnasium needs a higher ventilation rate than a library. The model codes give minimum requirements for ventilation, either by specifying minimum operable window areas, minimum mechanical ventilation rates, or both. The UBC states these requirements in each of the chapters dealing with specific occupancy groups.

Building codes specify the minimum amount of fresh, outdoor air that must be circulated in cubic feet per minute and the total circulated air, also in cubic feet per minute. Mechanical systems are designed to filter and recirculate much of the conditioned air, but to also introduce a certain percentage of outdoor air along with the recirculated air.

Where exhausting of air is required, such as in toilet rooms, kitchens, and spaces where noxious fumes are present, additional requirements are given. Codes state minimum exhaust rates in cubic feet per minute per square foot of floor area or say how often a complete air change must be made. In these situations, the ventilation system must exhaust directly to the outside; none of the exhausted air can be recirculated. In the design portion of the exam, you should show or note that exhaust from toilet rooms and other required areas is directly to the outside.

2 MEASUREMENT SYSTEMS

Because the relationships between temperature, humidity, radiation, and other factors are complex, various methods have been developed to show these relationships and to assist in designing mechanical systems. Two of the more common ones are discussed in the following sections.

A. Comfort Charts

Comfort charts show the relationship between temperature, humidity, and other comfort factors. A simplified version is shown in Figure 8.2. It shows the comfort zones for both winter and summer for temperate zones in the United States (about 40 degrees latitude) for elevations below 1000 feet above sea level, and for people normally dressed engaged in sedentary or light work.

The tolerable humidity limits of about 20 percent and 75 percent are shown but with limits between 30 and 65 percent preferred. The chart shows that as humidity increases, the air temperature must decrease to provide the same amount of comfort as lower humidity levels.

As the temperature drops below the recommended levels, radiation in the form of sunshine or mechanical radiation is needed to maintain comfort. The lower the temperature, the more radiation is required. As the humidity and temperature increase, air movement is required to maintain comfort levels.

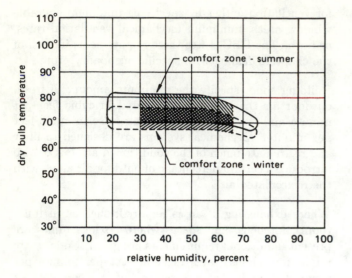

Figure 8.2 Comfort Chart for Temperate Zones

B. Psychrometric Chart

The psychrometric chart is a graphic representation of the thermodynamic properties of moist air. It is used for a wide variety of applications in heating and air conditioning design, including finding dew point temperatures, determining relative humidity, calculating enthalpy, and determining humidity ratios. These values are needed to compute the relationships of heat and air flow in air conditioning design. Figure 8.3 shows an abbreviated version of the more complex full version of the chart. The thermal comfort zone can also be plotted on this chart and is shown in Figure 8.3.

3   EXTERNAL AND INTERNAL LOADS

In order to maintain human comfort, a building must resist either the loss of heat to the outside during cold weather or the gain of heat during hot weather. Any excess heat gain or loss must be compensated for with passive energy conservation measures or with mechanical heating and cooling systems.

External factors that cause heat loss include air temperature and wind. External factors causing heat gain include air temperature and sunlight. Internal factors that produce heat loads include people, lights, and equipment.

Heat is transferred between the outside and inside of a building through conduction, convection, and radiation. Conduction is the transfer of heat through direct contact between molecules. Convection is the transfer of heat through the movement of air. Radiation is the transfer of heat energy through electromagnetic waves from one surface to a colder surface.

A. Heat Loss Calculations

In order to determine the size of a heating system for a building, the total amount of heat lost per hour must be calculated. Heat is lost in two basic ways: through the building envelope and through air infiltration. The building envelope consists of the walls, roof, doors, windows, and foundation. Each of the materials or groups of materials comprising these building elements resists the transfer of heat that occurs through the processes of conduction, convection, and radiation.

Every material has a unique property known as its conductivity, k, which is the amount of heat lost through one square foot of a one-inch thickness of the material when the temperature differential is one degree Fahrenheit. Conductance, C, is the same property, but when the material is a thickness other than one inch. The resistance, R, of a material is the number of hours needed for one BTU to pass through a material of given thickness when the temperature differential is one degree Fahrenheit. Conductance and resistance are related by the formula

$$R = \frac{1}{C} \qquad 8.1$$

Values for k, C, and R for various materials are given in standard reference texts as well as in the American Society of Heating, Refrigerating and Air-Conditioning Engineers (ASHRAE) Handbook of Fundamentals. If you are required to perform any heat loss calculations on the exam, the necessary tables will be included in the test information booklet.

When a building assembly consists of more than one material, the value used to calculate heat loss is the coefficient of heat transmission, U. However, the value of U is not simply the sum of all the conductances of the individual materials. Instead, the coefficient of heat loss must be calculated according to the formula:

$$U = \frac{1}{\sum R} \qquad 8.2$$

The amount of heat loss through a square foot of building material or assembly is dependent on the coefficient of heat transmission of the material or assembly and the temperature differential between the inside and outside. For an entire area of one type of material, this value is multiplied by the square footage to get the total heat loss. The formula is:

$$q = (U \times A) \times \Delta t \qquad 8.3$$

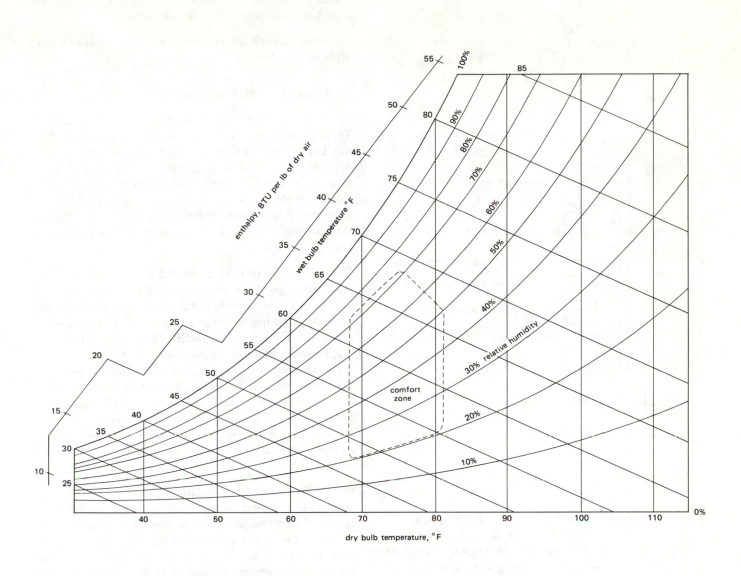

Figure 8.3 Psychrometric Chart

In order to calculate the heat loss for an entire room or building, the heat losses of all the different types of assemblies—walls, windows, roofs, and so forth—must be determined and then added together.

Example 8.1

Find the coefficient of heat transmission for the wall assembly shown in the sketch on the following page.

The R and C values for the various components are given in the sketch. However, they must all be converted to conductances for the thicknesses used. Remember that air spaces and the thin layer of air on the exterior and interior of buildings have some thermal resistance. If the brick has an R value of 0.11 per inch and it is 3 5/8 inches thick (3.625), then its total R value is 0.40. The conductance of the gypsum board is 2.22, so its resistance is 1/2.22 or 0.45.

The summation of the R values of the assembly is:

exterior air film	0.17
brick	0.40
air space	1.15
sheathing	4.3
insulation	13.0
gypsum board	0.45
interior air film	0.68
	———
total R	20.15

The overall coefficient of transmission is then,

$$U = \frac{1}{\sum R}$$
$$= \frac{1}{20.15}$$
$$= 0.05 \text{ BTU/hr-ft}^2\text{-}°\text{F}$$

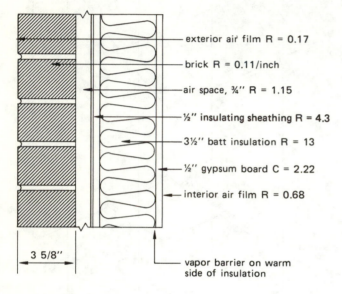

exterior air film R = 0.17

brick R = 0.11/inch

air space, ¾″ R = 1.15

½″ insulating sheathing R = 4.3

3½″ batt insulation R = 13

½″ gypsum board C = 2.22

interior air film R = 0.68

3 5/8″

vapor barrier on warm side of insulation

The value for Δt is determined by subtracting the outdoor design temperature from the desired indoor temperature in the winter, usually 70 degrees. Outdoor design temperatures vary with geographical region and are found in the ASHRAE Handbook or are set by local building codes.

One important aspect of heat loss calculations and the use of the psychrometric chart is to determine the dew point of the moisture in the air to avoid condensation on interior surfaces and especially inside building construction. For example, air at 70 °F and 35 percent relative humidity has a dew point of 41 °F. Moisture will condense on surfaces at or below this temperature.

In Example 8.1, if the outdoor temperature is zero degrees and the indoor temperature 70 degrees, somewhere inside the wall assembly the temperature is 41 degrees or less. Water vapor from inside the building permeating the construction would condense on this surface, damaging the wood construction and possibly negating the effectiveness of the insulation. To avoid this problem, a vapor barrier must be placed on the

warm side of the insulation, as shown in Example 8.1. Vapor barriers can be thin plastic films, or they can be a part of sheathing or insulation batts.

Heat loss through infiltration will be discussed in a separate section below.

B. Heat Gain Calculations

There are several sources of heat gain in buildings. There is, of course, heat gain produced when the outside temperature is high and heat is transferred by conduction, convection, and radiation, just as with heat loss. Heat gain through infiltration is also a factor when outside temperatures are high. In addition, heat is produced by the radiation of the sun on glazing, by the building's occupants, by lighting, and by equipment such as motors.

The percentage of heat generated by each of these factors varies with the occupancy of the building. For example, a residence is dominated by gains from the building envelope and through glazing. The number of occupants and lighting is negligible. A large office building, however, has a great many occupants, each producing a minimum of 400 BTUh at rest, a large number of light fixtures, and a significant amount of equipment. The ratio of room and wall surface may be quite low for such an office building compared with a residence. Because of these types of conditions, it is not unusual in many occupancies for air conditioning to be required even in the winter months.

Heat gain through the building envelope is calculated in a manner similar to heat loss, using the overall coefficient of heat transmission and the area of the building assembly (as shown in formula 8.3), but the temperature differential is not used directly. Instead, a value known as the *design equivalent temperature difference* (DETD) must be used. This value, calculated through complex formulae, takes into account the air temperature differences, effects of the sun, thermal mass storage effects of materials, colors of finishes exposed to the sun, and the daily temperature range. These values are published in tables produced by ASHRAE.

Heat gain through glazing can be a very significant factor. It is calculated by multiplying the area of the glazing by the *design cooling load factor* (DCLF). Like the design equivalent temperature difference, the DCLF takes into account several variables that affect how solar heat gain occurs, including the type of glazing, the compass orientation of the glazing, the type of interior shading, and the outdoor design temperature. Design cooling load factors are also published by ASHRAE.

The occupants of a building produce two kinds of heat: sensible heat and latent heat in the form of moisture from breathing and perspiration. Sensible heat gain from occupants can be assumed to be about 225 BTUh, although this varies slightly with occupancy type. Total sensible heat is calculated by simply multiplying the number of occupants by 225 BTUh.

Heat gains from lighting can be found by using the fact that one watt equals 3.41 BTU per hour. Simply multiply the total wattage load of the building's lighting by 3.41. For fluorescent and other discharge lights, the energy used by the ballast must also be included. A general rule of thumb is to multiply the BTUh generated by these types of fixtures by 1.25.

Heat generated by equipment such as motors, elevators, appliances, water heaters, and cooking equipment can be a significant factor in commercial buildings. The methods of calculating such heat are complex and depend on such variables as horsepower ratings and efficiencies of motors, load factors, and any latent heat produced.

Latent heat must be accounted for in calculating heat gains because for cooling purposes moisture in the air (latent heat) must be removed to maintain a comfortable relative humidity level while the sensible heat level is being reduced. In heat gain calculations, latent heat gain is either accounted for separately or by multiplying the total sensible heat gain in a building by a certain percentage derived through experience. Latent heat gain in residential and many other occupancies is about 30 percent of the sensible heat gain.

One effective passive method to mitigate the effects of heat gain from solar radiation and air temperature is to use building materials with high mass. Materials such as masonry, concrete, and tile slow the transmission of heat into a building. During the day, these materials absorb the heat energy and store it. During the night, when the air temperature is cooler than the surface of the mass, much of this energy is lost to the atmosphere instead of being transmitted into the building.

C. Infiltration

Infiltration is the transfer of air into and out of a building through open doors, through cracks around windows and other openings, through flues and vents, and through other gaps in the exterior construction. Unless a building is well sealed, infiltration can account for more heat loss than transmission through the walls and roof. However, no building is perfectly sealed; there is always some infiltration.

Heat loss through infiltration is calculated by the formula:

$$q_v = V \times 1.08 \times \Delta t \qquad 8.4$$

The factor of 1.08 accounts for the specific heat of air; that is, the amount of heat air at a certain density can hold. The value of V can be calculated in detail based on the air lost through cracks, doors, and other openings, or it can be estimated with the use of tables that give air changes per hour based on certain criteria.

Calculating sensible heat gain through infiltration is similar to calculating heat loss. The total heat gain is found by multiplying the total area by an infiltration factor. If a building is being mechanically ventilated, however, the volume of air being introduced into the building is multiplied by the amount of heat that must be extracted both to cool the air and to remove excess humidity (latent heat). In humid climates, the energy required to do this can be substantial.

SAMPLE QUESTIONS

1. Heat gain is most affected by:

    I.   motors

    II. sunlight

    III. people

    IV. fluorescent lighting

    V. humidity

      A. II and III
      B. II, III, and V
      C. I, II, III, and IV
      D. all of the above

2. A sling psychrometer measures:

    A. one of the factors shown in the psychrometric chart
    B. dry bulb temperature
    C. relative humidity
    D. the level of the dew point in humid climates

The answers to questions 3 through 6 can be found on the following key list. Select only one answer for each question.

    A0 coefficient of heat transfer
    A1 conductance
    A2 conduction
    A3 conductivity
    A4 convection
    A5 design cooling load factor
    A6 dew point
    A7 effective temperature
    A8 enthalpy
    A9 equivalent temperature difference

    B0 infiltration
    B1 latent heat
    B2 mean radiant temperature
    B3 psychrometric chart
    B4 radiation
    B5 resistance
    B6 sensible heat
    B7 thermodynamics
    B8 ventilation

3. Heat is lost through insulating glass by what process?

4. In calculating solar heat gain, what value must you have in addition to the area of the glass?

5. A high value of what property is desirable in heat loss calculations?

6. Weatherstripping is a good energy conservation strategy because it affects what?

7. Select the incorrect statement:

    A. Relative humidity is a measure of thermal comfort.
    B. People feel more comfortable in the winter if the MRT is high.
    C. There are differences in comfort level between different cultural groups.
    D. The range of comfortable dry bulb temperature is dependent on air movement.

8. A roof covers an area 40 feet wide and 80 feet long. With heavy insulation the resistance has been calculated as 38 and the design equivalent temperature difference as 44. If the design temperature is $-5°$ and it is desired to maintain a 70° indoor temperature, what is the heat loss through the roof?

    A. 3661 BTUh

    B. 5455 BTUh

    C. 5824 BTUh

    D. 6240 BTUh

9. Melting ice requires:

    A. enthalpy

    B. sensible heat

    C. dew point temperature

    D. latent heat

10. What would be the best design strategy for passive cooling during the summer in a hot-humid climate?

A. Design a series of pools and fountains to cool by evaporation.

B. Include broad overhangs to shield glass and outdoor activities from the sun.

C. Orient the building to catch summer breezes.

D. Use light-colored surfaces to reflect sunlight and solar gain.

9 HVAC SYSTEMS

1 ENERGY SOURCES

Regardless of what energy conservation measures are adopted for a building, either the primary or back-up energy source will be one of the conventional fuels. The selection of which fuel to use depends on its availability and dependability of supply, cost, cleanliness, convenience of storage, and requirements of the equipment needed to use it. For example, in an urban area steam may be readily available as a by-product of a local utility company, while in a suburban area oil may have to be the energy source. In some parts of the country electricity is inexpensive and readily available; in other locations its use for heating is cost prohibitive.

A. Natural Gas

Of all the fossil fuels, natural gas is the most efficient. It is clean burning and relatively low in cost. Depending on geographic location and local market conditions, however, it is not always available or the price fluctuates widely. In remote locations it may not be available at all. It has a heating value of about 1050 BTU per cubic foot.

Propane is another type of gas that can be used in remote areas or where natural gas is not available. It is delivered and stored in pressurized tanks and has a heating value of about 21,560 BTU per pound, or 2500 BTU per cubic foot.

B. Oil

Oil is widely used in some parts of the country, but because it is a petroleum product, its cost and availability are dependent on world and local market conditions. It must be stored in or near the building where it is used, and the equipment needed for burning it is subject to more maintenance than gas-fired boilers.

Oil is produced in six grades for residential and commercial heating use: No. 1, No. 2, No. 4, No. 5 light, No. 5 heavy, and No. 6. The lower the number, the more refined and the more expensive the oil is. No. 2 fuel oil is the grade most commonly used in residential and light commercial boilers, while No. 4 and No. 5 grades are used in larger commercial applications. The heat value for No. 2 oil is from 137,000 to 141,800 BTU per gallon while that for No. 5 is from 146,800 to 152,000 BTU per gallon.

C. Electricity

Electricity has the advantages of being easy to install, low in installation cost, simple to operate, easy to control, and flexible in zoning; and it does not require storage facilities, exhaust flues, or supply air. Its primary disadvantage is its cost in most parts of the country compared with other fuels. Since most electric utilities now charge more for peak use as well as total electricity consumed, heating during a cold period can be very expensive.

Electricity is ideal for radiant heating, either in a ceiling or in individual panels. It can be used in baseboard units as well as to operate electric furnaces for forced air systems. One of its most prevalent uses is for supplemental space heating. Electricity has an equivalent heating value of 3.14 BTU per hour per watt.

D. Steam

Steam is not considered a basic fuel as gas and oil are, but in many urban locations it is available from a central plant or as a by-product of the generation of electricity. Once piped into a building, it is not used directly for heating but can be used to heat water for water or air heating systems and to drive absorption-type water chillers for air conditioning.

E. Heat Pumps

A heat pump is a device that can either heat in the winter or cool in the summer. It works by transferring heat from one place to another, using the principles of refrigeration as discussed in a later section. In the summer a heat pump acts as a standard air conditioner, pumping refrigerant to the condenser where it loses heat and then to the evaporator indoors where it absorbs heat. By means of a special valve, the refrigerant flow is reversed in the winter so the heat pump absorbs available heat from the air outside and transfers it to the indoor space.

Because of this process, however, the efficiency of a heat pump for heating decreases as the outdoor air temperature decreases. Below about 40 °F a heat pump is not competitive with oil or gas as an energy source. It is more effective in mild climates where winter temperatures are usually moderate. For supplemental heating, electrical resistance coils are often placed in supply ductwork.

The efficiency of a heat pump can be extended by connecting it to a solar energy system. With this approach, solar energy provides heat when the outdoor temperature is between 47 °F and 65 °F. Below the lower extreme, a heat pump automatically turns on and provides heat until the temperature becomes too cold for its efficient use. Then both systems are used, the heat pump to preheat air and the solar energy system to raise the temperature high enough for space heating. Electrical resistance heating is also available for very cold or cloudy days.

F. Natural Energy Sources

Other energy sources include solar energy, either passive or active, photovoltaic, geothermal, wind, and tidal. Of these, solar energy is the one that has been developed to the point where it is readily available and efficient for residential and some commercial uses.

Photovoltaic panels are available, but the cost per kilowatt hour is still rather high and their general use is limited. This is likely to change as more research is conducted and more efficient panels are manufactured.

Use of the other natural energy sources is still in the research and development stage and limited to large-scale generation rather than use with individual buildings.

G. Selection of Fuel Sources

In addition to the considerations mentioned previously in the selection of a fuel source, the number of degree days in a building's location and the efficiency of the fuel must be taken into account.

Degree days are a measure of the approximate average yearly temperature difference between outside and inside in a particular location. The number of degree days for a day is found by taking the difference between an indoor temperature of 65 °F and the average outside temperature for a 24-hour period. For example, if the 24-hour average is 36 degrees, then the number of degree days is $65 - 36 = 29$. The values for each day of the year are added to get the total number of degree days for the year. Degree days are used to calculate yearly fuel consumption, to size some passive solar energy systems, and in other heating computations.

Since various fuels differ in the efficiency with which energy can be converted into heat, this is an important consideration in selection, assuming all fuels are available. Table 9.1 shows the typical efficiency ranges of several fuels.

Table 9.1
Approximate Efficiencies of Fuels

fuel	efficiency in percent
natural gas	70–80
propane	70–90
no. 2 oil	65–85
anthracite coal	65–75
electricity	100

2   ENERGY CONVERSION

Whatever type of fuel is selected for heating and cooling, it must be converted into a useful form for distribution throughout a building. This usually requires additional energy such as electricity to operate fans, motors, and other components of the system. This fact applies to conventional fuels as well as to natural energy sources like solar energy.

A. Heat Generation Equipment

Two of the most common devices for converting fuel to heat are the furnace and the boiler. Furnaces burn either gas or oil to heat air, which is then distributed throughout the building. Boilers burn gas or oil to heat water, in some instances using steam as the fuel.

A furnace burns fuel inside a combustion chamber around which air is circulated by a fan. As the cool air from return air ducts passes over the combustion chamber, it is heated for distribution to the building. The hot exhaust gases pass through a flue which is vented to the outside. Replaceable filters are used on the return air side of the furnace to trap dust and dirt in the system.

Forced air furnaces may be upflow, downflow, or horizontal. In an upflow furnace, the return air is supplied at the bottom of the unit and the heated air is delivered to the bonnet above the furnace where it is distributed through ductwork. A downflow furnace operates in exactly the opposite way and is used where ductwork is in a basement or crawl space and the furnace is on the first floor. A horizontal furnace is designed to be used in areas such as crawl spaces where headroom is limited.

Boilers convert fuel to hot water or steam. The fuel source can be gas, oil, electricity, or steam. In the typical boiler, tubes containing the water to be heated are situated within the combustion chamber where the heat exchange takes place. As with furnaces, the gases and other products of combustion are carried away through breeching into the flue or chimney. Of course, if the primary fuel source is electricity or steam, there is no need for an exhaust flue.

B. Principles of Refrigeration

There are two types of refrigeration processes that can produce chilled air or water: compressive refrigeration and absorption. A third type, evaporative cooling, can be used to produce cool air in some climates.

Compressive refrigeration is based on the transfer of heat during the liquification and evaporation of a refrigerant such as Freon. As a refrigerant in a gaseous form is compressed, it liquifies and releases latent heat as it changes state. As the same liquid expands and vaporizes back to a gas, it absorbs latent heat from the surroundings into the gas. These principles are used in the basic refrigeration cycle shown in Figure 9.1.

There are three basic components of a compressive refrigeration cycle: the compressor, the condenser, and the evaporator. The compressor takes the refrigerant in a gaseous form and compresses it to a liquid. The refrigerant passes through the condenser where the latent heat is released. This is usually on the outside of the building and the heat is released to the outside air or to water. The refrigerant flows out of the condenser into the evaporator where it is allowed to expand. As it expands, it vaporizes back to a gas and in the process absorbs heat from the surroundings (either air or water) and then enters the compressor where it is cycled through the process again.

For many small cooling units, air is forced over the evaporator coils with a fan, and it is this cool air that is circulated through the space. However, water is a much more efficient medium to carry heat than air. In larger units and in large buildings, water is pumped over the evaporator coils to produce chilled water, which is then pumped to remote cooling units where air is circulated over the chilled water pipes. On the condenser side, water is used to extract the heat from condenser pipes and carry it to remote cooling towers where the heat is released to the air.

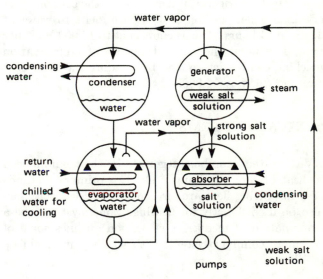

Figure 9.2 Absorption Cooling

Refrigeration by absorption produces chilled water and is accomplished by the loss of heat when water evaporates. This evaporation is produced in a closed system by a salt solution that draws water vapor from the evaporator. See Figure 9.2.

As the salt solution absorbs water it dilutes and must be regenerated by boiling off the water and returning the

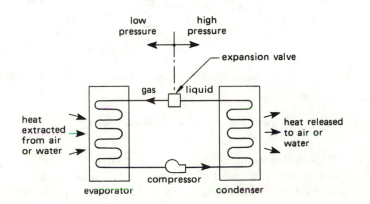

Figure 9.1 Compressive Refrigeration

strong salt solution back to the absorber. This is most often done with steam, but it can also be done with high-temperature water produced by solar collectors. The water boiled off in the generator is returned to a liquid state in the condenser and then returned to the evaporator. Both the condenser and absorber require condensing water, which removes the waste heat and carries it to cooling towers. Absorption systems are less efficient than compressive systems and are most often used when waste heat is available for energy input to the generator.

A third type of conditioning is evaporative cooling. Water is dripped over pads or fin tubes through which outdoor air or water is circulated. As the free water is evaporated to vapor, heat is drawn from the air or circulating water, which is then distributed to the indoor spaces. This type of cooling only works in hot, humid climates where the outdoor air has a low enough humidity level to allow the moistened air to evaporate. It is a more economic alternative in some instances to refrigeration cooling since there is only one motor used instead of three. An evaporative cooler is also simpler in construction and operation since there is no refrigerant line and fewer parts.

A "ton of refrigeration" is a term used to describe the capacity of a refrigeration system. It is the cooling effect obtained when one ton of 32 °F ice melts to water at 32 °F in 24 hours. This is equivalent to 12,000 BTU per hour. In general, the required capacity of a refrigeration machine can be determined by dividing the total heat gain in BTUh by 12,000.

3 HVAC SYSTEMS

HVAC systems can be categorized by the medium used to heat or cool a building. The two primary methods of transporting heat are air and water. Electricity can also be used directly for heating. Some systems use a combination of media. This section outlines some of the more common systems with which you should be familiar.

A. Direct Expansion

The simplest type of system is the direct expansion system (DX), also known as an incremental unit. This is a self-contained unit that passes non-ducted air to be cooled over the evaporator and back into the room. The condenser uses outdoor air directly so these units are typically placed in an exterior wall.

Smaller units with 1/3- to 2-ton capacity are adequate for individual rooms while larger units with over a 2-ton capacity can serve several rooms in a single zone.

With the addition of a heating coil, a DX system can serve both heating and cooling. Ventilation comes directly from the outside. Direct expansion units can be through-wall types, roof mounted, or packaged.

B. All-Air Systems

All-air systems cool or heat spaces by conditioned air alone. Heat is transported to the space with supply and return air ducts. There are four basic types.

1. Variable air volume: For large buildings and situations where temperature regulation is required, humidity control is needed, and energy conservation is a concern, the variable air volume (VAV) system is often used. See Figure 9.3.

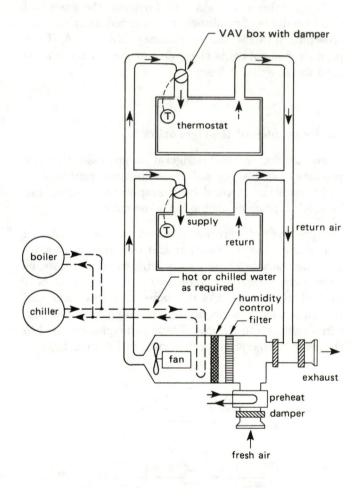

Figure 9.3 Variable Air Volume System

With this system, air is heated or cooled as required in a central plant and distributed to the building at a constant temperature through a single duct. At each zone, a thermostat controls a damper that varies the volume of conditioned air entering the space to respond to the user's needs. Dampers on the return air side of the system allow variable amounts of fresh air, up to 100 percent, to be introduced into the building for ventilation and for cooling when outdoor conditions make it unnecessary to mechanically condition the air. This system is somewhat limited in its ability to compensate for extremes in simultaneous heating and cooling demands in a building, but it offers a very efficient means of air conditioning large buildings.

2. High-velocity dual duct: Where more flexibility is required, a high-velocity dual duct system can be used. This system provides two parallel ducts, one with hot air and one with cool air. These two streams of air are joined in a mixing box in proportions to suit the temperature requirements of the conditioned space. A thermostat controls pneumatic valves in the mixing box to create the proper mixture. Figure 9.4 shows a simplified diagram of this type of system.

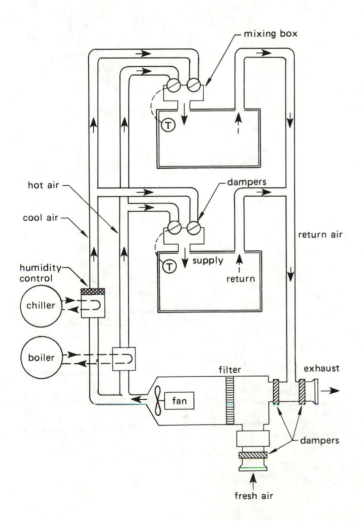

Figure 9.4 High-Velocity Dual Duct System

Because both hot and cool air is available anywhere in the building, a dual duct system can respond to varying requirements. For example, during a cold day on the north side of a structure with a high percentage of glazing, heating may be required. On the south side of the same building the combination of solar heat gain, lighting, and occupancy may create a need for cooling. Since the air travels at a high velocity, about 3000 feet per minute, the ducts can be smaller, which saves space in high-rise buildings.

In spite of these advantages, a high-velocity dual duct system has some disadvantages. It is inherently inefficient because both hot and cool air have to be supplied winter or summer and previously cooled air may need to be heated or previously heated air may need to be cooled. In addition, the high velocity requires larger, more powerful fans to move the air, which requires more energy. Also, the high velocity can cause noise problems in the ductwork. Initial cost is high because of the quantity of ductwork.

3. Constant volume with reheat: A reheat system takes return air and fresh outdoor air and cools and dehumidifies the mixture, which is distributed in a constant volume at low temperature throughout the building. At or near the spaces to be conditioned, the air is reheated as required by the cooling load of the space. See Figure 9.5.

Reheating of the air is accomplished most often with heated water, but it can also be done with electricity. If the reheating equipment is located near the conditioned space, it is called a *terminal reheat system*. If the reheating coils are located in ductwork to serve an entire zone, it is called a *zone reheat system*. Thermostats control valves in the water supply line to regulate the temperature.

In many cases, an economizer cycle is used. This allows outdoor air to be used for cooling when temperatures are low enough. The economizer works by adjusting dampers on the return air ducts and fresh air intakes.

The advantage of the reheat system is that humidity and temperature can be carefully controlled and the low supply temperature means smaller duct sizes and fan horsepower. However, it does use more energy than some systems because as the heat load decreases the energy required for the reheating increases.

4. Multizone: The multizone system, Figure 9.6, supplies air to a central mixing unit where separate heating and cooling coils produce hot and cold air streams. These are mixed with dampers controlled by zone thermostats, and the resulting tempered air is delivered to the zones.

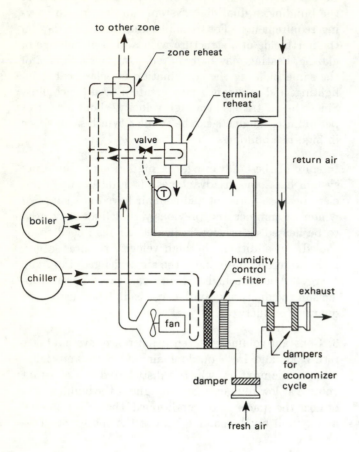

Figure 9.5   Constant Volume With Reheat

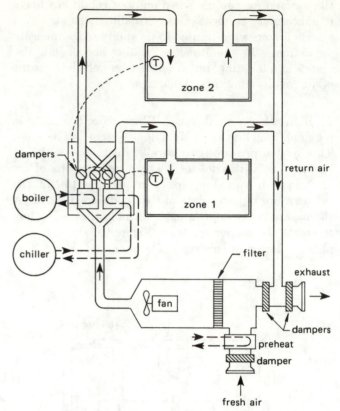

Figure 9.6   Multizone System

Multizone units offer the same advantage as a dual duct system in that simultaneous cooling and heating of different zones can be accommodated. Each unit can supply a maximum of eight zones.

C. All-Water Systems

An all-water system uses a fan coil unit in each conditioned space. The fan coils are connected to one or two water circuits. Ventilation is provided with openings through the wall where the fan coil unit is located, from interior zone air heating, or by simple infiltration. In a two-pipe system, either hot or chilled water is pumped through one pipe and returned in another. In a four-pipe system, as shown in Figure 9.7, one circuit is provided for chilled water and one for hot water. There are two supply pipes and two return pipes. A three-pipe system uses a single return pipe for both hot and cold water.

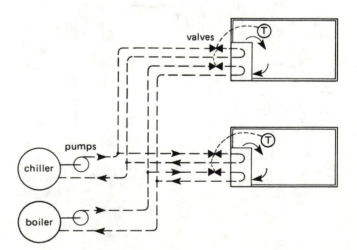

Figure 9.7   Four-Pipe All-Water System

All-water systems are an efficient way to transfer heat and are easily controlled, with a thermostat in each room regulating the amount of water flowing through the coils. However, humidity control is not possible at the central unit.

D. Air-Water Systems

Air-water systems rely on a central air system to provide humidity control and ventilation air to conditioned spaces. However, the majority of the heating and cooling is provided by fan coil units in each space. Air-water systems are often used where return air cannot be recirculated, such as hospitals and laboratories. In these cases, 100 percent outside air is supplied and return air completely exhausted to the exterior.

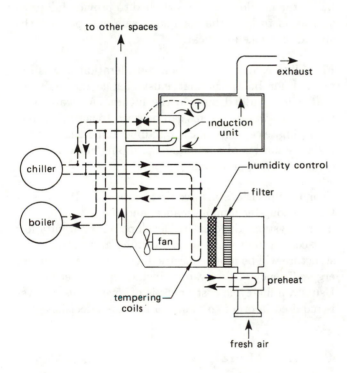

Figure 9.8 Air-Water Induction System

With an induction system, shown in Figure 9.8, air is supplied throughout the building under high pressure and velocity to each induction unit, where the velocity and noise are attenuated before the air passes over the coils and is heated or cooled as required. The water supply system may be either a two- or four-pipe system. Thermostatic control is provided by regulating the amount of water flowing through the coils. Another type of air-water system uses a fan coil unit for primary heating and cooling but has a separate constant volume, tempered air supply for humidity control, and ventilation air. See Figure 9.9.

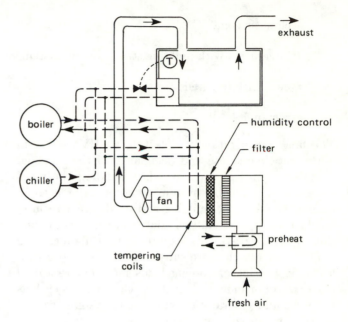

Figure 9.9 Fan Coil With Supplementary Air

E. Electric Systems

Electric heating is most often accomplished by laying a grid of wires in the ceiling of a room to provide radiant heating. Electric baseboard radiators are also available. This type of system provides a uniform, clean, inconspicuous form of heating that can easily be controlled with a separate thermostat in each room. No space is required for piping or ductwork. The big disadvantage is that electric heat is generally not economical except in areas where electricity is inexpensive. Most often, electric heat is used for supplemental heating in localized radiant panels or where water or air systems need a boost in temperature.

F. Selection of Systems

The selection of the most appropriate HVAC system for a building depends on several, interrelated variables. These include the following.

- use profile of the building

- building scale

- control requirements

- fuels available

- climatic zone

- integration with building structure and systems

- flexibility required

- economics

The first consideration in selecting an HVAC system is the anticipated use and occupancy of the building. Some occupancies, such as office buildings or retail stores, need a flexible system to account for changes during the life of the building and for different requirements of multiple tenants. Variable air volume or induction systems satisfy this requirement. Buildings with multiple uses or that are subject to simultaneous variations in heating or cooling loads may require a dual duct system or multizone system. Occupancies such as hospitals and laboratories will require systems like induction or fan coils with supplementary air so all air supply is 100 percent fresh with complete exhaust to the outside.

The size of the building helps determine whether to use a central system or individual units. If the air conditioning load is under about 25 tons, direct expansion units or heat pumps can usually be used, either rooftop mounted or the through-wall variety. For larger cooling needs, a central station is more economical and provides the required flexibility.

The third consideration is the kind of control that is required. Hotels, motels, apartments, and some office buildings need the ability for individual room or area thermostatic control while other uses such as theaters need less individual control.

Although chillers, boilers, and furnaces are available that operate with a variety of fuels, whichever system is most readily and economically available will help the designer select an HVAC system. If steam is adjacent to the building site, for example, absorption type chillers may be more appropriate than refrigeration equipment.

The climatic zone will also affect the system selection. If the proposed building is in a hot, arid climate, the requirement for dehumidification will not be as great so an all-water system may be appropriate. Locations that experience a wide swing in temperatures during the day may need a dual duct system or four-pipe system to provide flexibility and quick response as outdoor conditions change.

The consideration of integrating the mechanical system with other building systems is one with which the architect is most closely involved. The system must work with the building's structure; the location of the mechanical equipment room; provisions for piping and duct runs; the location and appearance of terminal units, such as fan coils or induction boxes; the choice of return air methods, either ducted or above a suspended ceiling; the means of air supply and location of supply air diffusers; and the location and appearance of air intakes or exhaust grills on the exterior of the building.

In addition, the mechanical system may have to be integrated with the method of fire protection and smoke control required for the structure. For example, smoke control in a high-rise building can be accomplished by providing a separate fan room on each floor. In the event of fire, the air supply on the fire floor can be switched off and all return air exhausted to the outside. At the same time, the dampers on the floors above and below the fire floor can be switched to provide full pressurization to keep the occupants safe and prevent the spread of smoke and heat.

Flexibility is another selection consideration that is important for buildings that must change internally or that will be added onto in the future. All-water systems or air-water systems can be sized to accommodate the ultimate capacity of the building. Expansion is then a simple matter of extending the piping runs from the central heating and cooling plant.

Economic decisions involve first costs of an HVAC system, its long-term maintenance, and the cost of operating the system. Speculative developers may want a low first-cost system while people owning and occupying a structure will be more concerned with the long-term energy efficiency of the system, including the cost of fuel. Usually, a life-cycle cost analysis of several alternatives is required in order to make an informed decision.

4   SYSTEM SIZING

Calculating the size of an HVAC system involves determining the required capacity of the heating and cooling equipment, determining the size of the mechanical spaces to house the equipment, and figuring the space needs and layout of the distribution system of pipes and ducts.

A. System Capacity

The primary determinants in sizing equipment are the total heat gains and losses the building will experience in the most extreme conditions. These are calculated according to the procedures discussed in Chapter 8, and then equipment is selected to offset these gains or losses. In some cases, cooling equipment is undersized slightly to lower initial costs, with the knowledge that some occasional minor extremes in indoor design temperature will be tolerated.

B. Mechanical Room Space Requirements

For preliminary sizing of mechanical rooms for medium- to large-size buildings using all-air or air-water systems, allow from 6 to 9 percent of the gross building area. This includes space for boilers, chillers, fans, and related pumps and piping. All-water systems will require about 2 percent of the total gross area.

Boilers and chillers require rooms long enough to allow for the removal of the tubes, so the room has to be slightly longer than twice the length of the equipment. Equipment rooms need to be from 12 to 18 feet high.

C. Ductwork Distribution and Sizing

Supply ductwork for all-air and air-water systems must run from the central air handling unit to each terminal unit or supply air diffuser. Since ductwork can occupy a significant amount of space, a logical, simple, and direct route must be planned and coordinated with the other building systems. Either round or rectangular ducts are used. Round ducts are the most efficient and produce the least amount of pressure loss for air delivered, but rectangular ducts make better use of available space above ceilings and in vertical duct chases.

In most cases, main trunk ducts can follow the path of circulation systems since these must serve every space just as hallways do. The ductwork can be located above the ceiling in the corridors or between structural beams. Some structural systems, such as open-web steel joists, allow ductwork to run both parallel and perpendicular to the direction of the structure.

In air ducts, there is a loss of pressure due to the friction of the air moving through the ducts, fittings, registers, and other components. The pressure required to overcome this friction loss is called the *static head* and is measured in inches of water. As this pressure increases, larger ducts and fans are required to overcome it, resulting in higher first costs as well as higher operating costs.

For preliminary sizing of low-pressure duct space, allow about 3 to 4 square feet for every 1000 square feet of floor space served for both vertical and horizontal duct runs. This figure includes supply and return ducts. Of course, high-pressure supply ducts will require less space.

SAMPLE QUESTIONS

Questions 1 through 3 are based on the following situation.

A developer in a midsize Arizona city is planning to build a small shopping mall for resale. You have been hired as the architect. The mall will consist of 40,000 square feet of rentable area on one level surrounding a small enclosed courtyard. Existing utilities adjacent to the site include water, sanitary sewer, storm sewer, natural gas, and electricity.

1. Which mechanical system for the lease area would you recommend?

    A. a multizone system with economizer cycle

    B. an active solar energy system for heating and evaporative cooling

    C. a direct expansion system with passive solar design of the building

    D. individual rooftop heat pumps

2. What cooling system would work best for the enclosed courtyard?

    A. evaporative cooling with a closed water loop

    B. absorption cooling with solar assist

    C. compressive refrigeration

    D. passive cooling

3. Which of the following would be most important in the selection of an HVAC system for this project?

    I. flexibility

    II. climatic zone

    III. economics

    IV. the tenant's preference

    V. building scale

        A. I, II, and V

        B. II, III, and IV

        C. II, III, and V

        D. all of the above

4. A seven-story office building is to have a variable air volume system. The building will have 105,000 square feet of net space and an estimated 126,000 square feet of gross area. About how much space should be allowed for HVAC systems?

    A. 2500 square feet

    B. 3800 square feet

    C. 6300 square feet

    D. 7600 square feet

5. Select the incorrect statement.

    A. A health center would probably use no. 4 or no. 5 fuel oil.

    B. Heat pumps rely on solar energy more than electricity.

    C. Natural gas has a higher heating value than propane.

    D. Electricity is not a good choice for powering boilers in remote areas.

6. A main trunk duct is to be placed above a suspended ceiling and below the structural framing. If ceiling space for the duct is not a problem, which of the following shapes of ducts would be best to use assuming equal capacities?

    A. rectangular, with the long dimension horizontal

    B. rectangular, with the long dimension vertical

    C. square

    D. round

7. A standard gas furnace has all of the following except:

    A. flue

    B. damper

    C. combustion chamber

    D. filters

8. The heat gain for a building has been calculated at 108,000 BTUh. What size compressive refrigeration machine should be specified?

A. 9 tons

B. 12 tons

C. 36 tons

D. 54 tons

9. An economizer cycle:

A. only cools as much chilled water as required by the demand load

B. uses outdoor air to cool a building

C. automatically reduces the amount of time the compressor runs

D. uses air and water to cool the condenser coils

10. The cooling system for a restaurant kitchen must remove which of the following?

A. sensible heat only

B. latent heat only

C. sensible and latent heat

D. sensible heat and latent heat at 30% of sensible heat

10 PLUMBING SYSTEMS

1 WATER SUPPLY

Depending on geographic location, water is available from a variety of sources. It comes from rivers, lakes, wells, surface runoff, oceans, and even recycled wastewater. In some cases, water may be pure enough in its natural state for immediate human use. In most instances, however, it must be treated to remove impurities. Water suitable for human drinking is called *potable water*. If it is not suitable for drinking, it is called *nonpotable*, but this type of water may be used for irrigation, flushing toilets, and the like.

Two of the most common sources of large water supplies for cities are surface and groundwater. Surface water comes from rain and snow that runs off into rivers and lakes. Groundwater is that which seeps into the ground until it hits an impervious layer of rock or soil. It then forms a water table that is tapped by drilling. Large regions of subsurface water are called *aquifers*.

Generally, the best sources for water are those that require little or no treatment, including water from deep wells, relatively clean rivers, and surface runoff. This type of water can be easily treated in most cases and made available in large quantities. However, with increasing pollution and scarcity of water in some locations, greater use of treated seawater or recycled wastewater will be necessary. The means are available to do this, but the processing is more expensive than other methods.

Regardless of the source of water, there are several types of water quality problems that may exist. The first is hardness. Hard water has a pH level over 7 (alkaline), a result of calcium and magnesium in the water, and if untreated it can cause clogged pipes and corrosion of boilers and can make clothes washing difficult. It can be treated by running the water through a water softener prior to distribution and use.

If the water has a pH under 7 it is acidic and, along with entrained oxygen, can cause rusting of iron and steel pipes. It can be corrected by adding a neutralizer to raise the alkaline content. Other common problems with water quality include pollution from organic matter, turbidity caused by suspended matter, poor taste and odor caused by organic matter, and coloring caused by iron and manganese.

A. Private Water Supply

Private water supplies include wells, springs, or collected rainwater. The most common, however, is the well, which is used for residences and small buildings where a municipal supply is not available. Wells are most commonly drilled or bored. A rotary bit is used for drilled wells, which is the only method possible for going through rock, and a bored well uses a rotary auger to make the hole.

Two of the most important considerations in drilling a well are depth and yield. The depth of a well may range from less than 25 feet, known as a shallow well, to several hundred feet. Of course, the depth affects the cost of the well and there is no sure way of knowing prior to drilling how deep it may have to be. Before drilling, you should talk to neighbors, local well drillers, and geologists to see what their experience has been.

The yield of a well is the number of gallons per minute (gpm) it provides. A yield of from 5 to 10 gpm is about the minimum required for a private residence. If a yield is too low for the project, the system may need to include a large storage tank that can be filled during periods of low use, such as during the night, so enough water is available during peak periods.

As a well is drilled or bored, a pipe casing is lowered into the hole to prevent the hole from cave-ins and to prevent seepage of surface contamination into the well.

The casing is a steel pipe from 4 to 6 inches in diameter. Lower in the well, perforated casings are used to allow the water to seep into the well from which it is pumped out.

B. Pumps

Several kinds of pumps are used in wells. These include the suction, deep-well jet, turbine, and submersible pumps. Suction pumps are only suitable for water tables less than 25 feet while deep-well jet pumps can operate at depths from 25 to over 100 feet. Turbine pumps are used for high-capacity systems with deep wells. One of the most common types for moderate to deep wells serving private residences or small buildings is the submersible pump. This type has a waterproof motor and pump which are placed below the water line and pump water to a pressure tank.

Jet pumps have the pump and motor aboveground and lift water by the venturi principle. Water is forced through a pipe in the well where a jet stream of small diameter is created in another pipe. The low pressure sucks up the well water and drives it to the surface. In both types of pumps, water is pumped to a pressure tank where air pressure circulates the water and operates fixtures.

C. Municipal Water Supply

Most cities get their water from rivers or lakes. It is filtered and treated as required to eliminate turbidity, organic matter, and hardness and piped through water mains at a pressure of about 50 pounds per square inch (psi), although this can vary from 40 to 80 psi depending on location and other factors. If the pressure is too high, a pressure-reducing valve is used between the water main and the building meter.

One of the first tasks in a building project is to determine the location of the water main, its size, its pressure, and the cost for tapping it. This information is available from the local water company. If a main is not adjacent to the property, the property owner is often required to extend the line at his or her own cost. If the water main is a substantial distance from the proposed building, the cost impact can be significant. The pressure in the line is needed to determine what kind of supply system can be used, as described in a later section.

2 WATER SUPPLY DESIGN

Designing a water supply system involves selecting the type of system; deciding on the type of piping, fittings, and fixtures of the system; and sizing the pipe. Each of these will be discussed in turn. Hot water supply is outlined in a later section.

A. Supply Systems

There are two primary types of water supply systems: the upfeed and the downfeed. The choice between the two is usually based on the height of the building and the pressure required to operate the fixtures.

Water supplied from a city main or from a pressure tank with a private well comes from the pipe under a certain pressure; in city mains it is about 50 psi. This pressure must be sufficient to overcome friction in the piping, fittings, meter, and static head and still be high enough to operate fixtures. A flush valve, for example, requires from 10 to 20 psi to operate properly; a shower needs about 12 psi.

The static head is the pressure required to push water vertically, or the pressure caused at the bottom of a column of water. It requires 0.434 psi to lift water up one foot. Viewed another way, one psi will lift water 2.3 feet.

Example 10.1

How much pressure is lost in static head at a fixture 40 feet above a water main with a pressure of 45 psi? Ignoring friction loss, how much pressure is available to operate a fixture at this level?

If 0.434 psi = 1 foot, then the pressure loss is:

$$40 \times 0.434 = 17.36 \text{ psi}$$

Ignoring friction loss, the remaining pressure at the 45 foot level is:

$$45 - 17.36 = 27.64 \text{ psi}$$

An upfeed system uses pressure in the water main directly to supply the fixtures. See Figure 10.1 (a). Since there is always some friction in the system and some pressure must be available to work the highest fixtures, the practical limit is about 40 to 60 feet.

If a building is too tall for an upfeed system, a downfeed system is most often used. In this case, water from the main is pumped to storage tanks near the top of the building or at the top of the zone served and flows by gravity to the fixtures. See Figure 10.1 (b). The pressure at any fixture or point in the system is determined by the distance from the outlet of the tank to the fixture, using the equivalency of 0.434 psi for every foot.

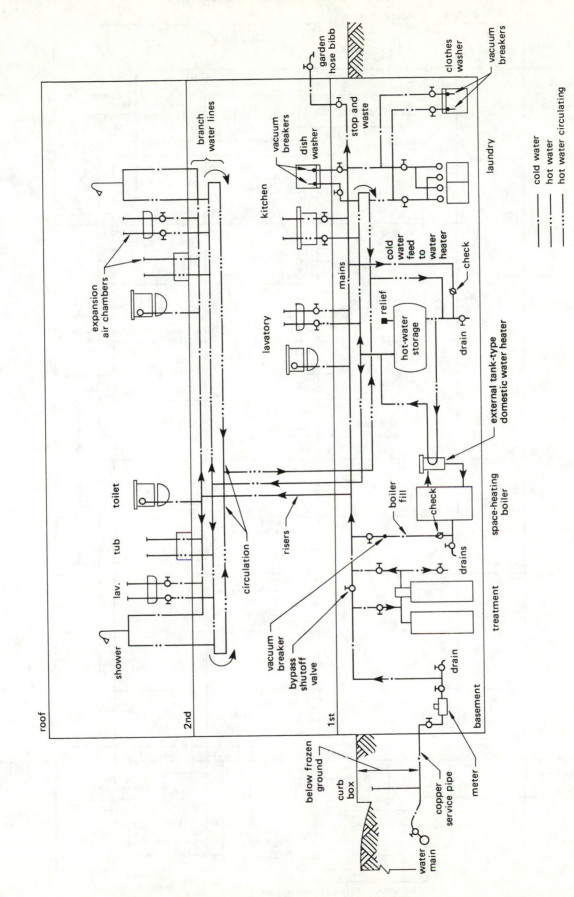

Figure 10.1 Upfeed and Downfeed Systems

PROFESSIONAL PUBLICATIONS ● Belmont, CA

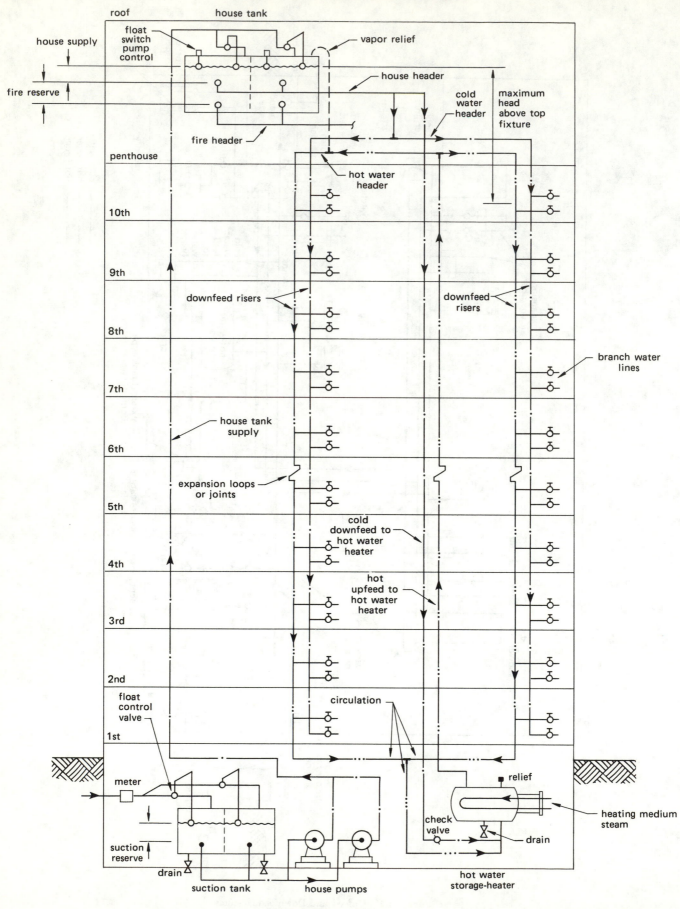

Figure 10.1 (cont'd)

The height of the zone served by a downfeed system is determined by the maximum allowable pressure on the fixtures at the bottom of the zone, allowing for friction loss in the piping. Depending on the fixture and manufacturer, this maximum pressure is from 45 to 60 psi. Therefore, the maximum height of a zone is 60 divided by 0.434 psi, or about 138 feet. Beyond this, pressure-reducing valves are required.

Conversely, the pressure at the fixtures at the top of a downfeed system is also of concern because there must be a minimum pressure to make fixtures work properly. For example, if a flush toilet needs 15 psi, then the water tank must be a minimum of 15/0.434, or about 35 feet above the fixture. Actually, the distance would have to be a little greater to overcome friction loss in the piping.

In some cases, the lower floors of a high-rise building are served by an upfeed system and the upper floors by a downfeed system.

Another type of supply system that can be used for tall buildings is direct upfeed pumping. Several pumps are used together controlled by a pressure sensor. When demand is light, only one pump operates to supply the needed pressure. As demand increases and is detected by the pressure sensor, another pump automatically starts.

B. Components and Materials

A water supply system is comprised of piping, fittings, valves, and other specialized components. Piping can be copper, steel, plastic, or brass. Copper is most commonly used because of its corrosion resistance, strength, low friction loss, and small outside diameter. Where the water is not corrosive, steel or galvanized steel pipe can be used, but these materials are more difficult to assemble because of their screw fittings.

Copper is available in three grades: K, L, and M. DWV copper is also used for drainage, waste, and vent piping that is not subject to pressure as supply pipe is, but it is rarely used. Type K has the thickest walls and comes in straight lengths (hard temper) or in coils (soft temper). It is used for underground supply pipe where greater strength is required. Type L has thinner walls than type K and also comes in straight lengths or coils. It is the grade most commonly used for the majority of the plumbing system in a building. Type M is the thinnest of the three types and is available in straight lengths (hard temper) only. It is only used where low pressure is involved, such as branch supply lines, chilled water systems, exposed lines in heating systems, and drainage piping.

Plastic pipe has generally gained acceptance as a material suitable for supply piping although some codes still restrict its use. Four types are used for cold water:

PE	polyethylene
ABS	acrilylonitrile-butadiene styrene
PVC	polyvinyl chloride
PVDC	polyvinyl dichloride

Of these, only PVDC is suitable for hot water.

Supply piping is connected with a variety of fittings, valves, and other components to form a complete system. Fittings connect pipes where lengths must be joined, where a change in direction occurs, where three pipes join, and where a change in size occurs. Figure 10.2 shows some common fittings.

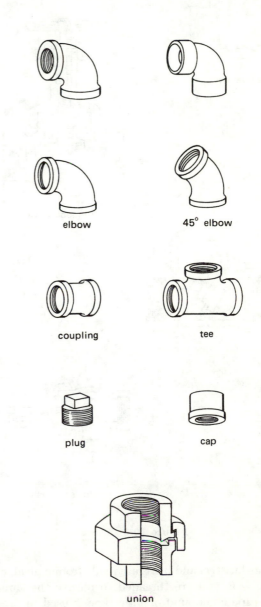

elbow   45° elbow

coupling   tee

plug   cap

union

Figure 10.2 Plumbing Fittings

A union is a special fitting that connects two rigid sections of pipe and that can be easily unscrewed to allow for repairs or additions to the piping system. Unions are also used between piping and devices like water heaters that may need to be replaced. Adapters are also available that allow two different piping materials to be joined.

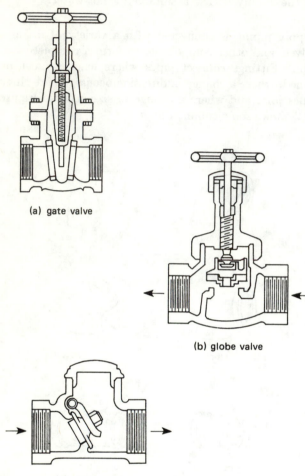

(a) gate valve

(b) globe valve

(c) check valve

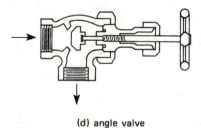

(d) angle valve

Figure 10.3 Valves

Fittings for steel and brass are made from maleable iron or cast iron and are threaded to receive the threaded pipe. Pipe compound or pipe tape is used to produce a watertight seal when the two are joined. Copper and plastic fittings are slightly larger than the pipe to allow

it to be slipped in. Copper joints are sealed by soldering and plastic pipes by using a solvent that "melts" the plastic together.

Valves are used to control water flow. They are located at risers, horizontal branch lines, and pipe connections to fixtures and equipment such as water heaters and sinks. Valves allow selective shutdown of the system for repairs without affecting the entire building. Four common valve types are shown in Figure 10.3.

The *globe valve* is used where water flow is variably and frequently controlled, such as with faucets or hose bibbs. A handle operates a stem that compresses a washer against a metal seat. Since the water must make two 90 degree turns, the friction loss in this type of valve is high. A *gate valve* seats a metal wedge against two metal parts of the valve. It is used where control is either completely on or off. Since there are no turns, it has a low friction loss. A *check valve* works automatically and allows water flow in only one direction where, for example, backflow might contaminate a potable water supply.

Other types of components include air chambers, shock absorbers, pressure reducers, and flow restrictors. Air chambers and shock absorbers are used to prevent water hammer. This is the noise caused when a valve or faucet is closed quickly, causing the water moving in the system to stop abruptly and the pipes to rattle. An air chamber is a length of pipe installed above the connection to the faucet that cushions the surge of water. A shock absorber performs the same function with a manufactured expansion device.

C. System Design

Designing a plumbing system involves sizing the pipes and laying out the required fittings, valves, and other components. As previously mentioned, there must be adequate pressure at the most remote fixture after deducting various pressure losses from the available pressure at the water main. Stated another way, the sum of all these values must equal or be less than the water main pressure:

    pressure at most remote fixture
+   pressure loss from static head
+   pressure loss by friction in piping and fittings
+   pressure loss through water meter
_____
=   total street water main pressure

The pressure required for fixtures can be found in Table 10.1. The pressure loss from static head is found by multiplying the total height by 0.434. The water main pressure is found by consulting the local water company. What remains is to determine the pressure losses through the piping and water meter, which is most often a process of trial and error.

Table 10.1

Minimum Flow Pressure for Various Fixtures

fixture	min. pressure, psi
standard lavatory	8
self-closing faucet	12
sink faucet, 3/8 in.	10
kitchen sink	8
service sink	8
flush tank toilet	8
flush valve toilet	15
flush valve urinal	15
bathtub	5
shower	12
dishwasher	8
clothes washer	8
drinking fountain	15
hose bibb	30
fire hose	30

Table 10.2

Demand Weight of Fixtures in Fixture Units

Fixture Type[2]	Weight in Fixture Units[3]		Minimum Connections	
	Private	Public	Cold Water	Hot Water
Bathtub[4]	2	4	½	½
Bedpan washer		10	1	
Bidet	2	4	½	½
Combination sink and tray	3		½	½
Dental unit or cuspidor		1	⅜	
Dental lavatory	1	2	½	½
Drinking fountain	1	2	⅜	
Kitchen sink	2	4	½	½
Lavatory	1	2	⅜	⅜
Laundry tray (1 or 2 compartments)	2	4	½	½
Shower, each head[4]	2	4	½	½
Sink, service	2	4	½	½
Urinal, pedestal		10	1	
Urinal (wall lip)		5	½	
Urinal stall		5	¾	
Urinal with flush tank		3		
Wash sink, circular or multiple (each set of faucets)		2	½	½
Water closet:				
Flushometer valve	6	10	1	
Flush tank	3	5	⅜	

[1] For supply outlets likely to impose continuous demands, estimate continuous supply separately and add to total demand for fixtures.

[2] For fixtures not listed, weights may be assumed by comparing the fixture to a listed one using water in similar quantities and at similar rates.

[3] The given weights are for total demand for fixtures with both hot and cold water supplies. The weights for maximum separate demands may be taken as seventy-five (75) per cent of the listed demand for the supply.

[4] Shower over bathtub does not add fixture unit to group.

Pressure loss in pipes depends on the diameter of the pipe and the flow in gallons per minute. The probable demand flow is found by first determining the demand load of the entire system or individual parts of the system. Probable demand is defined by fixture units; a fixture unit is a unit flow rate approximately equal to one cubic foot per minute. Fixture units for various fixtures have been established and are listed in Table 10.2.

Since it is unlikely that all the fixtures in a building would be in use at the same time, charts are available that relate fixture units to flow in gallons per minute. Figure 10.4 shows an enlarged portion of the chart commonly used, which is based on experience and illustrates that flow does not increase in direct proportion to an increase in fixture units.

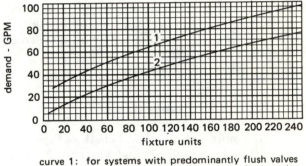

curve 1: for systems with predominantly flush valves
curve 2: for systems with predominantly flush tanks

Figure 10.4   Estimate Curves for Demand Load

Example 10.2

What is the flow rate for a group of plumbing fixtures in a small office building consisting of five flush valve toilets, two urinals, four lavatories, two service sinks, and a drinking fountain?

From Table 10.2, the fixture units are calculated as follows:

toilets	$5 \times 10 = 50$	
urinals	$2 \times 5 = 10$	
lavatories	$4 \times 2 = 8$	
sinks	$2 \times 3 = 6$	
fountain	$1 \times 2 = 2$	
total	76 fixture units	

Find 76 along the bottom of Figure 10.4; read up until you intersect curve 1 for predominately flush valves and read across to find about 60 gallons per minute.

Once you have the probable flow rate, other charts are used that relate flow, pipe size, and friction loss in static head in pounds per square inch per 100-foot length of pipe. The goal in pipe sizing is to select the smallest size that will do the job within the pressure loss limits. The smallest possible pipe size is desired because cost increases with pipe size. Several charts are available for different types of pipe. One such chart is shown in Figure 10.5.

To use the chart, find the flow in gallons per minute determined from the fixture unit demand and read across until you intersect one of the pipe diameter lines. You may have to assume a pipe size at first and then determine the total friction loss. If it is too great, select a larger pipe size and perform the calculation again. Using Example 10.2, the pressure loss for 60 gpm in a 1 1/2 inch pipe is about 13 psi per 100 feet.

Table 10.3

Allowance in Equivalent Length of Pipe for Friction Loss in Valves and Threaded Fittings

Diameter of fitting (inches)	90° Standard Elbow	45° Standard Elbow	Standard T 90°	Coupling or Straight Run of T	Gate Valve	Globe Valve	Angle Valve
	Feet	Feet	Feet	Feet	Feet	Feet	Feet
⅜	1	0.6	1.5	0.3	0.2	8	4
½	2	1.2	3	0.6	0.4	15	8
¾	2.5	1.5	4	0.8	0.5	20	12
1	3	1.8	5	0.9	0.6	25	15
1¼	4	2.4	6	1.2	0.8	35	18
1½	5	3	7	1.5	1	45	22
2	7	4	10	2	1.3	55	28
2½	8	5	12	2.5	1.6	65	34
3	10	6	15	3	2	80	40
4	14	8	21	4	2.7	125	55
5	17	10	25	5	3.3	140	70
6	20	12	30	6	4	165	80

Reproduced from the Uniform Plumbing Code, 1988 Edition, by permission of the copyright holder, International Association of Plumbing and Mechanical Officials. Copyright ©1988.

To find the total friction loss in the piping and fittings, calculate the total length of piping from the meter to the fixture under consideration. Friction loss in fittings is calculated by referring to tables that give the loss for various diameter fittings in equivalent lengths of pipe. Table 10.3 is one such table.

If the layout of the plumbing system has not been completely determined, you may have to estimate the number and location of fittings. Friction loss for pipe and fittings are then added together to get the total loss in pounds per square inch.

The final step is to calculate the loss through the water meter. Charts that relate pressure loss to meter size and flow rate in gallons per minute are also available for this. When the supply main is 1 1/2 inches or greater, the typical meter size is one pipe size smaller than the main.

One critical part of plumbing design in large buildings is allowance for the expansion of piping. This is especially important in high-rise buildings where long lengths of piping are encountered. For example, a 100-foot length of copper pipe can expand well over 1/2 inch with a 60 degree temperature change. Figure 10.6 shows two common methods of providing for expansion.

D. Hot Water Supply

Hot water is supplied with tank-type water heaters or boilers in which water is heated with gas, oil, electricity, or steam. In residences and small buildings, a single supply pipe is provided from the heater to the fixtures. This minimizes the cost of piping but can result in long waits for hot water when the fixture has not been turned on for a while. The water in the pipes cools and must be run until fresh hot water from the heater travels the distance to the fixture.

This problem can be solved with a two-pipe circulating system. All fixtures needing hot water are connected with a supply pipe and a return pipe. The natural convection in the system keeps the water slowly circulating; hot water rises to the uppermost fixtures and as it cools falls down to the water heater to be reheated. When a circulating system is used in long, low buildings, or where natural convection may not provide enough circulation, pumps are used.

The size of the water heater is based on the total daily and peak hourly hot water demands of a building. This can range from 0.4 gallons per person in a peak hour for an office building to 12 gallons per unit for a small apartment building. The peak hourly demand is used because at certain times of the day it is likely that most occupants will want hot water at the same time. For residences and small buildings, the capacity for the peak hourly demand will be the size of the water heater. For large buildings, a separate storage tank is required to meet demand while a smaller boiler actually heats the water.

friction loss lbs. per sq. in. head per 100 ft. length

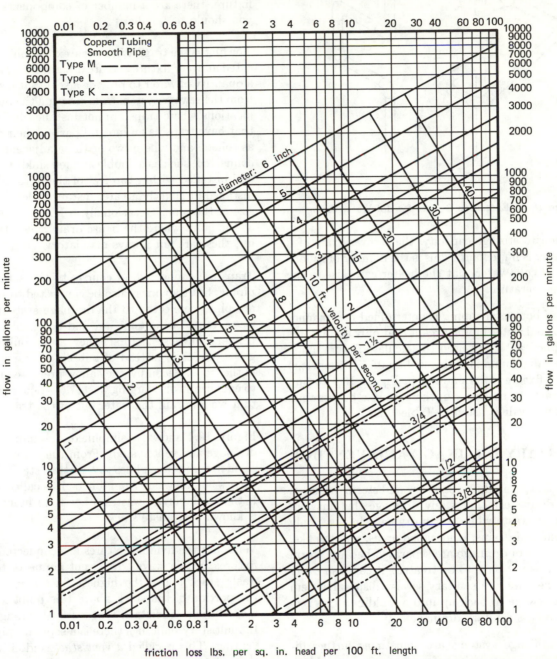

friction loss lbs. per sq. in. head per 100 ft. length

Figure 10.5 Flow Chart for Copper Pipe

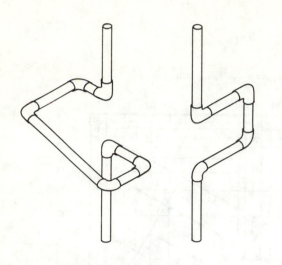

Figure 10.6 Expansion Devices for Hot Water Piping

In addition to storage capacity, the recovery rate of a water heater is important. This is the number of gallons per hour of cold water that the heater can raise to the desired temperature.

The size of hot water piping is determined in a manner similar to cold water piping except that only the fixtures requiring hot water are used to calculate fixture units. Then the value found is multiplied by 0.75 (75 percent) to get the fixture units entered in Figure 10.4 to find the flow rate. In no case can the pipe size be less than the minimum values listed in Table 10.2.

3   SANITARY DRAINAGE AND VENTING

Drainage is separated into sanitary and storm drainage. Sanitary drainage includes any drainage that may include human waste while storm drainage involves only runoff from roof drains, landscaped areas, and the like. The two types of drainage are separated because storm drainage does not have to be treated. It can also easily overload the lines of a sanitary sewage disposal system and cause sewage to back up into a building. This section will discuss sanitary drainage only.

Sanitary drainage systems are sometimes further divided into the categories of grey water and black water. Black water is sewage including human waste and grey water is sewage not including human waste, such as from kitchen sinks, dishwashers, and lavatories. In some conservation systems this distinction is made because grey water can often be recycled directly or with very little treatment for use in irrigation and other purposes, while black water needs more extensive treatment prior to recycling or disposal.

A. Drainage Systems

A drainage system consists of a number of components designed to safely carry away sewage to a private or municipal disposal system. Beginning with an individual fixture, there are a number of components with which you should be familiar.

The first is the trap. With a few exceptions, traps are located at every fixture and are designed to catch and hold a quantity of water to provide a seal that prevents gases from the sewage system from entering the building. The locations where traps are not installed include fixtures that have traps as an integral part of their design, such as toilets, and where two or three adjacent fixtures are connected, such as a double kitchen sink. Traps are usually installed within two feet of the fixture but may be installed at slightly greater distances depending on the size of the pipe. Occasionally, a house trap is installed at the point where the house drain leaves the building, but these are not always mandatory.

Traps are connected, of course, to the actual drainage piping, but they must also be connected to vents. Vents are pipes connected to the drainage system in various ways, vented to outside air, and designed to serve two primary purposes. First, they allow built-up sewage gases to escape instead of bubbling through the water in the traps. Secondly, they allow pressure in the system to equalize so discharging waste does not create a siphon that would drain the water out of the traps.

Figure 10.7 shows a simplified diagram of a typical drainage and vent system. From the trap, sewage travels in fixture branch lines to a vertical stack. If the stack carries human waste from toilets, it is called a *soil stack*. If the stack carries wastes other than human waste, it is known as a *waste stack*.

Vents from individual fixtures are connected above the fixtures in two ways. If a vent connects to a soil or waste stack above the highest fixture in the system, the portion of the stack above this point is known as a *stack vent*. The stack vent extends through the roof. In multistory buildings there is a separate pipe used for venting. This is called a *vent stack* and either extends through the roof or connects with the stack vent above the highest fixture, as shown in Figure 10.7.

The stacks connect at the bottom of the building to a horizontal drain. Within the building and to a point three feet outside the building this is the house drain (also known as the *building drain*). From a point three feet outside the building to the main sewer line or private disposal system, the horizontal pipe is known as the *house sewer* (also known as the *building sewer*).

Cleanouts are provided at the intersections of the stacks and house drain to allow for maintenance of the drain.

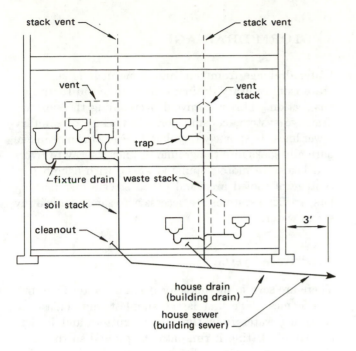

Figure 10.7 Drainage and Vent System

Horizontal drains must be sloped to allow for gravity drainage. The usual minimum for branch lines of house drains and sewers is 1/4 inch per foot, but for pipes larger than 3 inches, 1/8 inch per foot is sometimes allowed. Changes in direction must be made with easy bends rather than right angle fittings.

B. Components and Materials

Piping for drainage systems may be copper, cast iron, or plastic. Plastic has become very popular because it is less expensive and less labor intensive to install than other types. Occasionally, vitrified clay tile may be used for building sewers if allowed by the local code, but the joints in these pipes allow tree roots to grow into them so they are seldom used.

Cast iron piping can be connected with hub and spigot joints or hubless joints. In the hub and spigot fitting, the end of one pipe is slipped into an enlarged hub of another pipe and the joint sealed with a gasket. A hubless joint uses a gasket held in place with a stainless steel retaining clamp. Cast iron pipe is required for the

house sewer. Copper and plastic piping is joined just as supply water piping.

Other parts of a drainage system may include the following components.

Backflow preventers or *backwater valves* prevent sewage from upper stories or from the building sewer from reversing flow and backing up into fixtures set at a lower elevation.

When plumbing fixtures must be below the level of the house drain and house sewer, a *sump pit* is installed. This device collects the sewage and pumps it to a higher level where it can flow by gravity into the sewer.

Floor drains collect water in shower rooms or in places where overflow is likely. Because some floor drains are seldom used, special care must be taken so that the water seal does not evaporate and allow sewer gases to penetrate the building. The traps of floor drains are usually required to have a deeper seal than other types of traps.

Interceptors are devices that collect foreign matter at the source instead of allowing it to get into the sewer system. Some of the more common types include grease traps, plaster traps, and lubricating oil traps. Interceptors have provisions for periodic cleanout of the foreign matter.

C. System Design

The sizing of drainage pipes is based on the idea of fixture units, just as water supply piping is, although with different values of fixture units for each type of fixture. For example, a lavatory is assigned a drainage fixture unit of 1 and a public water closet is considered 6 fixture units. There are also certain minimum sizes of trap arms for individual fixtures; a single lavatory must have at least a 1 1/4-inch drain and a single toilet must have at least a 3-inch trap arm. These values are given in tables from the plumbing code.

Design of a drainage system begins with the individual fixtures and branch lines and proceeds to the sizing of stacks and building drains. Tables in the plumbing code give the maximum number of fixture units and the maximum vertical and horizontal lengths of piping based on pipe diameter. It is thus a simple matter to accumulate fixture units served by a particular stack or drain and increase the size as needed as more fixtures are added to it.

The plumbing code also states the minimum size and length of vents based on fixture units connected. It also gives the maximum horizontal distance of trap arms based on size.

4   WASTE DISPOSAL AND TREATMENT

Once sewage leaves the building, it is either transported by the house sewer to a municipal collection system or to a private disposal system. Private systems generally consist of a septic tank and leaching field. The septic tank collects the sewage and allows the solid matter to settle to the bottom and the effluent (liquid portion) to drain into the distribution system where it seeps into the ground. See Figure 10.8.

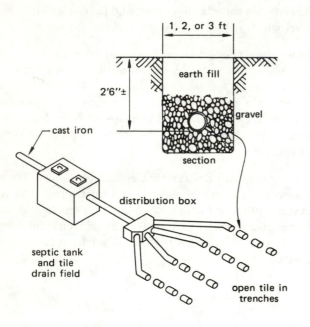

Figure 10.8   Private Sewage Disposal

The size of the septic tank is determined by the amount of daily flow. For residences this is usually based on the number of bedrooms and baths. For larger installations, it is based on the calculated sewage flow in gallons per day. The size and length of the leaching field system are based on the ability of the soil to absorb the effluent. This is determined by a percolation test, which measures the amount of time it takes water in a test hole to drop one inch. Tables give the minimum length of piping in leaching fields based on percolation and volume handled.

Since there is the potential for septic tanks and leaching fields to contaminate potable water supplies, mainly wells, plumbing codes give minimum required distances between various parts of the system and other features of the site such as wells, property lines, rivers, and buildings. For example, there must be a minimum of 100 feet between a leaching field and a well, 50 feet between a septic tank and a well, and 10 feet between a leaching field and a building.

5   STORM DRAINAGE

Water drainage from rain and snow melt is kept separate from sanitary drainage, as outlined in the previous section. This is to avoid overloading the sanitary drainage system, causing possible backup of sanitary sewer lines. In sparsely populated areas, storm drainage normally soaks into the ground or finds its way to rivers and lakes. In more populated areas, with a high percentage of roofed area and paved streets and parking lots, artificial systems are necessary to safely carry away storm water.

A.   Private Systems

There are several methods for draining water from private homes. The first is the simplest and consists of collecting water from the roof in gutters and leaders and simply letting it run onto the ground surrounding the house, where it soaks in. Splash blocks and other devices are used to carry the water far enough from the building to avoid excess water seeping into the foundation.

If this is not adequate, drywells are connected to the drain leaders with underground pipes. A drywell is a large, porous, underground container where water collects and seeps into the soil. If a drywell is not adequate or the ground is not sufficiently porous, a drain field, similar to a leaching field, can be used. In addition to draining water from the roof, the land around the building must be graded to divert water away from the foundation.

B.   Municipal Systems

Municipal storm sewer systems are laid out in a manner similar to the sanitary sewage system, collecting runoff from street gutters, catch basins, and individual taps from private buildings and land developments. The system carries the water by gravity to natural drainage areas such as rivers, lakes, or oceans.

C.   Gutter and Downspout Sizing

The size of gutters, downspouts, and horizontal drain pipes is determined based on the area of the roof or paved area drained and the maximum hourly rainfall. For gutters and horizontal piping, the slope of the pipe is also a factor, lower slopes requiring a greater size.

Gutter slopes range from 1/16 inch per foot to 1/2 inch per foot.

Rainfall rates are available from the local weather service or from published maps of the United States. When calculating the roof area of a sloped roof, the projected area is used. This is the horizontal area defined by the edges of the roof without regard to the slope. Knowing the maximum hourly rainfall rate, roof area, and proposed slope of gutter, tables are available that give the minimum required diameter of gutter.

6   FIRE PROTECTION

There are two principal means of fire protection with plumbing systems: sprinklers and standpipes. Which system or combination of systems is selected depends primarily on code requirements and insurance needs.

A. Sprinkler Systems

Fire sprinkler systems are becoming more prevalent in construction because of increasingly more stringent building code regulations and the awareness of owners and insurance companies of the systems' ability to minimize property damage and improve life safety. For example, the Uniform Building Code requires sprinklers in buildings over 75 feet high.

Fire sprinkler systems can be either wet pipe or dry pipe. Wet pipe systems are constantly filled with water and can respond immediately to a rise in temperature at any sprinkler head of from 135 to 160 degrees. Dry systems are typically used in unheated buildings and attic spaces and require a valve to automatically open when a fire is detected.

In tall buildings, water for a sprinkler system can either be supplied in a tank near the top of the building or zone just as the water supply is or it can be supplied with pumps connected to an emergency power supply. When tanks are used, they are designed to provide firefighting capability for a certain percentage of sprinklers for a given time until firefighters can arrive. Siamese connections are provided on the exterior of the building so the fire department can connect fire pumps to the sprinkler system.

The installation of fire sprinkler systems is governed by each local building code, but most codes refer to NFPA-13, Standard for the Installation of Sprinkler Systems, published by the National Fire Protection Association. This standard classifies the relative fire hazard of buildings into three groups: light, ordinary, and extra

hazard. Each hazard classification is further divide[d] into groups. The hazard classification determines th[e] required spacing of sprinklers and other regulations.

For example, light hazard includes occupancies such [as] residences, offices, hospitals, schools, and restauran[ts]. In these occupancies there must be one sprinkler f[or] each 200 square feet, or 225 square feet if the design [of] the system is hydraulically calculated. For open wo[od] joist ceilings, the area drops to 130 square feet. Ma[xi]mum spacing between sprinkler heads is 15 feet for [the] 225-square-foot coverage requirement, with the ma[xi]mum distance from a wall being one-half the requi[red] spacing.

B. Standpipes

Standpipes are pipes that run the height of a bu[ild]ing and provide water outlets at each floor to w[hich] fire fighting hoses can be connected. They are loc[ated] within the stairway or, in the case of smokeproof e[nclo]sures, within the vestibule.

The UBC defines three classes of standpipes. Class [I is a] dry standpipe system without a directly connecte[d wa]ter supply and equipped with 2 1/2-inch outlets fo[r use] by fire department personnel. Class II is a wet s[tand]pipe system directly connected to a water suppl[y and] equipped with 1 1/2-inch outlets intended for u[se by] building occupants. Class III is a combination s[ystem] directly connected to a water supply and equippe[d with] both 1 1/2-inch and 2 1/2-inch outlets.

The UBC defines where each class of standpipe [is re]quired. Buildings four stories or more in height or [those] over 150 feet must have standpipes as must certa[in oc]cupancies when the square footage exceeds a c[ertain] figure. In nonsprinklered buildings, hoses are re[quired] as part of the standpipe assembly.

Water is supplied in two ways: from storage tan[ks or] through siamese connections at ground level for c[onnec]tion with fire department pumps.

Like a sprinkler system, the standpipes can be eith[er dry] or wet. In a wet system the standpipes are cons[tantly] filled with water and are connected to a tank of w[ater at] the top of the building that provides a supply of [water] for immediate use. Once firefighters arrive, w[ater is] pumped from fire hydrants through the fire truck [and in]to the standpipes. In a dry system, there is no [water] standing in the pipe. In the event of a fire, i[t will] be charged with pumps in the building or by t[he fire] department through siamese connections.

SAMPLE QUESTIONS

The answers to questions 1 through 3 can be found on the following key list. Select only one answer for each question.

    A0 building sewer
    A1 casing
    A2 deep well
    A3 drywell
    A4 fixture pressure
    A5 fixture units
    A6 friction loss
    A7 grey water
    A8 hardness
    A9 hard temper pipe

    B0 percolation test
    B1 potable water
    B2 pressure tank
    B3 static head
    B4 submersible pump
    B5 union
    B6 water table

1. What determines the size of a leaching field?

2. What is an important concern in private water supply?

3. What part of water supply design is affected by building height?

4. Select the incorrect statements:

I. Dry pipe sprinkler systems are more efficient than wet pipe systems.

II. Siamese connections serve both sprinklers and standpipes.

III. The hazard classification does not necessarily affect sprinkler layout.

IV. Standpipes must be located within stairways or vestibules of smokeproof enclosures.

V. Standpipes are required in buildings four or more stories high or those exceeding 150 feet.

    A. I, II, and IV
    B. II, III, and V

    C. II, IV, and V
    D. III, IV, and V

5. The pressure in a city water main is 57 psi. If the pressure loss through piping, fittings, and the water meter has been calculated as 23 psi and the highest fixture requires 12 psi to operate, what is the maximum height the fixture can be above the water main?

    A. 9 feet
    B. 24 feet
    C. 50 feet
    D. 78 feet

6. You have been retained by a client to design a house in a suburban location. The nearest water main is one block away (about 300 feet) and the city has no plans to extend the line in the near future. City and county regulations do permit the drilling of wells. What should you recommend to your client regarding water supply?

    A. Estimate the cost of extending the municipal line, since the water quality is known and it would ensure a long-term supply. Consult with nearby property owners who plan to build in the area to see if they would be willing to share the cost of extending the line.

    B. Drill a test bore to determine the depth, potential yield, and water quality of a well and compare this information with the cost of extending the municipal line.

    C. Assist the owner in petitioning the city to extend the water line to serve new development sooner than they had planned to.

    D. Consult with nearby property owners who use wells and with well drillers to estimate the depth and yield of wells in the area. Compare the estimated cost and feasibility of drilling with the feasibility of extending the municipal line at the owner's cost.

7. Which statements about drainage are correct?

I. Drains should always slope at a minimum of 1/8 inch per foot.

II. The vent stack extends through the roof.

III. Vents help prevent the drainage of water from traps.

IV. The house drain cannot also be called the building sewer.

V. Cleanouts are always a necessary part of a drainage system.

    A. I, II, and V

    B. I, III, and IV

    C. II, III, and V

    D. III, IV, and V

8. Water hammer most often occurs when:

    A. the incorrect type of valve is used

    B. water suddenly stops when flow is turned off

    C. expansion joints are not installed in water lines

    D. water flows backward against a check valve

9. One component of a plumbing system that every building has is a:

    A. stack vent

    B. vent stack

    C. backflow preventer

    D. house trap

10. Select the incorrect statement:

    A. Several types of plastic can be used for cold water piping, but only PVDC is used for hot water supply where allowed by local codes.

    B. Steel pipe is more labor intensive and requires more space than copper pipes in plumbing chases.

    C. Type M pipe is normally specified for most interior plumbing.

    D. ABS is suitable for water supply.

11

ELECTRICAL SYSTEMS

d	distance	feet
E	illumination	footcandles
I	current (electrical circuits)	amperes (amps)
I	luminous intensity (lighting design)	candlepower
pf	power factor	
R	resistance	ohms
t	time	hours
V	voltage	volts
W	power	watts
Z	impedance	ohms

1 ELECTRICAL FUNDAMENTALS

A. Definitions

Ampere: the unit flow of electrons in a conductor equal to 6.251×10^{18} electrons passing a given section in one second.

Energy: the product of power and time, also called work.

Impedance: the resistance in an alternating current (AC) circuit measured in ohms.

Ohm: the unit of resistance in an electrical circuit.

Power factor: the phase difference between voltage and current in an alternating current circuit.

Reactance: part of the electrical resistance in an alternating current circuit caused by inductance and capacitance.

Volt: the unit of electromotive force or potential difference that will cause a current of one ampere to flow through a conductor whose resistance is one ohm.

Watt: the unit of electrical power.

B. Formulas

Ohm's law relates current, voltage, and resistance in direct current (DC) circuits according to the formula:

$$I = \frac{V}{R} \qquad 11.1$$

This states that the current in a circuit is directly proportional to the voltage and inversely proportional to the resistance.

Wattage in DC circuits is the product of volts times current, or:

$$W = VI \qquad 11.2$$

In AC circuits, resistance is known as *impedance*, which comprises resistance and reactance and causes a phase change difference between voltage and current. The difference is represented by the power factor and can be a significant factor in calculating power in an AC circuit. For circuits with only resistive loads, such as incandescent lights or electric heating elements, the power factor is 1.0.

For AC circuits, Ohm's law is similar to formula 11.1:

$$I = \frac{V}{Z} \qquad 11.3$$

Power in AC circuits is similar to formula 11.2 but with the power factor added:

$$W = VI(pf) \qquad 11.4$$

Example 11.1

Find the current in a 120-volt circuit serving nine 150-watt downlights.

2400/4160 v, three-phase, four-wire systems are available for very large commercial buildings and factories with a great deal of machinery.

B. Transformers

Transformers are used to change alternating current voltages, either up or down. In most cases, power is supplied to a building at a high voltage because the lines can be smaller and there is less voltage drop. The building owner must supply the transformer to provide one of the types of service described in the previous section. For residences and very small buildings, the utility company usually supplies step-down transformers to serve a small group of houses with 120/240 volt service.

Transformers are rated on their kilovolt-amperes capacity (kva) and described by their type, phase, voltages, method of cooling, insulation type, and noise level. For cooling, transformers are either dry, oil filled, or silicone filled. When there is a possibility of fire, as with oil-filled transformers, the equipment must be placed in a fire-resistive transformer vault room. Because transformers generate a great deal of heat, the vault must be at an exterior wall and vented to the outside. Locating a transformer vault near the exterior wall also makes it easier to move the large, heavy device into place and replace it when necessary.

C. Metering and Load Control

Metering must be provided at the service entrance to a building to allow the utility company to charge for energy used. For residences and other single-use buildings, one meter is typically used. For multiple-occupancy buildings, such as shopping centers and apartments, banks of meters are installed so each unit can be metered independently. One of the reasons for this is to encourage energy conservation, since every tenant must pay for the energy used.

The most common meter is the watt-hour meter. This registers the use of power over time in kilowatt-hours. The meter is placed on the incoming power line in front of any master service switch so it can operate continuously.

In order to encourage the conservation of energy and pay for the cost of providing power to customers, many energy companies levy energy charges based not only on the total amount of energy used (kilowatt-hours) but also on peak demand. The reasoning behind this is that if a customer uses a nominal amount of energy (power multiplied by time) over a billing period, but uses a great deal of energy only at certain times, the utility company must still provide facilities to supply the peak demand. The total amount of energy used can be relatively low even though the utility company must be ready to supply the occasional maximum amount.

To compensate for this, most utility companies make charges based on the maximum interval demand, the average amount of energy used in a certain time period, such as 15 or 30 minutes. The ratio of the average power used to the maximum power demand is called the *load factor*. A low load factor implies an inefficient use of energy and a high demand charge.

From the user's standpoint, a building's electrical system should be designed to avoid peak use of electricity. There are several methods of doing this, which are called *load control*. Other terms used include load shedding, peak demand control, and peak load regulation.

Manual and automatic devices are available to accomplish load control. With automatic load shedding, for example, a device automatically monitors the use of energy and when a certain point is reached it shuts off non-essential electrical loads. Such loads can include non-essential lighting, water heating, and space heating. Load scheduling can also be used if the energy consumption characteristics of the building are known. With this method, different electrical loads are automatically scheduled to operate at different times to control the peak demand.

D. Primary Distribution

For large buildings, a central electrical distribution center is required. Called *switchgear*, this center consists of an assembly of switches, circuit breakers, and cables or bus ducts that distribute power to other parts of the building. A transformer and metering are also often included with the switchgear. The equipment is usually housed in a separate room depending on the type of transformer used and the security required.

Power coming through the meter and transformer is split into separate circuits, each with a master switch and fuse or circuit breaker to protect the circuit from overload or short circuits. From the switchgear, power is distributed to substations for further transforming and distribution, to motor control centers, to elevator controls, and to individual panel boxes as part of the secondary distribution system.

E. Secondary Distribution and Branch Circuits

Power from the main switchgear is distributed to individual panelboards where it is further split into individual branch circuits used for power, lighting, motors, and other electrical needs of the building. Secondary distribution involves the typical lower voltages of 120v, 240v, and 277v. Secondary distribution is made with wires in conduit, various types of underfloor raceways, or flexible cabling systems.

Each circuit is protected with circuit breakers in the panelboard. These are rated for the amperage the circuit is expected to carry, ranging from 15- and 20-amp circuits for general lighting and power circuits to 100 amps or more for main disconnect switches or large loads.

There are two important kinds of protection for electric circuits: grounding and ground fault protection. All new construction is grounded, with a separate wire in addition to the hot and neutral wiring of each circuit. One of the primary purposes for providing a ground is to prevent a dangerous shock if someone touches an appliance with a short circuit and simultaneously touches a ground path such as a water pipe. The ground provides a path for the fault. The ground wire and the neutral wire are both grounded at the building service entrance to either a grounding electrode buried in the earth or to a buried cold water pipe.

A ground fault, however, can create other problems, since the current required to trip a circuit breaker is high and small leaks of current can continue unnoticed until someone receives a dangerous shock or a fire develops. Ground fault interrupters (GFI) are devices to detect small current leaks and disconnect the hot wire to the circuit or appliance. GFIs can be part of a circuit breaker or installed as an outlet. Ground fault interrupters are required for outdoor outlets and in bathrooms as well as other locations specified in the National Electrical Code. They are recommended on appliance circuits as well.

F. Emergency Power Supply

Emergency power is required for electrical systems that relate to the safety of occupants or community needs. This includes such things as exit lighting, alarm systems, elevators, telephone systems, and fire pumps, as well as equipment that could have life-threatening implications if power were lost, such as some medical equipment. Standby power, on the other hand, provides electricity for functions that the building owner requires to avoid an interruption in business. This often includes computer operations or industrial processes.

Emergency power is supplied by generators or batteries. Generators provide the capacity for large electrical loads for long periods of time, limited only by the available emergency fuel supply. However, they are expensive to install and must be maintained and checked periodically for proper operation.

Batteries are used for smaller loads for shorter time periods. Emergency lighting often consists of separate lighting packs with their own batteries placed in strategic locations such as in corridors and stairways. Large installations have racks of batteries in separate rooms connected to lights and other equipment with wiring.

3   LIGHTING FUNDAMENTALS

Light is defined as visually evaluated radiant energy. Visible light is a form of electromagnetic radiation with wavelengths that range from about 400 nanometers (10^{-9} meters) for violet light to about 700 nanometers for red light. White light is produced when a source emits approximately equal quantities of energy over the entire visible spectrum.

A. Definitions

There is a relationship between several illumination definitions with which you should be familiar. Figure 11.2 shows these units of light.

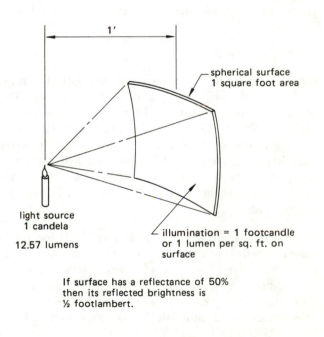

Figure 11.2   Relationship of Light Source and Illumination

Candlepower: the unit of luminous intensity approximately equal to the horizontal light output from an ordinary wax candle. In the SI system of measurement, this unit is the candela.

Illuminance: the density of luminous flux incident on a surface in lumens per unit area. One lumen uniformly incident on 1 square foot of area produces an illuminance of one footcandle.

Lumen: the unit of luminous flux equal to the flux in a unit solid angle of one steradian from a uniform point source of one candlepower. On a unit sphere (1-foot radius), an area of 1 square foot will subtend an angle of one steradian. Since the area of a unit sphere is 4 times π, a source of one candlepower produces 12.57 lumens.

Luminance: the luminous flux per unit of projected (apparent) area and unit solid angle leaving a surface, either reflected or transmitted. The unit is the footlambert (fL) where one footlambert equals $1/\pi$ candelas per square foot. Luminance takes into account the reflectance and transmittance properties of materials and the direction in which they are viewed. Thus, 100 footcandles striking a surface with 50 percent reflectance would result in a luminance of 50 footlamberts. Luminance is sometimes called *brightness.* A surface emitting, transmitting, or reflecting one lumen per square foot in the direction being viewed has a luminance of one footlambert.

Luminous intensity: the solid angular flux density in a given direction measured in candlepower or candelas.

B. Light Levels

Good lighting design involves providing both the proper quantity and quality of light to perform a task. This section discusses quantity; the next discusses quality. Different visual tasks under different conditions require varying levels of illumination. The variables involved include the nature of the task itself, the age of the person performing the task, the reflectances of the room, and the demand for speed and/or accuracy in performing the task.

The Illuminating Engineering Society (IES) has established a method for determining a range of illumination levels in footcandles appropriate to particular design conditions. Various areas and activities are assigned an illuminance category, and these categories are used with other variables to establish the recommended task and background illuminances.

In order to conserve energy, most codes require designers to develop a power budget for a project based on the building type and to design lighting systems within that budget. This most often requires that the recommended illumination level be provided for task areas only and that general background illumination be less, about one-third of the task level. Further, non-critical areas such as corridors are usually provided with less light than the background levels.

C. Design Considerations

The quality of light is just as important as the amount of light provided. Important considerations are glare, contrast, uniformity, and color.

There are two types of glare: direct and reflected. Direct glare results when a light source in the field of vision causes discomfort and interference with the visual task. Not all visible light sources cause direct glare problems. The extent of the problems depends on the brightness of the source, its position, the background illumination, and the adaptation of the eye to the environment.

In order to evaluate the direct glare problem, the visual comfort probability (VCP) factor was developed. This factor is the percent of normal vision for observers to be comfortable in a particular environment with a particular lighting situation. Although the calculations are complex, some simplifications are made and many manufacturers publish the VCP rating for their light fixtures when used under certain conditions.

For most situations, the critical zone for direct glare is in the area above a 45-degree angle from the light source. See Figure 11.3. This is because the field of vision when looking straight ahead includes an area approximately 45 degrees above a horizontal line. Many direct glare problems can be solved by using a luminaire with a 45-degree cut-off angle or by moving the luminaire out of the offending field of view.

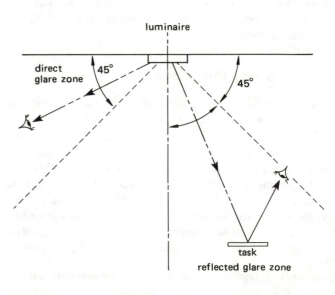

Figure 11.3 Glare Zones

Reflected glare occurs when a light source is reflected from a viewed surface into the eye. If it interferes with the viewing task, it is also called *veiling reflection*. The effect of reflected glare is to decrease the contrast of the task and its background. For example, a strong light on paper with pencil writing can bounce off the relatively reflective graphite, making it almost as bright as the paper, and effectively obliterate the writing.

Veiling reflections are a complex interaction of light source and brightness, position of the task, reflectivity of the task, and the position of the eye. One of the simplest ways to correct veiling reflections is to move the position of the task or the light source. Since for light the angle of incidence is equal to the angle of reflection, this is easy to calculate. It is not always possible, however, since the exact use of a room and its furniture position is not always known. Another approach is to provide general background illumination and specific task lighting, the position of which can be controlled by the user.

Contrast is the difference in illumination level between one point and nearby points. Since contrast is the way people see, it is vitally important to the quality of an environment. A printed word on a page is only visible because it contrasts with the brightness of the surrounding paper. However, too much contrast can be detrimental. It is difficult to see fine detail on a small, dark object when viewed against a bright background because the eye has adapted (the iris of the eye is smaller) to the brighter background and cannot admit enough light to see the darker object. The eye adapts by opening and closing the iris, but this causes eye strain and fatigue.

In most situations, brightness ratios should be limited to 1:1/3 between the task and adjacent surroundings, to 1:1/10 between the task and more remote darker surfaces, and to 1:10 between the task and more remote lighter surfaces.

Uniformity of lighting affects a person's perception of a space as being comfortable and pleasant to be in. Complete uniformity is usually not desirable except for certain tasks like drafting or machine shop work. Since people see by contrast, some amount of shade and shadow provides highlight and interest to a space.

Color in lighting is an interaction between the color of the light source (lamp or daylighting) and the color of the objects that reflect the light. Color in lighting is a complex subject but one which can affect the comfort of people and their impression of an environment. For example, most people think of reds and yellows as "warm" colors and greens and blues as "cool" colors. Colors of light sources will be discussed in the next section and the use of color in lighting design in Section 5.

4 LIGHT SOURCES

In addition to daylight, there are three types of light sources: incandescent, fluorescent, and high-intensity discharge. Some of the considerations that influence the type of light source used include its color rendition characteristics, initial cost, operating cost, efficacy, size, operating life, and the ability to control its output from a luminaire. *Efficacy* is the ratio of luminous flux emitted to the total power input to the source and is measured in lumens per watt. It is an important measure of the energy efficiency of a light source. The amount of heat generated by a light source is also an important selection consideration since waste heat usually needs to be removed or compensated for with the air conditioning system, which can add to the total energy load of a building.

A. Incandescent

An incandescent lamp consists of a tungsten filament placed within a sealed bulb containing an inert gas. When electricity is passed through the lamp the filament glows, producing light. Incandescent lamps are produced in a wide variety of shapes, sizes, and wattages for different applications. Some of the more common shapes are shown in Figure 11.4. A typical designation of an incandescent lamp is a letter followed by a number, such as A-21. This means that the shape is the standard arbitrary shape and the diameter of the bulb at its widest point is 21/8 of an inch, or 2 5/8 inches.

Incandescent lamps are inexpensive, compact, easy to dim, can be repeatedly started without a decrease in lamp life, and have a warm color rendition. In addition, their light output can be easily controlled with reflectors and lenses. Their disadvantages include low efficacy, short lamp life, and high heat output. The combination of low efficacy and heat production makes incandescent lamps undesirable for large, energy-efficient installations. For example, a 150-watt lamp produces less than 20 lumens per watt while a 40-watt cool white fluorescent lamp has an efficacy of about 80 lumens per watt with much less heat output.

Another type of incandescent lamp is the tungsten halogen. Light is produced by the incandescence of the filament, but there is a small amount of a halogen, such as iodine or bromine, in the bulb with the inert gas. Through a recurring cycle, part of the tungsten filament is burned off as the lamp operates, but it mixes with the halogen and is redeposited on the filament instead of on the wall of the bulb as in standard incandescent lamps. This results in longer bulb life, low lumen depreciation

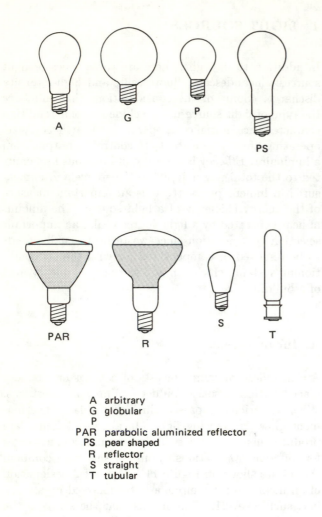

A   arbitrary
G   globular
P
PAR parabolic aluminized reflector
PS pear shaped
R   reflector
S   straight
T   tubular

Figure 11.4 Incandescent Lamp Types

over the life of the bulb, and a more uniform light color. Because the filament burns under higher pressure and temperature, the bulb is made from quartz and is much smaller than standard incandescent lamps.

B. Fluorescent

Fluorescent lamps contain a mixture of an inert gas and low-pressure mercury vapor. When the lamp is energized, a mercury arc is formed that creates ultraviolet light. This invisible light, in turn, strikes the phosphor-coated bulb causing it to fluoresce and produce visible light. The three types of fluorescent lamps are preheat, rapid start, and instant start, according to their circuitry. Preheat lamps have been supplanted by rapid start types. These types maintain a constant, low current in the cathode that allows it to start within about two seconds. Instant start lamps use voltage high enough to start the arc in the tube directly without preheating of the cathode.

All fluorescent lamps have a ballast, a device that supplies the proper starting and operating voltages to the lamp as well as limiting the current. Since ballasts produce noise and heat, their correct selection is critical for a successful lighting design. Ballasts are sound rated by letters. Class A is appropriate for spaces with the lowest ambient noise levels, and Class F is suitable only for noisy environments.

Lamps are produced in tubular shapes, normally straight, but U-shaped and circular lamps are also produced. They are designated according to their type, wattage, diameter, color, and type of starting. Thus, an F40T12WW/RS describes a fluorescent lamp, 40 watts, tubular, 12/8 of an inch in diameter (1 1/2 inches), warm white color, with a rapid start circuit. Like incandescent lamps, size is designated in eighths of an inch. A T8 lamp is one inch in diameter, for example. Fluorescent lamps come in a variety of lengths, 4 feet being the most common. Two-, 3-, and 8-foot lengths are also available as well as special U-shaped sizes and energy-conserving types that are designed to be screwed into normal incandescent sockets.

In the past, one of the objections to fluorescent lighting was that it was too "cold." Actually, lamps are available in a wide range of color temperatures, ranging from a "cool" FL/D (daylight) lamp of 6500K color temperature to a WWD (warm white deluxe) with a color temperature of 2800K, which has a large percentage of red in its spectral output.

Fluorescent lamps have a high efficacy (about 80 lumens per watt), relatively low initial cost, and long life, and they come in a variety of color temperatures. They can also be dimmed, although dimmers are more expensive than their incandescent counterparts. Because fluorescent lamps are larger than incandescent, it is more difficult to control them precisely, so they are usually more suitable for general illumination.

C. High-Intensity Discharge

High-intensity discharge (HID) lamps include mercury vapor, metal halide, and high-pressure sodium. In the mercury vapor lamp, an electric arc is passed through high-pressure mercury vapor, which causes it to produce both ultraviolet light and visible light, primarily in the blue-green band. For improved color rendition, various phosphors can be applied to the inside of the lamp to produce more light in the yellow and red bands. Mercury lamps have a moderately high efficacy, in the range of 30 to 50 lumens per watt depending on voltage and the type of color correction included.

Metal halide lamps, which produce about 80 to 100 lumens per watt, are similar to mercury except that halides of metals are added to the arc tube. This increases the efficacy and improves color rendition but decreases lamp life.

High-pressure sodium lamps produce light by passing an electric arc through hot sodium vapor. The arc tube must be made of a special ceramic material to resist attack by the hot sodium. High-pressure sodium (HPS) lamps have efficacies from 80 to 140 lumens per watt, making them one of the most efficient lamps available. Color rendition is also acceptable for a wide variety of applications.

Low-pressure sodium lamps have an even higher efficacy, about 150 lumens per watt, but produce a monochromatic light of a deep yellow color. Therefore, they are suitable only for uses where color rendition is not important, such as street lighting.

5 LIGHTING DESIGN

Lighting design is both an art and a science. There must be a sufficient amount of light to perform a task without glare and other discomfort, but the lighting should also enhance the architectural design of the space or landscaping. Lighting must also be designed to minimize energy use.

A. Lighting Systems

There are several general types of lighting systems. The terms used to describe them can refer to individual luminaires or to the entire lighting installation. They are broadly described as direct, semidirect, direct-indirect, semi-indirect, and indirect.

Direct lighting systems provide all light output on the task. A recessed fluorescent luminaire is an example of direct lighting. Semidirect systems put a majority of the light down and a small percentage toward the ceiling. Obviously, fixtures for this type of system must be surface mounted or suspended. Indirect systems throw all the light toward a reflective ceiling where it illuminates the room by reflection.

Another common lighting system is task ambient. This approach to lighting design recognizes that it is inefficient to try to illuminate an entire room to the level required for individual tasks scattered around the room. Instead, a general background level of illumination is provided and separate light fixtures used to increase the light level at individual work stations. This can be done with desk lamps, directed spotlights, or more fixtures near the tasks requiring more illumination. In addition to being energy efficient and responding to individual lighting needs, task-ambient systems usually create a more pleasant work environment.

B. Quality of Light

Lighting design requires the selection of luminaires, lamps, and fixture arrangement to provide the correct quantity of light. However, quality of light is just as important. The topics of glare and contrast were discussed in Section 3. Color quality depends on the color of the light source and its interaction with objects.

Every lamp has a characteristic spectral energy distribution. This is a measure of the energy output at different wavelengths, or colors. One such energy distribution curve is shown in Figure 11.5.

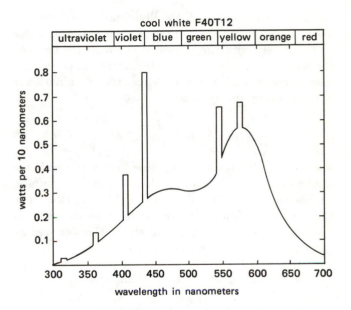

Figure 11.5 Spectral Energy Distribution Curve

Sources are also given a single number rating of their dominant color based on the temperature in degrees Kelvin to which a black body radiator would have to be heated to produce that color. Lower temperatures, such as 3100K, are relatively warm colors like a warm white fluorescent light. Higher color temperatures, such as 5000K to 6000K, are cool colors with a high percentage of blue. A daylight fluorescent lamp has a color temperature of 6600K, for example.

Sources are also rated with a number known as the color rendering index (CRI). This is a measure of how closely the perceived colors of an object illuminated with a test source match the colors of the object when it is illuminated with daylight of the same color temperature.

It is important to know the color characteristics of a light source when designing a lighting system because the light color can affect the color of objects. For example, using a lamp with a high complement of blue and violet will make finishes and furniture with the warmer colors of red in them appear dull and washed out. Where color appearance is important, finishes and materials should be selected under the same lighting that will be used in the finished space.

C. Lighting Calculations

Lighting calculations involve determining the quantity of light in a space. These calculations can be complex because illumination is a result of several variables.

For point sources of light, the illumination on a surface varies directly with the luminous intensity of the source and inversely with the square of the distance between the source and the point. If the surface is perpendicular to the direction of the source, the illumination is determined by the formula:

$$E = \frac{I}{d^2} \qquad 11.6$$

For spaces with several luminaires, other methods are used to calculate the illumination on the work surface, or, knowing the desired illumination level, to determine the number of luminaires required. One of the most common is the zonal cavity method. This procedure takes into account several variables:

- the lumen output of the lamps used

- the number of lamps in each luminaire

- the efficiency of the luminaire. The rating given a particular luminaire is known as the *coefficient of utilization* (CU) and represents the fact that not all of the lumens produced by the lamps reach the work surface. The CU is a number from 0.01 to 1.00 and depends on the design of the light fixture as well as the characteristics of the room in which it is placed, including the room size and surface reflectances. Manufacturers publish tables that give the CU for each of their luminaires under various conditions.

- the light loss factor, LLF. This is a fraction that represents the amount of light that will be lost due to several additional factors. Among these are lamp lumen depreciation, which is light loss with age, and luminaire dirt depreciation, which is light loss due to accumulated dirt on lamps based on the kind of environment they operate in. Additional factors include lamp burnout, room surface dirt, operating voltage of the lamps, ambient operating temperature of the lamps, and accumulated dirt on the luminaire.

To calculate the number of luminaires required in a room to maintain a given illumination level, the following formula is used:

number of luminaires =

$$\frac{\text{footcandles} \times \text{area of room}}{\text{number of lamps} \times \text{lumen per lamp} \times \text{CU} \times \text{LLF}}$$

11.7

D. Energy Budgets

Most jurisdictions have code requirements concerning the maximum amount of power that can be consumed in a building for lighting. The maximum amount of power for a particular building type is determined according to certain procedures developed by the Illuminating Engineering Society, and the designer must work within the guidelines so the total power budget is not exceeded. This allows for flexibility in design while conserving energy. Although the total power budget will vary with building type, a figure of approximately 2.3 watts per square foot is often considered a maximum.

E. Emergency Lighting

The UBC, National Electrical Code, and the Life Safety Code all include provisions for emergency lighting. Since each jurisdiction differs slightly in its requirements, the local codes in force must be reviewed. Generally, however, all codes require that in the event of a power failure, sufficient lighting must be available to safely evacuate building occupants.

Emergency lighting is required in exit stairs and corridors as well as in certain occupancies such as places of assembly, educational facilities, hazardous locations, and other places where occupancy loads exceed a given number. The usual minimum lighting level required is one footcandle at the floor level. Illuminated exit signs are also required in many situations.

As discussed in a previous section, the emergency power supply may come from a central generator connected to a separate emergency power circuit throughout the building or from batteries.

6 SIGNAL AND SAFETY ALARM SYSTEMS

Contemporary buildings contain a complex variety of signal and communication systems. These are low-voltage circuits connecting various types of devices, which make it possible for the building to function properly and which protect the occupants. In addition to communication systems, such as telephone lines, building automation systems control the mechanical, electrical, and security systems from one central station and continuously monitor their operation.

A. Communications Systems

Communication systems include telephone systems, intercom systems, paging and sound systems, television, closed circuit television (CCTV), and most recently, computer systems, as well as local area networks (LANs) that connect computers within one building or in a complex of buildings.

Telephone systems are the most prevalent type of communication system. In most buildings, main telephone lines enter the structure in a main cable and connect to the terminal room where they are split into riser cables. These risers are generally located near the core and connect telephone equipment rooms on each floor. From these equipment rooms the lines branch out to serve individual spaces.

In the past, there was one telephone equipment room on each floor, which contained relay panels and other equipment. With the proliferation of separate telephone companies in recent years, each tenant space in a large building usually needs its own equipment room. The size of the room is dependent on the type of equipment used and the number of telephone lines connected.

Other types of communication systems are typically prewired as the building is constructed. Cabling terminates at electrical boxes in the wall or floor with a jack into which individual equipment can be connected. Most signal cabling is run in metal conduit like electrical cable unless the local building code allows it to be exposed. Conduit protects the cable and prevents it from burning in a fire and giving off dangerous gases.

B. Security Systems

Security systems include methods for detecting intruders, for preventing entry, for controlling access to secure areas, and for notification in the event of unauthorized entry or other emergencies.

There are a wide variety of intrusion detection devices. Motion detectors and heat detectors sense the presence of someone in a room or within the field of view. Microwave and infrared beams trip a circuit when the path of their beam is interrupted. Pressure sensors detect weight on a floor or other surface. Other types of systems can be installed on glass, in door openings, and on fences and screens to set off an alarm when unauthorized entry is made through the opening.

Access to secure areas can be controlled with a number of devices. Locks can be connected to card readers. A plastic card containing a coded magnetic strip is used that allows entry when a valid card is passed over the reader. Numbered keyboards can serve the same purpose. In order to unlock a door, the user must enter the correct numerical code into the keyboard. New devices are now being developed that can read individual biological features such as the retina of the eye or the palm of a hand, providing a counterfeit-proof method of identification.

In the event of an unauthorized entry or other emergency, alarm systems can include simple noise alarms, notification of the breach of security at a monitored central guard station, or automatic notification over phone lines to a central security service.

C. Fire Detection and Alarms

There are four basic types of fire detection devices. The first is the ionization detector, which responds to products of combustion-ionized particles rather than smoke. They are not appropriate where fires may produce a lot of smoke but few particles. Because they can detect particles from a smoldering fire before it bursts into flames, these devices are considered early warning detectors.

Photoelectric detectors respond to smoke, which obscures a light beam in the device. These are useful where potential fires may produce a great deal of smoke before bursting into flame.

Rise-of-temperature devices detect the presence of heat and can be set to trip an alarm when a particular temperature is reached in the room. The major disadvantage is that flame must usually be present before the alarm temperature is reached. By that time it may be too late, since a fire can smolder and produce deadly smoke long before it reaches the flame stage.

There are also flame detectors that respond to infrared or ultraviolet radiation given off by flames. However, like rise-of-temperature detectors, they do not give an early warning of smoldering fires.

In many buildings, a combination of fire-detection devices must be used depending on the particular type of space they are placed in. For example, an ionization device would not operate properly where air currents or other circumstances would prevent the products of combustion from entering the device.

The building code states the required types and locations of fire detectors. They are required near fire doors, in exit corridors, in individual hotel rooms, and in places of public assembly. They are also often required in main supply and return air ducts. Codes usually require them in other spaces based on a given area coverage.

When activated, they can be wired to trigger a general audible alarm as well as visual alarm lights for the deaf. They can also activate a central monitoring station or a municipal fire station. In large buildings with a central station, the detection of a fire also activates fire dampers, exhaust systems, closing of fire doors, and other preventive measures as the alarm is being signaled to fire officials.

SAMPLE QUESTIONS

1. What steps could an architect take to increase the anticipated lighting level of a room if a selected fluorescent luminaire could not be replaced with another with a higher CU?

    A. change lamp types

    B. suggest to the owner that the lamps be replaced often

    C. use finishes with a higher reflection value

    D. all of the above

2. A spotlight shining perpendicular to a wall 15 feet away has a candlepower output of 3500 candelas. If the wall is painted to a reflectance of 75 percent, what is the luminance of the wall at the point perpendicular to the direction of light?

    A. 4.9 footlamberts

    B. 11.7 footlamberts

    C. 15.56 footcandles

    D. 55.7 footcandles

3. What precautions should be taken if aluminum conductors are used in a building?

    I. Leads should be cleaned prior to making connections.

    II. Special conduit should be specified.

    III. Licensed electricians should be required to make the installation.

    IV. All joints should be soldered.

    V. Larger sizes should be used.

    A. I, II, and III

    B. I, III, and V

    C. II, III, and V

    D. III and V

4. Which of the following would an architect be most concerned about when designing the lighting for an office space with computer work stations and standard desks?

    I. color-rendering index

    II. visual comfort probability

    III. veiling reflection

    IV. reflected glare

    V. task/surrounds brightness ratio

    A. I, II, IV, and V

    B. II, III, and IV

    C. III, IV, and V

    D. all of the above

5. High voltages are used in commercial buildings because:

    A. conductors and conduit can be smaller

    B. a wider variety of loads can be accommodated

    C. commercial buildings require more power

    D. transformers can step down the voltages to whatever is required

6. Which would be the best location for a transformer for a large school building?

    A. on the power pole serving the building

    B. in a separate room at the exterior wall

    C. outside, on a transformer pad close to the main switchgear

    D. in a protective shed where power from the utility company enters the property

7. Which of the following would not be appropriate for fire protection in an elementary school?

    A. ionization detector

    B. temperature-rise detector

    C. photoelectric detector

    D. none of the above

8. The brightness of daylight coming through a window would be measured in:

    A. footcandles

    B. candelas

    C. footlamberts

    D. candlepower

9. What combination of lighting would an architect probably recommend for a moderate-sized womens' clothing store?

    A. color-improved mercury lamps with metal halide accent lighting

    B. limited natural daylight, warm white deluxe fluorescent for general illumination, and tungsten halogen for accent lighting

    C. incandescent general lighting with low-voltage accent lighting on displays

    D. daylighting for general illumination and PAR lamps for dressing areas and display lighting

10. Why should high-pressure instead of low-pressure sodium lamps be used in a storage warehouse?

    A. They are less expensive.

    B. They have a longer lamp life.

    C. They can operate at higher, more efficient voltages.

    D. They have better color-rendering properties.

12 ACOUSTICS

Nomenclature

a	coefficient of absorption	
A	total acoustical absorption	Sabins
c	velocity of sound	feet per second
f	frequency of sound	Hertz (cycles per second)
I	sound intensity	watts/cm^2
I_o	minimum sound intensity audible to the average human ear	10^{-16} watts/cm^2
IL	sound intensity level	decibels (dB)
NR	noise reduction	decibels (dB)
P	acoustic power	watts
r	distance from the source	centimeters
S	area of barrier or component between rooms	ft^2
t	coefficient of transmission	
T	reverberation time	seconds
TL	transmission loss	decibels
V	room volume	ft^3
w	wavelength	feet

1 DEFINITIONS

Amplification: the increased intensity of sound by mechanical and/or electrical means.

Articulation index: a measure of speech intelligibility calculated from the number of words read from a selected list that are understood by an audience. A low articulation index (less than 0.15) is desirable for speech privacy while a high articulation index (above 0.6) is desired for good communication.

Attenuation: the reduction of sound.

Decibel: ten times the common logarithm of the ratio of a quantity to a reference quantity of the same kind such as power, intensity, or energy density. It is often used as the unit of sound intensity according to the formula:

$$IL = 10 \log \frac{I}{I_o} \qquad 12.1$$

dBA: the unit of sound intensity measurement that is weighted to account for the response of the human ear to various frequencies.

Frequency: the number of pressure fluctuations or cycles occurring in one second, expressed in Hertz (Hz).

Hertz: the unit of frequency; one cycle per second equals one Hertz (Hz).

Impact insulation class (IIC): a single-number rating of a floor/ceiling's impact sound transmission performance at various frequencies.

Intensity: the amount of sound energy per second across a unit area.

Intensity level: ten times the common logarithm of the ratio of a sound intensity to a reference intensity. See definition of decibel.

Noise: any unwanted sound.

Noise criteria (NC): a set of single-number ratings of acceptable background noise corresponding to a set of curves specifying sound pressure levels across octave bands. Noise criteria curves can be used to specify continuous background noise, to achieve sound isolation, and to evaluate existing noise situations.

Noise insulation class (NIC): a single-number rating of noise reduction.

Noise reduction (NR): the arithmetic difference, in decibels, between the intensity levels in two rooms separated by a barrier of a given transmission loss. It is dependent on the transmission loss of the barrier, the area of the barrier, and the absorption of the surfaces of the receiving room.

Noise reduction coefficient (NRC): the average sound absorption coefficient to the nearest 0.05 measured at the four one-third octave band center frequencies of 250, 500, 1000, and 2000 Hertz.

Octave band: a range of frequencies in which the upper frequency is twice that of the lower.

Phon: a unit of loudness level of a sound equal to the sound pressure level of a 1000-Hz tone judged to be as loud.

Reverberation: the persistence of a sound in a room after the sound has stopped.

Reverberation time: the time it takes the sound level to decrease 60 dB after the source has stopped producing the sound.

Sabin: the unit of absorption; theoretically, one square foot of surface having an absorption coefficient of 1.00.

Sabin formula: the formula that relates reverberation time to a room's volume and total acoustical absorption.

$$T = 0.05 \frac{V}{A} \qquad 12.2$$

Sound: a small compressional disturbance from equilibrium in an elastic medium that causes the sensation of hearing.

Sound absorption coefficient: the ratio of the sound intensity absorbed by a material to the total intensity reaching the material. 1.00 is theoretically the maximum possible value of the sound absorption coefficient.

Sound power: the total sound energy radiated by a source per second, in watts.

Sound transmission class (STC): a single-number average over several frequency bands of a barrier's ability to reduce sound. The higher the STC rating, the better the barrier's ability to control sound transmission.

Transmission loss (TL): The difference, in decibels, between the sound power incident on a barrier in a source room and the sound power radiated into a receiving room on the opposite side of the barrier. The transmission loss varies with the frequency being tested.

2 FUNDAMENTALS OF SOUND AND HUMAN HEARING

A. Qualities of Sound

Sound has three basic qualities: velocity, frequency, and power.

Velocity of sound depends on the medium in which it is traveling and the temperature of the medium. In air at sea level the velocity of sound is approximately 1130 feet per second (344 m/sec). For acoustical purposes in buildings, the temperature effect on velocity is not significant.

Frequency is the number of cycles completed per second; it is measured in Hertz (Hz). 1 Hz = 1 cycle per second.

Frequency and velocity are related by the formula:

$$f = \frac{c}{w} \qquad 12.3$$

Power is the quality of acoustical energy as measured in watts. Since a point source emits waves in a spherical shape in free space, the sound intensity (watts per unit area) is given by the formula:

$$I = \frac{P}{4\pi r^2} \qquad 12.4$$

Since 1 square foot = 930 square centimeters, the formula can be rewritten for English units as:

$$I = \frac{P}{(930)4\pi r^2} \qquad 12.5$$

B. Inverse Square Law

The basic inverse square law is derived from formula 12.5 where sound intensity is inversely proportional to the square of the distance from the source:

$$\frac{I_1}{I_2} = \frac{r_2^2}{r_1^2} \qquad 12.6$$

C. Sound Intensity

The sensitivity of the human ear covers a vast range (from 10^{-16} w/cm^2 to 10^{-3} w/cm^2). Because of this and the fact that the sensation of hearing is proportional to the logarithm of the source intensity, the decibel is used in acoustical descriptions and calculations. The decibel conveniently relates actual sound intensity to the way humans experience sound. By definition, zero decibels is the threshold of human hearing while 130 decibels is the threshold of pain.

In mathematical terms, this relationship is expressed by the formula:

$$IL = 10 \log \frac{I}{I_o} \qquad 12.7$$

Table 12.1
Common Sound Intensity Levels

IL dB	example	subjective evaluation	intensity w/cm^2
140	jet plane takeoff		
130	gun fire	threshold of pain	10^{-3}
120	hard rock band, siren at 100 ft.	deafening	10^{-4}
110	accelerating motorcycle	sound can be felt	10^{-5}
100	auto horn at 10 ft.	conversation difficult to hear	10^{-6}
90	loud street noise, kitchen blender	very loud	10^{-7}
80	noisy office, average factory	difficult to use phone	10^{-8}
70	average street noise, quiet typewriter, average radio	loud	10^{-9}
60	average office, noisy home	usual background	10^{-10}
50	average conversation, quiet radio	moderate	10^{-11}
40	quiet home, private office	noticeably quiet	10^{-12}
30	quiet conversation	faint	10^{-13}
20	whisper		10^{-14}
10	rustling leaves, sound proof room	very faint	10^{-15}
0	threshold of hearing		10^{-16}

Some common sound intensity levels and their subjective evaluations are shown in Table 12.1.

D. Loudness

The sensation of loudness is subjective, but some common guidelines are shown in Table 12.2. These are useful in evaluating the effects of increased or decreased decibel levels in architectural situations. For example, spending money to modify a partition to increase its sound transmission class by three decibels probably would not be worth the expense because it would hardly be noticeable.

Table 12.2
Subjective Change in Loudness
Based on Decibel Level Change

change in intensity level in dB	change in apparent loudness
1	almost imperceptible
3	just perceptible
5	clearly noticeable
6	change when distance to source in a free field is doubled or halved
10	twice or half as loud
18	very much louder or quieter
20	four times or one-fourth as loud

E. Addition of Decibels of Uncorrelated Sounds

Because decibels are logarithmic they cannot be added directly. A detailed calculation can be performed but a convenient rule of thumb gives results accurate to within 1 percent. Given two decibel values, use the values in Table 12.3 to add decibels.

Table 12.3
Addition of Decibels

when difference between the two values is:	add this value to the higher value
0 or 1 dB	3 dB
2 or 3 dB	2 dB
4 to 8 dB	1 dB
9 or more	0 dB

For three or more sources, first add two, then the result to the third number, and so on.

Example 12.1

Find the combined intensity level of two office machines, one generating 70 dB and the other generating 76 dB.

Use the rule of thumb shown in Table 12.3. The difference between 76 and 70 = 7; therefore, add 1 dB to 76, which gives 77 dB.

For the addition of several sources of identical value, use the formula:

$$IL \text{ (total)} = IL \text{ (source)} + 10 \log \text{(number of sources)}$$
$$12.8$$

Example 12.2

What would the sound level be in a room of eight typewriters, each producing 73 dB?

$$IL \text{ (total)} = 73 + 10 \log 8$$
$$= 82 \text{ dB}$$

F. Human Sensitivity to Sound

Although human response to sound is subjective and varies with age, physical condition of the ear, background, and other factors, some common guidelines are useful to remember:

The normal human ear of a healthy young person can hear sounds in the range of 20 to 20,000 Hz and is most sensitive to frequencies in the 3000 to 4000 Hz range. Speech is composed of sounds primarily in the range of 125 to 8000 Hz, with most in the range of 200 to 5000 Hz.

The human ear is less sensitive to low frequencies than to middle and high frequencies for sounds of equal energy.

Most common sound sources contain energy over a wide range of frequencies. Since frequency is an important variable in how a sound is transmitted or absorbed, it must be taken into account in building acoustics. For convenience, measurement and analysis is often divided into eight octave frequency bands identified by the center frequency. These are 63, 125, 250, 500, 1000, 2000, 4000, and 8000 Hz. For detailed purposes, smaller bands are often used.

3 SOUND TRANSMISSION

A. Transmission Loss and Noise Reduction

One of the primary concerns of architectural acoustics is reducing the transmission of sound from one space to another. Transmission of sound is primarily retarded by the mass of the barrier. In addition, the stiffness of the barrier is also important. Given two barriers of the same weight per square foot, the one with the smaller stiffness will perform better than the other.

There are two important concepts in noise reduction: transmission loss and actual noise reduction. Transmission loss (TL) is the difference (in decibels) between the

sound power incident on a barrier in a source room and the sound power radiated into a receiving room on the opposite side of the barrier. This is the measurement typically derived in a testing laboratory.

Noise reduction (NR) is the arithmetic difference (in decibels) between the intensity levels in two rooms separated by a barrier of a given transmission loss. Noise reduction is dependent on the transmission loss of the barrier, the area of the barrier, and the absorption of the surfaces in the receiving room.

Noise reduction is calculated by the formula:

$$NR = TL + 10 \log \frac{A}{S} \qquad 12.9$$

This formula shows that noise reduction can be increased by increasing the transmission loss of the barrier, by increasing the absorption in the receiving room, by decreasing the area of the barrier separating the two rooms, or by some combination of the three.

The actual transmission loss of a barrier varies with the frequencies of the sounds being tested. Test reports are often published with manufacturer's literature including the transmission loss over six or more octave bands. A single-number rating that is often used is the sound transmission class (STC). The higher the STC rating, the better the barrier is (theoretically) in stopping sound.

There are many times when a partition will be comprised of two or more types of constructions; for example, a door in a wall or a glass panel in a wall. The combined transmission loss can be found by the formula:

$$TL_{\text{composite}} = 10 \log \frac{\text{total area}}{\Sigma tS} \qquad 12.10$$

In finding the value of t, if you know the value of the transmission loss of individual materials, the following formula can be used:

$$t = 10^{-(TL/10)} \qquad 12.11$$

Example 12.3

A conference room and an office are separated by a common wall 13 feet long and 9 feet high with an STC rating of 54. The total absorption of the office has been calculated to be 220 Sabins. What is the total noise reduction from the conference room to the office?

$$NR = 54 + 10 \log \frac{220}{9 \times 13}$$
$$= 54 + 10 \log 1.88$$
$$= 54 + 2.7$$
$$= 57 \text{ dB}$$

Notice that the second term of formula 12.9 can be a negative number, resulting in a noise reduction less than the transmission loss of the wall.

Example 12.4

What is the combined transmission loss of a wall 9 feet high and 15 feet long with a 3 foot by 7 foot door in it? Assume TL of the wall is 54 and the door with full perimeter seals is 29.

total wall area: $9 \times 15 = 135$ square feet

area of door: 21 square feet

area of partition: $135 - 21 = 114$ square feet

t of partition $= 10^{-5.4}$

t of door $= 10^{-2.9}$

$$TL_{composite} = 10 \log \frac{135}{(10^{-5.4} \times 114) + (10^{-2.9} \times 21)}$$
$$= 10 \log 5020$$
$$= 37 \text{ dB}$$

Remember that STC ratings represent the ideal loss under laboratory conditions. Walls, partitions, and floors built in the field are seldom constructed as well as those in the laboratory. Also, breaks in the barrier such as cracks, electrical outlets, doors, and the like will significantly reduce the overall noise reduction.

In critical situations, transmission loss and selection of barriers should be calculated using the values for the various frequencies rather than the single STC average value. Some materials may allow an acoustical "hole," stopping most frequencies but allowing transmission of a certain range of frequencies. This often happens with very low or very high frequencies. However, for preliminary design purposes in typical situations the STC value is adequate.

B. Noise Criteria Curves

All normally occupied spaces have some amount of background noise. This is not undesirable because some noise is necessary to avoid the feeling of a "dead" space and to help mask other sounds. However, the acceptable amount of background noise varies with the type of space and the frequency of sound. For example, people are generally less tolerant of background noise in bedrooms than they are in public lobbies, and they are generally more tolerant of higher levels of low-frequency sound than of high-frequency sound.

These variables have been consolidated into a set of noise criteria curves relating frequency in eight octave bands to noise level. See Figure 12.1. Accompanying these curves are noise criteria ratings for various types of space and listening requirements. A representative sampling is shown in Table 12.4. Noise criteria curves can be used to specify the maximum amount of continuous background noise allowable in a space, to establish a minimum amount of noise desired to help mask sounds, and to evaluate an existing condition.

Table 12.4
Some Representative Noise Criteria

type of space	preferred NC (dB)
concert halls, opera houses, recording studios	15–20
bedrooms, apartments, hospitals	20–30
private offices, small conference rooms	30–35
large offices, retail stores, restaurants	35–40
lobbies, drafting rooms, laboratory work spaces	40–45
kitchens, computer rooms, light maintenance shops	45–55

For example, if the noise spectrum of an air conditioning system was plotted on the NC chart, as shown in Figure 12.1, the noise criteria rating would be defined by that curve that was not exceeded by the air conditioning spectrum curve at any frequency.

C. Rules of Thumb

In addition to using calculations for acoustical design, there are many rules of thumb that can be used for preliminary estimating and for non-critical situations.

- In general, transmission loss through a barrier tends to increase with the frequency of sound.

- A wall with 0.1 percent open area (from cracks, holes, undercut doors, etc.) will have a maximum transmission loss of about 30 dB. A wall with 1 percent open area will have a maximum of about 20 dB.

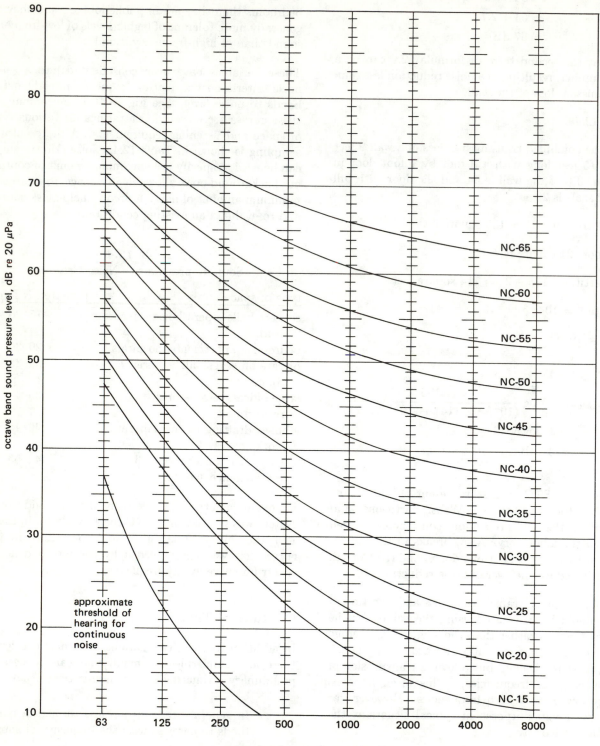

Figure 12.1   NC (Noise Criteria) Curves

- A hairline crack will decrease a partition's transmission loss by about 6 dB. A 1-square-inch opening in a 100-square-foot gypsum board partition can transmit as much sound as the entire partition.

- Although placing fibrous insulation in a wall cavity increases its STC rating, the density of the insulation is not a significant variable.

- In determining the required STC rating of a barrier, the guidelines in Table 12.5 may be used.

Table 12.5
Effect of Barrier STC on Hearing

STC	effect on hearing
25	normal speech can clearly be heard through barrier
30	loud speech can be heard and understood fairly well; normal speech can be heard but barely understood
35	loud speech is not intelligible but can be heard
42–45	loud speech can only be faintly heard; normal speech cannot be heard
46–50	loud speech not audible; loud sounds other than speech can only be heard faintly, if at all

4 SOUND ABSORPTION

A. Fundamentals

Controlling sound transmission is only part of good acoustical design. The proper amount of sound absorption must also be included. Although sound intensity level decreases about 6 dB for each doubling of distance from the source in free space, this is not the case in a room or semienclosed outdoor area. In a room, sound level decreases very near the source as it does in free space, but then it begins to reflect and levels out at a particular intensity.

In addition to reducing this intensity level of sound within a space, sound absorption is used to control unwanted sound reflections, to improve speech privacy, and to decrease or enhance reverberation.

The absorption of a material is defined by the coefficient of absorption, a, which is the ratio of the sound intensity absorbed by the material to the total intensity reaching the material. The maximum absorption possible, therefore, is 1, that of free space. Generally, a material with a coefficient below 0.2 is considered to be reflective and one with a coefficient above 0.2 is considered sound absorbing.

The coefficient of absorption varies with the frequency of the sound, and some materials are better at absorbing some frequencies than others. For critical applications all frequencies should be checked, but for convenience the single-number noise reduction coefficient (NRC) is used. The NRC is the average of a material's absorption coefficients at the four frequencies of 250, 500, 1000, and 2000 Hz, rounded to the nearest multiple of 0.05.

The total absorption of a material is dependent on its coefficient of absorption and the area of the material.

$$A = Sa \qquad 12.12$$

Since most rooms have several materials of different areas, the total absorption in a room is the sum of the various individual material absorptions.

B. Noise Reduction Within a Space

Increasing sound absorption within a space will result in a noise reduction according to the formula:

$$NR = 10 \log \frac{A_2}{A_1} \qquad 12.13$$

$A(1)$ = total original room absorption in Sabins

$A(2)$ = total room absorption after increase of absorption

Note that this formula relates to overall reverberant noise level in a room and does not affect noise level very near the source.

Example 12.5

A room 15 feet by 20 feet with a 9-foot ceiling has a carpeted floor with 44 oz. carpet on pad ($a = 0.40$), gypsum board walls, and a gypsum board ceiling ($a = 0.05$). What would be the noise reduction achieved by directly attaching acoustical tile with a given NRC of 0.70 to the ceiling?

Original total absorption of room:

$$
\begin{aligned}
\text{floor: } 15 \times 20 &= 300 \times 0.40 = 120 \\
\text{walls: } 2 \times 15 \times 9 &= 270 \times 0.05 = 14 \\
2 \times 20 \times 9 &= 360 \times 0.05 = 18 \\
\text{ceiling: } 15 \times 20 &= 300 \times 0.05 = 15 \\
\hline
\text{total} &= 167 \text{ Sabins}
\end{aligned}
$$

Absorption after treatment:

ceiling $= 15 \times 20 = 300 \times 0.70 = 210$ Sabins

Subtracting 15 from the old value and adding 210 as a new value, the net total is 362 Sabins.

$$\begin{aligned} NR &= 10 \log \frac{362}{167} \\ &= 10 \log(2.17) \\ &= 3.4 \text{ dB} \end{aligned}$$

Increasing the absorption by this amount helps a little but the difference would be just perceptible (see Table 12.2). Tripling the absorption would be clearly noticeable.

C. Rules of Thumb

There are several rules of thumb related to sound absorption that are useful to remember.

- The average absorption coefficient of a room should be at least 0.20. An average absorption above 0.50 is usually not desirable, nor is it economically justified. A lower value is suitable for large rooms, larger values for small or noisy rooms.

- Each doubling of the amount of absorption in a room results in a noise deduction of only 3 dB.

- If additional absorptive material is being added to a room, the total absorption should be increased at least three times (amounting to a change in about 5 dB, which is clearly noticeable). The increase may need to be more or less than three times to bring absorption to between 0.20 and 0.50.

- In adding extra absorption, an increase of ten times is about the practical limit. Beyond this (representing a reverberant noise reduction of 10 dB), more absorption results in a decreasing amount of noise reduction and reaching the practical limit of 0.50 total average absorption coefficient.

- Each doubling of the absorption in a room reduces reverberation time by one-half.

- Although absorptive materials can be placed anywhere, ceiling treatment for sound absorption is more effective in large rooms while wall treatment is more effective in small rooms.

- Generally, absorption increases with an increase in thickness of a porous absorber, except for low-frequency situations that require special design treatment.

- The amount of absorption of a porous type of sound absorber such as fiberglass or mineral wool is dependent on (1) the thickness of the material, (2) its density, (3) its porosity, and (4) the orientation of the fibers in the material. A porous sound absorber should be composed of open, interconnected voids.

D. Reverberation

Reverberation is an important quality of the acoustical environment of a space. It is the one quality that affects the intelligibility of speech and the quality of conditions for music of all types. Reverberation time is the time it takes the sound level to decrease 60 dB after the source has stopped producing the sound. Reverberation time is found by the following formula:

$$T = 0.05 \frac{V}{A} \qquad\qquad 12.14$$

Each type of use has its own preferred range of reverberation time, shorter times being best for smaller spaces and longer times working best for larger spaces. See Table 12.6.

Table 12.6
Recommended Reverberation Times

space	time, seconds
auditoriums (speech and music)	1.5–1.8
broadcast studios (speech only)	0.4–0.6
churches	1.4–3.4
elementary classrooms	0.6–0.8
lecture/conference rooms	0.9–1.1
movie theaters	0.8–1.2
offices, small rooms for speech	0.3–0.6
opera halls	1.5–1.8
symphony concert halls	1.6–2.1
theaters (small dramatic)	0.9–1.4

5   SOUND CONTROL

A. Control of Room Noise

There are three primary ways sound can be controlled within a space: by reducing the level of the sound source, by modifying the absorption in the space, and by introducing non-intrusive background noise to mask the sound.

Reducing the level of the sound source is not always possible if the source is a fixed piece of machinery, people are talking, or some similar situation. However, if the source is noise from the outside or an adjacent room, the transmission loss of the enclosing walls can be improved. If a machine is producing the noise, it can often be enclosed or modified to reduce its noise output.

Modifying the absorption of the space can achieve some noise reduction, but there are practical limits to adding absorptive materials. This approach is most useful when the problem room has a large percentage of hard, reflective surfaces.

In most cases, introducing non-intrusive background noise is desirable because it can mask unwanted noise. Some amount of background noise is always present. This may come from the steady hum of HVAC systems, from business machines, from traffic, from conversation, or from other sources. For example, in an office, if the sound level on one side of a partition with an STC rating of 45 is 75 dB and the background noise on the other side of the partition is 35 dB, the noise will not be heard (theoretically) on the "quiet" side of the wall. See Figure 12.2. If the background noise level is decreased to 25 dB, then sounds will be heard.

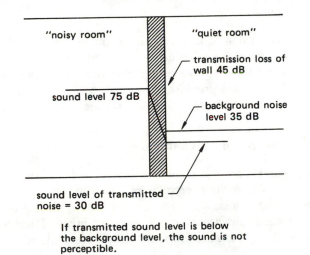

Figure 12.2 Noise Reduction

This phenomenon is used to purposely introduce carefully controlled sound into a space rather than rely only on random background noise. Often called white sound, random noise, or acoustical perfume, speakers are placed in the ceiling of a space and connected to a sound generator which produces a continuous, unnoticeable sound at particular levels across the frequency spectrum. The sound generator can be tuned to produce the frequencies and sound levels appropri-

ate to mask the desired sounds. White sound is often used in open offices to provide speech privacy and to help mask office machine noise.

B. Control of Sound Transmission

As mentioned previously, control of sound transmission through barriers is primarily dependent on the mass of the barrier, and to a lesser extent on its stiffness. Walls and floors are generally rated with their STC value; the higher the STC rating, the better the barrier is in reducing transmitted sound. Manufacturer's literature, testing laboratories, and reference literature typically give the transmission loss at different frequencies.

In addition to the construction of the barrier itself, other variables are critical to control of sound transmission.

Gaps in the barrier must be sealed. Edges at the floor, ceiling, and intersecting walls should be caulked. Penetrations of the barrier should be avoided, but if absolutely necessary they should be sealed as well. For example, electrical outlets should not be placed back to back but staggered in separate stud spaces and caulked.

Penetrations through the barrier should be avoided. Pipes, ducts, and similar penetrations provide a path for both airborne sound and mechanical vibration. If they are unavoidable, they should not be rigidly connected to the barrier, and any gaps should be sealed and caulked.

"Weaker" construction within the barrier should be avoided or given special treatment. Construction with a lower STC rating than the barrier itself will decrease the overall rating of the barrier. Doors placed in an otherwise well-built sound wall are a common problem and can be dealt with in several ways. The perimeter should be completely sealed with weatherstripping specifically designed for sound sealing at the jamb and head and with a threshold or automatic door bottom at the sill. The door itself should be as heavy as possible, preferably a solid core wood door. Often, two doors are used, separated by a small air gap.

Interior glass lights can be designed with laminated glass set in resilient framing. Laminated glass provides more mass and the plastic interlayer improves the damping characteristics of the barrier. If additional transmission loss is required, two or more layers can be installed with an air gap between them.

Flanking paths for sound to travel should be eliminated or treated appropriately, including air conditioning ducts, plenum spaces above ceilings, hallways, and open windows in adjacent rooms.

Unusual sound conditions or frequencies must be given special consideration and design. Low-frequency rumbling or high frequencies are often not stopped, even with a wall with a high STC rating.

C. Speech Privacy

In many architectural situations, the critical acoustical concern is not eliminating all noise or designing a room for music but providing for a certain level of privacy while still allowing people to talk at a normal level. In many cases, speech privacy is regarded as a condition in which talking may be heard as a general background sound but not easily understood.

Of course, speech privacy is subjective and depends on circumstances. People involved in highly confidential conversations may need greater privacy than those conducting normal, non-confidential business in an open office. Also, one person may be annoyed by adjacent conversations more than another person.

Speech privacy in areas divided by partitions is usually achieved by attenuation of the partitions and, to a lesser extent, by the proper use of sound-absorbing surfaces. In open areas, such as an open-plan office, speech privacy is more difficult to achieve. There are five important factors in designing for speech privacy in an open area. All of these must be present to achieve an optimum possible acoustical environment.

1. The ceiling must be highly absorptive. The idea is to create a "clear sky" condition so that sounds are not reflected from their source to other parts of the environment.

2. There must be space dividers that reduce the transmission of sound from one space to the adjacent space. The dividers should have a combination of absorptive surfaces to minimize sound reflections placed over a solid liner (septum).

3. Other surfaces, such as the floor, furniture, windows, and light fixtures, must be designed or arranged to minimize sound reflections. A window, for example, can provide a clear path for reflected noise around a partial height partition.

4. If possible, activities should be distanced to take advantage of the normal attenuation of sound with distance.

5. There must be a properly designed background masking system. If the right number of sound-absorbing surfaces are provided, they absorb all sounds in the space, not just the unwanted sounds. Background sound must then be reintroduced to maintain the right balance between speech sound and the background noise. This is referred to as the signal-to-noise ratio. If the signal-to-noise ratio is too great (as a result of either loud talking or minimal background noise), speech privacy will be compromised.

D. Control of Impact Noise

Impact noise, or sound resulting from direct contact of an object with a sound barrier, can occur on any surface, but it generally occurs on a floor and ceiling assembly. It is usually caused by footfalls, shuffled furniture, or dropped objects.

Impact noise is quantified by the Impact Insulation Class (IIC) number, a single-number rating of a floor/ceiling's impact sound performance. A given construction is analyzed in accordance with a standardized test over 16 third-octave bands and the results compared to a reference plot much as noise criteria ratings are established. The higher the IIC rating, the better the floor performs in reducing impact sounds in the test frequency range.

The IIC value of a floor can be increased by adding carpet, providing a resiliently suspended ceiling below, floating a finished floor on resilient pads over the structural floor, and providing sound-absorbing material in the air space between the floor and the finished ceiling.

E. Control of Mechanical Noise

Mechanical noise is similar to impact noise in that the cause is due to direct contact with the barrier. However, mechanical noise occurs when a vibrating device is in continuous direct contact with the structure. There are several ways mechanical noise can be transmitted:

*   Rigidly attached equipment can vibrate the building structure or pipes, which in turn radiates sound into occupied spaces.

*   The airborne noise of equipment can be transmitted through walls and floors to occupied spaces.

*   Noise can be transmitted through ductwork.

*   The movement of air or water through ducts and pipes can cause undesirable noise. This is especially true of high-velocity air systems or situations where the air or water changes velocity rapidly.

Depending on the circumstances, mechanical noise can be controlled several ways:

- Mechanical equipment should be mounted on springs or resilient pads (isolaters).

- Connections between equipment and ducts and pipes should be made with flexible connectors.

- Ducts should be lined or provided with mufflers where noise control is critical.

- The location of noise-producing equipment can be arranged away from quiet, occupied spaces.

- Walls, ceilings, and floors of mechanical rooms should be designed to attenuate airborne noise.

- Mechanical and plumbing systems should be designed to minimize high-velocity flow and sudden changes in fluid velocity.

6   ROOM ACOUSTICS

A. Reflection, Diffusion, and Diffraction

Reflection is the return of sound waves from a surface. If a surface is greater than or equal to four times the wavelength of a sound striking it, the angle of incidence will equal the angle of reflection. Wavelength, of course, varies with frequency according to formula 12.1. Assuming a velocity of 1130 feet per second, Table 12.7 gives wavelengths of certain frequencies.

Table 12.7
Wavelengths Based on Frequency

frequency (Hz)	wavelength (feet)
50	23
100	11
250	4.5
500	2.25
1000	1.13
2000	0.57
5000	0.23
10,000	0.11

Reflection can be useful for reinforcing sound in lecture rooms and concert halls and for directing sound where it is wanted. It can also be annoying if it produces echos, which occur when a reflected sound reaches a listener later than about 1/17 second after the direct sound. Assuming a sound speed of 1130 feet per second, an echo will occur whenever the reflected sound path exceeds the direct sound path by 70 feet or more.

Diffusion is the random distribution of sound from a surface. It occurs when the surface dimension equals the wavelength of the sound striking it.

Diffraction is the bending of sound waves around an object or through an opening. Diffraction explains why sounds can be heard around corners and why even small holes in partitions allow so much sound to be heard.

B. Room Geometry and Planning Concepts

There are many ways the acoustical performance of a building or individual room can be affected by floor plan layout and the size and shape of the room itself. In addition to designing walls and floors to retard sound transmission and proper use of sound absorption, you can use the following ideas to help minimize acoustical problems.

- Plan similar use areas next to each other. For example, placing bedrooms next to each other in an apartment complex is better than placing a bedroom next to the adjacent unit's kitchen. This concept is applicable for vertical organization as well as horizontal (plan) organization.

- Use buffer spaces such as closets and hallways to separate noise-producing spaces whenever possible. Using closets between bedrooms at a common wall is one example of this method.

- Locate noise-producing areas such as mechanical rooms, laundries, and playrooms away from "quiet" areas.

- Stagger doorways in halls and other areas to avoid providing a straight-line path for noise.

- Locate operable windows as far from each other as possible.

- If possible, try to locate furniture and other potential noise-producing objects away from the wall separating spaces.

- Minimize the area of the common wall between two rooms where a reduction in sound transmission is desired.

- Avoid room shapes that reflect or focus sound. Barrel vaulted hallways and circular rooms, for example, produce undesirable focused sounds. Rooms that focus sound also deprive some listeners of useful reflections.

- Avoid parallel walls with hard surfaces in small rooms. Repeated echos, called *flutter echos*, can be generated that result in a perceived "buzzing" sound of higher frequencies. This is why small music practice rooms have splayed walls. Standing waves can also be produced in small rooms, which occurs when parallel walls are some integral multiple of one-half wavelength apart and a steady tone is introduced in the room.

SAMPLE QUESTIONS

1. Which of the following are not true?

I. Sensitivity to sound varies between sexes.

II. People are generally more sensitive to middle and high frequencies than to low frequencies for sounds of equal energy.

III. Most healthy young people can hear sounds in the range of 15 to 25,000 Hz.

IV. Practically all common sounds are made up of energy in a wide range of frequencies.

V. Speech is composed of frequencies in the range of 125 to 8000 Hz.

    A. I and V

    B. III and V

    C. I and III

    D. II and III

2. The construction assembly shown would be best for controlling which of the following kinds of acoustic situations?

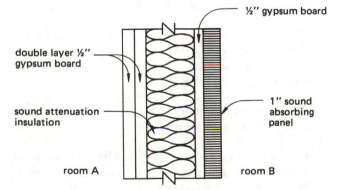

I. impact noise

II. excessive reverberation in room B

III. transmission from room A to room B

IV. transmission from room B to room A

V. mechanical vibration

    A. II and IV

    B. II and III

    C. III and IV

    D. I and II

3. In an office a copy machine is found to produce 65 dB. If a computer printer is added to the room and it produces a sound intensity of 69 dB, what will be the resulting sound level?

    A. 70 dB

    B. 71 dB

    C. 72 dB

    D. 73 dB

The answers to questions 4 through 6 can be found on the following key list. Select only one answer for each question.

    A0 amplification
    A1 attenuation
    A2 decibel
    A3 frequency
    A4 impact insulation class
    A5 intensity level
    A6 inverse square law
    A7 noise criteria
    A8 noise insulation class
    A9 noise reduction

    B0 noise reduction coefficient
    B1 phon
    B2 reverberation
    B3 room volume
    B4 sound absorption coefficient
    B5 sound intensity
    B6 sound transmission class
    B7 transmission loss

4. What is the single number often used to evaluate partitions?

5. What method is used to specify the maximum allowable intensity of background sounds?

6. What is one variable affecting reverberation time?

7. Which of the following is not true about noise reduction between two rooms?

    A. Noise reduction increases with an increase in the transmission loss of the wall separating the two rooms.

    B. The stiffness of the wall has little effect on noise reduction.

C. To improve noise reduction, you should place absorptive materials on both sides of the wall.

D. An increase in wall area separating the two rooms is detrimental.

8. A room 15 feet wide by 20 feet long by 8 1/2 feet high is finished with the following materials of listed absorptions. There is a window on one wall 3 1/2 feet high by 8 feet long. What is the total absorption of the room?

	NRC	125	250	500	1000	2000	4000
floor, wood	0.10	0.15	0.11	0.10	0.07	0.06	0.07
walls, gypsum board	0.05	0.10	0.08	0.05	0.03	0.03	0.03
ceiling, acoustical tile	0.60	0.29	0.29	0.55	0.75	0.73	0.57
window, glass	0.15	0.35	0.25	0.18	0.12	0.07	0.04

    A. 228 Sabins

    B. 244 Sabins

    C. 266 Sabins

    D. 242 Sabins

9. If a material supplier told you that adding his product to a wall assembly in a critical acoustical situation would increase the noise reduction (STC rating) between two spaces by more than 3 dB, what should your reaction be?

    A. Determine what the additional cost would be and then decide whether or not to use the product.

    B. Thank him for stopping by but explain that you probably will not be using his product because that amount of noise reduction does not make it worth the effort or cost.

    C. Specify the product as long as it does not affect the design or construction cost by more than 5%.

    D. Inquire whether some modification can be made to the product to increase its rating to 6 dB and say that then you might consider it.

10. During your design development presentation to the building committee of a middle school, one of the teachers on the committee mentions that there might be a noise problem between the classrooms shown in the partial plan because the larger classroom will be used for open discussions, movies, lab work, and other loud activities. Both classrooms are scheduled to have gypsum board partitions, vinyl tile floors, and suspended acoustical ceilings.

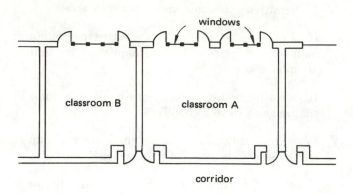

If cost is a consideration, what changes in the design should you suggest, in order of priority from most important to least important?

    I. Substitute carpeting for tile in both rooms.

    II. Move the operable windows near the separating wall so they are not so close together, and change the direction of the swing.

    III. Reroute the ductwork and conduit penetrations through the separating wall above the suspended ceiling and write specifications to direct that any remaining penetrations be tightly sealed.

    IV. Replan the layout so there is a small audiovisual storage room between the classrooms.

    V. Add an extra layer of gypsum board to each side of the separating partition and specify that the cavity be filled with sound-attenuating insulation.

    VI. Hire an acoustical consultant to determine the special frequency problems associated with the activities planned for the larger classroom, and design custom sound-absorbing surfaces and partitions accordingly.

    A. III, II, V, I, VI, IV

    B. IV, II, III, V, VI, I

    C. II, III, V, I, IV, VI

    D. V, III, II, I, IV, VI

13 SITE WORK

Site work includes demolition and clearing of land, earthwork, installation of piles and caissons, paving and other types of surfacing, drainage, site improvements, and landscaping. Included in this chapter are those aspects of site work encountered on almost any architectural project.

1 SOIL

Since all aspects of site work depend on the nature of the soil, the architect must have a basic understanding of this element. *Soil* is a general term used to describe the material that supports a building. It is generally classified into four groups: sands and gravels, clays, silts, and organics. *Sands* and *gravels* are granular materials that are low in plasticity. *Clays* are composed of smaller particles that have some cohesion, or tensile strength, and are plastic in their behavior. *Silts* are of intermediate size between clays and sands and behave as granular materials but are sometimes slightly plastic in their behavior. *Organics* are materials of vegetable or other organic matter.

In addition to these general types, there is solid rock, which has the highest bearing capacity of all soil types.

A. Soil Tests

Prior to design and construction, the exact nature of the soil must be determined. This is done with one of a variety of soil tests used to determine such things as the bearing capacity, water table level, and porosity. Porosity must be known if the land is used for private sewage disposal systems. Two of the most common soil tests for bearing capacity are borings and test pits.

With typical core borings, undisturbed samples of the soil are removed at regular intervals with the type of material recovered recorded in a *boring log*. This log shows the material, the depth at which it was encountered, its standard designation, and other information such as moisture content, density, and the results of any borehole tests that might have been conducted at the bore site.

One of the most common borehole tests is the *Standard Penetration Test* (SPT), which is a measure of the density of granular soils and consistency of some clays. In this test, a 2-inch diameter sampler is driven into the bottom of the borehole by a 140-pound hammer falling 30 inches. The number of blows, N, required to drive the cylinder 12 inches is recorded. A typical boring log is shown in Figure 13.1.

The recovered bore samples can be tested in the laboratory. Some of the tests include strength tests of bearing capacity, resistance to lateral pressure, and slope stability. In addition, compressibility, grain size, specific gravity, and density tests are sometimes performed. Since laboratory tests are expensive and not always necessary, they are not performed for every building project.

The number of borings taken at a building site is determined by many factors, such as the size of the building, suspected subsurface geological conditions, and requirements by local codes. Usually, a minimum of four borings is taken, one near each corner of the proposed building. If wide variations are found in the initial boring logs, additional tests may be warranted.

Test pits are the second common type of subsurface exploration. These are trenches dug at the job site that allow visual inspection of the soil strata and direct collection of undisturbed samples. Because they are open pits, the practical limit on depth is about 10 feet, so the soil below that cannot be directly examined.

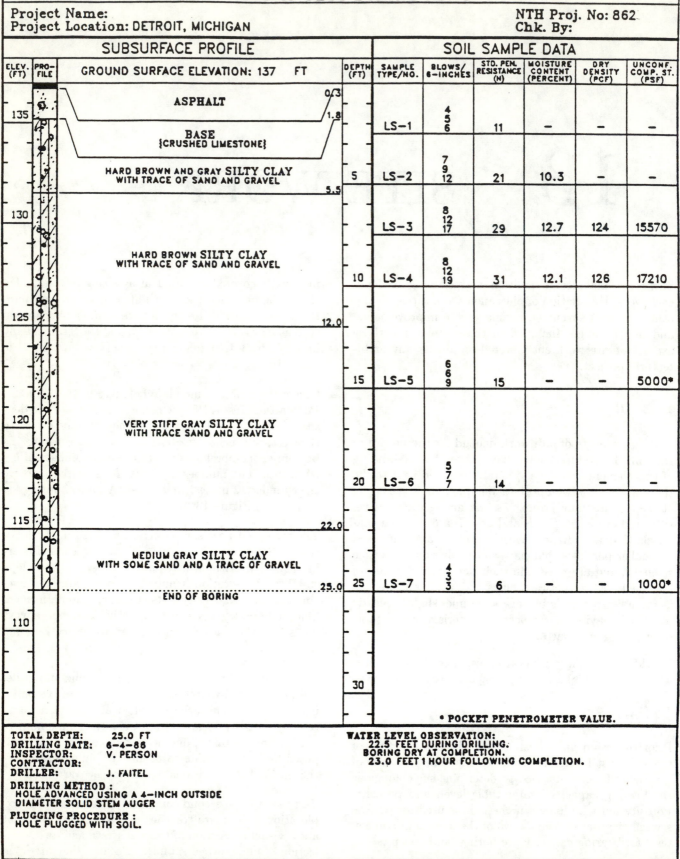

LOG OF TEST BORING NO. 3

Project Name:
Project Location: DETROIT, MICHIGAN

NTH Proj. No: 862
Chk. By:

SUBSURFACE PROFILE

GROUND SURFACE ELEVATION: 137 FT

ELEV. (FT)	PRO-FILE	Description	DEPTH (FT)
135		ASPHALT — 0.3	0.3
		— 1.8	1.8
		BASE {CRUSHED LIMESTONE}	
		HARD BROWN AND GRAY SILTY CLAY WITH TRACE OF SAND AND GRAVEL	5
130		— 5.5	5.5
		HARD BROWN SILTY CLAY WITH TRACE OF SAND AND GRAVEL	10
125		— 12.0	12.0
120		VERY STIFF GRAY SILTY CLAY WITH TRACE SAND AND GRAVEL	15
115		— 22.0	20 / 22.0
		MEDIUM GRAY SILTY CLAY WITH SOME SAND AND A TRACE OF GRAVEL	25 / 25.0
110		END OF BORING	
			30

SOIL SAMPLE DATA

SAMPLE TYPE/NO.	BLOWS/ 6-INCHES	STD. PEN. RESISTANCE (N)	MOISTURE CONTENT (PERCENT)	DRY DENSITY (PCF)	UNCONF. COMP. ST. (PSF)
LS-1	4 5 6	11	–	–	–
LS-2	7 9 12	21	10.3	–	–
LS-3	8 12 17	29	12.7	124	15570
LS-4	8 12 19	31	12.1	126	17210
LS-5	6 6 9	15	–	–	5000*
LS-6	5 7 7	14	–	–	–
LS-7	4 3 3	6	–	–	1000*

* POCKET PENETROMETER VALUE.

TOTAL DEPTH: 25.0 FT
DRILLING DATE: 6-4-86
INSPECTOR: V. PERSON
CONTRACTOR:
DRILLER: J. FAITEL
DRILLING METHOD:
 HOLE ADVANCED USING A 4-INCH OUTSIDE DIAMETER SOLID STEM AUGER
PLUGGING PROCEDURE:
 HOLE PLUGGED WITH SOIL.

WATER LEVEL OBSERVATION:
 22.5 FEET DURING DRILLING.
 BORING DRY AT COMPLETION.
 23.0 FEET 1 HOUR FOLLOWING COMPLETION.

Figure 13.1   Typical Boring Log

The location of each test boring or test pit is shown on the plot plan and given a number corresponding to the boring log in the soil test report. Soil tests are usually requested by the architect but paid for by the owner. They are typically shown on the drawings for information only. However, soil tests are not part of the contract documents.

Other types of tests include auger borings, wash borings, and soil load tests. *Auger borings* raise samples of the soil by using a standard auger bit. The test is best used in sand or clay for shallow or intermediate depths since the auger cannot penetrate hard obstructions such as bedrock or hardpan soil.

Wash borings are made with a 2- to 4-inch-diameter pipe through which a water jet is maintained to force up the soil material. The resulting samples are so thoroughly mixed that analysis is difficult, but the test is useful for soils too hard for an auger test.

Soil load tests involve building a platform on the site, placing incremental loads on it, and observing the amount of settlement during given time periods.

B. Soil Types

Soils are classified according to the *Unified Soil Classification System*. This system divides soils into major divisions and subdivisions based on grain size and laboratory tests of physical characteristics and provides standardized names and symbols. A summary chart of the USCS is shown in Figure 13.2.

coarse grained soils more than 50% of material is larger than No. 200 sieve	gravels more than 50% of coarse fraction retained on No. 4 sieve	clean gravels less than 5% fines	GW	well-graded gravel
			GP	poorly graded gravel
		gravels with fines more than 12% fines	GM	silty gravel
			GC	clayey gravel
	sands 50% or more of coarse fraction passes No. 4 sieve	clean sands less than 5% fines	SW	well-graded sand
			SP	poorly graded sand
		sands with fines more than 12% fines	SM	silty sand
			SC	clayey sand
fine grained soils 50% or more passes the No. 200 sieve	silts and clays liquid limit less than 50	inorganic	CL	lean clay
			ML	silt
		organic	OL	organic silty
	silts and clays liquid limit 50 or more	inorganic	CH	fat clay
			MH	elastic silt
		organic	OH	organic clay
highly organic soils	primary organic matter, dark in color, and organic odor		PT	peat

Figure 13.2 Unified Soil Classification System

Bearing capacities are generally specified by the building code based on the soil type. Other bearing capacities may be used if acceptable tests are conducted that show higher values are appropriate.

C. Water in Soil

The presence of water in soil can cause several problems for foundations as well as other parts of the site. Water can reduce the load-carrying capacity of the soil in general so larger or more expensive foundation systems may be necessary. If more moisture is present under one area of the building than another, differential settlement may occur, causing cracking and weakening of structural and non-structural components. In the worst case, structural failure may occur. Improperly prepared soil can also cause heaving or settling of paving, fences, and other parts of the site.

Foundations below the groundwater line, often called the *water table*, are also subjected to hydrostatic pressure. This pressure from the force of water-saturated soil can occur against vertical foundation walls as well as under the floor slabs. Hydrostatic pressure creates two difficulties: it puts additional loads on the structural elements, and it makes waterproofing more difficult because the pressure tends to force water into any crack or imperfection in the structure.

Even if hydrostatic pressure is not present, moisture in the soil can leak into the below-grade structure if not properly dampproofed and can cause general deterioration of materials.

D. Soil Treatment

In order to increase bearing capacity or decrease settlement, or both, several methods of soil treatment are used.

- *Drainage:* as mentioned in the previous section, proper drainage can solve several types of problems. It can increase the strength of the soil and prevent hydrostatic pressure.

- *Fill:* if existing soil is unsuitable for building, the undesirable material is removed and new engineered fill is brought in. This may be soil, sand, gravel, or other material as appropriate. In nearly all situations, the engineered fill must be compacted before building commences. Controlled compaction requires moisture to lubricate the particles. With all types of fill, there is an optimum relationship between the fill's density and its optimum moisture content. The method for determining this is the Proctor test,

with which fill samples are tested in the laboratory to determine a standard for compaction. Specifications are then written that call for fill to be compacted between 95 percent and 100 percent of the optimum Proctor density; higher values are necessary for heavily loaded structures, and lower values are appropriate for other loadings. Moisture contents within 2 to 4 percent of the optimum moisture content at the time of compaction must also be specified. Fill is usually placed in lifts of 8 to 12 inches, with each lift compacted before placement of the next.

- *Compaction:* sometimes existing soil can simply be compacted to provide the required base for construction. The same requirements for compaction of fill material apply to compaction of existing soil.

- *Densification:* this is a type of on-site compaction of existing material using one of several techniques involving vibration, dropping of heavy weights, or pounding piles into the ground and filling the voids with sand. The specific technique used depends on the grain size of the soil.

- *Surcharging:* surcharging is the preloading of the ground with fill material to cause consolidation and settlement of the underlying soil before building. Once the required settlement has taken place, the fill is removed and construction begins. Although suitable for large areas, the time and cost required for sufficient settlement often preclude this method of soil improvement.

- *Mixing:* in lieu of complete replacement of the soil, a layer of sand or gravel can be placed on less stable soil and mixed in, thus improving its bearing capacity. By varying the type of added material, a soil with required properties can be created.

2 EARTHWORK

Earthwork includes excavating soil for the construction of a building foundation, water and sewer lines, and other buried items as well as modifying the site's land contours.

A. Excavation

Excavation is the removal of soil to allow construction of foundations and other permanent features below the finished level of the grade. It is usually done with machinery, although small areas may be excavated by hand. When a relatively narrow, long excavation is done for piping or for narrow footings and foundation walls, it is called *trenching*.

Since excavations can pose a hazard to workers, unshored sides of soil should be no steeper than their natural angle of repose or not greater than a slope of 1 1/2 horizontal to 1 vertical. Where this is not possible, the earth must be temporarily shored as discussed in the next section.

For large excavations, excess soil has to be removed from the site. However, to minimize cost, it is best to use the soil elsewhere on the site for backfill or in contour modification.

B. Grading

Grading is the modification of the contours of the site according to the grading plan. *Rough grading* involves the moving of soil prior to construction to approximate levels of the final grades. It also includes adding or removing soil after construction to the approximate final grades. In both of these operations, the grade is usually within about 6 inches to 1 foot of the desired level. Often, excavating is part of the rough grading as soil removed for the building is placed in low spots where the grade must be built up.

Finish grading is the final moving of soil prior to landscaping or paving, where the level of the earth is brought to within 1 inch of the desired grades. This operation is done with machines and by hand and often includes the placement of topsoil.

3 SHORING AND BRACING

For shallow excavations in open areas, the sides of the excavation can be sloped without the need for some supporting structure. However, as the depth increases or the excavation walls need to be vertical in confined locations, temporary support is required. There are two common methods of doing this.

The first method employs a system of vertical beams and horizontal timbers. See Figure 13.3 (a). Prior to excavation, wide-flange soldier beams are driven at 6- to 10-foot intervals to a length slightly deeper than the anticipated excavation. As soil is removed, horizontal timbers 2 to 4 inches thick, called *breast boards* or *cribbing*, are placed between the soldier beams so they bear against the inside face of the flange.

When the excavation reaches a certain point, holes are drilled into the earth or deeper rock. Rods or tendons are inserted into the holes and grouted into place. These tiebacks are connected to horizontal wales that hold the soldier beams back against the pressure of the excavation. As the excavation proceeds, more breast boards and tiebacks are added. The advantage of this method of shoring is that the excavation is free from bracing and allows drilling of piers, forming of foundation walls, and other construction to proceed unimpeded.

The second method uses vertical sheeting, either wood or steel, supported by diagonal braces, as shown in Figure 13.3 (b). Steel sheeting is composed of interlocking Z-shaped sections supported by continuous horizontal members called *wales*. The wales, in turn, are supported by diagonal rakers anchored to the bottom of the excavation with steel or concrete heels. For very small excavations the diagonal rakers can be replaced with horizontal braces connecting opposite sides of the excavation.

Shoring and bracing are used to temporarily support adjacent buildings and other construction with posts, timbers, and beams when excavation is proceeding and to temporarily support the sides of an excavation.

Underpinning is a method to temporarily support existing foundations while they are being repaired or strengthened or when they are being extended to a lower level.

4 SITE DRAINAGE

Water must be properly drained from a site to carry off excess rain and other surface water, to avoid leakage into the building and to make other parts of the site, such as walks, parking areas, and outdoor activity areas, usable. There are two primary types of drainage to consider: subsurface and surface.

A. Subsurface Drainage

Water below ground can reduce the load-carrying capacity of the soil, cause differential settlement, and leak into a building. For these reasons, the site for a building must be examined and tested for potential water problems and steps taken to drain excess water.

A small amount of moisture in the soil normally does not pose significant problems. However, if there is a high percentage of water in the soil or the water table is high, these problems must be dealt with. The *water table* is the level below which the soil is saturated with groundwater. If any part of a structure is below this level, it is subject to hydrostatic pressure, putting additional loads on the structural elements of the foundation and making waterproofing more difficult.

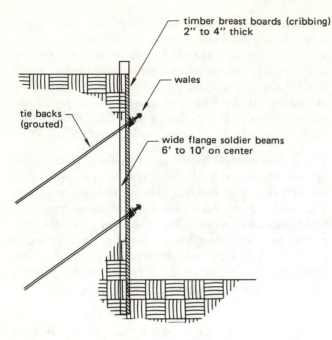

(a) soldier beams and breast boards

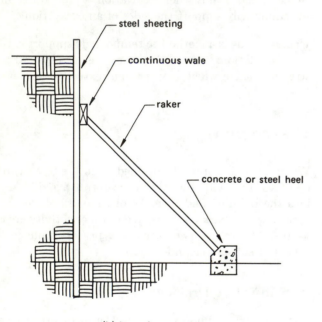

(b) braced excavation

Figure 13.3 Excavation Shoring

In order to minimize subsurface water, the land around the building must be sloped to drain surface water before it soaks into the ground near the structure. A minimum slope of 1/4 inch per foot is recommended. All water from roofs and decks should also be drained away from the building with gutters and drain pipes.

Below ground, perforated drain tile should be laid around the footings at least 6 inches below the floor slab to collect water and carry it away to a storm sewer

system, drywell, or some natural drainage area. The drain tile is set in a gravel setting bed and more gravel placed above the drain. This is commonly known as a "French drain."

If hydrostatic pressure against the wall is a problem, a layer of gravel can be placed next to the wall. Open web matting can also be used. With either of these methods, when water is forced against gravel or matting, it loses its pressure and drips to the drain tile.

To relieve pressure against floor slabs, a layer of large gravel can be placed below the slab. If the presence of water is a significant problem, the gravel layer can be used in conjunction with a waterproofing membrane and drain tiles placed below the slab.

B. Surface Water Drainage

Surface water should be drained away from a building by sloping the land and otherwise modifying the finish contours to divert water into natural drainage patterns or man-made drains. Gutters can be built into curbing to collect water from paved areas. In some cases, large paved or landscaped areas need to be sloped to drain inlets or catch basins that connect with storm sewers.

A drain inlet allows storm water to run directly into the storm sewer. A catch basin has a sump built into it so that debris will settle instead of flowing down the sewer. The sump can be cleaned out periodically. Large storm sewer systems require manholes for service access, located wherever the sewer changes direction, or a maximum of 500 feet apart.

5 SITE IMPROVEMENTS

Site improvements include items not connected to the building, such as parking areas, walks, paving, landscaping, sprinkler systems, outdoor lighting, fences, retaining walls, and various types of outdoor furnishings.

A. Paving

Paving is used for parking areas, driveways, and large, hard-surfaced activity areas. Paving is normally constructed of concrete, asphaltic concrete, or unit pavers.

Concrete paving is placed on compacted soil or a gravel bed and is normally reinforced with welded wire fabric to resist temperature stresses. If heavy loading is anticipated, the concrete is often reinforced with standard reinforcing bars. Concrete paving should be a minimum of 5 inches thick, but the actual thickness required depends on the anticipated loading. Concrete paving is poured in sections with joints between the sections. Expansion joints should be located every 20 feet separated with a 1/2-inch premolded joint filler. Construction joints or control joints are placed where separate sections of concrete are poured, and they are intended to control the location of the inevitable minor cracking that occurs in concrete.

Asphaltic concrete paving is a general term that includes several types of bituminous paving. The most common type of asphaltic concrete consists of asphalt cement and graded aggregates. This is laid on the base and rolled and compacted while still hot. Cold-laid asphalt is the same except that cold liquid asphalt is used. Before the asphalt is applied, a sub-base of coarse gravel is overlaid with finer aggregate and compacted and rolled to the desired grade. The asphalt is laid over this base to a depth of two or three inches.

Unit pavers can be any of a number of types of materials, including concrete, brick, granite, and flagstone. Unit pavers should be laid on a level, compacted base of sand over crushed gravel. For greater stability they may also be laid on a bituminous setting bed over a poured concrete slab.

B. Walks

Walks are common site improvements. Like paving, walks can be constructed of a number of materials, but the most common is concrete because of its strength and durability. Concrete walks should be laid over a gravel subbase with control joints every 5 feet and expansion joints every 20 feet. These are usually 4 inches thick. Additionally, expansion joints should be located where walks abut buildings, curbs, paving, and other permanent structures.

SAMPLE QUESTIONS

Sample questions for Chapters 13 through 22 are included in Chapter 23.

14 CONCRETE

Concrete is one of the most versatile basic building materials. It is durable, strong, weather resistant, and it can be molded into a wide variety of shapes and finished in a number of ways. It can be used in structural or non-structural applications. Concrete has existed since the Roman empire in one form or another, but in the latter part of this century it has been developed to a highly sophisticated level.

Although concrete has many advantages, its use requires a knowledge of many variables and construction steps. These include formwork, reinforcing, placing, curing, testing, and finishing.

1 FORMWORK

Formwork refers to the system of boards, ties, and bracing required to construct the mold in which wet concrete is placed. Formwork must be strong enough to withstand the weight and pressure created by the wet concrete and easy to erect and remove.

A. Types of Forms

Forms are constructed out of a variety of materials. Unless the concrete is finished in some way, the shape and pattern of the formwork will affect the appearance of the final product. Wood grain, knotholes, joints, and other imperfections in the form will show in their negative image when the form is removed.

Plywood is the most common forming material. It is usually 3/4-inch thick with one side coated with oil, a water-resistant glue, or plastic to prevent water from penetrating the wood and to increase the reusability of the form. Oil on forms also prevents adhesion of the concrete so the forms are easier to remove. The plywood is supported with solid wood framing, which is braced

or shored as required. Figure 14.1 shows two typical wood-framed forms.

Prefabricated steel forms are often used because of their strength and reusability. They are often employed for forming one-way joist systems, waffle slabs, round columns, and other special shapes.

Other types of forms include glass-fiber reinforced plastic, hardboard, and various kinds of proprietary systems. Plastic forms are manufactured with a variety of patterns embedded in them. These patterns are transferred to the concrete and constitute the final surface. Special form liners can also be used to impart a deeply embossed pattern.

For exposed architectural surfaces, a great deal of consideration must be given to the method and design of the formwork because the pattern of joints and form ties will be visible. Joints are often emphasized with rustication strips, continuous pieces of neoprene, wood, or other material that when removed shows a deep reveal in the concrete.

Form ties are metal wires or rods used to hold opposite sides of the form together and also to prevent their collapse. When the forms are removed, the wire remains in the concrete and the excess is twisted or cut off. Some form ties are threaded rods that can be unscrewed and reused. Tie holes are made with cone-shaped heads placed against the concrete form. When these are removed, a deep, round hole is left that allows the tie to be cut off below the surface of the concrete. These holes can remain exposed as a design feature or can be patched with grout.

B. Special Forms

Most formwork is designed and constructed to remain in place until the concrete cures sufficiently to stand

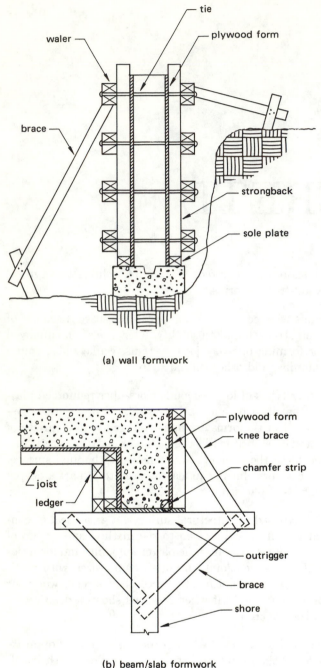

(a) wall formwork

(b) beam/slab formwork

Figure 14.1   Concrete Formwork

on its own. However, one method, called *slip forming*, moves as the concrete cures. Slip forming is used to form continuous surfaces such as tunnels and high-rise building cores. The entire form is constructed along with working platforms and supports for the jacking assembly. The form moves continuously at about 6 to 12 inches per hour. Various types of jacking systems are used to support the form as it moves upward.

Flying forms are large fabricated sections of formwork that are removed once the concrete has cured to be reused in forming an identical section above. They are often used in buildings with highly repetitive units, such as hotels and apartments. After forming the floor for a hotel, for example, the form assembly is slid outside the edge of the building where it is lifted by crane to the story above. Once that floor is poured, the process is repeated.

C. Economy in Formwork

Since one of the biggest expenses for cast-in-place concrete is formwork, the architect can minimize overall cost by following some basic guidelines. To begin with, forms should be reusable as much as possible. This implies uniform bay sizes, beam depths, column widths, opening sizes, and other major elements. Slab thicknesses should be kept constant without offsets, as should walls. Of course, structural requirements will necessitate variations in many elements, but it is often less expensive to use a little more concrete to maintain a uniform dimension than to form offsets.

D. Accuracy Standards

Because of the nature of the material and forming methods, concrete construction cannot be perfect; there are certain tolerances that are industry standards. Construction attached to concrete must be capable of accommodating these tolerances. For columns, piers, and walls, the maximum variation in plumb will be plus or minus 1/4 inch in any 10-foot length. The same tolerance applies for horizontal elements such as ceilings, beam soffits, and slab soffits.

The maximum variation out of plumb for the total height of the structure is 1 inch, while the maximum variation for the total length of the building is plus or minus 3/4 inch. Elevation control points for slabs on grade can vary up to 3/8 inch in any 20-foot bay and plus or minus 3/4 inch for the total length of the structure. However, for finished slabs the tolerance is 1/8 inch in 10 feet for a Class A slab, 1/4 inch in 10 feet for a Class B slab, and 1/4 inch in 2 feet for a Class C slab.

2   REINFORCEMENT

Concrete is very strong in compression but weak in tension. As a result, reinforcing is required to resist the tensile stresses in beams, slabs, and columns, and to reduce the size of columns. There are two types of reinforcing steel for cast-in-place concrete: deformed bars and welded wire fabric for reinforcement of slabs.

A. Reinforcing Bars

Reinforcing bars, often called *rebars*, are available in diameters from 3/8 inch to 2 1/4 inches in 1/8-inch increments up to 1 3/8 inches, and then two special large sizes of 1 3/4 inches and 2 1/4 inches. Bars are designated by numbers which represent the number of 1/8-inch increments in the nominal diameter of the bar. Thus, a no. 6 bar is 6/8 inch in diameter, or 3/4 inch.

Because reinforcing steel and concrete must be bonded together to provide maximum strength, rebars are deformed to provide a mechanical interlocking of the two materials. Additional bonding is provided by the chemical adhesion of the concrete to steel and by the normal roughness of the steel. There are several different types of deformation patterns depending on the mill that manufactures the bar, but they all serve the same purpose.

Rebars come in two common grades: grade 40 and grade 60. Grades 50 and 75 are also sometimes available. These numbers refer to the yield strengths in kips per square inch. Grade 60 is the type most used in construction. Wire for prestressing has a much higher tensile strength, up to 250 or 270 kips per square inch. Rebars are classified as axle, rail, and billet, with billet the most commonly used.

In order to protect the reinforcing, there are certain minimum clearances between the steel and the exposed face of the concrete under various conditions. These are listed in Table 14.1. There are also minimum clearances between rebars to allow the coarse aggregate to pass through as the concrete is poured.

Table 14.1
Minimum Concrete Protection for Reinforcement
(distance from edge of rebar to face of concrete)

location	distance
surfaces not exposed directly to the weather or ground:	
slabs and walls	3/4 inch
beams and columns	1 1/2 inches
surfaces exposed to the weather or in contact with the ground:	
no. 5 bars and smaller	1 1/2 inches
larger than no. 5 bars	2 inches
concrete poured directly on the ground	3 inches

B. Welded Wire Fabric

Welded wire fabric is used for temperature reinforcement in slabs and consists of cold-drawn steel wires, at right angles to each other, which are welded at their intersections. The wires are usually in a square pattern with spacings of 4 and 6 inches. Designations for welded wire fabric consist of the size first and then the gage.

A new system is currently replacing the old system but both are in use. The old system uses a designation grid size and gage. For example, 6×6—10/10 means the grid is 6 inches by 6 inches and both wires are 10 gage. The new designation for the same material is 6×6—$W1.4 \times 1.4$. The first part is still the grid size, but the gage designation has been replaced with a letter, either W or D to indicate smooth (W) or deformed (D), and a number which gives the cross-sectional wire area in hundredths of a square inch. The 1.4 in the example means that the area is 1.4 hundredths of a square inch, or 0.014 in^2.

C. Accessories

Before concrete is poured into the forms, various types of embedded items must be placed in addition to the reinforcing. These include welding plates for attachment of steel and other structural members, electrical boxes and conduit, sleeves for pipes to pass through the concrete, and other types of anchoring devices for suspended components and finish walls. Embedded items must be accurately placed and are temporarily held in position by wiring to the reinforcing, with nails, or with other proprietary devices until secured by the concrete.

Other accessories are used to hold the reinforcing bars in their proper location. Intersecting reinforcing bars are wired together and held in place with spacers in walls and chairs in slabs. *Chairs* are metal wire devices placed on the form to hold the rebars above the bottom of the form at the proper distance.

3 CONCRETE MATERIALS

A. Basic Components

Concrete is a combination of cement, fine and coarse aggregates, and water mixed in the proper portions and allowed to cure to form a hard, durable material. In addition, admixtures are used to impart particular qualities to the mix. Since the strength of concrete depends on the materials and their proportions, it is important to understand the relationship between the constituent parts.

Cement is the binding agent in concrete. It chemically interacts with water to form a paste that binds the other aggregate particles together in a solid mass. Portland cement is a finely powdered material manufactured primarily from limestones and clays or shales. It is supplied in bulk or in 94-pound bags containing one cubic foot.

There are five different types of cement, all used for specific purposes. Type I is called *standard* or *normal* cement, and is used for most general construction where the other types are not needed. Type II is called *modified*, and is used in places where a modest amount of sulfate resistance is needed and where the heat of hydration needs to be controlled, such as in dams or other massive structures. Type III is *high-early-strength* and is used where a quick set is needed. Type III also has a higher heat of hydration, so it is suitable for cold weather concreting. Type IV, used in massive structures to minimize cracking, is called *low heat*, and is very slow setting. Type V is *sulfate resisting* and is used for structures that will be exposed to water or soil with a high alkaline content.

Although water is required for *hydration* (the chemical hardening of concrete) and to make it possible to mix and place the concrete into forms, too much water can decrease its strength. This is because excess water not used in the chemical process remains in the paste and forms pores that cannot resist compressive forces. Generally, for complete hydration to occur, an amount of water equal to 25 percent of the weight of the cement is required. An extra 10 to 15 percent or more is required to make a workable mix. The water itself must be potable, or drinkable, to ensure that it is free of any foreign matter that could interfere with adhesion of the aggregates to the cement paste.

For most concrete mixes the minimum water-cement ratio is about 0.35 to 0.40 by weight. Based on the weight of water, this works out to about 4 to 4.5 gallons of water per 94-pound sack of cement. Because of the way water and cement interact, the water-cement ratio is the most critical factor in determining the strength of concrete. For a given mix, there should be just enough water to give a workable mix without being excessive.

Aggregates consist of coarse and fine aggregates; *fine aggregates* are those that pass through a No. 4 sieve (one with four openings per linear inch). Since cement is the most expensive component of concrete, the best mix is one that uses a combination of aggregate sizes that fill most of the volume with a minimum amount of cement while still achieving the desired strength. Typically, aggregates occupy about 70 to 75 percent of the total volume of the concrete.

Generally, aggregates are sand and gravel, but others are used. Materials such as expanded clays, slags, and shales are used for lightweight structural concrete. Pumice or cinders are used for insulating concretes. While standard stone concrete weighs about 150 pounds per cubic foot, lightweight mixes can range from 50 pounds per cubic foot for insulating concretes to 120 pounds per cubic foot for lightweight structural concrete.

The size of coarse aggregates is determined by the size of the forms and the spacing between the reinforcing. In most instances, it should not be larger than three-fourths of the smallest distance between reinforcing bars nor larger than one-fifth of the smallest dimension of forms, nor more than one-third of the depth of slabs.

B. Proportioning

Several methods are used to specify the proportions of the concrete mix. One is to define the ratio of cement to sand to gravel by weight using three numbers such as 1:2:4, which means one part cement, 2 parts sand, and 4 parts gravel. In addition, the amount of water must also be specified. Another method is to specify the weight of materials, including water, per 94-pound bag of cement. Yet another method, useful for large batch quantities, is to define the weight of the materials needed to make up one cubic yard of concrete.

The strength of the final mix is specified by the compressive strength of the concrete after it has cured and hardened for 28 days—this is known as the *design strength* of concrete. Typical specified design strengths, indicated with the symbol, f'_c, are 2000 psi, 3000 psi (one of the most common), and 4000 psi. Higher strengths, up to 12,000 psi, are now available for special applications but are more expensive than the standard mixes.

C. Admixtures

Admixtures are chemicals or other material added to concrete to impart certain qualities. Admixtures are used to speed hydration, retard hardening, improve workability, add color, improve durability, and for a variety of other purposes. Some of the more common admixtures include:

- *Air-entraining agents* form tiny, dispersed bubbles in the concrete. These agents increase the workability and durability of the concrete and improve its resistance to freezing and thawing cycles. They also help reduce segregation of the components during placing of the mix into forms.

- *Accelerators* speed up the hydration of the cement so the concrete achieves strength faster. This allows for faster construction and reduces the length of time needed for protection in cold weather.

- *Plasticizers* reduce the amount of water needed while maintaining the necessary consistency for correct placement and compaction. Reducing the water, of course, makes it possible to mix higher-strength concrete.

D. Poured Gypsum Decks

Poured gypsum decks are used for roofs and are similar to concrete in that a liquid mixture is poured on reinforcing material. In typical gypsum deck construction, purlins support fiber plank or rigid insulation. Wire mesh reinforcing is placed over this and gypsum poured on the assembly to a minimum depth of 2 1/2 inches. Gypsum provides a highly fire-resistant roof deck.

Precast gypsum planks with tongue and groove edges are also available in 2- and 4-inch thicknesses. They are reinforced with wire fabric and span up to 10 feet.

4 CURING AND TESTING

A. Curing Concrete

Since concrete hardens and gains strength by curing through chemical reaction between the water and the cement rather than by drying, it is critical that the proper conditions of moisture and temperature be maintained for at least seven days and up to two weeks for critical work. If concrete dries out too fast, it can lose strength, up to 30 percent or more in some instances. With high-early-strength cements, of course, the time can be reduced. This is because concrete gains about 70 percent of its strength during the first week of curing and the final 28-day design strength depends on the initial curing conditions.

There are many techniques for maintaining proper moisture levels, including covering with plastic, using sealing compounds, or by continually sprinkling the surfaces with water.

Concrete must also be kept from freezing while curing or it will lose strength, sometimes as much as half. Since concrete produces heat while it cures (known as *heat of hydration*) it is often sufficient to cover the fresh material with insulated plastic sheets for a few days.

In very cold conditions, Type III cement may be used and external heat supplied. In addition, the water and aggregate may be heated prior to mixing.

B. Testing Concrete

Because there are so many variables in concrete construction, the material must be continually tested at various stages to maintain quality. There are three tests that the architect must be familiar with: the slump test, the cylinder test, and the core cylinder test.

The *slump test* measures the consistency of the concrete, usually at the job site. In this test, concrete is placed in a 12-inch-high truncated cone, 8 inches at the base and 4 inches at the top. It is compacted by hand with a rod and then the mold is removed from the concrete and placed next to it. The distance the concrete slumps from the original 12-inch height is then measured in inches. The amount of slump desired depends on how the concrete is going to be used, but it is typically in the range of 2 to 6 inches. Too much slump indicates excessive water in the mix and a very small slump indicates the mixture will be difficult to place properly.

The *cylinder test* measures compressive strength. As the concrete is being placed, samples are put in cylinder molds, 6 inches in diameter and 12 inches high, and are moist cured and tested in the laboratory according to standardized procedures. The compressive strength in pounds per square inch is calculated and compared with the f'_c value used in the design of the structure. Cylinders are tested at a specified number of days, normally 7 and 28 days. Seven-day tests are usually about 60 to 70 percent of the 28-day strength.

The *core cylinder test* is used when a portion of the structure is in place and cured but needs to be tested. A cylinder is drilled out of the concrete and tested in the laboratory to determine its compressive strength.

Other tests include the Kelly ball test and the K-slump test. In the *Kelly ball test*, also known as the *ball penetration test*, a hemispheric mass of steel with a calibrated stem is dropped onto a slab of freshly laid concrete. The amount of penetration of the ball into the concrete is measured and compared to one-half the values of the slump test.

The *K-slump test* uses a 3/4-inch tube that contains a floating scale. The tube is placed on the wet concrete and the scale is pushed into the mixture and released. The distance the scale floats out is read directly and is a measure of the consistency of the concrete, comparable to the slump.

5   PLACING AND FINISHING

A. Concrete Placement

Placing concrete involves several steps from transporting the material from the truck or mixer to the forms. First, it must be conveyed to the formwork. This is done with bottom-dump buckets, by pumping, or in small buggies or wheelbarrows. Which method is used depends on the available equipment, the quantity of concrete, and the physical size and layout of the job. Concrete can even be placed underwater with a long, cylindrical steel chute called a *tremie*.

Once at the formwork the concrete must be placed in such a way as to avoid *segregation*, which is the separation of the aggregates, water, and sand from each other. Dropping concrete long distances from the conveying device to the forms is one of the typical causes of segregation. Typically, 5 feet is the maximum distance that concrete should be dropped. Excessive lateral movement of the concrete in forms or slab work is another practice that should be minimized.

After placement, the concrete must be compacted to make sure the wet material has flowed into all the forms and around all of the rebars, that it has made complete contact with the steel, and to prevent *honeycombing*, the formation of air pockets within the concrete and next to the forms. For small jobs, hand compaction can be used. More typically, it is done with vibrators.

B. As-Cast Finishes

Concrete can be finished in a variety of ways. The simplest is to leave the concrete as it is when the forms are removed. A *rough form finish* shows the pattern of the formwork and joints between forms. Defects and tie holes may be left unfinished or finished. This is the roughest finish and is usually used for concrete that will not be visible.

Smooth form finish is similar, but smooth forms of wood, metal, or hardboard are used, and joints and tie holes are planned so they are symmetrical. Any fins left from concrete seeping into joints between forms are removed.

C. Architectural Finishes

Architectural finishes are used where concrete will be exposed and appearance is a consideration. There are several varieties of these finishes:

- *Form liner:* the concrete is shaped with liners of plastic, wood, or metal. Parallel rib liners are a common type. Joints and form tie holes are treated as desired, either left exposed or patched.

- *Scrubbed:* the surface of the concrete is wetted and scrubbed with a wire or fiber brush to remove some of the surface mortar and expose the coarse aggregate.

- *Acid wash:* the surface of the concrete is wetted with muriatic acid to expose and bring out the full color of the aggregate.

- *Water jet:* a high-pressure water jet mixed with air is used to remove some of the mortar and expose the aggregate.

D. Tooled and Sandblasted Finishes

Tooled finishes are produced by mechanically modifying the concrete surface.

- *Bush hammering:* a bush-hammered finish gives a rugged, heavy texture by removing a portion of the surface made with form liners. The type of texture depends on the form liner used.

- *Grinding:* this finishing technique smooths out the surface of the concrete. It is similar to terrazzo in appearance.

- *Applied:* applied finishes include the application of other materials, such as stucco, to the concrete.

- *Sandblasted finishes:* these are produced by removing surface material from the concrete. This exposes the fine and coarse aggregate to varying degrees, depending on whether the sandblasted finish is specified as light, medium, or heavy.

E. Rubbed Finishes

- *Smooth:* the surface of the concrete is wetted and rubbed with a carborundum brick to produce a smooth, uniform color and texture.

- *Grout cleaned:* grout is applied over the concrete and smoothed out. This results in a uniform surface with defects concealed.

6   JOINTS AND ACCESSORIES

A. Purposes and Types of Concrete Joints

There are four primary types of concrete joints: control, construction, expansion, and isolation. They all serve different functions and are constructed differently. See Figure 14.2.

(a) control joint

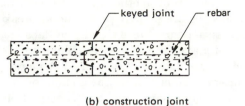

(b) construction joint

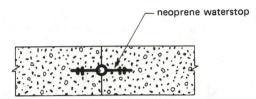

(c) construction joint with waterstop

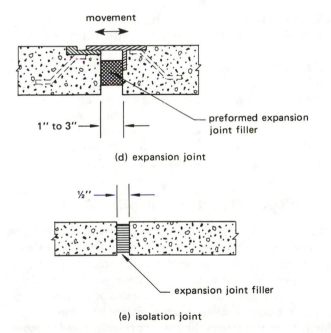

(d) expansion joint

(e) isolation joint

Figure 14.2 Concrete Joints

Control joints create a weak section so that normal temperature and stress cracking occur along the joint instead of at random. They are normally formed by tooling when the concrete is still wet, by sawcutting, or by using premolded sections in the formwork.

Construction joints occur wherever two successive pours occur; that is, a new pour against a cured section of

concrete. Since a construction joint creates a plane of weakness, it should be located at points of minimum shear. Normally, reinforcing extends from one pour to another to tie the two sections together. Construction joints are also a point where water leakage can occur. To prevent this, prefabricated waterstops are inserted in the first pour that extend into the second pour, as shown in Figure 14.2.

Expansion joints allow entire sections of a concrete structure to move independently of one another. The movement can be caused by shrinkage of the concrete or temperature changes. Since the movement can be cyclical, the expansion joint must be capable of moving in two directions. Expansion joints are complex fabrications, portions of which are embedded in the concrete and portions of which are exposed. In most instances, the expansion joint extends through the entire structure so there is no rigid connection between any two components of adjacent building sections.

Isolation joints also allow two adjacent sections to move independently of one another, but they are not as complex as expansion joints. Typically, they simply consist of two separate pours of concrete separated with a premolded joint material. They are often used to separate columns from slabs and slabs from foundations and other types of walls.

B. Inserts

Concrete inserts include a wide range of anchoring devices used to attach other materials and components to concrete construction. For example, *weld plates* are steel plates cast flush with the surface of concrete, to which steel members are welded. The weld plate is attached to a steel anchor that extends into the concrete for positive anchorage. In some cases, the anchors are welded to the reinforcing bars.

7 PRECAST CONCRETE

Precast concrete consists of components cast in separate forms in a place other than their final position. Precast concrete can be cast on site or in fabricating plants where conditions can be more carefully controlled and where work can proceed regardless of the weather.

A. Beams and Columns

Precast concrete beams for buildings are usually rectangular, T-shaped, or L-shaped as shown in Figure 14.3. T-shaped and L-shaped beams allow the floor structure to be flush with the top of the beam and minimize the total depth needed for the structure. Two very efficient sections that are widely used are the single-T and double-T. These combine a deep section for efficient beam action and a wide flange for the floor structure. When T-sections are used, a topping slab is poured to cover the joints and provide a level floor. T-sections are often used with T-shaped and L-shaped beams in precast buildings.

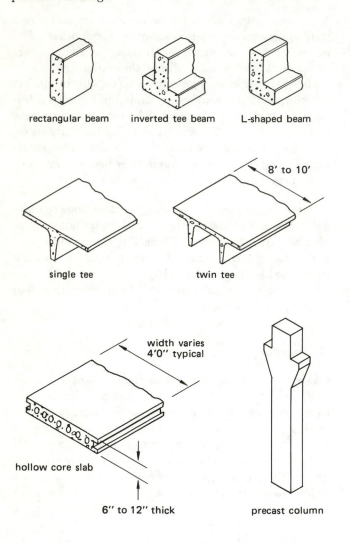

Figure 14.3 Typical Precast Concrete Shapes

Precast columns are usually rectangular in shape, cast with welding plates at the top and bottom. They are often cast with haunches that support beams, as shown in Figure 14.3.

B. Floor and Roof Panels

In addition to precast T-sections that serve as floor and roof structures, simple reinforced concrete slabs are cast for this purpose. For light loads and short spans the slabs may be solid; for heavier loads and longer spans,

hollow, cored slabs are used. These allow the depth of the slab to be increased for more efficient load-carrying capability while still minimizing weight. Cored slabs are 6 to 12 inches thick and normally 4 feet wide. They can span up to 36 feet.

Lift slab construction is a technique for multistory construction in which entire floor sections are cast on the ground, one on top of another around preerected columns. The slabs are poured with a bond breaker between successive pours. Once cured, the slabs are lifted into place with jacks attached to the columns. The slabs are connected to the columns with weld plates. This type of construction minimizes the amount of formwork required and generally reduces total construction time.

C. Wall Panels

Wall panels can be cast in a variety of sizes and shapes. For greatest economy, the number of types of panels and openings should be minimized. Wall panels are generally 5 to 8 inches thick (although they can be thicker) and long enough to span between columns or between beams. If the panels span between beams, greater cost savings can be achieved in multistory buildings by casting panels to span between two floors.

Wall panels can be cast in a precasting plant or on site. A typical method of building is with tilt-up construction. With this procedure the panels are cast in a horizontal position near their final location and lifted into place when sufficiently cured. In many cases the panels are cast directly on the building's floor slab with temporary boards forming the edges. A bond breaker is used to prevent the wall panel from sticking to the casting surface. A bond breaker may be a liquid solution or a sheet of plastic, but liquids result in a better finish.

8 PRECAST, PRESTRESSED CONCRETE

Prestressed concrete consists of members that have internal stresses applied to them before they are subjected to service loads. The prestressing consists of compressive forces applied where the member would normally be in tension. This effectively eliminates or greatly reduces tensile forces that the member is not capable of carrying. In addition to making a more efficient and economical structural section, prestressing reduces cracking and deflection, increases shear strength, and allows longer spans and greater loads. Prestressing is accomplished in one of two ways: pretensioning and post-tensioning.

A. Pretensioning

With this system, concrete members are produced in a precasting plant. High-strength pretensioning stranded cable or wire is draped in forms according to the required stress pattern, and a tensile force is applied. The concrete is then poured and allowed to cure. Once the concrete cures, the cables are cut and the resulting compressive force transferred to the concrete through the bond between cable and concrete.

B. Post-Tensioning

In post-tensioned construction, hollow sleeves or conduits are placed in the forms on the site and concrete is poured around them. Within the sleeves are high-strength steel tendons, which are stressed with hydraulic jacks after the concrete has cured. Once the desired stress has been applied, the ends of the cables are secured to the concrete and the jacks are removed. If the tendons are to be unbonded, no further action is taken. In bonded construction, the sleeves are removed and grout is forced into the space between the tendons and the concrete.

15 MASONRY

Masonry construction is one of the oldest building techniques known to man. It has survived through the centuries because of its many advantages: masonry is durable and strong, it can be formed into a variety of building shapes, and the raw materials are available in most parts of the world. Combined with modern materials such as improved mortars, reinforcing, and flashing, brick remains a timeless material.

In simplest terms, masonry consists of an assembly of relatively small units of stone, burned clay, or other manufactured material held in place with mortar. Traditionally, masonry has been considered a material to be used to support loads in compression, since stone, brick, and mortar have negligible resistance to tensile or bending forces. Horizontal spanning with masonry was always accomplished with some form of arch.

However, with steel reinforcing, high-strength mortars, steel lintels, and the like, brick and unit masonry can be used in an ever wider variety of situations, both horizontally and vertically. Philosophically, however, many designers still feel that the inherent nature of masonry is compressive and it should be used in the traditional way.

1 MORTAR

Mortar is the cementitious material used to hold masonry units together. It must be compatible with the masonry units being used, the strength required, and the environmental conditions.

A. Components of Mortar

Mortar is a mixture of cement, lime, sand, and water. Normally, portland cement is used. Lime is added to plasticize the cement so it is more workable, to add resilience, and to increase the water retention of the mortar. Resilience is important to accommodate movement caused by temperature change and brick swell. Water

retention is important to improve the hydration of the cement as it sets.

Masonry cement is a prepared mixture of portland cement and pulverized limestone. It is not as strong or expensive as portland cement but has greater plasticity. It is suitable for low-rise building veneers and for interior, non–load-bearing applications.

Various other types of cements are available for special applications. One of the most common is non-staining cement, which should be used for marble, limestone, terra cotta, cut stone, and glazed brick.

B. Types of Mortar

There are four basic types of mortar: Type M, S, N, and O. Each has a different proportion of cement, lime, and aggregate, and each has a different compressive strength. These are summarized in Table 15.1. Which mortar is specified depends on the type of masonry unit being used and the conditions of use. Generally, you should never use a mortar that is stronger in compression than is required for the job. In addition, since lime helps retain water in the mortar for hydration, a mortar with a high lime content is appropriate for bricks with a high initial rate of absorption or for summer construction where evaporation is a factor. Table 15.2 summarizes some guidelines for mortar selection.

C. Grout

Grout is similar to mortar, but it is mixed to a pouring consistency and used to fill wall cavities or cores of hollow masonry units and to bond masonry to reinforcement. Grout may be fine or coarse. Coarse grout includes no. 4 aggregate (pea gravel). Fine grout is used when the dimensions of the space in which the grout is placed are less than 2 inches.

Table 15.1
Types of Mortar

cement	type	portland cement	masonry cement			hydrated lime or lime putty	aggregate ratio– measured in a damp, loose condition	min. average 28-day compressive strength
			M	S	N			
cement-lime	M	1	–			1/4		2500 psi
	S	1	–			over 1/4 to 1/2	not less than 2 1/4 and not more than 3	1800 psi
	N	1	–			over 1/2 to 1 1/4	times the sum of the separate volumes of	750 psi
	O	1	–			over 1 1/2 to 2 1/2	cementitious materials	350 psi
masonry cement	M	1	–	–	1	–		2500 psi
	M	–	1	–	–			
	S	1/2	–	–	1	–		1800 psi
	S	–	–	1	–			
	N	–	–	–	1	–		750 psi
	O	–	–	–	1	–		350 psi

Table 15.2
Selection of Mortar

location	building component	mortar type	
		1st choice	alternate
exterior, above grade	load-bearing wall	N	S or M
	non–load-bearing wall	O*	N or S
	parapet wall	N	S
exterior, at or below grade	foundation walls, retaining walls, pavements, walks, manholes	S or M	N
interior	load-bearing walls	N	S or M
	non–load-bearing walls	O	N

* Use Type O mortar only where masonry is unlikely to be frozen when wet or unlikely to be exposed to high winds or other lateral loads.

2 BRICK

A. Types of Brick

A *brick* is a relatively small masonry unit made from burned clay, shale, or a mixture of these materials, which is not less than 75 percent solid. The two basic types of brick are *facing brick* and *building brick* (also called *common brick*). As the name implies, facing brick is used for exposed locations where appearance and uniformity of size are important. Building brick is made without regard to color or special finish.

Building brick is graded according to resistance to exposure: SW (severe weathering), MW (moderate weathering), and NW (negligible weathering). Among other things, these grades reflect the ability of brick to resist freeze-thaw cycles. Facing brick is available in SW and MW grades and is further classified into three types: FBS, FBX, and FBA. FBS is for general use where a wide range of color and variation in sizes are acceptable or required. FBX is used when a high degree of mechanical perfection, narrow color range, and minimal variation in size are required. FBA is non-uniform in color, size, and texture.

There are many sizes of brick, but not all of them are available from all manufacturers. Some typical sizes are shown in Figure 15.1 along with the common terms used to describe the various surfaces. The most common size is manufactured to an actual dimension of 3 5/8 inches thick, 2 1/4 inches high, and 7 5/8 inches long. With a mortar joint of 3/8 inch, this gives a modular size of 4 inches thick and 8 inches long. Three courses equal 8 inches, the same as a standard concrete block course.

B. Brick Coursing

Brick can be laid in a variety of patterns depending on which surface is oriented to the outside and what position it is in. Figure 15.2 illustrates the methods of laying brick courses and the terms used to describe them. (A *course* is one continuous horizontal layer of masonry.)

The method of laying several courses in a wall is called the *bonding pattern*. A brick wall is stronger if the joints do not align and the bricks overlap. Before steel joint reinforcing was used, bonding patterns were a way to accomplish this and to tie several wythes of brick together. A *wythe* is a continuous vertical section of a wall one masonry unit in thickness. For example, a header course was designed to hold a two-wythe wall together, since the length of the brick was as long as the thickness of the double wall.

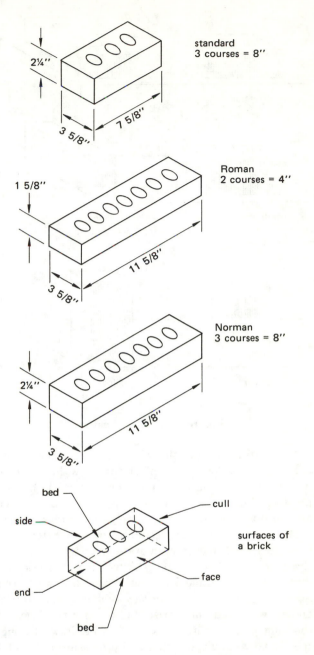

Figure 15.1 Sizes and Faces of Brick

With joint reinforcement, metal wall ties, and veneer walls, bonding patterns are not as important as they once were for structural reasons, although overlapping bricks still form a stronger wall than one with joints aligned. Some common bonding patterns are shown in Figure 15.3.

C. Brick Joints

Joints are a critical part of any masonry wall. Not only does the mortar in the joints hold the entire wall together, it also prevents infiltration of water and air. Bricks should be set in full beds of mortar, on both the bed joints and head joints.

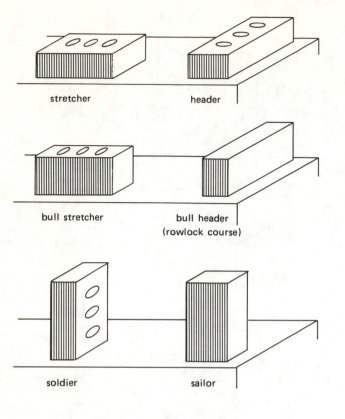

Figure 15.2   Brick Courses

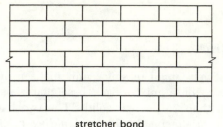

stretcher bond
(also known as running bond)

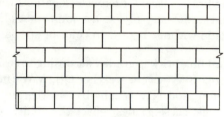

common bond

English bond

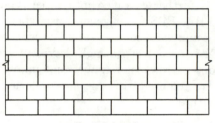

cross bond

Flemish bond

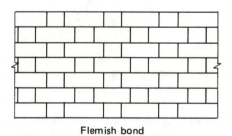

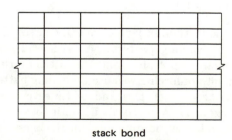

stack bond

Figure 15.3   Brick Bond Patterns

After the brick is laid, the joints must be tooled. *Tooling* imparts a decorative effect to the wall, but more importantly, it makes the joint more watertight by compressing the mortar near the exposed surface. There are various types of mortar joints, as shown in Figure 15.4, but only a few are recommended for exterior use because they shed water more effectively. These are the concave and the V joint. A weather-struck joint is sometimes acceptable for exterior use, but water running down the brick above the joint may not drip off and may instead run horizontally under the brick. If the joint is not tight, the water can be drawn through the joint by capillary action or by pressure differential between the outside and inside of the wall.

In addition to the joints between individual masonry units, there must be horizontal and vertical joints to accommodate building movement caused by differential movement between materials and by temperature changes. If joints are not provided for such movement, cracking can occur in the joints or in the bricks themselves, resulting in water and air leakage and unsightly appearance. In the worst case, stresses can be great enough without joints that the brick can crack and spall off.

There are several types of joints. Construction joints isolate the masonry from through-wall elements such as doors and windows. Control joints accommodate thermal expansion and contraction. Vertical control

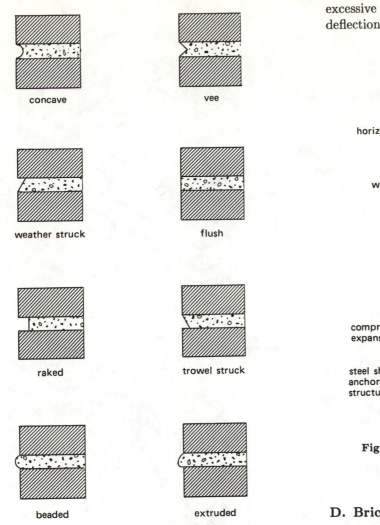

Figure 15.4 Brick Joints

excessive stress from being placed on the brick from the deflection of the angle or beam above.

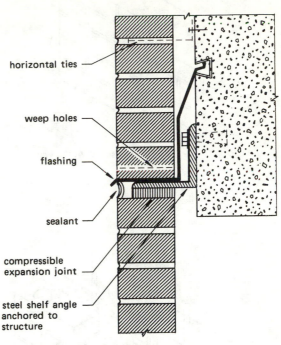

Figure 15.5 Typical Attachment of Brick Facing at Intermediate Floor

joints are constructed by separating two sections of masonry by about 3/8 to 1/2 inch and filling the joint with a backing covered with a sealant. In many cases, a neoprene gasket is placed within the wall between the two sections of masonry. Expansion joints are similar to control joints and accommodate expansion from swelling of the brick. Through-building expansion joints are much larger and are used to completely separate two sections of a building.

Major expansion joints are usually spaced every 100 to 150 feet in large buildings. Expansion and control joints are spaced about every 20 feet and at places where the wall changes direction, height, or thickness.

Horizontal expansion joints should be placed below shelf angles that support intermediate sections of brick and below beams and slabs above brick. One such detail is shown in Figure 15.5. These types of joints prevent

D. Brick Construction

Although brick is a basic, simple construction material, it must be designed, detailed, and installed correctly in order to function properly. There are many types of brick and masonry walls. The more common ones are shown in Figure 15.6.

A *single wythe wall* consists of one layer of brick that acts as either a load-bearing or non–load-bearing wall. Since it is unreinforced, the maximum ratio of unsupported height or length to thickness cannot exceed 20 for a solid wall or 18 for a hollow masonry wall.

A *cavity wall* consists of two wythes of brick separated by an air space. The two sections must be tied together. This is most often done with galvanized metal wall ties or continuous horizontal reinforcement placed 16 inches on center vertically.

A *reinforced grouted wall* also consists of two wythes of brick, but the cavity contains vertical and horizontal reinforcing bars and is completely filled with grout. Compared with cavity walls, grouted walls can carry heavier loads, have higher unsupported heights, and are better able to resist lateral loading.

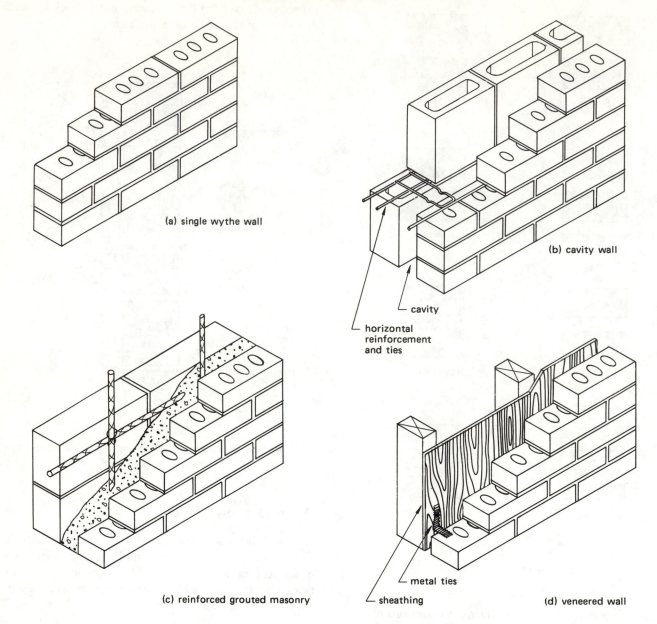

Figure 15.6 Types of Brick Walls

A *veneer wall* is a single wythe of brick attached to some other type of construction, normally a wood-frame wall, as shown in Figure 15.6. In a veneer wall, the masonry is for decorative and weatherproofing purposes, rather than for structural support.

One of the most important considerations in designing a brick wall is water tightness. In order to accomplish this, the brick and mortar must first be properly selected for the climate conditions and loading, as previously discussed. The brick joints must be tooled correctly to shed water and expansion, with control joints located correctly to allow the wall to move without opening up cracks.

Next, the wall must be flashed and finished to prevent water from entering and to allow water that does enter to flow out. See Figure 15.7. The tops of walls and parapets should be flashed and capped with coping, which should extend beyond the face of the wall and include drips to allow water to drain off instead of running down the wall.

Base flashing should be installed at the bottom of the exterior wythe, extend up about 8 to 10 inches, and be set in a reglet or masonry joint in the interior wythe, as shown in Figure 15.7. Weep holes should be located 24 inches on center horizontally in the lowest course of brick to allow any water that penetrates the wall to drip out. This type of detail should be used over windows and at shelf angles, as shown in Figure 15.5.

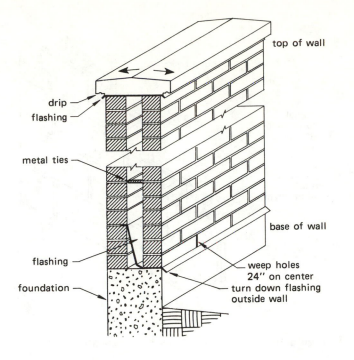

Figure 15.7 Brick Wall Construction

E. Efflorescence

Efflorescence is a white, crystalline deposit of water-soluble salts on the surface of brick masonry. It is caused when water seeps into the masonry and dissolves soluble salts present in the masonry, backup wall, mortar, or anything in contact with the wall. The dissolved salts are brought to the surface of the brick and appear when the water evaporates. Although unsightly, efflorescence is usually not harmful to the brick.

Efflorescence can be prevented or minimized by using materials with little or no soluble salts, by forming tight joints, and by detailing the wall to avoid water penetration. Both brick and mortar can be specified to contain no or limited amounts of soluble salts. If efflorescence does occur, it can be removed by dry brushing or by washing with a 5 percent solution of muriatic acid. A simple water wash can also be used, but this should be done in warm, dry weather so additional moisture is not added to the problem.

F. Cleaning and Restoration

At the completion of a job, brick should be cleaned with a mild 5 to 10 percent solution of muriatic acid in water and then washed off with clean water. A stiff brush can be used to remove loose mortar pieces, stains, and efflorescence.

Restoration of brick is more difficult. Over time, many problems can develop with brick. It can be physically damaged, mortar joints can deteriorate, and the entire surface can become dirty and stained. Damaged units must be carefully removed and replaced with new brick that matches the existing surface as closely as possible. If mortar has fallen out, it must be replaced with a process known as *tuck pointing* or *repointing*. In this process, the mortar in the areas to be redone is removed to about 2 1/2 times the depth of the joint. The joint is then cleaned and wetted with water. New mortar is pressed into the joint with a special tuck pointing tool. High-lime mortar is best and should be applied in layers, each one applied after the previous one becomes thumbprint hard.

There are several ways to clean brick. The one used should be selected for compatibility with the nature of the soiling, the amount of cleaning desired, the surrounding environment in which the cleaning must take place, and the type of brick involved. High-pressure water washing is often effective but can wash away mortar and create swirl marks across the surface of the wall. Simply scrubbing the wall by hand with a brush and water may be required for soft brick. Acid solutions and other types of chemicals may be used to remove stubborn dirt and stains, but this, too, is not always appropriate for some brick and can damage surrounding surfaces. Abrasive cleaning using sand, glass beads, or walnut shells can be used in certain circumstances, but this can erode both brick and mortar.

3   UNIT MASONRY

Unit masonry is a term used to describe various types of building products assembled with mortar, of which brick is one kind. Other types of unit masonry include concrete block, clay tiles, ceramic veneer, stone, terra cotta, gypsum block, and glass block.

A. Concrete Block

Concrete block is the common term for concrete unit masonry, also known as *concrete masonry units (CMU)*. This building product is manufactured with cement, water, and various types of aggregate, including gravel, expanded shale or slate, expanded slag or pumice, and limestone cinders.

Concrete block is classified as hollow, load bearing; solid, load bearing; hollow, non-load bearing; and solid, non-load bearing. Solid units are those that are 75 percent or more solid material in any general cross section.

Hollow units are those with less than 75 percent solid material.

CMU dimensions are based on a nominal 4-inch module with actual dimensions being 3/8 inch less than the nominal dimension to allow for mortar joints. Unit dimensions are referred to by width, height, and then the length. One of the most common sizes is an 8 × 8 × 16 inch unit which is actually 7 5/8 inches wide and high and 15 5/8 inches long. Common thicknesses are 4, 6, 8, 10, and 12 inches and common lengths are 8, 12, and 16 inches. Concrete block is manufactured in a wide variety of shapes to suit particular applications. A few of the most common shapes are shown in Figure 15.8.

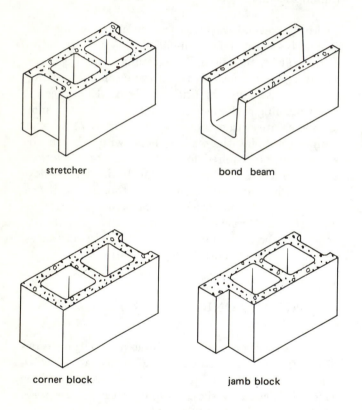

stretcher   bond beam

corner block   jamb block

Figure 15.8 Typical Concrete Block Shapes

Concrete block walls can be either single or double wythe, but they are normally single thickness for greater economy and speed of construction. The cores allow walls to be reinforced and grouted if additional strength is required for vertical or lateral load bearing. As with brick walls, horizontal reinforcing is required every 16 inches on center. Walls can simply be grouted if additional fire or sound resistance is required. Figure 15.9 shows a typical reinforced, grouted concrete masonry wall. It also shows the use of a bond beam at the top of the wall which can serve as a lintel over openings, to provide bearing for floor and roof structure, and to resist lateral loads from floor and roof diaphragms.

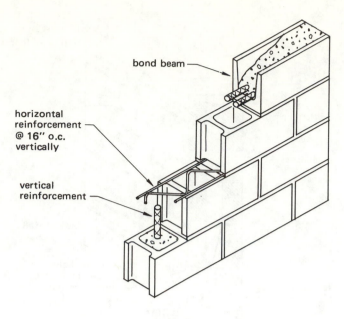

bond beam

horizontal reinforcement @ 16" o.c. vertically

vertical reinforcement

Figure 15.9 Reinforced, Grouted Concrete Masonry Wall

Since most concrete block walls consist of hollow units, it is important to understand equivalent thickness. Equivalent thickness is the solid thickness that would be obtained if the same amount of concrete contained in a hollow unit were recast without core holes. The value is calculated from the actual thickness of the block and the percentage of solid materials.

Example 15.1

What is the equivalent thickness of an 8-inch-thick concrete block that is 60 percent solids?

Actual thickness is 7 5/8 (7.625) inches. Equivalent thickness is then $7.625 \times 0.60 = 4.58$ inches.

Fire ratings for masonry walls are based on this value and the type of material used in the manufacture of the block. Building codes give the required equivalent thicknesses for various hourly fire ratings. The designer must determine whether the thickness and type of concrete block being used meet the required fire rating.

B. Structural Clay Tile

Structural clay tile is made from burned clay and is formed into hollow units with parallel cells. Various sizes are produced in nominal 4-, 6-, and 8-inch widths and 6-, 8-, and 16-inch heights and lengths. Two types are produced: side construction and end construction. Side-construction tile is designed to receive its principal stress at right angles to the axis of the cells and end-construction tile is designed to receive principal stress parallel to the axis of the cells.

Structural clay tile is used for load-bearing masonry walls that will be finished with other materials, as backup for exterior walls, and as non–load-bearing interior partitions. Units are also available with various glazed surfaces appropriate for finished exterior or interior walls.

C. Terra Cotta

Terra cotta is a molded, fired clay tile product used for decorative purposes. It can either be machine made or hand molded in a variety of shapes and sculptured faces, with a natural clay finish or applied glazed finishes. It is installed with corrosive-resistant anchors and mortar.

D. Gypsum Block

Gypsum block or tile is solid or cored units cast of gypsum plaster that are used for non–load-bearing partitions and for fire protection of structural elements. They are available in thicknesses from 1 1/2 inches to 6 inches with a standard face size of 12 inches high and 30 inches long. Gypsum block cannot be used for exterior applications or in areas subject to wetting.

E. Glass Block

Glass block is manufactured as hollow units with clear, textured, or patterned faces. The area inside the block is under a partial vacuum that improves the thermal insulating properties of the material. This property, along with the light-transmitting value and availability of obscuring patterns, makes glass block useful in applications where a combination of light transmission, privacy, and insulation is needed.

Glass blocks are manufactured in a nominal thickness of 4 inches and in face sizes of 6 × 6, 8 × 8, 12 × 12, and 4 × 8 inches. Block walls are laid in stack bond with mortar and horizontal and vertical reinforcement in the joints. Because of the coefficient of expansion of glass, special attention must be paid to providing expansion joints around the perimeter of glass block walls.

Since glass block cannot be load bearing, individual panels are usually limited to about 144 square feet. Each panel must be supported with suitable structure both horizontally and vertically and with expansion joints provided at the structural support points.

4   STONE

Stone is a construction material made from various types of naturally occurring rock. Rock is a geologic term meaning solid and unconsolidated material in the earth's crust, while small, quarried pieces of rock are called stone.

There are three classifications of rock: igneous, sedimentary, and metamorphic. Igneous rocks are formed from the solidification of molten rock. Granite is a type of igneous rock. Sedimentary rocks consist of consolidated products of rock disintegration, sea shells, and various clays and silts. Sandstone and limestone are examples of common sedimentary rocks. Metamorphic rocks are formed of either igneous or sedimentary rocks that have been altered by pressure or intrusion of molten rock or other liquids over a long period of time. Marble and slate are metamorphic rocks.

A. Types of Construction Stone

Stone is one of man's oldest building materials. In the past stone has been used as both a structural material and a finish material; however, with increased cost of stone and the labor to place it, solid stone is seldom used any longer for structural purposes. Stone is now used in the form of thin slabs for exterior and interior finish, as flooring, counter tops, stair treads, and various types of trim pieces in masonry construction. Stone chips are widely used with cement for terrazzo.

Five of the most common stones used in construction include granite, marble, limestone, slate, and sandstone. Table 15.3 lists the most common uses of the various types of stone.

B. Stone Finishes

There is a wide variety of available finishes for the different types of stone used in construction. Each type of stone has its own nomenclature, which is summarized in Table 15.4.

Stone finishes should be selected for the conditions under which they will be used. For example, highly polished surfaces are not appropriate for flooring or stairs where a small amount of water will make them very slippery. Rough finishes may not be appropriate for exterior walls in an environment where dirt and pollution may collect and be difficult to clean off.

C. Stone Coursing

Stone is classified by the way it is shaped and prepared prior to installation. Stone used with little or no shaping is called rubble, stone with slightly shaped edges resulting in vertical joints is called squared stone, while highly shaped stone is called ashlar. Ashlar is also referred to as cut stone and consists of thick pieces of stone.

Table 15.3
Stones Used in Construction

types	uses
granite	exterior wall panels
	interior finish panels
	flooring
	base
	trim
	water courses
	counter tops
	thresholds
	lintels
	window sills
	stair treads
	hearths
	sculpture
	chips for terrazzo
marble	exterior wall panels
	interior finish panels
	flooring
	base
	trim
	toilet partitions
	thresholds
	table tops
	stair treads
	hearths
	window sills
	sculpture
	chips for terrazzo
limestone	exterior wall panels
	coping
	lintels
	sculptured trim
slate	flooring
	stair treads
	roofing
	blackboards
	counter tops
sandstone	flooring
	exterior paving

uncoursed rubble
(random rubble)

uncoursed roughly squared

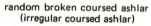

random broken coursed ashlar
(irregular coursed ashlar)

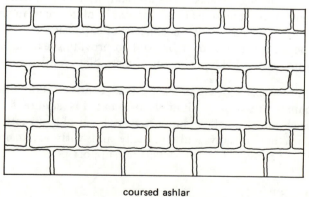

coursed ashlar
(regular coursed ashlar)

Figure 15.10   Stone Patterns

Several methods are used to arrange stones in a wall. They are categorized into range, broken range, and random. *Range masonry* arranges stones in uniform courses for the entire length of the wall. In *broken range masonry*, stones are coursed for short distances. *Random masonry* is devoid of coursing or any attempt to align vertical joints. Figure 15.10 shows some common stone wall patterns.

Table 15.4
Types of Stone Finishes

<u>marble finishes</u>

polished: a glossy surface, which brings out the full color and character of the marble (not recommended for floor finishes)

honed: a satin-smooth surface, with little or no gloss (recommended for commercial floors)

sandblasted: a matte-textured surface with no gloss (recommended for exterior use)

abrasive: a flat, non-reflective surface suitable for exterior use, stair treads, and other non-slip surfaces

wet-sand: a smooth surface suitable for stair treads and other non-slip surfaces

<u>granite finishes</u>

polished: mirror gloss, with sharp reflections

honed: dull sheen, without reflections

fine-rubbed: smooth and free from scratches; no sheen

rubbed: plane surface with occasional slight "trails" or scratches

shot-ground: plane surface with pronounced circular markings or trails having no regular pattern

thermal: plane surface with flame finish applied by mechanically controlled means to ensure uniformity;
(flame) surface coarseness varies, depending upon grain structure of granite

sandblasted: plane surface, slightly pebbled, with occasional slight trails or scratches
fine stipple

sandblasted: coarse plane surface produced by blasting with an abrasive; coarseness varies with type of
coarse stipple preparatory finish and grain structure of granite

8-cut: fine bush-hammered; interrupted parallel markings not over 3/32 inch apart; a corrugated finish

6-cut: medium bush-hammered; markings not more than 1/8 inch apart

4-cut: coarse bush-hammered; markings not more than 7/32 inch apart

sawn: relatively plane surface, with texture ranging from wire sawn (a close approximation of rubbed finish) to shot sawn, with scorings 3/32 inch in depth; gang saws produce parallel scorings; rotary or cirular saws make circular scorings; shot-sawn surfaces are sandblasted to remove all rust stains and iron particles

<u>limestone finishes</u>

smooth finish: machine finish producing a uniform honed finish; uses only select grade or standard grade

plucked: rough texture produced by rough planing the surface of the stone

machine tooled: finish made by cutting parallel, concave grooves in the stone with 4, 6, or 8 grooves to the inch; depth of the grooves range from 1/32 inch–1/16 inch

chat-sawed: coarse, pebbled surface that closely resembles the appearance of sandblasting; sometimes contains shallow saw marks or parallel scores; direction of score or saw marks will be vertical and/or horizontal in the wall unless the direction is specified

shot-sawed: coarse, uneven finish ranging from a pebbled surface to one rippled with irregular, roughly parallel grooves; steel shot used during gang-sawing rusts during process, adding permanent brown tones to the natural color variations

split face: rough, uneven, concave-convex finish produced by splitting action; limits stone sizes to 1 foot 4 inches high by 4 feet 0 inches long; available in ashlar or similar stone veneer only

rock face: similar to split face except the face of the stone has been dressed by machine or by hand to produce bold convex projection along the face of the stone

Another commonly used classification of stone is *veneer stone*, so called because it is applied in relatively thin sheets, approximately 3/4 inch thick, over a structural support system. With improved cutting methods, it is also possible to cut very thin slabs, about 3/8 inch thick, that can be mastic applied to a suitable back-up wall. These tiles are commonly manufactured in small shapes, normally 12 × 12 inches or similar sizes.

D. Stone Construction

Some types of stone work, such as steps, trim, coping, and belt courses, still employ cut stone. However, since the majority of stone wall finishes use veneer, it is important to know how such work is applied and anchored to structural back-up walls. There are many types of metal clamps and anchors used to attach cut stone and veneer stone to concrete, masonry, and steel construction. A few of the common methods of anchoring and forming corner joints are shown in Figures 15.11 and 15.12. In many cases, the space around the anchoring device between the back of the stone and the structural wall is filled with plaster of paris spots to plumb the stone and hold it away from the wall. The joints of stone should be filled with non-staining portland cement mortar.

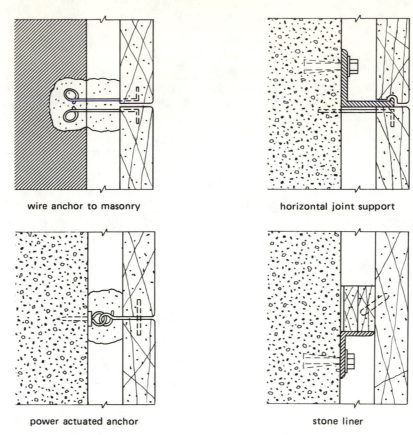

wire anchor to masonry   horizontal joint support

power actuated anchor   stone liner

Figure 15.11   Veneer Stone Anchoring Details

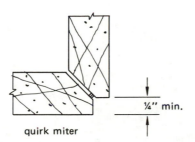

quirk miter

¼" min.

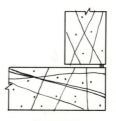

butt joint

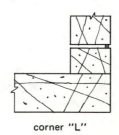

corner "L"

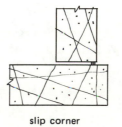

slip corner

Figure 15.12   Veneer Stone Corner Joints

16 METALS

Metals are the most versatile of all construction materials. Although they begin as natural elements, the process of refining, manufacturing, forming, and finishing metals allows an almost unlimited variety of forms and uses. Metals have been used in construction in a limited way for centuries, from the lead pipes of the Romans to the decorative grilles and doors of the English Medieval period. However, it has only been in the last 200 years that metals have seen widespread use in both structural and decorative applications.

1 BASIC MATERIALS AND PROCESSES

In their natural form, metals exist in combination with other elements and substances in metallic ores. *Smelting* is the process of refining the ores to extract the pure metal. Once the basic metal is obtained, it usually undergoes further treatment to eliminate any impurities that might affect its use.

Metals for construction are seldom used in their pure form but are combined with other elements to form alloys. The addition of other substances to the base metal imparts desirable characteristics. For example, adding chromium and nickel to steel makes it corrosion resistant or stainless. It is the ability to form alloys that makes metals so versatile.

A. Fabricating Metals

Fabrication is the process of forming and shaping refined metal into the desired condition. The most basic fabrication method is *casting*, which has been used for centuries. In this process, molten metal is poured into a form where it is allowed to cool and harden into the desired shape. The iron columns used in the nineteenth century were cast shapes. Today, the casting process is still used for decorative shapes, pipe valves, and some hardware.

Rolling is the process of passing metal through rollers to produce the needed shape. Rolling can be done while the metal is hot or cold. Hot rolling tends to eliminate flaws in the metal while cold rolling increases its strength and elastic limit but decreases its ductility. Most of the structural steel shapes such as wide-flange beams and channel sections are hot rolled. Many smaller, relatively thin steel shapes are cold rolled for increased strength. All metals except iron can be formed by this method.

Extruding pushes metal through a die to form a shape. Many aluminum sections are formed this way, especially decorative sections and those used for door and window frames. One advantage to the extruding process is that if a sufficiently large quantity is required, special dies can be made and custom shapes extruded for a particular job.

Drawing is similar to extruding, but the metal is pulled through a die instead of being pushed through. The drawing process usually reduces the size of the piece or changes its shape and also improves the strength and surface qualities of the metal. Drawing is applicable for all metals except iron.

There are also many ways metal can be fabricated with mechanical forming. *Bending* changes the shape of tubes and extruded shapes by passing them through various kinds of rolling machines and presses. *Brake forming* takes plates and sheets of metal and makes successive one-directional bends to fabricate the shape. *Spinning* forms round shapes on a lathe. *Embossing* makes patterns on flat sheets of metal by passing them through a machine with the embossing pattern on rollers.

Part of the fabrication process of many metals includes some type of heat treatment. Thermal treatments are used to change the strength or workability of the material. Although any metal can be heat treated, the process is most often used with steel for various structural purposes.

Annealing is a process in which the metal is reheated and slowly cooled to obtain a more ductile metal, which will improve its machinability and cold forming characteristics.

Quenching involves heating the metal (most often steel) to a certain temperature and then rapidly cooling it by complete submersion in water or some other liquid. This strengthens the steel.

Tempering is similar to quenching but does not involve the rapid cooling. It is also used to improve the strength and workability of steel.

Casehardening produces a hard-surface steel over a relatively softer core.

B. Finishing Metals

There are three general types of metal finishes. Not all of them are used on all metals, but the classification helps in understanding the processes involved. For each metal type, there are particular finishing systems and terminology, which will be discussed in the individual sections concerning each metal.

Mechanical finishes alter the surface of the metal in some way. This may be as simple as the way the metal comes from the final forming process to more refined finishing, such as grinding or buffing.

Chemical finishes are produced by altering the surface of the metal with some type of chemical process. They may simply clean and prepare the surface for other types of finishes or they may protect or color the metal. Anodizing of aluminum is one type of chemical finish in which the metal is immersed in an electrolytic bath and a current applied to the metal. In the process, the finish, which can include various colors, becomes an integral part of the aluminum structure, producing a very durable surface.

Coatings are finishes that consist of applied materials that may be for protection of the metal or for purely decorative reasons. Coatings may be clear or opaque.

In deciding on the type of finish, several considerations should be reviewed. These include appearance, the amount of protection required, first cost, long-term or life-cycle cost, and required maintenance.

C. Joining Metals

There are several methods of joining metals. The selection depends on the type of metal being joined, the working space available for the operation, and the final appearance desired.

All metals can be mechanically joined using accessories such as screws, bolts, and clips. It is common to use high-strength bolts in fastening structural steel. Bolts can also be used to fasten lighter metals such as aluminum and bronze. Bolts are useful when it is necessary to join two dissimilar metals. If potentially damaging galvanic action (electrolysis) might take place between the two metals, a plastic or rubber washer is used to separate them.

Screws can be used to join light gage metal. Self-tapping screws are typically used to fasten metal or other materials to steel studs or other light framing. Screws are also appropriate for securing light gage metals to other substrates, such as wood. However, heavier metals must be tapped with threads before screws can be used.

Welding is the joining of two metals by heating them above their melting point. When they cool, the metals physically form one piece of metal. Welding is commonly used for joining structural steel. Welding is not appropriate for thin metals or situations where appearance is important unless the weld can be ground smooth and finished to match the adjacent metal.

Brazing is the joining of two metals at an intermediate temperature using a non-ferrous filler metal with a melting point above 800 °F but lower than welding. Brazing is usually used for brass, bronze, and some aluminums. It results in a clean joint, although some buffing may be required if a completely smooth joint is desired.

Soldering is the joining of two metals using lead-based or tin-based alloy solder filler metal, which melts below 500 °F.

Metals can also be fastened with adhesives. This method is usually reserved for small trim pieces and sheet stock where strength of bond is not required. Normally, adhesives are used when fastening metals to other substrates such as plywood and particle board.

D. Properties of Metals

In selecting, detailing, and specifying metals, the architect must have a rudimentary knowledge of several of the unique properties of the various metals. These include gage sizing, galvanic action, and coefficients of expansion.

The thickness of large steel members is usually expressed in fractions or decimals of an inch. However, sheet steel and non-ferrous metals of tubing, strips, and sheets are expressed with a gage number. Gage sizing to indicate the thickness of metal started in the early days of the metal industries and was based on the weight of a square foot of a metal. Obviously, the weight would depend on the density of the metal and whether there were any coatings, such as galvanized steel. To confuse matters, different companies had their own gages and different standards have been adopted over the years. As a result, gage is only a rough approximation of a metal's thickness. Even within the same company, the actual thickness may vary even though the gage is the same.

Table 16.1 shows gage numbers and the equivalent thicknesses in decimals of an inch for the various systems currently used. Because of the variations, it is preferable to call out the actual thickness you want in decimals of an inch.

Galvanic action is the corrosion resulting when dissimilar metals come in contact with each other in the presence of an electrolyte such as moisture. In the process, called *electrolysis*, a mild electric current is set up between the two metals, gradually corroding one while the other remains intact.

The following list represents the galvanic series; the metals are listed in the order of their susceptibility to corrosion. The farther apart the metals are from each other on the list, the greater the possibility for corrosion.

- zinc
- aluminum
- steel and iron
- stainless steel
- lead
- tin
- copper alloys
- copper

To avoid galvanic action, you should use identical metals when they must be in contact or separate the metals with non-conducting materials such as neoprene, plastic, or rubber. If these precautions are not possible, you should use metals as close to each other on the galvanic series as possible. Electrolysis is most severe in humid, marine environments where there is an abundance of sea water and less severe in dry climates.

Metals expand and contract with changes in temperature more than many other materials, so it is important to allow for changes in size when designing and detailing metal building components. Table 16.2 lists some of the coefficients of thermal expansion for various metals, along with a few other materials for comparison. Most often, slip joints or expansion joints are provided to accommodate such movement when the building assembly is primarily comprised of metal. When metal is used within other materials, such as an aluminum frame within a concrete opening, allowances must be made for the differential movement.

2 FERROUS METALS

There are two major classifications of metals: ferrous and non-ferrous. *Ferrous* metals are those that contain a substantial amount of iron, *non-ferrous* metals are those that do not. The primary types of ferrous metals used in the construction industry include iron, steel, stainless steel, and other special steel alloys.

A. Wrought and Cast Iron

All ferrous metals contain a majority of iron, some carbon, and other elements in the form of impurities or components mixed with the iron to form an alloy. The amount of carbon and other elements determines the strength, ductility, and other properties of the ferrous metal.

Wrought iron is iron with a very low carbon content (less than about 0.30 percent) and a substantial amount of slag. It is similar in chemical composition to low-carbon steel, but most of the impurities are in the slag, which is mechanically mixed with the iron. Because of its low carbon content, wrought iron is soft, ductile, and resistant to corrosion. Its use in construction is limited to ornamental iron work such as gates, grilles, and fences.

Cast iron is iron with a carbon content above 2 percent. With this high percentage of carbon, it is very hard, but brittle. Cast iron was used extensively in the nineteenth century for columns and beams in such structures as the Crystal Palace, mill buildings in New England, and some of the early commercial buildings in New York City.

Cast iron with a low silicon content is called *white cast iron* and has little use in construction unless it is processed in such a way as to produce malleable iron. Cast iron with a high silicon content is called *grey cast iron* and is the type used for various types of castings such as plumbing valves, pipes, and hardware.

Table 16.1
Comparative Metal Gages

gage no.	aluminum, copper, brass, bronze sheets, strips, and wire; small copper and brass tubing	stainless steel sheets	stainless steel, aluminum, bronze, and large copper and brass tubing; stainless strip	steel sheets
	B&S and AWG	USG	BWG	MSG
3	0.2294	0.2500	0.259	0.2391
4	0.2043	0.2344	0.238	0.2242
5	0.1819	0.2187	0.220	0.2092
6	0.1620	0.2031	0.203	0.1943
7	0.1443	0.1875	0.180	0.1793
8	0.1285	0.1719	0.165	0.1644
9	0.1144	0.1562	0.148	0.1495
10	0.1019	0.1406	0.134	0.1345
11	0.0907	0.1250	0.120	0.1196
12	0.0808	0.1094	0.109	0.1046
13	0.0719	0.0938	0.095	0.0897
14	0.0640	0.0781	0.083	0.0747
15	0.0571	0.0703	0.072	0.0673
16	0.0508	0.0625	0.065	0.0598
17	0.0453	0.0562	0.058	0.0538
18	0.0403	0.0500	0.049	0.0478
19	0.0359	0.0437	0.042	0.0418
20	0.0320	0.0375	0.035	0.0359
21	0.0285	0.0344	0.032	0.0329
22	0.0253	0.0312	0.028	0.0299
23	0.0226	0.0281	0.025	0.0269
24	0.0201	0.0250	0.022	0.0239
25	0.0179	0.0219	0.020	0.0209
26	0.0159	0.0187	0.018	0.0179
27	0.0142	0.0172	0.016	0.0164
28	0.0126	0.0156	0.014	0.0149
29	0.0113	0.0141	0.013	0.0135
30	0.0100	0.0125	0.012	0.0120

B & S = Brown and Sharp
AWG = American Wire Gage
USG = United States Standard Gage
BWG = Birmingham Wire Gage
MSG = Manufacturer's Standard Gage

Table 16.2
Coefficients of Thermal Expansion for Metals
Temperature Range 68° – 212°

metal	coefficient of expansion
stainless steel, 430	5.8×10^{-6} in/°F
structural steel	6.7
nickel silver, alloy 745	9.1
copper, alloy 110	9.4
stainless steel, 304	9.6
commercial bronze, alloy 220	10.2
red brass, alloy 230	10.2
Muntz metal, alloy 280	11.0
architectural bronze, alloy 385	11.6
aluminum	12.9
lead	15.9
other materials	
wood	2.5
glass	5.1
concrete	6.5

B. Steel

Steel is one of the most widely used metals because of its many advantages, which include high strength, ductility, uniformity of manufacture, variety of shapes and sizes, and ease and speed of erection. *Ductility* of steel is a property that allows it to withstand excessive deformations due to high tensile stresses without failure. This property makes it useful for earthquake-resistant structures. Steel is used in a variety of structural and non-structural applications, including columns, beams, concrete reinforcement, fasteners of all types, curtain wall panels, interior finish panels and trim, pipes, flashing, electrical conduit, among many others.

Because steel is manufactured under carefully controlled conditions, the composition, size, and strength can be uniformly predicted. Therefore, structures do not have to be overdesigned to compensate for manufacturing or erection variables as with concrete or timber.

In spite of the advantages, however, steel does have properties that must be accounted for. Most notable are its reduction in strength when subjected to fire and its tendency to corrode in the presence of moisture. Steel itself does not burn, but it deforms when exposed to high temperatures. As a result, steel must be protected with fire-resistant materials, such as sprayed-on cementitious material, gypsum board, or concrete. This adds to the overall cost but is usually justified when the many advantages are considered.

As with any ferrous material, steel will rust and otherwise corrode if not protected. This can be accomplished by including other elements in the steel to resist corrosion, such as with stainless steel, or by covering it with paint or some other type of protective coating.

Steel is composed primarily of iron with small amounts of carbon and other elements that are part of the alloy, either as impurities left over from manufacturing or deliberately added to impart certain desired qualities to the alloy. In medium-carbon steel used in construction, these other elements include manganese (from 0.5 to 1.0 percent), silicon (from 0.25 to 0.75 percent), phosphorus, and sulfur. Phosphorus and sulfur in excessive amounts are harmful because they affect weldability and make steel brittle.

The percentage of carbon present affects the strength and ductility of steel. As carbon is added, the strength increases but the ductility decreases. *Low-carbon* steel contains from 0.06 to 0.30 percent carbon, *medium-carbon* steel has from 0.30 to 0.50 percent of the element, and *high-carbon* steel contains from 0.50 to 0.80 percent carbon. *Standard structural* steel has from 0.20 to 0.50 percent carbon.

The most common type of steel for structural use is ASTM A36, which means that the steel is manufactured according to the American Society for Testing and Materials (ASTM) specification number A36. The yield point for this steel is 36 kips per square inch (ksi). Other high-strength steels include A242, A440, and A441 steel, which have yield points of 46 ksi or 50 ksi.

C. Stainless Steel

Stainless steel is a steel alloy containing a minimum of 11 percent chromium. In addition, nickel is often added to increase the corrosion resistance and improve cold workability. Additional trace elements such as manganese, molybdenum, and aluminum are added to impart certain characteristics.

Stainless steel is highly corrosion resistant and stronger than other architectural metals. Its resistance to corrosion results from the formation of a chromium oxide film on the surface of the metal. If the film is scratched or otherwise damaged it will re-form as the metal is exposed to oxygen in the air.

Of the nearly forty types of stainless steel produced, only eight are used for building purposes, six for products, and two for fasteners. They are labeled by number designation of the American Iron and Steel Institute (AISI) and include the following, which are the most commonly used in construction:

- *Type 302:* this contains 18 percent chromium and 8 percent nickel and has traditionally been one of the most widely used stainless steel types. It is highly resistant to corrosion, very strong and hard, and can be easily fabricated by all standard techniques.

- *Type 304:* type 304 has largely replaced type 302 for architectural uses because of its improved weldability. Its other properties are identical to 302.

- *Type 301:* this alloy is similar to type 302, but with slightly smaller amounts of chromium and nickel. It is still very corrosion resistant. Its advantage is its improved work hardening properties, which can result in very high tensile strengths.

- *Type 316:* for extreme corrosive environments such as industrial plants and marine locations, this type is often used. It has a higher percentage of nickel than the other alloys and includes molybdenum.

- *Type 430:* this type does not contain any nickel so is less corrosion resistant than the other types. Its use is generally limited to interior applications.

Stainless steel is available in a variety of forms including sheets, wire, bars, and plates. Structural shapes of H sections, channels, tees, and angles are also available as are custom extrusions. It can be finished in a variety of ways, including mechanical and coatings.

The most common polished finishes for architectural work include:

- *No. 3 finish:* an intermediate, dull finish, coarser than No. 4.

- *No. 4 finish:* a general-purpose polished finish which is dull and prevents mirror reflection. It is one of the most frequently used architectural finishes.

- *No. 6 finish:* a dull satin finish.

- *No. 7 finish:* a highly reflective polished surface.

- *No. 8 finish:* the most reflective finish, used for mirrors and reflectors. It is seldom used for general architectural applications; a No. 7 finish is usually used instead.

There are also patterned finishes available that are produced by passing a sheet between patterned rollers. Color coatings are also available. Organic coatings consist of acrylic or other plastic-based enamels, which are fairly elastic, that can be applied to the metal prior to forming. Inorganic coatings such as porcelain enamel are less elastic but add color to the metal.

D. Other Alloy Steels

Various elements can be added to steel to impart certain qualities. In addition to stainless steel as described above, many types of alloy structural steel are produced, which are designated by specification numbers of the American Society of Testing and Materials (ASTM).

ASTM A36 is the most common type of structural steel. It has a minimum yield point of 36,000 pounds per square inch and a carbon content from 0.25 to 0.29 percent. ASTM A440 is a high-strength structural steel used for bolted or riveted structures. ASTM A441 is a high-strength, low-alloy manganese vanadium steel intended for welded construction.

Weathering steel is an alloy that contains a small amount of copper. When exposed to moisture in the air or from rain, it develops a protective oxide coating with a distinctive sepia-colored finish. It is used in structures where it is difficult to maintain the steel, or it is used simply for its appearance. However, since small amounts of oxide are carried off by rain, structures using weathering steel should be detailed so the runoff does not stain other materials.

3   NON-FERROUS METALS

Non-ferrous metals are those that do not contain iron. The types most often used in construction include aluminum, copper, and copper alloys such as bronze and brass. Other non-ferrous metals such as zinc, lead, and gold are of limited use in their pure state or are used in conjunction with other metals and materials.

A. Aluminum

Aluminum is an abundant element. The primary source of aluminum is bauxite, which is hydrated oxide of aluminum and iron with small amounts of silicon. Aluminum by itself is soft and weak; however, alloying it with manganese, zinc, magnesium, and copper improves its strength and hardness.

Aluminum is used in a wide variety of applications including structure, wall panels, curtain walls, window and door frames, and other decorative uses. In most uses, its high strength-to-weight ratio makes aluminum a desirable building material. It can be formed by casting, drawing, and rolling, although it is most often formed by extruding.

Aluminum can be finished mechanically, chemically, and with coatings. Mechanical finishes include:

- *Buffed finishes:* smooth specular and specular.

- *Directional textured finishes* (satin sheen with tiny, parallel scratches): fine satin, medium satin, coarse satin, hand rubbed, and brushed.

- *Non-directional textured finishes* (formed by abrasion methods, not applicable to thicknesses under 1/4 inch): extra-fine matte, fine matte, medium matte, coarse matte, fine shot blast, medium shot blast, coarse shot blast.

- *Patterned finishes:* formed by rollers and other methods.

Chemical finishes for aluminum are usually an intermediate process for some other final finish such as cleaning, etching, or preparing for some other coating.

Coating finishes for aluminum include the most familiar *anodizing process*, which is an electro-chemical process that deposits an integral coating on the metal. It is called an anodic coating and can include the familiar silvery color of aluminum or a number of colors in the black and brown ranges. The problem with this finish is that it can be scratched.

Other finishes include impregnated color coatings such as baked enamel, vitreous coatings, and laminated coatings.

B. Copper and Copper Alloys

Copper is widely used in construction because of its resistance to corrosion, its workability, and its high electrical conductivity. The two primary alloys of copper are bronze and brass. Bronze, by definition, is an alloy of copper and tin, while brass is an alloy of copper and zinc. However, traditional nomenclature calls many true brasses by the name bronze. The confusion is clarified by referring to the alloys by their standard designation numbers developed by the Copper Development Association (CDA). Table 16.3 lists some of the alloys used in construction, including their number designations and common names, as well as their nominal compositions.

Copper and copper alloys are used in a variety of applications. Of course, copper is used for electrical wiring because of its high electrical conductivity. The copper alloys are also used for hardware, curtain walls, piping, gutters, roofing, window and door frames, wall panels, railings, and many other ornamental purposes.

Table 16.3
Composition and Description of Copper Alloys

alloy #	name	nominal composition
110	copper	99.9% copper
220	commercial bronze	90% copper 10% zinc
230	red brass	85% copper 15% zinc
260	cartridge brass	70% copper 30% zinc
280	Muntz metal	60% copper 40% zinc
385	architectural bronze	57% copper 40% zinc 3% lead
655	silicon bronze	97% copper 3% silicon
745	nickel silver	65% copper 25% zinc 10% nickel

Copper and copper alloys can be formed by casting, rolling, bending, brake forming, extrusion, spinning, and several other methods. They are joined by mechanical fasteners, brazing, and adhesive bonding.

As with aluminum, copper alloys can be finished several ways using the three methods of mechanical finishes, chemical finishes, and coatings.

Mechanical finishes include: buffed, directional textured (in a variety of grain sizes), non-directional textured, and patterned.

Chemical processing is usually used as an intermediate step in a total finishing process, but it can also be used to color the copper alloy.

Coatings can involve clear organic coatings, metallics, and oils and waxes. Although one of the advantages of copper, brass, and bronze is their ability to resist corrosion, if left unprotected many of the alloys develop a patina which is very different in color from the original finish of the metal. The distinctive green color of aged copper is the most notable example. In some cases, this is undesirable, especially in interior applications. To prevent this, various types of thin, clear organic coatings can be applied to the metal. In other situations, a

coat of oil or wax can bring out the rich luster of the
metal, although continued maintenance is required.

One special alloy, used primarily for roofing, is *Monel
metal* (a trade name), which is a combination of copper
and nickel with small amounts of other elements. It is
also highly resistant to corrosion and is easily worked.

C. Miscellaneous Non-Ferrous Metals

Zinc is resistant to corrosion and is sometimes used
for sheet roofing and flashing. Zinc fasteners are also
made. The metal is more commonly used to coat steel
to produce galvanized steel.

Lead is also resistant to corrosion and is occasionally
used to cover complex roofing shapes because it is very
easy to form around irregularities. However, its density makes it ideal for acoustical insulation, vibration
control, and radiation shielding. An alloy of 75 percent
lead and 25 percent tin can be used to plate steel for
roofing. This is known as *terneplate*.

4 STRUCTURAL METALS

The two metals used in structural applications are steel
and aluminum, although steel is by far the most common. The structural use of aluminum is limited to small
structures or minor portions of structures. Steel is used
for beams, columns, and plates; in light gage framing
such as steel studs; for floor and roof decking; as prefabricated truss joists; and for many types of fasteners.

Structural steel comes in a variety of shapes, sizes, and
weights, giving the designer a great deal of flexibility in
selecting an economical member that is geometrically
correct for any given situation. Figure 16.1 shows the
most common shapes of structural steel.

Wide-flange members are H-shaped sections used for
both beams and columns. They are called wide flange
because the width of the flange is greater than that of
standard I-beams. Many of the wide-flange shapes are
particularly suited for columns because the width of the
flange is very nearly equal to the depth of the section
so they have about the same rigidity in both axes.

Wide-flange sections are designated with the letter W
followed by the nominal depth in inches and the weight
in pounds per linear foot. For example, a W 18 × 85
is a wide flange nominally 18 inches deep and weighing
85 pounds per linear foot. Because of the way these
sections are rolled in the mill, the actual depth varies
slightly from the nominal depth.

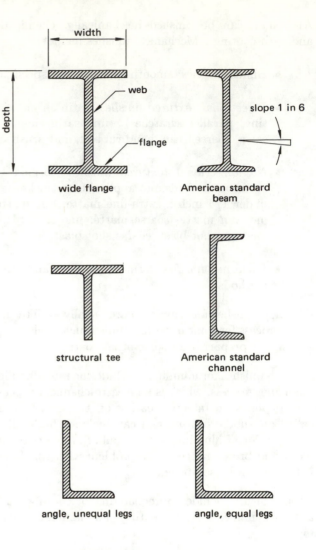

Figure 16.1 Structural Steel Shapes

American Standard I-beams have a relatively narrow
flange width in relation to their depth, and the inside
face of the flanges have a slope of one in six. Unlike the
wide flanges, the actual depth of an I-beam in any size
group is also the nominal depth. The designation of
depth and weight per foot for these sections is preceded
with the letter S. These sections are usually used for
beams only.

American Standard channel sections have a flange on
one side of the web only and are designated with the
letter C followed by the depth and weight per foot. Like
the American Standard I-beams, the depth is constant
for any size group; extra weight is added by increasing the thickness of the web and the inside face of the
flanges. Channel sections are typically used to frame
openings, to form stair stringers, or in other applications where a flush side is required. They are seldom
used by themselves for beams or columns because they
tend to buckle due to their asymmetrical shape.

Structural tees are made by cutting either a wide-flange section or I-beam in half. If cut from a wide-flange section, a tee is given the prefix designation WT and, if cut from an American Standard I-beam, it is given the designation ST. A WT 9 × 57, for example, is cut from a W 18 × 114. Because they are symmetrical about one axis and have an open flange, tees are often used for chords of steel trusses.

Steel angles are available either with equal or unequal legs. They are designated by the letter L followed by the lengths of the angles and then followed by the thickness of the legs. Angles are used in pairs for members for steel trusses or singly as lintels in a variety of applications. They are also used for miscellaneous bracing of other structural members.

Square and rectangular tube sections and round pipe are also available. These are often used for light columns and as members of large trusses or space frames. Structural tubing of various sizes is available in several different wall thicknesses, while structural pipe is available in standard weight, extra strong, and double-extra strong. Each of the three weights has a standard wall thickness depending on the size. Pipe is designated by its nominal diameter, although the actual outside dimension is slightly larger, while the size designation for square or rectangular tubing refers to its actual outside dimensions.

Finally, steel is available in bars and plates. Bars are considered any rectangular section 6 inches or less in width with a thickness of 0.203 inches and greater or sections 6 to 8 inches in width with a thickness of 0.230 and greater.

Plates are considered any section over 8 inches in width with a thickness of 0.230 inches and over or sections over 48 inches in width with a thickness of 0.180 inches and over.

5   ORNAMENTAL METALS

This class of metals includes non-structural applications such as spiral stairs, handrails, railings, decorative trim, and similar prefabricated assemblies. Although steel is sometimes used for ornamental work, especially in fences and gates, ornamental metal is usually formed of stainless steel, brass, and bronze.

Since ornamental metal work is usually expensive, the detailing should be kept simple and the amount of metal should be minimized. Buffed or other highly polished finishes on large, flat sheets should also be avoided to prevent "oil canning" which is an uneven, bowed appearance of flat metal. In addition, finishes should be selected to minimize maintenance and reduce fabrication expense. Usually, costs increase with increased finishing.

17 STRUCTURAL AND ROUGH CARPENTRY

There are two broad categories of wood use in construction: rough carpentry and finish carpentry. *Rough carpentry* includes the structural framing, sheathing, blocking, and miscellaneous pieces necessary to prepare the building for finish work. Most rough carpentry is hidden once construction is complete, but exposed lumber such as heavy timber beams, glued laminated members, and outdoor deck frames are considered rough carpentry.

As the name implies, *finish carpentry* includes the exposed, finished pieces of lumber necessary to complete a job, including such things as window and door trim, base, wood paneling, cabinets, and shelving. Finish carpentry work is normally done on the job site, but it also includes millwork, which is the fabrication of wood items in a manufacturing plant. Finish carpentry and millwork are reviewed in Chapter 18.

This chapter includes a general review of wood as a structural material. However, methods for calculating sizes of members and fasteners are not included.

When discussing wood as a construction material, several terms are often used interchangeably, but there is a distinction. *Wood* is the fibrous substance forming the trunk, stems, and branches of the tree. *Lumber* is the product of sawing, planing, and otherwise preparing wood to be used as construction members. *Timber* is lumber with a 5-inch minimum sectional dimension.

1 CHARACTERISTICS OF LUMBER

Lumber is a very versatile building material and has many advantages — it is plentiful, relatively low in cost, easy to shape and assemble, has good thermal insulating qualities, and is aesthetically pleasing. As a natural material, however, it does not have uniform characteristics of appearance and strength that other manufactured materials have. Also, because of its cellular structure, it is susceptible to dimensional changes when its moisture content changes.

These disadvantages can be overcome with some of the manufactured wood products available today. A few examples of these products include plywood, glued laminated timber, and wood I-joists.

A. Types and Species

There are two general classifications of wood: softwood and hardwood. These terms have nothing to do with the actual hardness of the wood, but refer to whether the wood comes from a coniferous tree or a deciduous tree. *Conifers* are cone-bearing, needle-leaved trees that hold their foliage in the winter, such as fir, spruce, and pine. *Deciduous* trees are broad-leaved trees that lose their leaves in the winter, such as oak, walnut, and maple. Softwoods are used for structural and rough carpentry because of their greater availability and lower cost. Finish carpentry and millwork utilize both hardwoods and softwoods.

There are literally hundreds of species of softwood and hardwood available throughout the world. However, only a few are used in this country for rough carpentry, primarily due to local availability and cost. For example, southern pine is used in the southeastern portion of the United States, while Douglas fir or Douglas fir-larch is used in the western region. Other commonly used species for rough carpentry include hem-fir, eastern white pine, and hemlock. Redwood and cedar are commonly used for exterior applications where resistance to moisture is required.

B. Strength

The strength of lumber is dependent on the direction of the load relative to the direction of the wood's grain. Lumber is strongest when the load is parallel to the direction of the grain, such as with a compressive load on a wood column. Wood can resist slightly less tensile stress parallel to the grain and even less when compressive forces are perpendicular to the grain.

Wood is weakest when horizontal shear force is induced, which occurs when bending forces are applied to a beam and the fibers tend to slip apart parallel to the grain. Allowable forces used in structural calculations are lowest for horizontal shear, and this quite often governs the design of bending members.

C. Defects

Since wood is a natural material, there are several types of defects that can be present in lumber. There are also many types of defects that can occur during manufacture. These affect the strength, appearance, and use of lumber and are reflected in how an individual piece of lumber is graded. Figure 17.1 shows some of the more common wood defects.

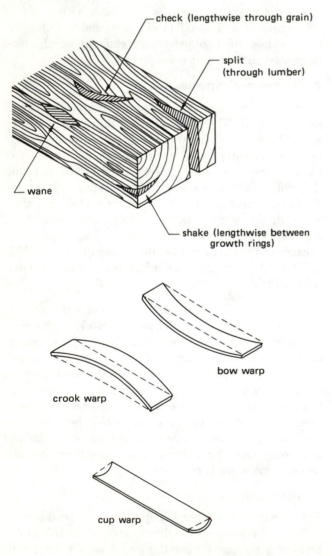

Figure 17.1 Common Wood Defects

- *Knots* are the most common natural defect. A knot is a branch or limb embedded in the tree that is cut through in the process of lumber manufacture. Knots are classified according to quality, size, and occurrence. There are over ten different types of knots.

- A *check* is a separation of the wood fibers occurring across or through the annual growth rings, a result of improper seasoning.

- A *shake* is a lengthwise separation of the wood that usually occurs between or through the annual growth rings.

- A *split* is similar to a check except the separation extends completely through a piece of lumber, usually at the ends.

- A *wane* is the presence of bark or lack of wood from any cause on the edge or corner of a piece of lumber.

Warping is a common manufacturing defect. A *warp* is any variation from a true or plane surface and is usually caused by the natural shrinkage characteristics of wood and uneven drying during processing. A *bow* is a deviation parallel to the length of the lumber in line with its flat side. A *crook* is a deviation parallel to the length of the lumber perpendicular to the flat side of the piece. A *cup* is a deviation from true plane along the width of the board.

D. Grading

Since a log yields lumber of varying quality, the individual sawn pieces must be categorized to allow selection of boards that are best suited for a particular purpose. For structural lumber, the primary concern is the amount of stress that a grade of lumber of a specific species can carry. For finish lumber, the primary concern is the appearance of the wood and how it accepts stain, paint, and other finishes. Load-carrying ability is affected by such things as size and number of knots, splits, and other defects.

Grading of lumber used for structural and rough carpentry purposes is done under standard rules established by several agencies certified by the American Lumber Standards Committee. The grading is done at the sawmill, either by visual inspection or machine, if the lumber is to be used for structural purposes. The resulting allowable stress values are published in tables that are used when making structural calculations.

There are two primary classifications of softwood lumber: "yard lumber," used for structural purposes and rough framing, and "factory and shop" lumber, used for making door frames, windows, and finish items.

Yard lumber is further classified as boards, dimension, and timber, as shown in Figure 17.2. Dimension lumber and timber are the two classifications used for structural purposes, and these are further classified into groups based on nominal size and use. With this system the same grade of lumber in a species may have different allowable stresses depending on which category it is in. This can be confusing, but it is critical in selecting the correct allowable stress for a particular design condition.

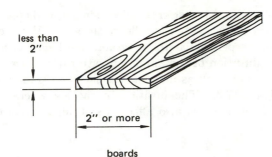

boards

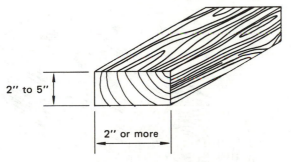

dimension lumber

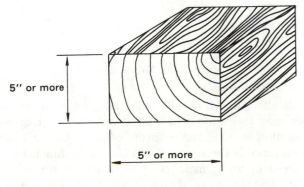

timber

Figure 17.2 Yard Lumber Types

The five size groups (based on nominal dimensions) are:

1. 2 inches to 4 inches thick, 2 inches to 4 inches wide. This includes members such as 2 × 2's.

2. 2 inches to 4 inches thick, 4 inches wide. This is the category for 2 × 4's, which are usually subdivided into grades of construction, standard, and utility.

3. 2 inches to 4 inches thick, 5 inches and wider. This includes wood members like 2 × 6's, 2 × 8's, and the like, but not 2 × 4's.

4. *Beams and stringers.* Beams and stringers are defined as members 5 inches and wider, having a depth more than 2 inches greater than the width.

5. *Posts and timbers.* Posts and timbers are defined as members 5 inches by 5 inches and larger with a depth not more than 2 inches greater than the width.

These five size categories are further subdivided into smaller groups such as select structural, no. 1, no. 2, and so on. The exact nomenclature and method of subdivision vary with each grading agency and the wood species.

Machine-stress-rated lumber is based on grade designations that depend on the allowable bending stress and modulus of elasticity of the wood.

Factory and shop lumber for boards (less than 1-inch nominal thickness) is graded according to defects that affect the appearance and use of the wood. Exact classifications vary with the grading agency and the species of lumber, but in general factory and shop lumber is divided into select and common grades. The three select grade categories are B & better, C select, and D select, with B & better being the best and free of knots.

Common grades available include no. 1, no. 2, no. 3, no. 4, and no. 5, with no. 1 common being the best. The individual grades are determined by the size and character of the knots.

E. Dimensioning

Lumber for rough carpentry is referred to by its nominal dimension in inches, such as 2 × 4 or 2 × 10. However, after surfacing at the mill and drying, its actual dimension is somewhat less. Table 17.1 gives the actual dimensions for various nominal sizes of sawn lumber.

Table 17.1
Nominal and Actual Sizes of Lumber

nominal size	standard dressed size, inches width × depth
1 × 2	3/4 × 1 1/2
1 × 4	3/4 × 3 1/2
1 × 6	3/4 × 5 1/2
1 × 8	3/4 × 7 1/4
2 × 2	1 1/2 × 1 1/2
2 × 4	1 1/2 × 3 1/2
2 × 6	1 1/2 × 5 1/2
2 × 8	1 1/2 × 7 1/4
2 × 10	1 1/2 × 9 1/4
2 × 12	1 1/2 × 11 1/4
4 × 4	3 1/2 × 3 1/2
4 × 6	3 1/2 × 5 1/2
4 × 8	3 1/2 × 7 1/4
4 × 10	3 1/2 × 9 1/4
4 × 12	3 1/2 × 11 1/4
4 × 14	3 1/2 × 13 1/4
6 × 6	5 1/2 × 5 1/2
6 × 8	5 1/2 × 7 1/2
6 × 10	5 1/2 × 9 1/2

Lumber is ordered and priced by the board foot. This is a measure of a quantity of lumber equal to a piece 12 inches wide by 12 inches long by 1 inch thick. Nominal sizes are used so an actual sized piece of lumber 3/4 inch thick, 11 1/4 inches wide, and 2 feet long contains 2 board feet.

F. Moisture Content

Moisture content is defined as the weight of water in wood as a fraction of the weight of ovendry wood. It is an important variable because it affects the amount of shrinkage, weight, and strength of the lumber, as well as the withdrawal resistance of nails.

Moisture exists in wood both in the individual cell cavities and bound chemically within cell walls. When the cell walls are completely saturated, but no water exists in the cell cavities, the wood is said to have reached its *fiber saturation point*. This point averages about 30 percent moisture content in all woods. Above this point the wood is dimensionally stable, but as the wood dries below this point it begins to shrink.

When wood is used for structural framing and other construction purposes, it tends to absorb or lose

moisture in response to the temperature and humidity of the surrounding air. As it loses moisture it shrinks, and as it gains moisture it swells. Ideally, the moisture content of wood when it is installed should be the same as the prevailing humidity to which it will be exposed. However, this is seldom possible so lumber needs to be seasoned, either by air drying or kiln drying, to reduce the moisture content to acceptable levels.

To be considered dry lumber, moisture content cannot exceed 19 percent. To be grademarked "kiln dry," the maximum moisture content permitted is 15 percent. Design values found in structural tables assume that the maximum moisture content will not exceed 19 percent. If it does, the allowable stresses must be decreased slightly.

Wood shrinks most in the direction perpendicular to the grain and very little parallel to the grain. When considered perpendicular to the grain, wood shrinks most in the direction of the annual growth rings (tangentially) and about half as much across the rings (radially). See Figure 17.3. The position in the log where a piece of lumber is cut also affects its shrinkage characteristics.

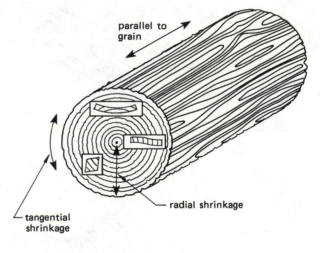

Figure 17.3   Wood Shrinkage

In detailing wood, an allowance must be made for the fact that the wood will shrink and swell during use regardless of its initial moisture content. Of particular importance is the accumulated change in dimension of a series of wood members placed one on top of the next. The shrinkage of an individual member may not be significant, but the total shrinkage of several pieces may result in problems such as sagging floors, cracked plaster, distortion of door openings, and nail pops in gypsum board walls.

2 FRAMING

Framing is the assembly of lumber and timber components to construct a building. Because of code restrictions, structural limitations, and construction techniques, most wood construction is limited to small to moderate-sized buildings. This section discusses light frame construction while the next section reviews heavy timber construction used for larger structures.

A. Light Frame Construction

Light frame construction uses small, closely spaced members such as 2-inch × 4-inch or 2-inch × 6-inch studs for walls and partitions and nominal 2-inch thick members for floor and roof joists. Beams may be built-up sections of nominal 2-inch lumber, or heavy timber or steel.

Two systems of wall framing include the platform frame and the balloon frame. The essential difference is that the platform frame uses separate studs for each floor of the building, with the top plates, floor joists, and floor framing of the second level being constructed before the second-floor wall studs are erected. The balloon frame uses continuous wall studs from foundation to second floor ceiling. Figure 17.4 shows the two types of framing systems.

One advantage of the platform frame is that each floor can be completed and used for constructing the next floor, and shorter studs cost less. The advantage of the balloon frame is that vertical shrinkage is minimized because most of the construction is parallel to the direction of the grain where wood shrinkage is the least.

When wood joists are framed into masonry walls instead of wood stud walls, they must rest on metal hangers attached to wood ledger strips anchored to the masonry or be fire cut, as shown in Figure 17.5. A fire cut is required to prevent the masonry from being pushed up and out if the wood member should collapse during a fire.

B. Framing Openings

Openings in wood construction are required for doors, windows, stairs, and similar conditions. Since light frame construction consists of many small, closely spaced members carrying the loads, eliminating any of these studs or joists affects the structural integrity of the building. As a result, framing of openings must be capable of transferring loads from one cut member to other members. Two typical methods of framing vertical and horizontal openings are shown in Figure 17.6. The size of header over a window opening depends on

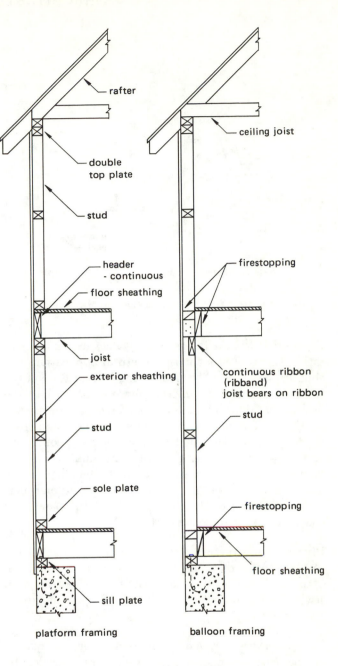

Figure 17.4 Light Frame Construction

the span and usually consists of a double 2-inch-wide member (commonly expressed as 2 ×) bearing on a stud at either side of the opening.

C. Plywood

Plywood consists of sheets of thin veneer glued together to form a rigid panel. Sheets are made in standard 4 foot × 8 foot sizes in thicknesses of 1/4 inch, 3/8 inch, 1/2 inch, 5/8 inch, and 3/4 inch. Other panel sizes and thicknesses are available, but these are the ones most readily available.

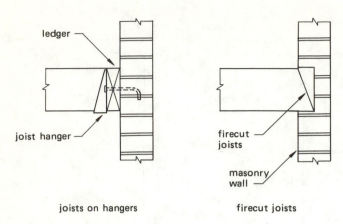

Figure 17.5 Wood Framing into Masonry

Plywood is graded in two ways. The first is by span rating and is used for most structural applications, including sheathing. The span rating is a measure of the strength and stiffness of the plywood parallel to the face grain. The rating consists of two numbers, such as 32/24. The first number gives the maximum spacing for roof supports under average loading conditions and the second number gives the maximum spacing for floor supports under average residential loading. These spacings are allowed if the face grain is perpendicular to the direction of the supports and if the panels are continuous over three supports.

Plywood for structural uses is also classified according to the species of wood used. There are five groups. Structural I plywood is made only from woods in group 1 while Structural II can be made from woods in groups 1, 2, and 3.

The other way plywood is graded is by the quality of the face veneer. Veneer grades are classified by the letters N, A, B, C, and D. *N grade* is intended for a natural finish and is made from all heartwood or all sapwood. It is free from defects but is only available on special order. *A grade* is smooth and paintable with few knots or other defects and is the best grade commonly available. *B grade* allows for plugged knotholes but has a smooth surface. *C grade* allows small knotholes and some splits, while *D grade* allows for larger knotholes. Plywood should be specified with exterior glue for outdoor locations.

Special types of plywood are also produced. These include patterned panels for exterior finish siding, marine plywood that has special glues, and overlaid plywood with a surface of resin-impregnated paper to provide a smooth surface.

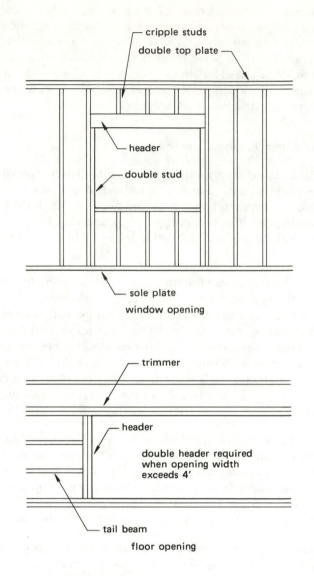

Figure 17.6 Framing for Openings

D. Sheathing and Miscellaneous Wood Framing Members

Sheathing is thin panel material attached to framing to provide lateral support, increase rigidity, and provide a base for applying exterior finishes. For structural purposes, sheathing most often consists of plywood or particle board nailed to the wood studs or joists. In situations where lateral stability is not critical, insulating sheathing may be used.

Blocking is wood framing installed between main structural members such as studs or joists to provide extra rigidity or to provide a base for nailing other materials. For example, short pieces of lumber are often placed perpendicular to joists under the locations of interior partitions. Edge blocking is also placed at the intersection of wall and ceiling framing to provide a nailing base for the application of gypsum wallboard.

Bridging is bracing between joists that prevents the joist from buckling under load. Bridging may be solid wood blocking, 1-inch by 3-inch wood cross members, or metal cross bridging. It is installed at intervals not exceeding 8 feet unless both the top and bottom edges of the joists are supported for their entire length.

Firestops are barriers installed in concealed spaces of combustible construction to prevent the spread of fire caused by drafts. Allowable materials include nominal 2-inch thick wood members, gypsum board, or mineral wool. In most cases, wood blocking is used. The building code specifies where and when firestops must be installed, but in general firestopping is used in concealed spaces between floors, between a floor and ceiling or attic space, between floors under stairs, and in vertical openings around vents, chimneys, and ducts between floors.

3 HEAVY TIMBER CONSTRUCTION

Heavy timber construction consists of exterior walls of non-combustible masonry or concrete and interior columns, girders, beams, and planking manufactured of large solid or laminated timbers. The Uniform Building Code requires that interior columns be at least 8 inches by 8 inches in nominal size and that beams and girders supporting floors be at least 6 inches wide and 10 inches deep. Girders framed into masonry walls must be fire cut similar to the joists shown in Figure 17.5. Floor decking must be at least 3 inches in nominal thickness with no concealed spaces below. Roof decking must be at least 2 inches in nominal thickness.

Due to the expense and limited availability of large, solid timbers today, new heavy timber construction is most typically built with glued laminated members.

A. Glued Laminated Construction

Glued laminated wood members are built up from a number of individual pieces of lumber glued together and finished under factory conditions for use as beams, columns, purlins, and other structural components. *Glue-lam*, as it is usually referred to, is used where larger wood members are required for heavy loads or long spans and simple sawn timber pieces are not available or cannot meet the strength requirements. Glue-lam construction is also used where unusual structural shapes are required and appearance is a consideration. In addition to being fabricated in simple rectangular

shapes, glue-lam members can be formed into arches, tapered forms, and pitched shapes.

Glue-lam members are manufactured in standard widths and depths. In most cases, 1 1/2-inch actual depth pieces are used, so the overall depth is some multiple of 1 1/2, depending on how many laminations are used. 3/4-inch thick pieces are used if a tight curve must be formed. Standard actual widths include 3 1/8 inches, 5 1/8 inches, 6 3/4 inches, 8 3/4 inches, 10 3/4 inches, and 12 1/4 inches.

Because individual pieces can be selected free from certain defects and seasoned to the proper moisture content and the entire manufacturing process is conducted under carefully controlled conditions, the allowable stresses for glue-lam construction are higher than for solid, sawn timber. Although glue-lam beams are usually loaded in the direction perpendicular to the laminations, they can be loaded in either direction to suit the requirements of the design.

For structural purposes, glue-lams are designated by size and a commonly used symbol that specifies the stress rating. Glue-lams are available in three appearance grades: industrial, architectural, and premium. These do not affect the structural properties but only designate the final look and finishing of the member. Industrial grade is used where appearance is not a primary concern, while premium is used where the finest appearance is important. Architectural grade is used where appearance is a factor but the best grade is not required.

B. Planking

Wood planking, or *decking* as it is often called, is solid or laminated timber that spans between beams. It is available in nominal thicknesses of 2, 3, 4, and 5 inches with actual sizes varying with the manufacturer and whether the piece is solid or laminated. All planking has some type of tongue-and-groove edging so the pieces fit solidly together and load can be distributed among adjacent pieces. Unlike sheathing, planking is intended to span greater distances between beams rather than between closely spaced joists. Common spans range from 4 feet to 20 feet, depending on the planking thickness and loads carried.

In addition to satisfying the code requirements for heavy timber construction, planking has the advantages of easy installation, attractive appearance, and efficient use of material, since the planking serves as floor structure, finish floor, and finish ceiling below. Its primary disadvantage is that there is no place to conceal insulation, electrical conduit, and mechanical services.

4 FASTENERS

There are many types of fasteners used for carpentry, including nails, screws, bolts, and fabricated metal fasteners.

A. Nails

Although they are the weakest of wood connectors, nails are the most commonly used connectors in light frame construction. The types used most frequently for structural applications include common wire nails, box nails, and common wire spikes. *Wire nails* range in size from six penny (6d) to sixty penny (60d). *Box nails* range from 6d to 40d — 6d nails are 2 inches in length, while 60d nails are 6 inches long. Common *wire spikes* range from 10d (3 inches long) to 8 1/2 inches long and 3/8 inch diameter. For the same penny weight, box nails have the smallest diameter, common wire nails the next largest diameter, and wire spikes the greatest diameter.

For engineered applications, that is, where each nailed joint is specifically designed, there are tables of values giving the allowable withdrawal resistance and lateral load (shear) resistance for different sizes and penetrations of nails depending on the type of wood used. The more typical situation of most nailed wood construction is to simply use nailing schedules found in the building code. These give the minimum size, number, and penetration of nails for specific applications such as nailing studs to sole plates, joists to headers, and so forth.

There are several orientations that nails (as well as screws and lag screws) can have with wood members, which affect the holding power of the fastener. The preferable orientation is to have the fastener loaded laterally in side grain where the holding power is the greatest. The least desirable orientation is to have the nail or fastener parallel to the grain.

B. Screws

Wood screws are available in sizes from no. 0 (0.060 inch shank diameter) to no. 24 (0.372 inch shank diameter) and in lengths from 1/4 inch to 5 inches. The most common types are flat head and round head. Because of the threaded design of screws, they offer better holding power and can be removed and replaced more easily than nails. As with nails, screws are best used laterally loaded in side grain rather than in withdrawal from side grain or end grain.

Lead holes, slightly smaller than the diameter of the screw, must be drilled into the wood to permit the proper insertion of the screw and to prevent splitting of the wood.

A lag screw is threaded with a pointed end like a wood screw but has a head like a bolt. It is inserted by drilling lead holes and screwing the fastener into the wood with a wrench. A washer is used between the head and the wood. Lag screws are sometimes called lag bolts.

Sizes range from 1/4 inch to 1 1/4 inches in diameter and from 1 inch to 16 inches in length. Diameters are measured at the non-threaded shank portion of the screw.

C. Bolts

Bolts are one of the most common forms of wood connectors for joints of moderate to heavy loading. Bolt sizes range from 1/4 inch to 1 inch in diameter and from 1/2 to 6 inches in length. Washers must be used under the head and nut of the bolt to prevent crushing the wood and to distribute the load.

The design requirements for bolted joints are a little more complicated than those for screwed or nailed joints. The allowable design values and the spacing of bolts are affected by such variables as the thicknesses of the main and side members, the ratio of bolt length in the main member to the bolt diameter, and the number of members joined.

D. Metal Fasteners

Because wood is such a common building material, there are dozens of types of special fasteners and connectors especially designed to make assembly easy, fast, and structurally sound. Hardware is available for both standard sizes of wood members and special members such as wood truss joists. Some of the common types of connection hardware are shown in Figure 17.7.

In addition to the lightweight connectors shown in Figure 17.8, there are also special timber connectors used for heavy timber construction and for assembling wood trusses. Two of the most common types are split rings and shear plates. Split rings are either 21/2 inches or 4 inches in diameter and are cut through in one place in the circumference to form a tongue and slot. The ring is beveled from the central portion toward the edges. Grooves are cut in each piece of the wood members to be joined so that half the ring is in each section. The members are held together with a bolt concentric with the ring, as shown in Figure 17.8.

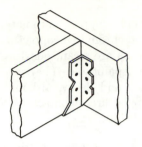

joist hanger

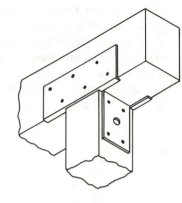

post cap

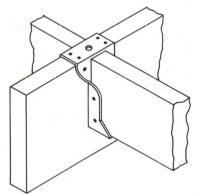

saddle hanger

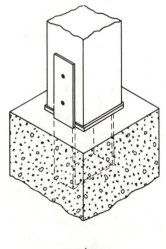

post base

Figure 17.7 Special Connection Hardware

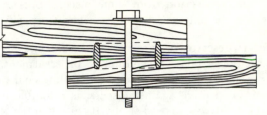

(a) split ring connector

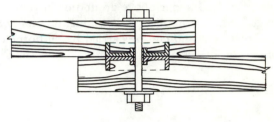

(b) shear plate connector

Figure 17.8 Timber Connectors

Shear plates are either 2 5/8 inches or 4 inches in diameter and are flat plates with a flange extending from the face of the plate. There is a hole in the middle through which either a 3/4 inch or 7/8 inch bolt is placed to hold the two members together. Shear plates are inserted in precut grooves in a piece of wood so that the plate is flush with one surface. (See Figure 17.8.) Because of this configuration, shear plate connections can hold either two pieces of wood together or one piece of wood and a steel plate.

Split ring connectors and shear plates can transfer larger loads than bolts or screws alone and are often used in connecting truss members. Shear plates are particularly suited for constructions that must be disassembled.

5   WOOD TREATMENT

As a natural material wood is a relatively durable material if kept dry. Some woods, such as cedar and redwood, have naturally occurring resins that make them resistant to moisture and insect attack. However, most wood is subject to damage and decay from a number of sources and must be protected. The most common sources of attack and damage include fungi when moisture is present, insects such as termites and marine borers, and fire.

Preservatives may be applied by brushing, dipping, or pressure treatment. The most effective is pressure treatment because the preservative is forced deep into the cells of the wood. For some applications such as marine use and protection from some insects, pressure treatment is the only satisfactory method to specify.

Wood preservatives are of two basic types: oils and water-borne salts. One common oil treatment is coal-tar creosote, which is made by distilling coal tar. Creosote is effective against insects, is insoluble in water, and is relatively easy to apply. Its disadvantages include the unpleasant odor it produces, the dark appearance on the timber, and the fact that it cannot be painted.

Pentachlorophenol is one of the water-repellent solutions used for lumber above ground or in contact with the ground. It is applied by brushing, dipping, or pressure treatment and can be carried by oil-borne or gas-borne solutions. Gas-borne solutions leave the wood in a condition that can be painted and glued.

Water-borne salts include acid copper chromate, ammoniacal copper arsenate, and chromated copper arsenate. These types of treatments are clean, odorless, non-staining, and leave the wood paintable. They provide protection against termites and decay, although some do not perform well when in direct contact with the ground under very wet conditions.

There are two general types of fire protective treatments. The first includes salt solutions containing ammonium and phosphates that penetrate the wood. The other type is intumescent paint, which coats the surface of the lumber. When exposed to fire, the intumescent coating forms a layer of inert gas bubbles that insulates the wood and retards combustion.

18 FINISH CARPENTRY AND MILLWORK

Finish carpentry is the final, exposed wood construction done on the job site. It is usually non-structural in nature. This class of work includes exterior wood siding, interior trim, door and window framing, stair framing, shelving and cabinetry, paneling, and similar finish items.

Although finish carpentry overlaps somewhat with millwork, the latter term refers to finish lumber items fabricated in a manufacturing plant and brought to the job site for installation. Millwork items normally include fine finished cabinetry, wall paneling, custom doors, and other items that can be better made under controlled factory conditions.

1 FINISH CARPENTRY

A. Wood Species and Grading

As stated in Chapter 17, wood is classified as softwood or hardwood. *Softwoods* are those cut from coniferous trees, while *hardwoods* are those coming from deciduous trees. Finish carpentry employs both. Lower cost interior trim is usually made from the better grades of pine and fir, but when appearance is important, hardwoods such as oak, mahogany, or birch are used. Hardwoods are used almost exclusively for millwork because of their superior appearance and durability.

There are hundreds of domestic and imported wood species available for finish carpentry and millwork. However, because of cost and availability, only a few are generally used for finish carpentry and several dozen for millwork. Some of the common hardwood species include red and white oak, ash, walnut, cherry, mahogany, birch, poplar, maple, and redwood.

Finish carpentry lumber is graded differently than millwork and structural lumber. The grading varies slightly from species to species, but in general the Western Wood Products Association (WWPA) classifies finish lumber into selects, finish, paneling, and commons, along with grades for siding and what the WWPA terms alternate boards. Selects are divided into B & better (the best grade in this category), C select, and D select. Finish is subdivided into superior, prime, and E grades. Western red cedar, redwood, and a few other domestic species have their own grading rules.

In addition to these grades, finish lumber may be specified as heartwood or sapwood. *Heartwood* comes from the center of the tree and *sapwood* from the perimeter. In some species, such as redwood, there is a marked color variance and resistance to decay between the two types of lumber. In some circumstances it is important to differentiate between the two.

For many types of softwood trim there is another category called *fingerjointed*. This is not really a grade but a method of manufacturing lengths of trim from shorter pieces of lumber. The ends of the short pieces are cut with finger-like projections, glued, and joined together. Fingerjointed material is less expensive than continuous molding but is only appropriate for a paint finish where the joints will be covered.

B. Lumber Cutting

The way lumber is cut from a log determines the final appearance of the grain pattern. There are three ways boards (also called solid stock) are cut from a log. Thin veneers are sliced in similar ways, but these are discussed in the next section on millwork. The three methods used are plain sawing (also called flat sawing), quartersawing, and rift sawing. These methods are illustrated in Figure 18.1.

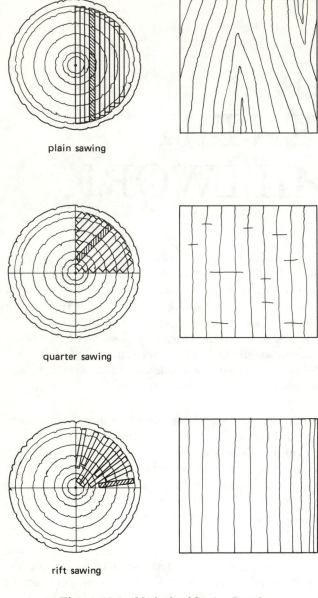

plain sawing

quarter sawing

rift sawing

Figure 18.1   Methods of Sawing Boards

Plain sawing makes the most efficient use of the log and is the least expensive of the three methods. Because the wood is cut with various orientations to the grain of the tree, plain sawing results in a finished surface with the characteristic cathedral pattern shown in Figure 18.1.

Quartersawing is produced by cutting the log into quarters and then sawing perpendicular to a diameter line. Since the saw cut is more or less perpendicular to the grain, the resulting grain pattern is more uniformly vertical. Not only does this result in a different appearance than plain sawing, but quartersawn boards also tend to twist and cup less, shrink less in width, hold paint better, and have fewer defects.

As illustrated in Figure 18.1, quartersawn boards cut from the edges of the log do not have the grain exactly

at a 90-degree angle to the saw cut as do those in the middle. For an even more consistent vertical grain, *rift sawing* is used. With this method, the saw cuts from a quartered log are always made radially to the center of the tree. Since the log must be shifted after each cut and since there is a great deal of waste, rift cutting is more expensive than quartersawing.

Because of the limited availability of some species of wood and the expense of making certain cuts, not all types of lumber cutting are available in all species. In some cases, for a particular species, a veneer cut (discussed in the next section) will be available, but not the corresponding solid stock cut. The availability of cuts in the desired species should be verified before specifications are written.

C. Wood Siding

Wood siding consists of individual boards applied horizontally, diagonally, or vertically. When the siding is applied over wood sheathing (either plywood or particle board), a layer of asphalt-impregnated building paper is placed under the sheathing to minimize air infiltration and improve the water resistance of the wall. When the siding is applied over fiberboard or insulating sheathing, an air infiltration barrier of high-density polyethylene is often used under the siding. This allows moisture vapor to pass through but minimizes air leakage.

Wood siding is milled from redwood, cedar, Douglas fir, pine, and several other species. Some, such as redwood, cedar, and cypress, are naturally resistant to moisture and require less protection than varieties like pine. Siding comes in several shapes, as shown in Figure 18.2. All are milled to allow one board to overlap the one below to shed water.

D. Wood Stairs and Trim

The construction of wood stairs is considered a finish carpentry item. Stairs can range from simple utilitarian assemblies to elaborate, ornate, crafted works. A simple form of stair construction is shown in Figure 18.3 with the primary construction elements identified.

Interior and exterior trim is used to finish off the joints between dissimilar materials, close construction gaps between building elements, and provide decorative treatment. Simple, rectangular shapes are used for a great deal of construction trim, but there are dozens of standard, shaped molding pieces used for particular applications. Some of the more common types of interior trim are shown in Figure 18.4.

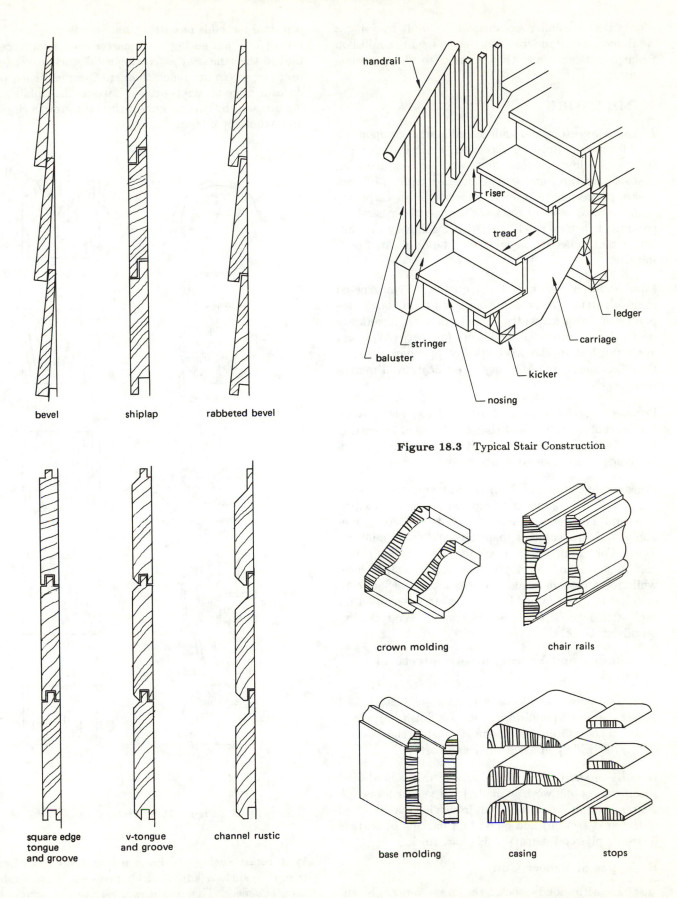

bevel   shiplap   rabbeted bevel

handrail

riser

tread

ledger

carriage

stringer

baluster

kicker

nosing

Figure 18.3 Typical Stair Construction

square edge
tongue
and groove

v-tongue
and groove

channel rustic

crown molding   chair rails

base molding   casing   stops

Figure 18.2 Wood Siding

Figure 18.4 Interior Trim

More ornate molding sections can be built by using a combination of standard shapes or by having a millshop make a cutting blade that is used to shape special profiles.

2   MILLWORK

Millwork is custom, shop-fabricated lumber components used for interior finish construction, which includes cabinetry, paneling, custom doors and frames, shelving, custom furniture, and special interior trim. Millwork makes it possible to produce superior finish carpentry items because most of the work is done under carefully controlled factory conditions with machinery and finishing techniques that could never be duplicated on a job site.

Lumber for millwork and the quality of constructed millwork items are graded differently than rough carpentry or finish carpentry. Standards for millwork are set by the Architectural Woodwork Institute (AWI) and are published in the AWI Quality Standards, Guide Specifications, and Quality Certification Program booklet.

Lumber is classed as Grade I, II, and III and is based on the percentage of a board that can be used by cutting out defects. There are also limitations on the types of defects that are allowed in any grade.

Construction standards, tolerances, and the finished appearance of completed components are specified as premium, custom, and economy grades. These grades apply to doors, cabinets, paneling, and other millwork items. For example, the maximum gap between a cabinet door and frame in premium grade is 3/32 inch, while for a custom grade it is 1/8 inch, and for economy grade it is 5/32 inch. A complete description for each item in each grade is given in the AWI Quality Standards booklet.

A. Lumber and Veneers for Architectural Millwork

Architects have a wider selection of solid stock and veneer for use in millwork than for finish carpentry. Material comes from both domestic and foreign sources and varies widely in availability and cost.

Because of the limited availability of many hardwood species, most millwork is made from veneer stock. A *veneer* is a thin slice of wood cut from a log (as described in the next section) and glued to a backing of particle board or plywood, normally 3/4 inch thick.

B. Types of Veneer Cuts

Just as with solid stock, the way veneer is cut from a log affects its final appearance. There are five principal methods of cutting veneers, as shown in Figure 18.5. Plain slicing and quarter slicing are accomplished the same way as cutting solid stock, except the resulting pieces are much thinner. Quarter slicing produces a more straight-grained pattern than plain slicing because the cutting knife strikes the growth rings at approximately a 90-degree angle.

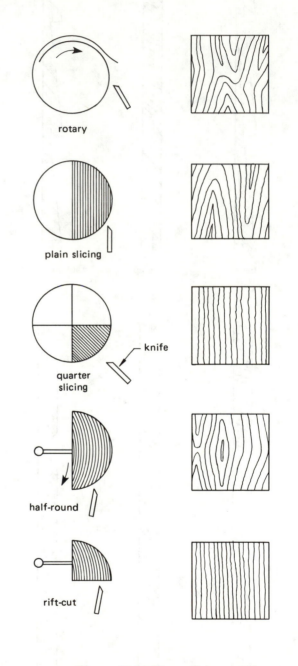

rotary

plain slicing

quarter slicing

knife

half-round

rift-cut

Figure 18.5   Veneer Cuts

With *rotary slicing*, the log is mounted on a lathe and turned against a knife, which peels off a continuous layer of veneer. This produces a very pronounced grain pattern that is often undesirable in fine quality wood finishes, although it does produce the most veneer with the least waste.

Half-round slicing is similar to rotary slicing, but the log is cut in half and the veneer cut slightly across the annular growth rings. This results in a pronounced grain pattern showing characteristics of both rotary-sliced and plain-sliced veneers.

Rift slicing is accomplished by quartering a log and cutting at about a 15-degree angle to the growth rings. Like quarter slicing, it results in a straight-grain pattern and is often used with oak to eliminate the appearance of markings perpendicular to the direction of the grain. These markings in oak are caused by *medullary rays*, which are radial cells extending from the center of the tree to its circumference.

Since the width of a piece of veneer is limited by the diameter of log or portion of log from which it is cut, several veneers must be put together on a backing panel to make up the needed size of a finished piece. The individual veneers come from the same piece of log, which is called a *flitch*. The word "flitch" is sometimes also used to describe the particular sequence in which the veneers are taken off the log as it is cut. The method of matching veneers is discussed below.

C. Joinery Details

Various types of joints are used for millwork construction to increase the strength of the joint and improve the appearance by eliminating mechanical fasteners such as screws. With the availability of high-strength adhesives, screws and other mechanical fasteners are seldom needed for the majority of the work produced in the shop. Field attachment, however, often requires the use of blind nailing or other concealed fastening to maintain the quality look of the work. Some of the common joints used in both millwork and finish carpentry are shown in Figure 18.6.

D. Cabinetwork

Millwork cabinets are built in the shop as complete assemblies and simply set in place and attached to surrounding construction at the job site. There are several methods of detailing door and drawer fronts on cabinets, but the construction of the cabinet frames is fairly standard, as shown in Figure 18.7.

The two basic types of door and drawer front construction are overlay and face frame. With *overlay construction*, the fronts of the doors and drawers stop in front of the face frame of the cabinet. Edges of adjacent fronts may almost touch or be separated enough to show the face frame with a reveal. In *face frame construction*,

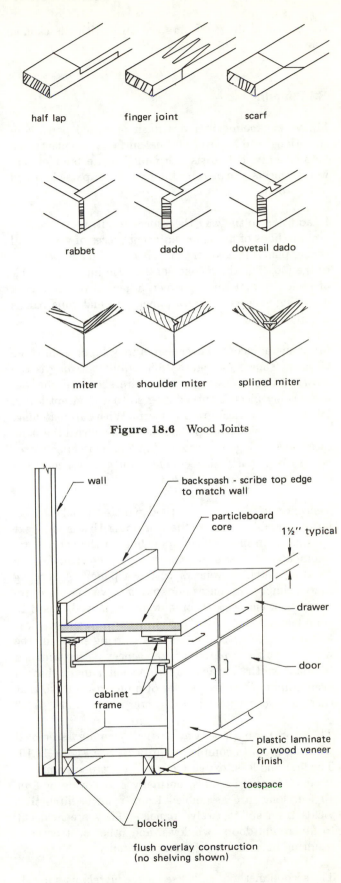

Figure 18.6 Wood Joints

half lap   finger joint   scarf

rabbet   dado   dovetail dado

miter   shoulder miter   splined miter

Figure 18.7 Typical Wood Cabinet

wall

backsplash - scribe top edge to match wall

particleboard core

1½" typical

drawer

door

plastic laminate or wood veneer finish

toespace

cabinet frame

blocking

flush overlay construction (no shelving shown)

the door and drawer fronts are flush with the cabinet frame.

E. Paneling

Millwork paneling includes flush or raised panel constructions used to cover vertical surfaces. As mentioned before, large, flat areas like paneling are built of thin wood veneers glued to backing panels of particle board or plywood.

In addition to the way the veneer is cut, there are several methods of matching adjacent pieces of veneer and veneer panels in a room that affect the final appearance of the job. The three considerations in increasing order of scale are matching between adjacent veneer leaves, matching veneers within a panel, and matching panels within a room.

Matching adjacent veneer leaves may be done in three ways, as shown in Figure 18.8. *Bookmatching* is the most common. As the veneers are sliced off the log, every other piece is turned over so that adjacent leaves form a symmetrical grain pattern. With *slip matching*, consecutive pieces are placed side by side with the same face sides being exposed. *Random matching* places veneers in no particular sequence, and even veneers from different flitches may be used.

Veneers must be glued to rigid panels to make installation possible. The method of doing this is the next consideration in specifying paneling. If the veneers are bookmatched, there are three ways, shown in Figure 18.9, of matching veneers within a panel. A *running match* simply alternates bookmatched veneer pieces regardless of their width or how many must be used to complete a panel. Any portion left over from the last leaf of one panel is used as the starting piece for the next. A *balance match* utilizes veneer pieces trimmed to equal widths in each panel. A *center match* has an even number of veneer leaves of uniform width so that there is a veneer joint in the center of the panel.

There are also three ways panels can be assembled within a room to complete a project. See Figure 18.10. The first and least expensive is called *warehouse match*. Premanufactured panels, normally 4 feet wide by 8 or 10 feet long, are assembled from a single flitch that yields from six to twelve panels. They are field cut to fit around doors, windows, and other obstructions, resulting in some loss of grain continuity.

The second method, called *sequence match*, uses panels of uniform width manufactured for a specific job and with the veneers arranged in sequence. If some panels

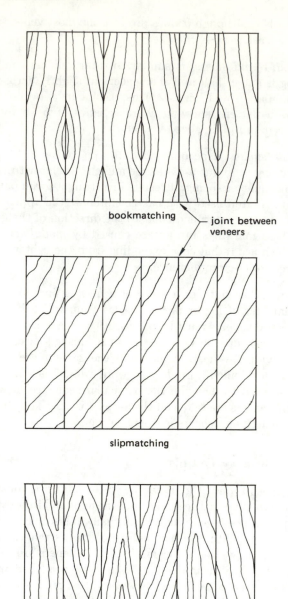

bookmatching — joint between veneers

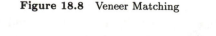

slipmatching

random matching

Figure 18.8   Veneer Matching

must be trimmed to fit around doors or other obstructions, there is a moderate loss of grain continuity.

The third and most expensive method is called *blueprint matching*. Here, the panels are manufactured to precisely fit the room and line up with every obstruction so grain continuity is not interrupted. Veneers from the same flitch are matched over doors, cabinets, and other items covered with paneling.

random widths of veneer

running match

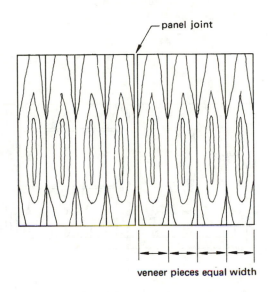

panel joint

veneer pieces equal width

balance match

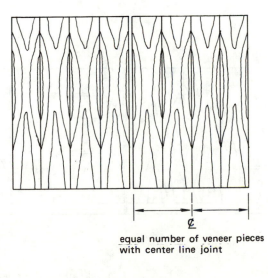

equal number of veneer pieces
with center line joint

center match

Figure 18.9 Panel Matching Veneers

Joints of flush paneling may be constructed in a number of ways depending on the finish appearance desired, shown in Figure 18.11. Paneling is hung on a wall with either steel Z-clips or wood cleats cut at an angle to allow the individual panels to be slipped over the hanger, which is anchored to the wall structure. These methods are also illustrated in Figure 18.11.

F. Laminates

A common finishing material used with millwork is *high-pressure plastic laminate*. This is a thin sheet material made by impregnating several layers of kraft paper with phenolic resins and overlaying the paper with a patterned or colored sheet and a layer of melamine resin. The entire assembly is placed in a hot press under high pressure where the various layers fuse together. Plastic laminates are used for counter tops, wall paneling, cabinets, shelving, and furniture.

Since laminates are very thin, they must be adhered to panel substrates such as plywood or particle board. Smaller pieces can be glued to solid pieces of lumber. There are several types and thicknesses of plastic laminate, the most common being a general-purpose type which is 0.050 inches thick. It is used for both vertical and horizontal applications. A post-forming type, 0.040 inches thick, is manufactured so it can be heated and bent to a small radius.

When plastic laminate is applied to large surfaces of paneling, it must be balanced with a backing sheet to inhibit moisture absorption and to attain structural balance so the panel does not warp.

G. Moisture Content and Shrinkage

Shrinkage and swelling of lumber in millwork is not as much of a problem as for rough and finish carpentry because of the improved manufacturing methods available in the shop and the fact that solid stock and veneer can be dried or acclimated to a particular region.

However, there are some general guidelines that should be followed. For most of the United States the optimum moisture content of millwork for interior applications is from 5 to 10 percent. The relative humidity necessary to maintain this optimum level is from 25 to 55 percent. In the more humid southern coastal areas the optimum moisture content is from 8 to 13 percent, while in the dry Southwest the corresponding values are from 4 to 9 percent.

H. Code Requirements

The various model building codes set limits on the flame spread ratings of interior finishes and occasionally on

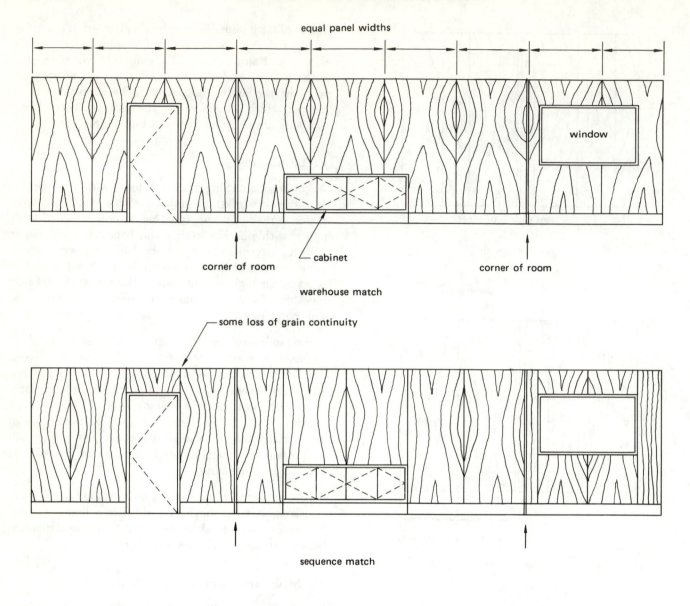

equal panel widths

window

corner of room

cabinet

corner of room

warehouse match

some loss of grain continuity

sequence match

blueprint match

Note: elevations of 3 sides of room shown "unfolded"

Figure 18.10   Matching Panels Within a Room

PROFESSIONAL PUBLICATIONS ● Belmont, CA

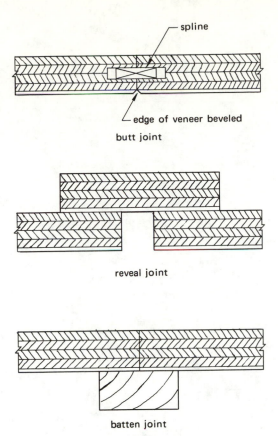

butt joint

reveal joint

batten joint

(a) vertical panel joints

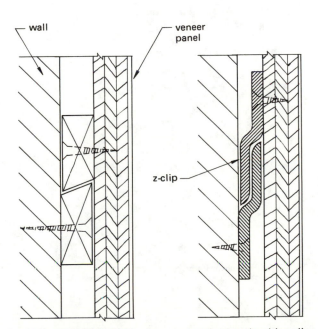

hanging panels with cleats   hanging panels with z-clips

(b) methods of hanging panels

Figure 18.11 Flush Panel Joints

trim, based on the occupancy of the building and the use area within the building. *Finish* is defined as wall coverings, paneling, grille work, ceilings, and other finishes applied to the wall and ceiling surfaces of a building. *Trim* includes items like moldings, railings, and door and window trim. Furniture, cabinets, shelving, doors, and windows are not considered interior finish and are not regulated by the finish provisions of the codes.

As discussed in Chapter 7, there are three flame spread groupings. In the Uniform Building Code these are I, II, and III, corresponding to flame spread ratings of 0–25, 26–75, and 76–200, respectively.

Different wood species have different flame spread ratings, but very few have ratings less than 75, so wood is generally considered a class III material unless it is treated with a fire retardant. However, treating often darkens the wood and makes it more difficult to finish.

3 FINISHES

Millwork can either be field finished or factory finished. More control can be achieved with a factory finish and this is the preferred method. Transparent finishes include penetrating oils, shellac, lacquer, and varnish. Oil finishes are easily applied and have a rich luster, but they have a short life and tend to darken with age. Shellac and lacquer become brittle and darken with age.

Other transparent finishes include the hard plastics such as polyurethane. They are very durable and will not darken with age but cost more and have a high gloss, which may not be desirable in some installations.

Prior to applying the final finish, wood may be stained to change its color. The two types of stains are water-based and solvent-based. Water-based stains yield a uniform color but raise the grain; solvent-based stains dry quickly and do not raise the grain, but are less uniform.

On many open-grain woods such as oak, mahogany, and teak, a filler should be applied prior to finishing to give a more uniform appearance to the millwork.

MOISTURE PROTECTION AND THERMAL INSULATION

19

Protecting buildings from water leakage and temperature transmission are two of the most troublesome technical problems an architect must solve. Water can leak into a building from underground moisture and groundwater and from precipitation on the roof and exterior walls. It can find its way into a building through a surface material such as roofing or a basement slab or through joints and penetrations between materials. Moisture can also be generated within a building from cooking, showering, or simple human habitation. This moisture must also be prevented from permeating the structure.

This chapter discusses the methods and materials used to protect a building from moisture and to control heat loss or heat gain.

1 DAMPPROOFING

Dampproofing is the control of moisture that is not under hydrostatic pressure. This includes water-repellent coatings on concrete, masonry, and wood walls above grade, but the most typical use of the term is for describing protection of slabs and foundation walls below grade that are subject to continuous exposure to moisture.

The following types of dampproofing may be used:

- *Admixtures:* various types of admixtures can be added to concrete to make it water repellent. These include materials such as salts of fatty acids, mineral oil, and powdered iron. They may reduce the strength of the concrete, but they make it much less permeable to water.

- *Bituminous coatings:* these are asphalt or coal-tar pitch materials applied to the exterior side of the foundation wall. They may be brushed on or sprayed, applied either hot or cold (depending on the type), and should be applied to smooth surfaces. They do not, however, seal cracks that develop after they are applied.

- *Cementitious coatings:* one or two coats of portland cement mortar can be troweled over the surface of masonry or concrete foundation walls. Mortar coatings are often used over very rough walls to provide a smooth surface for other dampproofing materials or by themselves. Powdered iron is often added as an admixture to the mortar. As the iron oxidizes it expands and limits the amount of shrinkage of the material, making a tighter seal.

- *Membranes:* these methods include built-up layers of hot or cold applied asphalt felts or membranes of butyl, polyvinyl chloride, and other synthetic materials. However, membranes are usually used for waterproofing walls subject to hydrostatic pressure and their cost and difficulty of application is usually not warranted for simple dampproofing.

- *Plastics:* silicone and polyurethane coatings are available, but they are usually reserved for above-grade dampproofing.

2 WATERPROOFING

Waterproofing is the control of moisture and water that is subject to hydrostatic pressure. This may include protecting structures below the water table. Waterproofing is a more difficult technical problem than dampproofing because of the water pressure and the need to create a continuous seal over all walls, slabs, and joints in the structure.

In most cases, waterproofing membranes are used on the exterior of the walls and slabs. These may be built-up layers of bituminous saturated felts similar to roofing, or single-ply membranes of synthetic materials such as butyl, polyvinyl chloride, or other proprietary products. When membranes are used, they are subject to puncture during backfilling operations. For this reason, a protection surface is placed over the waterproofing prior to backfilling. Figure 19.1 shows a typical installation of a waterproofed slab and foundation wall.

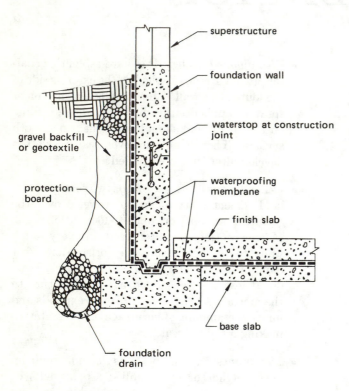

Figure 19.1 Waterproofed Wall and Slab

Joints in waterproofed walls are particularly subject to leakage. In concrete walls, *waterstops* are used to seal construction joints. Waterstops are dumbbell-shaped, continuous rubber or neoprene extrusions. Half of the waterstop is placed in the form during the first pour of concrete and the other half is allowed to extend into the second pour.

Another method of waterproofing is the use of *bentonite panels*. These are flat packages of bentonite clay inside kraft paper packages. They are placed under slabs and against walls. After backfilling, the kraft paper

deteriorates and the clay expands in the presence of moisture to form a waterproof barrier.

Of course, whether dampproofing or waterproofing a wall below grade, good construction design should include creating a positive slope away from the building to minimize water penetration around the foundation and provide some type of perimeter drainage if a heavy concentration of water is anticipated. This may include backfilling with gravel and placing perimeter foundation drains at the footing line, as discussed in Chapter 13. Hydrostatic pressure buildup can also be alleviated by using a geotextile matting over the waterproofing.

3 BUILDING INSULATION

Insulation is used to control unwanted heat flow, which can be from a warm building to a cold exterior or from a hot climate into a habitable space. Selecting and detailing insulation for buildings requires an understanding of the processes of heat gain and heat loss because different kinds of insulation are used to control them.

A. Methods of Heat Transfer

Heat is transferred in three ways: conduction, convection, and radiation. *Conduction* is the flow of heat within a material or between materials without displacement of the particles of the material. *Convection* is the transfer of heat within a fluid, either gas or liquid, by the movement of the fluid from an area of higher temperature to an area of lower temperature. *Radiation* is the transfer of heat energy through electromagnetic waves from one surface to a colder surface.

The best insulation is a vacuum. The next best insulation is air kept absolutely motionless in a space between two materials. However, this does not usually occur because convection currents carry warm air in one part of the space to the cooler parts of the space where heat is transferred by conduction. Most insulations are designed to create very small air pockets small enough to prevent convection but large enough to prevent the direct transfer of heat by conduction between the insulating material.

B. Measuring Thermal Resistance

Thermal resistance is described with several terms, as outlined in Chapter 8. The quantity of heat used to measure transfer is the *British thermal unit* (BTU), which is the amount of heat required to raise the temperature of 1 pound of water by 1 degree Fahrenheit. The basic unit of conductance is a material's *k* value, or *conductivity*. This is the number of BTUs per hour that pass through 1 square foot of homogeneous material 1 inch thick when the temperature differential is 1 degree Fahrenheit. When the material is more than 1 inch thick, the unit is conductance, or the C value.

The more common term used is the R value, or resistance of a material. *Resistance* is the number of hours needed for 1 BTU to pass through 1 square foot of a material of a given thickness when the temperature differential is 1 degree Fahrenheit. It is the reciprocal of conductance. Thus, the lower a material's k or C value, the better insulator it is, while higher R values also indicate a better insulating value.

There are three general types of insulation used to control heat transfer by conduction and convection: loose, batt, and rigid.

C. Loose Insulation

Loose insulation, or fill insulation, as it is sometimes called, is made from several materials. *Rock wool* is a fibrous material formed by blowing molten rock under pressure; *perlite* is volcanic rock expanded by heating; and *vermiculite* is mica expanded by heating. Rock wool, perlite, and vermiculite are all non-combustible and have good thermal resistance.

Cellulose is shredded waste paper or wood fibers. By itself, cellulose is combustible, but chemicals are added to make it fire resistant and to inhibit the growth of fungus and repel rodents. Granular pellets of foamed plastic, such as polystyrene are also available as fill insulation.

Loose insulation is used for pouring into cavities such as cells of concrete block walls and other hard-to-reach places. It is also widely used in retrofit applications because it can be blown into wall and ceiling cavities where other types of insulation cannot be installed without great difficulty.

D. Batt Insulation

Batt insulation consists of fibrous material placed on or within a kraft paper carrier. The insulation is usually mineral fiber or glass fiber. In addition to providing a means of installation and holding the insulation in place, the kraft paper also serves as a vapor barrier. Some batt insulation also comes with a reflective surface. Batts come in standard widths designed to fit within stud and joist spacings of 16 inches or 24 inches on center. It is either friction fitted or attached by stapling the paper flanges to the studs. Various thicknesses are available to suit the size of the cavity and the R value required.

If an integral vapor barrier is included, it should be placed on the warm side of the insulation (that side facing the heated room) to prevent condensation of moisture vapor from the interior from forming on the insulation, thus decreasing its effectiveness.

E. Rigid Insulation

Rigid insulation comprises two types: boards and sprayed-on. Organic board insulation is made from wood or cane fiber sandwiched between coatings of bituminous material, paper, foil, or other materials. Rigid boards can also be made with perlite or cork. However, organic board insulation has generally given way to the inorganic plastics, which have much higher insulating values.

Inorganic foamed insulation is made from polyurethane, polystyrene, or polyisocyanurate. If the insulation is formed with closed cells, it has a much higher resistance to moisture. These are the types appropriate for foundation insulation and other situations where water may be present.

Fiberglass and perlite rigid board are also available for use as wall or roof insulation. Rigid insulation may be purchased with foil coverings to act as vapor barriers and as reflective insulation.

F. Reflective Insulation

Reflective surfaces have two properties that make them good for insulation. The first is *reflectivity*, which simply means that the surface reflects radiant heat and strikes it back to the source. The other property is emissivity. *Emissivity* is a measure of the ability of a material to absorb, and then radiate, heat. A foil-faced insulation will emit very little heat it happens to receive by conduction.

To be most effective, reflective insulation should be used in conjunction with a closed air space on at least one side of the material.

G. Vapor Barriers

A *vapor barrier* is a material used to prevent the transmission of water vapor between spaces. Vapor barriers are not themselves insulation but play an important role in the effectiveness of other insulating materials.

Water vapor is produced in all buildings by human respiration and perspiration, by cooking, and by other activities that involve water. In addition, there is always a certain amount of humidity present in the air. Warm air is capable of holding more water than cold air. If the temperature of the air containing a certain amount of water vapor drops, the relative humidity rises until the saturation point is reached. This is known as the *dew point*, the point at which water condenses from the vapor.

During a cold day, water vapor in the air can pass through many building materials into the wall and ceiling cavities. If the temperature is cold enough the water condenses, wetting the insulation and greatly reducing its effectiveness. In addition, the water can soak wood and other materials, promoting their deterioration.

To avoid this, vapor barriers are placed on the warm side of the insulation to prevent the water from reaching the dew point temperature. Some vapor barriers are integral with the insulation; others, such as polyethylene films, are applied as separate sheets.

4   SHINGLES AND ROOFING TILE

Shingles and tiles are two of the oldest types of roofing materials. They consist of small, individual pieces of material placed on a sloped surface in order to shed water.

A. Types of Roofs

Roofs are classified according to their shape. Some of the more common types are illustrated in Figure 19.2, along with the common terms used to describe the various parts.

The amount of slope of a roof is designated by its *pitch*, which is the number of inches of rise for every 12 inches of horizontal projection or run. For example, a 5/12 pitch rises 5 inches vertically for every foot of horizontal projection.

Not all roofing materials are appropriate for all pitches, although the exact pitch for any one material may affect how the roofing is detailed and installed. For example, low-slope roofs for asphalt shingles require a double layer of roofing felt rather than the normal single layer. Some general guidelines are given in Table 19.1.

When describing size, estimating, and ordering materials, roofing area is referred to in squares. A square is simply equal to 100 square feet.

B. Shingles

Shingles are small, rectangular or shaped units intended to shed water rather than form a watertight seal. Asphalt shingles are made from a composition of felt, asphalt, mineral stabilizers, and mineral granules. They

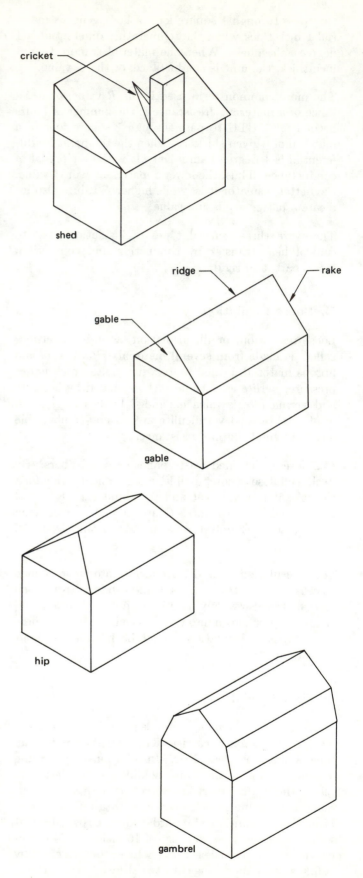

Figure 19.2   Roof Types

Table 19.1
Recommended Slopes for Roofing

roofing type	slope–vertical rise in inches per 12 inches	
	minimum slope	maximum slope
asplhalt shingles, low slope	2	4
asphalt shingles, normal	4	12
asphalt roll roofing	1	4
wood shingles	4	–
clay tile	4	–
slate tile	4	–
metal roofing	3	–
built up roofing	1/4	1
single-ply membranes	1/4	6
(varies with type and method of attachment)		

are available in a variety of colors and shapes and are laid over an asphalt-impregnated roofing felt that is nailed to wood sheathing.

Wood shakes are normally manufactured from cedar and are available in a variety of grades (no. 1, blue label being the best) and finishes including smooth face, and handsplit face. A typical installation is shown in Figure 19.3. Wood shingles are typically laid over spaced sheathing so that they can breathe without a buildup of moisture.

Wood shingles are laid so only a certain portion is visible. This is called the *exposure*, and the dimension varies with the pitch of the roof. The edges are staggered so joints do not coincide, and 30-pound asphalt felt is used as an underlayment.

C. Roofing Tile

Roofing tile consists of slate, clay tile, and concrete tile. Since each type is heavy (10 pounds per square foot or more), the roof structure must be sized accordingly.

Slate tile is made by splitting quarried slate into rectangular pieces from 6 to 14 inches wide and from 16 to 24 inches long. Slate tile is about 1/4 inch in thickness. It is laid over 30-pound asphalt-saturated roofing felt on wood or nailable concrete decking. The pieces are laid like other shingles, with the sides and ends overlapping, attached with copper or galvanized nails driven through prepunched holes in the slate. Slate is very expensive as a roofing material, but it is fire resistant and very durable, with most slate roofs lasting over 100 years.

Clay tile, available in many colors, patterns, and textures, is made from the same clay as brick and is formed into various shapes. Like slate, it is laid on roofing felt over a sloped wood or nailable deck and attached by nailing through prepunched holes. Also like slate, clay tile is expensive, but very durable, fire resistant, and attractive. Some of the available shapes are shown in Figure 19.4.

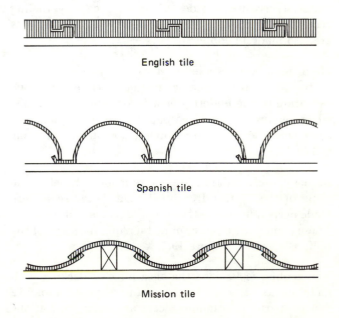

English tile

Spanish tile

Mission tile

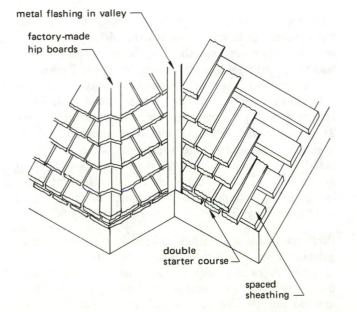

Figure 19.3 Wood Shingle Installation

Figure 19.4 Clay Roofing Tile Profiles

Concrete tile, manufactured from portland cement and fine aggregates, is available in several styles, some flat and others formed to look like clay tile. It is also available in several colors. Concrete tile is less expensive than clay tile, but it is still durable and fire resistant.

5   PREFORMED ROOFING AND SIDING

A. Sheet Metal Roofing

Metal roofing is durable, attractive, and can conform to a wide variety of roof shapes. Its disadvantages include high cost and the difficulty of installing it properly. Sheet metal roofs are fabricated of individual sheets of metal joined with various types of interlocking joints. Because of the high coefficient of expansion of metals used for roofing, these joints and other parts of the roofing system must be designed to allow for expansion and contraction.

Metals used for roofing include copper, galvanized iron, aluminum, and terne plate. *Terne plate* is steel sheet coated with lead and tin. Terne-coated stainless steel is also available. Other metals that are sometimes used include stainless steel, zinc, and lead. Stainless steel is expensive, but very durable and maintenance free.

Copper roofs are popular because of their long life and the attractive green patina that forms after a few years of weathering. Copper is also a good metal roofing material because a wide variety of necessary roofing accessories such as gutters, flashing, and downspouts are also made in copper.

Metal roofs are installed over asphalt roofing felt laid on top of wood or nailable concrete decking. The one exception to the underlayment is for terne or tin roofs, which require a rosin-sized paper since the asphalt can react with the tin. The minimum slope for metal roofs is 3 in 12.

In most cases, standing seams are made parallel to the slope of the roof and crimped tight. Flat seams are made perpendicular to the standing seams and soldered. These connect two pieces of metal along the slope of the roof, as shown in Figure 19.5.

The roofing is held to the sheathing or decking with metal cleats attached to the roof and spaced about 12 inches apart. Continuous cleats are often used at the eaves, rakes (gable ends), and flashing. In all cases, cleats, nails, and other fasteners must be of the same type of metal to avoid galvanic action.

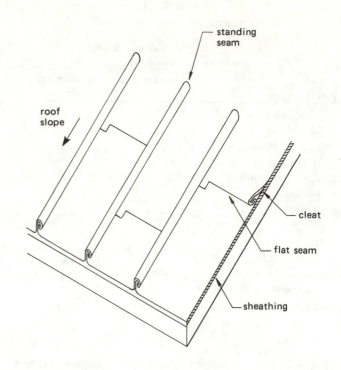

Figure 19.5   Standing Seam Metal Roof

B. Preformed Roof and Wall Panels

Preformed panels are shaped pieces of metal or assemblies of metal facing with insulation between that are self-supporting and span between intermediate supports. Roof panels span between purlins and wall panels span between horizontal girts.

The simplest preformed panels are simply corrugated or fluted sheets of metal of standard widths and varying lengths. They are assembled by lapping one corrugation at the edges and overlapping the ends. Preformed panels are also made as sandwich assemblies with insulation between two finished faces, joined with interlocking edges and a weather seal. Common widths are 24 inches, 30 inches, and 36 inches, although others are available. These types of sandwich panels are fabricated in lengths to match the requirements of the job and usually span from the foundation to the roof framing in one-story buildings. If two panels must be placed end to end they are butt-jointed with flashing between.

Preformed panels are made primarily from aluminum, galvanized steel, and porcelain enamel steel. They are attached to framing with screws, clips, and proprietary fasteners. They are durable, easy and quick to install, and do not require on-site finishing. For industrial buildings and some other types of structures, a sandwich panel can serve as the interior finish as well as the exterior finish. However, they are most economical when used on large, flat, unbroken expanses of walls or roofs.

6 MEMBRANE ROOFING

Membrane roofing includes those materials applied in thin sheets to nearly flat roofs. It also includes liquid applied products that can be applied to any roof slope. Although some manufacturers claim that their products are suitable for flat roofs, every roof should have at least a 1/4-inch-per-foot slope to avoid standing water and the possibility of ponding. *Ponding* occurs when standing water causes a flat roof to deflect a little, allowing more water to collect that causes more deflection that, in turn, allows more water to collect. The process continues until the roof fails.

A. Built-Up Bituminous Roofing

Built-up roofing consists of several overlapping layers of bituminous saturated roofing felts cemented together with roofing cement. The bituminous material can be either asphalt or coal tar pitch. The basic construction of such a roof is illustrated in Figure 19.6.

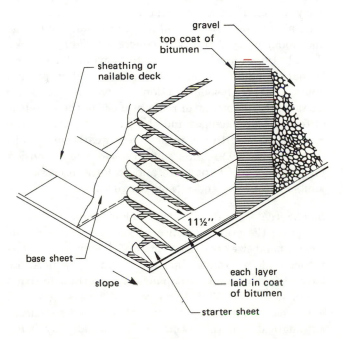

Figure 19.6 3-Ply Built-up Roof

Built-up roofs can be installed over nailable or non-nailable decks; the exact construction procedure changes slightly depending on which type is present. For nailable decks, a base sheet of unsaturated felt is nailed to the deck and covered with a coating of roofing cement. On non-nailable decks the base sheet is omitted and a base coat applied.

Three, four, or five layers of saturated roofing felts are then laid on top of each other with each layer being bedded in roofing cement so felt does not touch felt. The number of layers is determined by the type of deck used and the length of guarantee period desired. Five-ply roofs provide the most protection. A final coating of bituminous material is placed over the entire roof and covered with gravel or crushed slag. The purpose of the gravel is to protect the roofing from sunlight and other effects of weathering.

A variation of the built-up roof is the *inverted membrane roof*. Here, the built-up roof is placed on the structural decking and rigid, closed-cell insulation placed over the roof rather than under it. The insulation is held down with gravel ballast. The purpose of this type of construction is to protect the membrane from the normal deleterious effects of expansion and contraction, drying, ultraviolet rays, and foot traffic that can cause leaks.

B. Built-Up Roofing Construction Details

As with any roof, built-up roofs must be designed to provide for positive drainage. As mentioned above, the minimum roof slope should be 1/4 inch per foot. Nearly flat membrane roofs may be drained to interior drains, to perimeter drains, or to gutters on the low side of the roof. Crickets should be used to provide positive drainage in all directions. When a roof is surrounded on four sides with a parapet or walls, there should be scuppers (also called overflow drains) through the parapet positioned with their low edge slightly above the top of the roof to provide a second means of drainage should the primary drains become clogged. These are usually required by building codes.

At the intersection of the roof and any vertical surface such as a wall or parapet, continuous triangular cant strips are placed in the intersection to provide positive drainage away from the joint and to give a smooth transition surface for the installation of the flashing at these points.

When objects project through a roof or roof-mounted equipment needs to be supported, the intersection of the roofing and these projections must be waterproofed. One traditional way is to provide a pitch pan, a small metal enclosure around the projection that is filled with bituminous material. This method, however, is usually not recommended because of its tendency to leak. Projections should be treated like other joints and installed with cant strips and flashing. Roof-mounted equipment should be placed on wood curbs that are likewise flashed.

C. Single-Ply Roofing

Single-ply roofing is a single membrane layer of various types of materials. Because the quality of built-up roofing is labor intensive and largely dependent on proper installation, single-ply roofing has come into widespread use. Although it too must be applied carefully, there are usually installation problems. In addition, single-ply roofing is more resistant to slight building movement and the damaging effects of the weather.

There are several types of single-ply membranes. *Modified bitumens* are sheets about 50 mils thick comprised of bitumen, a chemical additive to enhance the elastic properties of the bitumen, and a reinforcing fabric to add tensile strength. The bitumen sheet is laid over insulation or insulating decks with a separator sheet between the deck and the membrane. These sheets allow the roof to move independently of the structure, and some sheets are designed to allow water vapor from the building to escape to the perimeter of the roof. To protect the membrane from ultraviolet degradation and anchor it, the surface is covered with gravel ballast.

Other types of membranes include EPDM (ethylene propylene diene monomer), PVC (polyvinyl chloride), and CPE (chlorinated polyethylene). These come in large sheets, the edges of which are sealed with chemicals or by heating the lapped edges. Depending on the material and type of system, they are applied either loose laid or adhered. Loose-laid sheets are free to move separately from the roof deck, while adhered sheets are either fully adhered to the deck with bonding adhesive or attached with mechanical fasteners.

D. Elastic Liquid Roofing

Liquid-applied roofings include butyl, neoprene, hypalon, and other products. They are applied in liquid form in one or two coats by brushing or spraying and air-cured to form an elastic, waterproof surface. Liquid-applied membranes are also used for below-grade waterproofing on foundation walls, tanks, pools, and for similar applications. These products are particularly suited for roofs with complex shapes such as thin shell concrete domes.

7 FLASHING

Flashing prevents water penetration and directs any water that does get into construction back to the outside.

Flashing is made of galvanized steel, stainless steel, aluminum, copper, plastic, and elastomeric materials. Material selection depends on the other metals or materials it is in contact with, the configuration of the joint, the durability desired, and the cost.

Flashing protects joints wherever water penetration is anticipated or where two dissimilar surfaces meet at an angle. This may include the intersection of roofs with parapets, above windows, above steel lintels supporting masonry, between butt joints of preformed siding, and elsewhere. Figure 19.7 shows some common metal flashing details, and Figure 19.8 illustrates flashing for single-ply roofing installations. Masonry flashing details are shown in Figures 15.5 and 15.7. In all cases, the flashing detail should allow joint movement without destroying the integrity of the flashing connection.

8 ROOF ACCESSORIES

Roof accessories include items in addition to the roofing itself or flashing necessary to form a complete installation. This may involve expansion joints, copings, roof hatches, smoke vents, and similar fabrications.

Expansion joints are required in buildings to allow for movement caused by temperature changes in materials and differential movement between building sections. They are required at frequent intervals in long buildings; about every 100 to 150 feet in masonry buildings and about every 200 feet in concrete buildings. They should also be located at the junctions of T-, L-, and U-shaped buildings and where a low building portion abuts a higher, heavier section. Expansion joints are particularly important in roofs because of the extremes of temperature changes and the fact that joints in the roof are exposed to the most severe weathering conditions. Figure 19.9 shows some typical roof expansion joints. Refer to Chapters 14 and 15 for a discussion of joints for concrete and masonry structures.

Smoke vents are devices that allow excess smoke to escape in the event of a fire. Exact requirements for location and size of smoke vents are given in the various model building codes, but in general they must be located in hazardous occupancies, in certain business occupancies over 50,000 square feet, over stages, and above elevator shafts. Vents are designed to release automatically in the event of fire, usually by being spring-loaded and connected to a fusible link.

9 CAULKING AND SEALANTS

Sealants are flexible materials used to close joints between materials. The word "sealant" is the more correct

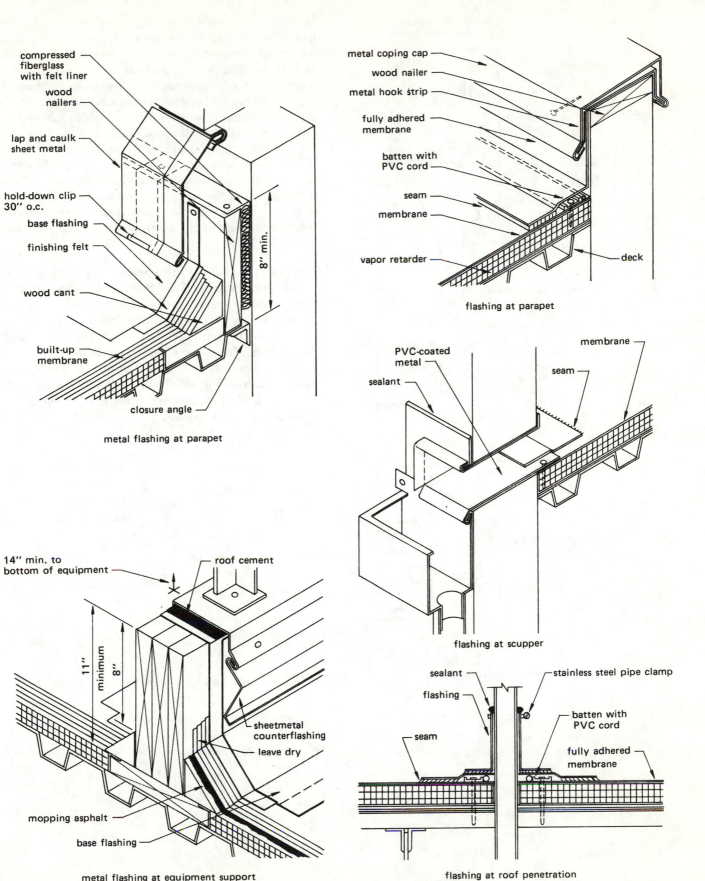

Figure 19.7 Metal Flashing Details

Figure 19.8 Elastomeric Flashing Details

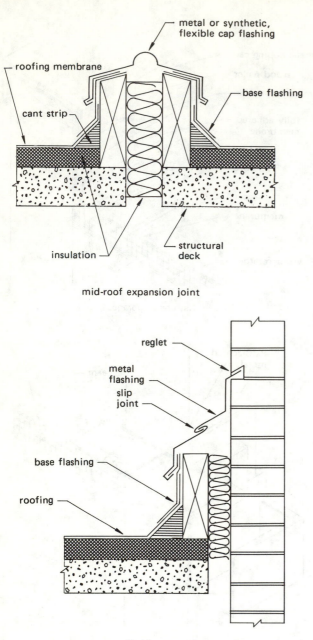

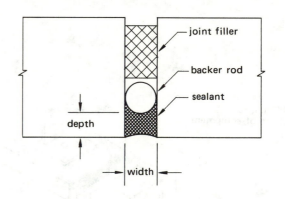

term, but the word "caulking" is often used to designate low-performance sealants employed where little movement is expected, such as between a window frame and an exterior wall. Sealants must be capable of adhering to the joints while remaining elastic and weatherproof. There are several types of sealants, each having slightly different properties and uses under various conditions. Sealants are classified as low, intermediate, and high performance, depending on the maximum amount of joint movement they can tolerate. Low-performance sealants are used in joints with plus or minus 5 percent movement, intermediate-performance sealants for plus or minus 12.5 percent movement, and high-performance sealants for joints with up to about 25 percent movement.

The width and depth of a sealant are critical to its proper performance. See Figure 19.10. The width is determined by the expected joint movement. The depth should be equal to the width for joints up to 1/2 inch wide; for joints from 1/2 inch to 1 inch, the depth should be 1/2 inch. For wider joints the sealant depth should not be greater than one-half the width. Joint fillers are used behind the sealant to control the depth of the sealant. Table 19.2 lists some of the common sealant types and their properties.

Figure 19.9   Expansion Joints

Figure 19.10   Typical Joint with Sealant

Table 19.2
Comparative Properties of Sealants

	sealant types									
	oil base	butyl	acrylic, water base	acrylic, solvent base	polysulfide, one part	polysulfide, two part	polyurethane, one part	polyurethane, two part	silicone	notes
recommended maximum joint movement, %	±5	±7.5	±7.5	±12.5	±12.5 to ±25	±25	±12.5 to ±15	±25	±25	(1)
life expectancy (in years)	5–10	10+	10	15–20	20	20	20+	20+	20+	
maximum joint width (in inches)	1/4	1/2	1/2	3/4	3/4	1	3/4	1–2	3/4	(2)
weight shrinkage (in %)	10+	5–10	15	15	10	10	10	10	4	
adhesion to: wood	•	•	•	•	•	•	•	•	•	(3)
metal	•	•	•	•	•	•	•	•	•'	
masonry	•	•	•	•	•	•	•	•	•	(3)
glass	•	•	•	•	•	•	•	•	•	
plastic		•	•	•					•	
curing time (in days)	120	120	5	14	14+	7	7+	3–5	5	
maximum elongation (in %)	15	40	60	60+	300	600	300+	400+	250+	
self-leveling available	n/a	n/a		•	•	•		•	•	
non-sag available	n/a	n/a	•	•	•	•	•	•	•	
resistance to: (see legend) ultraviolet	1–2	2–3	1–3	3–4	2	2–3	3	3	5	
cut/tear	1	2	1–2	1	3	3	4–5	4–5	1–2	
abrasion	1	2	1–2	1–2	1	1	3	3	1	
weathering	1–2	2	1–3	3–4	3	3	3–4	3–4	4–5	
oil/grease	2	1–2	2	3	3	3	3	3	2	
compression	1	2–3	1–2	1	3	3	4	4	4–5	
extension	1	1	1–2	1	2–3	2–3	4–5	4–5	4–5	
water immersion	2	2–3	1	1–2	3	3	1	1	3	

(1) Some high performance urethanes and silicones have movement capabilities as high as ±50%.
(2) Figures given are conservative. Verify manufacturers' literature for specific recommendations.
(3) Primer may be required.

Legend:
1 = Poor
2 = Fair
3 = Good
4 = Very good
5 = Excellent

20 DOORS, WINDOWS, AND GLAZING

With the materials and construction systems available today, doors and windows no longer simply serve to provide passage between spaces or to admit light. Openings can be designed and specified to fulfill certain functions selectively. For example, a window can admit light but be designed to minimize sound transmission while still providing security. Or a door passage can be designed as an unobtrusive, clear opening while still providing fire protection in the event of an emergency.

1 DOOR OPENINGS

Both metal and wood doors can serve a variety of functions. They can control passage, provide visual and sound privacy, maintain security, supply fire resistance and weather protection, control light, and serve as radiation shielding. It is important to understand what kind of control you want in order to select the most appropriate type of door. Considerations of durability, cost, appearance, ease of use, method of construction, and availability are also important in door selection.

There are three major components of a door system: the door itself, the frame, and the hardware. Each must be coordinated with the other components and be appropriate for the circumstances and design intent.

The common parts of a door opening are illustrated in Figure 20.1. To differentiate the two jambs, the side where the hinge or pivot is installed is called the *hinge jamb* and the jamb where the door closes is called the *strike side* or *strike jamb*.

There is also a standard method of referring to the way a door swings, called the *door hand* or the *handing* of a door. Handing is used by specifiers and hardware suppliers and manufacturers to indicate exactly what kind of hardware must be supplied for a specific opening. Some hardware will only work on a door that swings a

particular way because of the way the strike side of the door is beveled. Hardware that can work on any hand of door is called reversible or non-handed.

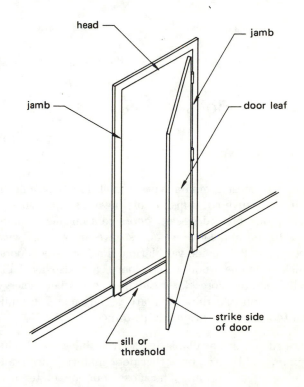

Figure 20.1 Parts of a Door

The hand of a door is determined by standing on the outside of the door, as shown in Figure 20.2. The exterior of a building is considered the outside, as is the hallway side of a room door, or the lobby side of a door opening into a room. In situations where the distinction is not clear, the outside is considered the side of the door where the hinge is not visible. When standing on the outside looking at the door, if the door hinges on the left and swings away from you, it is a *left-hand door*. If it hinges on the right and swings away from you, it is a *right-hand door*. If the door swings toward you, it is considered a *left-hand reverse* or a *right-hand reverse*, depending on the location of the hinge or pivot.

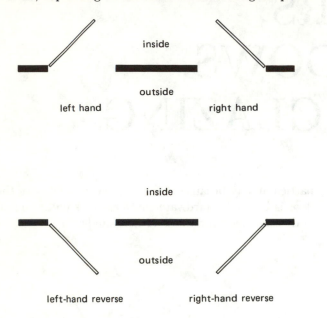

Figure 20.2 Door Handing

2 METAL DOORS AND FRAMES

A. Door Types

The three most common types of metal doors are flush, sash, and louvered. *Flush doors* have a single, smooth surface on both sides; *sash doors* contain one or more glass lights; and *louvered doors* have an opening with metal slats to provide ventilation. Paneled steel doors, which resemble wood panel doors, are also available with insulated cores for residential use where energy conservation and durability are requirements in addition to a more traditional appearance.

Metal doors are available in steel, stainless steel, aluminum, and bronze, but other door materials are available on special order. The most common material is steel with a painted finish.

B. Construction

Steel doors are constructed with faces of cold rolled sheet steel. 18 gage steel is used for light-duty doors while 16 gage is most common. Heavier gages are used for special needs. The steel face is attached to cores of honeycomb kraft paper, steel ribs, hardboard, or other materials. The edges are made of steel channels, with the locations for hardware reinforced with heavier gage steel. Mineral wool or other materials are used to provide sound-deadening qualities, if required.

C. Sizes

Although metal doors can be custom made in almost any practical size, standard widths are 2 feet 0 inches, 2 feet 4 inches, 2 feet 6 inches, 2 feet 8 inches, 3 feet 0 inches, 3 feet 4 inches, 3 feet 6 inches, 3 feet 8 inches, and 4 feet 0 inches. Standard heights are 6 feet 8 inches, 7 feet 0 inches, and 8 feet 0 inches. The standard thickness is 1 3/4 inches.

D. Frames

Steel door frames can be used for either steel doors or wood doors and are made from sheet steel bent into the shape required for the door installation. Frames are made from 12, 14, or 16 gage steel, depending on location and use. The frame is mortised for the installation of hinges and door strikes and is reinforced at these points with heavier gage steel. Two of the most common frame profiles are shown in Figure 20.3 along with some standard dimensions and the terminology used to describe the parts. Various types of anchoring devices are used inside the frame to attach it to gypsum board, masonry, concrete, and other materials. Where a fire rating over 20 minutes is required, steel frames are used almost exclusively.

Aluminum frames are used for both aluminum doors and wood doors. They are constructed of extruded sections and as a consequence can have thinner face dimensions and more elaborate shapes than are possible with bent steel.

Steel frames are painted, either in the shop or on site. Aluminum frames are anodized with the standard anodized colors or can be factory coated with a variety of colors with baked acrylic paints and other finishes.

3 WOOD DOORS AND FRAMES

Wood doors are the most common types for both residential and commercial construction. They are available in a variety of styles, sizes, finishes, and methods of operation.

A. Door Types

Wood doors can be classed according to their operation. *Swinging doors* are the most typical type and function by being hinged or pivoted on one side. They

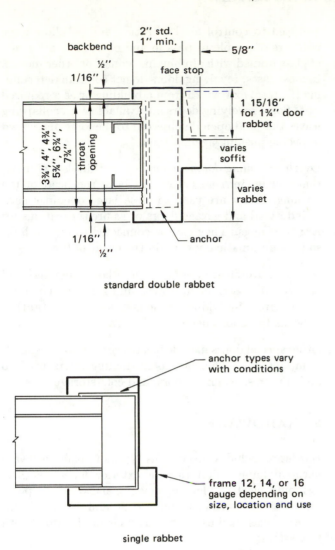

Figure 20.3 Standard Steel Door Frames

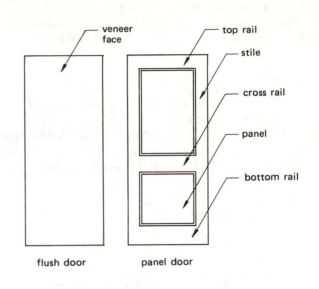

Figure 20.4 Types of Wood Doors

cores as described below. *Panel doors* consist of solid vertical stiles and horizontal rails that serve as a frame for flat or raised panels.

B. Construction

Wood doors are either hollow core or solid core. *Hollow core doors* are made of one or three plies of veneer on each side of a cellular cardboard interior. The stile and rails frame is made of solid wood with larger blocks of solid wood where the locksets or latchsets are installed. Hollow core doors are used in interior applications where only light use is expected and where cost is a consideration. They have no fire resistive capabilities.

Solid core doors are made with a variety of core types depending on the functional requirements of the door. Cores may be particle board, stave core (solid blocks of wood), or mineral core for fire-rated doors. Solid core doors are used for their fire-resistive properties, as acoustical barriers, for security, and for their superior durability. Solid core doors may have a fire rating from 20 minutes to 1 1/2 hours.

The face veneers of wood doors can be made from any available hardwood species using rotary-cut, plain-sliced, quarter-sliced, or rift-cut methods, just like wood panels. The veneers can be bookmatched, slip matched, or random matched, although bookmatching is the most common. Veneers of hardboard suitable for painting and plastic laminate are also available.

C. Sizes

Like metal doors, wood doors can be custom made to any size, but the standard widths are 2 feet 0 inches,

are relatively inexpensive, easy to install, and can accommodate a large volume of traffic. *Double-acting doors* swing in both directions when mounted on pivot hardware or special double-acting hinges.

Pocket sliding doors travel on a top track and move horizontally into a pocket built into the wall. They are good for limited space, but they are awkward to operate and latching and sealing are difficult.

Bypass sliding doors also travel on a top or bottom rail and are often used for closet doors where space is limited. Bifolding and multifolding doors are also used for closets and other large openings where full access needs to be provided when the doors are open.

The two primary types of wood doors are the flush door and the panel door. See Figure 20.4. *Flush doors* consist of a thin, flat veneer laminated to various types of

2 feet 4 inches, 2 feet 6 inches, 2 feet 8 inches, 3 feet 0 inches, and 3 feet 4 inches. Standard heights are 6 feet 8 inches and 7 feet 0 inches, although higher doors, often used in commercial construction, are available. Hollow core doors are 1 3/8 inches thick and solid core doors 1 3/4 inches thick; 2 1/4 inches thick doors are available for large, exterior doors and special applications.

D. Frames

Frames for wood doors are made from wood, steel (hollow metal), and aluminum. A common wood frame jamb is illustrated in Figure 20.5. Although the stop and casing are shown as rectangular pieces, several different profiles of trim are available and frequently used.

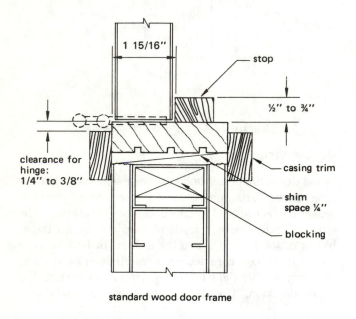

standard wood door frame

Figure 20.5 Standard Wood Door Frame

The decision concerning the type of frame to use for a wood door depends on the appearance desired, the type of partition the opening is being installed in, the fire rating requirements, the security needed, and the durability desired. For example, wood frames may be used in 20-, 30-, and 45-minute fire door assemblies, but a one-hour-rated door must be installed in a rated metal frame.

4 SPECIAL DOORS

Special doors have a wide variety of applications where a special closing assembly is required. Some of the more common types of special doors include the following:

Revolving doors are assemblies of four leaves connected at a central point that rotate within an enclosure. They are used to control air infiltration and to allow large numbers of people to pass in and out. They are made of glass framed with aluminum, bronze, or other metals. In most cases, revolving doors do not count in determining the total exit width from a building or as a required exit. Some revolving doors are available with collapsing leaves that fold open if subjected to the force of a crowd of people pushing against them.

Overhead coiling doors are made from thin slats of metal that roll up into an enclosure above the head of the opening. They are used to close large openings such as industrial and garage doors or as fire separations for large openings. They can be connected to fusible links so they automatically close in the event of fire.

Sectional overhead doors also close large openings and are typically used for industrial and garages. The door is made from individual sections of wood or metal that hinge as the door opened.

Other special doors include blast-resistant doors, sound-retardant doors, hangar doors, folding doors used to divide rooms, security doors, and cold-storage doors.

5 HARDWARE

Hardware includes the various types of finish hardware normally found on interior and exterior doors, weather-stripping, electrical locking devices, and window operators. Cabinet hardware and curtain and drapery hardware are classified as a different type and included with those items.

A. Functions of Hardware

Hardware is a vital part of any door opening assembly. In general, hardware can be grouped according to the function it serves based on the following list:

- Hanging the door: hinges, pivots, and combination pivots and closers.

- Operating the door: handles, latchsets, push plates, and pull bars.

- Closing the door: door closers and combination pivots and closers.

- Locking the door: locksets, dead bolts, flush bolts, electric locks, and other special devices.

- Sealing the door: weatherstripping, sound seals, smoke seals.

- Protecting the door: kick plates, corner protection, and similar materials.

B. Hinges

Hinges are the most common method of attaching a door to its frame. They are also referred to as *butts* because they are usually attached to the butt edge of a door. Hinges consist of two leaves with an odd number of knuckles on one leaf and an even number of knuckles on the other. The knuckles are attached with a pin. The pin and knuckles form the barrel of the hinge, which is finished with a tip.

There are four basic types of hinges: full mortise, half mortise, full surface, and half surface. These are shown in Figure 20.6.

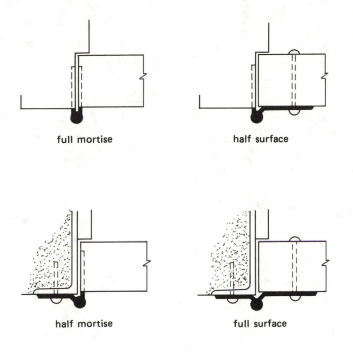

full mortise   half surface

half mortise   full surface

Figure 20.6   Types of Hinges

Full mortise is the most common type and has both leaves fully mortised into the frame and edge of the door. *Half-surface* hinges have one leaf mounted on the face of the door and the other leaf mortised into the frame. *Half-mortise* hinge leaves are surface applied to the frame and mortised into the edge of the door. *Full-surface* hinges are applied to the face of both the door and frame. The various types of hinges are used when either the door or frame cannot be mortised. For example, a half-mortise hinge may be bolted or welded to a heavy steel frame.

There are also special types of hinges. Raised barrel hinges are used when there is not room for the barrel to extend past the trim. The barrel is offset to allow one leaf to be mortised into the frame. Swing clear hinges have a special shape that allows the door to swing 90 degrees so the full opening of the doorway is available.

Without a swing clear hinge, standard hardware decreases the opening width by the thickness of the door when it is open 90 degrees.

Hinges are available with or without ball bearings and in three weights. Which type to use depends on the door weight and frequency of use. *Low-frequency* doors like residential doors can use standard weight, plain-bearing hinges. Most commercial applications require standard weight, ball-bearing hinges. *High-frequency* applications such as office building entrances, theaters, and so forth require heavy weight, ball bearing hinges. In addition, ball bearing hinges are required for fire-rated assemblies and on all doors with closers.

The size and number of hinges for a door depend on a number of factors. The size is given by two numbers such as $4 \times 4\ 1/2$. The first number is the length, which is the length of the barrel, and the second number is the width, which is the dimension when the hinge is open.

The width of the hinge is determined by the width of the door and the clearance required around jamb trim. One rule of thumb is that the width of the hinge equals twice the door thickness, plus trim projection, minus 1/2 inch. If a fraction falls between standard sizes, use the next larger size. Common hinge widths for 1 3/4 inch doors are 4 inches and 4 1/2 inches.

The length of the hinge is determined by the door thickness and the door width, as shown in Table 20.1.

Table 20.1
How to Determine Hinge Lengths

door thickness	door width	length of hinges
3/4 to 1 1/8″	to 24″	2 1/2″
1 3/8″	to 32 ″	3 1/3″
1 3/8″	over 32″ to 37″	4″
1 3/4″	to 36″	4 1/2″
1 3/4″	over 36″ to 48″	5″
1 3/4″	over 48″	6″
2, 2 1/4, 2 1/2″	to 42″	5″ heavy wt.
2, 2 1/4, 2 1/2″	over 42″	6″ heavy wt.

The number of hinges is determined by the height of the door. Numbers of hinges are commonly referred to by pairs; one pair being two hinges. Doors up to 60 inches high require 2 hinges (1 pair). Doors from 60 inches to 90 inches require 3 hinges (1 1/2 pair), and doors 90 inches to 120 inches require 4 hinges (2 pair).

C. Latchsets and Locksets

Latchsets and locksets are devices to hold a door in the closed position and lock it. A *latchset* only holds the door in place with no provision for locking. It has a beveled latch extending from the face of the door edge and automatically engages the strike mounted in the frame when the door is closed. A *lockset* has a special mechanism that allows the door to be locked with a key or thumbturn.

The most common types of locks and latchsets are the cylindrical lock, mortise lock, and unit lock, as shown in Figure 20.7. The cylindrical lock is simple to install in holes drilled in the door, and it is relatively inexpensive.

A *mortise* lock is installed in a rectangular area cut out of the door. It is generally more secure than cylindrical locks and offers a wider variety of locking options.

A *unit lock* has its mechanism in a rectangular box that fits within a notch cut in the edge of the door. Because of this, it is easier to install than a mortise lock.

With all types of latches and locks, either a door knob or lever handle may be used to operate the latch. In most cases, a lever handle is required to meet handicapped code requirements.

The distance from the edge of the door to the center line of the door knob or pivot of a lever handle is called the *backset*. Standard backsets are 2 3/4 inches and 5 inches, although others are available on special order.

D. Other Types of Hardware

- *Pivots:* pivots provide an alternative way to hang doors where the visual appearance of hinges is objectionable or where a frameless door design may make it impossible to use hinges. Pivots may be center hung or offset and are mounted in the floor and head of the door. For large or heavy doors an intermediate pivot is often required for offset hung doors only. Center-hung pivots allow the door to swing in either direction and can be completely concealed, but they allow only a 90-degree swing. Offset pivots allow the door to swing 180 degrees.

- *Panic hardware:* this type of operating hardware is used where required by the building code for safe egress during a panic situation. Push bars extending across the width of the door operate vertical rods that disengage latches at the top and bottom. The vertical rods can be surface mounted or concealed.

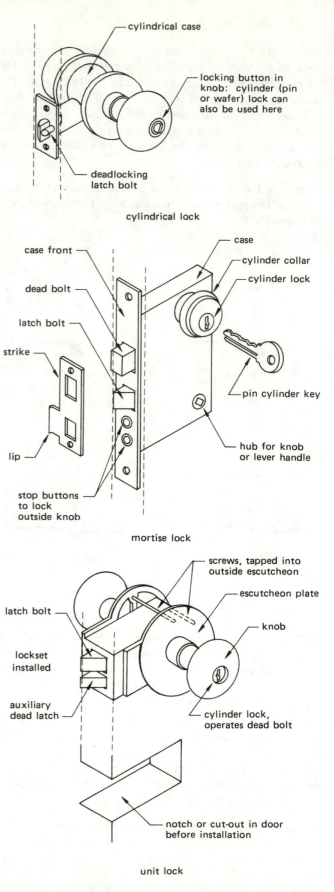

Figure 20.7　Types of Locksets

- *Push plates and pull bars:* these are used to operate a door that does not require automatic latching. They are also used to lock such doors to toilet rooms and commercial kitchens.

- *Closers:* closers are devices that automatically return a door to its closed position after it is opened. They also control the distance a door can be opened and thereby protect the door and surrounding construction from damage. Closers can be surface mounted on the door or head frame or concealed in the frame or door. Selection of a closer depends on the type, size, and weight of the door, the frequency of operation, the visual appearance desired and the door height clearance required. Closers can also be integral with pivots mounted in the floor or ceiling, either center hung or offset.

  Closers are available that have integral fire and smoke detectors built in so a door may be held open during normal operation but will close when smoke is sensed.

- *Door stops and bumpers:* some method of keeping a door from damaging adjacent construction should be provided. Closers will do this to some extent, but floor stops or wall bumpers provide more positive protection. These devices are small metal fabrications with rubber bumpers attached.

- *Astragals:* astragals are vertical members used between double doors to seal the opening, act as a door stop, or provide extra security when the doors are closed. Astragals may be fixed or removable to allow for a wide opening when moving furniture.

- *Coordinators:* a door coordinator is a device used with double doors that are rabbeted or that have an astragal on the active leaf. The coordinator is mounted in or on the head of the frame coordinating the closing sequence of the two doors so that they close completely, rather than having the leaf with the astragal close first and preventing the other leaf from closing.

- *Flush bolts:* these are used on the inactive leaf of a pair of doors to lock the door. They may be surface mounted or mortised into the edge of the door. The active leaf then closes to the locked inactive leaf, but both can be opened when needed.

- *Automatic door bottoms:* these are devices that are mortised or surface applied to the bottom of

the door to provide a sound or light seal. When the door is open the seal is up; as the door is closed a plunger strikes the jamb and forces the seal down.

- *Weatherstripping:* weatherstripping is used along the edge and bottom of doors to provide a tight seal against water and air infiltration. Various types of door seals are also used to provide light and sound protection on interior doors as well as sealing against the passage of smoke around fire doors. Different types of neoprene, felt, metal, vinyl, and other materials are used.

- *Thresholds:* these are used where floor materials change at a door line, where weatherstripping is required, where a hard surface is required for an automatic door bottom, or where minor changes in floor level occur.

E. Finishes

Hardware is available in a variety of finishes, the choice of which is dependent primarily on the appearance desired, but also on its ability to withstand use and weathering. The finish is applied over a base metal from which the hardware is made. For most hardware items this is not critical, but for hinges and other operating hardware it can be significant.

There are five basic metals: steel, stainless steel, bronze, brass, and aluminum. Fire-rated doors must have steel or stainless steel hinges, and hardware in corrosive environments may require stainless steel or bronze base metals with compatible surface finishes.

Hardware finishes have been standardized according to numbers developed by the federal government (U.S. designations) and the Builders Hardware Manufacturer's Association (BHMA). These are listed in Table 20.2.

6 BUILDING CODE REQUIREMENTS

Doors and hardware are highly regulated by the building codes. The requirements generally fall into three major categories: exiting requirements, fire-rated assemblies, and handicapped requirements. Many of the exit door requirements are reviewed in Chapter 7. Additional regulations specifically related to doors and hardware are included here.

The building codes regulate under what circumstances a door must provide fire protection. If a partition must have a fire rating, the openings in that partition must also be fire rated. Typical places where fire-rated doors

Table 20.2
Hardware Finishes

BHMA #	US #	BHMA finish description
605	US3	bright brass, clear coated
606	US4	satin brass, clear coated
609	US5	satin brass, blackened, relieved, clear coated
611	US9	bright bronze, clear coated
612	US10	satin bronze, clear coated
613	US10B	satin bronze, dark oxidized, oil rubbed
616	US11	satin bronze, blackened, relieved, clear coated
618	US14	bright nickel, clear coated
619	US15	satin nickel-plated, clear coated
622	US19	flat black
623	US20	light oxidized, statuary bronze, clear coated
624	US20A	dark statuary bronze, clear coated
625	US26	bright chromium plate
626	US26D	satin chromium plate
627	US27	satin aluminum, clear coated
628	US28	satin aluminum, clear anodized
629	US32	bright stainless steel
630	US32D	satin stainless steel

are required include openings in stairways, in fire-rated corridors, in occupancy separation walls, and in certain hazardous locations.

The codes consider not just the door but the entire collection of door, frame, and hardware to be the fire door assembly. Every part of the assembly must be rated to make an approved opening. Doors, frames, and hardware are tested by Underwriters Laboratories (UL) and Factory Mutual (FM) according to standard ASTM tests. If the door meets the requirements of the standard fire test, a small metal label is attached to the door indicating its class and hourly rating. Thus, a fire-rated door is also called a labeled door.

Doors are rated according to the time they can withstand the standard fire test and according to the class of opening in which they can be installed. Time ratings, summarized in Table 20.3, range from 20 minutes to 3 hours.

Table 20.3
Fire Door Classifications

fire door rating (hours)	opening class	use of wall	rating of wall (hours)
3	A	fire walls occupancy separations	3 or 4
1 1/2	B	exit stairways vertical shafts fire separations	2
1	B	exit stairways vertical shafts fire separations	1
3/4	C	corridors fire resistive walls hazardous areas	1
1/3		corridors smoke barriers	1 or less
1 1/2	D	severe exterior	2 or more
3/4	E	moderate to light exterior exposure	1 or less

The class of door also implies requirements for the maximum amount of wire glass permitted. For example, no glass is permitted in 3-hour, A-label doors while up to 1296 square inches is permitted in 3/4-hour, C-label doors.

Additional requirements, based on the Uniform Building Code, are listed below. You should verify exact requirements with the model code used in your area.

- A fire-rated door assembly must have a label attached to the door and frame.

- A fire door must be self-latching.

- All hardware used must be UL listed.

- A fire door must have an automatic closer. In some cases the code permits the door to be held open if the hold open or closer is connected to an approved smoke or fire detector.

- A fire door must use steel hinges of the ball-bearing type.

- In some cases fire doors must have panic hardware.

- If a pair of doors is used, astragals or other required hardware must also be used.

- Glass (if permitted) must conform in maximum area and construction to requirements of the local code. Glass must be set in a steel frame with the glass stop made of steel.

- Louvers must conform to UL requirements for maximum size and construction.

Handicapped requirements for doors and hardware include the following:

- Minimum width, clear of hardware, of an opened door must be 32 inches.

- There must be adequate maneuvering clearance in front of and on the latch side of the door to operate it.

- There must be a minimum of 48 inches between two doors in a series.

- The maximum opening force required is specified by the code for various types of doors.

- Handles and latches must have a shape that is easy to grasp and use. This usually means lever handles or push-pull type mechanisms.

- Thresholds cannot exceed 3/4 inch in height for exterior doors or 1/2 inch for interior doors, and they must be beveled.

7   WINDOWS

A *window* is an opening in a wall used to provide vision, light transmission, and ventilation. The standard nomenclature of a window is shown in Figure 20.8 and the types of windows are illustrated in Figure 20.9.

A. Metal Windows

Metal windows are fabricated of aluminum, steel, or bronze. Aluminum is the most common because of its light weight, low cost, strength, and resistance to corrosion. A variety of finishes can be applied in the factory to make aluminum windows compatible with almost any building. Two disadvantages of aluminum are its susceptibility to galvanic action and its high heat conduction. However, both of these can be controlled: galvanic action can be minimized or eliminated with the proper selection of fasteners and flashing; heat transmission and condensation can be prevented by specifying

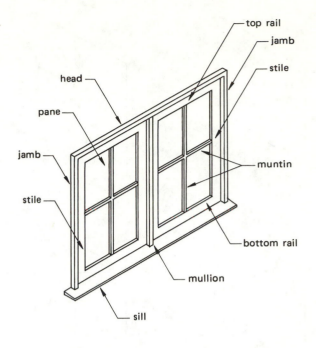

Figure 20.8   Parts of a Window

aluminum frames with thermal breaks. These are nonmetallic elements that connect the exterior and interior portions of a window.

Steel windows are fabricated from relatively small sections of hot rolled or cold rolled steel. Because of steel's greater strength, frame sections are small compared to aluminum. Steel windows are more expensive than aluminum and are used where high strength, security, and a minimum profile size is required. They are shop painted or bonderized to improve the adhesion of site-applied paint.

B. Wood Windows

Wood windows are very popular because of the variety of types and sizes available, their appearance, ease of installation, and good insulating properties. These windows are delivered to the job site as complete manufactured units including the exterior trim. They are simply placed in a rough opening and secured to the framing. Installation of interior trim finishes the window opening.

Common types of wood windows include fixed sash, double hung, casement, and horizontal pivoted, either the awning or hopper types. Horizontal sliding units are also available. Materials used are usually pine and fir, although some other species, such as redwood and cypress, are occasionally used. Many manufacturers

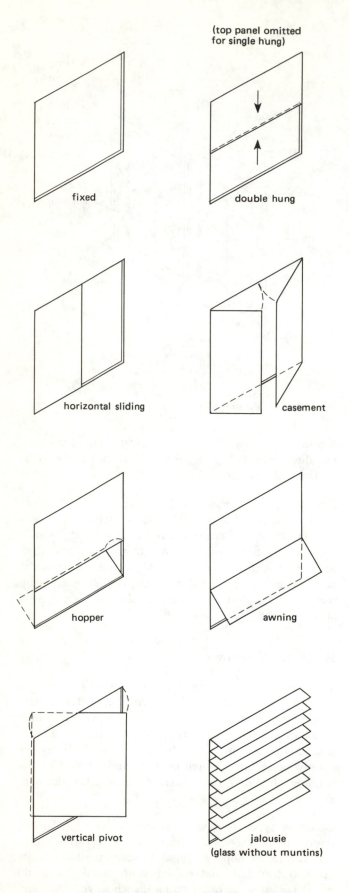

Figure 20.9 Types of Windows

now provide clad wood windows. The exterior, exposed wood members are covered with a thin layer of steel or vinyl to minimize maintenance while the interior portions are left exposed for painting or other types of wood finish.

Single-strength or double-strength glass is used for glazing windows, but some building codes now require glazing to be insulated glass, especially in cold climates.

C. Skylights

Skylights are glazed openings in roofs that allow light to penetrate the interior. They are sometimes operable to allow for ventilation. Skylights may be glazed with glass or plastic, but if plastic is used the building codes set restrictions on location and maximum size. If glazed with glass, the glass must be laminated or wire glass. If tempered or annealed glass is used, it must be protected from above and below with wire screening. These restrictions prevent objects from falling onto the glass, and so that broken glass cannot fall and injure someone below.

Skylights should be mounted on curbs to raise the bottom edge above the roof surface, especially if the roof is low slope. Because condensation of water vapor in a building can be a problem, the frames of skylights should be provided with a condensate gutter and weep holes, which allow collected water to drain to the outside.

8   GLASS AND GLAZING

Today's technology offers a wide variety of glass products to meet various glazing needs, ranging from simple, clear glass, to glass that can selectively transmit or reflect different wavelengths, to glass whose transparency can be switched on and off with electric current.

Glass is the term used to describe the actual material. Clear glass is a mixture of silica sand with small amounts of alkaline salts such as lime, potash, and soda. *Glazing* is the process of installing glass in the framing as well as installing the framing itself.

A. Types of Glass

In selecting the type of glass to be used in a particular situation, several parameters must be considered. These include the amount of light to be transmitted, the degree of transparency, strength and security, sound isolation, insulating qualities, cost, availability, and special qualities such as radiation shielding. The following are the common types of glass available.

- *Float glass:* float glass comprises the vast majority of glass produced in the United States. It is made by pouring molten glass on a bed of molten tin and allowing it to slowly cool, forming smooth, flat surfaces.

- *Heat-strengthened glass:* this glass is produced by heating glass to about 1100 °F and slowly cooling it. Heat strengthened glass has about twice the strength of annealed glass of the same thickness. This type of glass is used where the surface is subject to solar-induced thermal stresses and cyclic windloading.

- *Tempered glass:* tempered glass is produced by subjecting annealed glass to a special heat treatment in which it is heated to about 1150 °F and then quickly cooled. The process sets up compressive stresses on the outer surfaces and tensile stresses inside the glass. This glass is about four times stronger than annealed glass of the same thickness. Tempered glass is available in thickness from 1/8 inch to 7/8 inch.

  In addition to its extra strength for normal glazing, tempered glass is considered safety glass, so it can be used in hazardous locations (discussed in a later section). If it breaks, it falls into thousands of very small pieces instead of into dangerous shards.

- *Laminated glass:* laminated glass consists of two or more pieces of glass bonded together by an interlayer of polyvinyl butyral resin. When laminated glass is broken, the interlayer tends to hold the pieces together even though the glass itself may be severely cracked. This type of glass is used where very strong glazing is required. It can be bullet resistant and provides high security against intentional or accidental breakage. Like tempered glass, it is considered safety glazing and can be used in hazardous locations.

  Laminated glass is also used where sound control is required. In addition to the sound control provided by the extra glass thickness, the interlayer has a damping effect on the otherwise rigid material. This glass is available in thicknesses from 13/64 inch to 3 inches.

- *Tinted* or *heat-absorbing glass:* this is produced by adding various colorants to the glass material. The standard colors are bronze, gray, green, and blue. The purpose of tinted glass is to reduce the solar transmittance of the glass, which reduces the air conditioning load on the building, the brightness on the interior, and fading of fabrics and carpeting. Since tinted glass absorbs heat, it should not be used where portions of it are in direct sun and portions shaded. The differential expansion and contraction (thermal load) will crack the glass. Because of this phenomenon, tinted glass is often heat strengthened or tempered.

One of the important variables for tinted glass as well as other glass materials and sun blocking devices, is the shading coefficient. This is the ratio of the solar heat gain through a specific fenestration to the solar heat gain through a pane of 1/8-inch clear glass under identical conditions. It is used when calculating heat gain.

- *Reflective glass:* reflective glass is clear or tinted glass coated with an extremely thin layer of metal or metallic oxide. In insulating units, this reflective layer is placed on the inside of the exterior lite of glass. Its primary purpose is to save energy by reflecting solar radiation. In addition to this, the exterior of a building with reflective glass has a mirror-like surface which may have a desired aesthetic effect. Reflective coatings come in various silver, copper, golden, and earthtones that can be combined with the several colors of tinted glass.

- *Insulating glass:* insulating glass is fabricated of two or three sheets of glass separated by a hermetically sealed air space of from 1/4 inch to 1/2 inch. Insulating glass has a much lower U value than single-thickness glass and is used almost exclusively in regions where heat loss is a problem. Insulating glass can be made with heat-strengthened, tempered, reflective, tinted, and laminated glass.

- *Patterned glass:* this specialty glass is made by passing a sheet of glass through rollers on which the desired pattern is etched, which may be on one or both sides. Vision through the panel is diffused but not totally obscured; the degree of diffusion depends on the pattern and depth of etch.

- *Wire glass:* wire glass has a mesh of wire embedded in the middle of the sheet. The surface can be either smooth or patterned. Wire glass is used primarily in fire-rated assemblies where it is required by most building codes. It is approximately 50 percent stronger than annealed glass. Wire glass cannot be tempered and does not qualify as safety glazing for hazardous locations.

- *Spandrel glass:* spandrel glass is used as the opaque strip of glass that conceals the floor and ceiling structure in curtain wall construction. It is manufactured by permanently fusing a ceramic frit color to the back of heat-strengthened or tempered glass. It is normally manufactured and installed as a single sheet with insulation behind.

- *Low emissivity glass:* low emissivity glass, or *low-e* glass as it is sometimes referred to, selectively reflects and transmits certain wavelengths of the electromagnetic spectrum. It is manufactured by placing a very thin coating (just a few atoms) of metal or metal oxide on the surface of a piece of glass or a thin film. Low-e glass works by transmitting visible light and short-wave solar radiation but reflecting long-wave heat radiation from the air and warm objects.

Thus, in a cold climate, low-e glass will admit solar heat gain during the day but prevent the built-up heat inside the building from escaping at night. In the summer, the same glass will reflect much of the ambient long-wave infrared heat away from the glass. In warm climates, low-e glass can be combined with tinted or reflective glass to prevent even more heat from being transmitted to the interior of the building.

This type of glass is used in insulated units where it is placed on the interior surface of the inside lite to reflect building heat back to the inside before it crosses the air gap. Low-e glass can also be made by suspending a very thin layer of film in the center of the air gap, creating two air spaces. This is even more efficient than directly applying the coating to the glass, although it is more easily damaged.

An insulating low-e unit with 1/4 inch thick glass has a U value of about 0.31, while an insulating unit with a low-e film suspended in the middle has a U value of about 0.23. Standard double-pane insulating glass with a comparable air space has a U value of about 0.42.

- *Fire-rated glazing:* a fairly recent development in glass technology is a glazing system that is fire rated. The glass itself is not fire resistive but is fabricated with two or three panes of glass with a transparent gel between. Under normal conditions the glass is transparent, but when subjected to fire the gel foams and forms a heat shield. This type of fire protection glazing is available with 30-, 60-, and 90-minute ratings, but there are restrictions on the maximum size

of lites and the type of perimeter framing required.

B. Installation Details

There are several ways glass can be framed. Some of the more common ones are shown in Figure 20.10. The traditional way is to place the glass in a rabbeted frame, hold it temporarily with *glaziers points* (small triangular pieces of metal), and face putty the glass in place. This is shown in Figure 20.10 (a). This method is very labor intensive, and the putty dries and cracks with time and must be replaced often.

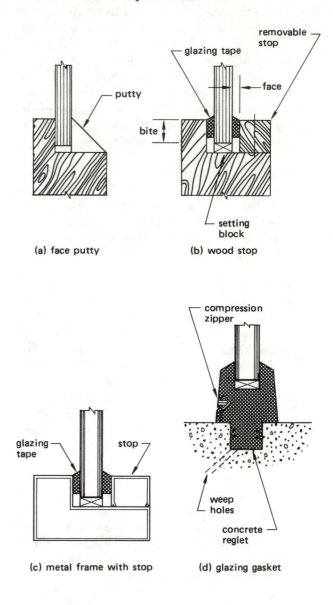

Figure 20.10   Methods of Glazing

Although this method is still used for single-pane glass on small residential jobs, it has been largely replaced with other methods. The glazing putty has been replaced with glazing compounds of various types that are applied like caulking and with *glazing tape*, a semirigid, formed material that is placed between the frame and the glass. See Figure 20.10 (b).

Glazing stops are usually required for most installations. These are removable pieces of framing that allow the glass to be installed and removed easily if it must be replaced.

Structural glazing gaskets are also used, fairly rigid strips of neoprene specifically designed to hold glass. Figure 20.10 (d) shows an application in a concrete reglet, but they can also be attached to metal frames. Once the glass is inserted, a compression strip is forced into a slot, which tightens the grip on the glass.

In all glazing installations, the glass should be placed on semirigid setting blocks of neoprene or other compatible elastomeric material. These prevent direct contact between the glass and frame and allow both to expand and contract and move without putting excessive stress on the glass.

Two dimensions of importance when installing exterior glazing are the face dimension and the bite, as illustrated in 20.10 (b). Since glass is subject to wind loading and deflects, effectively pulling partially out of the frame, the bite must be sufficiently deep to hold the glass in place.

Some glazing installations may also be made with a *frameless glazing system*. With this method, the glass is supported at the top and bottom and the edges simply butt-jointed and sealed with silicon sealant. With structural glazing systems, the vertical and horizontal framing members are entirely behind the glass (on the interior of the building) and the glass is attached to it with silicon sealant. From the exterior, the installation presents a smooth, uniform appearance, broken only by the thin, butt-jointed glass units.

The required thickness of exterior glass is dependent on the size of the glazed unit and the wind loading. Tables are given in the building code that determine the minimum thickness for various types of glass based on these variables.

C. Building Code Requirements for Glazing

There are three primary glazing situations that are regulated by the model codes. These are sizing of glass for wind loading, limitation on glass in fire-rated assemblies, and safety glazing subject to human impact in hazardous locations.

The codes specify the minimum thickness for glass depending on wind loading and the size of the glazed unit. The subject of maximum glass areas in fire doors has also been reviewed.

The Uniform Building Code places limits on the amount and type of glass in one-hour-rated corridors. Such glass is used to admit light from one space to another or to provide vision into a space. The glazed openings must be protected by 1/4-inch wired glass installed in steel frames. The maximum glazed area cannot exceed 25 percent of the area of the corridor wall of the room that it is separating from the corridor. In some cases, wire glass can be replaced with tempered glass if the building is fully sprinklered.

In order to prevent injuries from people accidentally walking through glass doors or other glazed openings, codes require safety glazing in hazardous locations. Hazardous locations are those subject to human impact such as glazing in doors, glass doors, shower and bath enclosures, and certain locations in walls. A composite drawing of where safety glazing is and is not required according to the UBC is shown in Figure 20.11.

The exact requirements are given in two references: The American National Standards Institute ANSI Z97.1, Performance Specifications and Methods of Test for Safety Glazing Material Used in Buildings and the Code of Federal Regulations, 16 CFR Part 1201, Safety Standard for Architectural Glazing Materials. *Safety glazing* is considered to be tempered or laminated glass.

9 CURTAIN WALL SYSTEMS

A *curtain wall* is an exterior wall system that is attached to the structural framework of a building and that carries no weight other than its own and wind loading that it transfers to the structure. Curtain walls can be made of preformed metal panels, precast concrete, and prefabricated marble, granite, or masonry panels, but they are usually built of aluminum framing and glass panels.

With aluminum and glass systems, the vertical mullions are attached to the floors or beams at every floor. Attachment devices allow the vertical mullions to be adjusted to provide a perfectly plumb and straight line for the entire height of the building. Horizontal mullions are attached to these vertical pieces according to the design of the system. Glass vision panels are used for window openings while spandrel glass is used where floor and column lines must be concealed.

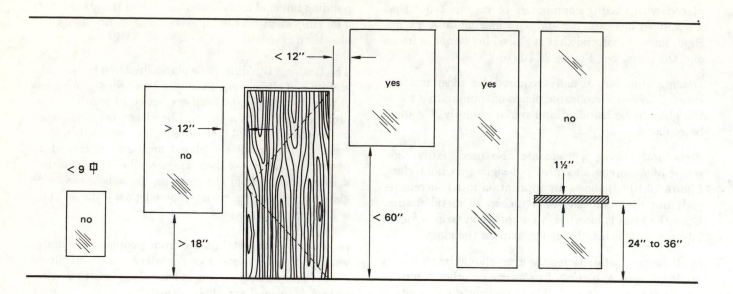

Figure 20.11 Safety Glazing Locations

21 FINISH MATERIALS

1 LATH AND PLASTER

Plaster is a finish material made from various types of cementing compounds, fine aggregate, and water. It is applied over several kinds of base materials in two or three coats to form a smooth, level surface. Plaster is a term commonly used to describe various types of finish materials of this type used for interior applications, while stucco is a term reserved for exterior applications of plaster made with portland cement.

Plaster is made from gypsum and lime, aggregates of sand, vermiculite, or perlite, and water. Vermiculite and perlite are used when a lightweight, fire-resistant plaster is needed. A special process is used to produce *Keene's cement*, which is a plaster that has a high resistance to abrasion and water penetration. It is used in wet areas or on walls subject to scratching or other abuse.

Stucco is made from portland cement, lime, sand, and water. It is used for exterior applications when a hard, non–water-absorbent plaster is needed. Portland cement plaster is also used as a backing for tile walls and as the scratch and brown coats under Keene's cement.

There are two common methods of applying plaster. The first is on metal lath that is attached to metal or wood studs. Metal lath is available in several types: expanded diamond mesh, paper-backed diamond mesh, flat-rib lath, and high-rib lath. Expanded diamond lath is a general-purpose type used for flat as well as curved surfaces. The paper-backed type has an asphalt-impregnated paper applied to it and is used as a base for portland cement plaster under ceramic tile. Rib lath is more rigid due to the one-way, vee-shaped ribs about 4 inches on center, and it is used for ceilings and solid partitions.

Metal lath provides a surface for the first coat of plaster to key into when the material flows around and behind the open mesh. This first coat is called the *scratch coat*. In standard plastering, the scratch coat is followed by the *brown coat* and then the final *finish coat*. The scratch and brown coats are about 1/4 inch thick, while the finish coat is about 1/8 inch thick. *Two-coat* work combines the scratch and brown coats.

The other method of plastering uses *gypsum board lath* instead of metal lath. This is a special gypsum product specifically designed for plastering. Gypsum lath comes in 16-inch by 48-inch boards that are applied horizontally to studs, or as 48-inch by 96-inch sheets. One or two coats of thin veneer plaster are applied over the boards. Veneer plastering reduces labor over the traditional method because only one coat is needed.

Edges of plaster and stucco work must be finished with various types of metal trim pieces. These provide a termination point for the work and serve as screeds to give the plasterers guides for maintaining the required thickness. Common profiles include corner beads to protect outside corners, casing beads to trim doors, windows, and other openings, base screeds to finish plaster at the base of a room, and expansion joints to control cracking in the plaster or stucco surface. Stucco requires expansion joints at a minimum of every 10 feet or where it is likely to crack, such as at the corners of door and window openings.

In general, gypsum drywall systems have largely supplanted lath and plaster work because of their lower cost and faster construction sequence. However, plaster is still used where curved shapes are required and where a hard, abrasion-resistant surface is required. Stucco is still used for exterior applications regardless of the surface form of the building. Veneer plaster walls can be constructed to provide a one-hour or two-hour fire-rated partition.

2 GYPSUM WALLBOARD

Gypsum wallboard construction is one of the most common methods for building partitions in commercial and residential structures. It is inexpensive and can satisfy most of the performance requirements for partitions found in today's construction. *Gypsum wallboard*, also known as *drywall*, is made of a gypsum plaster core sandwiched between sheets of paper or other materials.

The advantages of gypsum wallboard include:

- low installed cost

- quick and easy installation

- fire resistance

- sound control ability

- availability

- versatility: it can be used for partitions, shaft enclosures, ceilings, and elsewhere

- ease of finishing and decorating

- ease of installation of doors, windows and other openings

A. Gypsum Wallboard Materials

Gypsum wallboard normally comes in 4-foot by 8-foot sheets, although 10-foot and 12-foot lengths are available. 1-inch-thick coreboard comes in 2-foot widths. Thicknesses range from 1/4 inch to 5/8 inch; 1-inch core board is used for shaft lining.

Gypsum wallboard is available with square edges, tapered edges, and tongue-and-groove edges. The tapered edge is the most commonly used because the slight taper allows joint compound and tape to be applied without showing a bulge in the finished surface.

Other types available include Type X for fire-rated partitions, foil-backed for vapor barriers, water-resistant for use behind tile and in other moist conditions, exterior, backing board, and predecorated with vinyl wall covering already applied.

Gypsum board is applied by nailing or screwing it to wood or metal framing, or with mastic when applying it to concrete or masonry walls. The joints are finished by embedding paper or fiberglass tape in a special joint compound and allowing it to dry. Additional layers of joint compound are added and sanded smooth after each application to give a smooth finish wall surface.

Various types of textured finishes can be applied, or the surface can be left smooth for the application of other wall coverings.

B. Framing

Gypsum wallboard is attached to wood or metal framing. 2 × 4 and 2 × 6 inch studs are common framing members for residential construction while metal framing is typically used for commercial construction because it is non-combustible and easier to install. Metal framing consists of steel studs set in floor and ceiling runners, or C-shaped channels. See Figure 21.1. Steel studs come in standard depths of 1 5/8 inches, 2 1/2 inches, 3 5/8 inches, 4 inches, and 6 inches. Standard thickness for metal studs is 25 gage, although heavier gages are used for higher partitions or where other structural considerations are important. Hat-shaped furring channels are used for ceiling framing and to furr out from concrete or masonry walls. Resilient channels are used to improve the acoustical properties of a wall by isolating the wallboard from rigid attachment to the framing.

The depth of the stud depends on the height of the partition, gage of the stud, number of layers of wallboard and spacing of the studs. The most commonly used size is 2 1/2 inches, which is sufficient for normal ceiling heights and slab-to-slab partitions and also allows enough room for electrical boxes and small pipes. Metal studs are normally spaced 16 and 24 inches on center with 1/2-inch or 5/8-inch-thick gypsum board screw applied.

C. Wallboard Trim

Like plaster walls, gypsum wallboard must have fabricated edging. This includes cornerbead, which is used for all exterior corners not otherwise protected and various types of edge trim. These trim pieces are shown in Figure 21.2 and include the following:

- *LC bead:* edge trim requiring finishing with joint compound.

- *L bead:* edge trim without back flange; good for installation after the wallboard has been installed. It requires finishing with joint compound.

- *LK bead:* edge trim for use with kerfed jamb. It requires finishing with joint compound.

- *U bead:* edge trim that does not require finishing with joint compound, but the edge of the metal is noticeable. It is sometimes called J metal by contractors.

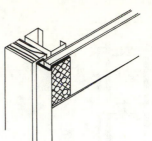

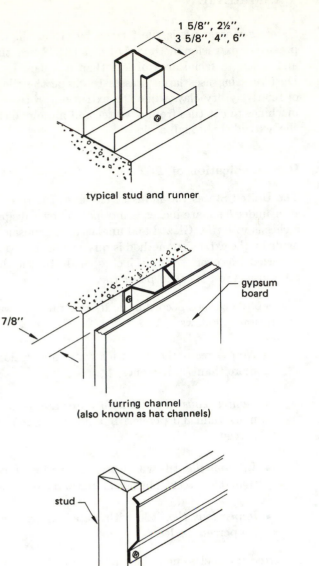

typical stud and runner

7/8''

gypsum board

furring channel
(also known as hat channels)

stud

resilient channel

Figure 21.1 Gypsum Wallboard Framing

LC bead

L bead

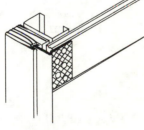

U bead

LK bead

Figure 21.2 Gypsum Wallboard Trim

Two of the most common types of gypsum wallboard construction on metal framing are shown in Figure 21.3. The standard partition is only built up to the suspended ceiling, while the slab-to-slab partition is used when a complete fire-rated barrier must be constructed or when sound control is needed. By adding additional layers of Type X wallboard, fire-resistive ratings of two, three, and four hours can be obtained. Gypsum wallboard is also used for ceilings and to provide fire protection for columns, stairways, and elevator shafts. It can also be used as a base for finishing by furring over other walls.

3 TILE

Tiles are small, flat finishing units made of clay or clay mixtures. The two primary types are ceramic tile and quarry tile. The advantages of tile include durability; water resistance (if glazed); ease of installation; ease of cleaning; a wide choice of colors, sizes and patterns; fire resistance; fade resistance; and the ability to store heat for passive solar collection.

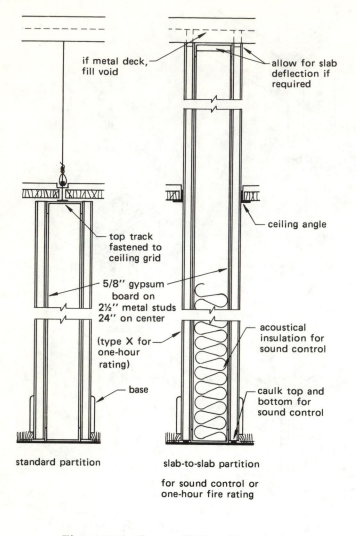

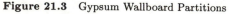

Figure 21.3 Gypsum Wallboard Partitions

A. Types of Tile

Ceramic tile is defined as a surfacing unit, usually relatively thin in relation to facial area, made from clay or a mixture of clay and other ceramic materials, having either a glazed or unglazed face, and fired above red heat in the course of manufacture to a temperature sufficiently high to produce specific physical properties and characteristics.

Quarry tile is glazed or unglazed tile, usually has 6 square inches or more of facial area, and is made by the extrusion process from natural clay or shale.

Some of the common types of tile include glazed wall tile, unglazed tile, ceramic mosaic tile, paver tile, quarry tile (glazed or unglazed), abrasive tile, and antistatic tile.

Ceramic mosaic tile is tile formed by either the dust-pressed or extrusion method, 1/4-inch to 3/8-inch thick, and having a facial area of less than 6 square inches. *Dust pressing* uses large presses to shape the tile out of relatively dry clay, while the extrusion process uses machines to cut tiles from a wetter and more malleable clay extruded through a die.

B. Classification of Tile

The United States tile industry classifies tile based on size: under 6 square inches is *mosaic tile*, over 6 square inches is *wall tile*. Glazed and unglazed non-mosaic tile made by the extrusion method is *quarry tile*; glazed and unglazed tile over 6 square inches made by the dust-pressed method is called *paver tile*.

Tile is often classed according to its resistance to water absorption as follows:

- *Non-vitreous tile:* tile with water absorption of more than 7.0 percent.

- *Semivitreous tile:* tile with water absorption of more than 3.0 percent but not more than 7.0 percent.

- *Vitreous tile:* tile with water absorption of more than 0.5 percent but not more than 3.0 percent.

- *Impervious tile:* tile with water absorption of 0.5 percent or less.

Imported tile is classified differently than tile produced in the United States. European manufacturers classify tile according to its production method, either the dust-press or extrusion method, its degree of water absorption, its finish, and whether it is glazed or unglazed.

The classifications of abrasion resistance are: Group I, light residential; Group II, moderate residential; Group III: maximum residential; Group IV, highest abrasion resistance—commercial.

C. Tile Sizes

Standard sizes of ceramic mosaic tile are 1 inch × 1 inch, 2 inches × 2 inches, and 1 inch × 2 inches, all 1/4 inch thick. Glazed wall tiles comes in normal sizes of 4 1/4 inches × 4 1/4 inches, 6 inches × 6 inches, 4 1/4 inches × 6 inches, in 5/16-inch thicknesses. Various other shapes are also available. Quarry tile comes in standard sizes of 3 inches × 3 inches, 4 inches × 4 inches, 6 inches × 6 inches, 8 inches × 8 inches, 3 inches × 6 inches, and 4 inches × 8 inches, in 1/2-inch and 3/4-inch thicknesses.

D. Tile Installation

Tile must be installed on firm, solid, flat substrates capable of supporting the weight of the material. The traditional method of installing tile is to lay it in a thick bed of mortar both on floors and walls. This is still the preferred method for quality installations and wet locations such as shower rooms, pools, and steam rooms. Tile may also be installed with the thin-set method using a thin layer of latex-portland cement mortar or other adhesive.

4 TERRAZZO

Terrazzo is a composite material poured in place or precast that is used for floors, walls, stairs, and other construction elements. It consists of marble, quartz, granite, or other suitable chips, in a matrix that is cementitious, chemical, or a combination of both. Terrazzo is poured, cured, ground, and polished to produce a uniformly textured surface.

Terrazzo has many of the same advantages of tile, which includes durability, water resistance, ease of cleaning, a wide choice of patterns and colors, and fire resistance.

A. Types of Terrazzo

There are four basic types of terrazzo. *Standard terrazzo* is the most common type, using small chips no larger than 3/8 inch. *Venetian terrazzo* uses chips larger than 3/8 inch. *Palladiana terrazzo* utilizes thin random-fractured slabs of marble with standard terrazzo between. *Rustic terrazzo* has the matrix depressed to expose the chips.

An unlimited number of terrazzo finishes can be achieved by specifying various combinations of chips and matrix colors.

B. Installation of Terrazzo

Terrazzo can be installed on walls as well as floors. The four common floor installations are shown in Figure 21.4. The sand cushion method is the best way to avoid cracking of the terrazzo because the finish system is physically separated from the structural slab with a membrane. Since the underbed is reinforced, the terrazzo system can move independently of the structure. If floor movement or deflection is not anticipated, the bonded method can be used. Where the thickness of the installation is a problem, a monolithic or thin-set method can be used.

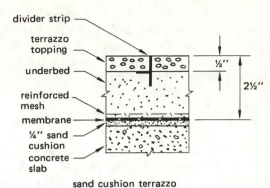
sand cushion terrazzo

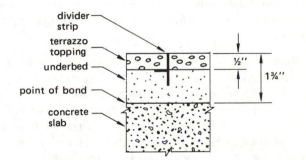
monolithic terrazzo

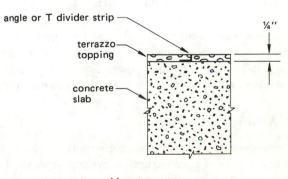
bonded terrazzo

thin-set terrazzo

Figure 21.4 Methods of Terrazzo Installation

Terrazzo is generally finished to a smooth surface with an 80-grit stone grinder, but it can be ground with a rough, 24-grit to achieve a more textured surface. Rustic terrazzo exposes some of the stone when the matrix is washed before it has set.

5   STONE FINISHES

Stone is often used for interior finishes of walls and floors. Commonly used types include marble, granite, and slate for flooring. Interior veneer stone is about 3/4 to 7/8 inches thick and is attached to wall substrates with stainless steel wires or ties. These are anchored to the substrate and hold the stone by being set in holes or slots cut into the back or sides of the panel. Lumps of plaster of paris, called *spots*, are placed between the substrate and the back of the stone panel at each anchor to hold the slab in place and to allow for precise alignment before they set.

Anchoring stone inside a building is simpler than exterior stone work because there is no wind load, precipitation, or freezing and thawing to contend with and panels are seldom stacked above each other so the weight of the panel can be carried by the floor. For high interior spaces many of the anchoring details are similar to exterior work, as shown in Figure 15.11.

Thin stone tiles are also used for interior finishing. These are about 3/8-inch thick and come in sizes of 1 foot × 1 foot and 1 foot × 2 foot, and are used for flooring and wall finish.

When stone is used for flooring it may be installed in a number of ways. These are illustrated in Figure 21.5. Like terrazzo, stone floors are subject to cracking if bonded to a subfloor that deflects excessively. To prevent this, a membrane is used so the subfloor and stone flooring can move separately. However, on rigid structures stone may also be thin set.

6   ACOUSTICAL TREATMENT

The three most common acoustical treatments for ordinary construction include ceilings, special acoustical wall panels, and carpeting. Special devices used in auditoriums and similar spaces are not discussed here.

A. Acoustical Ceilings

In contemporary commercial construction, the ceiling is almost always a construction system separate from the structure. This allows a smooth, flat ceiling surface for partition attachment, lights, and acoustical treatment while the space above the ceiling can be used for mechanical systems, wiring, and other services.

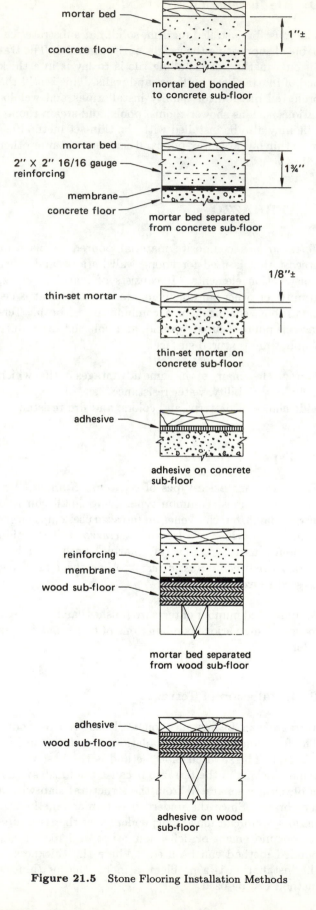

Figure 21.5   Stone Flooring Installation Methods

Acoustical ceilings consist of thin panels of wood fiber, mineral fiber, or glass fiber set in a support grid of metal framing that is suspended by wires from the structure above. The tiles are perforated or fissured in various ways to absorb sound, which is the basis for the term acoustical ceiling. It is important to remember that acoustical ceilings absorb sound, but they do not prevent sound transmission to any appreciable extent.

Acoustical ceiling tiles and the metal supporting grid are available in a variety of sizes and configurations. The most common type is the lay-in system in which tiles are simply laid on top of an exposed T-shaped grid system. See Figure 21.6 (a). A variation of this is the tegular system that uses tiles with rabbeted edges, as shown in Figure 21.6 (b). Systems are also available in which the grid is completely concealed. These systems use 1 foot × 1 foot or 1 foot × 2 foot tile sizes. See Figure 21.6 (c).

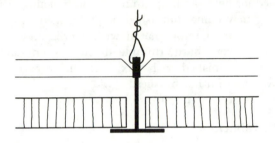

(a) lay-in exposed grid

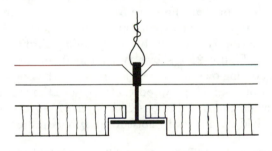

(b) lay-in tegular

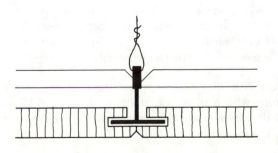

(c) concealed spline

Figure 21.6 Acoustical Ceiling Systems

Lay-in acoustical ceiling systems are available in sizes of 2 foot × 2 foot, 1 foot × 2 foot, 2 foot × 4 foot (the most common), and 20 inches × 60 inches. The 20-inch-by-60-inch system is used in buildings with a 5-foot working module. This allows partitions to be laid out on the 5-foot module lines without interfering with special 20 inch × 48 inch light fixtures located in the center of a module.

Other types of suspended systems that provide acoustical properties are also available. These include metal strip ceilings, wood grids, and fabric-covered acoustical batts. They all serve the same purpose: to absorb rather than reflect sound in order to reduce the noise level within a space.

Because suspended acoustical ceilings serve so many purposes in today's construction in addition to acoustical control, there are many elements that must be coordinated in their selection and detailing. These include determining required clearances for recessed lights; verifying clearances for duct work; locating sprinklers, fire alarm speakers, smoke detectors and similar items; and designing drapery pockets and other recessed fixtures.

In many cases, the space above a suspended ceiling is used as a return air plenum. Return air grilles are set in the grid and return air simply allowed to pass through the grilles, through the ceiling space, and back to a central return air duct or shaft that connects to the HVAC system. If this is the case, building codes require that no combustible material be placed above the ceiling and that all plastic wiring be run in metal conduit. Some codes allow wiring used for telephone, computer, low-voltage lighting, and signal systems to be exposed if it has an approved teflon-coated covering.

Suspended ceilings may be rated or non-rated. If they are fire rated, it means that they are part of a complete floor-ceiling or roof-ceiling assembly that is rated. Ceiling systems in themselves cannot be rated. Rated acoustical ceiling systems consist of rated mineral tiles, and rated grid systems, which include hold-down clips to keep the tiles in place and expansion slots to allow the grid to expand if subjected to heat.

B. Acoustical Wall Panels

Sound-absorbent panels can be purchased or constructed for use in spaces that require acoustical treatment in addition to acoustical ceilings and carpeting. These are made from a sound-absorbent material such as fiberglass, and are covered with a permeable material such as a loose-weave fabric. The acoustical material must be at least 1 inch thick in order to be effective.

7 WOOD FLOORING

Wood flooring offers a wide variety of appearances while providing a surface that is durable, wear resistant, and comfortable. It is available in several species and can be laid in dozens of different patterns.

Wood flooring is made from both hardwood and softwood, with the hardwoods predominating. Standard hardwoods used are red oak, white oak, maple, birch, beech, pecan, mahogany, and walnut. Softwoods used are yellow pine, fir, and western hemlock, among others.

A. Types of Wood Flooring

There are four basic types of wood flooring. *Strip flooring* is one of the most common and consists of thin strips from 3/8 inch to 25/32 inch thick of varying lengths with tongue-and-groove edges. *Plank flooring* comes in the same thicknesses as strip but is over 3 1/4 inches wide.

Block flooring is the third type and is made of preassembled wood flooring in three basic configurations. *Unit block flooring* is standard strip flooring assembled into a unit held together with steel or wood splines. Laminated block flooring is flooring made with from three to five plies of cross-laminated wood veneer. *Parquet flooring* is made of preassembled units of several small, thin slats of wood in a variety of patterns. It may be finished or unfinished. Parquet flooring is usually sold in 12-inch squares for mastic applications.

The fourth type of wood floor is made from solid end grain blocks. These are solid pieces of wood from 2 1/4 inches to 4 inches thick laid on end. Solid block floors are very durable and resistant to oils, mild chemicals, and indentation. They are often used for industrial floors.

B. Sizes of Wood Flooring

The common sizes of strip flooring include pieces 2 1/4 inches wide by 25/32 of an inch thick with tongue-and-groove edges. 1 1/2-inch-wide strips are also available. Plank flooring comes 3 inches to 8 inches wide by 25/32 inch thick. Block flooring is from 3/8 inch to 25/32 inch thick. Parquet flooring is usually 5/16 inch thick and comes in square tiles, usually 12 inches in length. Solid block flooring is from 2 1/4 inches to 4 inches thick in varying lengths and widths.

C. Grades of Wood Flooring

Wood flooring is graded differently than other wood products. Grading rules are set by the various trade associations such as the National Oak Flooring Manufacturers' Association, the Maple Flooring Manufacturers' Association, the Southern Pine Inspection Bureau, the West Coast Lumber Inspection Bureau, and the Western Wood Products Association.

Unfinished oak flooring is graded as clear, select, no. 1 common and no. 2 common. Clear is the best grade with the most uniform color. Plain sawn is standard, but quarter sawn is available on special order. Lengths of pieces are 1 1/4 feet and up with the average length being 3 3/4 feet.

Beech, birch, and maple are available in first, second, and third grades along with some combination grades.

D. Finishes

Wood strip and plank flooring is usually installed unfinished for field sanding, staining, and finishing. Block flooring may come unfinished or prefinished. Parquet flooring is often impregnated with acrylic and irradiated for a very hard, durable finish. Wood may be stained and finished with wax, varnish, polyurethane, or a variety of other finishes.

E. Installation

Wood flooring must be installed over a suitable nailable base. Since wood swells if it gets damp, provisions must be made to prevent moisture from seeping up from below and to allow for expansion of the completed floor. Strip flooring is installed by blind nailing through the tongue. Figure 21.7 shows two methods of installing wood flooring over a concrete subfloor. In the first case, a sheet of 3/4 inch plywood is attached to the concrete to provide the nailable base. A layer of polyethylene film is laid down first if moisture may be a problem.

In the second drawing, the wood flooring is laid on wood sleepers. This method of installation not only gives a more resilient floor that is more comfortable under foot, but it also provides an air space so any excess moisture can escape. In both instances, a gap of about 3/8 inch to 3/4 inch is left at the perimeter to allow for expansion and is concealed with the wood base.

Figure 21.8 shows the typical installation over wood framing with a plywood subfloor. A layer of 15-pound asphalt felt may be laid to prevent squeaking and act as a vapor barrier.

There are also resilient pads available that are used in place of sleepers for strip flooring installation. These provide an even more resilient floor and are often used for dance floors and gymnasium floors.

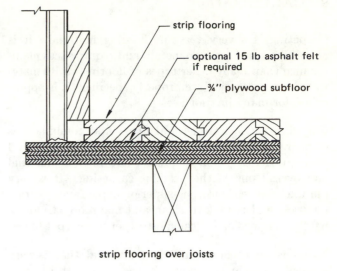

strip flooring over joists

Figure 21.8 Wood Flooring on Wood Framing

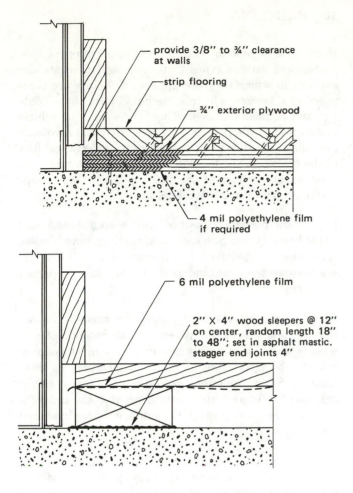

wood strip flooring over concrete

Figure 21.7 Wood Flooring Installation

8 RESILIENT FLOORING

Resilient flooring is a generic term describing several types of composition materials made from various resins, fibers, plasticizers, and fillers and formed under heat and pressure to produce a thin material either in sheets or tiles. Resilient flooring is applied to a subfloor of concrete, plywood, or other smooth underlayment with mastic. Some resilient floorings may only be installed above grade while others may be placed below, on, or above grade.

A. Vinyl Flooring

Vinyl is produced in sheet form or tiles in 1/16 inch or 1/8 inch thicknesses. It is a good, durable resilient flooring resistant to indentation, abrasion, grease, water, and alkalis. Vinyl comes in a variety of colors and patterns and is easy to install and inexpensive. It can be used below grade, on grade, or above grade. It must be installed over a clean, dry, and smooth surface.

B. Linoleum

Linoleum is made from oxidized linseed oil, resins, fillers, and pigments over a backing of burlap or asphalt-saturated felt. It is available in tiles but is more commonly used in sheet form. Although it is resistant to abrasion, grease, and dirt, it is not good where alkalis are present. Because its backing is susceptible to fungus, it should not be used where moisture is present, such as below grade or on concrete floors below or on grade. Linoleum must also be installed over a clean, dry, and smooth surface.

C. Rubber

This flooring is made from synthetic rubber and offers excellent resistance to deformation under loads, providing a very comfortable, quiet, resilient flooring. Rubber, however, is not very resistant to oils or grease. Rubber is often used as loose-laid matting in golf courses, skating rinks, and other areas subject to abuse from indentation.

D. Cork

Cork flooring is available in tile form and is used where acoustical control or resilience is desired. However, it is not resistant to staining, moisture, heavy loads, or concentrated foot traffic. It should only be used above grade and must be sealed and waxed to protect the surface.

9 CARPETING

Carpeting is a very versatile flooring material. It is attractive, quiet, easy to install, and requires less maintenance than many other types of flooring. If its material and construction are properly specified, it is appropriate for many interior uses.

Carpet is made from several fibers and combinations of fibers, including wool, nylon, acrylic, polyester, and polypropylene. Wool, of course, is a natural material and overall one of the best for carpeting. It is very durable and resilient, has superior appearance characteristics, and is easy to clean and maintain. Unfortunately, it is also one of the most expensive carpet fibers.

Nylon is an economical carpet material that is very strong and wear resistant. It has a high stain resistance and is easy to clean. However, its appearance is generally less appealing than that of other fibers.

Acrylic has moderate durability, but it has a more wool-like appearance than nylon. It is easy to maintain and has a fair crush resistance. Polyester has properties similar to acrylic.

Polypropylene is used for indoor-outdoor carpeting and has good durability and resistance to abrasion and fading, but it is less attractive and has poor resiliency.

Carpet is manufactured by tufting, weaving, needle punching, and fusion bonding. *Tufting* is the most common way of producing carpet and is done by inserting pile yarns through a prewoven backing. The tops of the yarns are then cut for cut pile carpet or left as is for level loop carpet. *Weaving* interlaces warp and weft yarns in the traditional manner, a method that produces a very attractive, durable carpet, but is the most expensive method of manufacturing carpet. *Needle punching* pulls fibers through a backing with barbed needles. It produces carpet of limited variation in texture and accounts for a very small percentage of the total carpet market. *Fusion bonding* embeds fabric in a synthetic backing. It is used to produce carpet tiles as well as other types.

The appearance and durability of carpet is affected by the amount of yarn in a given area, how tightly that yarn is packed, and the height of the yarn. The *pitch* of a carpet is the number of warp lines of yarn in a 27-inch width. The *stitch* is the number of lengthwise tufts in one inch. The higher the pitch and stitch numbers, the denser the carpet is. The *pile height* is the height of the fiber from the surface of the backing to the top of the pile. Generally, shorter and more tightly packed fibers result in a more durable carpet.

10 PAINTING

Painting is a generic term for the application of thin coatings of various types to protect and decorate the surfaces to which they are applied. Coatings are composed of a *vehicle*, which is the liquid part of the coating, and pigments if the coating is opaque. The vehicle has a non-volatile part called the *binder*, and a volatile part called the *solvent*. The binder forms the actual film of the coating while the solvent dissolves the binder to allow for application of the coating. The solvent evaporates or dries leaving the final finish.

Paints are broadly classified into solvent-based and water-based types. *Solvent-based* coatings have binders containing or dissolved in organic solvents while the *water-based* type has binders either soluble or dispersed in water.

Clear, solvent-based coatings include varnishes, shellac, silicone, and urethane. When a small amount of pigment is added, the coating becomes a *stain*, which gives color to the surface but allows the appearance to show through. Stains are often used on wood. Clear coatings are used for interior applications because the lack of a pigment does not protect the surface as a pigmented coating does.

Opaque, solvent-based coatings have a pigment added to the vehicle. *Pigments* are finely ground solids suspended in the vehicle that add color to the coating and provide the opacity needed to protect the substrate from ultraviolet light and other damaging effects of the environment.

Alkyds are one of the most common binders for solvent-based, opaque coatings. They are also used in water-based paints. Alkyds are often combined with other binders to improve their water resistance, color retention, and resistance to chalking.

Epoxy is used as a binder when resistance to corrosion and chemicals is required. Epoxies also resist abrasion and strongly adhere to concrete, metal, and wood.

Urethanes are used for superior resistance to abrasion, grease, alcohol, water, and fuels. They are often used for wood floors and for antigraffiti coatings.

Acrylic is a very good binder for water-based coatings and can be used for interior or exterior applications. Vinyl is also frequently used as a water-based binder.

Successful application of coatings depends not only on the correct selection for the intended use but also the surface preparation of the substrate, the primer used, and the method of application. Surfaces should be clean, dry, and free from grease, oils, and other foreign material. Application can be done by brushing, rolling, or spraying. The amount of coating material to be applied is normally specified as either wet or dry film thickness in mils for each coat needed. The coatings should be applied under dry conditions when the temperature is between 55 and 85 degrees.

22 VERTICAL TRANSPORTATION

Vertical transportation is a term that describes all the methods used to move people and materials vertically. This includes passenger and freight elevators, escalators, dumbwaiters, vertical conveyors, moving ramps, wheelchair lifts, and platform lifts.

1 HYDRAULIC ELEVATORS

Hydraulic elevators are one of the two major types used for the movement of people and freight; the other is electric elevators. These elevators are lifted by a plunger, or *ram*, set in the ground directly under the car and operated with oil as the pressure fluid. As a consequence, the cylinder for the ram must be extended into the ground as high as the elevator rises.

Because the ram must be set in the ground and speed is limited, hydraulic elevators are only used for passenger and freight loads in buildings from two to six stories high, or about 50 feet. They have much lower speeds than electric elevators, traveling from 25 to 150 feet per minute (fpm) and are therefore not appropriate for moving large numbers of people quickly. Single-ram elevators have weight capacities from 2000 to 20,000 pounds, and multiple-ram units can lift from 20,000 to 100,000 pounds.

A few variations of the standard hydraulic elevator are available. The holeless hydraulic uses a telescoping plunger set in the shaft next to the cab. Lift is provided by applying force to the upper members of the car frame. Another type uses a roller chain mounted over a wheel mounted on top of the hydraulic plunger. With this type, the plunger is mounted above the ground in the side of the shaft.

2 ELECTRIC ELEVATORS

Electric elevators are the most common type used for passenger service. They are capable of much higher lifts and greater speeds than hydraulic types and can be precisely controlled for accelerating and decelerating. The system employs a cab suspended by cables (known as ropes) that are draped over a sheave and attached to a counterweight. A motor drives the sheave, which transmits lifting power to the ropes by the friction of the ropes in grooves of the sheave. For this reason, electric elevators are also referred to as *traction elevators*. The common components of a traction elevator are shown in Figure 22.1.

Electric passenger elevators travel from 250 fpm to 1800 fpm and have capacities from 2000 pounds to 5000 pounds. Higher capacities are available for electric freight elevators.

A. Types

The two types of electric elevators are the gearless traction and the geared traction. *Gearless traction machines* use a direct current (dc) motor directly connected to the sheave. The brake is also mounted on the same shaft. Gearless machines that are dependable and easy to maintain are used on high-speed elevators.

The *geared traction elevator* is used for slow speeds from 25 to 450 fpm. A high-speed dc or ac motor drives a worm gear reduction assembly to provide a slow sheave speed with high torque. With the many possible variations in gear reduction ratios, sheave diameters, motor speeds, and roping arrangements, geared traction machines provide a great deal of flexibility for slow-speed, high-capacity elevators.

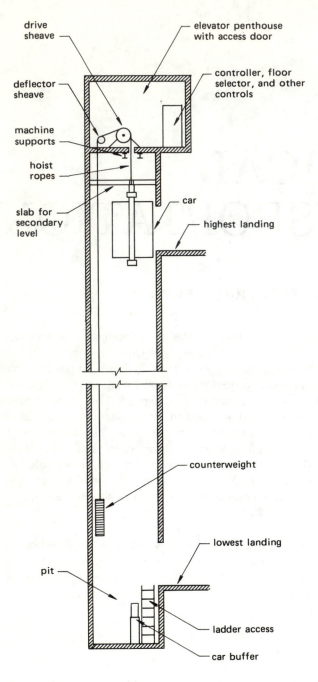

drive sheave

elevator penthouse with access door

deflector sheave

controller, floor selector, and other controls

machine supports

hoist ropes

slab for secondary level

car

highest landing

counterweight

lowest landing

pit

ladder access

car buffer

Figure 22.1 Traction Elevator

When the rope is directly connected to the counterweight, the cable travels just as far as the car, only in the opposite direction. This is known as 1:1 roping. When the rope is wrapped around a sheave on the counterweight and connected to the top of the shaft, the rope moves twice as far as the elevator cab. This is known as 2:1 roping and requires that less weight be lifted. Therefore, a smaller, higher-speed motor can be used, which is desirable for speeds up to 700 fpm.

C. Operation and Control

Operation is the term used to describe the way the electrical systems for an elevator or group of elevators answer calls for service. *Control* describes the method for coordinating and operating all the aspects of elevator service, such as travel speed, accelerating and decelerating, door opening speed and delay, leveling, and hall lantern signals.

Many types of operating methods are available. The purpose of an operating system is to coordinate elevator response to signal calls on each floor so that waiting time is minimized and the elevators operate in the most efficient manner possible.

The simplest type of system is the *single automatic*. This was the first type of automated system for elevators without attendants and consists of a single call button on each floor and a single button for each floor inside the car. The elevator can only be called if no one is using it, and once inside, the passenger has exclusive use of the car until the trip is complete. This type of system has limited use, and is therefore best for small buildings with little traffic where exclusive use is desired.

The most common type of system for many buildings is the *selective collective operation*. With this system, the elevator remembers and answers all calls in one direction and then reverses and answers all calls in the opposite direction. When the trip is complete, the elevator can be programmed to return to a home landing, usually the lobby.

The selective collective system works well for many installations, but for large buildings with many elevators, *group automatic operation* is employed. This is simply the control of all the elevators with programmable microprocessors to respond to calls in the most efficient manner possible, taking into account all the variables involved. In addition, things like the time of day or day of the week can be included in the programming. This provides very precise response to any building's unique needs.

B. Roping

Roping refers to the arrangement of cables supporting the elevator. The simplest type is the *single wrap*, in which the rope passes over the sheave only once and is then connected to the counterweight. For high-speed elevators, additional traction is usually required so the rope is wound over the sheave twice. This is known as a *double-wrap* arrangement. The disadvantage to double wrapping is that there are more bends in the cable and consequently a shorter rope life.

D. Safety Devices

There are many safety devices on modern elevators. The main brake on the sheave or motor shaft is normally operated by the control mechanism. If a power failure occurs, the brake is automatically applied. A governor also senses the speed of the car and if the limit is exceeded, the brake is applied. There is also a safety rail clamp that grips the side rails if there is an emergency. In the pit of the elevator below the lowest landing, car buffers stop a car's motion if it overtravels the lowest stop; however, they are not designed to stop a free-falling elevator cab.

Hoistway door interlocks prevent the elevator from operating unless the hoistway door is closed and locked. In addition, various devices prevent the doors from closing on someone in their path. *Safety edges* are movable strips on the leading edge of the door that activate a switch to reopen the door if something contacts it. Photoelectric devices serve the same purpose. There are also proximity detectors that sense the presence of a person near the door and can stop the closing motion.

To prevent overloading of a car, sensors under the floor detect when the maximum weight is reached by deflection of the floor. This then makes a warning noise with additional loading and prevents the elevator from picking up any more people. Additional safety devices include multiple ropes, escape hatches in the top of the cab, alarm buttons on the car control panel, and telephones for direct communication in an emergency.

Elevators must also be accessible to the handicapped. This includes placing controls within reach, visual and audio indicators, and minimum cab sizes.

3 ELEVATOR DESIGN

In simplest terms, elevator design involves selecting the capacity, speed, and number of elevators to adequately serve a particular building's population and then arranging the location of each elevator bank and the arrangement of the lobby. In addition, the roping method, machine room layout, control system, and cab decoration must also be determined.

A. Capacity and Speed

Determining the number, capacity, and arrangement of elevators to serve a building is a complex process because there is an optimum interrelationship between the number of people to be served in a given time period, the maximum waiting time desired, cost, and particular requirements of the building. For example, a hospital elevator moves large numbers of people but also must have provisions for stretchers and large quantities of supplies. Or the elevator in a corporate headquarters building may handle a great deal of interfloor traffic, while one in an apartment building will primarily move people from the lobby up to their floors and back down again.

For most buildings the *handling capacity*, or number of people to be served, is usually based on a five-minute peak period. For office buildings, this is usually the time in the morning when everyone is coming to work at about the same time. The number of people a car can carry is a function of its capacity, which is measured in weight. Through experience, there have been some general guidelines established for recommended capacities based on building types and rough building areas. These are shown in Table 22.1.

Table 22.1
Recommended Elevator Capacities

| building type | building size | | | service elevator |
	small	medium	large	
offices	2500/3000	3000/3500	3500/4000	4000–6500
garages	2500	3000	3500	—
retail	3500	3500	4000	4000–8000
hotels	3000	3500	3500	4000
apartments	2000/2500	2500	2500	4000
dormitories	3000	3000	3000	—
senior citizens	2500	2500	2500	4000

General recommended elevator speeds are also available based on the number of floors served and the general size of the building. The higher speed translates to shorter intervals or waiting time, but there are some limits due to overall travel distance (number of floors). Higher-speed elevators also generally cost more. Recommended elevator speeds are shown in Table 22.2.

B. Number of Elevators Required

Based on the car capacity and speed, along with the particular characteristics of the elevator functioning, such as door opening and closing time, delays at stops, and so forth, the average round trip time can be calculated and then the handling capacity of one car in a given five-minute period can be determined. The exact procedure for doing this is complicated and involves probability of number of stops, highest floor reached, and other variables.

The number of elevators required is then found by taking the total number of people to be accommodated in a five-minute peak period and dividing by the handling capacity of one car. The *interval*, or average waiting time, for an elevator to arrive can then be checked to see if it is acceptable. Recommended intervals vary with the type of building. For diversified offices the time is between 30 and 35 seconds. For hotels and apartments it is from 40 to 70 seconds or more.

Table 22.2
Recommended Elevator Speeds

offices	small	medium	large	service
number of floors				
2–5	250	300/400	400	200
5–10	400	400	500	300
10–15	400	400/500	500/700	400
15–25	500	500/700	700	500
25–35	–	800/1000	1000	500
35–45	–	1000/1200	1200	700
45–60	–	1200/1400	1400/1600	800
over 60	–	–	1800	800
garages				
2–5	200			
5–10	200–400			
10–15	300–500			
hotels				
2–6	150–300			200
6–12	200–500			300
12–20	400–500			400
20–25	500/700			500
25–30	700/800			500
30–40	700–1000			700
40–50	1000–1200			800
apartments/ dormitories senior citizen housing				
2–6	100/150			200
6–12	200/250			200
12–20	300–500			200
20–25	400/500			300
25–30	500			300

C. Location and Lobby Design

Elevators should be grouped near the center of a building whenever possible. At the lobby level, they should be easily accessible from the entrance and plainly visible from all points of access. In all but the smallest installations, there should be a minimum of two elevators so one is available if the other is being serviced. Consideration should also be given to obvious traffic generators such as subway entrances, parking garage doors, and the like. Service elevators may be located remote from passenger elevators as required by the building function.

Elevator lobbies should be designed so it is easy to see all the hall lanterns from one point and to minimize walking distance from any one point to the car that happens to arrive. This is especially important for handicapped accessibility. Adequate space must also be available so people can wait without interfering with other circulation. There should never be more than 8 cars

in a group. Figure 22.2 shows the recommended lobby layouts for various numbers of cars and the minimum space requirements based on the depth of the car.

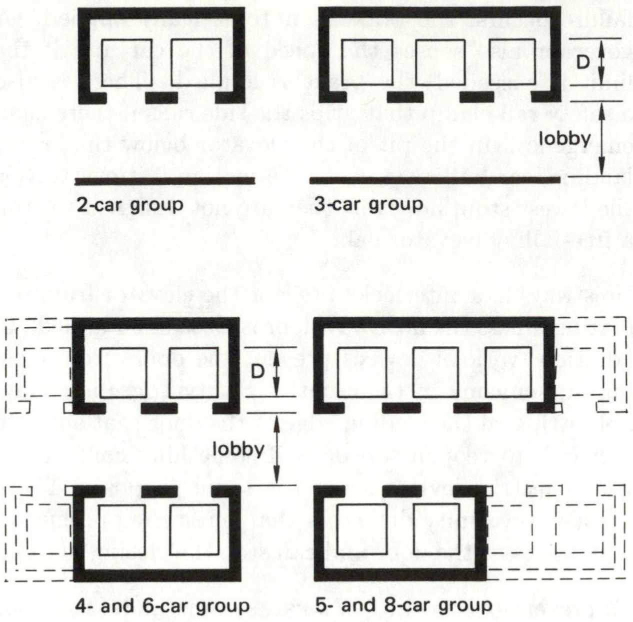

grouping	relative to D	but no less than	other
2 car	D		
3 car	1.5 × D	6 ft	
4 car	1.5 to 2 × D	10 ft	4 cars in line 1.5 × D, min. 8 ft
5 car	1.5 to 2 × D	10 ft	
6 car	1.75 to 2 × D	10 ft	
8 car	2 × D	max 14 ft	lobby open both ends

Note: Maximum of 5'0" from center line of lobby to wall for handicapped accessibility.

Figure 22.2 Elevator Lobby Space Requirements

D. Doors

Doors are an important part of elevator design because of their effect on passenger convenience and round trip time. If a car makes ten stops on a trip, a difference in opening and closing time of only one half-second can add ten seconds to the interval time and make an otherwise satisfactory design unacceptable. Doors can be either center opening or side opening and single speed or two speed. Single-speed, center-opening doors are common and allow faster passenger loading and unloading than side-opening doors.

Two-speed, side-opening doors have two leaves, one of which telescopes past the other as they move.

Two-speed, center-opening doors have four leaves. The minimum opening width is 3 feet 6 inches, but 4 feet 0 inches is better because it allows two people to easily and quickly enter or leave at the same time.

E. Machine Room

Machine rooms are best located directly above the hoistway and must provide adequate space for the motor, sheave, brake, controller board, speed governor, floor selector mechanism, and motor generator. All of these require minimum clearances for servicing and access. The exact size varies with manufacturer and type of elevator, but in general the machine room must be about as wide as the hoistway and from 12 to 16 feet deeper than the hoistway.

Minimum ceiling height ranges from 7 feet 6 inches to over 10 feet. In addition to this dimension, the distance from the floor of the top landing to the underside of the machine room floor can be substantial, from about 15 to 30 feet depending on the type, speed, and capacity of the elevator.

4 FREIGHT ELEVATORS

Freight elevators are designed and intended to transport only equipment and materials and those passengers needed to handle the freight. Elevator codes classify these into three groups, A, B, and C. *Class A* is for general freight and no item can exceed one-fourth of the rated capacity of the elevator. The rating cannot be less than 50 pounds per square foot of platform area. *Class B* elevators are those used for motor vehicle loading and are rated at no less than 30 pounds per square foot. *Class C* elevators are for industrial truck loading where the platform must be capable of supporting the freight as well as the weight of the truck used to load the elevator. The rating cannot be less than 50 pounds per square foot.

Freight elevators are commonly available in capacities from 2500 pounds to 8000 pounds, with some multiple ram hydraulic elevators capable of lifting up to 100,000 pounds. Speeds range from 50 fpm to 200 fpm with speeds up to 800 fpm available for very tall buildings. With freight elevators, interval time is not as important as capacity so the speeds are much less than passenger elevators.

5 ESCALATORS

Escalators are very efficient devices for transporting large numbers of people from one level to another. They are also useful for directing the flow of traffic where it is desired.

Escalators are rated by speed and width. The two available speeds are 90 fpm and 120 fpm. The two available widths (measured at approximately hip level) are 32 inches and 48 inches. Different combinations of these variables yield varying capacities in the number of people that can be carried per hour or per five-minute interval.

The actual observed capacity of people using escalators is somewhat less than the theoretical maximum capacity. This is due to the fact that, under crowded conditions, people tend to space themselves on every other step on 32-inch models and on an average of every step on 48-inch models. Observed capacity ranges from 2040 people per hour for a 90 fpm, 32-inch escalator to 5400 people per hour for a 120 fpm, 48-inch model.

Escalators are housed in a trussed assembly set at a 30-degree angle. The motors, drives, and other mechanism extend below the treads and floor at both the top and bottom of the assembly so head height clearance and floor-to-floor heights must take this into account. See Figure 22.3.

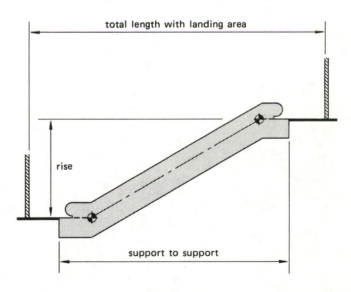

Figure 22.3 Escalator Configuration

If more than one floor is traversed by escalators, the directional flow of people should be maintained at each landing so it is possible to get off of one, turn, and step onto the next without having to backtrack the length of the opening. In addition, there must be sufficient space for people to bunch as they are waiting to get on and to disperse once they get off.

MATERIALS AND METHODS— SAMPLE QUESTIONS

23

This chapter contains sample questions related to materials and methods of construction that are reviewed in Chapters 13 through 22. To treat this chapter as a sample test, allow yourself about 50 minutes to answer the questions.

1. Which of the following is not a copper alloy?

    A. Monel metal

    B. Muntz metal

    C. nickel silver

    D. all are copper alloys

2. In the sketch shown, where should the vapor barrier be located?

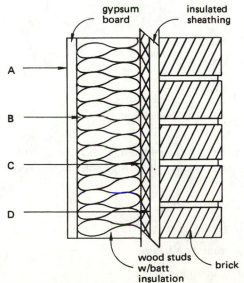

3. Which of these water-related soil problems would be the most important to solve for a large building being planned with a two-level basement used for meeting rooms?

    A. uplift pressure on the lowest slab

    B. moisture penetration caused by hydrostatic pressure

    C. deterioration of foundation insulation

    D. reduced load-carrying capacity of the soil

Questions 4 and 5 refer to the following sketch :

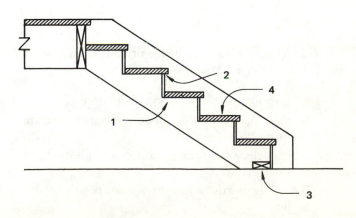

4. What is the purpose of the block shown at 3?

　　A. to counteract the thrust of the stair

　　B. to provide a nailing base for the riser board

　　C. to give lateral stability to the vertical supports

　　D. to help locate and lay out the stair

5. The parts identified as 1 and 2 respectively are:

　　I. tread

　　II. nosing

　　III. carriage

　　IV. ledger

　　V. stringer

　　　A. III and I

　　　B. V and I

　　　C. III and II

　　　D. IV and V

6. Tempered glass is required in:

　　A. entry doors

　　B. sidelights with sills below 18 inches

　　C. glazing within 1 foot of doors

　　D. all of the above

7. If a soil is analyzed as being primarily silty, what characteristics could you expect?

　　A. very fine material of organic matter

　　B. rigid particles with moderately high bearing capacity

　　C. particles with some cohesion and plasticity in their behavior

　　D. smaller particles with occasional plastic behavior

8. What type of glass would probably not be appropriate for a ten-story building?

　　A. tempered

　　B. annealed

　　C. heat-strengthened

　　D. laminated

9. A fire-rated gypsum board partition must always consist of:

　　A. type X gypsum board

　　B. full height construction

　　C. attachment according to testing laboratory standards

　　D. all of the above

10. Which mortar type has the highest compressive strength?

　　A. M

　　B. N

　　C. O

　　D. S

11. What type of brick would most likely be specified for an eastern exposure in New Hampshire?

　　A. NW

　　B. FBX

　　C. MW

　　D. SW

12. In order to achieve the most uniform, straight-grain appearance in wood paneling, you should specify:

　　A. plain slicing

　　B. rotary slicing

　　C. quarter slicing

　　D. half-round slicing

13. Asphalt-impregnated building paper is used under siding to:

    A. improve thermal resistance

    B. increase the water resistance of the wall

    C. act as a vapor barrier

    D. all of the above

14. Which area in the masonry wall assembly shown would be most susceptible to water penetration?

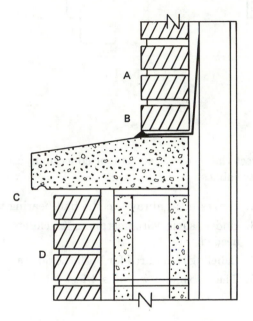

15. Concrete expansion joints should be located at a maximum spacing of:

    A. 5 feet

    B. 10 feet

    C. 20 feet

    D. 25 feet

16. Which of the following are characteristics of stainless steel?

    I. It cannot be welded.

    II. It should not be in contact with copper.

    III. It is an alloy of steel and chromium.

    IV. It is only available with mechanical and coated finishes.

    V. It is just as strong as bronze.

    A. I, II, and III

    B. II, III, and IV

    C. II, IV, and V

    D. III, IV, and V

17. The horizontal member that holds individual pieces of shoring in place is called a:

    A. wale

    B. breast board

    C. raker

    D. none of the above

18. When the architect is on the job observing concrete placement, what is most likely to be of least concern?

    A. the height of a bottom-dump bucket above the forms as the concrete is being placed

    B. the type of vibrator being used

    C. the location of the rebar in relation to the forms

    D. the method of support of the forms

19. A nominal $3'' \times 6''$ piece of lumber is classified as:

    A. timber

    B. board

    C. dimension

    D. yard

20. Select the incorrect statement from among the following:

    A. The larger the pennyweight, the longer the nail.

    B. Design values for bolts are dependent on the thickness of the wood in which they are located.

    C. Split ring connectors are often used for heavily loaded wood structures that must be disassembled.

    D. In general, lag bolts have more holding power than large screws.

21. What cement would be used in slip form construction?

    A. Type I
    B. Type II
    C. Type III
    D. Type IV

22. Which of the following most affects lumber strength?

    A. split
    B. wane
    C. check
    D. shake

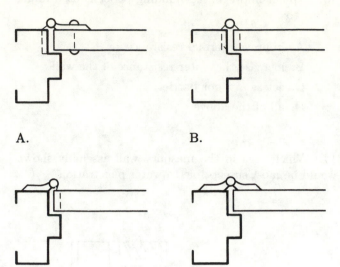

A.   B.

C.   D.

23. What is used to measure the rate of transfer in a thickness of material?

    A. k
    B. r
    C. R
    D. C

24. Which of the following would be least appropriate for insulating a steel stud wall?

    A. polystyrene boards
    B. rock wool
    C. fiberglass batts
    D. perlite boards

25. Three courses of a bull stretcher using a standard brick and standard mortar joints equals what dimension?

    A. 8 inches
    B. 12 inches
    C. 15 inches
    D. 24 inches

26. Which of the sketches depicts a half-surface hinge?

27. Select the incorrect statement concerning fire-rated door assemblies.

    A. Hinges must always be the ball-bearing type.
    B. Under some circumstances a closer is not needed.
    C. Labeling is required for both the door and frame.
    D. The maximum width is 4 feet 0 inches.

28. Which of the following would be most appropriate for dampproofing an above-grade concrete wall with a moderately rough surface?

    A. cementitious coating
    B. bituminous coating
    C. synthetic rubber
    D. silicone coating

29. The depth of elevator lobbies serving four or more cars should generally not be less than:

    A. 6 feet
    B. 1 1/2 times the depth of the car
    C. 10 feet
    D. 3 times the depth of the car

30. Which of the following would probably not be reasons for using a copper roof?

I. workability

II. resistance to denting

III. cost

IV. corrosion resistance

    A. I and II

    B. I and III

    C. II and III

    D. III and IV

31. If cracking occurred along the joints of a brick wall in a generally diagonal direction from a window corner up to the top of the wall, which of the following would most likely be the cause?

    A. lack of vertical control joints

    B. horizontal reinforcement placed too far apart

    C. poor grouting of the cavity

    D. inadequate mortar

32. What is used to keep water from penetrating an expansion joint at the intersection of a roof and wall?

    A. base flashing

    B. counter flashing

    C. sealant

    D. coping

33. The portion of paint that evaporates or dries is called the:

    A. binder

    B. pigment

    C. solvent

    D. vehicle

34. In the partial plan of a concrete basement shown, what would be the best way to improve the economy of the concrete form work?

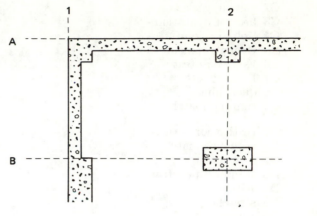

    A. make the column square

    B. separate the pilaster at A2 from the wall

    C. form the pilaster at A1 with a diagonal

    D. make the wall along grid line 1 a uniform thickness

35. Structural steel typically contains what percentage of carbon?

    A. above 2.0 percent

    B. from 0.50 to 0.80 percent

    C. from 0.20 to 0.50 percent

    D. from 0.06 to 0.3 percent

The answers to questions 36 through 40 can be found on the following key list. Select only one answer for each question.

    A0 admixtures
    A1 annealing
    A2 auger boring
    A3 backset
    A4 bentonite panels
    A5 blueprint match
    A6 bond beam
    A7 bond breaker
    A8 bookmatching
    A9 bush hammer

    B0 casehardening
    B1 cavity wall
    B2 chamfer strip
    B3 coordinator
    B4 cribbing
    B5 cylinder test
    B6 dampproofing
    B7 densification
    B8 efflorescence
    B9 equivalent thickness

C0 flush bolt
C1 flying form
C2 glazing gaskets
C3 heat of hydration
C4 isolation joint
C5 Keene's cement
C6 Kelly ball test
C7 Proctor test
C8 quenching
C9 running match

D0 rustication strips
D1 sequence match
D2 slump test
D3 standard penetration test
D4 stile
D5 stretcher
D6 strongback
D7 sump
D8 surcharging
D9 terne plate

E0 waterproofing
E1 weep holes
E2 wythe

36. What is used to minimize corner chipping of concrete?

37. What part of a panel door is the lockset mounted in?

38. What is the building code requirement for pairs of exit doors with astragals?

39. What is the most important fire-resistant property of a CMU partition?

40. What is a requirement for an opening for a door in a masonry partition?

41. Galvanic action can be avoided by:

    A. using neoprene spacers

    B. increasing the thickness of the materials

    C. reducing contact with dripping water

    D. all of the above

42. A geared traction elevator would be most appropriate for which of the following applications?

    A. a five-story medical office building

    B. a sixteen-story office building

    C. a four-story department store

    D. an eight-story apartment building

43. In determining the width and gage of gypsum board framing, what are some of the important considerations?

    I. thickness of the gypsum board

    II. spacing of studs

    III. height of the wall

    IV. size of piping and other built-in items

    V. number of layers to be supported

    A. I, III, IV, and V

    B. II, III, and IV

    C. II, III, IV, and V

    D. all of the above

44. What is the purpose of the gravel in the drawing shown?

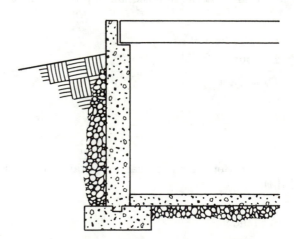

    A. to reduce hydrostatic pressure

    B. to keep the soil from direct contact with the concrete

    C. to provide a firm base for concrete bearing

    D. to hold the membrane in place and protect it

45. Joining two metals with heat and a filler metal with a melting point above 800 °F is called what?

    A. annealing

    B. soldering

    C. brazing

    D. welding

46. Which of the following is not true about veneer stone?

    A. It can be fabricated 3/8 inches thick.

    B. Copper or steel clamps are used to anchor the stone to the substrate.

    C. Only special types of portland cement mortar or sealants should be used in the joints.

    D. It can be supported on masonry, concrete, steel, or wood framing.

47. Which of the following is the most important consideration in detailing a wood strip floor?

    A. flame spread rating

    B. expansion space at the perimeter

    C. nailing method

    D. moisture protection from below

48. In the window elevation shown, what is represented at point 1?

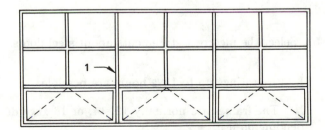

    A. mullion

    B. muntin

    C. stile

    D. rail

49. Which of the following are of most importance in wood frame construction?

    I. sheathing type

    II. differential shrinkage

    III. location of defects

    IV. firestops

    V. headers

    A. I, II, and III

    B. I, II, and IV

    C. II, III, and V

    D. III, IV, and V

50. Which type of lock would be most appropriate for an entry door into an office suite?

    A. cylindrical lock

    B. unit lock

    C. mortise lock

    D. rim lock

51. Which of the following are true about built-up roofing?

    I. It may be applied on slopes from 0 to 1 inch per foot.

    II. They are best applied only over nailable decks.

    III. The top layer should be protected from ultraviolet degradation.

    IV. Proper installation is more important than the number of plies.

    V. Roof insulation can either be placed above or below the roofing.

    A. I, III, and V only

    B. I, II, IV, and V only

    C. II, III, and IV only

    D. III, IV, and V only

52. Ceramic mosaic tile in a public shower room is best installed over:

    A. water-resistant gypsum board

    B. a bed of portland cement mortar

    C. concrete block walls coated with a waterproofing membrane

    D. rigid cement composition board made for this purpose

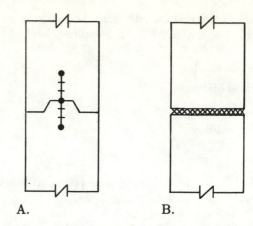

A.   B.

53. What are two important considerations in designing a fire-rated ceiling?

    I.   hold-down clips

    II.   the structural slab

    III.   thermal insulation

    IV.   composition of the floor/ceiling assembly

    V.   style of grid

    A. I and IV

    B. I and III

    C. II and IV

    D. III and V

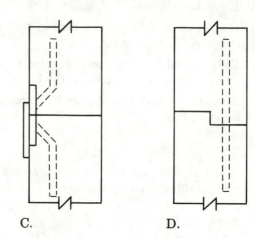

C.   D.

56. A reasonable elevator capacity for a medium-size office building is:

    A. 2000 pounds

    B. 3000 pounds

    C. 4000 pounds

    D. 6000 pounds

54. What is the primary purpose of the voids in a cored slab?

    A. to allow electrical services to be concealed in the slab

    B. to make a more efficient load-carrying member

    C. to make erection easier

    D. to minimize weight

57. Select the incorrect statements about steel doors.

    I.   Fire ratings up to 1 1/2 hours are possible.

    II.   The frames are normally 12, 14, or 16 gage depending on use.

    III.   Steel doors must be used with steel frames.

    IV.   Hinges or offset pivots can be used with steel doors.

    V.   The standard thickness is 1 3/8 inches.

    A. I and V

    B. I, III, and V

55. Which of the vertical joints shown would be appropriate for a concrete basement wall?

C. II and IV

D. II, III, and V

58. The allowable stress ratings for lumber in the building codes are based primarily on:

    A. size groups

    B. species

    C. types of defects

    D. all of the above

59. Millwork for installation in the southwestern part of the United States should have a maximum moisture content of:

    A. less than 5 percent

    B. 4 to 9 percent

    C. 5 to 10 percent

    D. 8 to 13 percent

60. On floors subject to deflection, both terrazzo and granite installations should include:

    A. a membrane

    B. a latex additive in the mortar

    C. thin-set mortar

    D. a sand cushion

24 CONSTRUCTION DRAWINGS AND DETAILS

Construction drawings represent the architect's final decisions concerning design, building methods, and construction technology. As such, they must show the technically correct ways of meeting the functional requirements of the design, such as keeping water out, distributing electricity, providing safe finishes, and satisfying thousands of other concerns. They must also clearly communicate the information to the contractor, material suppliers, and other people involved with the project. Finally, they must be coordinated with the specifications and the consultant's drawings.

This chapter reviews some of the functional criteria for selecting materials and evaluating or developing details based on design development decisions and drawings. It takes a broader look at building technology, while other chapters examine specific materials and construction techniques. This chapter also reviews some of the essentials in assembling a set of construction drawings and making sure they are correctly coordinated with the consultant's drawings and with the project specifications. Thorough coordination is vital in order to avoid errors, cost overruns, and scheduling delays, as well as to minimize the architect's exposure to liability.

1 DEVELOPING AND EVALUATING CONSTRUCTION DETAILS

A *building* is a complex collection of component parts, all of which are connected to other parts in various ways. The manner in which an assembly of several parts is organized and connected is commonly referred to as a detail. A detail may be as simple as two bricks connected with a mortar joint or as complex as the intersection of a curtain wall, roof, ceiling, structural beam, and parapet consisting of dozens of different materials.

There are certain common functional characteristics involved with almost every category of construction detail, and the correctness of the assembly can be developed or evaluated based on these characteristics. For example, the intersection of a roof and a parapet must be designed to fulfill several functions, one of which is to drain water and avoid leakage into the structure. This holds true regardless of what the roofing material is or how the wall is constructed. Different materials may influence certain aspects of the detail, but the intersection still needs a cant strip, it must have positive drainage, and material expansion and contraction must be taken into account.

The following parameters cover most of the common characteristics of a construction assembly that must be considered in its design or evaluation. Of course, not all of them relate to every detail, but combined with the specific information on materials given in other chapters, you should be able to make rational evaluations during the examination.

A. Compatability with Design Intent

All building configuration begins with the desire to satisfy the program requirements and specific needs arising from these requirements. They must be balanced against practical considerations such as code requirements, cost, and material limitations, but even with these types of constraints there are many ways to design. Sometimes, during the long process of design and detailing, the original design intent gets lost in the practicalities of solving functional problems and making changes. A detail may work but it is not what the client and designer originally intended it to look like.

Simple performance requirements can also be involved. This is simply the ability of the product to do its intended job. For instance, how well does an acoustical ceiling absorb sound? How slip resistant is a floor tile? In many cases, the criteria of performance can be judged against a standard test procedure.

The architect should constantly check the development of a detail against its original purpose, performance requirements, and desired appearance. For example, a client might have originally requested a simple, unobtrusive demountable partition system. Through material selection, cost analysis, and integration with other building systems, the final product may satisfy the requirements of demountability, sound transmission, cost, and finish but may not have the clean, simple look the client wanted.

B. Structural Integrity

Structural integrity refers to the ability of a material or construction component to withstand the forces applied to it. These include not only the obvious natural forces of gravity, snow, wind, and seismic loading, but also other forces such as impact. The particular type of detail will determine what kinds of forces it must resist, and each should be reviewed.

Some of the common forces on a detail can include the following:

- live and dead loads

- wind loads

- seismic loads

- hydrostatic pressure

- forces induced by building movement

- loads induced by human use (for example, the forces produced on a door jamb through the hinge from door operation)

- loads created by one material acting as the substrate for another

- forces caused by accidental or intentional abuse

- strength properties of a material or assembly that may be necessary to resist various forces include compression, tension, shear, torsion, rupture, hardness, and impact.

C. Safety

There are many aspects to safety, which is one of the most important elements of detailing, because the architect is responsible for protecting the health, safety, and welfare of the public. Some of the safety concerns you should be alert to include:

- *Structural safety:* will the material or detail physically collapse or otherwise fail, causing harm?

- *Fire safety:* is the material fire resistant enough for its intended use? Will it produce smoke or toxic fumes if burned? If it burns will its failure lead to failure of adjacent construction?

- *Safety with human contact:* is there a potential for harm when people come in contact with the material or detail? For example, will sharp edges cut people, wet floors promote slipping, or poorly designed stairs cause falls?

D. Durability and Maintainability

Most building materials and details are subject to a wide range of abuse during their life, both from natural forces and human use. To the extent possible, they must be able to withstand this abuse and be maintained and repaired over their lifetime.

For exterior materials, there must be resistance to ultraviolet radiation, temperature changes, pollution, water, and atmospheric corrosion. For materials and details within human reach, there must be resistance to scratching and abrasion, impact, and marking.

All details must be maintainable. Can a material be cleaned easily? How will it look if it is not regularly maintained? How costly will the maintenance be? Can part of a detail be easily replaced or repaired?

E. Code Requirements

Of course, all details and building components must satisfy the requirements of the local building code and other statutory regulations. Checking for compliance should be an automatic reaction when developing or reviewing construction drawings. Many of these requirements have been discussed in other chapters with reference to specific materials and areas of construction

F. Construction Trade Sequence

Since all building requires the involvement of many trades and material suppliers, the best details are those that allow for construction to proceed directly from one trade to another in a timely fashion. Since labor is one of the largest expenses of a building project, anything that can be done to minimize it saves money (within the bounds of adequate craftsmanship, of course). It is also desirable to organize the detailing of a building to allow for a clear division of the labor trades so there is a minimum amount of interference and potential conflicts.

Each detail should be reviewed to see if its construction can proceed from one trade to another with the least amount of overlap. For example, in building a standard partition, the drywallers can install the metal framing. Then the electricians and plumbers can install conduit and piping. Then the drywallers can return, finish the wall, and leave, making way for the painters. Partition details that deviate from this standard sequence will take more time to complete and will be more costly.

G. Fabrication and Installation Methods

All construction details should be reviewed to see if they present problems in building. This includes limitations on the size and shape of assemblies due to transportation restrictions, the ability to move materials into proper position, and possible difficulties in actual installation. It also includes problems with making connections and installing subsequent construction. For example, swinging a steel beam into position and then having enough room to tighten the bolts requires certain minimum clearances. Installing a door frame in an opening requires shim space to compensate for possible deviations in plumb of the rough door opening.

H. Tolerances

All elements of construction are built to a different closeness to perfection. This level of perfection is typically represented by the lines on the construction drawings. The amount of allowable variance from perfection is known as *tolerance*, and must be accounted for in detailing. Some construction items, such as millwork, have a very small tolerance, sometimes as small as 1/64 inch, while other elements like poured concrete footings may be oversized by as much as 2 inches and still be acceptable.

Tolerances for a great many construction components have been established by various trade organizations and are the accepted norms unless the architect specifies otherwise. However, requiring tighter tolerances than is industry standard usually requires better materials, more time, more labor, or a combination of all three. These also mean a higher cost.

Details should allow for expected tolerances. For example, a finished, wood panel wall installed over cast concrete must have enough space for shimming and blocking so the final wall surface can be plumb while the rough structural wall may be out of plumb by as much as 1/4 inch in a 10 foot height.

I. Costs

There are three major elements of cost involved with building: materials, labor, and equipment. There is also the cost of overhead and profit of the contractor which represent the first costs of the structure and may change as the other costs fluctuate. However, there are life-cycle costs with which the architect and client must be concerned. What may be a low initial cost of an assembly may end up being a very expensive detail to maintain and ultimately replace.

Cost control involves striking the proper balance between client needs, initial costs, and life-cycle costs. The client may want more than is affordable or may ask for the lowest first costs without realizing that inexpensive materials will cost more in the long run. If the building is a speculative venture, low first costs may be acceptable to the developer regardless of future consequences. It is up to the architect to make sure the client understands all the choices and ramifications of design and detailing decision.

The cost of a portion of a building in proportion to the total cost is also an important concept to understand. If the entire building is going to cost $2 million, it does not make much sense to spend a great deal of time and worry over saving $100 on one detail. On the other hand, if extensive research and study on a typical wall detail of the same building can save $30,000, then it is reasonable to make the effort. In another situation, saving a little money on quantity items is desirable. If just $100 can be trimmed from the construction of one hotel room, then saving this amount on a 2000-room hotel will add up to $200,000.

Of course, cost is directly related to the choice of materials, which is a function of the intended use, durability, strength, maintainability, and all the other considerations involved with designing a detail. Labor cost is largely determined by the effort required to build a detail so, in general, the cost of construction can be minimized by developing simple details that still satisfy all other criteria. Equipment costs involve the purchase or rental of specialized machinery needed to build the project. Prefabricated concrete components may require large, expensive cranes to set them in place, but this cost may be more than offset by the savings in formwork and time delays involved with cast-in-place concrete.

J. Material Availability

Construction is a very geographically localized industry. Not only does labor availability vary with location, but many different materials are found in different parts of the country. Of course, any material can be shipped anywhere else, but the cost may not be justified. Specifying southern pine for rough framing in Oregon just does not make any sense. Steel framing may be less expensive than concrete in some parts of the country near mills, while the same steel building would be prohibitively expensive in other locales where concrete would be the logical choice.

K. Building Movement and Substrate Attachment

Since all details consist of a number of components connected with each other, it is important to understand that one material must provide an appropriate base for the attachment of another. This attachment may be done in one of three ways. The first is rigid, such as plaster fixed to lath: if one material moves, both move. The second is rigid, but adjustable for installation, like a curtain wall anchored to a floor beam. The third is flexible, so movement is allowed. An expansion joint is a typical example of this attachment.

Within each detail there must be space for the attaching device as well as clearance for workers. Problems with incompatible materials must also be considered, such as possible galvanic action or deterioration of one material from water leakage through another. If the materials are chemically bonded with sealants, mastics, paint, or other coatings, the base material must be compatible with the coating or the joining material.

In all cases, the detail must provide for expected building movement, as discussed in other chapters. It is inevitable, whether it is from live, dead, or lateral loading, temperature changes, water absorption, or other causes. The amount of movement that will occur on a given detail varies, but it is always present.

L. Conformance to Industry Standards

There are certain common methods of building that are considered industry standards. These methods have been developed through practice and experience, from the recommendations of trade associations and testing organizations, and from building codes. A reinforced masonry wall should be built about the same way regardless of who designs it, who builds it, or what it is used for. The only things that may change to suit the particular needs of the building are the finish, the size of reinforcing, the type of mortar, and so on.

Conforming to these types of industry standards not only increases the likelihood that the detail will work but also minimizes potential liability if something goes wrong. This is not to say that the architect should not try new design approaches or be creative in solving unusual technical problems, but only do it when necessary.

Deviation from industry standards should be done only after precise definition of the performance requirements specified for the building assembly, after thorough research of the materials and construction techniques being proposed to meet the requirements, and by careful analysis of how the construction might actually perform. Then, the final decision should be made by the client based on information and recommendations provided by the architect.

M. Resistance to Moisture and Weathering

Controlling moisture is one of the most troublesome areas of construction design and detailing and one of the most error prone. Specific methods of waterproofing are discussed in Chapter 19. Whenever water might be a problem, the detail should be carefully reviewed. These situations include all roofing details, exterior walls and wall penetrations, below-grade walls and slabs, pools, areas under and around showers, tubs, kitchens, mechanical rooms, and in any other interior space where excess moisture is present.

Some of the things to consider include:

- *The permeability of the material itself:* can it resist moisture or must it be protected with a coating or by some other mechanical means?

- *The durability of the material:* will aging, building movement, and other forms of deterioration cause the material to crack or break up, allowing water to penetrate?

- *Aggravating circumstances:* will other conditions cause a normally water-resistant detail to leak? An exterior material may shed water but leak when wind-driven rain is forced in.

- *Joints:* are joints constructed, flashed, and sealed so water cannot enter? Will building movement damage the integrity of the joints?

- *Capillary action:* are tiny joints or holes inherent in the material, which can admit water? Brick mortar joints are a perfect example of this. The wrong type of joint can crack imperceptibly and let water that does not run off be sucked into the wall. A window sill or coping without a drip can allow water to flow up the underside and into the structure.

- *Outlets:* if water does get into the structure, as is normal in some situations, is there a way for it to drain back out? Weep holes in masonry walls and curtain walls allow this to happen.

- *Sealants:* have the proper types of sealants been selected for the type of material used and for the expected movement of the joint? Is the backup material correct and is the sealant installed with the correct dimensions?

In addition to precipitation, other forms of weathering include ultraviolet degradation, freeze-thaw cycles, and atmospheric corrosion. Materials must be selected to withstand the expected conditions.

N. Thermal Resistance

When necessitated by the detail's location, its resistance to heat transfer must be investigated, including both heat loss and heat gain. Of course, the resistance of the insulation must be checked, but in addition, the prudent architect will look for possible paths of air infiltration and insulation breaks where the full thickness of the insulation is not present. Exterior studs, pipes penetrating walls, and metal door frames are examples of areas where there is a weakness in the insulation value of the exterior wall.

O. Other Properties

There are many other properties of materials and construction details to review when developing or evaluating drawings. These include, when applicable, such things as acoustical properties, light reflection, abrasion resistance, resistance to termites and other insects, holding power of fasteners, resistance to fading, mildew resistance, color, and finish. Of course, no material will completely satisfy all criteria, but the architect must find the best balance.

2 ORGANIZATION AND LAYOUT OF CONSTRUCTION DRAWINGS

Construction drawings (also known as working drawings) are used the most often of all parts of the contract documents. In addition to representing a correctly designed and detailed building, the drawings themselves must be accurately produced and organized to clearly communicate the architect's intent.

A. Organization of Construction Drawings

Construction drawings are organized in a generally standardized sequence, which has been established based on the normal sequence of construction and through practice. The drawings are usually organized in the following way:

- title and index sheet
- site drawings
- civil engineering drawings (if any)
- architectural drawings
  · demolition plan (if any)
  · floor plans (may include schedules)
  · reflected ceiling plans
  · building sections
  · exterior elevations
  · exterior details
  · interior details
- structural drawings
- mechanical drawings
- plumbing drawings
- electrical drawings
- other consultants' drawings, such as kitchen, acoustical, etc.

Some offices vary the exact sequence of individual sheets in the architectural portion, but this is the usual method. The intent is to present the information in a logical sequence so that the contractors and others can find what they need without confusion.

B. Content of Construction Drawings

Drawings should show the general configuration, size, shape, and location of the components of construction with general notes to explain materials, construction requirements, dimensions, and similar explanations of the graphic material. Detailed requirements for material quality, workmanship, and other items are contained in the technical specifications of the project manual. The following is a brief description of some of the more common items that should be included with the architectural drawings. This list is by no means inclusive.

- *Site plan:* vicinity map, property description, property line locations with dimensions and bearings, bench marks, existing structures, new building location, landscaping, site improvements, fencing, roads, streets, right of way, drainage, and the limit of the work of the contract.

- *Floor plans:* building configuration with all walls shown, dimensions, grade elevations at the building line, construction to remain, references to other details and elevations, room names and numbers, door swings and door numbers, window numbers, floor material indications, plumbing fixtures, built-in fixtures, stairs, special equipment, vertical transportation, and notes as required to explain items on the plan.

- *Roof plans:* roof outline, overall dimensions and dimensions of setbacks, slope of roof, drainage, reference to other drawing details, roof materials, penetrations through roof, and roof-mounted equipment.

- *Reflected ceiling plans:* partitions extending to and through the ceiling, ceiling material and grid lines, ceiling height notes, changes in ceiling heights, locations of all lights including exit lights, location of diffusers, access panels, speakers and other equipment and ceiling penetrations, and expansion joints.

- *Exterior elevations:* structural grid center lines, vertical dimensions, floor-to-floor heights, opening heights, references to other details, floor lines, elevations of major elements, grade lines, foundation lines (dashed), material indications and notes, symbols for window schedule, gutters, signs and windows, doors, and all other openings.

- *Building sections:* vertical dimensions, elevations of the top of structural components and finish floor lines, general material indications, footings and foundations, reference to other details, ceiling lines, and major mechanical services.

- *Wall sections:* dimensions to grid center lines, face of wall dimensions to other components, vertical dimensions from foundations to parapet relating all elements to top of structural elements, material indications with notes, all connection methods, mechanical and electrical elements shown schematically, roof construction, floor construction, and foundation construction. Normally, the architect will orient all wall sections with the exterior on the left side.

- *Interior elevations:* vertical dimensions to critical elements, references to other details, openings in walls, wall finishes, built-in items, and locations of switches, thermostats, and other wall-mounted equipment.

- *Schedules:* room finish schedule, door schedule, window schedule, and hardware schedule are common schedules found on most drawings. Others are louver, millwork, piling, and equipment schedules.

In addition to these overall views of the construction, there are corresponding details for all portions of the work.

3   COORDINATION

Because the architectural construction drawings are only a part of the entire set of contract documents, they must be coordinated with other documents. Coordination is an ongoing effort during the design and production phases. Depending on how an individual office is organized, the responsibility may fall on the project architect, project manager, or job captain.

A.   Coordination With Consultants' Work

On nearly all projects there will be several consultants working with the architect. Small- to medium-size jobs will have structural, mechanical, and electrical consultants as a minimum. Larger projects may have additional consultants in fire protection, civil engineering, landscape architecture, food service, elevators, curtain walls, and interior design, among others.

Each discipline develops its own drawings, so coordination among everyone on the team is critical. Although all consultants must be diligent in their efforts to work with others, the primary responsibility for overall coordination is with the architect. In the office, this responsibility usually falls on the project manager, although in smaller firms or on smaller jobs the project architect may take on this task.

There are a number of ways to accomplish coordination during the design and production of contract documents. First, periodic meetings should be held to exchange information and alert everyone to the progress of the job. At these meetings, anyone can ask questions and raise issues that may affect the work of others. Second, progress prints should be exchanged between the architect and the consultants for ongoing comparison of work being produced. Third, the project manager must be responsible for notifying all consultants, in writing, of changes made as they occur. If overlay drafting or computer-aided drafting is being used, base sheets or electronic information can be exchanged according to the particular methods being employed. Finally, the architect must have a thorough method of checking and coordinating the entire drawing set prior to issue for bidding or negotiation.

B.   Correlation with the Specifications

The architectural drawings must also be coordinated with the specifications. These components of the contract documents are complementary; they both give necessary information about the design of the project. Either component alone is incomplete. They should work together without duplication or overlapping.

Specifications are part of the project manual and describe the types and quality of materials, quality of workmanship, methods of fabrication and installation, and general requirements related to the construction of the project. They are normally written after production of the drawings has started and materials have been selected. Because the specifications are usually written by someone not working on the drawings, there must also be close coordination within the architect's office. Again, this is usually the responsibility of the project manager. Specifications are discussed in more detail in Chapter 25.

If a computer-aided master specification system is used, there may be a sheet of drawing coordination notes produced by the system for each section of the specifications. These can be used for checking by the people producing the drawings.

SAMPLE QUESTIONS

1. Which of the following is probably of least concern to a subcontractor?

    A. the number of times equipment must be brought to the job site

    B. the types of tools required to build a project

    C. the level of skill of workers needed to complete the work

    D. other trades that will be working on the same part of the construction

2. You are reviewing a decorative wood grille wall covering in a building lobby. It is attached to a gypsum board partition with metal clips. In what probable order of importance would you check the following items?

I.   the spacing and size of the screws holding the clips to the partition

II.   the possibility of splintering due to the way the exposed surfaces are milled

III.   the flame spread rating

IV.   the method of cleaning the grill based on design and finish techniques used

V.   the local code requirements for surface finishes

    A. I, II, III, V, then IV

    B. III, V, II, IV, then I

    C. III, I, V, IV, then II

    D. V, III, I, II, then IV

Questions 3 and 4 refer to the accompanying wall detail at second floor.

3. If this detail is on an east-facing elevation in Boston, what recommendation would you make to the client?

    A. modify the drip detail at the top of the window frame

    B. change the glazing

    C. add seismic fasteners for the suspended ceiling

    D. increase the shim space

4. In the floor/ceiling detail shown, which of the following would be of most concern?

    A. attachment of exterior materials to the structure

    B. possible water leakage

    C. lack of tolerance for the storefront system

    D. cracking from differential movement of materials

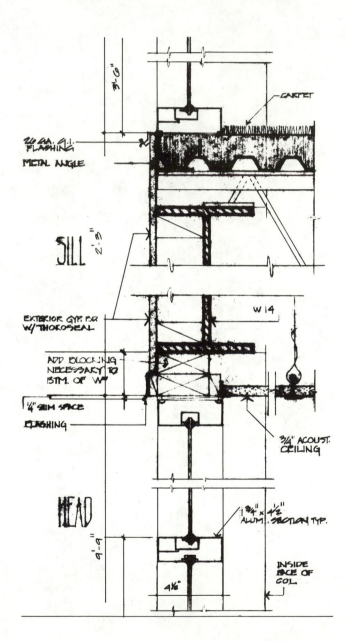

Wall Detail at Second Floor

5. During design development for a small corporate headquarters building, your client informs you that the estimated construction costs must be reduced. As far as the details are concerned, which of the following would most likely accomplish this?

I. Design and specify larger tolerances.

II. Examine areas subject to maintenance and improve the quality of these.

III. Review with the client changes to make custom details closer to industry standards.

IV. Examine ways to reduce the number of pieces in the details.

V. Try to reduce the number of different details involved in the project.

    A. I, IV, and V
    B. II, III, IV, and V
    C. III, IV, and V
    D. all of the above

6. Who is responsible for verifying that recessed down lights do not interfere with ductwork shown on the plans?

    A. the architect
    B. the electrical engineer
    C. the lighting designer
    D. the architect's drafting staff

7. As the project architect on a job, what would be one way you would ensure that the client's design goals were being satisfied by the final set of construction documents?

    A. Hold periodic meetings with the project designer, job captain, and programmer to compare the current status of the drawings with schematic design documents.

    B. Have another architect in the office review the drawings for compliance with the original program report.

    C. Send the client periodic check sets of drawings for review and request that any corrections be communicated to the architect's office within a set time period.

    D. Make up a checklist of design requirements based on the original design goals and give this to the people working on the job so they have a constant reminder of the client's needs.

THE PROJECT MANUAL AND SPECIFICATIONS

25

1 THE PROJECT MANUAL

The *project manual* is a bound book containing all the contract and non-contract documents for a construction project except the drawings. The project manual contains the technical specifications, but it also includes several other types of documents.

A. Organization of the Project Manual

The project manual is divided into four major parts: (1) bidding requirements; (2) parts of the contract itself, which will contain the agreement between owner and contractor, bond forms, and the like; (3) the general and supplementary conditions of the contract; and (4) the technical specifications.

A more detailed list of contents of the project might include some or all of the following:

- bidding requirements
  - · invitation to bid
  - · prequalification forms
  - · instructions to bidders
  - · information available to bidders
  - · bid forms
- supplements to bid forms
  - · bid security form
  - · subcontractor list
  - · substitution list
- contract forms
  - · agreement (contract between owner and contractor)
  - · performance bond
  - · labor and materials payment bond
  - · certificates of insurance
- general and supplementary conditions
  - · general conditions of the contract (such as AIA form 201)
  - · supplementary conditions
- technical specifications

Contracts, bidding documents, and general conditions of the contract are discussed in more detail in later chapters. This chapter focuses on the technical specifications.

B. Coordination With the Drawings

The technical specifications and the drawings are complementary. The *drawings* show the general configuration and layout of the building; the size, shape, and dimensions of the construction; and general notes to explain the graphic representation. The *technical specifications* describe the quality of materials and workmanship, along with general requirements for the execution of the work, standards, and other items that are more appropriately described in written, rather than graphic, form.

The drawings, technical specifications, and other parts of the project manual must be coordinated to avoid conflicting requirements, duplication, omissions, and errors. There are several areas of particular concern.

First, the specifications should contain requirements for all the materials and construction indicated on the drawings. A common checklist used by both the specifications writer and the project manager or job captain is one way to accomplish this.

Second, the terminology used in both documents should be the same. If the term "gypsum board" is used in the specifications, the term "drywall" should not be shown on the drawings.

Third, dimensions and thicknesses should only be indicated on one document. If the thickness of flashing is included in the technical specifications, there is no need to note it on the drawings.

Fourth, notes on the drawings should not describe methods of installation or material qualities; these belong in the specifications.

When there is a conflict between the drawings and specifications, the courts have held that the specifications are more binding and take precedence over the drawings.

2   SPECIFICATIONS

As previously described, specifications form part of the project manual and are legal documents. As such, they must be complete, accurate, unambiguous, and exact. Because of these needs and because specifications represent complex technical information, they are difficult to write correctly. Fortunately, some standard methods of preparing specifications are in general use. These will be described in the following sections.

In addition, master specifications are available that can be used as starting documents. A *master specification* is a prewritten text that includes the majority of requirements for a particular specification section. Master specifications are edited by deleting unnecessary portions, adding particular requirements for a specific job, and coordinating them with other specification sections and other parts of the project manual. They are available in written form and on computer disk from the American Institute of Architects (Masterspec), the Construction Specifications Institute (SpecText), and various other commercial sources.

Computer programs based on expert system technology are also becoming available. These generate specifications through interactive sessions with the specifier and with links to some computer-aided drafting software.

A. Types of Specifications

There are two broad categories of specifications, prescriptive and performance. Prescriptive specifications are sometimes called closed, while performance specifications are known as open.

Prescriptive specifications tell exactly what product or material you want the contractor to use by using brand names. *Performance specifications* tell what results you want the final construction assembly to achieve, but they give the contractor some choice in how they will be achieved. Most specifications fall somewhere between these two extremes.

The type you select will depend on several factors. Public projects almost always require open specifications in order to encourage competitive bidding. In other cases,

you may want to use a closed specification to ensure that only one particular product is used. Whether the job is bid or a negotiated contract may also affect your choice. With bidding, you want to allow the contractor as much choice as possible so he or she can find the lowest price within the context of the specification requirements.

The following types of specifications are the ones most commonly used.

Types of Prescriptive Specifications

Proprietary specifications are the most restrictive in that they call out a specific manufacturer's product. These give the architect complete control over what is installed. They are easier than other types to write and are generally shorter. However, they do not allow for competitive bidding and by limiting products you may force the contractor to get materials that may be difficult or expensive to procure in a certain geographical area or that require excessive delivery time. Further, the burden is on the specifier to call out products that meet code requirements, are within the budget, and are technically correct.

A base bid with alternates is a type of specification that calls out a proprietary product but allows the substitution of other products that the contractor thinks are equal to the one stated. This is a dangerous method of specifying because the contractor may substitute a less expensive item that he or she thinks is an equal, but which usually is not.

There are two variations of a base bid specification. The first lists several approved manufacturers of a product. The contractor is free to bid on any one listed. This type satisfies the requirements for public work where at least three different manufacturers must be listed, but it puts the burden on the architect to make sure that every one of the approved products or manufacturers listed is equal.

The second variation is a base bid with "approved equal" language. This specification states one product or an approved equal must be used . This means that the contractor may submit a proposed substitution but it is subject to review and approval by the architect before it can be incorporated into the bid. Although this gives the contractor some freedom in looking for lower-priced alternates, it also puts the burden for finding them on the contractor. However, the responsibility for fairly and accurately evaluating the proposed alternates is placed on the architect or owner. During a hectic bidding period this can be a large burden, so the specifications should clearly state how much lead time the contractor must give the architect and how alternates will be evaluated.

Types of Performance (Open) Specifications

A *descriptive specification* gives detailed written requirements for the material or product and the workmanship required for its fabrication and installation. It does not mention trade names. In its purest form, a descriptive specification is difficult to write because you must include all the pertinent requirements for the construction and installation of the product.

A variation of the descriptive type is a *reference standard* specification. This describes a material, product, or process based on requirements (reference standards) set by an accepted authority or test method. For example, a product type can be required to meet the testing standards produced by such organizations as the American Society for Testing and Materials (ASTM), the American National Standards Institute (ANSI), or Underwriter's Laboratories (UL). Reference can also be made to specific trade associations, such as the Architectural Woodwork Institute, The American Iron and Steel Institute, and the Gypsum Association.

For example, in specifying gypsum wallboard you can state that all gypsum wallboard products must meet the requirements of ASTM C36. This particular document describes in great detail the requirements for gypsum wallboard so you do not have to repeat it and can instead refer to a generally recognized industry standard.

Reference standard specifications are fairly easy to write and are generally short. Chances for errors are reduced and your liability minimized because you are using industry standards and generally recognized methods of building. However, you must know what is in the standard and how to refer to the appropriate part of the standard if it includes more provisions than you need for your job.

A pure performance specification is a statement setting criteria and results required of the item being specified, which can be verified by measurement, test evaluation, or other types of assurance that the final result meets the criteria. The means of achieving the required results are not specified, leaving that up to the person trying to meet the specification.

A true performance specification is often used for construction components when the specifier wants to encourage new ways of achieving a particular end result. For example, a movable partition system could be specified by stating its required fire rating, acoustical properties, finish, maximum thickness, tolerances, size required, and all the other required properties. It would then be up to the contractor and manufacturer to design and develop a system to meet the criteria.

Performance specifications are difficult to write because the specifier must know all the criteria, state the methods for testing compliance, and be prepared for the cost consequences.

B. Organization of the Technical Sections

The organization of the technical sections has been standardized through the general adoption of the *Masterformat* system. This has been developed by the Construction Specifications Institute and Construction Specifications Canada to standardize the numbering and format of project-related information for use in specifying, cost estimating, and data filing. The organization is based on sixteen broad divisions that represent major categories of work. Each division is subdivided into sections, each of which is assigned a five-digit number. The divisions and major sections are shown in Figure 25.1.

The sections shown in Figure 25.1 are considered *broadscope sections* in that they may cover several types of materials, products, or systems. If more specific classification is required, then a so-called *narrowscope section* is used. For example, Section 09900, Painting, is a broadscope section that can include many different types of painting. A project manual can also be written using the narrowscope sections of 09910, Exterior Painting, 09920, Interior Painting, and 09930, Transparent Finishes.

C. Technical Section Outline and Format

The *Masterformat* system also establishes a standard way of organizing any particular broadscope or narrowscope section. The first level of division within a section is the three-part format. This includes Part 1, General, Part 2, Products, and Part 3, Execution. All sections include these three parts while the specific articles within the parts vary with the type of material or product being specified.

Part 1 gives the general requirements for the section, such as the scope of the section, submittals required, quality assurance requirements, warranties, project conditions, and specifications for the delivery, storage, and handling of materials.

Part 2 details the specifications for the materials and products themselves, including acceptable manufacturers (if applicable), what standards and test methods the materials must conform to, how items are to be fabricated, and similar concerns.

BIDDING REQUIREMENTS, CONTRACT FORMS, AND CONDITIONS OF THE CONTRACT

00010	PRE-BID INFORMATION
00100	INSTRUCTIONS TO BIDDERS
00200	INFORMATION AVAILABLE TO BIDDERS
00300	BID FORMS
00400	SUPPLEMENTS TO BID FORMS
00500	AGREEMENT FORMS
00600	BONDS AND CERTIFICATES
00700	GENERAL CONDITIONS
00800	SUPPLEMENTARY CONDITIONS
00850	DRAWINGS AND SCHEDULES
00900	ADDENDA AND MODIFICATIONS

Note: Since the items listed above are not specification sections, they are referred to as "Documents" in lieu of "Sections" in the Master List of Section Titles, Numbers, and Broadscope Explanations.

SPECIFICATIONS

DIVISION 1—GENERAL REQUIREMENTS

01010	SUMMARY OF WORK
01020	ALLOWANCES
01025	MEASUREMENT AND PAYMENT
01030	ALTERNATES/ALTERNATIVES
01040	COORDINATION
01050	FIELD ENGINEERING
01060	REGULATORY REQUIREMENTS
01070	ABBREVIATIONS AND SYMBOLS
01080	IDENTIFICATION SYSTEMS
01090	REFERENCE STANDARDS
01100	SPECIAL PROJECT PROCEDURES
01200	PROJECT MEETINGS
01300	SUBMITTALS
01400	QUALITY CONTROL
01500	CONSTRUCTION FACILITIES AND TEMPORARY CONTROLS
01600	MATERIAL AND EQUIPMENT
01650	STARTING OF SYSTEMS/COMMISSIONING
01700	CONTRACT CLOSEOUT
01800	MAINTENANCE

DIVISION 2—SITEWORK

02010	SUBSURFACE INVESTIGATION
02050	DEMOLITION
02100	SITE PREPARATION
02140	DEWATERING
02150	SHORING AND UNDERPINNING
02160	EXCAVATION SUPPORT SYSTEMS
02170	COFFERDAMS
02200	EARTHWORK
02300	TUNNELING
02350	PILES AND CAISSONS
02450	RAILROAD WORK
02480	MARINE WORK
02500	PAVING AND SURFACING
02600	PIPED UTILITY MATERIALS
02660	WATER DISTRIBUTION
02680	FUEL DISTRIBUTION
02700	SEWERAGE AND DRAINAGE
02760	RESTORATION OF UNDERGROUND PIPELINES
02770	PONDS AND RESERVOIRS
02780	POWER AND COMMUNICATIONS
02800	SITE IMPROVEMENTS
02900	LANDSCAPING

DIVISION 3—CONCRETE

03100	CONCRETE FORMWORK
03200	CONCRETE REINFORCEMENT
03250	CONCRETE ACCESSORIES
03300	CAST-IN-PLACE CONCRETE
03370	CONCRETE CURING
03400	PRECAST CONCRETE
03500	CEMENTITIOUS DECKS
03600	GROUT
03700	CONCRETE RESTORATION AND CLEANING
03800	MASS CONCRETE

DIVISION 4—MASONRY

04100	MORTAR
04150	MASONRY ACCESSORIES
04200	UNIT MASONRY
04400	STONE
04500	MASONRY RESTORATION AND CLEANING
04550	REFRACTORIES
04600	CORROSION RESISTANT MASONRY

DIVISION 5—METALS

05010	METAL MATERIALS
05030	METAL FINISHES
05050	METAL FASTENING
05100	STRUCTURAL METAL FRAMING
05200	METAL JOISTS
05300	METAL DECKING
05400	COLD-FORMED METAL FRAMING
05500	METAL FABRICATIONS
05580	SHEET METAL FABRICATIONS
05700	ORNAMENTAL METAL
05800	EXPANSION CONTROL
05900	HYDRAULIC STRUCTURES

DIVISION 6—WOOD AND PLASTICS

06050	FASTENERS AND ADHESIVES
06100	ROUGH CARPENTRY
06130	HEAVY TIMBER CONSTRUCTION
06150	WOOD-METAL SYSTEMS
06170	PREFABRICATED STRUCTURAL WOOD
06200	FINISH CARPENTRY
06300	WOOD TREATMENT
06400	ARCHITECTURAL WOODWORK
06500	PREFABRICATED STRUCTURAL PLASTICS
06600	PLASTIC FABRICATIONS

DIVISION 7—THERMAL AND MOISTURE PROTECTION

07100	WATERPROOFING
07150	DAMPPROOFING
07190	VAPOR AND AIR RETARDERS
07200	INSULATION
07250	FIREPROOFING
07300	SHINGLES AND ROOFING TILES
07400	PREFORMED ROOFING AND CLADDING/SIDING
07500	MEMBRANE ROOFING
07570	TRAFFIC TOPPING
07600	FLASHING AND SHEET METAL
07700	ROOF SPECIALTIES AND ACCESSORIES
07800	SKYLIGHTS
07900	JOINT SEALERS

DIVISION 8—DOORS AND WINDOWS

08100	METAL DOORS AND FRAMES
08200	WOOD AND PLASTIC DOORS
08250	DOOR OPENING ASSEMBLIES
08300	SPECIAL DOORS
08400	ENTRANCES AND STOREFRONTS
08500	METAL WINDOWS
08600	WOOD AND PLASTIC WINDOWS
08650	SPECIAL WINDOWS
08700	HARDWARE
08800	GLAZING
08900	GLAZED CURTAIN WALLS

DIVISION 9—FINISHES

09100	METAL SUPPORT SYSTEMS
09200	LATH AND PLASTER
09230	AGGREGATE COATINGS
09250	GYPSUM BOARD
09300	TILE
09400	TERRAZZO
09500	ACOUSTICAL TREATMENT
09540	SPECIAL SURFACES
09550	WOOD FLOORING
09600	STONE FLOORING
09630	UNIT MASONRY FLOORING
09650	RESILIENT FLOORING
09680	CARPET
09700	SPECIAL FLOORING
09780	FLOOR TREATMENT
09800	SPECIAL COATINGS
09900	PAINTING
09950	WALL COVERINGS

Figure 25.1 Masterformat System
Reproduced with permission of the Construction Specifications Institute

DIVISION 10—SPECIALTIES

10100	CHALKBOARDS AND TACKBOARDS
10150	COMPARTMENTS AND CUBICLES
10200	LOUVERS AND VENTS
10240	GRILLES AND SCREENS
10250	SERVICE WALL SYSTEMS
10260	WALL AND CORNER GUARDS
10270	ACCESS FLOORING
10280	SPECIALTY MODULES
10290	PEST CONTROL
10300	FIREPLACES AND STOVES
10340	PREFABRICATED EXTERIOR SPECIALTIES
10350	FLAGPOLES
10400	IDENTIFYING DEVICES
10450	PEDESTRIAN CONTROL DEVICES
10500	LOCKERS
10520	FIRE PROTECTION SPECIALTIES
10530	PROTECTIVE COVERS
10550	POSTAL SPECIALTIES
10600	PARTITIONS
10650	OPERABLE PARTITIONS
10670	STORAGE SHELVING
10700	EXTERIOR SUN CONTROL DEVICES
10750	TELEPHONE SPECIALTIES
10800	TOILET AND BATH ACCESSORIES
10880	SCALES
10900	WARDROBE AND CLOSET SPECIALTIES

DIVISION 11—EQUIPMENT

11010	MAINTENANCE EQUIPMENT
11020	SECURITY AND VAULT EQUIPMENT
11030	TELLER AND SERVICE EQUIPMENT
11040	ECCLESIASTICAL EQUIPMENT
11050	LIBRARY EQUIPMENT
11060	THEATER AND STAGE EQUIPMENT
11070	INSTRUMENTAL EQUIPMENT
11080	REGISTRATION EQUIPMENT
11090	CHECKROOM EQUIPMENT
11100	MERCANTILE EQUIPMENT
11110	COMMERCIAL LAUNDRY AND DRY CLEANING EQUIPMENT
11120	VENDING EQUIPMENT
11130	AUDIO-VISUAL EQUIPMENT
11140	SERVICE STATION EQUIPMENT
11150	PARKING CONTROL EQUIPMENT
11160	LOADING DOCK EQUIPMENT
11170	SOLID WASTE HANDLING EQUIPMENT
11190	DETENTION EQUIPMENT
11200	WATER SUPPLY AND TREATMENT EQUIPMENT
11280	HYDRAULIC GATES AND VALVES
11300	FLUID WASTE TREATMENT AND DISPOSAL EQUIPMENT
11400	FOOD SERVICE EQUIPMENT
11450	RESIDENTIAL EQUIPMENT
11460	UNIT KITCHENS
11470	DARKROOM EQUIPMENT
11480	ATHLETIC, RECREATIONAL AND THERAPEUTIC EQUIPMENT
11500	INDUSTRIAL AND PROCESS EQUIPMENT
11600	LABORATORY EQUIPMENT
11650	PLANETARIUM EQUIPMENT
11660	OBSERVATORY EQUIPMENT
11700	MEDICAL EQUIPMENT
11780	MORTUARY EQUIPMENT
11850	NAVIGATION EQUIPMENT

DIVISION 12—FURNISHINGS

12050	FABRICS
12100	ARTWORK
12300	MANUFACTURED CASEWORK
12500	WINDOW TREATMENT
12600	FURNITURE AND ACCESSORIES
12670	RUGS AND MATS
12700	MULTIPLE SEATING
12800	INTERIOR PLANTS AND PLANTERS

DIVISION 13—SPECIAL CONSTRUCTION

13010	AIR SUPPORTED STRUCTURES
13020	INTEGRATED ASSEMBLIES
13030	SPECIAL PURPOSE ROOMS
13080	SOUND, VIBRATION, AND SEISMIC CONTROL
13090	RADIATION PROTECTION
13100	NUCLEAR REACTORS
13120	PRE-ENGINEERED STRUCTURES
13150	POOLS
13160	ICE RINKS
13170	KENNELS AND ANIMAL SHELTERS
13180	SITE CONSTRUCTED INCINERATORS
13200	LIQUID AND GAS STORAGE TANKS
13220	FILTER UNDERDRAINS AND MEDIA
13230	DIGESTION TANK COVERS AND APPURTENANCES
13240	OXYGENATION SYSTEMS
13260	SLUDGE CONDITIONING SYSTEMS
13300	UTILITY CONTROL SYSTEMS
13400	INDUSTRIAL AND PROCESS CONTROL SYSTEMS
13500	RECORDING INSTRUMENTATION
13550	TRANSPORTATION CONTROL INSTRUMENTATION
13600	SOLAR ENERGY SYSTEMS
13700	WIND ENERGY SYSTEMS
13800	BUILDING AUTOMATION SYSTEMS
13900	FIRE SUPPRESSION AND SUPERVISORY SYSTEMS

DIVISION 14—CONVEYING SYSTEMS

14100	DUMBWAITERS
14200	ELEVATORS
14300	MOVING STAIRS AND WALKS
14400	LIFTS
14500	MATERIAL HANDLING SYSTEMS
14600	HOISTS AND CRANES
14700	TURNTABLES
14800	SCAFFOLDING
14900	TRANSPORTATION SYSTEMS

DIVISION 15—MECHANICAL

15050	BASIC MECHANICAL MATERIALS AND METHODS
15250	MECHANICAL INSULATION
15300	FIRE PROTECTION
15400	PLUMBING
15500	HEATING, VENTILATING, AND AIR CONDITIONING (HVAC)
15550	HEAT GENERATION
15650	REFRIGERATION
15750	HEAT TRANSFER
15850	AIR HANDLING
15880	AIR DISTRIBUTION
15950	CONTROLS
15990	TESTING, ADJUSTING, AND BALANCING

DIVISION 16—ELECTRICAL

16050	BASIC ELECTRICAL MATERIALS AND METHODS
16200	POWER GENERATION
16300	HIGH VOLTAGE DISTRIBUTION (Above 600-Volt)
16400	SERVICE AND DISTRIBUTION (600-Volt and Below)
16500	LIGHTING
16600	SPECIAL SYSTEMS
16700	COMMUNICATIONS
16850	ELECTRIC RESISTANCE HEATING
16900	CONTROLS
16950	TESTING

Figure 25.1 (cont'd)

PROFESSIONAL PUBLICATIONS ● Belmont, CA

Part 3 tells how the products and materials are to be installed, applied, or otherwise put into place. This part also describes the examination and preparation required before installation, how quality control should be maintained in the field, and requirements for adjusting, cleaning, and protection of the finished work.

Figure 25.2 shows the section format outline listing all the possible articles of each part.

D. Specification Writing Guidelines

As previously mentioned, specifications are legal documents as well as a way of communicating very technical information to the contractor. Because of this, they must be complete, accurate, and unambiguous. The language must be precise. Some of the important things to remember include the following:

- Know what the standards and test methods referred to include and what parts of them are applicable to your project. They must also be the most current editions.

- Do not specify together the results and the methods proposed to achieve those results, as the result may be a conflict. For instance, if you specify that a brick must have certain absorption characteristics according to an ASTM test method and then specify a particular brick that does not meet the stated requirements, the specification will be impossible to comply with.

- Do not include standards that cannot be measured. For example, saying that the work should be done in "a first class manner" is subject to wide interpretation.

- Avoid *exculpatory clauses*. These are phrases that try to shift responsibility to the contractor or someone else in a very broad, general way. An example is something like "contractor shall be totally responsible for all . . . ." Unless the clause is generally accepted wording or makes sense in the context of the specification, current legal opinion disapproves of such clauses, especially when they favor the person who wrote them.

- Avoid words or phrases that are ambiguous. The combination "and/or," for example, is unclear and should be replaced with one word or the other. The abbreviation "etc." is also vague and implies that a list can go on forever and may include something you do not want it to include. The word "any" implies the contractor has a choice. This is acceptable if you want to allow a choice, but most often you do not.

- Keep the specifications as short as possible. Specification writing can be terse, even sometimes omitting unnecessary words like "all," "the," "an," and "a."

- Describe only one major idea in each paragraph. This makes reading easier and improves comprehension and it also makes changing the specification easier.

PART 1 GENERAL

SUMMARY
Section Includes
Products Furnished But Not
  Installed Under This Section
Products Installed But Not
  Furnished Under This Section
Related Sections
Allowances
Unit Prices
Alternates/Alternatives*

REFERENCES

DEFINITIONS

SYSTEM DESCRIPTION
Design Requirements
Performance Requirements

SUBMITTALS
Product Data
Shop Drawings
Samples
Quality Control Submittals
  Design Data
  Test Reports
  Certificates
  Manufacturer's Instructions
  Manufacturer's Field Reports
Contract Closeout Submittals
  Project Record Documents
  Operation and Maintenance Data
  Warranty

QUALITY ASSURANCE
Qualifications
Regulatory Requirements
Certifications
Field Samples
Mock-Ups
Pre-Installation Conference

DELIVERY, STORAGE, AND HANDLING
Packing and Shipping
Acceptance at Site
Storage and Protection

PROJECT/SITE* CONDITIONS
Environmental Requirements
Existing Conditions
Field Measurements

SEQUENCING AND SCHEDULING

WARRANTY
Special Warranty

MAINTENANCE
Maintenance Service
Extra Materials

PART 2 PRODUCTS

MANUFACTURERS

MATERIALS

MANUFACTURED UNITS

EQUIPMENT

COMPONENTS

ACCESSORIES

MIXES

FABRICATION
Shop Assembly
Shop/Factory Finishing
Tolerances

SOURCE QUALITY CONTROL
Tests
Inspection
Verification of Performance

PART 3 EXECUTION

EXAMINATION
Verification of Conditions

PREPARATION
Protection
Surface Preparation

ERECTION
INSTALLATION
APPLICATION
Special Techniques
Interface with Other Products
Tolerances

FIELD QUALITY CONTROL
Tests
Inspection
Manufacturer's Field Service

ADJUSTING

CLEANING

DEMONSTRATION

PROTECTION

SCHEDULES

Figure 25.2 Section Format Outline

Reproduced with permission of the Construction Specifications Institute

SAMPLE QUESTIONS

1. Which of the following would not be found in a project manual?

    A. bid log

    B. subsurface soil conditions report

    C. sitework specification

    D. bid bond

Question 2 refers to the following excerpt from a specification.

Part 2—Products

2.01 Metal Support Material

    General: To the extent not otherwise indicated, comply with ASTM C754 for metal system supporting gypsum wallboard.

    Ceiling suspension main runners: 1 1/2 inches steel channels, cold rolled.

    Hanger wire: ASTM A641, soft, Class 1 galvanized, prestretched; sized in accordance with ASTM C754.

    Hanger anchorage devices: size for 3 × calculated loads, except size direct-pull concrete inserts for 5 × calculated loads.

    Studs: ASTM C645; 25 gage, 2 1/2 inches deep, except as otherwise indicated.

        ASTM C645; 25 gage, 3 5/8 inches deep.

        ASTM C645; 20 gage, 6 inches deep.

    Runners: Match studs; type recommended by stud manufacturer for floor and ceiling support of studs, and for vertical abutment of drywall work at other work.

    Furring members: ASTM C65; 25 gage, hat-shaped.

    Fasteners: Type and size recommended by furring manufacturer for the substrate and application indicated.

2. Which item is described as a performance specification?

    A. fasteners

    B. hanger wire

    C. hanger anchorage devices

    D. ceiling suspension main runners

3. A performance specification:

    A. allows innovation by the contractor

    B. requires more work by the architect

    C. is not appropriate for normal building products

    D. all of the above

4. What is likely to occur if the drawings and specifications are not thoroughly coordinated?

    I. a decrease of the actual cost from the estimated cost because the contractor bid on a less expensive material shown on the drawings while the same material was called out as a more expensive type in the specifications

    II. a lawsuit

    III. the need for a change order during construction to account for modifications required to correct discrepancies in the two documents

    IV. a delay in construction

    V. an increase in cost because the contractor bid the least expensive choice between two conflicting requirements when the client wanted the more expensive option

        A. I, III, and IV

        B. I and III

        C. II, IV, and V

        D. III, IV, and V

5. In specifying asphalt roofing shingles, which of the following types of specifications would you probably not use?

    A. descriptive

    B. base bid or equal

    C. reference standard

    D. base bid with alternate approved manufacturers

6. Which of the following are generally true of specifications?

    I. Both narrowscope and broadscope sections can be used in the same project manual.

II. For the contractor, drawings are more binding than the specifications if there is a conflict.

III. Specifications show quality; drawings show quantity.

IV. Proprietary specifications are the same as prescriptive specifications.

V. They should not be open to interpretation if they are the base bid type.

    A. I, III, IV, and V
    B. I, III, and V

C. II, III, and IV

D. all of the above

7. Where would you find requirements for testing a plumbing system?

    A. in a section of Division 1 of the specifications
    B. in Part 1 of Section 15400, Plumbing
    C. in Part 2 of Section 15400, Plumbing
    D. in Part 3 of Section 15400, Plumbing

THE PRIMARY CONTRACTUAL DOCUMENTS

26

This chapter reviews the various approaches to project delivery and the primary contractual documents that formalize the delivery method selected. These include the owner-architect agreement, the owner-contractor agreement, and the general and supplementary conditions of the contract. Additional contractual documents, which include the drawings, specifications, change orders, and other types of forms are discussed in other chapters. You should remember that the various types of documents that are used in the project delivery process, which may establish contractual relationships between the many parties involved, should not be confused with the formal definition of contract documents.

The *contract documents* consist of the owner-contractor agreement, the general conditions of the contract, the supplementary conditions of the contract (if any), the drawings, specifications, addenda issued prior to execution of the contract, any other documents specifically listed in the agreement, and modifications issued after execution of the contract. A *modification* is a change order, a construction change directive, a written order for a minor change in the work issued by the architect, or a written amendment to the contract signed by both parties.

1 APPROACHES TO PROJECT DELIVERY

Project delivery is a term used to describe the entire sequence of events necessary to provide an owner with a completed building. It includes the selection of people who will design and construct the project, establishment of contractual relationships, and some method of organizing contractors to perform the work. This section reviews some of the elements of project delivery and discusses the three primary types.

A. Responsibility for Design and Construction

The traditional method available to owners is to hire an architect to design the project and to hire someone else, the contractor, to build the project. The architect acts as agent for the owner, looking after the owner's best interest with no financial stake in the project. The contractor, in turn, agrees to finish the project according to the plans and specifications for a fixed price within a certain time period. The owner has separate contracts with the architect and the contractor.

Another method is to have a single entity responsible for both designing and building a project. This approach has both advantages and disadvantages. It allows review by construction experts during design and often includes a guaranteed cost. However, it eliminates the advantages of competitive bidding and can set up potential conflicts because the goals of designers are usually at variance with the goals of contractors. Both of these delivery approaches will be discussed later in this section.

B. Agency

One of the key concepts in the traditional relationship between the architect, owner, and contractor is that of *agency*. The legal concept of agency involves three parties: the principal, the agent, and the third party. The owner is the *principal*, the architect is the *agent* of the owner, and the contractor is the *third party*. The agent acts on behalf of the principal and has the authority to perform certain duties. In the performance of these duties the agent can legally bind the principal to the third party (contractor). It is therefore important that the architect understand the full extent of his or her authority and what duties are expected.

In contrast to an agent, the contractor is considered a vendor. A *vendor* supplies a specific product for a fixed price. Unlike the architect/agent, vendors act primarily in their own self-interest.

C. Contract Types

In nearly any building project, regardless of size, there are a number of contractual relationships established between all the parties involved. Contract types are often classified by the primary relationship the owner has with the contractor (or contractors). This relationship is called the *prime contract*.

The most common type is the *single prime contract*, in which the owner has an agreement with a general contractor to build a project according to the plans and specifications. If other, specialized, contractors are needed, then the general contractor subcontracts with these parties. Typical subcontractors include mechanical, electrical, plumbing, concrete, roofing, and the like. On large projects there are dozens of subcontractors and many sub-subcontractors. However, the general contractor is responsible to the owner and must coordinate the other subcontractors. The primary advantage to this method is that the owner has single source responsibility, and it is easier for the architect to administer.

Another type is the *multiple prime contract*. With this method, major portions of the work, such as mechanical, electrical, and plumbing work, are contracted separately with the owner. Many specialty contractors favor this approach, but it is more difficult for the architect to coordinate.

A third type of contract arrangement is the *many prime contracts*. This is usually used in fast-track construction where one portion of the work needs to start before other elements are designed or ready to be priced. This arrangement is much more difficult to manage and often requires the use of a construction manager if the architect is unable to coordinate the effort.

D. Design-Award-Build

The design-award-build is the first and most traditional of the three common methods of project delivery. With this approach, the architect designs the project and prepares the construction drawings and specifications. These are used as the basis for costing the project and awarding a construction contract, either through competitive bidding or negotiating with one contractor. The contractor then builds the project with the architect providing contract administration services. The owner has separate contracts with both the architect and contractor.

This method of project delivery is fairly simple since all the roles are well-defined and the work proceeds in a linear fashion from selection of the architect to final build out. Coordination problems are minimized, contract relationships are straightforward, and the owner

can receive a fixed price before proceeding with construction. The disadvantages are that one phase must be completely finished before the next one proceeds. This can be a problem if the owner needs the building quickly or if extended design and construction time may result in higher financing costs.

E. Fast-Track

When the overall time for design and construction must be compressed, a *fast-track* method can be used. This overlaps some of the design process with some of the construction process to reduce the total time needed for project delivery. For example, based on design development drawings, construction drawings and specifications can be completed for foundations and this work begun before the architect has completed work on interior finish design. Fast-track construction requires multiple prime contracts and much more coordination, but it can substantially reduce the time and cost of a project.

Because of the extra management required, the architect may offer construction management services or the owner may contract with a separate construction management company. A construction manager usually works as the owner's agent (like the architect) to provide services of scheduling, early material purchasing, design review related to constructability, contract preparation, and many other services required in the fast-track process. In some cases, the construction manager may guarantee the cost and time delivery of the project.

F. Design-Build

With the *design-build* method, the owner contracts with one entity to provide both design and construction services. The design-build firm then subcontracts with others, as required. There are several variations of the design-build firm. It may have its own staff of architects and construction personnel. It may primarily have a construction staff and hire architects as subcontractors. It may be a joint venture of an architect and contractor. Or, it may subcontract both architecture and construction.

The design-build approach offers the owner several advantages. It is a single source of responsibility and administering the contract is direct. The owner also has a fixed price early in the process. In addition, the total time of design and construction is usually reduced over more traditional approaches.

There are also several disadvantages. First, the owner does not have the same amount of control over design once the contract is signed. Second, there can be disagreements concerning what was supposed to be included in the design since this is done after the contract is signed. Third, the design-build firm has control over the quality of the materials and construction methods used. Fourth, in order to get what is needed, the client must develop a specific set of performance requirements.

In many cases, the owner hires an architect to act as advisor. The architect acts as the owner's agent to help set up performance requirements, evaluate potential design-build firms, administer the contract, and evaluate the progress of the work against the contract and approved design.

Design-build contracts are typically used by owners who have building experience with multiple facilities and who have clearly defined needs that can be precisely stated in performance requirements.

2 OWNER-ARCHITECT AGREEMENTS

There are several types of owner-architect agreements published by the American Institute of Architects (AIA). The most common is AIA Document B141, Standard Form of Agreement Between Owner and Architect. This agreement is used on construction projects where services are based on the traditional five phases of schematic design, design development, construction documents, bidding or negotiation, and administration of the construction contract. When the architect is asked to perform more extensive services, AIA Document B161, Standard Form of Agreement Between Owner and Architect for Designated Services, is commonly used. Both of these documents are discussed in this section.

Additional AIA standard documents are available for projects of limited scope, for jobs where construction management services are performed, for interior design services, and for housing services.

Although AIA forms do not have to be used between either the owner and architect or the owner and contractor, they have been developed over many years and represent a general consensus concerning the rights and duties of the various parties involved with a construction project. If you understand the provisions in the AIA documents, you should have a very good idea of standard contractual relationships.

Because the various agreements discussed in this chapter are lengthy and cover a great deal of material, you should read through the primary ones prior to taking the exam. The remaining sections of this chapter will only highlight some of the more important provisions.

A. The Architect's Responsibilities

The first part of Document B141 outlines the architect's scope of basic services according to the standard five phases of a project: schematic design, design development, construction document preparation, bidding or negotiation, and administration of the construction contract. When beginning the schematic design phase, the program is furnished by the owner for review by the architect. The architect then proceeds to develop alternate approaches to design and to develop drawings and other documents illustrating the project. At the end of the first three phases the architect is to submit to the owner current information on the preliminary estimate of construction cost.

During the construction documents phase and the bidding or negotiation phase, the agreement states that the architect will assist the owner in the preparation of bidding documents, assist the owner in connection with the owner's responsibilities for filing documents required for various governmental approvals, and assist the owner in obtaining bids or negotiating proposals. The intent in all of this language is to make the owner an active participant in many of the critical parts of the process and to have the owner assume this responsibility.

The duties and responsibilities during the construction phase are rather detailed and correspond with the language in the general conditions of the contract. There are four especially important provisions with which you should be familiar.

The first concerns site visits. The architect's responsibility is to visit the site at intervals appropriate to the stage of construction and to determine in general if, when completed, the project will be in accordance with the contract documents. The architect must keep the owner informed of the progress and endeavor to protect the owner against defects.

The second important point is that the architect is not responsible for the means of construction, for building techniques, or for safety precautions. These are the sole responsibility of the contractor.

Third, the owner and contractor are supposed to communicate through the architect. The communications by and with the consultants are also supposed to be through the architect. Although this does not always happen in practice, the architect should be the central control point in this type of agreement.

Finally, the architect only reviews shop drawings for conformance with information given and the design concept expressed in the contract documents. The contractor is responsible for determining the accuracy and completeness of dimensions, details, quantities, and other aspects of the shop drawings.

One article of B141 lists services that are not part of the agreement unless specifically added. These include such things as programming, extensive site representation, or making revisions due to owner changes or changes in codes or regulations. The list is quite extensive and you should read through it prior to the exam. The purpose is to clearly communicate to the client what is not considered basic services, because there are often misunderstandings in this area.

B. The Owner's Responsibilities

Under the basic B141 agreement the owner must provide the architect with various information, such as the program, the desired schedule, a budget, the site survey, and soil tests when requested by the architect. The owner must also furnish the services of other consultants when they are reasonably required by the scope of the project and requested by the architect. may include structural, mechanical, and electrical engineers, among others. The architect is entitled to rely on the accuracy and completeness of the various reports provided by the owner. You should also read through the entire list of items that the owner is responsible for providing under normal circumstances.

C. Construction Cost

Construction cost is defined as the total cost or estimated cost to the owner of all components of the project, including items designed or specified by the architect, labor and materials furnished by the owner, and a reasonable allowance for the contractor's overhead and profit. Construction cost does not include professional fees, land cost, financing costs, or other costs, such as land surveys, that are the responsibility of the owner.

The architect does not warrant that bids or negotiated costs will not vary from the owner's budget or from any estimate prepared by the architect. The architect's estimated cost represents his or her best judgment as a design professional.

Language in the agreement specifically states that no fixed limit of construction cost shall be established as a condition of the agreement unless agreed to in writing by both parties. Only if the two parties thus agree to a fixed limit, and the lowest bid or negotiated price exceeds that limit, is the architect obligated to modify the drawings and specifications at no additional charge in order to reduce the construction cost.

D. Additional Services

As previously mentioned, B141 covers architectural services according to the standard five phases of a project. There is a long list of services not included unless written into the agreement. They are divided into three parts: project representation beyond basic services, contingent additional services, and optional additional services.

Contingent additional services are those that arise because of something else happening. For example, if drawings and specifications have to be prepared in connection with a change order, this is an additional service and the architect is due extra compensation. Optional additional services are those that the client might like the architect to provide but which are also beyond basic services and require extra payment by the owner. Examples of these services include such things as programming, providing financial feasibility studies, providing tenant planning, and providing services to verify the accuracy of drawings and other information provided by the owner.

If additional services are included in the agreement, they are written into the agreement along with the basis for compensation. If the list becomes extensive, you should consider using agreement B161 for designated services.

E. Other Provisions

There are many other important provisions in the owner-architect agreement. These include the following:

- *Arbitration:* claims and disputes are subject to arbitration according to the rules of the American Arbitration Association unless both parties mutually agree otherwise.

- *Architect's documents:* the drawings, specifications, and other documents prepared by the architect are instruments of service and belong to the architect, who retains copyright on them. Copyright is best protected if the work is recorded with the copyright office in Washington, D.C.. The owner is allowed to keep and use originals and copies in connection with the project, but cannot use them for other projects.

- *Termination:* either party can terminate the agreement on no less than seven days' written notice if the other party fails substantially to perform according to the terms of the agreement. The architect is also allowed to suspend performance of services on seven days' written notice to the owner if the owner fails to make fee payments when due.

- *Third party claims:* one provision states that nothing in the agreement shall create a contractual relationship with a third party against either the architect or owner. This is to reinforce the idea of privity, which states that one party to a contract is protected from claims from other parties with whom there is no direct contractual relationship. Ideally then, the architect is protected from claims by the contractor because the architect only has a contract with the owner. In practice, however, the design professional is often involved in third-party claims.

- *Hazardous materials:* the architect has no responsibility for the discovery, handling, removal, or disposal of, or exposure of persons to, hazardous materials such as asbestos, PCBs, or other toxic substances.

F. Compensation Methods

There are several methods of compensation that the owner and architect can negotiate. The following are the common types.

- *Stipulated sum:* this method states a fixed sum of money that the owner will pay to the architect for a specific set of services. The money is usually paid out monthly according to the proportion of the five basic phases of services previously described. With a stipulated sum, the architect must accurately estimate the cost for the office to do the job, as well as make a profit. Reimbursable expenses are in addition to fees for the basic services, and include such things as postage, reproduction, transportation, long-distance communication, computer-aided design and drafting equipment time, renderings, and models.

- *Cost plus fee:* with this approach the professional is compensated for the actual expense to do the job plus a reasonable fee for profit. The actual expenses include salaries, employee benefits, direct expenses, and office overhead. Several variations of the cost plus fee approach are used.

  With the *multiple of direct personnel expense,* the direct salary of employees is determined and multiplied by a factor to account for normal and required personnel expenses such as taxes, sick leave, health care, and so on. This is then increased by a multiplier that includes provisions for overhead and profit. For example, if a particular person's direct personnel expense is calculated at $30.00 per hour and the multiplier is 2.5, then the cost to the client for that person is $75.00 per hour.

  Multiple of direct salary expense is similar, except the multiplier is larger to provide for employee benefits.

  Hourly billing rates simply build in the multiplier to the hourly rate so the client only sees one number for each of the types of people working on the project.

- *Percentage of construction cost:* this method is not used as much as it once was. With it, the professional fee is tied to the cost of construction as a fixed percentage. However, from the client's standpoint, the architect may be encouraged to increase the cost of construction to increase the fee or, conversely, may lessen any incentive to reduce construction cost. From the architect's standpoint, the percentage method may not be good because an economical or low-cost project may require just as much or more work as an expensive project.

- *Unit cost method:* fees are based on a definable unit, such as on square footage for such work as tenant planning in a leased building or on a per-house basis in a large residential project.

The method of compensation to select depends on several factors. It should fairly compensate the architect for the actual work required and the value of that professional service. It should also provide for the rising cost of providing services, especially important when the project will be of long duration. Finally, the client should be comfortable with the method and understand where the money is being spent.

G. Designated Services Agreements

When the architect is to provide a more extensive range of services than is normal under the five-phase B141 agreement, AIA Document B161 can be used. This is the Standard Form of Agreement Between Owner and Architect for Designated Services. In this arrangement, services are divided into nine categories:

- predesign

- site analysis

- schematic design

- design development

- construction documents

- bidding or negotiation

- construction contract administration

- postconstruction

- supplemental services

Another form, B162, Scope of Designated Services, lists in great detail many of the possible tasks that might be included under each category. It is used by the owner and architect to check off exactly what services will be performed, whether the owner or architect will be responsible, and what method of compensation will be used. Forms B161 and B162 must be used together.

3   OWNER-CONTRACTOR AGREEMENTS

Although the owner enters into an agreement directly with the contractor for construction of the project, the architect must be familiar with the various types of agreements. The variations of agreements are usually based on the method of compensation for the contractor. These will be discussed in a later section. One common document used is AIA Document A101, Standard Form of Agreement Between Owner and Contractor, where the basis of payment is a stipulated sum. Many of the provisions of this agreement are used in other agreement types and in non-AIA agreements between owner and contractor.

A. Identification of Contract Documents

The first article specifies that the contract documents include the agreement, the general and supplementary conditions of the contract, the drawings, specifications, addenda, modifications, and other documents listed in the agreement. It makes reference to a later article in which all the documents are listed in detail. The purpose of this article is to include all the other documents by reference.

B. Basic Provisions

Some basic provisions are common to all contracts. These include a description of the work, the time of commencement and substantial completion, and the contract sum.

The work normally includes what is described in the contract documents, primarily the drawings and specifications. Any exclusions can be spelled out in the owner-contractor agreement as well as in the contract documents when they are identified as being the responsibility of others.

The *date of commencement* is an important time because it is from this date that construction completion time is measured. The date can be a specific calendar day or can be when the contractor is give a notice-to-proceed letter by the owner.

The time of substantial completion is expressed with a specific calendar date or by a number of calendar days from the date of commencement. *Substantial completion* is defined as the stage in the progress of the work when the work or designated portion thereof is sufficiently complete in accordance with the contract documents so the owner can occupy or utilize the work for its intended use.

Completion time may be extended as provided for in the general conditions when circumstances are beyond the control of the contractor. If a particular completion date is important to the owner, provisions for liquidated damages may be included. *Liquidated damages* are monies paid by the contractor to the owner for every day the project is late. They represent actual anticipated losses the owner will incur if the project is not completed on time. For example, if an owner cannot move and must pay double rent, the liquidated damages may be the amount of extra rent.

In many cases, a liquidated damage provision is accompanied by a bonus provision so the contractor receives a payment for early completion. This too is usually based on a realistic cost savings the owner will realize for early completion. If a penalty clause is included (which is something different from liquidated damages) a bonus provision *must* also be included.

The *contract sum*, of course, states the compensation the contractor will receive for the work. The various methods are discussed in a later section.

C. Progress Payments

Based on applications for payment submitted by the contractor, the owner makes periodic payments, usually monthly, to the contractor on account of the contract sum. The owner-contractor agreement defines how these payments are to be made.

In the AIA A101 agreement, the amount due in any time period is based on the percentage of completed work and any materials purchased and in approved storage. The percentage is based on a schedule of values that the contractor submits to the architect, which allocates the total contract sum to various portions of the work such as mechanical, electrical, foundations, and so forth. A certain percentage of each payment, usually 10 percent, called the retainage, is withheld until final completion of the work.

In order to receive payment, the contractor must submit an application for payment to the architect listing the completed work and stored materials according to the schedule of values. The architect then reviews the application, verifies that it is correct and recommends payment to the owner, who then makes payment. If there is work in dispute, the architect may choose not to certify payment of all or a portion of the amount until the problem is resolved.

D. Enumeration of Contract Documents

In this article, all of the documents are listed individually. Reference is made to the agreement itself, AIA Document A201, General Conditions of the Contract, any supplementary general conditions, each specification section, all the drawings, the addenda, if any, and any other documents made part of the contract.

E. Compensation Methods

There are several ways the contractor can be paid for the work. One of the most common is the *stipulated sum*, which is a fixed price the owner agrees to pay the contractor for the work as shown in the contract documents. This is a simple way to arrange things and owners like it because the cost is known when the bids are made or negotiation is completed. Competitive bidding always uses a stipulated-sum method.

Cost-plus-fee methods compensate the contractor for actual expenses of labor, materials, and subcontracts in addition to a fixed fee for overhead and profit. Cost-plus-fee contracts have more flexibility than fixed fees and allow construction to proceed before design is complete. Their disadvantage is that the cost is not known, a problem that can be mitigated with such things as guaranteed maximums, target prices with incentives, and partial cost guarantees. Target prices establish a likely project cost, and the contractor may share in a percentage of savings below the target price or be responsible for a percentage over the price. Partial cost guarantees involve obtaining fixed prices from certain subcontractors or material suppliers.

Construction can sometimes be based on unit prices. Entire projects are seldom based this way, but portions of a project may be. For example, in cases where it is not possible to firmly establish quantities at the time of bid, a unit price can be set. This happens quite frequently with excavation where a cost per cubic yard of material is stated. The final quantity is then multiplied by this unit price to arrive at the total cost. In other cases where changes or additions are anticipated, the contractor can be requested to include unit prices in the bid. These can then be used to evaluate the possible cost consequences of making a change and as a check against the final cost of a change order.

4 GENERAL CONDITIONS OF THE CONTRACT

The General Conditions of the Contract, AIA Form A201, 1987 edition, is one of the most important parts in the entire set of contract documents. It is incorporated by specific reference into the owner-architect agreement as well as the owner-contractor agreement. You should obtain a copy of the General Conditions and read the entire document prior to the test. Many of the most important provisions will be outlined in this section. Other portions that pertain to bidding and contract administration are discussed in the following two chapters.

A. The Owner

Article 2 outlines the duties, responsibilities, and rights of the owner. Among these is the responsibility of the owner to furnish evidence, at the request of the contractor, that financial arrangements have been made to fulfill the owner's obligations under the contract; in other words, to pay the contractor.

The owner must also furnish, free of charge, the necessary copies of the drawings and project manual required for the completion of the work.

If the contractor fails to correct work not in conformance with the contract documents or persistently fails to carry out such work, the owner may order the contractor to stop the work until the cause for the order is eliminated.

The owner also has the right to carry out the work if the contractor fails in his or her duties to correctly do so. The contractor has seven days from receiving written notice from the owner to commence corrections.

B. The Contractor

The *contractor* is solely responsible for the means, methods, and techniques of construction and for coordinating the work under the contract. This includes making sure that work already performed is in a proper condition to receive subsequent work. It also includes taking field measurements, controlling his or her work force, coordinating the subcontractors, and being responsible to the owner for acts and omissions of all people performing work under the contract.

The contractor is not liable to the owner or architect for damage resulting from errors or omissions in the contract documents unless the contractor recognized such error and knowingly failed to report it to the architect. It is also not the contractor's responsibility to ascertain that the contract documents are in accordance with building codes, ordinances, and other regulations. However, if the contractor notices some variance, he or she must notify the architect and owner in writing. If the contractor does not give this notice and proceeds to perform work knowingly in variance with some regulation, the contractor assumes full responsibility for such work.

The contractor is also obligated to provide a schedule for the owner's and architect's information, to keep it up to date, and to conform to it.

Under a section on indemnification, it is stated that, to the extent provided by law, the contractor shall indemnify and hold harmless the owner, architect, architect's consultants, and agents against claims, damages, and expenses arising out of performance of the work. However, this clause does not relieve the architect of his or her liability for errors with the drawings, specifications, or administration of the contract.

To *indemnify* is to secure against loss or damage. This clause is intended to protect the owner and architect against situations where a person is injured due to the negligence of the contractor or the contractor's agents. It also is intended to protect the owner and architect against claims from property damage other than to the work itself.

C. Administration of the Contract

Article 4 of the General Conditions states the architect's roles and responsibilities in contract administration. These are discussed in more detail in Chapter 28, but in general this article provides for the typical duties the architect performs as follows.

The architect visits the site regularly to become familiar with the progress of the work and to determine, in general, if it is proceeding in accordance with the contract documents.

It is reiterated in one paragraph that the architect does not have control over construction means, methods, techniques, or procedures, or safety precautions.

The architect has the authority to reject work that does not conform to the contract documents. However, this authority does not give rise to any duty or responsibility to the contractor, subcontractors, or others. In addition, the architect does not have the right to stop the work if something is wrong or the architect observes some safety problem. Instead, the architect should notify both the contractor and the owner.

The architect reviews shop drawings and other submittals but only for the limited purpose of checking for conformance with the design intent expressed in the contract documents.

The architect prepares change orders and may authorize minor changes in the work that do not involve adjusting either the contract sum or contract time and that are not inconsistent with the intent of the contract documents.

The architect interprets and decides on matters concerning the performance of the contract if the owner or contractor requests such interpretation.

The architect's decisions concerning matters related to aesthetic effect are final if consistent with the intent shown on the contract documents.

The procedures for dealing with claims and disputes, as well as requirements for arbitration, are covered in the article on administration of the contract. Both of these are discussed in Chapter 28.

D. Construction by Owner or by Separate Contractors

The owner has the right to perform construction on the project with the owner's own forces and to award separate contracts for certain work. However, exercising this right does require the owner to provide for coordination of his or her own forces and to act with the same obligations and rights as any contractor would have.

E. Changes in the Work

The General Conditions of the Contract allow for changes to be made in the work after execution of the contract. These changes are made by written change order, construction change directive, or minor change in the work.

A change order is based on written agreement among the owner, contractor, and architect concerning the extent of the change and how it affects construction cost and construction time. A construction change directive only requires agreement between the owner and architect and may or may not be agreed to by the contractor. A minor change can be made by the architect alone.

The ability to issue a construction change directive is a new procedure with the 1987 edition of A201. It directs the contractor to proceed with the required changes in the work even if the contractor does not agree with the basis for adjustment in contract sum or contract time. When final determination of cost and time changes are made through submittals by the contractor and review by the architect and owner, then a change order is issued.

The exact procedures the architect must follow for making changes is described in Chapter 28.

F. Time

The *contract time* is the period from the starting date established in the agreement to the time of substantial completion, including any authorized adjustments. The contractor is expected to proceed expeditiously with adequate work forces and complete the work within the allotted time.

G. Payments and Completion

As mentioned previously, the contractor makes monthly applications for payment based on the percentage of work complete in accordance with a schedule of values allocated to various portions of the work. The architect reviews these applications and issues to the owner a certificate for payment or decides to withhold issuance if there are valid reasons. The exact procedures the architect must follow are described in Chapter 28.

H. Liens

A *mechanics lien* is a claim by one party against the property of another party for the satisfaction of a debt and is a common method for a contractor or material supplier to gain payment. If a property has a mechanics lien on it, it cannot be sold or transferred until the lien is disposed of, except through foreclosure. If a contractor does not pay a subcontractor or material supplier and they file a mechanics lien against the property, the owner becomes responsible for payment. If the lien is not paid, the property can be foreclosed on by the lender or a taxing entity.

Since the owner has no responsibility for paying subcontractors or material suppliers, the General Conditions of the Contract provide ways to protect the owner from liens. This is done by requiring the contractor to submit a release or waiver of liens to the owner before final payment is made or retainages of previous payments are released. The contractor must also furnish to the owner and architect an affidavit of release of liens (a standard AIA form) stating that all obligations have been satisfied. The release or waiver of liens is attached to this affidavit.

The exact laws governing liens and the time period during which a lien may be filed vary from state to state, so the architect and owner must be familiar with local regulations.

I. Protection of Persons and Property

The contractor is exclusively responsible for on-site safety and precautions against damage to persons and property. This includes the contractor's employees, other people affected by the work, the work itself, and adjacent property. Provisions concerning the discovery of asbestos or PCBs are included in the General Conditions. In this case the contractor must stop work and report the condition to the owner and architect in writing, and work cannot start until the danger has been removed.

If any damage to the work is sustained due to inadequate protection, the contractor must repair or correct it. However, this does not include damages caused by acts of the owner or architect.

J. Insurance and Bonds

During the duration of the project both the owner and contractor must maintain insurance to protect against various types of losses. The provisions for insurance are spelled out in Article 11 of the General Conditions of the Contract. Additional provisions as required by the unique nature of each project are included in the Supplementary General Conditions.

Although insurance is required, the architect is not responsible for giving advice to either the owner or the contractor on matters related to insurance and bonds. In fact, architects' professional liability insurance policies exclude such advice from coverage. Both the owner and contractor should receive advice from their respective legal counsels and insurance advisers as required.

The contractor must provide liability insurance to provide coverage for the entities for whom the contractor is legally liable. This includes such coverage as worker's compensation, bodily injury or death of the contractor's employees and others, damages to the work, personal injury, motor vehicle insurance, and claims involving contractual liability. The contractor should require that all subcontractors carry similar insurance.

The amount of coverage should not be less than the limits of liability specified in the contract or required by law, whichever is greater. It must be maintained without interruption from the beginning of the work until the date of final payment.

At the beginning of the project, the architect should write a letter to the owner reminding him or her of the owner's responsibilities under the terms of the agreement and requesting that the owner determine, with the owner's legal and insurance advisers, the amount and type of coverage required. This information, including the owner's requirements on bonds, should be given to the architect for use in assisting the owner with preparing the contract documents.

The architect should also have certificates of insurance from the contractor on file and not issue any certificate of payment until such evidence is available or until he or she has been advised by the owner that such insurance has been obtained.

The owner must also purchase and maintain liability insurance needed to protect the owner against claims and losses arising from operations under the contract. This includes insurance for property damage and loss of use.

The owner's property insurance protects against fire, theft, vandalism, and other hazards. It must be an all-risk policy that insures against all perils that are not otherwise specifically excluded. The amount of coverage must be for the full value of the work, which is usually the contract sum plus any subsequent modifications.

This article of the General Conditions also gives the owner the right to require the contractor to furnish bonds covering faithful performance of the contract. A bond, often fully labeled a surety bond, is an agreement by which one party, called the surety (the bonding company), agrees to be responsible to another party, called the obligee (the owner), for the default or debts of a third party, called the principal (the contractor). Bonds are simply a protection for the owner against default by the contractor. Bonds are discussed in more detail in Chapter 27.

K. Uncovering and Correction of Work

If the contract documents state that certain portions of the work are to be observed by the architect prior to being covered or enclosed and the contractor proceeds with covering them, then the contractor must uncover them at no additional charge on request by the architect. If there is no specific mention of an item to be observed prior to covering and if the work is in accordance with the contract documents, the architect may ask that it be uncovered, but the cost is borne by the owner through a change order.

The contractor must correct work rejected by the architect for failing to conform to the requirements of the contract documents. The contractor must bear the cost of such corrections, including testing, inspections, and compensation for the architect's services connected with the corrections.

If the owner so chooses, he or she can accept nonconforming work. Since this entails a change in the contract, it must be done by written change order and, if appropriate, the contract sum may be reduced.

L. Termination or Suspension of the Contract

Either the owner or contractor may terminate the contract for valid reasons enumerated in Article 14 of the General Conditions of the Contract.

The contractor may terminate the contract if work has stopped for more than 30 days through no fault of the contractor, for any of the following causes: a court order, an act of government, failure by the architect to issue a certificate of payment without giving a reason, repeated suspensions by the owner, and failure of the owner to provide proper evidence that financial arrangements have been made to fulfill the owner's obligations. Seven days' written notice is required.

If the architect certifies that sufficient cause exists, the owner can give seven days' written notice and terminate the contract if the contractor fails to supply enough properly skilled workers or proper materials, fails to make payment to subcontractors, disregards laws and ordinances, or is guilty of substantial breach of a provision of the contract documents.

5   SUPPLEMENTARY CONDITIONS OF THE CONTRACT

Because of the unique nature of construction projects, not every condition can be covered in a standard document such as the General Conditions of the Contract. Each job must be customized to accommodate different clients, governmental regulations, and local laws. Information that is unique to each project can be included in one of four areas: in the bidding requirements if it relates to bidding, in the Owner-Contractor Agreement, in the Supplementary Conditions if it modifies the General Conditions, and in Division 1 (General Requirements) of the specifications.

For example, limits of insurance and other bonding and insurance requirements are very specific to each client and project type. These are often placed in the Supplementary General Conditions.

SAMPLE QUESTIONS

1. Which of the following may the owner not do?

   A. Stop work if the contractor's performance is not satisfactory or in variance with the contract documents.

   B. Carry on the work and deduct costs normally due to the contractor for these corrections.

   C. Stop the work if the architect reports safety problems on the site.

   D. Refuse, with good cause, to give the contractor proof that the owner can meet the financial obligations of the project.

The answers to questions 2 through 4 can be found on the following key list. Select only one answer for each question.

   A0 agency
   A1 arbitration
   A2 architect's services
   A3 contract sum
   A4 contingent additional services
   A5 designated services
   A6 duties to the contractor
   A7 fixed limit
   A8 liquidated damages
   A9 optional additional services

   B0 privity
   B1 project representation beyond basic services
   B2 substantial completion
   B3 third-party relationship
   B4 retainage
   B5 schedule of values
   B6 surety bond

2. If, during bidding, your client asked you to provide a full-time staff member on the job site during construction, you would be entitled to extra compensation under what provision of AIA Form B141?

3. The standard owner-architect agreement separates the architect from the contractor with what?

4. What is used to encourage the contractor to finish the job or to satisfy mechanics lien claims by subcontractors?

5. What fee method would you prefer if your client was doing their first architectural project and did not yet have a program?

   A. fixed sum

   B. multiple of direct personnel expense

   C. percentage of construction cost

   D. unit cost based on square footage

6. A project is about 60 percent complete when the owner begins receiving field reports from the architect stating that the contractor is failing to properly supervise the job, resulting in incorrect work. After several weeks of this the owner becomes worried and asks the architect what to do. What should be done if the work is being performed under the conditions of AIA Document A201?

   A. After receiving the architect's field reports, the owner should stop the work and arrange for a meeting between the owner, architect, and contractor to determine the cause of the problems and what the contractor intends to do. If the contractor does not correct the work, the owner should carry out the work with other contractors and deduct the cost by change order from the original contractor's construction cost.

   B. The architect should recommend that the owner give the contractor written notice of nonconformance with the contract documents and if, after seven days the contractor has not begun corrective measures, terminate the contract.

   C. The architect and owner should discuss the problem to see if the owner would be willing to accept it in exchange for a reduction in the contract sum. If not, the owner should give seven days' written notice to terminate the contract and find another contractor to finish the job.

   D. The architect should, with the owner's knowledge, reject non-conforming work and notify the contractor that it must be corrected promptly. The architect should then remind the owner that the owner can have the work corrected after giving the contractor two seven-day written notices to correct the work.

7. Which of the following describes agency?

   A. The architect acts on behalf of the owner, making decisions and expediting the work and taking on responsibilities the owner would normally have.

B. The architect mediates between the owner and the contractor and vendors for the benefit of the owner.

C. The architect is the principal of the relationship who balances the needs of the contractor and the owner.

D. The architect works for the owner in certain designated areas with the authority to act on the owner's behalf.

8. You have a client who owns a large manufacturing plant and needs to expand to new facilities without interruption in production. The owner has already arranged for a flexible line of credit to finance construction but wants to minimize project costs. If the new facility will be very similar to the previous one, only sized for greater production capacity, which type of construction would you recommend?

     A. design-build

     B. fast-track

     C. multiple prime contract

     D. design-award-build

9. Which of the following are part of the contract documents?

     I.   an addendum

     II.   a change order

     III.   special supplementary conditions

     IV.   the contractor's bid

     V.   a written amendment signed by owner and contractor

     A. I, III, and V

     B. I, II, III, and V

     C. II, III, IV, and V

     D. all of the above

10. Which one of the following is not an accurate statement?

     A. The architect is responsible for a defect in the work if she or he sees it but fails to report it to the contractor.

     B. The owner has the sole right to make changes in the work but must do it through the architect.

     C. The architect does not have to verify soil test reports given by the owner.

     D. By the time construction documents are almost completed, the architect still does not have to give a reasonably accurate construction price.

27 BIDDING PROCEDURES AND DOCUMENTS

Bidding is one of the primary ways contracts are awarded. After the architect has completed the contract documents, various acceptable or invited contractors review them and submit a price for doing the work. The contractor with the lowest bid is usually awarded the contract. Bidding is in contrast with *negotiation*, in which one contractor is selected and the final contract price worked out between the owner and contractor. In both cases, the architect assists the owner in preparing bidding documents and evaluating bids, or in the negotiation process.

Competitive bidding is popular with many owners because it usually results in the lowest construction cost. For most public agencies, bidding is mandatory. However, it must be done within clearly defined guidelines to protect the owner from disreputable contractors and unethical bidding practices.

1 BIDDING PROCEDURES

Through many years of practice the bidding procedure has generally been standardized and codified in various industry association documents. Everyone involved with the process knows the rules and what is expected of them. This chapter reviews the common procedures and documents used during this phase of the project delivery process.

A. Prequalification of Bidders

Bidding may be open to any contractor or restricted to a list of contractors who have been prequalified by the owner. The purpose of prequalification of bidders is to select only those contractors who meet certain standards of reliability, experience, financial stability, and performance. An owner contemplating the construction of a multimillion-dollar laboratory building would not be comfortable reviewing the bid of a small home contractor. Once these standards have been met, the owner is better able to review their bids based primarily on price, personnel, and completion time.

Prequalification is usually based on information submitted by contractors concerning their financial qualifications, personnel, experience, references, size, bonding capability, and any special qualities that make them particularly suited for the project under consideration. For public work, when prequalification is allowed, it is usually based on financial assets and the size of the firm.

B. Advertising for Bids

There are two ways to notify prospective bidders. The first is by advertising in newspapers and trade journals. This type of announcement simply states the project name and location and the fact that bids are being accepted. The advertisement further gives a brief description of the project, the time and place for receiving bids, where bid documents can be obtained, the conditions for bidding, and other pertinent information. Advertising for bids is usually required for public work although much private work is also advertised if it is open bidding.

For prequalified bidders, an invitation to bid is sent to the prospective bidders. The invitation contains the same information listed above for bid advertisements. Even with a prequalified list, there should be a sufficient number of bidders to encourage price competition.

C. Availability of Bid Documents

Bid documents are generally made available through the architect's office. Each bidder receives the required documents including prints of the drawings, specifications, bidding documents, bid forms, and other items as required. It is general practice to require that each bidder put down a deposit on each set of documents taken up to a certain number. The deposit may be returned when the documents are returned in usable condition after bidding. In some cases the documents are loaned with no deposit required. Extra sets of documents over a certain number can be purchased by the contractor. In most large cities, documents are also put on file in a central plan room where subcontractors and material suppliers can review them.

D. Substitutions

During bidding, many contractors request that substitution for some of the materials specified be considered. This most often happens when there are proprietary specifications or a very limited list of acceptable manufacturers. The conditions under which substitutions will be considered and the procedures for reviewing submissions are clearly defined in the instruction to bidders.

Generally, the bidder is required to submit a request for approval at least ten days prior to the bid opening date. The request must include the name of the material or equipment for which the substitution is submitted along with complete back-up information about the proposed substitution. The burden of proof of the merit of the substitution rests with the bidder. The architect then reviews the submission and may either reject it or approve it. If approved, the architect issues an addendum stating this fact and sends it to all the bidders.

E. Addenda

An *addendum* is a written or graphic document issued by the architect prior to the execution of the contract that modifies or interprets the bidding documents by additions, deletions, clarifications, or corrections. During the bidding process, there are always questions that need answers, errors that are discovered, and changes that the owner or architect decides to make. Addenda are instruments to do this. They are usually issued prior to bidding.

When an addendum is issued, it is sent to all registered bidders not later than four or five days before receipt of bids to give all the bidders ample opportunity to study the document and modify their proposals accordingly.

F. Prebid Conference

On some projects, it is advantageous to hold a prebid conference. This is a meeting with the architect, owner, and bidders during which the bidders can ask questions and the architect and owner can emphasize particularly important conditions of the project. On very large projects, there may be a separate conference for mechanical subcontract bidders, electrical bidders, and so on. During these conferences, the architect should have someone take complete notes concerning the items discussed. A copy of the notes should be sent to all bidders, whether or not they were in attendance.

G. Bid Opening

In the instructions to bidders, the date, time, and place of the bid opening is included. Unless modified by addenda, the bid opening time should be strictly adhered to as well as the method of submitting the bids. Bids received after the opening time should not be accepted, unless none of the bids have been opened and there are no objections from those bidders present.

Most bid openings are conducted by the architect with the owner and bidders present. The bids are read aloud and the presence or absence of any required supporting documentation is noted. The architect usually prepares a bid log to note the base bid amount, amounts of alternates (if any), whether receipt of addenda was acknowledged, and other pertinent information. This should be made available to the bidders in either open or private bidding.

There should be no announcement of the apparent low bid at the bid opening; the architect should thank everyone for submitting and state that the submissions will be evaluated and a decision of award made within a certain time, usually ten days. The decision should be sent to all the bidders.

If, after the bids have been opened, a bidder discovers that a clerical or mathematical error has been made and can support the claim, the bidder is usually allowed to withdraw the bid. If it was the low bid, the next lowest bidder is accepted.

H. Evaluation and Awarding of Bid

The architect assists the owner in evaluating the bids. This includes not only looking for the lowest proposed contract sum but also reviewing prices for alternates, substitutions, lists of proposed subcontractors, qualification statements, and other documentation required by the instruction to bidders.

The owner has the right to reject any or all bids, to reject bids not accompanied by the required bid bond or other documentation, and to reject a bid that is in any way incomplete or irregular.

If all of the bids exceed the project budget and the owner-architect agreement fixes a limit on construction, the owner has one of four courses of action:

1. to rebid (or renegotiate if a negotiated contract)

2. to authorize an increase in the construction cost and proceed with the project

3. to work with the architect in revising the scope of the project to reduce construction cost

4. to abandon the project

Rebidding seldom results in any significant reduction in cost unless the bidding marketplace is changing rapidly. If the project is revised, the extra cost of having the architect modify the documents may be borne by the owner. As discussed in a later section, alternates are often used as a flexible method of deleting or substituting alternative materials or construction elements to help reduce costs. Since the alternates are priced along with the base bid, the owner and architect can quickly evaluate the ramifications of selecting certain alternates.

2 BIDDING DOCUMENTS

Bidding documents are usually prepared by the architect using standard AIA forms or forms provided by the owner. Many commercial clients who engage in a great deal of building have developed their own forms and procedures, but they are typically similar in content to the AIA forms. The bidding documents are bound into the project manual, but they are not part of the contract documents.

The bidding documents usually include:

- the advertisement or invitation to bid

- instructions to bidders

- bid forms

- bid security information

- performance bond, if required

- labor and material payment bond, if required

Other documents that are sometimes added include: qualification forms, subcontractor list form, certificates of insurance, certificates of compliance with applicable laws and regulations, and information available to bidders such as geotechnical data.

In addition to the bidding documents that are not part of the contract documents, the bidding package also includes the drawings, specifications, general and supplementary conditions of the contract, addenda issued prior to the receipt of bids, and the form of agreement between owner and contractor.

A. Advertisement to Bid

As mentioned in the previous section, public bidding requires that bidding for the proposed building project be advertised in one or more newspapers and trade publications. If a list of prequalified bidders is being used, an invitation to bid is sent to those contractors. The advertisement or invitation to bid is also printed and bound into the project manual with the other bidding documents.

B. Instructions to Bidders

The instructions to bidders outline the procedures and requirements that the bidders must follow in submitting bids, how the bids will be considered, and submittals required of the successful bidder. AIA standard document A701, Instructions to Bidders, is often used. Other organizations also produce similar forms. Instructions to bidders normally include the following items. (If the AIA form is being used and additional requirements must be included, it is suggested that supplementary instructions to the bidders be written.)

- *Bidders representation:* in making a bid, the bidder represents that he or she has read and understood the documents, reviewed the plans and specifications, and visited the site to become familiar with the conditions under which the work will take place.

- *Bidding documents:* the form states where the documents may be obtained, provisions for bid security, and what the contractor and subcontractors should do if they discover an error or inconsistency. In such a case, they should make a written request to the architect for clarification at least seven days prior to bid opening. The architect will then issue an addendum to all bidders answering the questions.

- *Substitutions:* the procedures required for submitting substitution proposals and having them considered are outlined. No substitutions should be considered after the contract award.

- *Bidding procedures:* this portion specifies how the bid form is to be filled in, what kind of bid security is to accompany the bid, how the bid should be physically submitted, and provisions for modification and withdrawal of bids. Bids are normally submitted in sealed envelopes with the name of the party receiving the bid on the outside, along with the project name and the name of the entity submitting it.

- *Consideration of bids:* the procedure for opening bids and reviewing them is included, including under what conditions bids may be rejected, how they will be evaluated, and conditions for award of the contract.

- *Bonds:* the required bonds and the time during which they must be delivered are outlined. The cost of bonds is included in the bidder's price.

C. Bid Forms

There should be a standard form on which all the bidders enter the required information, to ensure that all bids will be in identical form, making it easier to compare and evaluate them. The bid form should contain space for the amount of the base bid written in both numbers and words, the price for the alternates (if any), unit prices (if any), and the number of calendar or work days in which the bidder proposes to complete the work. Space should be provided for the bidder to acknowledge receipt of any addenda. The bid form must be signed by someone legally empowered to bind the contractor to the owner in a contract.

D. Bid Security

Bid security is required to ensure that the successful bidder will enter into a contract with the owner. The form of the bid security may be a certified check, cashier's check, or bid bond. If the successful bidder does not enter into an agreement, the bid security may be retained and compensates for the difference between the low bid and the next lowest bidder. The amount of the bid security is either set as a fixed price or as a percentage of the bid; it is usually about 5 percent of the estimated cost of construction or the bid price.

E. Performance Bonds

A *performance bond* is a statement by a surety company that obligates the surety company to complete construction on the project should the contractor default on its obligations. If this happens, the surety company may complete construction by hiring another contractor or it may simply supply additional money to the defaulting contractor to allow construction to proceed.

Performance bonds are usually mandatory on public work and advisable on private work. The cost of the performance bond is paid by the owner and is usually written in the amount of the construction price. The architect or owner must verify that the bond is written by a surety acceptable to issue bonds in the particular state where the construction is to take place. Some states will not accept so-called "surplus lines" carriers who are not based in their state. Therefore, the bond may be no good.

F. Labor and Material Payment Bonds

Although a performance bond ensures the completion of the contract, it does not guarantee payment for labor and materials by the defaulting contractor. The result could be liens against the property or litigation by subcontractors and material suppliers. Because of this, a labor and material payment bond is usually required along with a performance bond to protect the owner against these possibilities.

3   COST CONTROL

Throughout the design process and up to completion of contract documents the construction cost is only an estimate by the architect. It is only with bidding or final negotiation that the owner finally receives a firm price on the project. If the architect has been doing a reasonable job of tracking design changes and has a good idea of component costs, the bid price should be fairly close to the estimated amount.

Although the architect does not (and cannot) guarantee that the final construction cost will not vary from the estimate, there are several variables with which you should be familiar that can affect the final bid price.

A. Bidding in the Marketplace

By its very definition, bidding is a competitive activity. The price a contractor is willing to submit to an owner is, of course, dependent on the actual cost of subcontractor bids, the cost of the contractor's own labor and materials, the cost of equipment rental, the contractor's indirect costs, overhead, and profit.

Bidding is also affected by the construction marketplace, which is itself competitive. For example, if the local economy is depressed, contractors, subcontractors, and material suppliers may be willing to lower prices or reduce profit margins in order to get work and simply stay in business. In good times when work is plentiful, contractors are more selective about what jobs to bid on and what profit allowance to put in their bids. They are not as concerned about reducing prices to get jobs.

Both the architect and owner should be sensitive to these types of market conditions. If there is some flexibility in the owner's schedule, it can be advantageous to either delay or accelerate design and bidding to match favorable market conditions.

B. Effects of Documents on Bids

One of the variables over which the architect and owner have control is the set of contract documents. These can affect the amount of bids by what they contain and how they are put together, beyond just the amount and quality of construction they represent.

Poorly prepared drawings and specifications can raise questions in the mind of the contractor about what is specifically required, what may simply be implied, and what is omitted. To cover possible unforeseen items, the contractor may add extra money in the bid to cover these unknowns. On the other hand, a complete and clearly coordinated set of documents gives the contractor confidence in the scope and quality of the work. The contractor can then bid with more confidence only those items shown.

C. Alternates

An *alternate* is a request included in the bidding documents asking the contractor to supply a price for some type of variation from the base bid. This may be a change in materials or level of quality of a material, a deletion of some component, or the addition of some construction element. For example, the base bid may include carpet as a floor covering while an alternate may be to substitute wood flooring for the carpet.

Alternates allow the owner some flexibility in modifying the cost of the project when the bids are in by varying the quantity or quality of the project. They also allow the owner to select certain options based on firm prices rather than preliminary estimates.

Alternates are called *add-alternates* if they add to the base bid or *deduct-alternates* if they reduce the base bid amount. Since alternates require more time for both the architect and bidders to prepare, they should be used carefully and should not be a substitute for conscientious cost estimating and reasonable design for the base bid amount.

For evaluating the bids, the selected alternates should be used to arrive at the lowest overall bid, but alternates should not be manipulated to favor one bidder over another.

D. Unit Prices

Unit prices are set costs for certain portions of work based on individual quantities. When required, they are listed on the bid form and provide a basis for determining changes to the contract. For example, a square foot cost for asphalt paving may be requested if the full extent of paving is unknown when bids are received. Even though the total cost may not be known, the unit costs of the bidders can be compared.

If unit prices are used when work is deleted from the contract, the amount of credit is usually less that the price for an additional quantity of the same item. Spaces should be provided in the bid form for both add and deduct amounts when applicable.

SAMPLE QUESTIONS

1. Which of the following would be used to formally incorporate a substitution into the work prior to the award of the contract?

    A. change order

    B. addendum

    C. alternate listing

    D. construction change directive

2. Which of the following are part of the bidding documents?

    I.   specifications

    II. invitation to bid

    III. list of subcontractors

    IV. owner-contractor agreement

    V. performance bond

        A. I, II, IV, and V

        B. II, III, and IV

        C. II, III, IV, and V

        D. all of the above

3. At the time scheduled for a bid opening, a contractor comes rushing into the room three minutes late with his bid. You have not begun to open the bids. What should you do?

    A. Refuse to accept the bid, stating that the deadline has passed.

    B. Ask if there are no objections from the other bidders to accepting the bid since none have been opened yet.

    C. Accept the bid with prejudice.

    D. Accept the bid since none have been opened but make a mental note to look on it with disfavor when you are evaluating it.

4. Which of the following is generally not true about bidding?

    A. Bidding procedures must be clearly and extensively outlined in the Instructions to Bidders because there are so many variations of the procedures.

    B. Bidding is nearly always necessary for federal government projects.

    C. Open bidding usually presents more problems than other types.

    D. Competitive bidding takes more time than negotiation but can result in a lower construction cost.

5. A performance bond is designed to:

    A. ensure that the subcontractors complete their work

    B. guarantee that the contractor will finish on time

    C. cover any possible liens that may be filed on the building

    D. protect the owner by having a third party responsible for completing the work if the contractor does not

6. If the lowest bid came in 20 percent over your client's construction budget, what would be the best advice you could give your client?

    A. that you revise the design at no cost to the client to reduce the construction cost

    B. that the project be rebid using another list of contractors

    C. that you and the client work to revise the scope of the project to reduce cost

    D. that all the deduct-alternates be accepted to reduce the bid, and that the client authorize a slight increase in construction cost to bring the two closer together

7. What variable affects a bid the most?

    A. the contractor's profit margin

    B. the influences of the construction marketplace

    C. labor and materials

    D. subcontract bids

28 CONSTRUCTION ADMINISTRATION SERVICES

Construction of the project is one of the most important phases of project delivery. It is the culmination of a great deal of planning, design, documentation, and organization. The architect should be closely involved with this phase of the project to the extent of his or her contractual responsibilities. During this phase the architect reviews and processes shop drawings and samples, manages requests for changes in the work, observes construction to make sure it is consistent with the contract documents, evaluates and processes the contractor's requests for payment, and administers the project closeout procedures.

1 SUBMITTALS

After the contract is awarded the contractor is responsible for providing submittals called for in the contract documents. These include shop drawings, samples, and product data. The submittals are sometimes prepared by the contractor, but most often they are prepared by the subcontractors, vendors, and material suppliers.

Shop drawings are drawings, diagrams, schedules, and other data prepared to show how a subcontractor or supplier proposes to supply and install work to conform to the requirements of the contract documents. As such, they are usually very detailed drawings showing how a portion of the work will be constructed.

Samples are physical examples of a portion of the work intended to show exactly how a material, finish, or piece of equipment will look in the completed job. They become standards of appearance and workmanship by which the final work will be judged.

Product data include brochures, charts, performance data, catalog pages, and other information that illustrates some portion of the work.

Although all submittals show in detail how much of the work is going to be built and installed, they are not contract documents.

When shop drawings and other submittals are prepared by the various subcontractors and material suppliers, they are sent to the general contractor who is responsible for reviewing and approving them. By reviewing them, the contractor represents that field measurements have been verified, materials checked, and other construction criteria have been coordinated. Only after this review should the contractor transmit the submittals to the architect. If they are not checked and signed by the contractor, the architect should immediately return them without review.

The architect's review of submittals is only for the limited purpose of checking for conformance with information given and to see if they conform to the design intent. The architect is not responsible for determining the accuracy of measurements, and completeness of details, verifying quantities, or checking fabrication or installation procedures. The architect's review does not relieve the contractor of his or her responsibilities under the contract documents.

If the submittals require the review of one of the architect's consultants, they are forwarded to the consultant, who returns them to the architect after review. The architect then reviews them and returns them to the contractor who, in turn, returns them to the subcontractor or material supplier who prepared them. The architect may indicate that no exceptions are taken, that marked corrections should be made, that they should be revised and resubmitted, or that they are rejected.

2 CHANGES IN THE WORK

During construction, changes in the work are always required. They may be necessitated by errors discovered in the drawings, by unforeseen site conditions, by design changes requested by the client, by rulings of building officials, and for many other reasons. During bidding and prior to contract award, changes are made by addenda. During construction, changes in the work are accomplished in one of three ways: by written order, by construction change directive, or by formal change order.

A. Written Order for Minor Changes

When a change does not involve a modification of the contract sum or time and is consistent with the contract documents, the architect may issue a written order directing the contractor to make a change. For example, moving a door opening over 6 inches before it is framed would be a minor change. The contractor may issue an order for such a minor change without the approval of either the owner or contractor.

B. Construction Change Directive

When a change needs to be made right away, but the owner and contractor cannot agree on a price, the architect may issue a *construction change directive*. This must be signed by both the architect and owner but does not have to be signed by the contractor. In addition to describing the changes required, it includes a proposed basis for determining the adjustment of cost or time or both.

Under the provisions of the AIA General Conditions of the Contract (A201), the contractor must proceed with the work and advise the architect of the contractor's agreement or disagreement with the basis for cost and time adjustment. If the contractor agrees, the change is recorded as a change order. If the contractor disagrees, the architect is responsible for determining the final adjustment, based on costs or savings attributable to the work plus costs of related equipment, supplies, premiums for bonds and insurance, field supervision, overhead, and profit.

C. Change Orders

A *change order* is a document authorizing a variation from the original contract documents that involves a change in contract price, contract time, or both. Technically, it is issued by the owner since the owner has the agreement with the contractor, but it is prepared by the architect. It must be signed by the owner, architect, and contractor.

Any of the three parties may suggest a change order, but normally the architect submits a proposal request to the contractor. This is accompanied by supporting drawings or other documents as required to fully describe the proposed change. The contractor submits his or her quotation of price and time change. If these are acceptable to the owner, the formal change order document is prepared and signed by all three parties.

3   FIELD ADMINISTRATION

Once the project actually gets underway the architect has a number of responsibilities under the Standard Form of Agreement Between Owner and Architect and in accordance with the General Conditions of the Contract.

A. Construction Observation

As part of basic services, the architect visits the site at intervals appropriate to the stage of construction or as agreed in writing. The purpose is to become generally familiar with the progress and quality of the work and to determine, in general, if the work is progressing in such a way that, when completed, it will be in accordance with the contract documents.

The number and timing of visits to a job site is left to the judgment of the architect, based on the size and complexity of the project, the type of construction contract being used, and the exact schedule of construction operations.

During each site visit the architect should make complete notes of the observations and include these in appropriate field reports. Copies of the field reports are sent to the owner to keep him or her informed on the progress of the work. Unless otherwise agreed to in writing in the owner-architect agreement, the architect is not responsible for exhaustive or continuous on-site inspections. Nor is the architect responsible for the contractor's failure to carry out the work or for the means, methods, techniques of construction, or safety precautions on the job.

B. Rejecting Work

The AIA General Conditions of the Contract give the architect the authority to reject work that does not conform to the contract documents. Since rejecting work means extra time and expense for the contractor, the causes and reasons for rejecting it should be carefully documented and the owner kept informed of the situation. If suspect work is covered contrary to the architect's request or to requirements specifically stated in the contract documents, the architect also has the authority to request that the contractor uncover the work for inspection. As mentioned in Chapter 26, the owner has the right to accept non-conforming work and to adjust the contract sum, if appropriate.

C. Safety

The contractor is solely responsible for safety on the job site. If the architect volunteers suggestions or directions concerning construction means and techniques in regard to safety issues, the architect may also assume legal responsibility and be held liable for accidents or other problems.

If the architect observes an obvious safety violation, he or she should call it to the attention of the contractor and follow up with a notice in writing but not suggest how it can be corrected. If the safety problem is not corrected, the architect should notify both the contractor and owner in writing.

D. Field Tests

When tests and inspections are required by the contract documents, the contractor is responsible for making arrangements with testing agencies acceptable to the owner or with the appropriate public authorities. The contractor pays for the tests and must give the architect timely notice of when and where the test is to be made so the architect can observe the procedure.

If the architect, owner, or public authorities require additional testing beyond what is required in the contract documents, the architect should instruct the contractor to make arrangements, but only after written authorization from the owner. In this case, the owner pays for the tests.

E. Documentation

During the entire construction administration phase (as well as during all phases of the architect's services), the architect should keep complete documentation of the progress of the job. This includes not only the standard forms used, such as change orders, certificates of payment, and the like, but also all correspondence, meeting notes, telephone logs, and similar written material that records the who, what, why, when, and how of the project. This kind of documentation is critical if disputes arise or the client objects to fee payments for extra services of the architect.

F. Claims

There are usually disputes and claims on any construction project, and these typically occur during the construction phase. The AIA General Conditions of the Contract specifically outlines the procedure to be followed if a claim or dispute arises.

The architect is responsible for reviewing claims and making decisions, such decisions being final but subject to arbitration. In the worst of cases, a claim may have to be decided by litigation.

If the owner or contractor has a dispute or makes a claim, the architect must take certain preliminary action within ten days of receipt of the claim. These actions may include: (1) rejecting the claim in whole or part along with the reasons, (2) requesting additional supporting data, (3) submitting a schedule to the parties indicating when the architect expects to take action, (4) recommending approval of the claim by the other party, or (5) suggesting a compromise.

If the claim is not immediately resolved, the party making the claim must then take action within ten days of receiving the architect's preliminary response. This action may include: (1) submitting additional data as requested by the architect, (2) modifying the initial claim, or (3) notifying the architect that the initial claim remains unchanged.

If the claim is still not resolved, the architect must notify the parties in writing that the architect's decision will be made within seven days. The decision is final and binding, but it is subject to arbitration.

G. Arbitration

Arbitration is a method of resolving disputes between the owner and architect and between the owner and contractor. It is an alternative to the lengthy and costly procedure of litigation. The General Conditions of the Contract require arbitration as the method of resolving claims between the owner and contractor if they are not resolved by the architect in the procedures outlined in the previous section.

The AIA standard documents require that arbitration proceedings be conducted under the Construction Industry Arbitration Rules of the American Arbitration Association and any applicable state laws.

Under arbitration, the two parties agree to submit their claims to an arbitrator or arbitrators and agree to abide by the arbitrator's decision. The arbitrator is someone knowledgeable in the construction industry and listens to evidence, reviews documents, and hears witnesses before making a decision.

Arbitration has the advantages over litigation of speed, economy, and privacy. However, unlike a trial, there are no rules of evidence and the decision cannot be appealed.

4 PROGRESS PAYMENTS

During the course of a job, the contractor requests periodic payments, usually monthly against the total contract sum. Under the General Conditions of the Contract, the architect is responsible for making sure that the amounts requested are consistent with the amount of work actually done and the amount of materials stored.

A. Intermediate Payments

In order to receive periodic payment, the contractor must submit to the architect a notarized application for payment at least ten days before the date established for each payment in the owner-contractor agreement. This application should include the value of work done to the date of the application in addition to the value of materials purchased and in acceptable storage, but not yet incorporated into the work.

Certification of the application for payment constitutes a representation by the architect that the work has progressed to the point indicated and that, to the best of the architect's knowledge, information, and belief, the quality of the work is in accordance with the contract documents. Certification is not a representation that the architect has made exhaustive on-site inspections or that the architect has reviewed construction methods, techniques, or procedures. Further, certification is not a representation that the architect has reviewed copies of requisitions received from subcontractors and material suppliers or that the architect has determined how and for what purpose the contractor has used money previously paid.

The amount due to the contractor is based on the schedule of values that the contractor submits to the architect after the award of the contract. This allocates the total contract sum to various portions of work, such as site work, foundations, framing, and so forth.

If the application for payment is approved, the architect signs it and sends it to the owner for payment. An amount, called the *retainage*, is withheld from each application until the end of the job or some other time during the work that is agreed on by both the contractor and owner. The retainage gives the owner leverage in making sure the job is completed and can be used to provide money to satisfy lien claims.

The architect may withhold all or a portion of the applications for payment in order to protect the owner if the architect cannot represent that the amount of work done or materials stored is in conformance with the application. The architect may also withhold payment for any of the following reasons:

- defective work

- third-party claims or evidence of probability of third-party claims

- failure of the contractor to make payments to subcontractors

- reasonable evidence that the work cannot be completed for the unpaid balance of the contract sum

- damage to the owner or another contractor

- reasonable evidence that the work will not be completed on time and that the unpaid balance will not be sufficient to cover damages due to the delay

- persistent failure of the contractor to carry out the work in accordance with the contract documents

B. Final Payment

After the final punch list inspection, the contractor notifies the architect in writing that the work is ready for final inspection and submits a final application for payment. If, after a final inspection, the architect determines that the work is complete and acceptable under the conditions of the contract documents, a final certificate for payment is issued to the owner.

Before the certificate can be issued, however, the contractor must submit to the architect the following items:

- an affidavit that payrolls, materials, and other indebtedness that the owner might be responsible for have been paid, (AIA document G706, Contractor's Affidavit of Payment of Debts and Claims, is often used)

- a certificate showing that insurance required by the contract documents to remain in force after final payment will not be canceled or allowed to expire until at least 30 days' written notice to the owner

- a written statement that the contractor knows of no reason that the insurance will not be renewable

- the consent of surety to final payment, if applicable, (AIA form G707, Consent of Surety Company to Final Payment, may be used for this purpose)

- any other data required by the owner that establish evidence of payment of obligations such as releases and waivers of liens

If final completion is delayed through no fault of the contractor, the owner may, with certification by the architect, make partial payment for that portion completed without terminating the contract.

5 PROJECT CLOSEOUT

Project closeout is an important part of the construction administration phase. It is during this time that the building work is completed, the structure is made ready for occupancy, and all remaining documentation takes place.

The contractor initiates closeout procedures by notifying the architect in writing and by submitting a comprehensive list of items to be completed or corrected. The contractor must proceed promptly to complete or correct these items. The architect then makes an inspection to determine if the work or a designated portion of it is substantially complete or if additional items need to be completed or corrected.

Substantial completion is defined as the stage of the work when it is sufficiently complete in accordance with the contract documents so the owner can occupy or utilize the work for its intended purpose. The date of substantial completion is important because it has legal implications. For example, in many states, the statute of limitation for errors possibly caused by the architect begins with the date of substantial completion. The date of substantial completion is also the termination of the contractor's schedule for the project. If there are bonuses or liquidated damages involved, they are based on this date.

The inspection and resulting list of items by the architect is called the *punch list*. It is during this inspection that the architect prepares a list of anything that needs to be completed or corrected if not in accordance with the contract documents. The contractor must correct these items, after which another inspection is called for. If the final inspection shows the work is substantially complete, the architect issues a certificate of substantial completion. It is at this time that the final application for payment is processed.

In addition to completing the work, the contractor must also submit to the owner certain other items, including the following:

- all warranties, maintenance contracts, operating instructions, certificates of inspection, and bonds

- all documentation required with the application for final payment as described above

- a set of record drawings if required by the owner-contractor agreement

- the certificate of occupancy as issued by the building department

- extra stock of materials as called for in the specifications

The contractor must also complete final cleaning, instruct the owner or owner's representatives in the operation of systems and equipment, complete the keying for locks and turn keys over to the owner, and restore all items damaged by the contractor.

If the work is not substantially complete based on the architect's inspection, the architect notifies the contractor of work that must be completed before a certificate of substantial completion can be prepared. The owner may wait for the entire project to be completed or, if appropriate, may agree with the contractor to occupy only a portion of the work.

The architect's basic services terminate when the final certificate for payment is issued.

SAMPLE QUESTIONS

1. In what order should the following activities take place during project closeout?

I. preparation of the final certificate for payment

II. punch list

III. issuance of the certificate of substantial completion

IV. notification by the contractor that the project is ready for final inspection

V. receipt of consent of surety

    A. II, III, V, IV, then I

    B. II, IV, III, V, then I

    C. IV, II, V, I, then III

    D. IV, V, II, III, then I

2. Substantial completion indicates that:

    A. the owner can make use of the work for its intended purpose and the requirements of the contract documents have been fulfilled

    B. the contractor has completed correcting punch list items

    C. the final certificate for payment is issued by the architect and all documentation has been delivered to the owner

    D. all of the above

3. During a periodic visit to the site the architect notices what appears to be an undersized variable air volume box being installed. What should the architect do?

    A. Notify the mechanical engineer to look at the situation during the next site visit by the engineer. Note the observation on a field report.

    B. Find the contractor and stop work on the installation until the size of the unit can be verified by the mechanical engineer and compared against the contract documents.

    C. Notify the owner in writing that the work is not proceeding according to the contract documents. Arrange a meeting with the mechanical engineer to resolve the situation.

    D. Notify the contractor that the equipment may be undersized and have the contractor check on it. Ask the mechanical engineer to verify the size of the unit against the specifications and report to the architect.

4. An architect would use which one of the following instruments if the building department required additional exit signs beyond those shown on the approved plans when the project was 90 percent complete?

    A. order for minor change

    B. addendum

    C. change order

    D. construction change directive

5. The contractor is solely responsible for:

I. field reports to the owner

II. field tests

III. scaffolding

IV. reviewing claims of subcontractors

V. reviewing shop drawings

    A. I, II, and III

    B. II and III

    C. II, III, and IV

    D. III and IV

6. Which of the following is not true about submittals?

    A. The architect must review them prior to checking by the contractor.

    B. The contractor is ultimately responsible for the accuracy of dimensions and quantities.

    C. They are not considered part of the contract documents.

    D. The contractor can reject them and request resubmittal.

7. If a contractor makes a claim for additional money due to extra work caused by unforeseen circumstances, under AIA Document A201, the architect must respond within:

A. 5 days

B. 7 days

C. 10 days

D. not until supporting data are submitted

29 SOLUTIONS

This chapter contains solutions and explanations for the sample questions in this book. The solutions to sample questions in Chapter 2 through Chapter 12 are listed first. (There are no sample questions or solutions for Chapter 6.) Chapter 23 contains sample questions for the subjects of materials and methods that are covered in Chapters 13 through 22. The solutions for Chapters 24 through 28 are included here.

2 PRE-DESIGN—ENVIRONMENTAL ANALYSIS

1. B, point 2, is correct.

Point 1 has a good view, but at the top of a hill it would be very windy. In addition, access to the lake is difficult due to the steep slope from this site to the lake. Point 3 is in a drainage pattern. This alone makes it unsuitable for development, but the location would also be cool due to its position at the bottom of two slopes and in the path of wind coming through the valley. Point 4 has a good view, easy access to the lake, and could be used for development, but the slightly steeper slope might complicate grading and site work. Point 2 has level ground, a good view of and access to the lake, and its location on a south-facing slope would capture the sun and minimize the detrimental effects of the wind.

2. C, 4 stories, is correct.

If the floor area ratio is 2, then the maximum amount of floor area that can be built is 120,000 square feet. The available ground area that can be covered within the setbacks is 270 feet times 130 feet, or 35,100 square feet. Dividing this figure into 120,000 gives 3.42 stories, which indicates that three full stories and a partial fourth story could be built. But this is usually not economical. Dividing 120,000 by 4 gives an area per story

of 30,000 square feet which would easily fit within the setbacks.

3. C is correct.

The Columbian Exposition revived interest in city planning and showed that desirable results could be achieved through organized efforts. It also prompted many cities to plan civic centers and parkways. The Ordinance of 1785 started the rectangular survey system which reinforced grid planning begun with the plan for Philadelphia. Garnier's plan was one of the responses to the Industrial Revolution and the first to use the idea of zoning. The Industrial Revolution prompted a reform movement which led to many ideas about planning, many of which influenced urban design in Europe and the United States.

Although L'Enfant's plan was widely praised and publicized as a major planning effort, its Baroque planning approach was never widely adopted.

4. A is the correct answer.

A freeway could be considered a path if traveling on it or an edge if it divided a district or enclosed an area. A popular neighborhood gathering spot would probably be considered a node because it can be entered and because it is a center of interest. It would most likely be the center of a neighborhood district as well. An area with many hospitals would be viewed as the hospital district. This image would be reinforced because of the likely support services, such as doctor's offices and pharmacies, that would also be nearby. A group of houses by themselves would have little image unless they formed an edge or surrounded a park or similar node.

5. D is correct.

A is incorrect because forcing too many people within close, personal space would be counterproductive. People would become uncomfortable and defensive. B is incorrect because the orientation of the benches would be sociofugal, requiring that people face away from each other. C is incorrect because the cooking and serving area would be one of the most popular gathering spaces and a destination for people. Here, people could watch food being prepared, serve themselves, and informally meet other people.

6. B is correct.

Using the scale on the drawing, the distance between the two points is about 15 feet. Using formula 2.1, the slope is:

$$G = \frac{8}{15}(100) = 53\%$$

7. C is correct.

B is not correct because a relatively thin layer of clay only 6 feet thick could either be removed and replaced with better soil or the foundations could be placed on the good underlying layer of sandy soil. Both A and D would pose minor problems, but these would probably not affect the final decision to build. A speculative office building depends on a wide catchment area, and lack of arterial roads in some portions of it would most likely not affect the marketability of the project. If there was strong objection to parking lots, the visual impact could be minimized through landscaping, or parking could be placed underground or in a well-designed parking structure. The vacancy rate is the one factor that would most affect the financial success of the project and the decision to build.

8. D is correct.

All of the conditions listed would create unusual excavating and foundation problems.

9. C is correct.

II, the size of utility easements, would be found on the site survey. If a site survey had not been performed, the information would come from the utility company. III, minimum lot size, is usually a part of a subdivision regulation. V, roof coverings, would be prescribed either in restrictive covenants for the property or as part of a building code. Covenants would dictate the type and appearance of the material for aesthetic reasons, while the building code would specify types of roofing based primarily on fire-resistive needs.

10. B is correct.

Point A is too close to another intersecting street. Point C intersects the street at an angle that is unsafe. Point D intersects an arterial street. While sometimes possible, it should be avoided, especially if it is as close to an intersection as this one is.

3 PRE-DESIGN—BUILDING PROGRAMMING

1. D is correct.

A multi-level system of pedestrian circulation implies a definite type of physical solution. This should not be confused with a programming statement. Such a statement that might preceed the design concept would be something like, "separate incompatible circulation functions."

2. A is correct.

None of the enclosed mall would be rentable, so subtract the 6 percent (5100 square feet) right off the top:

$$85,000 - 5100 = 79,900 \text{ square feet}$$

Then, take 75 percent of the remainder, which gives about 60,000 square feet (59,925 square feet exactly).

3. C is correct.

There are a number of ways of arriving at the same answer for this question. City B has a higher cost index so divide the lower into the higher:

$$\frac{1517}{1440} = 1.053$$

Multiply this factor by the cost in city A, $1,500,000, to get 1,580,208. Then, increase this by the 5 percent inflation factor:

$$1,580,208 \times 1.05 = 1,659,218$$
$$\sim \$1,659,000$$

You can also increase for inflation first, then use the cost index factor.

4. D is correct.

5. B is correct.

Grouping waiting areas to encourage interaction would probably be the least desirable for two reasons. People are usually a little nervous while waiting with strangers and prefer the option to avoid contact in sociofugal space. In addition, since there are different departments in a medium-sized facility, having everyone in one space would be inefficient as well as uncomfortable. One large waiting area would make people less at ease and therefore would be counterproductive to the client's goals.

6. D is correct.

Since the facility is expected to grow, and since there are several distinct departments, a radial organization would work for the first phase and allow for easy growth. Because the site is ample and flat, terrain would probably not restrict this type of organizational pattern. An axial pattern might work, but since everyone enters in one place for directions and orientation, the central focus of a radial pattern would probably be preferable.

7. C is correct.

For the first phase of this type of building, most functions would probably be fixed, requiring little need for convertibility in the future or multiple use initially. The primary need of expansibility would guide the structural framing system so the building could be added onto easily.

8. A is correct.

Reducing the total time by three months means about a 15 percent reduction. Fast-track construction could probably take this amount of time off the process. CPM scheduling would not help much, and negotiation rather than bidding would reduce the time a little but certainly not three months. In addition, negotiation would most likely result in a higher cost to the client, so answer B is not correct. Adding more people to the design process would only help a little, and overtime is not generally efficient, so C is incorrect. Streamlining the decision-making process would not reduce the time required and would probably not be acceptable to the client.

9. D is correct.

The architect can, of course, control his or her own fees, and, to a certain extent, negotiate with consultants, so C is incorrect. Since the architect can control building costs and site work through design, B is not correct. Although the rate of escalation cannot be controlled, the amount depends on the base cost of construction which can be controlled through design, so A is not correct, even though it is a tempting answer.

10. B is correct.

Since the amount is only 8 percent, this could probably be made up through a slight reduction in area (statement III) and modifying some levels of quality (statement IV). Since it is only the programming phase, value engineering is not possible, so statement II is not correct. Statements I and V are not appropriate because school districts cannot borrow money from other accounts and usually need to have schools completed as originally scheduled.

4 SITE ANALYSIS AND DESIGN

1. A6, crown, is correct.

All roads should have a crown, or high point, in the center to ensure positive drainage to either side.

2. B7, township, is correct.

A township contains 36 sections. A check is 24 miles square and consists of 16 townships.

3. A9, inverts, is correct.

The difference in elevation between the bottom of a sewer line at two points causes the water flow. The term invert is also used to call out the bottom elevation of drains, catch basins, and manholes.

4. B is correct.

Without knowing other conditions of the site, the best placement of the building and road is based on road grading and building construction on the existing topography. Roads should cut across slopes gradually to minimize steep grades, so this eliminates choice D where the road runs perpendicular to the slope. The road is well placed in C, but the length of the building runs perpendicular to the slope which would make construction more difficult and expensive. Choice A works fairly well, with a gradual slope for the road and the building on level ground, but the road is in a valley and on the north side of the building. Choice B places the building parallel to the contour lines, is on a south-facing slope, and has a road gently rising across the grade with curves following the direction of the contours, so this is the best choice.

5. D is the correct answer.

Most roads should be kept under a 10 percent grade except for very short distances or for parking garage ramps. In northern climates, where snow and ice are a problem, it is even more important to maintain gentle slopes. A 12 percent grade would not be safe and could make driving difficult. Refer to Table 2.1 for recommended site work slopes.

6. B is correct.

II is incorrect because automobile and pedestrian traffic should always be kept separate. IV may be considered partially correct due to the idea of separating parking from walks, but a single entrance may create conflicts with vehicles pulling into and out of parking spaces, and entering and leaving by the same drive. The other three statements are generally good guidelines for planning site circulation.

7. D is correct.

All three of these methods are used to describe property although the metes and bounds method is not used as much as the other two methods.

8. C is correct.

A is incorrect because overhangs are not effective on the west and east sides of a building due to the low sun angle. Vertical louvers or fins are more effective in these locations. B is incorrect because the south side actually receives less solar radiation than the east or west sides because the sun is high during the middle of the day. It would be more effective to minimize the roof area to cut down on solar radiation.

9. D is correct.

This pattern is characteristic of roads with a crown in the middle sloping toward curbs on either side. As with any contour map, contour lines representing a ridge (which is what a crown of a road is in miniature) point in the direction of the down slope, so this road slopes down from east to west (or up from west to east as the answer states). The contours pointing in the other direction represent a ditch. Just as with any valley on a contour map, the lines point in the direction of the up slope.

10. A is correct.

90 degree parking layouts are always the most efficient if space is limited, so answers B and C are incorrect. D is incorrect because a single-loaded circulation drive providing access to parking is not as efficient as two rows of parking sharing one drive.

5 SITE DESIGN

The accompanying sketch shows one possible solution to this problem.

From a reading of the problem, it is clear that most of the design effort will involve accommodating parking and the drive. There are no buildings to locate or complex landscaping to design. Since the site is so large and the existing grade changes are minimal, developing new contours should be fairly easy.

A reasonable first step is to determine how much area is needed for parking. Since time is short on the site design problem, you should use the simplest, most efficient parking layout possible. This is 90-degree parking on both sides of a drive. Since the program calls for equal distribution between compact car stalls and regular stalls, the total width can be determined as 19 feet plus 15 feet plus 24 feet as a minimum drive width. The total is 58 feet. This assumes compact cars parked on one side of the drive and standard cars on the other.

The most efficient orientation of parking is in the east-west direction since the site has its longest dimension in this direction. For a quick first calculation, find the length of parking lot needed if all 84 cars were parked off of one drive, or 42 on each side. Multiply 42 by the larger standard car stall width of 9 feet to get 378 feet. This is longer than the length of the site, so at least two parking bays will be required.

The program calls for the driveway to the drop-off area to be one-way and to be separate from the parking lot circulation. This means that you could either have an in-and-out curb cut for the driveway and a separate drive for the parking area, or combine the curb cut access. However, the program calls for only one entrance and exit. To avoid congestion with cars pulling in and out of the street, the site access points should be separated as much as possible.

The sample solution shows one way of resolving these requirements. The access drive is kept outside the double bay parking area, and a separate drive is provided for people driving around the lot looking for a space. Since the curb at the drop-off should be on the right side, the entrance is near the northwest corner and the exit near the northeast corner.

Handicapped parking is best located adjacent to the platform, both to satisfy the problem statement and to minimize grade changes that would have to be accommodated with ramps. In the site plan shown, a back-up space is required since the handicapped area is a dead end off the drive.

The solution shown satisfies all the functional requirements of the problem although there are some weaknesses. The trees and shrub indication along Evans Avenue provide a buffer between the site and adjacent property as required, but the separation could have been made a little stronger with berms or a low, decorative fence. This, however, would not be sufficient to fail the solution. Landscaping is also weak on the east and west ends of the site.

The grading is resolved well and is clearly shown with correct contour lines as well as spot elevations. There seem to be no problems with handicapped access, although it is not clear if there is a curb without a ramp between the parking lot and the sidewalk.

Note that most of the required elements such as the 6-inch curb and handicapped parking are clearly noted. The individual parking stalls are also indicated and the number of available spaces noted so the graders can quickly verify that you have met the requirements.

Graphically, this solution could be a little stronger, especially the difference between groundcover and paved areas and the landscaping indications, but this is not enough to fail the solution. Overall, it is a well thought out, workable solution to the problem.

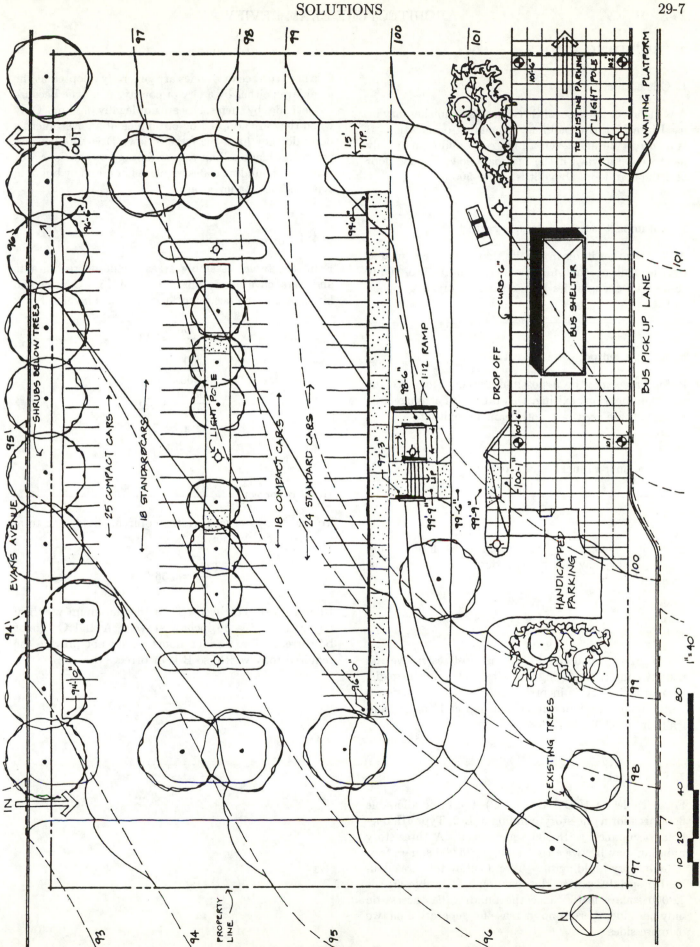

7 BUILDING CODES

1. C is correct.

A is incorrect because all three classes of finishes may be used in a high-rise building, depending on location. B is incorrect because even a high-rise building may only need two stairways if the occupant load for one floor and the two floors above it is under 500.

2. A6, impact isolation class, is correct.

All of the other items in the list that might be regulated by the code are not unique to residential use. Only residential occupancies have acoustical criteria applied to them.

3. B3, smokeproof tower, is correct.

Refuge area may be a possible answer, but since the question mentions exiting, this precludes a refuge area because these areas are not meant for exiting.

4. B4, Steiner tunnel test, is correct.

5. A is correct.

Exits may pass through reception areas, lobbies, and foyers. They may not pass through storage rooms or areas.

6. C is correct.

I is incorrect because zone 1 is the most restrictive and usually comprises the high density central business district of a city. IV is incorrect because the fire-resistive requirements are found in UBC Chapter 17 and specifically in UBC Table 17-A.

7. D is correct.

From Table 7.1 (UBC Table 5-C), the basic allowable floor area for a one-story building of B-2, Type III, one-hour occupancy is 18,000 square feet. A three-story building may be twice that area, or 36,000 square feet. A multistory building may have its allowable area doubled if sprinklered, so the maximum allowable area is 72,000 square feet. Since the building has access on only one side, there is no increase for separation on two or more sides.

8. C is the correct answer.

C is not true because codes are generally adopted at the local level, either by a city or county. A is true because model codes by themselves are not legally binding. Only when they are adopted by ordinance of a governmental body do they have the force of law. D is true because zoning ordinances limit square footage by the floor area ratios, and building codes regulate floor area by building type and occupancy group.

9. B is correct.

From the table, assembly areas including restaurants and bars have an occupant load of 15. Commercial kitchens have an occupant load of 200. Therefore,

$$\frac{3500}{15} = 233$$
$$\frac{1000}{200} = 5$$
$$\frac{1200}{15} = 80$$
$$\text{total} = 318$$

10. D is correct.

To find the total exit width required, divide the total occupant load by 50:

$$\frac{318}{50} = 6.36 \text{ feet}$$

Round up to $6\,1/2$ feet. Since the minimum width of any exit door is 36 inches, answers A and C cannot be correct. Two 36-inch doors would not provide the required total width, so B is incorrect.

8 HUMAN COMFORT AND MECHANICAL SYSTEM FUNDAMENTALS

1. C is correct.

Although motors, people, and lighting may be less critical in residences and some other types of occupancies, all of the items listed produce heat except humidity.

2. A is correct.

The sling psychrometer measures wet bulb temperature. As shown in the abbreviated psychrometric chart in Figure 8.3, wet bulb temperature is one of the ordinates on the chart. A sling psychrometer may have a dry bulb thermometer on it, but its primary purpose is to measure wet bulb temperatures. Likewise, relative humidity can be determined from the difference between dry and wet bulb levels, but this is not what the device measures directly.

3. A4, convection, is correct.

Although heat loss and gain through glazing is complex and results from a combination of conduction, convection, and radiation, insulating glass is separated by an air space. Therefore, most heat loss is through convection, and not conduction, because the air circulates within the glass picking up heat on the warm side and transferring it on the cold side where is lost to the outside through the glass by conduction. Even if the air space is evacuated, there is still some air present.

4. A5, design cooling load factor, is correct.

Equivalent temperature difference is incorrect because that value is used to calculate the heat gain through the building envelope, such as walls and roofs.

5. B5, resistance, is correct.

Since resistance is the number of hours it takes for one BTU to be transferred through one square foot of material when the temperature differential is one degree, the higher value is better.

6. B0, infiltration, is correct.

Weatherstripping serves to seal joints and cracks around doors and windows. Because infiltration is a large factor in heat loss, weatherstripping is always a good strategy.

7. A is the correct answer.

Although relative humidity affects human comfort, by itself it is not the only measure of comfort. For example, even at a high humidity of 75 percent, if the temperature is cool enough or there is enough of a breeze, most people will feel comfortable. Effective temperature (ET) is a better indicator of comfort because it takes all the variables into account.

8. D is correct.

The design equivalent temperature difference has no bearing on the solution to this problem. First, calculate the U value. Since the R value is given as 38, the U value is just the reciprocal, or

$$U = 1/38$$
$$= 0.026 \text{ BTUh/ft}^2\text{-}°\text{F}$$

The temperature difference, Δt, is 75 degrees.

The roof area is 40×80, or 3200 square feet. Using formula 8.3, the total heat loss can be calculated:

$$q = (U \times A) \times \Delta t$$
$$= (0.026 \times 3200) \times 75$$
$$= 6240 \text{ BTUh}$$

9. D is correct.

Latent heat is the heat required to produce a change in state of a material. Simply introducing sensible heat to raise the temperature from 32° to 33° would not melt ice. Additional heat is required which is the latent heat.

10. C is correct.

When the temperature is above about 80 °F, the body loses more heat through evaporation than convection or radiation. In a humid climate, this process is retarded, so encouraging air movement would be the best strategy although overhangs and light-colored surfaces would help minimize heat build-up in the structure itself.

9 HVAC SYSTEMS

1. C is correct.

Two of the primary concerns for this type of development would be low first cost and the ability for tenants to individually control their HVAC system. These criteria would preclude a multizone system and a more expensive first-cost active solar energy system, although evaporative cooling might be appropriate by itself. An economizer cycle is not useful where outside temperatures are normally high when cooling is needed. Therefore, answers A and B are not correct.

Individual rooftop heat pumps would work, but they are more expensive. The option that tips the choice to answer C is the provision for passive solar design. Even if it was a speculative building, simple passive design would be easy and inexpensive to accomplish, and would possibly minimize the required capacity of any HVAC unit. Further, since the primary concern will be cooling, a direct expansion system would be appropriate. It has low initial cost, is controllable by individual tenants, can be ducted, and can be roof-mounted or through wall mounted to avoid taking up rentable space. For occasional winter use, a heating coil can be included.

2. A is correct.

It is unlikely in the Arizona climate that passive cooling by itself would be acceptable or workable in this situation, so answer D is not correct. Absorption cooling is only economical if waste heat is available. Solar heated water might be used, but the system would be too expensive and not appropriate for this project, so answer B is not correct.

The choice is between A and C, both of which would work. However, if first cost is a concern as it would be for a speculative developer, evaporative cooling would be the best choice. A closed water loop running through the cooler instead of direct air would eliminate odor problems, and the cool water could be used in a ducted system.

3. C is correct.

The shopping mall would be planned for relatively fixed sizes of rental spaces. Although flexibility might be a concern, it would not be most important. I is not correct. Since the tenant mix would probably not be completely known at the time of design, the tenant's preference could not be solicited even if it was appropriate. In most cases, the tenants would not care what

the HVAC system was as long as it worked, so IV is not correct.

4. D is correct.

For most mid-size buildings, using an all air or air-water system needs about 6 to 9 percent of the gross area for HVAC system mechanical space. Six percent of the estimated 126,000 square feet gross area is 7560 square feet. This is rounded up to 7600, so D is correct as a minimum estimated area.

5. C is the correct answer.

Propane has a heating value of 2500 BTU per cubic foot, while natural gas has a heating value of 1050 BTU per cubic foot.

6. D is correct.

A round duct is the most efficient and offers the most area for the least perimeter area which causes friction and pressure loss. A square duct is the next most efficient shape, being the closest to a circle. A square shape would use the available space most efficiently, but it is not as efficient as a round duct. As ducts become more rectangular, they become less efficient and have increased friction loss. A rectangular duct with the long dimension horizontal would only be used if space was a problem.

7. B is correct.

A standard gas furnace does not have a damper. Only special energy-saving furnaces sometimes have a damper that automatically closes when the furnace is off.

8. A is correct.

A ton of air conditioning is equivalent to 12,000 BTUh. Dividing 108,000 by 12,000 gives 9 tons.

9. B is correct.

An economizer cycle uses outdoor air when its temperature is low enough to assist in cooling.

10. C is correct.

Cooking produces a change in state of water and other substances, so latent heat is required and must therefore be offset with air conditioning. Sensible heat is also present, so both types are present.

10 PLUMBING SYSTEMS

1. B0, percolation test, is correct.

The size of a leaching field is determined by the quantity of effluent that must be accommodated and the ability of the soil to let the effluent soak in. This permeability of the soil is measured by the percolation test, and since there is no answer related to quantity, this is the correct response.

2. A8, hardness, is correct.

Although there are many concerns in a private water supply related to both water quality and the method of pumping the water, of the answers provided, hardness is the most important.

3. B3, static head, is correct.

4. C is correct.

I is incorrect because the type of sprinkler system has nothing to do with its efficiency. III is incorrect because sprinkler spacing is dependent on which hazard classification exists.

5. C is correct.

In order to find the maximum height, you must first take the pressure in the water main and subtract other known pressure losses and the pressure required for the fixture to operate properly:

$$57 - 23 - 12 = 22 \text{ psi}$$

Since it requires one pound per square inch to lift water 2.3 feet, the maximum height is:

$$22 \times 2.3 = 50.6 \text{ feet}$$

6. A is correct.

Even though the nearest water line is 300 feet away, the best recommendation would be to use city water, where the quality and quantity are known and a long-term supply is assured. Although nearby property owners might or might not be willing to share the cost, the owner would still be best advised to extend the line.

Drilling a test bore could help determine the depth, potential yield, and water quality, but would cost almost as much as a complete well.

Petitioning the city to extend the line would be time-consuming and probably not successful if they have already decided against it.

Asking nearby property owners who use wells about their experience would yield useful information, but even if the cost and water quality were acceptable, extending the municipal line would still be the preferred course of action.

7. D is correct.

I is incorrect because the minimum slope of drains depends on the size of the pipe. II is incorrect because the vent stack may sometimes extend through the roof but does not always have to. In many cases, the vent stack connects with the stack vent above the highest fixture served by the stack.

8. B is correct.

Water hammer occurs when a valve is suddenly turned off and causes the water to stop, forcing the pipes to shake.

9. A is correct.

A stack vent extends a soil or waste stack to vent through the roof, and every stack must have one of these. A vent stack is a separate vent connected to a waste or soil stack in multistory buildings, so not every building has this. A house trap is not mandatory in many codes, and a backflow preventer is not required in many plumbing installations.

10. C is the correct answer.

Type M copper pipe is only used for low pressure piping. Type L is the one most commonly used in plumbing installations.

11 ELECTRICAL SYSTEMS

1. D is correct.

A is correct because lamps with a higher efficacy could be selected, although this would have to be balanced against the change in color temperature. B is correct because lumen output decreases as lamps age and as dirt accumulates on them. Changing lamps often would help maintain the initial footcandle level. C is correct because room finishes have a significant effect on the total light level in a room.

2. B is correct.

In this problem, the footcandle level must first be determined. Since the source is perpendicular to the wall, the inverse square law is used.

$$E = \frac{I}{d^2}$$
$$= \frac{3500}{(15)^2}$$
$$= 15.56 \text{ footcandles}$$

Once the footcandle level is determined, it is multiplied by the reflectance to find the brightness:

$$15.56 \times 0.75 = 11.7 \text{ footlamberts}$$

3. B is correct.

Because of the potential for oxidation, the leads of aluminum conductors must be cleaned prior to installation, so statement I is correct. III is correct because all the special requirements of aluminum conductors and the danger of incorrect installation require that a licensed electrician do the work. V is correct because larger conductors are required to carry the same amperage as copper conductors.

4. C is correct.

Although all of the choices listed should be considered and are potentially important, the question asks which ones are *most* important. For office space where video display tubes (VDTs) and standard office tasks are present, the architect should be concerned with two results of glare. Veiling reflection would be of concern for the standard office tasks like writing and reading, while reflected glare would be critical in using the VDTs. Therefore, statements III and IV are correct. Likewise, the brightness ratios between the tasks and their surroundings are important, especially with VDTs, so V is correct. The color rendering index is less important. Although visual comfort probability deals with sources of direct glare, this answer is not given in conjunction with the others.

5. A is correct.

As voltages increase, current decreases to provide the same amount of power. Lower currents require smaller conductors. For large commercial buildings, smaller conductors translates to less expense in conductors and conduit, as well as easier installation of smaller wires.

6. B is correct.

A large school building would require high voltage service from the utility and step-down transformers provided by the owner. This would rule out answer A. A transformer vault near the exterior wall would be the best choice for protection, ventilation, and ease of installation and removal. Although the transformer could be placed on a pad outside the building, this would leave it exposed to possible vandalism and might present a danger to the school children.

7. B is correct.

A temperature rise detector would not give early warning to the occupants. If properly located, either an ionization or photoelectric detector would work.

8. C is correct.

Footcandles is a measure of the light incident on a transmitting or reflecting surface. Footlamberts is a measure of the brightness (or luminance) of a surface and takes into account the transmittance properties of the glass. Candela is the SI unit for candlepower, which is the unit of luminous intensity.

9. B is correct.

Selection B offers the best balance between appropriate color rendering, accent lighting, and energy efficiency. Daylighting would provide natural light for viewing clothes, and warm white deluxe lamps would be efficient and provide a pleasant, overall light.

Selection A would not be appropriate because of the cooler colors of mercury lamps and metal halide lighting. Selection C is not good because of the potentially damaging effects of too much daylighting on fabrics. Selection D would not be energy efficient, and would also present the problem of daylight damaging the fabrics.

10. D is correct.

Low pressure sodium lamps produce a monochromatic yellow light which would not be appropriate in a storage warehouse where people may have to discriminate between colors.

12 ACOUSTICS

1. C is correct.

Sensitivity to sound is generally not dependent on sex, so statement I is not true. Although the lower end of sensitivity to sound is somewhere between 20 and 30 Hz, 15 Hz is too low. The generally accepted upper limit is about 20,000 Hz, so statement III is also incorrect.

2. B is correct.

The assembly shown would not be the best for controlling impact noise or mechanical vibration, so these two answers are incorrect. Since the sound absorbing panel is in room B, this would help control excessive reverberation, so statement II is correct. The decision to be made is between III and IV. Since noise reduction between two spaces is dependent on the transmission loss of the wall, the area of the wall, and the absorption of the surfaces in the receiving room, statement III is more correct. It is true that adding absorption to a space will result in a noise reduction within that space.

3. A is correct.

The rule of thumb is that if the difference between two sound sources is 4 to 8 decibels, you should add 1 dB to the higher value which in this case is 69 dB.

4. B6 is correct.

STC, or sound transmission class, gives the designer a quick way to evaluate tested partitions in the common frequency ranges.

5. A7 is correct.

Noise criteria curves are used to specify the allowable sound pressure levels at octave band center frequencies.

6. B3 is correct.

Even though reverberation is dependent on total room absorption and room volume, room volume is the only variable listed.

7. C is correct.

Although placing absorptive materials on both sides of the wall would not hurt and decrease the noise level in the "noisier" room, the three most important variables are the transmission loss of the wall, its stiffness (damping qualities), and minimizing the area of the separating barrier.

8. D is correct.

To find the total absorption when calculation at specific frequencies is not required, the NRC, or noise reduction coefficient, is used. The total absorption is the summation of all the individual absorptions according to the formula $A = \Sigma Sa$.

floor:	$15 \times 20 \times 0.10$	$= 30$ Sabins
walls:	$[(15 + 15 + 20 + 20) \times 8.5]$	
	$- [(3.5 \times 8)] \times 0.15$	$= 28$
window:	$3.5 \times 8 \times 0.15$	$= 4$
ceiling:	$15 \times 20 \times 0.60$	$= \underline{180}$
total		242 Sabins

9. B is correct.

Since a change in intensity level in decibels is considered "just perceptible" you would probably be better off not using the material regardless of how low the added cost was. Trying to modify the material to 6 dB would also probably not be worth the trouble. If you needed an STC rating 6 dB higher, you would be better off looking at another construction assembly instead of trying to make do with a modified material. Answer D could be correct if the material was such that simply doubling it would result in a 6 dB increase rather than modifying it.

10. C is correct.

In this question, the phrase "If cost is a consideration" affects the order of priority of the suggestions. Although adding an extra layer of gypsum board might be one of the best suggestions from an acoustical point of view, it would cost money. The simplest, least expensive suggestion during design development would be to reorient the operable windows so sound from one classroom did not reflect off an open window and onto the window in the adjacent classroom. Also, during design development, it is an easy matter to coordinate routing of mechanical and electrical work to minimize acoustical problems.

The third priority would be to add the extra layer of gypsum board to improve the transmission loss of the partition. For the small additional cost of materials and labor, sound transmission would be greatly reduced. Next, substituting carpeting for tile would reduce the noise in each room, but not so much the loss through the wall. The cost would probably be more than the gypsum board but still reasonable for the benefits obtained.

Statement IV would be the next to the least valid suggestion. Even though it would greatly limit sound transmission between the two rooms and would be easy to do during the early planning stages, it doesn't make sense to place a storage room along the windows when the potential acoustical problem can be solved by other means.

Least desirable is hiring an acoustical consultant for this situation only. The anticipated noise sources are not so unusual that the preceding steps would not sufficiently solve the problem.

23 MATERIALS AND METHODS

1. D is correct.

Monel metal is a trade name for an alloy of copper and nickel. Muntz metal is a common alloy of 60 percent copper and 40 percent tin. Nickel silver is a name given to an alloy of 65 percent copper, 25 percent zinc, and 10 percent nickel.

2. B is correct.

Vapor barriers should always be located on the warm side of insulation to prevent moisture from condensing when it cools and reaches the dew point. Moisture penetrating the insulation can reduce the insulation's effectiveness and damage other materials.

3. B is correct.

All of the answers listed would need to be addressed, but since the question asks which is *most* important you need to use some judgment. Answer D is unlikely since a large building would probably utilize piers or caissons for the foundation, so the load-carrying capacity of the soil would not be as critical. Foundation insulation could be easily selected to avoid deterioration problems, so C is an unlikely answer. Of the two remaining answers, hydrostatic pressure could cause the most problems so this is the primary problem to be solved.

4. A is correct.

If the block shown is not used, the carriages must be toe nailed to the floor which is a weaker construction detail than that shown.

5. C is correct.

The member supporting the treads is the carriage, and the member on either side of the stair is the stringer.

6. D is correct.

Safety glazing is required in all areas subject to human impact. This includes, of course, glass doors, and also any glass within one foot of doors. Glass farther than one foot from doors and with a sill over 18 inches above the floor does not have to be safety glazed.

7. D is correct.

Answer A describes organic material, answer B describes gravels, and answer C describes clays.

8. B is correct.

Annealed glass is the standard glass used in most non-critical glazing situations. All of the other types of glass listed have higher strengths and could be used in a tall building with large panels of glass subject to high wind loads and thermal cycling.

9. D is correct.

Fire-rated partitions must be constructed according to tested and approved methods which include using Type X gypsum board, the method of attachment to the framing, how the joints are finished, the type and size of studs and other details. In addition, the fire separation must extend from the slab to the rated slab above, not just to a suspended, finish ceiling.

10. A is correct.

Type M masonry has a compressive strength of 2500 psi. Types S and N have strengths of 1800 psi and 750 psi, respectively, while Type O is the lowest with a compressive strength of 350 psi.

11. D is correct.

SW stands for severe weathering and would be the type that should be specified for the northeastern part of the United States. NW is normal weathering, and type MW is moderate weathering. Type FBX refers to the finish appearance.

12. C is correct.

Plain slicing produces a figured pattern with the characteristic "cathedral" appearance. Rotary slicing produces the most varied grain pattern, and half-round slicing yields a moderate amount of pattern. Since quarter slicing cuts perpendicular to the growth rings, this gives the straightest pattern of the choices listed. Rift slicing would also give a very uniform grain pattern.

13. B is correct.

Although asphalt-impregnated paper can act as a vapor barrier, the fact that it is placed on the outside of the sheathing precludes answer C (and also answer D) from being correct. It does add a little to the thermal resistance but its primary purpose is to prevent any water that seeps behind the siding from getting into the structure. It also serves to prevent air infiltration.

14. A is correct.

A raked joint like that shown in the masonry wall above the ledge is not a good one to use because water running down the wall can seep into the joint by capillary action. The concave joint shown in D is preferred. The details at points B and C are correctly executed. The flashing and sealant at B would keep water out, and the drip at point C would prevent water from running under the ledge and into the masonry joint.

15. C is correct.

Control joints placed where separate sections of concrete are poured and in walks are placed 5 feet apart. Expansion joints with a joint filler are placed a maximum of 20 feet apart.

16. B is correct.

Stainless steel can be welded and it is stronger than bronze, so answers I and V are incorrect. It is primarily an alloy of steel and chromium, but sometimes nickel is added.

17. A is correct.

Breast boards are horizontal boards between soldier beams, and rakers are diagonal braces that support walers.

18. B is correct.

The height of the dump bucket is important because dropping concrete too far causes segregation, which should not be allowed. The location of rebar is important because of the minimum coverages required to protect the steel from moisture. The method of form support is important because unstable forms can affect the final appearance and size of the concrete. They can also be a safety hazard, but this is the contractor's responsibility.

19. C is correct.

Any piece of lumber from 2 inches to 5 inches nominal width is considered dimension lumber. Timber is lumber 6 inches and over, while boards are 1 inch or less.

20. C is correct.

Shear plates, not split ring connectors, are used for structures that must be disassembled. The face of the shear plate is flush with the face of the lumber, and the two pieces are connected with a bolt.

21. C is correct.

Type III cement is high-early-strength—the type needed for rapid slip form construction. Type I is normal cement. Type II is low heat and sulfate-resistant, while Type IV is slow-setting and low heat for massive structures.

22. A is correct.

A split extends completely through the wood, so this would affect both horizontal shear resistance and bending strength. The other defects listed extend only partially into the wood.

23. D is correct.

k is the unit of conductance for one inch of material, while C is the conductance through the total thickness of the material under consideration. r and R are units of resistance, or the amount of time it takes a certain amount of heat to pass through a material.

24. B is correct.

Rock wool is a loose insulation poured or blown into cavities. It is usually not used in commercial construction, and can settle when installed in any type of cavity wall. The other types of insulation listed would be more appropriate, although fiberglass batts would be difficult because the usual method of attaching them is by stapling the flanges of the insulation to wood studs. However, fiberglass batts could be fit in steel stud cavities by friction.

25. B is correct.

A bull stretcher is a brick laid on its face so the width of the brick is visible. With a width of 3 5/8 inches and a mortar joint of 3/8 inch, three courses would be 12 inches. Three standard stretcher courses equal 8 inches, while three soldier courses equal 24 inches.

26. A is correct.

Choice B is a full mortise hinge, choice C is a half mortise, and choice D is a full surface hinge.

27. B is correct.

Closers are always required for fire-rated doors. The other statements are correct.

28. D is correct.

Silicone coatings would provide the best coverage for rough walls since they can be sprayed, painted, or rolled on. If the wall was below grade, the correct choice would be a cementitious coating or a bituminous coating.

29. C is correct.

The depth should be at least 1 1/2 times the depth of the car, but no less than 10 feet. Since the question does not give any information about car depth, you should assume that the minimum depth is the correct answer.

30. C is correct.

The advantages of copper roofs include their workability and corrosion resistance so statements I and IV are correct. Since copper roofs are relatively soft and expensive, statements II and III are reasons for not using them.

31. A is correct.

Vertical cracking is usually an indication that the brick wall is not able to move laterally, which is a condition caused by lack of vertical expansion joints.

32. B is correct.

Base flashing extends from the roof over the cant strip and up the wall, so answer A is incorrect. Counter flashing covers the base flashing by extending from the wall over the base flashing and covering any expansion joint that may occur at this point. Coping protects the top of the parapet, so answer D is incorrect. Sealants by themselves are not adequate to cover a major expansion joint as would occur at the roof and wall intersection, so answer C is incorrect.

33. C is correct.

The vehicle consists of two parts: the nonvolatile part called the binder, which forms the final coating, and the volatile part called the solvent, which evaporates or dries. Pigments, if added, are part of the vehicle and form the color of the coating.

34. D is correct.

Forming corners in concrete always adds to the cost, so making the wall a uniform thickness would be most economical even though more concrete would be required. Making the column square would decrease the amount of concrete, but still require the same amount of forming. Separating the pilaster from the wall would actually increase the cost of form work. Forming the pilaster with a diagonal would not be appropriate because of the structural problems caused by decreasing the column area and placing reinforcement.

35. C is correct.

Steel with over 2.0 percent carbon is classified as cast iron. The other choices are all used, but answer C is considered medium-carbon steel and is most common.

36. B2, chamfer strip, is correct.

A chamfer strip is a small triangular piece of material placed in the corners for forms to prevent sharp 90 degree corners, which are difficult to cast and have a tendency to break off when the forms are removed or during use.

37. D4, stile, is correct.

38. B3, coordinator, is correct.

A coordinator prevents the door leaf with the astragal from closing before the other leaf, so the pair of doors seals properly.

39. B9, equivalent thickness, is correct.

Concrete masonry partitions are usually hollow, so the actual thickness of the solid material is used to rate the fire resistance of the unit, not the actual overall width.

40. A6, bond beam, is correct.

A bond beam is a masonry unit made to accommodate reinforcing and grout to span openings in masonry walls. These are often used in place of steel lintels.

41. A is correct.

Dissimilar metals should be physically separated by non-conducting materials in order to prevent galvanic action. Increasing the thickness of the materials may postpone the complete deterioration of the materials, but not prevent it, so answer B is incorrect. Reducing direct contact with water will minimize it, but moisture in the air is sufficient to cause galvanic action, so answer C is incorrect.

42. C is correct.

Geared traction elevators can be designed to serve a wide variety of slower speeds and high capacities, so they are ideal for low-rise buildings with heavy loads like department stores. A geared traction elevator could be used for a small medical office building, but a higher speed would offer better service. A 16-story office building would need a high-speed, moderate capacity elevator, so a geared traction type would be inappropriate. An apartment would require a low capacity, but higher speeds.

43. C is correct.

The thickness of the gypsum board is not critical because there is little difference in weight of 3/8-inch, 1/2-inch, or 5/8-inch board. The number of layers, on the other hand, can affect the total weight significantly.

44. A is correct.

The gravel provides open spaces for any water under hydrostatic pressure to lose its pressure and drip to drains near the footing. Although it does this by preventing direct contact of the soil with the wall, this is not the sole purpose.

45. C is correct.

Welding is joining two metals by heating them above their melting point. Soldering is joining two metals using lead-based or tin-based alloys as filler metals which melt below 500 °F.

46. B is correct.

Only non-corrosive metals, like stainless steel, should be used to anchor stone. Both copper and steel would deteriorate over time.

47. D is correct.

All of the choices listed are considerations in detailing wood floors, so you must select the *most* important. Moisture is one of the biggest problems with wood floors, so keeping moisture out in the first place would minimize other problems like expansion at the perimeter. Therefore, answer D is the best choice.

48. A is correct.

Mullions are members that separate large sections of glass, while muntins are framing that separates individual panes of glass. Stiles are vertical members of doors, and rails are horizontal members of doors.

49. B is correct.

Statement III is not as important because the characteristics of defects are implied in the grading of the lumber. Statement V is not of prime importance.

50. C is correct.

A mortise lock offers the most flexibility in the number of operating functions available and is a very durable type of lockset. The next best choice would be a cylindrical lock.

51. D is correct.

Statement I is partially correct because built-up roofs can be applied to flat roofs, but they should not be. There should be a minimum of 1/4 inch per foot of slope. Even if you select statement I as correct, there is no answer choice containing statement I and the other correct statements. II is incorrect because built-up roofs can be applied over nailable and non-nailable decks.

52. B is correct.

A full bed of portland cement mortar offers the best durability and water resistance for high-use, wet areas.

53. A is correct.

The structural slab is a consideration, but only as part of the entire floor/ceiling assembly, so II is an incorrect choice. III is not correct because thermal insulation is not a consideration in a ceiling's fire resistance. V is not correct because the style is not as important as whether or not the grid is rated.

54. B is correct.

As with any beam, the deeper the member, the more efficient it is. Using a cored slab rather than a solid slab allows the depth to be increased without increasing the weight in the center of the beam where it is not needed. Answers A and D are partially correct, but answer B is the best choice.

55. A is correct.

Selection A shows a strong keyed joint with a waterstop to prevent water penetration. The other selections show joints that are weak structurally or that do not provide for adequate waterproofing.

56. B is correct.

2000 pound elevators are only used for small apartments, and 6000 pound elevators are used for freight. A 4000 pound capacity is often used for large office buildings and retail stores, but 3000 pound is more common for small and medium-size buildings.

57. A is correct.

I is incorrect because ratings up to 3 hours are possible. III is incorrect because wood doors may be used with steel frames under some circumstances. V is incorrect because the standard thickness is 1 3/4 inches.

58. D is correct.

59. B is correct.

The southwestern portion of the United States is the driest, so moisture content should approximate the conditions in which the lumber will be used. However, it is difficult to reduce the moisture content much below 5 percent, so A is an unrealistic answer.

60. A is correct.

A membrane is part of a total assembly that also includes reinforcing and a thick bed of mortar on which the granite is laid or which is part of the terrazzo. The membrane allows the structural slab to move independently of the finish flooring so any deflection does not crack the floor.

24 CONSTRUCTION DRAWINGS AND DETAILS

1. B is correct.

A subcontractor would be most interested in the number of times equipment must be brought to a job site, what kinds of workers will be required to complete the work, and possible interference with other trades, because all of these have cost and time implications. The types of tools needed may, under some circumstances, have some bearing on cost if they must be purchased or rented, but normally tools are available and do not represent a significant portion of the total cost.

To a certain extent, the architect can control these variables and therefore exercise some control over cost by design and detailing so that construction proceeds in the most straightforward manner.

2. D is correct.

Of the four detailing considerations implied by the choices (structural integrity, safety from contact, fire safety, and maintainability), fire safety is the most important, so answer A is eliminated. The choice is then between III and V. Either the actual flame spread or the code requirements could be investigated first, but generally it is more important to know the performance requirements before you design or determine if a building assembly conforms to them. Answer D is therefore the better choice.

3. B is correct.

The most significant problem with this detail in a cold climate like Boston is the lack of insulating glazing. The detail only indicates a single pane of glass. Although the question does not address this issue, notice also that there is no insulation between the ceiling and the floor above.

4. B is correct.

Although flashing is shown and noted below the sill of the second floor framing, extending it under the framing to the edge of the carpet is questionable. In addition, there is no sealant called out for the joint between the sill and the flashing. Water dripping down the window could be drawn into the framing by capillary action. Answer D might be considered the correct answer, except the ceiling-to-floor dimension is small enough and the structure rigid enough that cracking would probably not occur.

5. C is correct.

I is not correct because there is not enough information given to determine if tolerances smaller than industry standard are called out. Simply increasing tolerances greater than normal will not decrease the cost because contractors will price standard tolerances unless specified otherwise.

II would be correct if life cycle costs were a concern. Although this is implied because it is a corporate office presumably owner-occupied and maintained, the question clearly states that "estimated construction costs" should be reduced which means first costs. Statements III, IV, and V would all help reduce costs.

6. A is correct.

The architect (or the architect's representative, such as the project manager on the job) is responsible for the overall coordination of all the contract documents.

7. A is correct.

Direct meetings with the people responsible for the programming, design, and execution of the project is the best way to facilitate communication. Having another architect look at the drawings may be a good way to do a technical check, but that person could not know what the client's design goals were. It is common to request from the client necessary information to design and complete the working drawings, but isolating the client in reviewing them (unless specifically requested) does not allow the architect to participate in the process. In addition, this is not a normal duty of the client. Making a checklist for the drafting staff is a good tool, and one that is often used, but in the context of the question, answer A is the method most likely to ensure the results desired.

25 THE PROJECT MANUAL AND SPECIFICATIONS

1. A is correct.

A bid log is used by the architect to record the bids as they are opened and to help the owner evaluate them. It is never included in the project manual. A subsurface soil conditions report, although not a part of the contract documents, may be included in the project manual for information only. A site work specification, as one of the technical sections, is also included in the manual as is a bid bond. The bid bond, however, is also not a part of the contract documents since it is a bidding document.

2. C is correct.

The specification simply states how the hangar anchorage devices must perform; that is, they must support a certain amount of weight. As long as they do this, they can be any type, size, or style that the contractor selects. The requirements for the fasteners are simply those selected as appropriate by the manufacturer. The hangar wire specification is a reference type since it refers to a particular industry standard specification. The ceiling suspension main runner is a descriptive specification since it describes various qualities (size, material, and method of fabrication) of the ceiling runner.

3. D is correct.

All of the responses are correct. A performance specification lets the contractor, material supplier, and fabricator decide how best to supply the required building component. Although performance specifications are detailed, there are still many ways to satisfy them. They are more difficult to research, write, and review, so there is more work for the architect. For ordinary materials, there is usually no need to write performance specifications because the requirements are so well established in the construction industry.

4. D is correct.

I is not correct because the specifications take precedence over the drawings, so the more expensive material in the specifications would be the one used. In general, any time there are conflicts in the project documents, the best that can happen is no change to the cost, but usually an increase results.

II is not correct because litigation would be a last result and other remedies would be sought and implemented

before a lawsuit occurred. Any conflicts in the documents can be corrected with an addendum prior to bidding or negotiation, by change order, or modification after the construction contract is signed.

5. B is correct.

You would most likely not want to use an "or equal" type of specification for asphalt roofing because, in general, strict "or equal" specifications leave too much to the discretion of the contractor with no review by the architect. This would be especially true with shingles where there are many inferior products available for such an important part of the building. A better specification would be the base bid with alternate manufacturer.

6. A is correct.

II is not correct because the specifications take precedence over the drawings. This fact is usually stated in the instructions to bidders and in the technical sections in Division 1, General Requirements of the Project Manual. Courts have also held that the specifications override the drawings in case of conflicts.

7. D is correct.

Testing of materials and equipment is in part 3 of each technical section if appropriate to the section. Refer to Figure 25.2 for an outline of the three-part format.

26 THE PRIMARY CONTRACTUAL DOCUMENTS

1. D is correct.

The owner is obligated to furnish the contractor reasonable evidence that financial arrangements have been made to fulfill the owner's obligations under the contract. This is contained in paragraph 2.2.1 of the 1987 edition of the General Conditions of the Contract. Therefore, the owner cannot refuse to do this, even with good cause.

2. B1, project representation beyond basic services, is correct.

The owner-architect agreement clearly defines what is included in the contract administration phase, which includes periodic visits to the site to become generally familiar with the progress of the work and to determine if it is being performed consistent with the contract documents. The additional services article (Article 3) specifically states that the architect will be compensated additionally for an on-site project representative.

3. B0, privity, is correct.

Paragraph 9.7 states that nothing in the owner-architect agreement shall create a contractual relationship with a third party against either the architect or the owner. This reinforces the idea of privity—two parties to a contract are not liable to a third party.

4. B4, retainage, is correct.

Witholding money gives the owner leverage to make the contractor finish the job and provides a reserve in case liens must be satisfied. Surety bond is not the correct answer because this involves a third party (the surety) who is insuring that they will complete the project if the contractor fails to meet his or her obligations.

5. B is correct.

It is very likely that a client undertaking his first construction project without a program would spend a great deal of his time and the architect's time in determining his needs and making decisions. A cost-plus-fee method like multiple of direct personnel expense would ensure that no matter how much time you spent on the project, you would still meet expenses and make a profit. This is the best answer since the question asked for what you, as the architect, would prefer. The client, of course, might prefer a fixed sum.

6. D is correct.

The first step is to officially notify the contractor that the work is incorrect. Although the architect may have done this during the site visits, it must be done in writing. As part of the architect's normal duties, the incorrect work should be rejected and the contractor told to promptly correct it in accordance with paragraph 12.2.1 of the General Conditions of the Contract. If the contractor does not correct the work, then the owner should be aware of the alternative courses of action available up to and including terminating the contract. However, it is a better course of action for the owner to correct the work (if the contractor refuses) than to first terminate the contract.

Answer A is not the best course because stopping the work always has a detrimental effect on the entire project and it does not provide for the normal notice to the contractor of non-conforming work.

Answer B is not correct because quick termination of the contract without trying other remedies is not according to the General Conditions of the Contract.

Answer C is not the best choice because the contractor, again, should be notified in writing of the problem and requested to correct the situation. Only then should the owner consider accepting non-conforming work. This is also not the best course of action because there is almost always a disagreement about what amount should be deducted from the contract sum for accepting non-conforming work.

7. D is correct.

An agent acts on behalf of another and assumes certain specified authority and duties, but does not take on responsibilities another person would normally have. Answer B is incorrect because agency does not involve mediation nor does it involve vendors. Answer C is incorrect because the architect is the agent, not the principal.

8. B is correct.

The fast-track method would help keep costs down and be appropriate for a client who must move to a new facility as soon as possible. In this situation, it is likely that the owner is familiar with the process, knows what is needed, and would be comfortable with letting early construction proceed before the final design was worked out. With a flexible line of credit, knowing a fixed price would not be as important as with some other types of clients.

9. B is correct.

The contractor's bid, like other bidding documents, is not part of the contract documents unless specifically stated in the agreement. Paragraph 1.1.1 of the General Conditions of the Contract outlines what is and is not included in the contract documents.

10. A is the correct answer.

The architect has a duty and ethical responsibility to keep the contractor informed of any non-conforming work and to cooperate in getting the job done, but may not be held legally responsible. Paragraph 3.3.3 of the General Conditions of the Contract states that the contractor shall not be relieved of obligations to perform the work in accordance with the contract documents by activities or duties of the architect. Paragraph 3.2.1 also states that if the contractor performs any construction activity knowing it involves an error the contractor shall assume responsibility.

27 BIDDING PROCEDURES AND DOCUMENTS

1. B is correct.

Addenda are used to make changes to the contract documents after they are issued for bidding, but before the contract is awarded. Change orders and construction change directives also modify the original contract documents, but are used after the contract is awarded. An alternate listing is simply the list of alternates that the contractor must include in the bid.

2. D is correct.

Although not all of the items listed are included in every set of bidding documents, they can all be used in bidding. Of the five, a list of subcontractors is used least frequently.

3. B is correct.

The most reasonable approach, in light of the fact that none of the bid has been opened and the contractor was only three minutes late, would be to ask the other bidders if there is an objection. If not, accept the bid. If one of the bids had been opened, you would certainly not want to accept any other late submittals. Nor should a bid that is three minutes late be prejudiced if it is accepted simply because it was late.

4. A is correct.

Bidding procedures should always be clearly and unambiguously stated, but not because there are so many variables. In fact, bidding procedures are fairly well established in the construction industry, regardless of whether there is open bidding or private bid openings.

Open bidding does usually present more problems because nearly anyone can bid, regardless of experience. Evaluating qualified bidders can be a problem. The extra advertising required can also add more complexity to the process.

5. D is correct.

A performance bond is issued by a surety company that obligates itself to finish a project should the contractor default. A labor and material payment bond is designed to pay liens if they occur. Other provisions of the owner-contractor agreement, such as liquidated damages, are designed to encourage the contractor to finish on time. The general contractor is responsible for the performance of the subcontractors under provisions of the owner-contractor agreement.

6. C is correct.

Since it is clearly stated in the owner-architect agreement that changes in the contract documents to reduce costs are not part of the basic services, answer A is not correct. Answer B is not correct because rebidding, even with new contractors, would probably not result in much, if any, cost savings. All the deduct alternates might not be a desirable course of action and may not even be enough to compensate for the cost overrun, so answer D is not the best.

7. C is correct.

This is the type of question that has an answer so simple it makes you wonder what the trick is. Labor and materials are by far the biggest influence on the cost of a job because they represent about 80 percent of the cost. Subcontract bids could be considered the correct answer, especially on jobs where most of the work of the general contractor is subcontracted, but labor and materials still account for subcontract bids.

28 CONSTRUCTION ADMINISTRATION SERVICES

1. B is correct.

Although the contractor must notify the architect when the project is ready for the punch list inspection, notification for final inspection comes after the punch list. It is during this final inspection that the architect verifies that the project has been completed according to the contract documents and the contractor is entitled to final payment. The issuance of a certificate of substantial completion comes only after the final inspection, and, if followed by the consent of surety, the payment certificate can be prepared.

2. A is correct.

All of the answers given are possible, but only answer A includes the technical definition of substantial completion. Answer D is not correct because answer B is not entirely correct. The job can be substantially complete and there can still be a few items left on the punch list that the contractor must correct.

3. D is correct.

Answer D is the best answer because the architect has a duty to cooperate with the contractor and should at least mention the potential problem during the site visit. The contractor may then check on the equipment while the architect is following up with the mechanical engineer. The observation should be noted on the architect's field report to keep the client informed of the progress of the work. If, in fact, the equipment being installed is incorrect, then corrective action may be taken. By notifying the contractor immediately, he or she can decide whether or not to suspend work on the installation of the equipment until the situation is resolved.

Answer B is not correct because the architect never stops the work. Answer C is not correct because notifying the owner first is a premature step. Answer A is not correct because by the time the mechanical engineer is notified and visits the site, the installation of the equipment may have proceeded to a point where it is difficult to remedy.

4. C is correct.

Since the additional exit signs would necessitate an increase in construction cost and possibly in contract time, an order for minor change would not be appropriate. An addendum is used before the contract is signed, so this is not the correct answer. It is possible that the contractor and owner might disagree with the cost of the additional exit signs and a construction change directive would be used initially, but it is more likely that everyone would realize the need for the extra signs and agree on a price. In any event, a change order would ultimately be needed.

5. B is correct.

I is not correct because field reports are the responsibility of the architect. IV is not correct because the architect is responsible for reviewing claims. A subcontractor may make a claim directly to the contractor, but the contractor, in turn, would have to make a claim to the owner. V is not correct because both the contractor and architect are responsible for reviewing shop drawings although only the contractor is responsible for the accuracy of the shop drawings.

Since scaffolding is part of the means of construction, the contractor is solely responsible for this. The General Conditions of the Contract specifically state the contractor is responsible for arranging and coordinating field tests.

6. A is the correct answer.

The contractor must review submittals prior to giving them to the architect.

7. C is correct.

The General Conditions specifically state that the architect must respond within 10 days of notification of the claim by the contractor. One of the responses of the architect may be to ask for supporting data.

BIBLIOGRAPHY

General Reference

American National Standards Institute. *ANSI A117.1-1986. Specifications for Making Buildings and Facilities Accessible to and Usable by Physically Handicapped People.* New York: American National Standards Institute, 1986.

Anchor, R. D., ed. *Design of Structures Against Fire.* New York: Elsevier Publishing Co., 1986.

Architectural and Transportation Barriers Compliance Board. *Minimum Guideline and Requirements for Accessible Design.* Washington, DC: Architectural and Transportation Barriers Compliance Board, 1981.

Callender, John Hancock. *Time-Saver Standards for Architectural Design Data.* New York: McGraw-Hill Book Company, 1982.

Goldberg, Alfred. *Design Guide to the 1988 Uniform Building Code.* Mill Valley, CA: GRDA Publications, 1988.

Healy, Richard J. *Design for Security.* 2nd ed. New York: John Wiley & Sons, 1983.

International Conference of Building Officials. *Uniform Building Code.* Whittier, CA: International Conference of Building Officials, 1988.

Kemper, Alfred M. *Architectural Handbook.* New York: John Wiley & Sons, 1979.

Liebing, Ralph W. *Construction Regulations Handbook.* New York: John Wiley & Sons, 1987.

Merritt, Frederick S., ed. *Building Design and Construction Handbook.* 4th ed. New York: McGraw-Hill Book Company, 1982.

National Council of Architectural Registration Boards. *NCARB Architect Registration Examination Handbook.* 2 vols. Washington, DC: National Council of Architectural Registration Boards, 1988.

National Fire Protection Association. *National Electric Code,* NFPA no. 70. Quincy, MA: National Fire Protection Association, 1984.

National Fire Protection Association. *Life Safety Code Handbook.* Quincy, MA: National Fire Protection Association, 1985.

National Fire Protection Association. *Life Safety Code,* NFPA no. 101. Quincy, MA: National Fire Protection Association, 1985.

National Fire Protection Association. *Fire Protection Handbook.* Quincy, MA: National Fire Protection Association, 1986.

Packard, Robert T., ed. *Architectural Graphic Standards.* 8th ed. New York: John Wiley & Sons, 1988.

Robinette, Gary O., ed. *Barrier-Free Exterior Design: Anyone Can Go Anywhere.* New York: Van Nostrand Reinhold, 1985.

Schultz, Neil. *Fire and Flammability Handbook.* New York: Van Nostrand Reinhold, 1985.

Pre-Design

Architectural License Seminars. *Pre-Design 1.* Los Angeles: Architectural License Seminars, 1985.

Architectural License Seminars. *Pre-Design 2.* Los Angeles: Architectural License Seminars, 1985.

Bacon, Edmund N. *Design of Cities.* Rev. ed. New York: Viking Press, 1974.

Barnett, Jonathan. *An Introduction to Urban Design.* New York: Harper & Row, 1982.

Catanese, Anthony, and Snyder, James. *Introduction to Urban Planning.* New York: McGraw-Hill Book Company, 1979.

Fletcher, Sir Banister. *A History of Architecture on the Comparative Method.* New York: Charles Scribner's Sons, 1963.

Hedman, Richard. *Fundamentals of Urban Design.* Chicago: Planners Press, 1984.

International City Management Association. *The Practice of Local Government Planning.* Washington, DC: International City Management Association, 1979.

Lynch, Kevin. *Image of the City.* Cambridge, MA: MIT Press, 1960.

_____. *Site Planning.* 3rd ed. Cambridge, MA: MIT Press, 1984.

Mumford, Lewis. *The City in History.* New York: Harcourt, Brace & World, 1961.

Newman, Oscar. *Defensible Space.* New York: Macmillan, 1972.

Peña, William. *Problem Seeking.* 3rd ed. Washington, DC: AIA Press, 1987.

Preiser, Wolfgang F. E. *Programming the Build Environment.* New York: Van Nostrand Reinhold, 1985.

Sanoff, Henry. *Methods of Architectural Programming.* Stroudsburg, PA: Dowden, Hutchinson & Ross, 1977.

Simonds, John O. *Earthscape: A Manual of Environmental Planning.* New York: McGraw-Hill Book Company, 1978.

_____. *Landscape Architecture: A Manual of Site Planning and Design.* 2nd ed. New York: McGraw-Hill Book Company, 1983.

White, Edward T. *Space Adjacency Analysis: Diagramming Information for Architectural Design*. Tucson, AZ: Architectural Media Ltd., 1986.

Site Design

Architectural License Seminars. *Site Design*. Los Angeles: Architectural License Seminars, 1984.

Brown, G. Z. *Sun, Wind, and Light: Architectural Design Strategies*. New York: John Wiley & Sons, 1985.

Clayton, George T. *The Site Plan in Architectural Working Drawings*. Champaign, IL: Stipes Publishing Co., 1983.

DeChiara, Joseph, and Koppelman, Lee. *Time Saver Standards for Site Planning*. New York: McGraw-Hill Book Company, 1984.

Gallion, Arthur B, and Eisner, Simon. *Urban Pattern: City Planning and Design*. New York: Van Nostrand Reinhold, 1975.

Giedion, Sigfried. *Space, Time and Architecture*. Cambridge, MA: Harvard University Press, 1967.

Lynch, Kevin. *Site Planning*. 3rd ed. Cambridge, MA: MIT Press, 1984.

Newton, Norman T. *Design on the Land: The Development of Landscape Architecture* (Chapters 21-24). Cambridge, MA: Harvard University Press, 1971.

Olgyay, Victor V. *Design with Climate*. Princeton, NJ: Princeton University Press, 1963.

Rubenstein, Harvey. *A Guide to Site and Environmental Planning*. 3rd ed. New York: John Wiley & Sons, 1987.

Untermann, Richard. *Grade Easy*. Washington, DC: Landscape Architect Foundation, 1976.

Watson, Donald, and Labs, Kenneth. *Climate Design: Energy Efficient Building Principles and Practices*. New York: McGraw-Hill Book Company, 1983.

White, Edward T. *Site Analysis: Diagramming Information for Architectural Design*. Tucson, AZ: Architectural Media Ltd., 1983.

Building Design

Architectural License Seminars. *Building Design*. Los Angeles: Architectural License Seminars, 1984.

Architectural License Seminars. *Design Exercise Handbook*. Los Angeles: Architectural License Seminars, n.d.

Bennett, Corwin. *Spaces for People*. Englewood Cliffs, NJ: Prentice-Hall, Inc., 1977.

Brebner, John. *Environmental Psychology in Building Design*. London: Applied Science Publishers, 1982.

Ching, Francis D. K. *Architecture: Form, Space & Order*. New York: Van Nostrand Reinhold, 1979.

Deasy, C. M. *Designing Places for People: A Handbook on Human Behavior for Architects, Designers, and Facility Managers*. New York: Whitney Library of Design, 1985.

DeChiara, Joseph, and Callender, John Hancock. *Time-Saver Standards for Building Types*. 2nd ed. New York: McGraw-Hill Book Company, 1980.

Lang, Jon, Burnette, Charles, Moleski, Walter, and Vachon, David. *Designing for Human Behavior*. Stroudsburg, PA: Dowden, Hutchinson & Ross, 1974.

Proshansky, Harold M., Ittelson, William H., and Rivlin, Leanne G., eds. *Environmental Psychology; Man and His Physical Setting*. New York: Holt, Rinehart & Winston, 1970.

Steven Winter Associates, Inc. *The Passive Construction Handbook*. Emmaus, PA: Rodale Press, 1983.

Watson, Donald, ed. *Energy Conservation Through Building Design*. New York: McGraw-Hill Book Company, 1979.

Building Systems

American Institute of Architects. *AIA Architect's Handbook of Energy Practice: Predesign/Climate and Site*. Washington, DC: American Institute of Architects, 1982.

American Society of Heating, Refrigerating and Air-conditioning Engineers, Inc. *ASHRAE Handbook—Fundamentals Volume*. Atlanta, GA: American Society of Heating, Refrigerating and Air-conditioning Engineers, Inc., 1985.

Architectural License Seminars. *Mechanical/Plumbing/Electrical/Life Safety*. Los Angeles: Architectural License Seminars, 1986.

Babbitt, Harold E. *Plumbing*. New York: McGraw-Hill Book Company, 1986.

Banham, Reyner. *The Architecture of the Well Tempered Environment*. 2nd ed. Chicago: University of Chicago Press, 1984.

Barney, G. C., ed. *Elevator Technology*. New York: John Wiley & Sons, 1986.

Cremer, Lothar. *Principles and Applications of Room Acoustics*. New York: Applied Science, 1982.

Dagostino, Frank R. *Mechanical and Electrical Systems in Buildings*. Reston, VA: Reston Publishing Company, 1982.

Egan, M. David. *Concepts in Architectural Acoustics*. New York: McGraw-Hill Book Company, 1972.

———. *Concepts in Lighting for Architecture*. New York: McGraw-Hill Book Company, 1984.

Flynn, John E., and Segil, Arthur W. *Architectural Interior Systems*. 2nd ed. New York: Van Nostrand Reinhold, 1987.

Illuminating Engineering Society of North America. *IES Lighting Handbook*. New York: Illuminating Engineering Society of North America, 1981.

Jones, Robert St. Claire. *Noise and Vibration Control in Buildings*. New York: McGraw-Hill Book Company, 1984.

Lam, William. *Sunlight as Formgiver for Architecture*. New York: Van Nostrand Reinhold, 1986.

Mazria, Edward. *The Passive Solar Energy Book*. Emmaus, PA: Rodale Press, Inc., 1979.

McPartland, Joseph F. *National Electrical Code Handbook*. New York: McGraw-Hill Book Company, 1984.

Moore, Fuller. *Concepts and Practice of Architectural Daylighting*. New York: Van Nostrand Reinhold, 1985.

Robbins, Claude. *Daylighting: Design and Analysis*. New York: Van Nostrand Reinhold, 1986.

Stein, Benjamin, Reynolds, John S., and McGuinness, W. J. *Mechanical and Electrical Equipment for Buildings*. 7th ed. New York: John Wiley & Sons, 1986.

Traister, John E. *Practical Lighting Applications for Building Construction*. New York: Van Nostrand Reinhold, 1982.

Traister, John E. *Heating, Ventilating, and Air-Conditioning: Design for Building Construction*. Englewood Cliffs, NJ: Prentice-Hall, Inc., 1987.

Materials and Methods of Construction

Architectural License Seminars. *Materials and Methods*. Los Angeles: Architectural License Seminars, 1986.

Architectural Woodwork Institute. *Architectural Woodwork Quality Standards, Guide Specifications and Quality Certifications Program*. Arlington, VA: Architectural Woodwork Institute, 1984.

Ching, Francis. *Building Construction Illustrated*. New York: Van Nostrand Reinhold, 1979.

Dagostino, Frank R. *Materials of Construction*. Reston, VA: Reston Publishing Company, 1981.

Dell'Isola, Alphonse, and Kirk, Stephen J. *Life Cycle Costing for Design Professionals*. New York: McGraw-Hill Book Company, 1981.

Ellison, Donald C., Mickadeit, Robert, and Huntington, W. C. *Building Construction, Materials and Types of Construction*. 6th ed. New York: John Wiley & Sons, 1987.

Harris, Cyril M. *Dictionary of Architecture and Construction*. New York: McGraw-Hill Book Company, 1975.

Marble Institute of America. *Design Manual III*. Farmington, MI: Marble Institute of America, 1985.

Merritt, Frederick S., ed. *Building Design and Construction Handbook*. 4th ed. New York: McGraw-Hill Book Company, 1982.

Olin, Harold Bennett. *Construction Principles, Materials and Methods*. 5th ed. Chicago: Institute of Financial Education, 1983.

Prestressed Concrete Institute. *Precast/Prestressed Concrete Design Handbook*. Chicago: Prestressed Concrete Institute, 1985.

Randall, R. A., and Panarese, W. C. *Concrete Masonry Handbook*. Skokie, IL: Portland Cement Association, 1985.

Rosen, Harold J. *Construction Materials for Architecture*. New York: John Wiley & Sons, 1985.

Stein, J. Stewart. *Construction Glossary*. New York: John Wiley & Sons, 1980.

Strakosh, George R. *Vertical Transportation: Elevators and Escalators*. New York: John Wiley & Sons, 1983.

Waddell, Joseph J. *Concrete Construction Handbook*. New York: McGraw-Hill Book Company, 1974.

_____. *Construction Materials Ready Reference Manual*. New York: McGraw-Hill Book Company, 1986.

Wakita, Osamu, and Linde, Richard M. *The Professional Handbook of Architectural Detailing*. 2nd ed. New York: John Wiley & Sons, 1987.

Construction Documents and Services

American Institute of Architects. *The Architect's Handbook of Professional Practice*. Washington, DC: American Institute of Architects, 1987.

Architectural License Seminars. *Construction Documents and Services 1, Documentation*. Los Angeles: Architectural License Seminars, 1985.

Architectural License Seminars. *Construction Documents and Services 2, Administration*. Los Angeles: Architectural License Seminars, 1985.

Ballast, David Kent. *The Architect's Handbook*. Englewood Cliffs, NJ: Prentice-Hall, Inc., 1984.

The Construction Specifications Institute. *Manual of Practice*. Alexandria, VA: The Construction Specifications Institute, 1985.

Dib, Albert, and Grant, James K., eds. *Legal Handbook for Architects, Engineers, and Contractors*. New York: Clark Boardman Co., 1985.

Greenstreet, Robert. *Legal and Contractual Procedures for Architects*. London: Architectural Press, 1984.

Greenstreet, Robert, and Greenstreet, Karen. *The Architect's Guide to Law and Practice*. New York: Van Nostrand Reinhold, 1984.

Haviland, David S. *Managing Architectural Projects: The Process*. Washington, DC: The American Institute of Architects Service Corporation, 1981.

Rosen, Harold. *Construction Specifications Writing: Principles and Procedures*. New York: John Wiley & Sons, 1981.

Sweet, Justin. *Legal Aspects of Architecture, Engineering, and the Construction Process*. 3rd ed. St. Paul, MN: West Publishing Co., 1985.

Wakita, Osamu A., and Linde, Richard M. *The Professional Handbook of Architectural Detailing*. New York: John Wiley & Sons, 1987.

INDEX

PROFESSIONAL PUBLICATIONS, INC. ● **Belmont, CA**

PROFESSIONAL PUBLICATIONS, INC. ● Belmont, CA